Daytrips

EASTERN AUSTRALIA

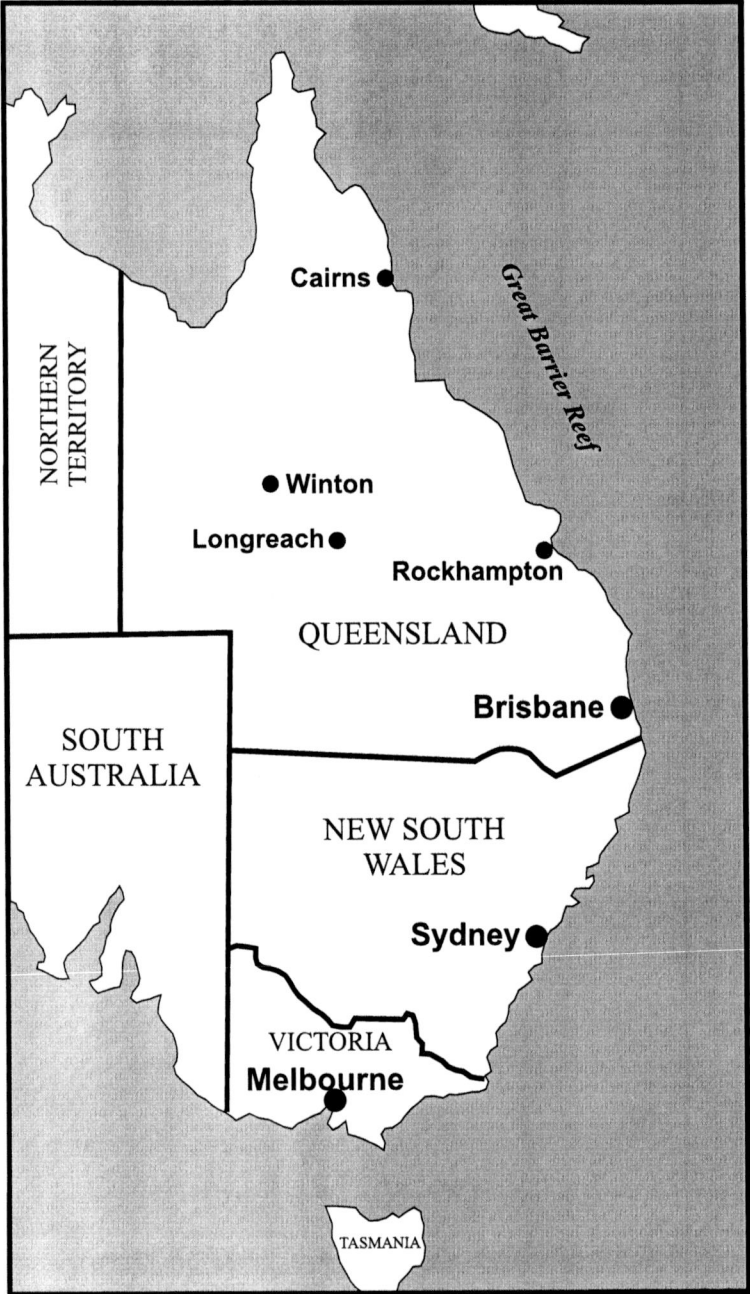

Daytrips

EASTERN AUSTRALIA

60 *one day adventures by car, rail or bus*

JAMES POSTELL

HASTINGS HOUSE
Book Publishers
Fern Park, Florida

Credits

Photos on pages 11, 27, 48, 57, 110, 127, 188, 214, and 307 are by Ann Rudden

Photos on pages 89, 146, 172, 177, 250, 270, 284, 320, 347 and 376 are by James Postell

Photo on page 338 is by Ron Postell

Photos on pages 224 and 229 are courtesy of Clarence River/NSW Tourism

Photo on page 327 is courtesy of Queensland Tourism

While every effort has been made to insure accuracy, neither the author nor the publisher assume legal responsibility for any consequences arising from the use of this book or the information it contains.

No gratuities were accepted in writing this guide, and the tours were chosen based simply on the fun factor.

ISBN: 0-8038-2051-8

Printed in the United States of America
10 9 8 7 6 5 4 3 2 1

Contents

6   CONTENTS

Introduction

G 'day and welcome to the world of Daytrips Australia, where you will experience this vast continent in the easiest way possible—on comfortable one-day excursions. Even for those lucky enough to live in this sunburnt land, seeing the country can be accomplished best by selecting a hub and traveling outwards to several chosen attractions. Because Oz (that's what we call Australia) is approximately the size of the continental United States, highlighted tours are clustered around convenient centers allowing you to enjoy the sights, sounds, and tastes without that harried feeing experienced by so many visitors.

Between the three main bases of Sydney, Melbourne, and Brisbane are wide-open spaces with plenty of kangaroos, red sand, and a hardy stock of people. All jumping-off points are based near the coast, but the trips outlined are nevertheless very different from each other. The tours will offer you a flavor of an Australia rarely advertised or promoted. You will become part of the cultural experience and not just witness it from the back end of a camera.

The suggested tours do not force you into a rigid and hurried visit to the land down under. Pick and choose from the varied attractions and get to meet the locals—including the roos, koalas, and crocodiles. Take the time to absorb the larrikin attitude, taste foods not found on many tables outside this country, and understand why this land is so unique.

The format of the book allows you to organize the trips in any order you wish or eliminate certain spots that just may not interest you. But it's likely you will want to spend more time in a favored location and just chill out. You have heaps to choose from including Sydney's freewheeling city life and its national icon the Sydney Opera House, the unbeatable markets and theater of conservative Melbourne, and the laidback lifestyle of Queensland's Great Barrier Reef, lush rainforests, and majestic Outback.

The mix of walking, driving, and biking tours provides a nice blend to seeing the wonders of Australia. A few organized tours are offered for the areas that are either too remote or are, ah, too dangerous to venture off on your own. They do have some fearsome critters here, but you are quite safe if you follow the ranger's advice and your own common sense. It does add to the adventure to see a crocodile swimming alongside your boat or greet a dingo face-to-face on the largest sand dune island in the world.

As far as the food, put away your Crocodile Dundee notions and she'll be right. The food is fantastic, fresh, and inexpensive. Don't expect great service as tipping is not the norm and the wait staff has no incentive to be overly attentive. But don't confuse slow service with bad service. The

Australians are baffled at the speed at which North American diners eat. Here, a three-hour dinner is not out of the ordinary with every person enjoying a bottle of wine.

There are plenty of ethnic foods to choose from, and Fusion is currently in vogue. Fusion is a blend of Asian and European flavors that will delight many of you. I would encourage you to at least try some of the wild-side foods like kangaroo steak, emu sausage, crocodile stew, and shark filet. Oh, and do not miss the bugs! Moreton Bay bugs are tasty morsels of shellfish that look like a cross between a crab and lobster and taste like heaven. It's fun to tell everyone back home that you loved to eat the Australian bugs. If you want to really eat some bugs, I have included some bush tucker tours where you can dine on Aboriginal treats like witchetty grubs (yep, larva), barramundi (great fish), and plants I can't even name. I must admit that I didn't have the nerve to try them, except for barramundi—and that was excellent.

Keep in mind that the seasons are reversed and North American winters are summers here and vice versa. Another rule of thumb is that the weather regions are also opposite. So, the south of Australia (closest to the South Pole) is the coolest and the northern sections (nearest the equator) are hot and humid. The center is very hot and very dry.

Although the official language of Australia is English, you may have a difficult time understanding Oz-speak. The intonations are different, the slang is uniquely Aussie, and some of the locals will throw a few phrases at you just to have a go at you—for fun. If you want to read up on the slang before you come down, try the book "Don't' Go the Raw Prawn" or "The Penguin Book of Australian Slang." They are both fun reads. Or just check the Glossary in the back of this book.

Finally some friendly cultural advice—and take it only as that. Since September 11, the Australians have identified with Americans and shared our suffering. The outpouring of support has been overwhelming, and it has been very touching. However, the recent Iraq conflict has tempered this attitude a bit. Most Australians will hear your accent and give you a polite nod or will want to chat with you. Australians tend to look you in the eye, especially in Queensland and in remote areas. On the other hand, they do not favor the loud, brash, and demanding American and will avoid you like the plague. And do expect to be questioned about US global attitudes, and to be held accountable for the government's behavior.

The information provided in this guide was accurate when I wrote it, but things do change including exchange rates, hotel tariffs, opening/closing times, and access to some exhibits. I have included web sites where they are available, and also phone numbers. So, please check ahead especially if you have to travel some distance to get to an attraction.

One last thought: Don't feel as if you have to see it all or photograph every koala in the country. Pick the areas and attractions that interest you the most and absorb them. There is so much to see and do, but it will not be fun if you're too tired to remember where you are. Stop, have a dip, enjoy a XXXX (Fourex) beer and become an Aussie—even if it's only for a few weeks.

Happy Daytriping Mates!

COMMENTS & FEEDBACK:

Crikey mates, if you have a bellyful of information to add or want to make some fair dinkum suggestions, I am all-ears. Ideas from readers have enhanced the Daytrip guides and helped to provide an even better read. If your suggestions are used in our next edition, we'll be as happy as a dog with two tails to send you a complimentary copy of any book in the series. Please send your ideas to Hastings House, Book Publishers, 2601 Wells Ave., #161, Fern Park, FL 32730, U.S.A., or E-mail to: Hastings_daytrips@earthlink.net Drop in at www.DaytripsBooks.com and say g'day.

Koala in a Gum Tree

Exploring the Great Outdoors at the Glass House Mountains

Section I

DAYTRIP STRATEGIES

The word "Daytrip" may not have made it into the dictionary yet, but for experienced travelers it represents the easiest, most logical, and often the most economical approach to exploring this planet's treasures. By basing yourself in a centralized area, whether it be a city or remote Outback town, allows you to get comfortable with one bed while setting a staging area to become familiar with the surrounding areas. Since Australia is a wide-open country, this is really the easiest way to see the continent. Plus, it provides choices to skip around and focus on the areas that interest you.

Being so remote from the rest of the world, Australia is a challenge and joy to visit. A challenge because it is a long haul by plane or ship and you need to prepare yourself for the inevitable jetlag. A pleasure because it is so different and truly unique from any other continent. The animals, accents, foods, and landscapes are magical. The people are the friendliest you'll come across on the planet. And for those who actually live in Australia, daytrips can be the key to discovering those out-of-the-way places that you never even thought of.

Taking those issues into consideration, these one-day excursions are organized to give you some time to acclimate to the time zone, get your bearings, and learn the language of Aussie—fair dinkum mates! The tours are mixed in length to give you a chance to chill out on the beach or let someone else do the driving while you gaze upon the rainforests. But for those who want to see it all, you can pace yourself to any speed, but please take time for a frosty pint of beer or a cool Australian chardonnay.

ADVANTAGES:
Freedom and flexibility to:
1. Go anywhere you feel like when the mood strikes you. No fixed itinerary.
2. Travel light. Stash your baggage in your hotel and daytrip with this guidebook, a camera, and a spring in your step.
3. Enjoy each day without worrying about finding a place to eat or sleep each night. Your pillow is where you left it in the morning.

4.   Change your mind to meet the evolving weather, indulge in newly discovered passions, or meet up with newfound friends.

5.   Chill out, take a break from the touring, sleep late, watch a cricket game on TV, or spend some time at the Internet café and visit with family back home.

6.   Try a new adventure without committing to more than a few hours or a day to it. If you don't fancy bush foods, you had a look-see and didn't waste lots of money or time to give it a go.

7.   Become a "temporary resident" of your newly found city, Outback ranch, or rainforest getaway. You get to know an area in depth, become familiar with the local pubs, shops, and recognize familiar faces.

8.   Refresh those travel clothes, unpack the bags and actually hang those clothes in a closet for more than one night.

9.   Be reachable by family and friends back home. By having a fixed address in your base resort or town, loved ones or business associates can ring you for fun or important news.

10. Save money by getting longer-term rates or arranging a package deal. Knowing that you will be in one area you have better chances of negotiating terms, and it won't even affect your travel plans.

CHOOSING YOUR BASE RESORTS

SYDNEY:

There are several areas to choose from when looking for a hub in the home of the Opera House. The upscale hotels are in the Central Business District (CBD) section surrounding the waterfront. The best deals are in "The Cross" or Kings Cross. It can be a bit intimidating with its nighttime clientele, and if you are planning to walk everywhere it might not be the best location. I don't mind the local celebrities or the walk, and you can get a suite for under AU $100 a night. Several specific options are provided in the Sydney Section, and the standard chains are also available.

MELBOURNE:

The walking tours are best started in the CBD. I like the hotels on Little Collins Street as they are central to everything. It is a very walkable town, and the trolleys can ease the feet if you choose to ride a bit. The road trips can be done from the city, but you may want to do a couple of overnighters when you drive. There are plenty of B&Bs and hotels along the way, and chain hotel/motels are also an option in the city and beyond. A few recommendations are made, if you trust me mates.

QUEENSLAND:

The large state of Queensland has been divided into six different sections to make the tours easy, safe, and enjoyable. To avoid sensory overload, the trips are clustered in very user-friendly areas with comfortable lodging options. The Brisbane & Surrounds, Gold Coast & Hinterlands, Southeast Queensland & Northern New South Wales, and the Sunshine Coast tours can all be based from either Brisbane or the Gold Coast. The choice depends on your interest in staying in a city environment or desire to enjoy your evening sundowner drink with the ocean waves breaking in the background. Either base is great. My pick would be the sandy one at the Gold Coast, but the most centrally based is from Brisbane.

Alternatively, accommodations have been included if you choose to stay two days or more in a local touring area. It depends on your interests, time schedules, budget, and lifestyles.

GETTING TO THE BASE RESORTS

All of the base cities listed have access to Australian airlines, trains, and buses. The best way to see the cities and the areas between is to drive, but this is a time-consuming effort. The rail is fantastic, but rather expensive. Check Out Country Link Trains at **W**: countrylink.info or ☎ 13-22-32 for prices. The preferred method is to fly to the major cities like Sydney, Melbourne, and Brisbane, and drive from those hubs. Ask your travel agent about a **Boomerang Pass** or **One World Air Pass** that offers a comprehensive list of options to fly, at will, around the country. See **Qantas** at ☎ 13-13-13, **W**: qantas.com.au or **Virgin Blue** at ☎ 13-67-89 domestic, ☎ 617-3295-2296 international, **W**: virginblue.com.au. You can do a cost comparison of flights on **W**: bigpond.com (under TRAVEL), or News Interactive at **W**: newstravel.com.au, or at **W**: ninemsn.com.au (under TRAVEL).

For the high rollers, there is an all-inclusive private aircraft charter available through **Bill Peach Aircruising**. You can book the AU $10,000+ trips at ☎ 1-800-252-053 or on **W**: billpeachjourneys.com.au

Another option is to **Go Greyhound** using their **Aussie Explorer Pass** or **Aussie Kilometer Pass** programs. The Explorer allows a pre-set and unlimited number of stops, free tours along the way, for a minimum of 48 days, traveling in one direction, for AU $2403. The Kilometer Pass allows an unlimited itinerary by purchasing from 1,242-12,420 miles (2,000-20,000 kilometers) in advance, is good for 12 months, and the cost is based on the number of miles purchased. Right now a Reef & Rock tour from Sydney to the Barrier Reef and to Ayers rock (approximately 9,800 kilometers) is AU $1,106. Check them out on **W**: greyhound.com.au. Catalogues with services and prices can be obtained at most bus stations.

If you do decide to drive, check out **W**: webcarhire.com to compare the rates of the major and unadvertised rental agencies. Many young

European travelers come here and buy a used car instead, and that may be the best way to get out there.

Specific airport and shuttle information on each base is provided in that section of the guide.

ACCOMMODATIONS

Most of the major hotel and motel chains are represented in Australia. If you have memberships with any of them you will be able to use them throughout the country. I recommend several options in each area from hostel to top-of-the-line lodging (where available). If you come to really see and feel the country, I strongly suggest that you stay in a pub or two during your travels. They are commonly a good value (around AU $80 a night), are quiet and have great counter meals. B&Bs are also available, which I prefer to the chain hotels. You can get a good B&B package for about AU $120. If you can find a copy, use the RACQ guides, and if you stay in the three-star range, you will get a comfortable stay for around AU $100 a night.

If you like to travel on a wing and a prayer you can get some great deals. Check out this website: **Last Minute Accommodation** at **W**: wotif.com.au, E-mail on Info@wotif.com, or ☎ 1-300-88-7979 or (07) 3839-7979.

CHOOSING DESTINATIONS

With over fifty trips to choose from, and numerous attractions for each location, deciding which might be the most enjoyable might be a worry. You could read through the entire guide and dog-ear the crocodile farms, koala parks, and nature reserves, but there's and easier way mates. Just turn to the index at the back of the book and check out the special interest categories set in **BOLD FACE** type. Things like Museums, Rainforests, Outback, Hiking Trails, Adventure Tours, Beaches and the like will be listed for you. Another option is to select attractions in the same area to customize your trip, suiting what you came to see. Use the maps in the book as a rough guide and check out the stuff you find on the Internet and in the brochures that you pick up along the way (see the website section and the references to the information booths in each area). Some of the trips are designed as **SCENIC DRIVES**, and that's what they are designed for. They are set up as a relaxing day in the car or bus to soak up the beauty of the rainforests, Outback, or cityscapes. You can redesign them to stop off in an area, and explore on foot when you find something that peaks your interests. As the Aussies say, it's "easy-peasy mate" and "she'll be right."

GETTING AROUND

Directions for each walking and driving trip assume that you are leaving from each of the base cities, towns, or resorts listed. Even if you choose to pick another location, it will be easy to find your bearings by referring to the maps provided.

The route maps scattered throughout the book show you approximately where the sites are, and which main roads lead to them. In many cases, however, you'll still need a good up-to-date road map. An excellent choice are the free/low-cost maps (free to some AAA members or a nominal fee of AU $15.00 for non-members) found at the RACQ outlets in most shopping areas. Also check with the car rental agencies, and all Yellow Pages books have detailed local maps that are quite good. But when asking for those types of maps, they are called a "refadex."

There is a mix of walking and driving included in this guide, providing you with a great deal of flexibility and mobility. Public transportation is good in Australia, and the tours are also a great alternative to making long drives. The tour bus drivers are usually quite interesting. These "Coach Captains" may entertain you with Aussie songs, colorful narratives, and encourage the riders to meet each other. Each section of the book lists reputable tour companies that can show you the sights.

Domestic planes, because the competition is limited, is pricey, as is rail travel. Taxicabs and buses are a good deal though. If you need a cab and have lots of gear, or if you require special attention like wheel chair accessibility, ask for a maxi taxi. Since most cities are on or near the water, water taxis are easy to find; the price ranges vary from city to city.

A fun way to get around Sydney is the monorail system, and Melbourne has a great tram program. Brisbane features the CityCat taxis that can glide you up and down the Brisbane River to many of your destinations.

FOOD AND DRINK

Don't believe the horror stories about food in Australia. Yes, you can eat kangaroo, emu, or bugs if you like, but the choices include fine dining to pub counter meals. Both are quite good, and don't forget the fish & chip shops when you're here. Each area of the country has it's own specialties, and all have delicious seafood treats. Pub meals are similar to food you might get in diners, but with the added bonus of a beer or wine to wash the hearty meal down with. Standard fare in all areas is the major fast food giants found around the world. Ethnic foods are abundant and offer a full range of choices. The major hotels offer foods that are familiar, ranging from inexpensive to very costly. With the dollar going so far, why not splurge a bit? But don't miss out on the local foods and sample Fusion foods—a mix of cultural tastes blended into an Aussie plate worth trying.

For the cost-conscious traveler, no worries. There are free barbeques in most towns and cities, which are heavily used. The Australians delight in the outdoors, and you will meet a few fair dinkum mates if you decide to throw a few prawns on the barbie. Snags (sausages) are the favorite grilled food, and it is common for picnickers to slide a sausage into a piece of white bread slathered with butter and loaded with onions. One word of warning though—the meats can be a bit gamey in taste, so try some first to see if you like it.

Drink is also varied and plentiful in Australia. Actually, that's an under-statement. If you like beer, you will be in heaven. If you want to blend in, don't order the obvious brand, but ask for Fourex (XXXX is the Budweiser of Oz), Crown Lager (think Michelob), Cascade (Molson), or VB (Victoria Bitter). Wine is inexpensive and delightful. You can get a good bottle of white for under US $7, and red for just a little more. Local wines are get-ting popular and though they are good, I personally prefer the Western Australia and South Australian brands.

Restaurants, cafés, pubs, and fast food establishments are listed in each section. At each information center, at the concierge desks, and in most resorts there is a brochure or two listing all the best spots to eat. The approximate price ranges are shown as:

$ – Inexpensive.
$$ – Reasonable.
$$$ –   Luxurious and expensive.
X: – Days closed.

PRACTICALITIES

SYDNEY WEATHER:

Sydney is moderately warm in summer (remembering that seasons are reversed south of the equator) and cool in winter, sort of like San Francisco. The breeze off the harbor can make it a bit cooler around the Quay area, but it is fairly constant throughout the city. Average tempera-tures in the winter are around 50°F (10°C) and summer hover around 71°F (22°C). If you venture out into the Blue Mountains, it is considerably cool-er.

Sydney's regional average temperatures are:

September – November	(Spring)	56°–72° F	(13°–22° C)
December – February	(Summer)	65°–78°F	(18°–26°C)
March – May	(Autumn)	58°–72°F	(14°–22°C)
June – August	(Winter)	47°–63°F	(9°–17°C)

MELBOURNE WEATHER:

I can't say it often enough, the weather in Melbourne is wacky. I compare it to Boston's weather with less snow. The good news is that it is an easy topic to start a conversation, and will always get a shake of the head or fatalistic smile. It is a great place to show off the winter gear, but shorts are not a typical piece of attire even in the middle of summer.

Melbourne's regional average temperatures are:

September – November	(Spring)	49°–67° F	(9°–19° C)
December – February	(Summer)	57°–78°F	(13°–25°C)
March – May	(Autumn)	52°–69°F	(11°–20°C)
June – August	(Winter)	44°–58° F	(6°–14°C)

QUEENSLAND WEATHER:

The temperatures listed below are relevant to Brisbane, Gold Coast, Southeast Queensland & Northern New South Wales, and the Sunshine Coast. The coastal areas are usually a few degrees cooler and the temperature gradually increases as you work your way north. The average water temperature in the Gold Coast area is 70°F (22°C). Being subtropical, the southern cities are humid in the summer and cooler and dryer in the winter months.

For the interior trips of Queensland and Outback adventures, you should refer to the sections for specific guidelines. It gets dry and unbearably hot in summer, and rainy between January and March. Cairns is much warmer and very humid, depending on the season. You will want to avoid the area in autumn when the county's heaviest rainfalls come in torrents and cyclones warnings are common.

Brisbane's regional average temperatures are:

September – November	(Spring)	59°–77° F	(15°–25° C)
December – February	(Summer)	68°–83°F	(20°–32°C)
March – May	(Autumn)	61°–77°F	(16°–25°C)
June – August	(Winter)	52°–70°F	(11°–21°C)

OPENING TIMES, FEES, and FACILITIES:

Australia has a more laid-back approach, even when it comes to tourism. Be sure to look at the times of operation under each section, and it would be a good idea to call ahead if you have a long drive to an attraction. Check the **PUBLIC HOLIDAYS** section page 383 too; there are holidays like Boxing Day and the Queen's Birthday that may interfere with your plans.

The same rule applies to entrance fees. The costs were accurate when the book went to press, but prices do change. Admission fees are reasonable, especially when you consider the strength of the currency you bring down with you. Look for discount coupons in travel brochures and in the newspapers. On your road trips don't worry too much about keeping change handy, as there are few toll roads. If the museum or park requests a "gold coin donation," that means a gold one-dollar or two-dollar coin. It does truly help to keep the volunteer and locally sponsored places open.

Special facilities offered at each location are listed in italics in each section. The websites listed will also provide information if assistance is available. Telephone numbers are indicated by the symbol ☎, Internet addresses are designated with a **W**, and wheelchair accessibility is shown with a ♿. To reduce your need to remember the area codes for each area, they are included as part of the number as two digits shown in parentheses.

SAFETY:

Each section will list particular safety issues, especially when it comes to potentially dangerous wildlife and weather conditions. If you use common sense, there is very little danger of jeopardizing your safety. The nationwide emergency phone number is 000 (not 911).

WEATHER: The rule of thumb is to always keep water on hand and hydrate even if you aren't thirsty. The heat is different here, though you may not notice a problem early. If you are anywhere other than the coastline, remember the layer thing. The temperature may change quickly, and you will enjoy the adventure more if you're comfortable.

CRITTERS: Respect them and they will generally respect you. It's as simple as that. The general rule is that if you don't see an Aussie doing something (like swimming at dusk, wandering off of hiking paths, or poking sticks in holes)—don't try it unless you ask a local if it's safe. Warnings of particular hazards are listed in each section if applicable.

WATER: If you swim between the flags that are posted on the beaches, you are safe. If you decide to swim in un-patrolled areas (and I really would not advise this) don't swim alone, and it would be best if you stayed in water not over your head. Read the signs at each beach and heed the warnings.

SUN: They don't call it the sunburnt land for nothing. Even if you have a good base tan, you can get burned if you don't use block. You actually get a better tan with block on. Listen to the radio for reports on UV levels and believe them. The slogan to be safe in the sun is Slip (on a shirt), Slop (sunscreen), Slap (a hat). Add sunglasses and you will be golden.

DRIVING: Seat belts are the law—as is not using mobile phones while driving. Both great ideas, especially since you will be on the opposite side of the road, cruising in kilometers, and reading road signs that are comical as well as informative. Car theft is real as in any country, so it is best to keep valuables in the boot (trunk) and out of sight.

CONSERVATION:

Remember you are a visitor and respect the land, water, and people. Water is a valuable resource here; do not waste or pollute it. If you smoke, please dispose of the butts properly. In some areas the fines are substantial if you are caught littering. Any of the World Heritage and conservation reserves are posted with rules and guidelines to preserve the sites. Again, please use common courtesy when visiting and don't pocket coral, plants, or any protected objects.

HANDICAPPED TRAVELERS:

Though not quite as accommodating as it should be, Australia is moving to make it easier for disabled travelers. The cities are generally easily accessible, while the interior areas are a bit more of a challenge. Attractions equipped with handicapped facilities are indicated with a &. If in doubt, call ahead or check with the front desk at your accommodation. The travel guide "Easy Access Australia" gives an in-depth review of handicapped services. Also **W**: toiletmap.gov.au provides a complete nationwide listing of public toilets.

TRAVELING WITH CHILDREN:

Make sure the kids are comfortable, first and foremost. Have plenty of water on hand along with sun protection. Most resorts have recreation for the young ones and are pretty good about making all ages comfortable. Some B&Bs and resorts discourage kids, so make sure you mention that you have children when booking ahead. Caravan (trailer/mobile home) parks have the best facilities for children, and pubs are probably the least favorable spot to choose. Some of the drives between locations can be long and tedious, so pack books and games for the kids. A good way to keep them entertained is to rent or borrow books on tape; you can all listen to a good story.

GROUP TRAVEL:

Group rates are available and most sites require an advanced booking to take advantage of the specials. Several attractions offer special tours if you call ahead asking for a group excursion. You will get extra treats if you travel in groups, as many areas will set up specialized demonstrations and events for you. Check with the web sites provided and E-mail ahead if you can plan in advance.

TAXES:

The prices listed in the book are the actual price, but are subject to change. The most notable tax is the Goods and Services Tax or GST, which varies from product to product. Most bookings, rentals, and food list the actual price with the GST included. There are now levies being attached to airline tickets, and there are some airport departure taxes. But don't expect too many hidden taxes to surprise you.

SUGGESTED TOURS

Two different approaches are provided to make your daytrips varied and more enjoyable. You may want to alter the methods laid out, but they have been selected based on the best way to see the most. The first, structured itineraries follow a planned walking, driving, cycling, or touring routes. The second, allowing you to pick and choose the attractions that suit you the best, is set up to just describe the local attractions. Either way you go, a detailed area map is provided to help the assigned navigator easily find your favorites.

Major attractions are described in a condensed format and pack details in a few paragraphs. Practical information is listed first to allow you to decide on how to best approach the visit. Additional sites are blended into the same section and offer more options to add or delete as time permits. All are arranged in a logical geographic sequence, and practical information is highlighted in italics.

Walking tours, where used, are easily defined on the accompanying map. Times and level of effort are indicated in each section. You can estimate the endeavor by calculating your fitness level against the distances on the scaled maps. The average person walks about 100 yards a minute or three miles an hour on a flat surface. The terrain is noted if there is a strenuous walk planned.

I have purposely included plenty of sites and interesting things to see at each location, so don't feel as though you have to see everything listed. Enjoy the tours by selecting the attractions that interest you the most. The guide is adaptable to individual tastes, and a variety of activities allow you to skip or add things as you go. No worries mate! And if you miss something, it's a good excuse to visit again.

Practical information, like prices and hours of operation, was spot on at the time of writing, but do verify the data if it will adversely impact your journeys.

*OUTSTANDING ATTRACTIONS:

An *asterisk before any attraction, either an entire daytrip or just one section of a trip, highlights a unique spot that is highly recommended. Some are out-of-the-way places offering a unique perspective of Australia that will remain one of your fondest memories. A few are the standard Aussie icons that must be seen. But both types are designed to give you a different perspective, a deeper understanding of the people and the culture of this wild and wonderful country.

VISITOR INFORMATION

Up-front research can mean the difference between just seeing a place or really experiencing it. The addresses, phone numbers and Internet sites selected in each section will allow you to get the full benefit from this journey. The **TOURIST INFORMATION** section provides a list of relevant sources of information. In addition, the information centers listed throughout the book will direct you to a wealth of free brochures, maps, and helpful hints from the locals.

Section II

Daytrips Within Sydney

Welcome to Australia's front door, the showcase of the country, and the harborside city that offers a freewheeling experience. The sights, history, food, and people will be an eye-opening adventure. There is so much to do, see, hear, and taste in Sydney that you are in danger of sensory overload. The tours listed will help you through the most popular, famous, and out-of-the-way spots. If you combine Plymouth Rock (first settlers) and San Francisco (city with spunk) you have Sydney.

In 1770 Captain Cook discovered the harbor, and in 1788 the first settlers landed. From there it has been an interesting ride for a city with a diverse population, a fresh-scrubbed look, and a very casual atmosphere.

Australia's largest city and the capital of New South Wales, Sydney is also a very walkable town. The strolls will allow you to brush elbows with many ethnic groups, and your ears will pick up exotic languages. Sydney is Australia's pride and joy, enticing many to visit. The 2000 Olympics created a spruced-up center city, and a tour of that internationally famous Olympic Park will be included in this section. The Eighth Wonder of the World is also highlighted, and you can easily spend a whole day in the Sydney Opera House. Remnants of the convict era are prevalent, the beaches are magnificent, and museums and galleries are top notch. But most of all, it's just a fun place to tour.

Despite being almost 700 square miles in size, the city can be properly explored by dividing the tours into the sections below. Most journeys will be on foot, but ferries, monorails, and buses will be part of the experience. The duration of the trips will be determined by how much you want to see on each, but plan on a day for each trip and add another for recovery. Here are the main areas of the Central Business District (CBD): The Harbour—This is Sydney's claim to fame and is boasted to be the best harbor in the world. It has a bay shoreline of 15 miles and is home to the Opera House. City Centre—The CBD, or Central Business District, is loaded with museums, plush garden walks populated with ibis, and Victorian-style buildings. The business section of town is on a rise overlooking the harbor. The Rocks and Circular Quay—This is the cove where the 11 convict ships docked in 1788 and a nation was begun. The Rocks area is dotted with convict cottages, warehouses, and cafés. The Quay (pronounced *key*), a man-made landing to which ships are tied for transferring goods, is home to the visitors center and is adjacent to the harbor. Paddington—The farthest city region from the harbor, it boasts some of the prettiest houses in the city and is the hub of the fashion district. Darling Harbour—This second harbor of the city is wrapped around Cockle Bay and is the entertainment center with IMAX, the Sydney Aquarium, Chinese Gardens, Powerhouse Museum, and the Maritime Museum. Manly and the Northern Beaches—A favorite beach escape for the city dwellers and visitors alike. Kings Cross, Bondi and the Eastern Suburbs—The Cross is the most famous nightspot in the country. It is a magnet for the gay population. Bondi *(Bon-dye)* and the Eastern Suburbs are home to the chic—and to the most expensive real estate in the country. The Olympic Village—A futuristic complex of sports stadiums and the home of the 2000 Olympics.

GETTING TO SYDNEY:

By Car: If you're driving from **Brisbane**, it's a good 2–3 day drive of 621 miles, providing a nice mix of stops along the way including the famous Big Banana at Coffs Harbour. From **Melbourne**, it's 554 miles along the rough-and-tumble Tasman Sea and past the capital of Canberra or across the mountains on the Hume Highway (Route 31).

By Bus: If you want to give it a go, call one of the two primary Australian bus lines: Greyhound Pioneer, ☎ 13-20-30 or **W**: greyhound.com.au; and McCafferty's, ☎ 13-14-99 or **W**: mccaffertys.com.au. The booking agent for both transportation organizations is **Travel Coach Australia** on ☎ 13-14-99.

By Train: Country Link, ☎ 13-22-32 or **W**: countrylink.info, is the train service around Australia. The fares to/from Brisbane (15 hours) and Melbourne (11 hours)are about AU $110 for a full-fare adult. There are 7 & 14-day discounts that are offered for around AU $66/$55.

By Plane: QANTAS, ☎ 13-13-13 or **W**: qantas.com.au, is the primary airline; and **Virgin Blue**, ☎ 13-67-89 domestic, ☎ 617-3295-2296 international, or **W**: virginblue.com.au, is the discount airline. Fares fluctuate weekly and specials run frequently, so check ahead and book early to save a few quid. The ride from the airport to downtown is only about six miles and about AU $40. There are taxis, buses, and Airport Link trains that run regularly into town. Airport Express buses can be arranged at ☎ 13-15-00 and Hotel Buses can be contacted on ☎ (02) 9666-9988.

GETTING AROUND:

The main contact numbers for all city transport is ☎ 13-15-00 or **W**: 131500.com.au. There is a **Sydney Pass** available for a three-day unlimited use of the buses, ferries, and trains for around AU $90 adult / AU $45 children. This does not include the harbor cruises. There are also packages that include Travel Ten (ten bus rides for AU $11.30-$39.80), Ferry Ten (ten boat rides for AU $26.50-$55.80), Travel Pass (7-day all-transport pass for AU $30-$64.50), Bus Tripper (all-day bus pass for AU $9.70), and the Day Tripper (all-day/all-transport for AU $21.20). The overall choices are fantastic in town with all major car rentals available—**Avis** on ☎ (02) 8374-2870, **Hertz** on ☎ (02) 9669-2444, **Thrifty** on ☎ (02) 9582-1701, **Budget** on ☎ 13-28-48, **Delta Europcar** on ☎ 13-13-90, and **Red Spot** on ☎ (02) 9317-2233. Taxis can be hailed on the street or near the taxi ranks at Circular Quay, Wynyard Station (Carrington Street), and near Town Hall (Park Street). Cab companies include **ABC Taxis**, ☎ 13-25-22; **Legion Cabs**, ☎ 13-14-51; or **Taxis Combined Services**, ☎ (02) 9361-8222. The buses have a wide coverage, even to the beaches and suburbs. The **Sydney Ferries**, ☎ 13-15-00 or **W**: sydneyferries.nsw.gov.au, are stationed at Circular Quay and cover most of the water stops that might interest you. Trains are quick, clean, and usually on time. Bus and train route maps are available at any information center and are included in most of the visitor guides. The **Light Rail** is a new system that connects City Central to Darling Harbour, the Star City Casino, and the Sydney Fish Market. A cool way to get your bearing and to save the legs a bit is the above-ground **Monorail**, ☎ (02) 9552-2288 or **W**: metromonorail.com.au, with stops at the shopping centers, Darling Harbour, and the Peking duck restaurants of Chinatown. It costs about AU $9 for an all-day Supervalue pass, AU $22 for a family pass, and AU $4 for a one-loop trip. Kids under five are free. But the best mode of transportation, to get the real flavor of the town, is your own two legs.

ACCOMMODATIONS:

There are over twenty pages of Sydney accommodations listed in the Royal Automobile Club of Queensland guide, ☎ (07) 3361-2802 or **W**: racq.com.au. Included are: The five-star **Sheraton on the Park**, ☎ (02) 9286-6000 or **W**: sheraton.com, will set you back AU $370-450/night for a center city spot. The **Westin Sydney**, ☎ (02) 8223-1111 or **W**: westin.com, also in the middle of town, is a bit more reasonable with a five-star room costing about AU $236. The 3-1/2-star **TraveLodge Wentworth Avenue Sydney**, ☎ (02) 8267-1700 or **W**: travelodge.com.au, is at the far end of Hyde Park so it's a longer walk to the Harbour, but runs about AU $119-$149/night. Even the **YWCA's on the Park**, ☎ 1-800-994-994 or **W**: ywca-sydney.com.au, costs about AU $108-$132 per night. The **Crest Hotel**, ☎ (02) 9358-2755 or **W**: cresthotel.com.au, is a hike into a riskier neighborhood, but a B&B-style room costs only AU $110-$154. B&Bs include **Bed & Breakfast Sydney Harbour**, ☎ (02) 9247-1130 or **W**: bedandbreakfastsydney.com.au, at The Rocks B&B for AU $110-$185; or the 2-star guesthouse of Sydney Central Private Hotel, ☎ (02) 9212-1005, for AU $45-$150/night.

PRACTICALITIES:

This is a fun city to have a wander, and it's easy to get to most attractions. If you do tire out, just jump on any of the mass transit systems to save your energy for the nightlife. Good walking shoes, camera, and even sunscreen are a must. You are in the city now, and like every big city in the world, you need to be aware of your surroundings. It's relatively safe in this town, but there is an element of crime to be aware of. Remember that 000 is the phone number for an emergency. On the fun side of things, there are great beaches here, and Bondi is a must see. Just remember to swim between the flags and use sun protection. Also look in the free travel guides handed out at the information centers—they often offer discounted coupons (usually 15-20% off) for the attractions.

Before you arrive, here are a few good websites to check out: **W**: sydney.com.au for general tourist information, **W**: cityofsydney.nsw.gov.au is the city council's page, **W**: viewsydney.com.au is loaded with photos and highlights the major attractions, **W**: visitnsw.co.au for the state government tourism data and the "Sydney The Official Guide," **W**: sydney.sidewalk.com.au for the current events schedule, and **W**: sydneyforchildren.com.au for all the kid's stuff. **Tourism New South Wales** can be contacted at ☎ 13-20-77 or **W**: tourism.nsw.gov.au

When you arrive into town, the **Information Centres**, ☎ 13-20-77, are located at 106 George Street, in the middle of the Royal Botanic Gardens, at the Circular Quay Terminals, and on Macquarie Street. The best is at The Rocks on George Street, open 9–6 daily.

SPECIAL EVENTS:

January—Australia Day to celebrate the landing of Governor Arthur Phillip in 1788 (**W**: adc.nsw.gov.au); The Sydney Festival (**W**: sydneyfestival.org.au); February—Chinese New Year; April—The Sydney Royal Easter Show to unite the city and country (**W**: eastershow.com.au), School Holidays in Sydney from April 14–25, Good Friday celebrations (**W**: newadvent.org/cathen/00643a.htm), ANZAC Day (**W**: cultureandrecreation.gov.au/articles/anzac); March—The Gay & Lesbian Mardi Gras (**W**: mardigras.org.au) is one of the largest gay and lesbian celebration anywhere and is quite a party.

FOOD AND DRINK:

The list of eateries is endless, and you can find any ethnic food you desire. Look at **W**: eatstreets.com.au for listings or call ☎ (02) 9327-6088 for hints. There are over 50 eateries just in The Rocks section of town, over 95 in Central Sydney, bunches of them clustered around Darling Harbour, fantastic flavors in Chinatown, and heaps of choices around the beaches and suburbs. A fantastic place to enjoy modern Australian food with a view of the Opera House is the **Veranda at the Park** ($$), ☎ (02) 9256-1660, at 7 Hickson Road (for around AU $45). A little-advertised, but highly recommended by local Asian friends is the **BBQ King** ($), ☎ (02) 9267-2586, at 18-20 Goulburn Street. It's the best Peking duck I have ever sampled and the atmosphere is definitely spot on for eating this food—simple, hectic, crowded with Asian-speaking people, and the smell alone is heaven. In the center of the Royal Botanic Gardens, near Gallery & Hospital Roads on the footpath is the tree-house-style **Botanic Gardens Restaurant & Café**, ☎ (02) 9241-2419. They serve beautiful meals during the daytime hours and it's a good spot for a break when you are touring the central part of the city. At the top of the town are the two **Sydney Tower Restaurants** ($$–$$$), ☎ (02) 9233-3722, with casual or upscale à la carte choices. Both are revolving dining experiences 984 feet above the harbor.

The night scene is varied, and Kings Cross comes alive at night. There are lots of clubs and adult cabarets sprinkled amongst the hotels and restaurants. Most of the hotels have late night hours and some are very popular, like the Club Bar in the Park Hyatt Hotel on Hickson Road. There are over 66 pubs and bars listed in one of the local visitor's handbooks, so you will not go dry. This is in addition to the over 40 nightclubs and late night wine cafés in town.

SHOPPING:

First, check out **W**: sydney-shopping.com.au for an overview, then just go for it. Shopping is such a major attraction that it has been given a separate walking tour in the "City Map Guide—City Host." It really is too much to do in a single day (though it's claimed the hike can be covered in 3–4 hours). Here are some of the top spots: Top of the list is the **Queen Victoria Building**, ☎ (02) 9264-9209 or **W**: qvb.com.au, at the corner of George & Park Streets. You'll feel like you are in jolly old England, and the eateries are great too. Across the street is the fashionable **The Galleries Victoria**, ☎ (02) 9286-3742, for leading fashion brands. **Pitt Street Mall** on King Street is where the chain stores hang their shingles. **Westfield Centrepoint**, ☎ (02) 9231-9300 or **W**: westfield.com/centrepoint, houses the needle-shaped observation tower and over 120 specialty stores. **Castlereagh Street** is loaded with upscale designer shops, department stores, and gourmet foods. The **MLC Centre**, ☎ (02) 9224-8333, at the corner of King & Castlereagh Streets is a large and modern shopping mall with varied stores from souvenirs to Gucci. The **Chifley Plaza**, ☎ (02) 9221-4500 or **W**: chifleyplaza.com.au, on Hunter Street is the Tiffany's version of shopping so; take a large credit card to this marble mansion. At the **Strand Arcade**, ☎ (02) 9232-4199 or **W**: strandarcade.com.au, next to Pitt Street Mall is a three-story mall with stained glass 1890's décor. It's a good place to find unusual gifts. **Martin Place** is a mix of stores with free entertainment at noon. **The Skygarden**, ☎ (02) 9231-1811 or **W**: skygarden.com.au, on Pitt Street is a good place to shop and eat. **Piccadilly Centre**, ☎ (02) 9267-3666 or **W**: stockland.com.au, also on Pitt Street is a fun place to hang out and spend a few Aussie dollars. **Harbourside** is a waterfront-shopping mecca in Darling Harbour and is a great place to just hang out. **Paddy's Markets** at Thomas & Hay Streets is perfect to do some shopping for the trip home. **Market City**, also on Darling Harbour, is the factory outlet complex. Grace Brothers, ☎ (02) 9238-9111 or **W**: gracebros.com.au, at 436

George Street is fragrance central. And for the guys, try **Growings**, ☎ (02) 9287-6394 or **W**: growings.com, at the corner of Market & George Streets.

Most major shopping centers are open 9–6*ish* with extended hours on Thursday nights. Craft markets are as follows: **The Rocks Markets** on the weekends, **Paddington Markets** on Saturday, **Sydney's Paddy Markets** on Thursdays-Sundays, **Balimain Market** on Saturday, **Glebe Market** on Sunday, and the sandy **Bondi Markets** on Sunday at the beach.

Sydney Opera House and Harbour Ferry

Sydney Harbour

Considered the most famous harbor in the world (by Sydneysiders), the 15-mile shoreline and water-bound sites are best seen by ferry-boat. If the Opera House is the heart of the city, the harbor is its soul. The trip from Circular Quay into the depths of the protected harbor reveals the history and beauty held in this waterfront area. Cruise past the city's old fortifications, gape at the mansions of the rich and famous (including Cruise and Kidman's old hideaway), and learn about the nation's beginnings.

The entire trip will take only three hours and allows plenty of time to wander the shops along the water, have a relaxing tea break, or soak in the sun at the steps of the Opera House. You can shop or take in another trip. There are walking excursions listed in the many visitors' guides and most are only 1–3 hours in length.

GETTING THERE:

By Car: Leave the car behind. Parking is expensive and difficult to find.

By Bus: Hop any bus to the Circular Quay (Sydney Explorer bus stops 1, 2, 24, 25, 26).

By Train: The Monorail and the city train stop at the Circular Quay.

By Foot: Simply follow Elizabeth, Pitt, and George streets downhill towards the water and the Cahill Expressway. Most streets that drop to the harbor have a peek of the water, so it's fairly easy to find.

GETTING AROUND:

Captain Cook Cruises, ☎ (02) 9206-1111 or **W:** captaincook.com.au, offers 1– to 2-1/2 hour cruises with food and tea starting at AU $20. They are sleek boats and have a top deck for good viewing. Others include the **Aussie Duck,** ☎ 13-10-07, AU $55 adult, $30 child, $145 family; **Bounty Cruises** ☎ (02) 9247-1789 or **W:** tehbounty.com —private charters only, for a tall ship experience; **Harbour Jet,** ☎ 1-300-887-373 or **W:** harbourjet.com —AU $50/$35 to $90/$60 for adult/child tours, for smooth and fast cruising; James Craig, ☎ (02) 9266-4800; **Matilda Cruises** and **Sail Venture Cruises,** ☎ (02) 9264-7377 or **W:** matilda.com.au —AU $20.50-$94.50; **Oz Jet Boating,** ☎ (02) 9808-3700 or **W:** ozjetboating.com —AU $45) for a thrill ride on the harbor; **Sydney Showboats,** ☎ (02) 9552-2722, AU $58-$99 lunch cruise or

AU $99-$175 for dinner rides; and **Vagabond Cruises,** ☎ (02) 9660-0388, AU $ 25 coffee cruise, AU $42 lunch, AU $66 dinner tour. Most harbor cruises can be booked through **Australian Travel Specialists** on ☎ (02) 9211-3192.

PRACTICALITIES:

Sunglasses and a hat are a good idea. There will be strolling on most tours, and this will put the least amount of wear on your walking shoes. The boat cruise is calm, but often windy. If you have a telephoto lens for your camera — take it along.

There are a bunch of competing cruise operators; the best advice is for you to walk along the Circular Quay and check the billboards that list the times, costs, and lengths of the tours. Let your schedule and pocket-book dictate the trip you want. For a quick overview, try the 1-1/2- hour Morning or Afternoon Harbour Cruise on the **Sydney Ferries,** ☎ 13-15-00 or **W**: sydneyferries.nsw.gov.au. There is an evening cruise also, but do the daytime version first. The prices range from AU $15 adults/$7.50 kids for the morning cruise, AU $22/$11 for afternoon cruises, and AU $19/$9.50 for evening rides. You get the feel of being close to the water, and even though the sound system might be a bit cranky, it's informative and enjoyable. The tour outlined below is based on that operator.

FOOD AND DRINK:

If you enjoy the hustle and bustle, you can graze along the waterfront at the many cafés, fast-food eateries, fine restaurants, and food offered on the cruise tours. For a more sophisticated approach, there are five pleasant culinary spots right at the Sydney Opera House. The Rocks also has a fine selection of eateries, but we will catch them later.

LOCAL ATTRACTIONS:

Circled numbers correspond to numbers on the map.

The tour boat operator will identify the attractions on this ride. These are some of the sights to soak in from the bow of the ship:

The journey begins at the **Circular Quay** ❶ — the hub of the water traffic and tours. It is nestled in a small inlet called Sydney Cove. Located at the bottom of the business district, it's the heart of many of the public transportation systems. Enjoy the street and sidewalks loaded with street musicians, mimes, and a mish-mash of interesting sights. After boarding the ship, you will cruise eastward towards Watsons Bay, pass the **Sydney Opera House** ❷, and duck in near the Botanical Gardens. The Opera House from this vantage point is the one seen in most of the glossy magazines; much more impressive up close. The next and most impressive historical site on the voyage is the tiny island in the middle of the Sydney Harbour called **Fort Denison** ❸. It's a brown rock that was used as a prison for the most dangerous of convicts, about a half-acre in size with fortified brown stonewalls to keep the waves from flooding the cells. No one ever escaped alive, and it was called Pinch Gut by the unlucky residents

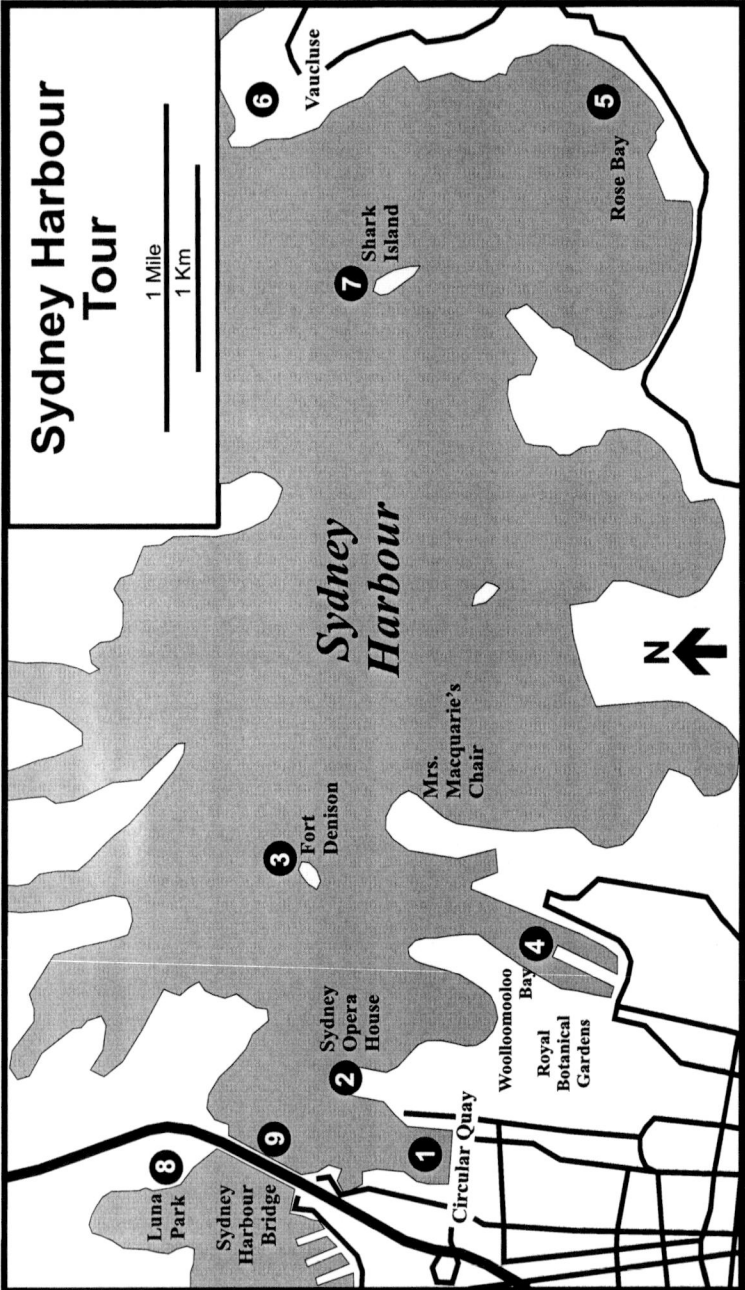

Sydney Harbour Tour

1 Mile
1 Km

Sydney Harbour

N

- 1 Circular Quay
- 2 Sydney Opera House
- 3 Fort Denison
- 4 Woolloomooloo Bay — Royal Botanical Gardens
- 5 Rose Bay
- 6 Vaucluse
- 7 Shark Island
- 8 Luna Park — Sydney Harbour Bridge
- 9

Mrs. Macquarie's Chair

because they had to tighten their belts due to extreme hunger and pinched what was left of their guts. One historic character was sentenced to hang from the gallows on that awful place and he was noted as saying, "That's alright lads, I like the view of the harbor from here." Because of his impertinence, the guards left him hang there for three years and the yardarm stands today!

Around the point and past Mrs. Macquarie's Chair, the cruise will take you along the little inlet called **Woolloomooloo Bay** ❹ or Garden Cove, home to the Royal Australian Navy. The harbor is usually lined with gray ships being tended by the largest crane in the Southern Hemisphere. This huge tinker toy towers over the boats and appears to be guarding the navy's ships.

The PA system will tell the story of the USS *Chicago* being sunk in the harbor by a Japanese mini-sub, and points out sights like Tom Cruise and Nicole Kidman's former house on the cliffs near **Rose Bay** ❺. **Vaucluse** ❻ is dotted with cliff-side houses and includes the one owned by the Bushell Tea Company. They are priced in the AU $30 million range and look it—constructed of stone and brick, some are covered in ivy, and all have lavish verandas, complete with porcelain-white statues that welcome guests at the water's edge.

Passing **Shark Island** ❼, originally set up as a quarantine station for animals entering Australia. It's now a nature reserve fondly known as the island that sunk the American Cup winner Dennis Connor. After Connor won the US Cup he good-naturedly challenged the Aussies to a race around Shark Island. The Aussies, knowing the underwater terrain, lured Connor in close to the island, and his boat ran aground. That spit of ground is now called Connor Island.

Nearing the end of the cruise you will pass by the **Luna Park** ❽ amusement park on the far shore. The park is a fanciful sight from the western bank with a large, wide-eyed clown grinning a welcome to the visitors, along with a multi-colored Ferris wheel and Disney-like rides packed into a small area. Finally you will see the underbelly of the widest bridge in the world—the **Sydney Harbour Bridge** ❾. The bridge is a network of girders, beams, and rivets. The first of the 1,400 construction workers arrived in 1920, and the ribbon was cut on March 19, 1932. Of those workers, 16 died in accidents during construction, but more of that later.

The Rocks and The Bridge

This is a flashback tour of the colony as it was back in the early 1800s. You can almost hear the ghostly groans as the convicts haul the goods from ships and lug them onto the wharf. Walking amongst the narrow streets and smelling the salt air will set the stage for an interesting tour of Sydney's beginnings.

This oldest part of Sydney is also the most visited section of town. It has in recent times undergone a major renovation to its Old World status. But it does have a wonderful mix of new and old with flashy modern cafés sitting next to historic brick facades. If you have read any of the historical accounts of this area, it was vividly described as a place to avoid in the early days. It was home to waterfront thugs, diseases ran rampant through the population, and prostitution was the main occupation. Described as dark and dangerous, it had a magnetic draw on the adventuresome.

Starting at the Rocks Heritage and Information Centre, your wanderings will pass old merchant homes, seamen's cottages, beautiful aromas wafting from old pub windows, and a unique view of the Sydney Harbour Bridge. For the daring, there are tours to the top of the latter.

When exploring this section of town, you might learn more than you want about the Sydney Harbor Bridge. Here are a few trivia facts: Prior to the bridge being built, the only arteries to keep the city alive were a ferry from the north and a 12-mile road with five separate bridges. The structure is supported by solid sandstone on each bank and is fastened by cable anchored in solid rock. The arch is 550 yards in length, was built in two spans, has 128 steel cables supporting it, and has hinges at each end to allow the metal to flex in the wind and to accommodate temperature changes. To pay for the £6.2 million building cost, the original toll was set at 6 pence for a car and 3 pence for a horse and rider. Tolls have been increased to cover the annual 5-million-dollar maintenance cost. The bridge is a dark blue/gray and is constantly being painted as it takes exactly one year to put on a layer of paint of 21,000 gallons; and by then it needs another coat. The Aussies have nicknamed the structure The Great Coat Hanger, and it does look like a metal hanger. Finally, Paul Hogan did a stint at painting the bridge before his Crocodile Dundee movie days.

GETTING THERE:

By Car: Don't even think of it.

By Bus: Hop any bus to the Circular Quay (Sydney Explorer bus stops 1, 2, 24, 25, 26).

By Train: The Monorail and the city train stop at The Rocks.

By Foot: Simply follow Elizabeth, Pitt, and George streets downhill towards the water and the Cahill Expressway. Most streets that angle towards the harbor have a peek of the water, so it's fairly easy to find. At the waterfront, turn left and then right onto Circular Quay West at First Fleet Park.

PRACTICALITIES:

There will be lots of walking on this tour, so wear good walking shoes. Most of the areas will be shaded with a fair amount of time spent indoors. But if you decide on the Sydney Bridge Climb, book well in advance. You need to be fit, are not bothered by strenuous climbing, or fearful of heights. It takes three hours for the climb; those who have taken it find it exhilarating.

Check out **W**: therocks.com for more information on the rocks and **W**: pylonlookout.com.au, **W**: bridgeclimb.com for bridge data.

FOOD AND DRINK:

This might become your favorite spot to munch. The restaurants are cozy and serve interesting Australasian and standard European fare with seafood as the main focus. Pick one of the small eateries along the wharf and enjoy the scenery too.

LOCAL ATTRACTIONS:

Circled numbers correspond to numbers on the map. Note: An alternative to this self-guided tour is the 1-1/2-hour narrated tour starting at Kendall Lane. Call The Rocks Walking Tour group at ☎ (02) 9247-6678 for times and prices (now costing AU $17.50 and running every two hours between 10:30-2:30).

Starting at the ***Sydney Visitor Centre ❶**, ☎ (02) 9255-1788, 106 George Street, you will find this 1864 old sailor's home one of the best spots to grab your tourist guides. Open daily from 9–6, you can book tours, find accommodations, and buy "The Rocks Self-Guided Tour" walking guide for a mere AU $2.20. This heritage stroll describes 31 different historically significant sites. Backtracking on Circular Quay West, just across the steps in the park, you can check out the 1816 cottage that houses Sydney Harbour National Parks. You can book tours of the harbor islands at **Cadman's Cottage ❷** as you get the feel for this oldest residence in the city. When you exit the building, take a short walk towards the mooring spaces of the giant cruise ships at the **Harbourfront ❸**. From this spot you can get some great portrait shots of the Sydney Opera House. When your happy

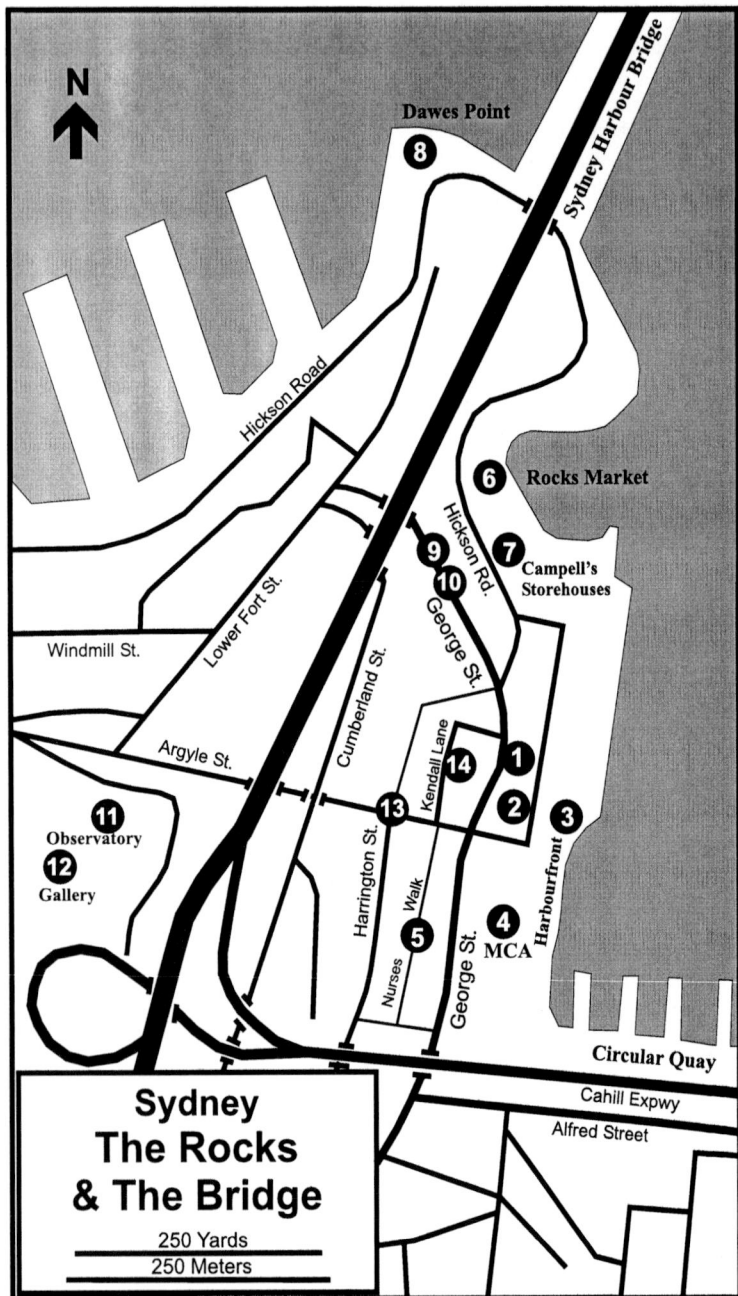

N

Dawes Point

8

Sydney Harbour Bridge

Hickson Road

6 Rocks Market

9
7 Campell's
10   Storehouses

Hickson Rd.

Lower Fort St.

George St.

Windmill St.

Cumberland St.

Argyle St.

Kendall Lane

14 1

13 2

11   3
Observatory

12

Gallery

Harrington St.

Nurses Walk

5

4 MCA

George St.

Harbourfront

Circular Quay

Cahill Expwy

Alfred Street

Sydney
The Rocks
& The Bridge

250 Yards
250 Meters

snaps are completed, enter the four levels of the *Museum of Contemporary Art or MCA ❹, ☎ (02) 9241-5892 or W: mca.com.au, between 10–5 daily, free. The 1930's Art Deco building is a mix of paintings, film, and multimedia exhibits to delight the lover of fine art.

Looping around the First Fleet Park, climb the steps near George Street and turn right to pass some of the neatest historical sites along Nurses Walk ❺. This narrow lane on the site of the first hospital in Sydney is now loaded with bistros, galleries, and gift shops. The long block includes an old seaman's chapel, one of the first police stations, the Australian Steamship Navigation Company, and The Rocks Market ❻ for fantastic souvenirs at Campell's Cove. Don't be surprised to be greeted by fanciful street musicians along the way. Next up is a stroll past Campell's Storehouses ❼ — the old warehouses that once stored sealskins and whale oils. Here Sydney's tall ship the HMAV *Bounty* is moored and ready for a tour. Continue along Hickson Road, under the bridge, and past Dawes Point 8. This former bastion of defense for the city with cannons from the First Fleet is now a grassy park with vistas that scan the harbor. Right near the Sydney Harbour Bridge on Cumberland and behind George Street is the *Harbour Bridge Exhibition & Pylon Lookout ❾, ☎ (02) 9247-3408 or W: pylonlookout.com.au. Climb the 200 steps, located at Observatory Hill (not accessible from Dawes Point Park), to one of the best views in the city. It costs AU $5 adult, AU $3 for 4-12 year olds, free for the younger ones. But before you do this one, try the 20-minute walk across the bridge to the north side and back. The only better view is on the tour to the top of the bridge and the *BridgeClimb ❿, ☎ (02) 8274-7777 or W: bridgeclimb.com. This hike takes three hours and is not for the meek. The trip includes safety gear, a jumpsuit, and narrative along the way. It is featured on many travel shows. The tour operates daily from 7–7 (weather permitting), with prices ranging from AU $100–$175 depending on day and time. See them at 5 Cumberland Street to book.

You may require a rest after the bridge tour, so why not stop at any of the cafés that caught your eye and have a sweet and a cuppa, or proceed to the highest point of the city called Observatory Park. There you can enter the site of an old fort and the see the colony's first windmill. It's now the home to the *Sydney Observatory ⓫, ☎ (02) 9217-0485 or W: phm.gov.au, open from 10–5 daily. It's free during the day, but a fee does apply for night tours to view the galaxies in its interactive astronomy museum. While in the area you can have tea and a browse in the S.H. Ervin Gallery ⓬, ☎ (02) 9258-0122 or W: nsw.nationaltrust.org.au

When you are refreshed, re-enter Argyle Street and head back towards Circular Quay. Turn right at Cumberland Street and left onto Gloucester Street until you arrive at the shopping area of Susannah Place ⓭ (open daily 10–5:30) and maybe have another sweet. It is also a museum depicting the realities of the working class in the early 1900s. Finally, you will end up on Kendall Lane at the Toy Museum and Puppet Cottage ⓮, ☎ (02) 9251-9793. You'll find it a fantastic place to get a gift for that special "child" in your life.

Sydney Central

The streetscape is actually the best attraction on this trip. Delve into the city and get a taste of this fresh vibrant lifestyle. This town does feel good, being a mix of business, street party, and sophistication. But the historical aspects are interesting and the harsh beginnings are often worn as a badge of honor for Sydney. The city, its parks and buildings all have a very British feel about them. The names will jog memories of the English influence like Hyde Park and the streets named after their kings and queens. This tour offers a blend of dark museums, airy art galleries, majestic government buildings, busy shopping complexes, and open-air parks. The museums, cathedrals, and art galleries will satisfy the urbanite in you, but the parks might be your preferred focus. The footpaths amongst the hustle and bustle will treat you to cool breezes, take you to the 1,000-foot golden Sydney Tower, past the Queen Victoria Building, amongst the over 200 boutique stores, and to the Aboriginal exhibit in the Australian Museum.

It can also be a chance for a shopping spree with choices of merchants to fill your suitcases with goodies. If you are not a shopper, go anyway as the buildings are truly amazing with ornate decorations and offering a regal approach to spending money.

The town does have defined rush hours; if you want to enjoy the city at a less busy pace, wait until after 9:30 to go out on the streets, and have a break around five in the afternoon to let the business crowds dissipate. But do try to find the giant bronze boar and give it a rub on its nose (think rum and hospitals).

This tour can be broken into several days if you wish, or simply pick and choose the attractions that most interest you. I would recommend at least one of each flavor—museum, art gallery, cathedral, and shopping mall. This will provide an overview of interests and if you find a favorite area or type of attraction, then proceed to others of a similar venue.

GETTING THERE:

If you are staying anywhere downtown, there is no need for a car, bus, or train. Put your feet into action. If you do get tired, just hail a cab at most any street corner.

PRACTICALITIES:

This is an urban tour with lots of pavement to cover and even more stops for food, coffee, or cold drinks,—and plenty of shady resting spots. It can get a bit steamy in the warmer months, so drink plenty of water as you soak in the city and hike to the attractions. Be a bit more wary at night, avoiding dark and vacant streets. Remember, this is a city with all of its advantages and trappings.

FOOD AND DRINK:

The city is your oyster, where you will have the pick of the best foods as well as quick meals on the street. Five highly recommended eateries include **Sydney Tower's** ($$-$$$) at the top of the AMP Building, ☎ (02) 9231-1000; **Banc** ($$-$$$) at 53 Martin Place, ☎ (02) 9233-5300 for French cuisine; the **CBD** ($$-$$$) at 75 York Street, ☎ (02) 9299-8911 for a bistro setting; **Forty One** ($$-$$$) on Chifley Square, ☎ (02) 9221-2500 for high-class dining; and **Café Sydney** ($), ☎ (02) 9251-8683 for casual eats.

LOCAL ATTRACTIONS:

Circled numbers correspond to numbers on the map. For convenience, the tours will be broken into three manageable sectors. The attractions will be clustered by location starting with the AMP Centrepoint Tower area, then the Queen Victoria Building trip, and the Royal Botanic Gardens walk. Pick from the list as you like, but I have added an asterisk to the recommended sites.

Sector #1:

The first stop is the ***AMP Centrepoint Tower ❶**, at 100 Market Street, ☎ 02-9231-9300 or **W**: gdaysydney.com/centrepoint.html, for a grand view of the city. This upside-down teacup is 1,001 feet above the pavement and is the tallest observation deck in the Southern Hemisphere. The Tower, completed in 1981, now houses an attraction on the first floor called **Skytour**. The movie experience treats you to a 40-minute tour of the Rainforest, the Outback, the Urban, and the Seashores of Australia. Overhead, the turret, weighing over 2,200 tons, is secured with 392 tons of steel cable, and has a built-in water tank to assist in balancing the tower. The enclosed viewing platform is open daily 9:30am–10:30pm, and until 11:30 on Sat. Adults AU $22.00, children AU $13.20, and family AU $55.00. If you don't like heights, there are over 100 stores in the building to keep you happy. Or try the nearby **Pitt Street Mall ❷**, a shopping mall with **The Imperial Arcade**, ☎ (02) 9233-5662 or **W**: stockland.com.au, for affordable goods and services; **Skygarden**, ☎ (02) 9231-1811 or **W**: skygarden.com.au, for international designer clothing; **Mid City Central**, the **Glasshouse**, and **Westfield Centrepoint**, ☎ (02) 9231-9300 or **W**: Westfield.com/centrepoint. **The Strand Arcade ❸**, ☎ (02) 9232-4199 or **W**: strandarcade.com.au, is the most magnificent shopping mall in the area. with specialty shops housed in an 1892 Victorian masterpiece of a building with intricate wrought-iron

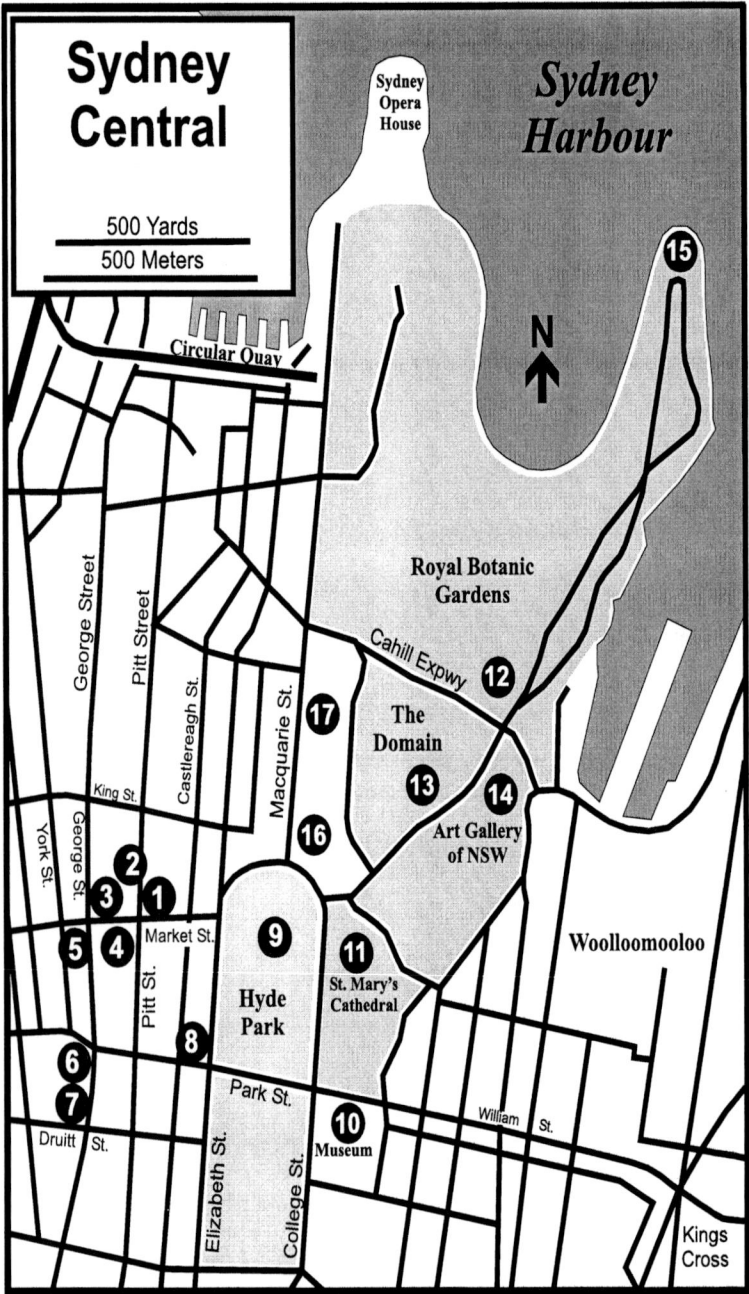

Sydney Central

500 Yards
500 Meters

Sydney Opera House

Sydney Harbour

Circular Quay

N

George Street

Pitt Street

Castlereagh St.

Macquarie St.

King St.

York St.

George St.

Market St.

Pitt St.

Elizabeth St.

College St.

Druitt St.

Park St.

Hyde Park

St. Mary's Cathedral

Royal Botanic Gardens

Cahill Expwy

The Domain

Art Gallery of NSW

Woolloomooloo

William St.

Museum

Kings Cross

2 3 1 5 4 6 7 8 9 10 11 12 13 14 15 16 17

balconies brightened by the skylights. Also nearby on Market Street are **Grace Brothers**, ☎ (02) 9238-9111 or **W**: gracebros.com.au; **Growings**; and **David Jones**, ☎ (02) 9266-5544 or **W**: davidjones.com.au

With the shopping done for now, try a peek in the *State Theatre ❹, at the corner of Market & Pitt Streets, ☎ (02) 9373-6655 or **W**: statetheatre.com.au. You can view the second-largest cut-glass chandelier in the world on a free self-guided tour (with the aid of an audio guide if you like). Open Mon.–Sat. from 10–4 (unless there is a performance on). Opened in 1929, it has a mix of Gothic, Art Deco, and Italian influences on its design. There is a Dress Circle Gallery that displays many notable Australian artworks, and the four-ton chandelier in auditorium is a spellbinder. The 2,000-seat venue is host to the annual Sydney Film Festival as well as many live performances throughout the year.

Sector #2:

After a rest or a refreshment, either shop or gawk at the incredible *Queen Victoria Building ❺, 455 George St., ☎ (02) 9264-9209 or **W**: qvb.com.au. Built in 1898, this Byzantine shopping center encompasses an entire block. The multi-level mall is decorated with antique clocks, replicas of British jewels, and a series of royal paintings. The Royal clock is the real showpiece. It has a revolving stage depicting scenes of King John signing the Magna Carta, King Henry and his wives, the beheading of King Charles I, and the knighting of Sir Francis Drake. Rich wood panels, exquisite stained-glass windows, and clear dome ceilings accentuate the 200 shops. And if you want a fine luncheon, stay awhile and sample the taste delights.

For a breath of fresh air, it's time for some street strolling. Near the corner of George and Druitt Street is the Town Hall with its two levels of shops and food court, and right next door is the **Sydney Town Hall ❻**, ☎ (02) 9265-9007, and *St. Andrew's Cathedral ❼, ☎ (02) 9265-1661 or **W**: sydney.Anglican.asn.au/andrews. The Victorian-style Town Hall has a massive 8,000-pipe organ, and there are midday concerts with the giant instrument as an accompaniment. It's free to have a wander inside from 9–5 each day. The cathedral is a 19th-century building in the Neo-Gothic style, and is the oldest cathedral in Australia. Now wander past The Galleries Victoria at the corner of Park & Pitt Streets (unless you really need more shopping), stop at 187 Elizabeth Street, and enter the *Great Synagogue ❽, ☎ (02) 9267-2477 or **W**: greatsynagogue.org.au. The free self-guided tours and introductory movie introduces you to this 1878 place of worship. There you will learn of the 16 Jews who sailed here from England with the First Fleet, then petitioned for a house of worship in 1825, established a congregation in 1831, and raised one-fifth of the building cost (£5,000) in a six-day bazaar in Martin Place. The building is of Byzantine/Gothic design, has a massive front façade of 64 feet, and is 140-feet deep. When you enter make sure you notice the "Wheel Window" and "The Ark."

Exit the synagogue, pass though a small park, past the Piccadilly

Centre (more shopping) and into the beautifully landscaped wonderland of *Hyde Park ❾. The common area was the site of the first Australian cricket match in 1804, is home to the ANZAC Memorial, and features the Archibald Fountain that looks like it came from Old Europe. The mix of grand old maple trees, palms, and curved flowerbeds makes it a favorite for daytrippers and the lunch crowd.

The final two spots in this sector will take a bit of time to explore properly. The *Australian Museum ❿, 6 College St., ☎ (02) 9320-6000 or W: austmus.gov.au, has a large collection of natural history artifacts of Australia including the standard dinosaur bones and, more importantly, the anthropological history of the Aboriginal peoples of the land. Open daily, 9:30–5. Adults AU $8, kids AU $3, seniors AU $4, families AU $19 Closed Christmas.

Just opposite the museum is the glorious *St. Mary's Cathedral ⓫, ☎ (02) 9220-0400. The free guided-tours (noon on Sundays) will astound you with the revelation of a mosaic floor reflecting The Creation. You can quietly walk in the crypt and amongst the pews from 10–4 daily. The geometrical Gothic giant has twin towers that are visible from the opposite end of Hyde Park. It is the second cathedral built on this site—the first had burnt to the ground in 1865. The final work on the current structure was only competed in 2000 with the stone spires finally covered in stone. The stonework is of dressed Pyrmont stone and is 350 by 80 feet of pure beauty.

Sector #3:

This might be your favorite sector of the City Central with open parks, old goals (jails), and views of the harbor. The first, and probably the majority of the trek will be among the varied trees and plants of the *Royal Botanic Gardens ⓬, ☎ (02) 9231-8111 or W: rbgsyd.gov.au. The 24-hour-a-day park is free and is probably the prettiest spot in town. The walkways meander through more than one million plant specimens and 7,500 trees from all over the world. Try to take a break in the Botanic Gardens Café Restaurant or pay the AU $2.20/$1.10 to enter the pyramid called the Tropical Centre. It houses miniature ecosystems that are amazing and educational. Open daily 10–5 in Oct.–March and 10–4 the rest of the year. The original garden was called "nine acres of corn" in 1788. Governor Macquarie and his botanist friend Charles Fraser formally established the gardens in 1816. The gardens housed a zoo at one time and the generations of gardeners have created a fine escape within the city. There are over 13 special niches amongst the well-groomed gardens; make sure you pass the Wollemi Pine (one of 38 rare and ancient ferns), the Rare and Threatened Plants of the World (learn how you can help to save them), the Cadi Jam Ora: First Encounters with it's Aboriginal gardens, the desert landscape of the Succulent Garden, the fragrant Rose Garden, the medical and culinary displays at the Herb Garden, the Sydney Fernery (9–4:30 daily), the 1853 Palm Grove, the Macquarie Wall that is a 951-foot wall built to separate the convict population from the "good" citizens, the National Herbarium, and soak in the formal gardens of the Government House Grounds (10–4 daily). If you want to come back at night, try dinner at the **Pavilion on the Park Restaurant** ($$-$$$), ☎ (02) 9232-1322, for fine food and views of the skyline. Other lunch options include the **Palace Gate Kiosk** ($) near Macquarie Street and the **Gardens Café** ($) in the heart of the gardens.

Still in the gardens is **The Domain** ⓭ and the *****Art Gallery of NSW** ⓮, ☎ (02) 9225-1744 or **W**: artgallery.nsw.gov.au. The Domain is an open space used for free concerts and outdoor movies. The art gallery is a free maze of Asian, Aboriginal, and Australian masterpieces. It was originally constructed for the International Exhibition of 1879 and was a magnificent crystal palace, but the art committee objected to the gaudy structure. The building eventually succumbed to fire, termites, and mold, was reconstructed, and now is the pride of Sydney. There are guided tours available, but some exhibits require an entry fee.

A bit farther and on the point is the famous *****Mrs. Macquaries Chair** ⓯. This is an incredible monument to Governor Macquarie's wife, an inscribed chair that was carved from solid rock in the early 1800s. The story has it that Elizabeth Macquarie would sit in the chair and await her husband's return. The rock is perched at a vantage point to see the entrance of the harbor so she could spot her husband's ship as it approached. This is a fantastic location to sit and view the Opera House, Fort Denison, the Sydney Bridge, and the far shores of North Sydney.

Double back to the streets and duck into the *****Hyde Park Barracks Museum** ⓰, ☎ (02) 9223-8922 or **W**: hht.nsw.gov.au. It is a frightening experience to see the conditions provided to the male convicts in the early 1800s. An admission of AU $7 adult and AU $3 for kids and seniors grants entry to the dark world that the early convicts tolerated. Built by the prisoners between 1817–19, it is a fine Georgian structure that housed the men until 1848. It later became an orphanage for Irish children and unsupervised girls, then a holding station for immigrants, an insane asylum, court, and offices. It now houses art collections and offers a good history lesson of life at the start of the colony.

Rounding out this section is a quick look at some of the government buildings including the **Government House**; the **State Library of NSW**, ☎ (02) 9273-1414 or **W**: slnsw.gov.au; the **Parliament House of NSW**; the **Mint**, **W**: hht.nsw.gov.au; and the **Sydney Hospital** ⓱. Some offer tours and interesting tidbits of history—like the Mint was originally the Rum Hospital when it was used as a monopoly on rum running (think boar).

The Sydney Opera House

The Sydney Opera House can be an all-day affair, and if you take in a show it could extend your visit late into the evening. It is a stunning building with amazing architectural feats. Not only the most recognizable landmark in Australia, it hosts over 3,000 performances each year, and more than 300,000 people tour the building annually. Take you time on this trip and go through the building slowly. I would urge you to take a tour; the options and prices are listed below. Reserve tickets well in advance for the day you want to have a look around.

GETTING THERE:

It's best to walk to the point and enjoy the experience of coming upon the white shells from the street. You can also take any mass transportation to Circular Quay, exit, and turn right along the waterfront until your reach the big house.

PRACTICALITIES:

There are lots of steps on this tour; if you have bad knees, you will have a rough time with the walk. The tours are worth every Aussie penny (no longer in circulation), and you will learn so much from your leader. Plus you gain entry to sections of the Opera House not open to the public. You can shop at the four boutique gift shops, or spend you money on a quality show. The small theaters are the best buy and are usually very interesting.

FOOD AND DRINK:

The Opera House contains five eateries, ranging from an Espresso Bar to top-end dining before or after a show. Prices range from moderate to expensive.

LOCAL ATTRACTIONS:

*THE SYDNEY OPERA HOUSE, Bennelong Point, ☎ (02) 9250-7250, **W:** soh.nsw.gov.au. *Open daily 9–5 (until 11 pm on nights of a show). Free to* *have a walk around. Guided tours cost between AU $16.20–$25 and are all available when performances permit. Gift shops. Cafés and restaurants. Special events. Partially &.*

Approach from the monumental steps leading to the front doors of the Opera House for the one-hour tour through the building. The polished wood halls open into the five massive theaters. The **Concert Hall** is the most dramatic, with 2,679 seats. It has 18 acrylic rings or clouds above the stage to reverberate the sound of the instruments back to the artists so they can hear their music and keep things in tune. It also has the largest mechanical tracker-action organ in the world with 10,500 pipes and six keyboards. The **Opera Theatre** seats 1,547 people and is the center of all opera and dramatic performances. The **Drama Theatre** has a capacity for 544 wide-eyed people who witness the double revolving stage that is utilized to change scenery and create special effects. The **Playhouse** seats 398 spellbound spectators for intimate plays and recitals, while the Broadwalk Studio hosts experimental theatre.

Some of the fast, hard facts of the Opera House that I learned on the guided tour include: The four large roofs (shells or sails) were designed for visual rather than acoustical benefit; one nickname of the building is "a bunch of mussels stuck in the mud;" the building was built on a solid bed of Sydney sandstone; the designer was a Dane named Joern Utzon; the proposed building cost and construction time was $17 million and 6 years—actual cost and time was $102 million and 15 years; the building was paid for by implementing a legal state lottery, and the rental fees of the 3,000 events staged there each year maintain the building; the highest shell is ten feet higher than the Harbour Bridge and the lowest seat in the building is below the harbor; the Opera House has no productions of its own and rents exclusively to outside production companies; there are over 1,000 rooms in the four-and-a-half-acre building; the roofs are made of 2,194 pre-cast concrete sections, weigh 15.5 tons each, and are held together by 217 miles of steel cable; the total weight of the roofs is 27,230 tons; there are 20,418 square feet of glass placed in two layers—one clear and one tinted to reduce glare.

Probably the most interesting fact about the entire visit to the House was the ceramic tiles covering the outer shells like diamonds. I asked the question about the two different glazings of the tiles and the response was that the flat white tiles give the roof a flat color and the shiny white tiles make it shine. I never noticed the difference until I viewed them up close.

Darling Harbour

Starting at dawn, visit the Fish Market with over 180 fishmongers bidding for the best catch of the day. Then walk over to the live exhibits at the Sydney Aquarium, stroll through the Chinese Garden, and play at the Powerhouse Museum—the city's largest. This is the touristy part of town with many of the new attractions, more shopping, upscale bistros, and museums. You can plan on a whole day in this harbor, which is more of a showcase than the working Sydney Cove and Circular Quay. It's also more of a nighttime hangout than its sister area near the Opera House. This is the place for the kids to hang out and the young at heart to play in the museums and be wowed by the colorful exhibits. For the ladies, there are heaps of stores, markets, and cafés. For everyone there are great food courts, the best ethnic foods in town in Chinatown, and fun pubs too. The harbor is lined with colorful flags, a miniature train transporting the foot-weary, and small boats chugging under the many bridges of the harbor. The buildings in this area are very futuristic and are of the nautical theme. All the sights are pleasing to the eye, especially the innovative and interactive water fountains in the plazas. One is a circular stream that ripples over small two-inch-wide steps into a central pond. The kids play like mini-salmon by hopping up and down the stream. It will be tempting on a hot afternoon.

There are way too many things to cover in one day, so I have highlighted the best of the best, and then listed the other favorites. Just two of the attractions—the Fish Market and either the Powerhouse Museum or the Sydney Aquarium could consume an entire day. So pick the two or three things that interest you the most and make sure you do them justice.

GETTING THERE:

It's only a short walk from the center of the city, but I would recommend a little help from the public transport system on this one. By train, exit at Town Hall and walk a block on Druitt Street, turning right on Kent, left on Market, and across Pyrmont Bridge into the harbor complex. From the monorail, just choose your exit point, as there are a few around this section of attractions. You can take the ferry from Circular Quay into Darling Harbour's Pyrmont Bay Wharf or the Aquarium Wharf, taking about 30 minutes. You can also hop a bus to stops 17, 19, 20, 21, 22, or 23.

PRACTICALITIES:

Once you get there it will be easy walking with lots of stops for food, rest, and a cool drink. Use the monorail to save your legs, as there will be a full day of strolling the museums. This will probably be the most expensive of the Sydney tours. But you can simply choose to stroll the harbor side walkways and enjoy the scenery for free. On Wednesday — Sunday night, make sure you hang around for the free laser show. They run every half hour and are a mix of movie, water screens, light and sound beamed over Cockle Bay.

More information can be had at **W**: darlingharbour.com

FOOD AND DRINK:

This area offers maybe the most diverse and enjoyable waterfront dining in the city. The four areas to consider are Cockle Bay Wharf for upmarket food, Harbourside for food courts and cheap eats, King Street Wharf for a good mix of expensive and kid's favorites, and Chinatown for great Asian foods at very reasonable prices.

LOCAL ATTRACTIONS:

Circled numbers correspond to numbers on the map.

*SYDNEY FISH MARKET ❶, Blackwattle Bay, Wattle Street & Pyrmont Bridge Road, ☎ (02) 9660-1611 or ☎ (02) 9004-1122 for tours, **W**: sydney fishmarket.com.au or **W**: sfmlive.com. *Open daily 7–4, closed Christmas. Free to enter and have a look around or the 1-1/2-hour tours for AU $20 are every first Thursday of the month (but check ahead). Gift shops. Cafés and restaurants. Special events.* ♿.

This market of ocean delights is the largest in the Southern Hemisphere and is set up like a big amphitheater with school-sized desks lined up across the back. The desktops had bidding buttons set into the top for the buyers to make a selection of over 100 species and lock in a price. In the center of the auction floor is a giant clock dial with lot numbers displayed. This Dutch Clock has been used since 1989 and was adopted from the Dutch tulip auction system. As the time ticks by, prices drop for a lot of fish. But if the buyers wait too long, a competitor may scoop the fresh fish. The auctions begin at 5:30 a.m. every weekday and over 1,000 crates of fish are sold every hour. About 2,700 crates weighing 50 pounds each are sold every auction. Of the 600 registered buyers, about 180 arrive at 4:30 a.m. to inspect the seafood. On the upper deck are a series of classrooms where you can take cooking classes at the Seafood School. The tours run at 7a.m., but the times/dates do change frequently. Self-guided tours offer a good chance to see the hall at your own leisure, and the viewing platform is full of plaques describing the operations and equipment down below. There are shops adjacent to the market, and you can grab a bottle of wine and some fresh seafood and enjoy the sunshine.

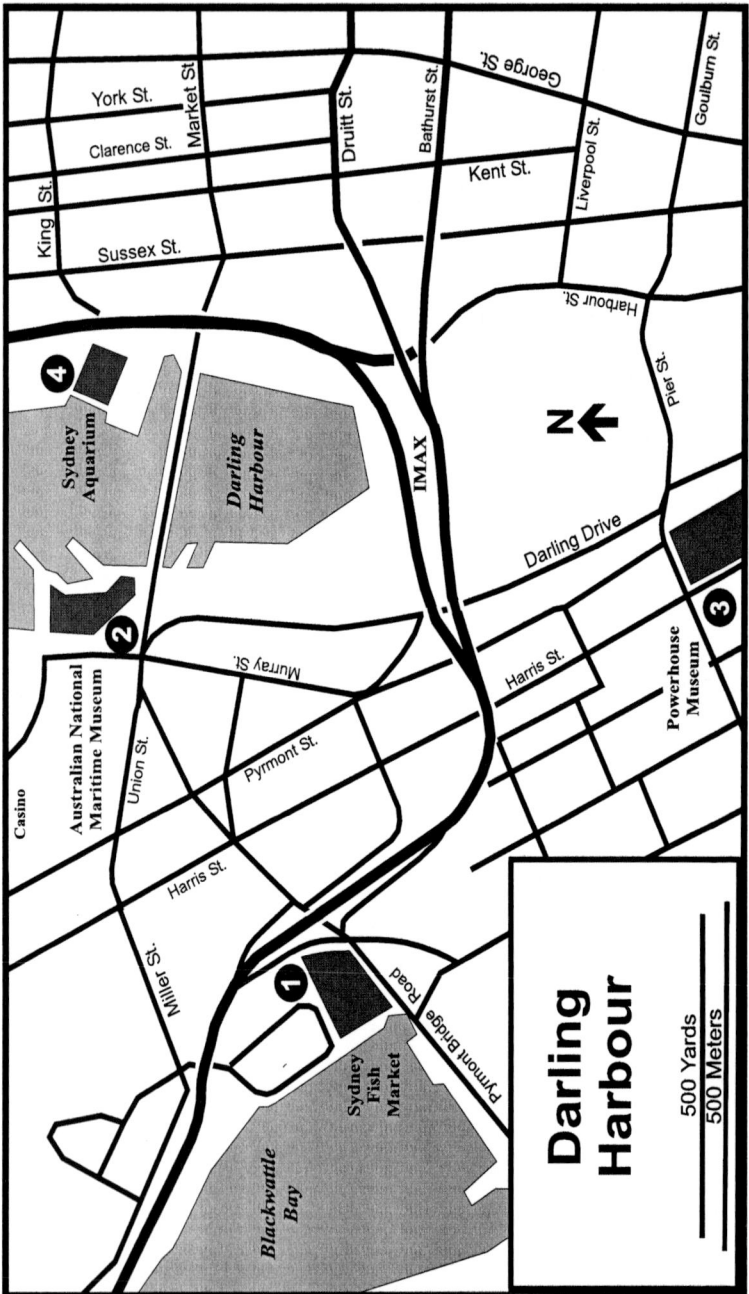

Darling Harbour

500 Yards
500 Meters

York St.
Clarence St.
Market St.
King St.
Sussex St.
Druitt St.
Bathurst St.
George St.
Kent St.
Liverpool St.
Goulburn St.
Harbour St.
Pier St.

N

Sydney Aquarium

Darling Harbour

IMAX

Darling Drive

Harris St.

Murray St.

Australian National Maritime Museum

Casino

Union St.

Pyrmont St.

Harris St.

Miller St.

Powerhouse Museum

Pyrmont Bridge Road

Sydney Fish Market

Blackwattle Bay

The market is a bit of a walk, so you may want to consider the Light Rail system and get off at The Fish Market stop.

*THE AUSTRALIAN NATIONAL MARITIME MUSEUM ❷, 2 Murray Street, ☎ (02) 9298-3777, **W**: anmm.gov.au. *Open daily 9:30–5, till 6 in Jan. Admission prices range from AU $6–$45 depending on the package sought. Guided tours, self-guided tours. Gift shop. Café. Special events.* &.

Look for the building that actually looks like the sails of a ship with various boats moored alongside. The **HMAS** *Vampire* (a huge gun destroyer) is on site, as well as the Cape Bowling Green Lighthouse. For the sea dog in you this is a good two-hour tour. There are outdoor exhibits, indoor galleries, hands-on displays, movies, and audio guides. The free tours include the Highlight Gallery Tour with audio stories, the *Vampire* Tour with battle sounds and action from the bridge, and the Fleet Lighthouse Tour for an overview of the boats on display. Boats in sight include racing cutters, pearl luggers, a Vietnamese refugee boat, patrol boats, commando raider craft, and tugboats. Some indoor favorites include the *Spirit of Australia* speed boat that holds the record at 317.5696 mph, the Nariyarrku bark canoe made from the bark of a messmate tree, and the dugout canoe that is commonly used by Indonesian Makassens for trepang fishing.

*THE POWERHOUSE MUSEUM ❸, 500 Harris Street, ☎ (02) 9217-0111, **W**: phm.gov.au. *Open daily 10–5, closed Christmas. Adults AU $10, children AU $3, seniors AU $3, and family AU $23. Guided tours, self guided tours. Gift shop. Café. Special events.* &.

Built in the old powerhouse station, this is a Smithsonian-style museum where you can spend a good half of a day among the over 380,000 displayed items. From seaplanes to spaceships, the collections mix Aboriginal weapons, musical instruments, and special exhibits. The 22 permanent exhibitions include Australian Social History with a cinema from the 1930s; the Boulton and Watt Engine with the world's oldest rotative engine; Transport displays from steam to solar power; Success and Innovation showing manufacturing ideas on interactive computers; Experimentations of heat, light, magnetism and gravity; and Space: Beyond This World and the various international successes. Guided tours run every 15 minutes from 10–1 weekdays. There may be a bit of a queue at the 250 interactive stations around the museum floor, but they are definitely worth the wait. You will find very cool gifts in the gift shop too.

*SYDNEY AQUARIUM ❹, Aquarium Pier, Darling Harbour, ☎ (02) 9262-2300, **W**: sydneyaquarium.com.au. *Open daily 9–10 p.m. Adults AU $23, children AU $11, families $27–$49. Guided tours, self-guided tours. Gift shop. Café. Special events.* &.

Enjoy the sharks, crocodiles, and colorful fish safely behind thick walls of glass. If you can't make it to the Great Barrier Reef, have a look at the replica of the reef here. There are touch pools for the kids and lots of interactive displays. Educational sections are provided as well as the all-popular seal pool (closes at dusk).

These four stops will take you at least a day to cover. Allow a bit of time to sit back and enjoy the fine eateries in the area—especially the flavors of Chinatown. If you are a speedster, here are a few more choices to think about:

IMAX Theatres, ☎ (02) 9281-3300 or **W**: imax.com.au, an eight-story screen with 3D, animation, nature, sport, and tourism shows every hour from 10–10. **Star City Casino**, ☎ (02) 9777-9000 or **W**: starcity.com.au, with 200 gaming tables, cinemas, eateries, pubs and 1,500 pokies (slots). **Australia's Northern Territory and Outback Centre**, ☎ (02) 9283-7477 or **W**: outbackcentre.com.au, for free live shows, movies of the Outback, and Aboriginal arts and crafts. The **Chinese Garden of Friendship**, ☎ (02) 9281-6863 to book the tours for AU $4.50, for a quiet walk among water gardens, amongst the waterfalls and the traditional teahouse. **Paddy's Markets**, ☎ 1-300-361-589 or **W**: paddysmarkets.com.au, are a must on Thursdays–Sundays. Or just wander around **Harbourside**, ☎ (02) 9281-3999 or **W**: harbourside.com.au, for food, fashion, and people watching.

AMP Tower and ANZAC Memorial

Sydney Surrounds

This section will allow choices of some beach time at Australia's most famous beaches (and maybe one not too well known), a bizarre walk around the infamous Kings Cross, or a flashback to the 2000 Sydney Olympics. Each selection will take at least a half-day to satisfy your tourist appetite. I would recommend the beach tours over the two city-bound excursions. You might want to top up the tan a bit, or at least the waterside stops will give you bragging rights for posing with the Sydneysiders' at their favorite hangouts. And there are two great walking tours at Bondi Beach.

Although some travel guides warn tourists away from Kings Cross, it is worthy of a pass through during the day (admittedly, at night it is not for the faint-hearted). This is one of the best people-watching tours of the entire book—just think of it as a bizarre trip to Greenwich Village in New York. Predominately and openly gay with the gay and lesbian Mardi Gras as one of the big events of the year. Bondi Beach and The Cross are the heart and soul of the event.

The Olympic Park is the newly constructed complex that was the center of the 2000 Olympics. The tours are the best way to get around as they allow access to areas exempt from public view.

GETTING THERE:

The beaches can be reached by car, cab, bus, or ferry. Bondi also has a train station only a couple of blocks from the surf. The Olympic Village is accessed via the Olympic Park train station or by Rivercat, ☎ 13-15-00. Kings Cross has car, bus, train, and cab service and is easily walked.

PRACTICALITIES:

Take a towel, swimming suit good enough to pose in, and sun protection for the beach. The Olympic tours are easy, and air-conditioned transport is provided. Kings Cross is a city sidewalk tour with quite a bit of walking.

FOOD AND DRINK:

Food and drink will be abundant on all of the tours as will the range of selections. Probably the most enjoyable spot to eat will be at Bondi Beach.

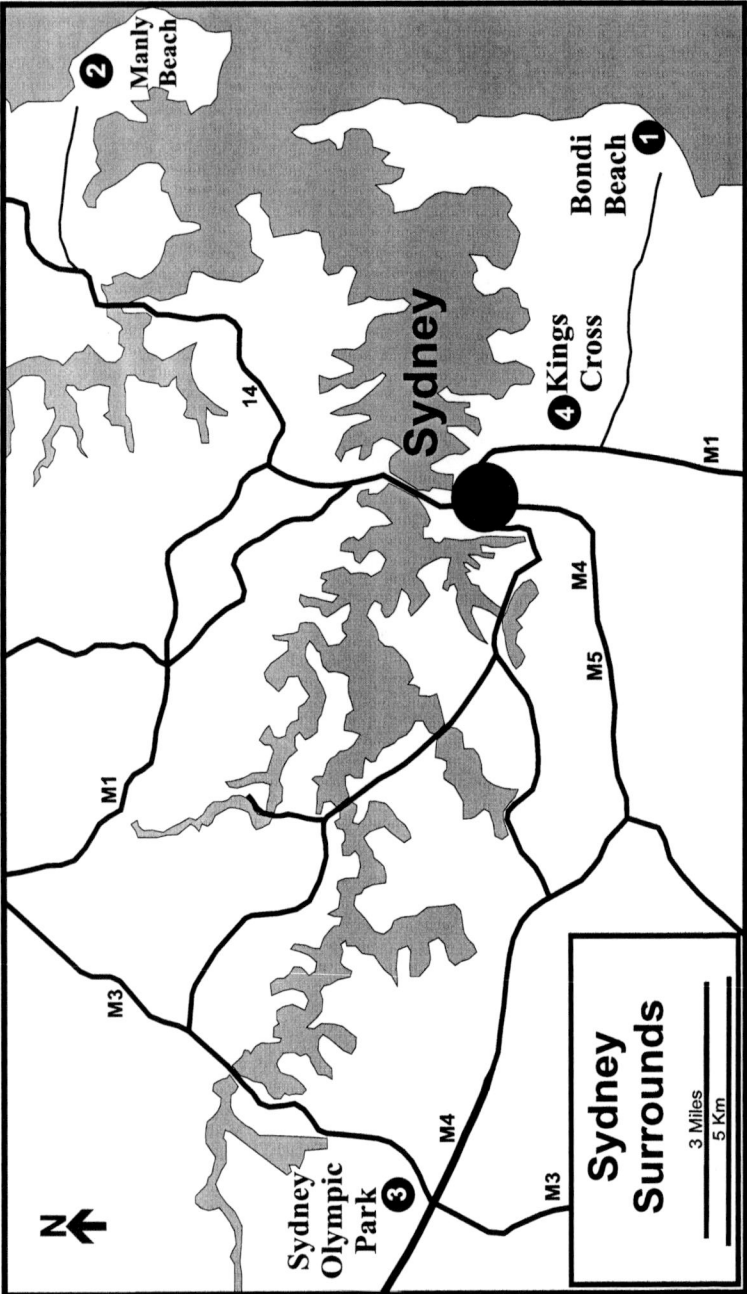

Sydney Surrounds

3 Miles
5 Km

LOCAL ATTRACTIONS:
Circled numbers correspond to numbers on the map.

The Beaches:
   *Bondi Beach ❶ is probably the most accessible and most popular, with the majority of the beautiful people hanging about. It is just 2-1/2 miles east of the center of the city and is the nation's beach as well as the home to the Sydney Cricket Ground. It is also claimed to be the origination point for Australia's Surf Life Saving Clubs. The one-mile-long shoreline is usually packed with sun worshipers posing for each other. I thought of the scene as a mixture of New Jersey and St. Tropez with lots of kids mixed in with the topless single ladies. The beach is horseshoe-shaped, and the rock cliffs are stacked with high-rise condos. The little town behind the beach is a 50's-style vacation spot with the retaining wall decorated with local graffiti. There are two great ocean view walks in the area. The first is the 3-mile Bondi-to-Bronte hike past the Bondi Pavilion (originally a 1920's bathhouse with Turkish baths and a gymnasium), through Marks Point and the Aboriginal rock carvings, around Mackenzies Bay and Tamarama Beach, and ends at North Bronte Cliffs. The second return hike is called Bronte Beach-to-Waverley Cemetery, starting at the Bronte Baths (opened in 1887) and the natural swimming hole right next door. Passing picnic areas, waterfalls, and historical sites, you end up at the Waverley Cemetery—a virtual history lesson carved in headstones.
   *Manly Beach ❷ is in the northern suburbs and is the off-the-beaten-track spot favored by many locals. With 18 beaches, 80 restaurants, craft markets, hidden coves and inlets to explore, this is a full-day trip. It's also home to **Oceanworld**, ☎ (02) 9949-2644 or **W**: oceanworldmanly.com.au, and the **Quarantine Station*, ☎ (02) 9247-5033 or **W**: npws.nsw.gov.au. Oceanworld is open daily 10–5:30. To see the sea critters, including the deadly blue-ringed octopus, costs only AU $15.90 adults/$8 kids/$11 seniors/$25–$39.90 families. The Quarantine Station can be toured by appointment, so call ahead. There is a great ghost tour available, and you can see the fortifications by moonlight. Great walks along the beaches are easily found in this protected cove. You can view cabbage trees, snorkel near Shelly Beach and Fairy Bower, shop at South Steyne, and stroll to the northern beaches fondly called the desert outpost by the locals. It is a nice place to relax and enjoy the dunes and surf.

Sydney Olympic Park:
   The **Sydney Olympic Park** ❸ section is another full-day trip, one that mixes walking and bus tours. Start your sporting adventure at the Visitor Centre, ☎ (02) 9714-7545, ☎ (02) 9714-7958 for tours, or **W**: sydney-olympicpark.nsw.gov.au. If you call well in advance, you can enjoy a private mini-bus tour of the entire complex for AU $110–$220. The 45-minute walking tour (AU $7.50–$10) is guided and covers the central district. The Explorer tour (AU $5–$10) has a ten-stop guided tour and allows you a full

day in the park. The Sydney SuperDome (**W**: superdome.com.au) tour includes a weekday trip for about AU $11.50–$15.40. A SuperPass is a mix of guided and self-guided tours of the Telstra Stadium, the Sydney Aquatic Centre, and the Observation Centre. And you get a chance for a free swim in the Olympic pool where all the records were set. The People Mover can transport you between the Olympic Park Station to the Olympic Park for a mere AU $2.20–$11 (10–5 daily). Other stand-alone tours include the Aquatic Centre Tour—covers the fitness center, the swim school, massage rooms, and recreational swimming areas, the Bicentennial Park Tour—an educational trip for the school kids, the Telstra Stadium, the Observation Tour—great views from the top of the Novotel Hotel, and the Hall of Champions—loaded with photographs and memorabilia of the legends.

Kings Cross:

It's not all bizarre stuff in **Kings Cross** ❹, what with the **Elizabeth House** (☎ (02) 9356-3022) on Onslow Avenue and its spectacular views from the 1839 colonial estate bedroom windows, and the **Sydney Jewish Museum** at the corner of Darlinghurst Road & Burton Street (☎ (02) 9360-7999). But if you get a few hours, please have a walk around and do a bit of New Age shopping, or have a stroll around Fitzroy gardens.

Other Stuff:

There are organized biking, walking, ballooning, horseback rides, and coach tours offered in the area that cover the city and surrounds. Call **Australian Travel Specialists** on ☎ (02) 9211-3192 or **W**: atstravel.com.au. Finally, Paddington is a good spot to shop and stroll among the old homes. It is the farthest city region from the harbor, boasts some of the prettiest houses in the city, and is the hub of the fashion district.

Section III

Daytrips in and Around
Melbourne

Get ready for a city filled with a varied culture, innovative theater, and Victorian architecture (not to mention strange new ethnic foods) on this trip to Australia's second most inhabited town. Melbourne (pronounced *Mel-bin*) boasts a population of around three million people whose stock, unlike Sydney's, was founded by free men and women in 1835. The people of this city love to stick this fact in the collective face of Sydney folk and are proud of the many differences between the two capitals. Victoria's capital is the cultural center of the Land Down Under and home of the event that stops the nation—the Melbourne Cup horserace. This city is also easy to navigate and is a walking haven for sightseers. But be warned that it has dramatic daily weather changes all year-round; so be prepared for changes in temperatures and humidity. If you like food you will adore this town as the markets and eateries are some of the best in the world. On the more chilling side of things, the gallows that sent the famous bushranger Ned Kelly to his grave is a must-see, mates, and a ghost is still visible on the third tier of the Melbourne Gaol (pronounced jail). Within a day's drive, tours are available to see fairy penguins, gaze upon the Twelve Apostles, and enjoy wineries plentiful enough to keep a monk happy.

The city is divided into precincts including Uptown, Hardware, Collins Street, Flinders Quarter, Chinatown, St. Kilda Road, Greek, Magnificent Seven City Arcades, The Market, Southbank, Swanston Street, and Yarra River. I have segmented it a bit differently combining a few of the precincts to create the tours in the Central Business District (CBD) with its historic buildings and museums, Southbank with the arts, theater and gardens, Queen Victoria Market & The Gaol with hundreds of stalls crowded with magnificent goods, and if you haven't had enough, driving tours outside the city limits on the Country Driving and The Great Ocean Road trip. The activities are very different from each other and most are constantly changing.

Lodging has been selected to accommodate most of the city tours that are easily walked from your lobby, but you can catch the trams to save the legs. You will need at least four days to comfortably cover the

Melbourne Central attractions. The Surrounds tour will add an additional two or three days unless you simply take the Port Phillip trek as a daytrip.

GETTING TO MELBOURNE:

For travel information in the Melbourne area have a look at **W**: victrip.com.au for general times, prices, and areas of public transport service.

By Car: If you're driving from **Brisbane**, it's a good 3–4 day drive of 1,045 miles. You have several driving options and the most direct is via Newell Highway (Route 39). From **Sydney**, it's 554 miles past the capital of Canberra and along the rough-and-tumble Tasman Sea or across the mountains on the Hume Highway (Route 31).

By Bus: If you want to give it a go, call one of the two primary Australian bus lines: **Greyhound Pioneer**, ☎ 13-20-30 or **W**: greyhound.com.au; and **McCafferty's**, ☎ 13-14-99 or **W**: mccaffertys.com.au. The booking agent for both transportation organizations is **Travel Coach Australia** on ☎ 13-14-99.

By Train: Country Link, ☎ 13-22-32 or **W**: countrylink.info, is the train service around Australia. The fares to/from Brisbane and Sydney are about AU $110 for a full fare adult. There are 7 & 14-day pre-booked discounts offered for around AU $66/$55.

By Plane: QANTAS, ☎ 13-13-13 or **W**: Qantas.com.au, is the primary airline, and **Virgin Blue** ☎ 13-67-89 domestic, ☎ 617-3295-2296 international, or **W**: virginblue.com.au, is the discount airline. Fares fluctuate weekly and specials run frequently, so check ahead and book early to save a few quid. Flight information is listed on **W**: melair.com.au. The ride from the airport to downtown is only about a half-hour or 13 miles, and costs about AU $45. There are taxis, buses, and rental cars available from the terminal. **Skybus**, ☎ (03) 9335-3066 or **W**: skybus.com.au, service runs into the city every half hour for about AU $13/$22 (roundtrip) adult, AU $5/$10 child, and AU $26 family.

GETTING AROUND:

The main city transport is the **Tram System**, ☎ 13-16-38 or **W**: bigtrip.com.au. They crisscross the city and offer an inexpensive and fun way to get about the city sights. The charges are based on zones and daily usage of the trams/buses/met trains within the city are about AU $5.10–$2.65 (seniors). There is the Free City Circle Tram that runs at ten-minute intervals, stops at every major intersection around the CBD, and operates daily from 10–6. All major car rentals are available from the airport or at the hotels. But for most of the tours, it's best to walk it and get the flavor of this vibrant town. Taxis include **Arrow**, ☎ 13-22-11; **Black Cabs**, ☎ 13-22-27; and **Silver Top**, ☎ 13-10-08.

If you want to try other options to see the town, there is a large selection of tours available. A complete list can be found in the Melbourne Events brochure available at the information centers. The most comprehensive group seems to be **White Hat Tours**, ☎ (05) 0050-0655 or **W**: white hat.com.au. Specific tours include **Chocolate & Coffee Tours**, ☎ (03) 9815-1228 or **W**: chocoholictours.com.au, for AU $25; **Chinatown Heritage Walks**, ☎ (03) 9662-2888; **Aboriginal Heritage Walk** through the Botanic Gardens, ☎ (03) 9252-2300; **Melbourne City Walks**, ☎ (03) 9376-6558; the highly recommended **Melbourne Cricket Ground Tours**, ☎ (03) 9657-8879 or **W**: mcg.org.au, from AU $16–$44 (book well in advance); free half-day tours from the **Melbourne Greeter Service**, ☎ (03) 9658-9036 or **W**: thatsmelbourne.com.au; and make sure you book three days in advance for the **Melbourne Town Hall Tours**, ☎ (03) 9658-9658; the popular **Night Tours at the Old Melbourne Goal**, ☎ (03) 9663-7228; **Queen Victoria Market Foodies Dream Tour**, ☎ (03) 9320-5822; the pink bus **Shopping Spree Tours**, ☎ (03) 9596-6600 or **W**: shoppingspree.com.au, for AU $60 adult and AU $16.50 children; **Mystery & Murders Tour**, ☎ (05) 0050-0655; **The Haunted Melbourne Ghost Tour**, ☎ (03) 9670-2585; personalized limo tours on **Timesaver Guided Tours**, ☎ (03) 9848-8599; and **Victoria Winery Tours**, ☎ (03) 9621-2089. The tour operators for Port Phillip and the Twelve Apostles include **AAT King Tours** (book through a travel agent or your hotel); **Go West Tours**, ☎ (03) 9828-2008; and the tour rated the best by some of the hostels and information centers is **Eco Platypus Tours**, ☎ 1-800-819-091, (03) 5570-8331, or **W**: ecoplatypustours.com

ACCOMMODATIONS:

The choices are incredible with varying ranges of prices and star ratings. The key to accommodations for the tours in this section is location. My choice is the 3-star **The Victoria Hotel**, ☎ (03) 9653-0441, at 215 Little Collins Street. The rooms are small and the lobby is a bit crowded and hurried, but it is central to most tours and at AU $75–$155/night, it's a bargain. Other choices in the area include the 5-star **The Windsor**, ☎ (03) 9633-6000, at 103 Spring Street ranging from AU $299–$1,306 a night. The **Radisson Hotel**, ☎ (03) 9322-8000, at 380 William Street for AU $179–$299. The 3-star **Hotel Y**, ☎ (03) 9329-5188, at 489 Elizabeth Street for around AU $77–$115. The **B&B of Charsfield** on St Kilda, ☎ (03) 9866-5511, is a bit out of the way, but a fine choice for AU $75–$140. A fantastic backpackers' experience is **The Friendly Backpacker**, ☎ (03) 9670-1111, or **W**: friendlygroup.com.au, for a mere AU $24/night or AU $154/week to crash in a four-to-six-bed room. It is right across from the Spencer Street Station and all the public transportation systems. If you decide to stay out near the Twelve Apostles, see that section for your preferred accommodation.

PRACTICALITIES:

Expect the unexpected in weather conditions; it is claimed that most days can have all four seasons rolled into 24 hours. That includes rain, sun, hail, snow, and high winds. Most of the tours are indoors, but there is quite a bit of walking between attractions. It really isn't that bad and it is a bit of a badge of courage for the locals to talk of the unpredictable skies. You can get sunburned too, so take precautions in that department. There will be plenty of shopping and lots of walking, so dig out the comfortable shoes. This is probably the dressiest town in the book. If you have fine threads, now is the time to use them. The shows, eateries, and shopping malls are showcases for fashion.

Before heading down to this fun-filled city, take a peek at some of the local websites: **W**: visitvictoria.com.au—Victoria Tourism; **W**: thatsmelbourne.com.au—Melbourne Tourism; **W**: melbourne.vic.gov.au —City of Melbourne hotline; **W**: melbourne.citysearch.com.au—entertainment and services in the city; **W**: melbourne.org—shops, entertainment and dining; **W**: victrip.vic.gov.au—commuting and mass transit info; **W**: theage.com.au—weather and news; and **W**: parks.vic.gov.au—information on the national parks in the state. And if you get into difficulties in finding your way around, the City Ambassadors (dressed in red with a green CITY patch) or the Greeter Services can help you out. They are usually on the city streets or can be contacted at ☎ (03) 9658-9658 or **W**: melbourne.vic.gov.au. A website that has a great map of the city is the City Circle site at **W**: victrip.com.au/city circle/routes.html

SPECIAL EVENTS:

There is probably an event each week in the Melbourne area. Check the website **W**: thatsmelbourne.com.au for a complete listing. The annual events are as follows and are found on **W**: visitvictoria.com.au at Hallmark Events: January—Australian Open Tennis Championships; February—Australian International Airshow; March—Foster's Australian Grand Prix, The Melbourne Food & Wine Festival, Melbourne International Comedy festival; April—Melbourne International Flower & Garden Show, Rip Curl Pro & SunSmart Classic; September—Mt. Buller World Aerials (aerial skiers), Australian Football League Finals Series (rugby-like sport); October—Spring Racing Festival (horses), Melbourne Festival, Skyy Vodka Australian Motorcycle Grand Prix, Wangarate Festival of Jazz' November—The Melbourne Cup, Equitana Asia Pacific (horse show); December—Melbourne Orange Boxing Day Test Match (cricket).

FOOD AND DRINK:

Sorry Brisbane, Sydney, and the Gold Coast—I think Melbourne has the best, most varied, and tastiest foods in Australia. The choices are incredible, from street vendors, food courts, pubs, Chinatown noodle shops, to the Italian and Greek sections, and the mouthwatering stalls located in the Victoria Market. You can even have a fine meal on the 1927 **Colonial Tramcar Restaurant**, ☎ (03) 9696-4000 or **W**: tramrestaurant.com.au, and sip a nice wine while you circle the city. Prices for the 1-1/2-circuit, 3-course meal is AU $66; the 3-hour, 5-course dinner is AU $93.50–$104.50. The drinks-included ride starts at Southbank at Normanby Road (near the Exhibition Centre). Nightclubs abound and this city seems to go on till the wee hours allowing only a few hours of sleep.

Look in the free brochures at the Information Centres and they will list a few of the city's favorites. For food, I found it best to just wander and stop when you're hungry. I would recommend at least one night at Lygon Street. It's crammed with Italian eateries trying to drown each other out in smells of garlic. At night, the area becomes a great block party.

SHOPPING:

You generally have from 9–5 weekdays and 10–5 on weekends to cover the massive number of stores in this town. Take your passport for duty-free shopping and receive a healthy discount. The shopping centers include **Bourke Street Mall, Melbourne Shopping Centre,** ☎ (03) 9922-1100, on Latrobe Street and its over 200 specialty stores under a giant glass cone; **The Block & Royal Arcades,** ☎ (03) 9650-4355; and **Galleria Plaza,** ☎ (03) 9675-6416 on Collins Street; the **Crown Complex,** ☎ (03) 9292-8888; the **Armadale Antique Centre,** ☎ (03) 9822-7788, on High Street for those precious collectables; **Collins Place,** ☎ (03) 9655-3600; and **Collins 234,** ☎ (03) 9650-4373, along Collins Street; **Chadstone Fashion Capital,** ☎ (03) 9563-3355, a bit out of town. The streets are also filled with small shops, souvenir stalls, and department stores. The markets are dominated by **Queen Victoria Market,** ☎ (03) 9320-5822 or **W**: qvm.com.au, with over 1,000 stalls of produce and fun stuff. Open Tues.–Thurs. 6–2, Fri. 6–6, Sat. 6–3, and Sun. 9–4. This is at least a four-hour excursion, so be prepared and do not miss it. Weekend markets are usually found at St Kilda's Esplanade as well as along the Yarra River.

Flinders Street Railway Station

Melbourne Central

Since Melbourne is basically a square grid consisting of wide streets adorned with rich-smelling tropical gardens, clacking cable cars, hurrying people dressed in basic black, and an international representation of cuisine—this will be a walking pleasure. The CBD is a mere 6/10 of a mile radius; squared-off by Latrobe, Spencer, Spring, and Flinders streets. The Melbourne Central and Southbank are split by the muddy Yarra River and are spanned by Spencer Street Bridge, Queens Bridge, and the Princess Bridge. If you decide to stay on Little Collins Street, you will be smack dab in the heart of the town and right behind Town Hall. Some sights I earmarked as must-see include the observation deck of the Rialto Towers—the tallest office building in the Southern Hemisphere; Cook's Cottage, nestled in the pristine Fitzroy Gardens; enjoying high tea at the elegant Windsor Hotel; inspirational views at St. Patrick's Cathedral; and the shopping hub under the Glass Cone—complete with a full-sized hot air balloon and Coops' Shot Tower. The walking tour will offer a good mix of shopping, museums, garden strolls, and a chance to scope out the eating and drinking establishments in center city.

Consider this walking tour a treasure hunt rather than a scenic venture to merely visit the attractions. Although specific sites have been listed, you will find prizes of your own along the streets of center city. I would recommend first taking the free tram ride along the perimeter of the CBD. That way you can get your bearings and actually start the tour at an area that peaks your interest. The attractions are laid out so you can stop and start at any location, skip a section, or jump around as you wish. Where sufficient background information was available, it has been included to help you decide which attractions most interest you.

GETTING THERE:

All you have to do is walk to the Information Center at Federation Square and start the stroll from there. If you are staying out of town, catch the train/tram to Flinders Street Station and walk the three blocks up Swanston Street.

PRACTICALITIES:

There will be loads of walking and as mentioned earlier, the weather changes quickly. Take some small bills or change for the tram system if you decide to hop the green trolleys for a ride.

FOOD AND DRINK:

There are food courts in the shopping centers, and Melbourne Central is my favorite spot for mall food. All the hotels have restaurants and cafés, and the streets are loaded with good choices. If you like Chinese and noodle bars, you will be in luck in this section of town. Favorite pubs include **Sherlock Holmes**, ☎ (03) 9629-1146 at 415 Collins Street; **Bridie O'Reilly's** ($-$$), ☎ (03) 9650-0840 at 62 Little Collins Street; and **The Charles Dickens Tavern** ($-$$) ☎ (03) 9654-1821 at 290 Collins Street. Recommended restaurants include **Il Barco** ($$-$$$), ☎ (03) 9654-6778 at 170 Little Collins Street; **Le Restaurant** ($$-$$$) ☎ (03) 9653-0000 at 25 Collins Street; **Stella Restaurant** ($$-$$$), ☎ (03) 9639-1555 at 159 Spring Street; and my favorite—**The Windsor** ($$$) on Spring Street. **The Red Ant** on Little Collins Street is a funky hangout and close to the hotels. A great noodle bar is the **Mekong Vietnam** right around the corner. You can also search for food selections on **W**: melbourne.citysearch.com.au

LOCAL ATTRACTIONS:

Circled numbers correspond to numbers on the map.

Start with the *__Information Centre__ ❶, ☎ (03) 9658-9933, Federation Square (Melbourne Town Hall) on the corner of Little Collins & Swanston Streets. Here you will find all the brochures, attraction data, and maps you might need to navigate the city. It is open Mondays through Fridays from 9–6, and weekends from 9–5. If you can't find the spot or get stuck along the way, simply look for an easily identifiable City Ambassador and they will direct you to your location. Other information booths are located at Bourke Street Mall and on the corner of Flinders & Swanston streets near Flinders Street Station.

Continue along Swanston Street for three big blocks and you will come upon **St Paul's Anglican Cathedral** ❷, ☎ (03) 9650-3791 at the corner of Flinders & Swanston streets. You can't miss it with its central spire pointing straight to the heavens, 315 feet above the sidewalk. The construction of this Gothic-style church began in 1880, but was only completed in 1933. As you will notice in some of the historical buildings, the massive organ is the showcase and this site is no exception. If you walk by in the evenings, you might be lucky enough to hear the nightly choir accompanying the massive musical pipes. Right across the street is the historical **Young and Jackson's Hotel** ❸, ☎ (03) 9650-3884 or **W**: youngandjackson.com.au, with the scandalous nude of Chloe. Considered Melbourne's oldest and most famous pub, it has been in operation for over 140 years. It is a really cool, classy bar and home to the beautiful 19-year-old brunette—Chloe. The 1875 French painting was very popular in the 19th century as it was the only chance to have a peek at a nude woman. Under the famous work of the Master Jules Lefebrue, US Marines drank and brawled, business deals have been struck, and love has been found. The most notable story of Chloe is that she was an artist's model and at the age of 21, threw a huge party for her friends. Afterwards

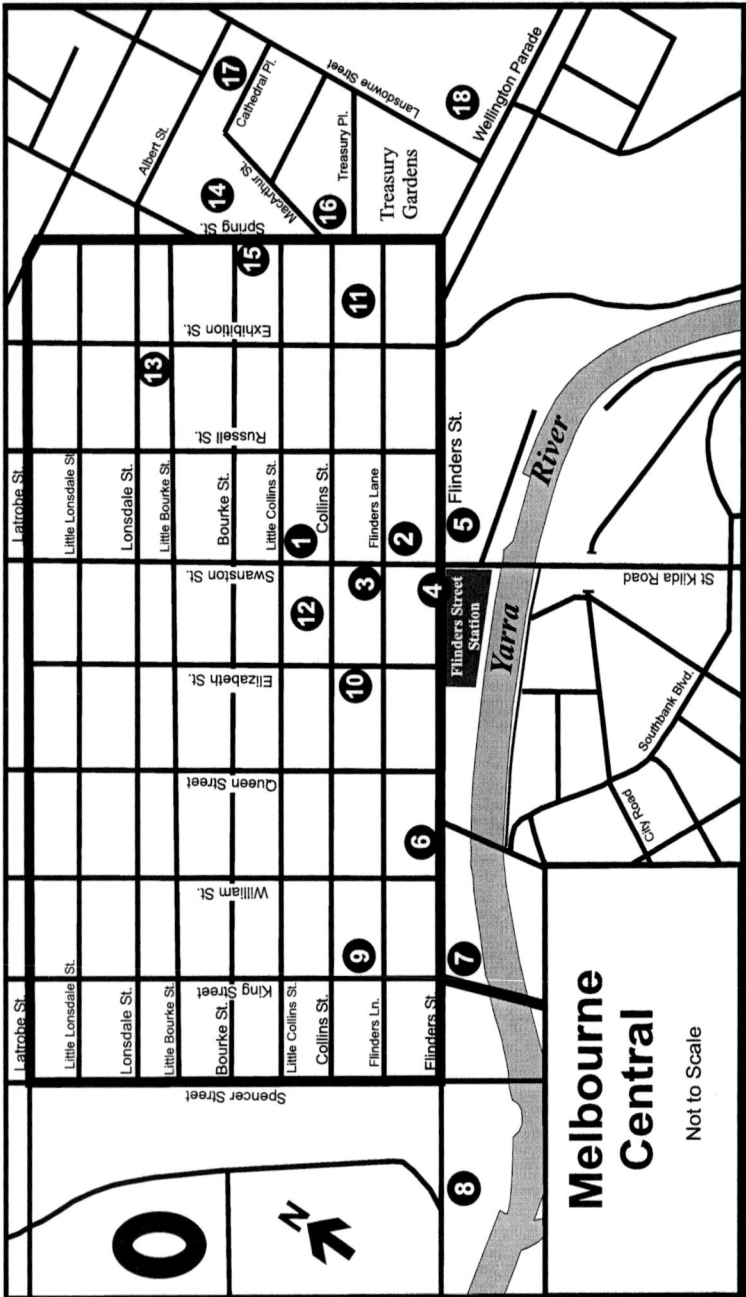

Melbourne
Central

Not to Scale

she drank a poisonous potion of boiled matches, and died destitute. Under her image, soldiers from three wars have shared a pint, and unfortunately a GI was so smitten by her that he drunkenly threw a beer in her face to remember him by. The pub and the painting have been fully restored and they continue to cut a handsome swath through history.

Crossing to the river side of the street is the *Flinders Street Station ❹. This main railroad hub in Melbourne will be buzzing with mobs of commuters disappearing through the shiny turnstiles and descending into the subway maze. Over 260,000 people pass through this oldest metropolitan train station in Australia each day. It is a grand old dame with her notable clock, French Renaissance architecture, noble blackened bronze dome, and yellowish brick facade. Named after the famous explorer Mathew Flinders, it was first opened in 1854 and the current building was finished in 1910. The huge clocks above the entrance show train departure times from the station's 15 platforms. Originally the site of a fish market, it is now one of the most visited icons in the city.

Right across the street and adjacent to Chloe's hangout is the unmistakable, controversial, and monumental:

*FEDERATION SQUARE ❺, ☎ (03) 8662-1555, W: federationsquare.com.au. *Open 10–5 Mon.–Thurs., 10–9 Fri., 10–6 weekends. Closed Christmas, Good Friday, and closed until noon on April 25th. Free with fees for some exhibits.*

The Ian Potter Centre or National Gallery of Victoria is a 10-acre square that has recently opened to a massive public fervor. It seems that half the city loves the strange architectural design unveiled in November 2002—and the other half despised the mix of Star Trek (think the Borg ship), camouflaged panels, glass portals, and angular beauty. The AU $440-million building is home to over 22,000 works of art including special rotating exhibits, and houses the largest collection of Australian art in the world. Even if you are not into the arts scene, have a wander around and make up your own mind on the claim that this building (like the Sydney Opera House) is the most stunning architectural design in Australia.

Walk five blocks west on Flinders Street to the:

*IMMIGRATION MUSEUM ❻, ☎ (03) 9927-2700 or W: immigration.muse um.vic.gov.au. *Open daily 10–5, closed Christmas & Good Friday. AU $7 adult, AU $5.50 seniors, AU $3.50 kids.*

This three-story white 19th-century building was once the Customs house and is now a showcase of the city's history. Multiculturalism is the main theme—how it has created the strong bond among the current Melbournians. The museum highlights life from the early 1800s through movies, photos, and memorabilia. The coolest exhibit is the 56-foot boat set up to demonstrate how it felt to travel to Australia via steamship. There are haunting views of the early immigrants, and you can actually scan the roles in the Discovery Centre to find an ancestor.

Weave your way under the highway through Enterprize Park and to the **Melbourne Aquarium** ❼, ☎ (03) 9620-0999 or **W:** melbourneaquarium .com.au. Open daily 9–6. AU $22 adults, AU $12 kids, AU $14 seniors, and AU $55 families. Plunked right on the Yarra River, this museum is full of interactive displays hosted by an electronic fish, and is a great spot for those who like simulator rides. You can continue on to **The Victoria Police Museum** ❽, ☎ (03) 9247-5215, just past Batman Park at 637 Flinders Street or double back to Flinders Street. The small museum depicts the history of the police forces of the state and memorabilia of their nemesis—Ned Kelly. Free.

Walking two blocks up King Street to 525 Collins Street, you will be confronted by the:

*RIALTO   TOWERS   ❾,   ☎   (03)   9629-8222   or   W: rialtoobservationdeck.com.au. *Open daily 10–10. AU $11.80 adults, AU $6.80 kids, AU $7.50 seniors, and AU $33.80 families.*

The Towers' Observation Deck is 55 floors up and opens up to a 360-degree vantage point. This 830-foot structure is the tallest office building in the Southern Hemisphere, and some athletes actually climb the steps in less than six minutes. Completed in 1994, it's one of the highest observation towers in the world. With ears popping you pass 706 door openings in one of the 36 lifts, and arrive at the platform in 38 seconds. The view is a magnificent panorama of Port Phillip Bay in the south, the city below, and the Dandenong Ranges to the north. The platform is equipped with multi-language computers with animated descriptions of each view providing a brief history of them while pointing out significant landmarks. A separate camera allows you to scan the city and zoom in on specific areas of interest. Your can actually see the faces of people walking across the Queens Street Bridge. At the base of the elevators is the RialtoVision Theatre and a movie of "the best of Melbourne and Victoria in just 20 minutes."

Double back onto Little Collins Street to the shopping section of the tour, starting at the ***Block Arcade** ❿, ☎ (03) 9654-5244 at 282 Collins Street; **Australia on Collins** at the corner of Elizabeth & Collins Street; **Collins Place** ⓫, ☎ (03) 9655-3600 or **W:** collinsplace.com.au; and the **Melbourne Athenaeum** ⓬, ☎ (03) 9650-3100 or **W:** athenaeumlibrary.city search.com.au, at 188 Collins Street. The **Block Arcade** has over 30 shops housed in a National Trust historic building. **Australia on Collins** is a sixty-store complex with a food court and a fine mix of merchants. **Collins Place** is the multi-purpose mall with fashion, services, movie theaters, food, and hotels. **The Athenaeum** is a book lover's paradise. It is an Old World bookstore with a café, designer stores, opal gallery, and Ticketmaster—for those evening plans. Nearby is the **Bourke Street Mall**, an eight-block street full of stores, restaurants, and just plain fun.

Right around the corner is the old familiar **Town Hall** where you can pick up more information, cool off, or take a break and stroll the lobby.

The next three spots are for a quick look around. If you like what is show-ing, book an evening at the **Regent Theatre** at 191 Collins Street; **Her Majesty's Theatre** at the corner of Little Bourke & Exhibition Streets; or the **Princess Theatre** at the corner of Little Bourke and Spring Streets.

Make your way to the corner of Lonsdale and Exhibition Street to the *Chinese Museum ⓭, ☎ (03) 9662-2888. Open Sun.–Fri 10–4:30, Sat. 12–4:30. There are five levels of uniquely interesting showcases filled with infor-mation of the Chinese immigration, their contributions and struggles dur-ing the gold rush years, and ancestral artifacts. This incredible building has on display the world's largest dragon—Dai Loong, a queue (pigtail) from the 19th century, and urns found in the gold fields of Victoria. It's worthy of a couple of hour's inspection.

At the outer edge of the circuit on Spring Street (near Bourke Street) is **Parliament House** ⓮, ☎ (03) 9651-8568. This is the original site of Australia's Federal Government founded in 1901, before it was moved to the current capital of Canberra in 1927. It's claimed to have the most extravagant decorations of any public building on the continent. You can get free tours around the cool interiors when sessions are not proceeding or sit in on a hearing in the public gallery. Tours run Tue. 2–11, Wed. 10–11, and Thurs. 10–5:30.

Try planning your visit to this part of town around lunch or high tea time. When you need a break cross the street to the *Windsor Hotel ⓯, ☎ (03) 9633-6000 or **W**: thewindsor.com.au. This is Australia's last and only remaining Grand Hotel, and temporary home to foreign dignitaries, royal-ty, and international travelers. Opening in 1883, it was later purchased in the late 1880s as The Grand (its original name) by a leader of the Temperance Party who burned the liquor license, after which it became the Grand Coffee Palace. The drinking rights were restored by the Duke of Windsor, and he renamed it in his own honor. You will be ushered through the double-glass doors to the lobby of a grand hotel complete with lush carpets, huge paintings staring from the walls (worth over $3 mil-lion), the feel of old money, and impeccable service. There will probably be a massive bouquet of native flowers perched atop an antique circular table strategically placed under a beaming crystal chandelier and enhanced by highly polished mirrors behind them. Persian rugs are right at home in the darkly paneled foyer as floor-to-ceiling paintings of Scottish pipers watch you enter the dining area. There you will probably notice a table or two stacked with obscenely rich pastries. Expect extreme-ly good service for a reasonable price. And make sure you check out the telephone booths adjacent to the dining area. They are gilded wrought-iron cages that were obviously the old lifts (elevators). The tiny rooms are fitted with a burgundy leather chair, an end table stacked with phone books, and an ugly orange payphone common here in Australia.

After refreshments cross back across the street, pass the **Old Treasury Building** ⓰, and enter the **Treasury Gardens**. If you time it right (9–5 week-days and 10–4 weekends), you can stop in and have a walkabout in the

Gold Treasury Museum with the historic gold vaults, and witness the legacy of the gold rush. Outside, have a stroll and soak in the shaded park as you make your way north on Lansdowne Street, turn left onto Cathedral Place and enter *St Patrick's Cathedral ⓱, ☎ (03) 9662-2233. This might be the most impressive and most beautiful church I have ever seen. It is built right in the center of a huge botanical garden that is surrounded by the hustle and bustle of city life. The massive, old brownstone cathedral, complete with gargoyles, pointed spires, and wrought-iron lattice is placed right in the middle of multi-colored flowerbeds, and is tucked under lush green palm trees. It looks like an old castle protected by a moat of flowers. The newly consecrated statues of St Francis of Assisi and St Catherine of Siena are located in the side courtyard as the centerpieces of the churchyard. The construction on this church began in 1858, taking 82 years to complete. Amber glass windows cast a mystical glow on the 28 wooden angels peering down from their perch 200 feet above the black-and-tan diamond-shaped marble floor tiles. The plain stone pillars are painted a sandy color and rise to meet the angelic carved figurines 45-feet up. Round stained-glass windows are set at the front and the back of the church, looking like opposing kaleidoscopes.

Stepping back into the daylight, continue into the *Fitzroy Gardens and Captain Cook's Cottage ⓲, ☎ (03) 9419-4677. Open daily 9–5. Fitzroy Gardens are over 150 years old, and were named after the Governor of New South Wales—Sir Charles Augustus Fitzroy (1796–1858). On the garden grounds is Cook's cottage, a conservatory filled with flowers and ponds, a Tudor village, Sinclair's cottage, and the famous Fairies Tree. As it is a mystical forest, the Fairies Tree seemed appropriate. To check it out look at W: fitzroygardens.com and click on The Fairies Tree icon. The Cook family, known as the greatest navigators of the Southern Hemisphere, built the cottage in 1755 and fitted the house with furniture typical of the homes in the North of England in the 1700s. The small stable area to the rear, now the gift shop, shows how James Cook lived in this oldest building in Australia. Ivy covering the cottage was started as a cutting from his original cottage site in Great Ayton. The gardens depict the working garden as it was during his lifetime and has herbs for medicinal uses, fruits and vegetables, as well as some ornamental shrubs. This cottage of the famous pacific navigator was transported, stone-by-stone from Great Ayton in Yorkshire England, and reassembled on the grounds. He apparently enjoyed the small, cramped style of this house that he lived in between voyages, as it closely resembled the way he lived on board ship.

End the day at one of the many bistros, pubs, or restaurants on Little Collins Street.

Southbank & The Royal Botanic Gardens

T ime to chill out and smell the roses in the vast parklands of Southbank (also referred to as Southgate). The café in the middle of the botanic gardens is a great place to break for lunch, too. This tour focuses on the gardens, the theaters, and will also sneak in some relaxing time along the promenade adjacent to the Yarra River. The museums are worth a peek, and if you save the theaters until after dark, you can easily fit everything into your schedule. The parks and gardens could be covered first as you may want to spend the entire day wandering around the massive landscaped lawns. Plus if the weather becomes uncooperative, you can head inside to nearby museums, shops, and galleries. If the cultural aspects are more to your liking, then check a few days before you might want to see a show or concert to assure seating that pleases. There is shopping on the southern shores too, and the shop in the gardens has a few intriguing items on the shelves. The mall at Southgate is loaded with shops, cafés, wine clubs, and fine dining spots.

The area has numerous names, but is commonly referred to as the Southgate Arts & Leisure Precinct. It is a popular place both day and night with street performances, craft markets, top restaurants, and parkland walks that go on forever.

GETTING THERE:

I would suggest walking to Southbank and enjoy the transition from metropolitan attitudes to the relaxed feelings of massive parks and gardens. It's only about five (long) blocks passing Flinders Street Station, across the Princess Bridge (St Kilda Road), and over the Yarra River into the Arts Precinct. Public transportation is available if you need a bit of assistance.

PRACTICALITIES:

There will be lots of walking in this section. The paths are easily navigated and provide shaded strolls along gently sloping paths. Wear comfortable shoes and check the weather predictions to estimate what to wear. If your main interest is culture, then check the free brochures, talk to the concierge, or contact **Ticketek**, ☎ 13-28-49, ☎ 1-800-062-849 or **W**: ticketek.com for the current shows and times. A good free newsletter that contains interesting things to do is "Melbourne's Great Indoors;" visit their web page at **W**: visitvictoria.com/mgi

FOOD AND DRINK:

Most of the eateries are clustered around the Yarra River and the Southgate Promenade. There are about 20 of them at the Food Wharf and over 40 retail stores to explore after your meal. The museums, galleries, casino, and theaters provide varying levels of refreshments and are a bit less crowded than the riverfront cafés. The Royal Botanic Gardens has a fantastic **Tearoom Restaurant** right next to a pond full of swans; I would recommend lunching at this beautiful location. Other award-winning eateries include **Mecca**, ☎ (03) 9682-2999, $$-$$$; **Red Emperor**, ☎ (03) 9699-4170, $$; **Scusa Mi Ristorante**, ☎ (03) 9699-4111, $$-$$$; and **Walter's Wine Bar**, ☎ (03) 9690-9211, $$-$$$.

LOCAL ATTRACTIONS:

Circled numbers correspond to numbers on the map. To provide a systematic approach to this section, I will list the attractions in the order in which they reside—from the river to the far end of the gardens. Mix and match as you wish. I have put an asterisk next to the more popular spots.

As you walk across the Princess Bridge from the center of the city you will see gardens on your left, the theaters straight ahead, and the Southgate shopping area to the right under the bridge. At this point you can decide to head to the theaters and book a show, veer off to explore the gardens, or walk for the store sales. For the first option start at Melbourne Concert Hall attraction below, for the second choice go to the Queen Victoria Gardens description, and to start your exploration of Southbank riverfront beginning at the Polly Woodside Museum.

As you reach Southbank, descend the stairs, walk along the boardwalk, past the stores to the far end of the boardwalk, enter Riverside park, walk to Lorimer Street, and turn right into the:

POLLY WOODSIDE MUSEUM ❶, ☎ (03) 9699-9760. *Open daily 10–4, closed Christmas. AU $9 adult/AU $6 child/AU $7 senior/AU $25 family).*

The highlight of the museum is the tallship named *Irish*, an iron barque boat built in 1885. You can walk the gangplank in search of ghosts on its ancient decks. The ship is dry-docked in the only wooden-walled dry dock in the world. It is an interesting tour with old photographs, relics of the mariners, and a chance to get a taste of what it must have been like sailing in the 1880s.

Across the street is the **Melbourne Exhibition Hall ❷**, ☎ (03) 9205-6400,

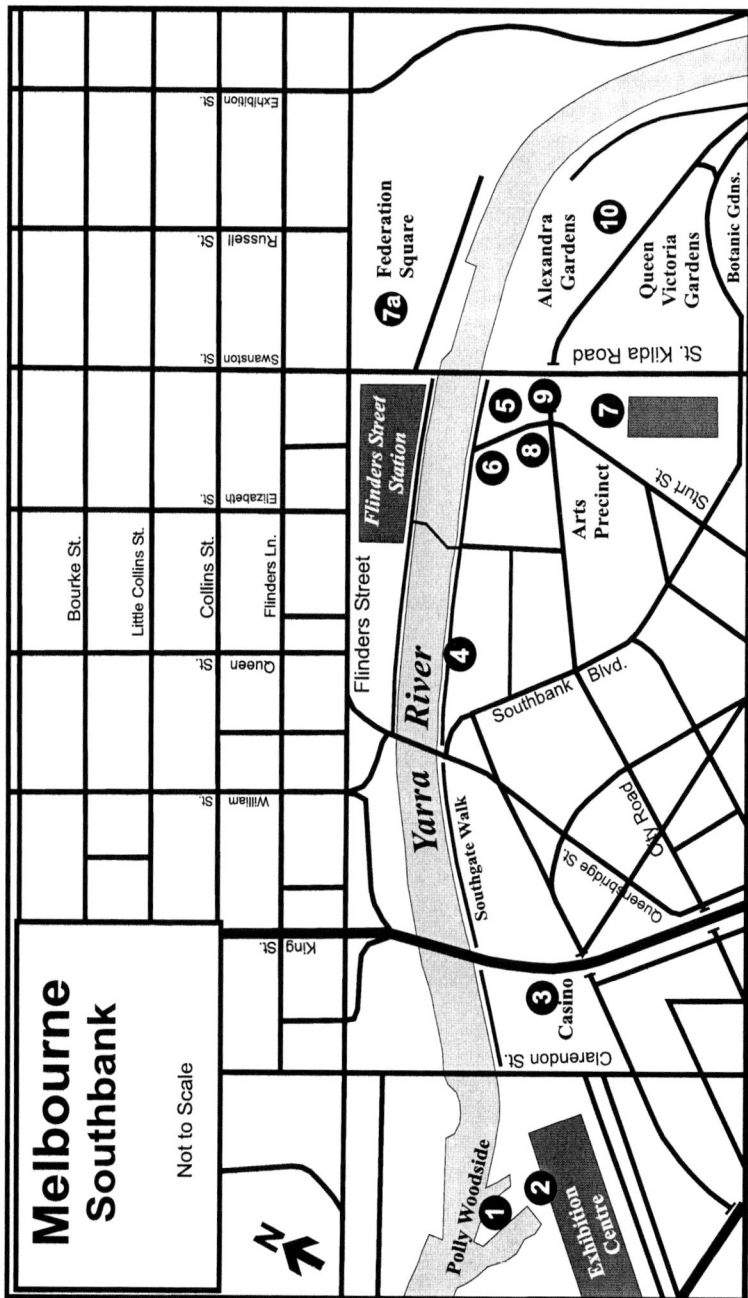

Melbourne
Southbank

Not to Scale

Exhibition St.

Russell St.

Swanston St.

Bourke St.

Little Collins St.

Collins St.

Flinders Ln.

Elizabeth St.

Queen St.

William St.

King St.

Flinders Street

Flinders Street Station

Federation Square

7a

Alexandra Gardens

10

Queen Victoria Gardens

Botanic Gdns.

St. Kilda Road

5
9
6
8

7

Arts Precinct

Sturt St.

Yarra River

4

Southbank Blvd.

Southgate Walk

Queensbridge St.

City Road

3 Casino

Clarendon St.

Polly Woodside

1
2

Exhibition Centre

and as you double back towards Princess Bridge you may want to stop for a few games of blackjack at the **Crown Casino & Entertainment Complex** ❸, ☎ (03) 9292-8888. This huge entertainment center has 14 movie theaters, 17 bars, and 35 restaurants in addition to its gaming floors. Continuing along the *Southgate Walk ❹, ☎ (03) 9699-4311, stop in at the shopping strip, watch the street buskers and mimes, or enjoy a chilled glass of wine and a cheese plate at Water's Wine Bar. The 40 retail outlets are in a compact area making it easy for quick shopping, and there is a brochure of all the stores at the riverside entrance. When you had your fill of food and buying, head up the stairs to the theaters and galleries on St Kilda Road.

The **Melbourne Concert Hall** ❺, ☎ (03) 9281-8000 or **W**: vicartscentre.com.au, The *Victorian Arts Centre ❻, ☎ (03) 9281-8000, the *National Gallery of Victoria ❼, ☎ (03) 8662-1555 or **W**: ngv.vic.gov.au, open 10–5, the **Opera Australia Centre** ❽, and the **Australian Ballet Centre** ❾ are all clustered between St Kilda Road and Sturt Street. The plays, concerts, and exhibits are magnificent even if they are not very well advertised. Try to pick up an events schedule to plan a matinee or evening of culture. Inquiries are taken at **Ticketek**, ☎ 13-28-49, ☎ 1-800-062-849 or **W**: ticketek.com. They provide information on the current shows and times. The **Concert Hall** opened its doors in 1982 with 2,677 seats arranged in three sets of stalls, circle, and balcony-level views. The 22 wooden acoustic baffles, 30 sound shells hanging from the ceiling, and surrounding walls painted like Australian gemstones make for a perfect spot to witness a show. From opera to rock to symphonies, this is a great place for an evening. The **Victorian Arts Gallery** building is unmistakable as it looks like something from the Jetson's cartoon show, with a futuristic (even now) spire and silver facades. It's home to some of Australia's top performers and welcomes international stars to present some fantastic. If you don't have time for entertainment, try to get one of the tours of the building. They will introduce you to the galleries with displays of over 400 works of art, explain why the spire had to be replaced, and be allowed to check out the Soundhouse. Tours cost about AU $10–$23, take about an hour, and usually start around noon. You can get tickets at the foyer or call ☎ (03) 9281-8608. If you are lucky enough to be around on Sunday, check out the 150 stalls of the **Sunday Market** right outside the building. There are some far-out goods to be purchased. The **National Gallery** is on three levels, and the 20 galleries now house an international display of artwork. The Australian collection has been transferred to the Federation Square annex of the gallery. Masterpieces are rotated with approximately 800 pieces on display at one time. The gallery hosts education studios, a great gift shop, multimedia displays, a theater, a bistro and cafés. There are free tours and self-guided audio tours (AU $5), and they usually run for 30 minutes.

Now for the gentle strolls amongst the fragrant flowers of the gardens. Right across the street from the arts area are the city's pride and joy of the *Queen Victoria Gardens, the **Alexandria Gardens**, the **Sidney Music Bowl**, the **Ice Rink**, **Kings Domain**, the **Herb Gardens**, and the *Royal Botanic

Garden ⑩, ☎ (03) 9252-2300 or **W**: rbgmelb.org.au or **W**: rbg.vic.gov.au. The Royal Botanic Garden has over 12,000 species of native and imported flora with a total of 51,000 individual plants. Established in 1846, it has shaded pathways along the river, with joggers everywhere. The free walks can begin at 7:30 and end at dusk when the park is open. The scents vary as you pass through each section of the gardens, and multi-colored flowers are scattered all over the park. The crisp-cut lawns and manicured flower gardens are almost too perfect to be real. Some highlights of the sections include the Alexandria Gardens with its monuments; the Queen Victoria Gardens complete with a floral clock, Kings Domain that has King George V's statue, the old Government House, and the newly renovated Sidney Myer Music Bowl for outdoor concerts. The **Shrine of Remembrance** is a must-see as it is one of the largest war memorials in the world. Volunteers are available, ☎ (03) 9654-8415, to explain the unique features like the ray of light.

Designer and curator of the Royal Botanic Gardens was W.R. Guilfoyle (1873–1910). The 100 acres, over 12,000 species of native plants, flocks of swans and ducks paddling the ponds, and imported flora are a testament to his foresight. Tennyson Lawn has four 120-year-old English elm trees; near the old billabong (pond) is the tallest tree—an American swamp cypress. Lynch Gate is an interesting site—it's a narrow iron-gated arch with sharp pikes protruding from every possible nook and cranny. The stone masonry is topped with two-inch black iron prods and appears that they really don't want you in the place when the gate is secured. As you pass through the gate you will meander down a path to the Temple of Winds, the huge Ornamental Lake with stoic black swans paddling about the clear waters, and come upon the Rose Pavilion. But beware of Fern Gully with its hundreds (maybe thousands) of bats hanging from the trees. Have a break down at the William Tell Rest House. The small green and yellow building looks like an enchanted-forest bus stop with an open section for visitors to sit and rest. Just past the cottage you will come upon the Southern Lawn and a little tearoom by the edge of the Nymphaea Lake. It's a perfect spot for lunch and to purchase a fun gardening gadget at the gift shop.

Queen Victoria Market & the Gaol

The highlight of this trip will be the Queen Victoria Market with its astounding assortment of food stalls, hawking vendors, and fantastic people-watching opportunities. As you join the crowds at this 17-acre festival, you will be hard pressed to walk away without a bagful of goods. Expect to spend at least thee hours amongst multi-cultural vendors, and to have a grand time watching them hawk their wares. This will be a delightful experience for the eyes, nose, and taste buds. Your ears will take some time to get used to the constant onslaught of sales pitches originating from the heavy-accented vendors.

On the opposite spectrum is the creepy Old Melbourne Gaol (jail), with Ned Kelly's death mask and full armor; a stark reminder of how things got started in Melbourne—at least for a few unfortunate souls. And to mix the tour up a bit, there is a great shopping center housed under a giant glass pyramid between the two contrasting attractions. It would be best to spend the time between those three as they could actually take the entire day to see properly.

GETTING THERE:

This can also be easily walked from the center of town, but the tram stops right at the corner of the market square, which may save a bit of time. Buses also stop at the Victoria Street side. The jail, museum, and shopping center are all on the tram lines too.

PRACTICALITIES:

Expect lots of walking, but there will be plenty of shade and stops to rest. Casual clothes and comfortable shoes are a good idea. If you decide to buy instead of shop, take the trams back home and maybe do the jail and other attractions before the markets.

FOOD AND DRINK:

Food is the center of this section, and you can graze as you walk the market, sit and relax in the many cafés and restaurants, or save your appetite for dinner at Lygon Street. Since you are in the neighborhood, this is a good time to have a hearty meal at this famous block of Italian taste delights.

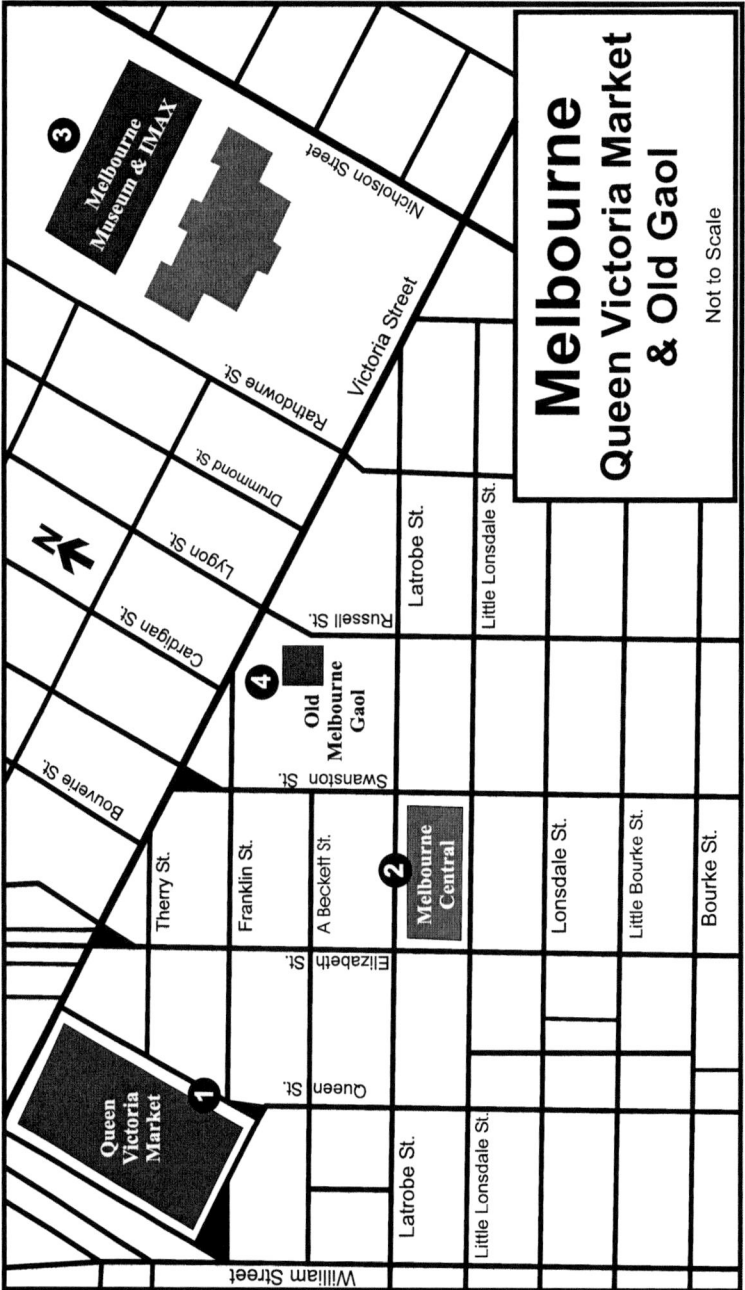

Melbourne
Queen Victoria Market & Old Gaol

Not to Scale

Melbourne Museum & IMAX **3**

Nicholson Street

Victoria Street

Rathdowne St.

Drummond St.

Lygon St.

Cardigan St.

Bouverie St.

Therry St.

Franklin St.

A Beckett St.

Elizabeth St.

Queen St.

William Street

Latrobe St.

Little Lonsdale St.

Russell St.

Old Melbourne Gaol **4**

Swanston St.

Melbourne Central **2**

Lonsdale St.

Little Bourke St.

Bourke St.

Queen Victoria Market **1**

LOCAL ATTRACTIONS:
Circled numbers correspond to numbers on the map.

*QUEEN VICTORIA MARKET ❶, 513 Elizabeth Street, ☎ (03) 9320-5838 or (03) 9320-5822, **W**: qvm.com.au. *Open Tues.–Thurs. 6–2, Fri. 6–6, Sat. 6–3, Sun. 9–4, closed holidays. Free. Guided tours—Foodies Dream Tour on Tues., Thurs. Fri., and Sat. 10am for AU $22 (includes sampling), or the Heritage Market Tour on Tues., Thurs., Fri., and Sat. 10:30am for AU $16 (includes brunch); self-guided tours. Cafés, food court, and restaurants. Special events. &.*

Officially opened in 1878, the market is a triangular city block that is joined by another section making it about 2–3 blocks in size. The pyramid-shaped block is host to organics, fruits and vegetables, seafood, cheese displays, deli treats, and a food court. Shops facing Elizabeth Street and Therry Street are comprised of coffee and trinket marts. You will be one of the 130,000 weekly visitors to this century-old market that includes almost 17 acres of stores and over 1,000 traders. The stalls are laid out in rows from A to LL and are broken out into the various goods being sold—veggies, meats, and clothing. The butchers seem to be all big European men (few women) with balding heads and serious looks as they hawked their wares. Fishmongers wear weather-beaten faces and smells of the sea. Vegetable farmers are earthy Anglos with strong honest hands and faces that showed the trials of farming. The mix of men and women who peddle cheese and pastries look French to me. Carpet salesmen are predominately Middle Eastern and will attempt to lure you in to just touch the quality of their rugs. Finally the Asians seemed to corner the market in souvenirs and general wares. Many of the stalls have been handed down for generations, since the market opened. A little-known fact is that the market was built on the original site of the city's first graveyard. No wonder they open after sunrise and close at 4pm! The massive clean rows of aisles are full of locals as well as tourists. The natives seem immune to the haranguing of the vendors, and most are equipped with little handcarts filled with fresh strawberries, newly cut flowers, and meats. No trinkets in those trolleys. The out-of-towners carry bags full of stuffed koala toys, Aussie hats, and hand-painted boomerangs.

The market offers cooking classes that feature the specialty foods sold by their vendors. For around AU $65 you can learn Spanish, Middle Eastern, Italian, Seafood, Indian, Cantonese, and baking preparation. This section is so rich in culture, making it a blast to soak in the sights, noise, and especially the smells.

*MELBOURNE CENTRAL ❷, 211 LaTrobe Street, ☎ (03) 9922-1100. *Open Mon.–Thurs. 10–6, Fri. 10–9, Sat. 10–6, Sun. 11–6, closed major holidays. Free. Self guided tours. Cafés and restaurants. Special events. &.*

Opened in 1991, Melbourne Central can be identified by its large aluminum and glass pyramid dome filtering light onto the massive shopping area below. The **Glass Cone**, as it's called, is the largest glass structure of its kind in the world, with 20 stories, 924 glass panes, and weighing 490 tons. A full-sized hot air balloon, a replica of the Wright Brothers biplane, and a gigantic marionette watch decorate its interior. At the striking of the hour the white-and-brass watch opens and galahs, cockatoos, koalas, and two minstrels dance to Waltzing Matilda. The centerpiece of the sparkling mall is **Coops' Shot Tower**, constructed in 1890. The British Romanesque/Art Nouveau Shot Tower was built to manufacture ammunition. In employing the gravity method by dropping hot lead from the top of a nine-story perch, perfectly rounded shot was produced. As it cooled on its way down, the shot separated and was finally drenched in three feet of cool water. At the height of operations, over six tons of shot was sold per week. You can visit over 160 shops in an area the size of two city blocks. If you can't decide what to do next, check out the Superscreen in the center area or stop in at the information booth near the Marionette Watch.

*MELBOURNE MUSEUM & IMAX THEATRE ❸, Carlton Gardens (corner of Victoria & Nicholson Streets), ☎ 13-11-02, **W**: melbourne.museum .vic.gov.au. *Open daily 10–6, closed Christmas and Good Friday. AU $12 adult, AU $9 seniors, AU $6.60 child, and AU $33 family. Self-guided tours. Gift shops. Cafés. Special events.* ♿.

Australia's largest museum has tons of interactive displays, virtual reality shows, and out-of-the-ordinary stuff. The highlight for many is the famous Phar Lap. This fully stuffed and preserved racehorse was a legend in Australia, and there were rumors that the American mob poisoned this record-breaking horse. Kids will love this building, full of touch & climb exhibits, and the adults will be fascinated with the Aboriginal Centre and special shows throughout the complex. There is a cool forest gallery that is a living testament to Victoria's woodlands.

IMAX is next door, where you can experience one of the many big-screen shows, the free information research center, and see some of the live shows. The Royal Exhibition Building is also on the grounds of the museum and is a great place to wander around.

Nearby is the:

*OLD MELBOURNE GAOL ❹, Russell Street, ☎ (03) 9663-7228, **W**: nat trust.com.au. *Open daily 9–5, closed Christmas and Good Friday. Adults AU $12.50, seniors AU $9.50, kids AU $7.50, and family AU $33.50. Self-guided tours (guides are available for questions). Nightly tours are AU $20 and can be booked at* ☎ *136-100. Gift shop. Café. Special events. Partially* ♿.

This, the home of Victoria's oldest surviving prison, might be the creepiest place you will see in Australia. Constructed in 1841, the jail was designed to accommodate short-term prisoners sentenced for minor offences such as drunkenness, lunacy, vagrancy, and those awaiting execution. With the 1851 gold rush and the increase of lawlessness, the jail was expanded in 1864 to become one of the largest buildings in

Melbourne. Closed in 1929 and reopened briefly as a military detention barracks from 1942–46, it was finally converted to a museum in 1972. The three tiers of cages built of solid bluestone are lit only by small openings in the door that received rays of sun from a series of skylights on the roof. The rooms are about five feet by ten feet and have only a straw filled rag that was used as a bed. A few did have a small rudimentary writing table and stool. Castings of the 135 executed faces stared blankly ahead as you can read their stories. The masks were used to study common characteristics of criminals to determine if evil behavior could be predicted. Most of the prisoner vaults have the death masks of their former inhabitants along with a description of their offenses. Many were children held for stealing food, women were often jailed for killing their abusive husbands, and quite a few were insane.

It is also the resting place of Ned Kelly's armor. Ned was the leader of the bushrangers called the Kelly Gang. Bushrangers were outback highwaymen who chose the outlaw life and defied the poorly-equipped law enforcement agencies in the 1800s. The death mask of Ned Kelly, his full armor, and the beam that hung him remains in the Melbourne Goal. As legend has it, just before he was hung he told the magistrate that he would soon follow him to the grave and his last words were, "Such is Life." The magistrate died two weeks later of a heart attack. At the end of the dim corridor is the hangman's scaffold, a figure depicting the death pose of Ned Kelly, and the lashing triangle. The rope still hangs from the oaken beam two stories from the lashing rack that faced the noose. A glass enclosure displays his full armor and his trusty 45 revolver. The armor is an ingenious piece of work with a helmet similar to a knight's headgear including a horizontal slit cut in the metal for vision. The breastplate is about four pieces of brownish metal riveted with heavy bolts and looks as though a ballpein hammer was used to make the final alterations. Finally, look to the top tier for the ghost of the woman who was executed at the jail.

Mornington Peninsula & the Great Ocean Road

West of Melbourne proper your drive will take you past some of the most spectacular ocean views anywhere. Like California's Pacific Highway, it is winding and has lots of ups and downs. You can double back at any time, but the tour is set to take you as far as the Twelve Apostles, 150 miles west of Melbourne in Port Campbell National Park. On the windswept coastline enjoy Bells' Beach and the world-famous surf waves, and stopover at the shearer's huts at the National Wool Museum. The road itself is a major attraction and many find it enjoyable to put the top down and cruise along the sheer cliffs at the water's edge without stopping. This tour will culminate with the appearance of the Twelve Apostles rock formations surrounded by the boiling waters of the Southern Ocean. In the same area you can also hike the Port Campbell National Park and visit the Lord Ard Gorge, the Blowhole, and the deafening Thunder Cave. Some tour companies also bring you back to Melbourne through the interior and past the mountain range called the Grampions.

If you decide to drive out towards Port Phillip Bay first, you will pass strange timber bathhouses that are remnants of the Victorian bathing customs, and miles of tea-trees. Stops along the way will allow you to dip your toe in the Southern Ocean at secluded beaches. The coastline will open up and you will have camera stops at the Sorrento Marine Aquarium, the span carved by the waves at London Bridge, and watch the violent seas from Cape Schanck Lighthouse and Museum. Crossing onto Phillip Island you will be in the homeland of the fairy penguins and the spectacular sights of the rock formations that face the Bass Strait. The bird life is varied and overwhelming, and you can also view the Australian fur seals on Seal Rocks.

You can drive the route, but I would strongly recommend that you arrange one of the bus tours. The road is very treacherous, winding, and if you keep your eyes on the road, you will miss the whole reason for this trip. The trip can be completed and arrive back into Melbourne in one day, but it is not recommended. This should be a two-day tour with plenty of stops and stares over the Bass Strait.

GETTING THERE:

By Car: I would not recommend this as a course of action. It's a precarious jaunt and you will miss the sights of the ocean as you drive. You have three distinct routes available, but the path along the **Great Ocean Road** is the best with breathtaking scenery. The quickest is via the inland **Princess Highway**. If you take the 78-mile Phillip Island Trek, leave the city via the **Monash Freeway**, south to the South Gippsland Highway, through Cranbourne, and onto the Bass Highway. Take the Phillip Island (San Reno) exit and cross the bridge to the island. You can also drive to the point via the Nepean Highway and travel to the island in a counterclockwise fashion. Upon your return from the island, go to Sorrento for the ferry to Queenscliff. From there follow signs to the B100 and Torquay. The Great Ocean Road Drive is about 177 miles from Melbourne and will take about 5–6 hours (with a few stops). Leave the city via the M1 or Princess Highway towards Geelong. From Geelong, proceed due south on Torquay Road into Torquay, then just keep the ocean on your left and enjoy the sights. The Princess Highway Inland Tour is 150 miles and three hours to the 12 Apostles. Exit the city via Princess Highway to Geelong and continue inland to Colac. At Colac take the Simpson-Timboon Road and follow signs to the Great Ocean Road and Princetown.

By Bus: Public transport can be organized from **V-line** in Melbourne, ☎ 13-61-96 or **W**: vline.vic.gov.au, but they only take you to the island or to Port Campbell and no tours are available from there. Bus tours are the best option and are offered by **AAT King Tours** (only through a travel agent or your concierge) or **Go West Tours**, ☎ (03) 9828-2008 or **W**: gowest.com.au, for around AU $65—with morning tea. The tour rated the best by some of the hostels and information centers is **Eco Platypus Tours**, ☎ 1-800-819-091, ☎ (03) 5570-8331, or **W**. ecoplatypustours.com. They cater to a younger backpack crowd, but offer accommodations and tours for all ages. For AU $120 (tour), AU $20 (accommodation and breakfast), and AU $7 (dinner BBQ) you get a two-day package with all the sights to the 12 Apostles (not the Phillip Island section) and back through the Grampians. The tour may not be for everyone as they pack two 12-hour days into the adventure. It is full of kangaroos, koalas, hiking in bushland, touring the falls, and 12 Apostles, and an overnight homestay at Karramar.

By Train: Trains do not run to the specific areas and attractions of this trip.

PRACTICALITIES:

This will be primarily a bus coach tour with short breaks for hikes, soaking in the scenery, and refreshments. If you take the recommended bus tour, all will be provided and you just have to relax and watch the world go by. If you drive, take plenty of rest stops and take your time. Also beware of animals on the roadway, the marsupials are notorious for wandering on the road after dark. If you do injure an animal, call the Wildlife Emergency Service on ☎ (04) 1738-0687.

The tour options can be booked around the Mornington and Sorrento or straight out along the Great Ocean Road. A comprehensive web site related to the Great Ocean Road can be found at **W**: greatocean road.org

FOOD AND DRINK:

There is food all along the roadway; here are a few recommendations. Mornington offers a trio of eateries at **Arthur's** ($-$$$), ☎ (03) 5981-4444, in Arthur's Rock—daily for lunch and Wed.–Sat. for dinner; Phillip Island has **The Jetty Restaurant** ($-$$), ☎ (03) 5952-2060, at Thompson Avenue; **Carmichaels**, ☎ (03) 5952-1300 at The Esplanade; and **George Bass Hotel** ($$) ☎ (03) 5678-2206, at Hade Avenue. The choices at Port Campbell include **Neptune's Realm** ($$), ☎ (03) 5598-6059, at 34 Lord Street; **Port Campbell Take Away** ($), ☎ (03) 5598-6237, at 16 Lord Street; **Twelve Apostles Country Retreat** ($$), ☎ 1-800-351-233, at the entrance to the car park; **Waves** ($-$$), ☎ (03) 5598-6111 at 29 Lord Street; and the **Information Center** ($).

ACCOMMODATIONS:

If you decide to spend the night out in Port Campbell, here are a few choices: **Great Ocean Road Motor Inn**, ☎ (03) 5598-6522—four-star motel for AU $105–$175 at 10 Great Ocean Road; **Loch Ard Motor Inn**, ☎ (03) 5598-6328—three-stars for AU $88–$120 on Lord Street; **Daysy Hill Country Cottages**, ☎ (03) 5598-6226—four-stars for AU $115–$140 on Port Campbell Road; **Port Campbell Shearwater Haven B&B**, ☎ (03) 5598-6532, at 12 Pleasant Drive for AU $80–$140; Port Bayou, ☎ (03) 5598-6403, at 52 Lord Street for AU $55–$90.

If you use the Eco Platypus Tours, you will be staying at a comfortable and modest accommodation that is more of a homestay than a hotel. The **Karramar Homestay** is run by an Australian family, and the experience is full of good food, interesting yarns, and wildlife. For AU $20 (dorm) or AU $25 for a twin or double share, you get breakfast, linens, and marshmallows over the campfire.

LOCAL ATTRACTIONS:

Circled numbers correspond to numbers on the map.

These are listings of attractions along the Great Ocean Road. If you take a coach tour, they may vary a bit, but are considered the highlights for most travelers. The attractions begin in the Port Phillip Bay area and continue around the eastern side to the tip. From there you can hop the ferry across to Queenscliff and continue the journey towards the 12 Apostles. If you choose to bypass the penguins and Phillip Island, start the attractions with Geelong and continue out to the 12 Apostles.

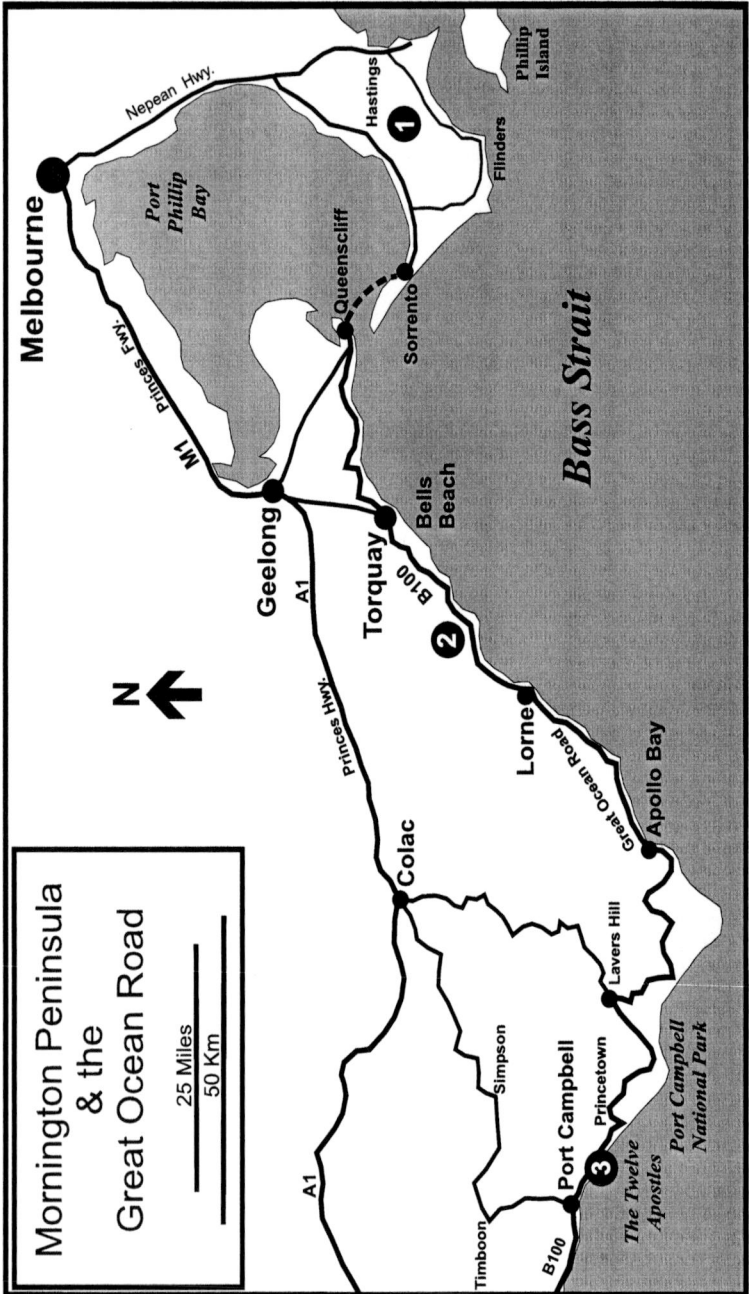

Mornington Peninsula & the Great Ocean Road

25 Miles
50 Km

N

Melbourne
Port Phillip Bay
Nepean Hwy.
Princes Fwy.
M1
Hastings
❶
Flinders
Phillip Island
Queenscliff
Sorrento
Bass Strait
Geelong
A1
Princes Hwy.
Torquay
Bells Beach
B100
❷
Lorne
Great Ocean Road
Apollo Bay
Colac
Lavers Hill
Simpson
Timboon
A1
B100
Port Campbell
Princetown
Port Campbell National Park
The Twelve Apostles
❸

*THE MORNINGTON PENNINSULA ❶

Home to the **Sorrento Marine Aquarium's** (☎ (03) 5984-4478) seal feeding program, the natural bridge called **London Bridge** at Back Beach, **Arthur's Seat National Park** and its summit views over the bay, and the famous **Cape Schanck Lighthouse and Museum** right on the furious coastline. The peninsula has been a long-time favorite summer spot for the city dwellers, and offers a quaint and homey feel to everyone who visits. Just beware if you venture into the waters around the peninsula, and swim only in patrolled areas.

The highlight of this tour is *Phillip Island Nature Park (☎ (03) 5951-2800 or **W**: penguins.org.au) and the fairy penguins. You can start at the Information Centre, ☎ (03) 5956-7447 or 1-300-366-422, at Tourist Road on the island. Grab a map or two, get the latest news, and head out. You can also arrange your tours from there. Tour operators are: **Bay Connections**, ☎ (03) 5678-5642, from San Remo with 1–5 hour tours from seal watching, French Island, and sunset cruises; **Melbourne's Best Tours**, ☎ 1-300-130-550 or (03) 9338-6822, from Melbourne with small bus tours; and **Amaroo Park Tours**, ☎ (03) 5952-2548, on the island at 97 Church Street.

The island nature park is a 6,795-acre home to the *Penguin Parade and the **Koala Conservation Centre**. Its 16-by-6-mile landmass is a bit commercialized, but well worth the trip out to meander along the elevated boardwalks, informative footpaths, miles of beaches, and numerous bike paths. The fairy penguins are the big hit, though, and their nightly antics are closely supervised at the reserve area. More private viewing can be had in more remote areas of the island. But please keep your distance. There also tours out to Seal Rocks for the spectacle of hundreds to thousands of Australian fur seals hanging around or swimming about the island.

When you are done playing with the penguins, take the ferry from Sorrento to Queenscliff. The options include the **Sorrento Car & Passenger Ferry**, ☎ (03) 5258-1877 or **W**: searoad.com.au, for AU $38 cars, AU $4 adult, AU $2 kids 5–15, and AU $1 for under 5. The M.V. *Queenscliff* runs every hour on the hour from 7–6. The **Sorrento Ferry**, ☎ (04) 0854-5714, (03) 5984-1602 or **W**: sorrentoferryco.com.au, costs AU $8/14/45 for one-way adult/return adult/family, AU $7/$12 for one-way senior/return senior, and AU $6/$11 for one-way child/return child. You will cross The Rip (the narrow entrance to the bay) and exit on the western side of Port Phillip Bay at Queenscliff. You can stop for a quick tour of the town and Fort Queenscliff or continue your journey towards the 12 Apostles and the first town of Torquay.

If you are driving directly from Melbourne, your first stop might be **Geelong**, ☎ (03) 5222-2900, Victoria's second-largest town. This the former sheep grazing area boasts the **National Wool Museum**, ☎ (03) 5226-4660, with replicated wool shearers and manufacturing exhibits, an interesting *Military Museum** that also has relics as well as background on the shipwrecks in the area, and a fabulous bayside walk past bollards that represent the events and characters of the maritime town. You can find heaps of eateries along the refreshing Bayside Bollard Walk. Pick up Torquay Road and drive 13 miles to **Torquay**, ☎ (03) 5261-4219. This seaside town is known as the Surf Capital of Australia, and has a grand range of underwater reefs for diving enthusiasts. Bells Beach is the home to the first surfing reserve in the world. If you can break away from the beautiful beaches, have a look at the **Surfworld Surfing Museum** at Surf City Plaza, just off Beach Road. If you need to stretch the legs a bit, this is the place to have a hike around the coast and a bit inland. Stop at the Torquay Visitor Information Centre at Surf City Plaza (near the Quicksilver Shop) and pick up a map of the six planned walking treks. And since this is just short of the halfway point to the 12 Apostles, have a bite to eat at the **Nocturnal Donkey Café** ($-$$) at 15 Bell Street, the **Sandbah Café** ($-$$) at 21 Gilbert Street, or one of the may eateries at the Surf City Plaza.

Continue the drive west along the Shipwreck Coast and enjoy the various lookouts along the way, the waterfalls in **Otway National Park**, hidden beach alcoves, and the numerous lighthouses that dot the coastline (some offer tours). You will pass through the towns of Anglesea, pass the lighthouse at Aireys Inlet, and stop for more information at Lorne or Apollo Bay, cross through Otway National Park, and approach Port Campbell National Park and The Twelve Apostles near Port Campbell. What you will experience is:

*THE GREAT OCEAN ROAD ❷, Melbourne to Adelaide, ☎ 13-28-42, **W**: vis itvictoria.com.au

The construction of The Great Ocean Road began in 1918 and the highway was opened to traffic in 1932. Prior to the establishment of this major artery from Melbourne to Adelaide, the only mode of transport was via the treacherous Bass Strait. But the main reason for the building of the road was the need to employ the soldiers who had just returned from the trenches of WWI and to open a tourist route between major cities. Imagine, as you drive along the winding roads overlooking sheer cliffs— this was built with picks, shovels, and a few sticks of dynamite. Testimony of the dangers before the road was built is the 300 ships resting on the ocean floor along the coast. The only commuters who were safe in these journeys were the whales. The local waters are also deemed the Southern Right Whale Nursery and from June to October the giant mammals come north from Antarctica to give birth. If you travel the coastline at that time, it is common to see the pods and calves swimming only yards from the viewing platforms. The other critters to keep watch for (September to April) are the odd mutton birds that arrive at Port Campbell National Park.

At the far end of your trip you will come upon:

*PORT CAMPBELL NATIONAL PARK & THE TWELVE APOSTLES ❸,

Information Center at 26 Morris Street, Port Campbell, ☎ (03) 5237-6529, ☎ (03) 5598-6053, or ☎ 13-19-63, **W**: greatoceanroad.org, **W**: 12apostlesnatpark.org, or **W**: parkweb.vic.gov.au. *Open daily Wed.–Mon. 10–5, closed holidays. Free. Guided tours, self-guided tours. Gift shops. Cafés. Special events. Partially* &.

This coastline was part of the early shipping routes, and the soft limestone cliffs have been sculptured to form spectacular arches, blowholes, narrow inlets, and the amazing Twelve Apostles. The cliffs are about 11 million years old, reaching about 200 feet out of the boiling sea. Walkways are a bit scary as the railings allow you a close and personal view of the vistas and crashing waves below. From the viewing platforms you will witness the Twelve Apostles, climb down the Gibson Steps to face the ocean, explore the walking tracks at Loch Ard Gorge, look down upon The Arch, see the penguin trails near London Bridge, and take the 1,312-foot trail to The Grotto. There are several easy hiking trails to explore on your own or link up with a guide to describe the intimate details of the nooks and crannies of this natural wonder.

The Twelve Apostles are the centerpiece, grace many calendars, and are the subject of numerous maritime and nature documentaries. There is now a new interpretive center at the visitor center containing geologic, historic, and fun information available for free and some to purchase. Learn about the famous 1878 Loch Ard shipwreck and the harrowing story of the survival of only two of the 54 souls. Make sure you have your camera loaded to capture the changing sea and sky vistas.

Section IV

Daytrips in
Queensland

Take your pick mates, because Queensland does have it all. The diversity of this Sunshine State includes: Over 2,700 miles of sparkling opal-blue ocean waters lapping a pristine white sand coastline. Prehistoric paths that lead you into lush tropical rainforests decorated with bright-colored parrots. Mars-like landscape of the Outback complete with opal mines, remnants of Bushrangers, millions of kangaroos, and miles of open space. One of the most famous natural wonders of the world is the Great Barrier Reef with its magical coral and colorful marine life. Animals unique to the rest of the planet like the playful kangaroo, the loveable koala, and the strange cassowary. And home to the friendliest folks to wish you a g'day.

Queenslanders love to repeat their state motto—"Beautiful one day, perfect the next." And this holiday hotspot is not only the favorite destination of the Aussies and their Oceanic neighbors, it is now attracting over four million North Americans who have discovered the wonders of this lucky land each year. A recent newspaper series listed 101 tourist attractions within this sunshine state, and that merely scratched the surface of things to see.

Queensland's 667,180 square miles is about the size of the northeastern quadrant of the United States. But to make your visit manageable, the touring areas are broken into six regions—Brisbane & Surrounds, Gold Coast & Hinterlands, Southeast Queensland & Northern New South Wales, Sunshine Coast, Queensland Outback, and Tropical North. Each has a different character and unusual allure.

BRISBANE & SURROUNDS

The river town of Brisbane (pronounced *Briz-bin*) is not only the capital of the second-largest state in the country; it is the gateway to the holiday region for all of Australia. Located in the northeast part of the country, the subtropical cityscape is lush with palms, mango-laden trees, and fragrantly purple-colored shrubs. It is a stroller's paradise with the relatively flat walkways making it a very accessible city.

Even though Brisbane is the third-largest populated city in Australia, it is unhurried, uncluttered, and friendly. The Central Business District (CBD), a common term to describe the center of most cities and towns in Australia, is segmented into four walking tours—the Queen Street Shopping Mall with major landmarks as well as great souvenir gathering, the Riverside Precinct with its scenic gardens, the exotic and funky Chinatown & Fortitude Valley, and the sprawling parklands of the South Bank Precinct. Added to them is a driving/walking tour and a boating excursion to feed the wild dolphins.

Your visit will thrill your eyes with sleek CityCat taxis speeding past old-time paddlewheel boats, delight your taste buds with Fusion eateries (a mix of Asian, European, and Aussie), make you dizzy with the aromatic smells from the tropical gardens, and immerse you in otherworldly sounds played by street buskers on their didgeridoos. It is the perfect first stop for your adventure into the wild and wonderful state of Queensland.

All tours in the Brisbane & Surrounds section are based from central-ly-located lodging in the vicinity of the Treasury Casino and near the Queen Street Mall. This allows for easy access to public transport as well. Some alternative lodging ideas are included if you want a different atmos-phere.

The duration of the Brisbane series of trips is between four and five days each, and will allow for plenty of rest and relaxation in between. Each tour can be covered in one day, while Day 1 & 2 of Trip 11 can be combined into a one-day tour to save time—but only if you drop some of the more time-consuming attractions like the Sciencecentre. Many of you may not want to stop at each attraction, and that is OK. But review each agenda before trekking out and allow a bit more than a day if you choose to absorb each and every spot.

GETTING AROUND BRISBANE & QUEENSLAND

Since this section combines walking and driving tours, you might need to utilize some form of transportation to get to the starting points and back again. You can avoid renting a car while stationed at specific hubs, but may want the freedom of having a car to get from one location to another—depending on your time restraints. You will probably want to fly between the different states (between Queensland, New South Wales' Sydney, and Victoria's Melbourne), and I would suggest air travel to/from Cairns and maybe the same for the Outback trips. Here are some of your options:

Air Transport: Not much to choose from here as the country has only two major airlines, Qantas and Virgin Blue. The good news is that the ser-vice is generally great, the access is less frantic with fewer people to serve, and you don't have to lug your bags too far to the car or taxi stand. Make you reservations with an agent to get the best deals or book direct with **Qantas** at ☎ 13-13-13 or **W:** qantas.com.au; and **Virgin Blue** at ☎ 13-67-89 or

W: virginblue.com.au

By Car: You will arrive at either the international terminal or domestic station at the Brisbane International Airport. If you are renting a car, get good directions from the rental agency and follow the signs. The twenty-minute drive into Brisbane is easy, and only six miles to the CBD. You might want to hold off on a car until you are ready to move your base location from Brisbane to another hub. It will save you some money, you won't need the car in the city, and the mass transit is easy and relatively cheap. Plus parking is a real hassle in Brissy, and parking tickets don't come cheap. Most major rental car agencies are represented including: **National** at ☎ 13-10-45 or **W**: nationalcar.com.au; **Thrifty** on ☎ 1-300-367-227 or **W**: thrifty.com.au; **Budget** on ☎ 1-300-362-848 or **W**: budget.com.au; **Avis** on ☎ 13-63-33 or **W**: avis.com.au; and **Hertz** on ☎ 13-30-39 or **W**: hertz.com.au

Driving around Queensland is also easy as there are a limited number of roads to choose from. Traffic jams are not prevalent, but they do occasionally happen. Don't underestimate the amount of time to get from one location to another, as the distances are deceiving.

Ride the Rails: City Train is the way to go from the airport, and the newly connected **Airtrain** gets you into town in 22 minutes. The one-way, single adult ticket is AU $9.00 and runs four times an hour; or the 90-minute ride to the Gold Coast is AU $20.00 and departs 27 times daily (AU $35 with limo connections). You can obtain information at ☎ (07) 3216-3308, **W**: airtrain.com.au, or by E-mail on info@airtrain.com.au

The **City Train** operates in the suburban and inter-urban areas; the Yellow Line will take you from the airport into the center of town. The trains are clean, fast, and run on schedule. Pick up a brochure listing the stops and times at any of the rail stations, City Hall, or information booths in the city. The hub of the rail system is at Roma Street, just next to the fabulous new gardens. You can pick up information there, ☎ 13-12-30 or (07) 3235-5555 or at **W**: qr.com.au

Riding the rails around Queensland is a great option, but it is expensive and can be time consuming. However, many locals recommend this mode of travel, especially into the Outback. Some great packages include **Outback Rail Holidays,** ☎ 1-800-627-655 or **W**: traveltrain.qr.com.au; **Queensland Rail Adventures,** ☎ 1-800-809-992, **W**: sunloverholidays.com.au; and **Ritz Rail,** ☎ 1-300-655-808, E-mail: nrail@bigpond.com

Buses: Since the city is so easily walked and the trains are simple to use, I have rarely used the buses. But when I did, they were clean, prompt, and the drivers helpful in getting you where you should be going. The fares are based on zones and sectors, and run from AU $1.80 to $3.80. Concession rates are available for students and senior citizens (pensioners), and not all discounted fares are available on public holidays. You can save heaps of money if you choose one of these options:

Off-Peak Saver—weekend and non-rush times, providing unlimited travel between 9am and 3:30 on weekends and after 7pm Monday thru

Queensland Rail Network

Stations Listed for Reference Only

Chillagoe

Kuranda

Cairns

Normanton   Croydon

Forsayth

Great Barrier Reef

Townsville

Mt Isa

Hughenden

Mackay

Winton

Barcaldine

Longreach   Emerald   **Rockhampton**

Queensland Outback

Gladstone

Bundaberg

Charleville   Roma

Quilpie

Toowoomba

Cunnamulla   **Brisbane**

To Sydney

Map Information Provided by Queensland Rail

Friday, all for just AU $4.60.

Day Rover—gives unlimited one-day travel on all buses, ferries, CityCats (except tours) for only AU $8.40.

Ten Trip Saver—offers ten trips for the price of eight.

The bus schedules, fares and routes can be found in the "Bus& Ferry Fares" brochure found at the information booths,at City Hall, or at the Transport locations. Call **TRANS Public Transport Information** at ☎ 13-12-30 for help in obtaining ticket stall locations and station information.

You may want to check out the **Greyhound Pass** options, ☎ 13-20-30 or **W**: greyhound.com.au, for travel around the state. It is inexpensive and alleviates the stress of getting from one hub to another. As I mentioned before, the drivers are usually full of good information and often narrate or sing as they drive along the highway.

Taxis: Yellow Cab is the predominate service in the area, and their orange cars (not yellow) are easy to spot. One thing you will notice about the cabs in this city—they don't honk the horns very often and they are polite for the most part. One bit of advice though—it is customary for at least one passenger to sit in the front next to the driver. No protective glass barriers here mates and the cabbie doesn't want to feel like a servant, so sit next to him/her, have a yarn or two and enjoy the sights up front. If you need handicap access and need a van-style cab or want limo service, call ☎ (07) 3391-1000 and 13-22-27 respectively to book a ride. Yellow Cabs can be contacted from the concierge's desk, found at cab ranks (not easily hailed in the street) or called on ☎ 13-19-24.

Water Taxi: The Brisbane River offers a different perspective to the city and is not to be missed. Even if you don't need to be transported up/down the river to a specific destination, ride the water just for the fun of it. The ferries cruise the snake-shaped river that cuts the city in half, making twelve stops from Bretts Warf to the University of Queensland. The sleek boats hover along the cityscape at quiet and deceptively fast speeds, and you can get your tickets onboard. To go the full distance will set you back only AU $3.80, while the average price from stop-to-stop is about AU $2.90. More information and a brochure listing maps, CityCat stops, special tours available, and local attractions at each waterway stop can be found at the information booths, ☎ (07) 3229-5918 or contact the Brisbane City Council at ☎ (07) 3403-8888 or **W**: brisbane.qld.gov.au

INFORMATION CENTRES:

Tourism Queensland has developed a system of visitor information centers throughout the state. The staff is extremely helpful and patient with questions. Look for signs with a blue square with a yellow **i** to find a friendly face and heaps of help.

ORGANIZED TOURS:

There are a host of tours offered in the city, both on water and land, during the days and into the night, and even historical or comedic trips.

Some of the operators are: **City Sights Tours** that give you a great value and cover most of the city by bus for AU $20 for an entire day. See the information centers or call ☎ 13-12-30. **Club Crocodile River Queen** paddle-wheeler on ☎ (07) 3221-1300; **Mirimar Cruises** to the Lone Pine Koala Sanctuary on ☎ (07) 3221-0300; **Personally Yours Tours** on ☎ (04) 1774-0489; **Australian Day Tours** to the Woolshed on ☎ (07) 3236-4155; **Brian Ogden's Historical Walking Tours** on ☎ (07) 3217-3673; **Day and Night Tours** on ☎ (04) 1873-5141; **Boggo Road Gaol Ghost Tours** on ☎ (07) 844-6606 or **W**: ghost-tours.com.au; and a host of half to full-day boat tours out into Moreton Bay.

SHOPPING:

With the greenback so strong against the Australian dollar, shopping is hard to resist. All of the tours offer shopping opportunities and each one will offer something a bit different. The first tour includes one of the best shopping areas in southern Queensland, but don't spend all your money at once. Each area offers specialties not found in other spots, like inexpensive crocodile goods near Cairns, so choose carefully. The prices don't vary a great deal between stores in one general area, so there is not much of a need to shop around. In general though, Surfers Paradise on the Gold Coast has some of the least expensive goods to be found. An entire section is dedicated to shopping, including a tour of some of the discount malls.

FESTIVITIES:

It's not really necessary for an Australian to have a holiday to party, and there are lots of special events to get blotto with you new-found mates. Check out the upcoming events at any of the information sites and scan the websites of **W**: ourbrisbane.com; **W**: brisbanemarketing.com.au; **W**: citysearch.com.au; or **W**: whatson.com.au

A few of the most notable include:

The River Festival, August - September timeframe. Music, fireworks and water parades.

Brisbane Festival, date varies from year-to-year. Giant block party.

International Film Festival, late July early August. Gathering of stars and movie greats.

Queensland Day, early June. Go to the party and get your show bag.

Brisbane Exhibition or the Ekka, in mid August. The huge agricultural show—a giant 4H.

Anzac Day, April 25. Parades and memorial services to honor the war veterans.

Australia Day, late January. More fireworks, music, and dance.

Christmas and New Year Celebrations. Festival of lanterns, fireworks and the greeting of the New Year.

ACCOMMODATIONS:

If you choose Brisbane as your hub, try to book ahead of time to assure that you can get the hotel, motel, B&B, or backpacker resort that suits your fancy. It is usually not a problem getting a room, but it's wise to assure you get that non-smoking bed, with river views, on the top floor. In this town, as well as any city or shire, look for discount deals through AAA, your airline, and credit card memberships. And don't forget to ask about the frequent flyer points as many programs are honored here. Standby rates can be found at **W**: ratestogo.com

Three different-style accommodations have been recommended for you to get started in the city. All are in the CBD and are good spots for the walking tours. In addition, several chain hotels are listed for your convenience along with contact numbers. They are preferred listings in the Royal Automobile Club of Queensland (RACQ) catalogue. The RACQ is similar to AAA; their web site is **W**: racq.com.au

The Chifley Hotel on George is one of my favorites, and the **** 1/2 hotel is also reasonably priced. Breakfast is usually included in the tariff, which will save you AU $15 to AU $20 per person right off the bat. However, the morning queue to the buffet is often long, so get there early if you can. Your pick of 99 rooms/suites are comfortable, and the service is good. Listed prices: AU $143 to AU $156, but specials start as low as AU $123 with breakfast included. ☎ (07) 3221-6044 or toll-free at 1-300-650-464, E-mail: reservations.george@chifleyhotels.com, **W**: chifleyhotels.com

Stamford Plaza is a top-of-the-line, 6-star luxury experience. The rooms overlook the Brisbane River and the Botanical Gardens, and it offers special packages well below their standard rates of AU $380-$580. The 232 rooms (20 suites) and the fantastic Siggi's Restaurant located across from the lobby are found at the corner of Margaret & Edward Streets. ☎ (07) 3221-3535, 1-800-773-700, or **W**: stamford.com.au

Diana Plaza Hotel is a boutique hotel tucked in a suburb called Wooloongaba (or Gabba for short). It is close to the transport system, offers 67 rooms (9 suites) and is only a short walk from South Bank. Listed prices for this **** hotel is: AU $109-$155, but there is a weekend special that includes a breakfast buffet for $115, an Indulgence Package with spas and meals for AU $225, and a Relaxation Package with discounted spa treatments and meals for AU $175. ☎ (07) 3391-2911, fax: (07) 3391-2944, E-mail: info@dianaplaza.com.au, **W**: plazahotels.com.au

The Thornbury House is a great little B&B off the beaten path of the city. This cute Queenslander home has six rooms, with three of them being ensuites (bathroom/toilet in the room). The *** 1/2 lodge is quiet, cozy, and breakfast is served in a secluded garden. Listed prices: AU $77–$99 or a week for AU $420. ☎ (07) 3832-5985, fax: (07) 3832-7255, E-mail: thornburyhouse@primus.com, **W**: babs.com.au/thornbury.htm

I have not tried **New Brisbane City YHA**, but the RACQ recommends it. Listed prices: AU $40 to $56 and dormitories at AU $16–$20. ☎ (07) 3236-1004, fax (07) 3236-1947 or contact YHA Queensland, ☎ (07) 3236-4999, E-mail: yha@yhaqld.org, **W**: yha.com.au

Chain hotels include: **Sheraton Brisbane Hotel & Towers**, ☎ (07) 3835-3535, fax: (07) 3835-4960; **Best Western's Wickham Terrace**, ☎ (07) 3839-9611, fax: (07) 3833-5348; and **Quality Inn's Albert Park Hotel**, ☎ (07) 3831-3111, fax: (07) 3832-1290.

Street Scene on the Gold Coast

Queen Street Mall and Central Brisbane

Although it is an urban shopping area, Queen Street Mall will provide an introduction to the easygoing lifestyle found in this northern urban city. Unlike its sister cities to the south, it lacks the hustle and bustle that you are probably used to. There is something for everyone, but try to soak up the history that makes this city so interesting. You will find it fun, safe, easy to navigate, and the people unusually friendly (especially when they hear your accent). But beware, there are no short conversations and a quick request for directions may take you a half-hour while making a new friend.

GETTING THERE:

By Airtrain, take the train right from the airport terminal and zoom right into your choice of stations for about AU $9. Central Station is the preferred stop for the Chifley Hotel, South Bank for Hotel Diana, and the main station at Roma Street for both the Thornbury and Youth Hostel. All are within reasonable walking distance, but if you're carrying a bunch of luggage, hail a cab for the short hop.

By Car, not recommended, but get directions straight to the hotel of your choice and park it. All selected homes-away-from-home are within walking distance and parking is usually included with the lodging package. If you are staying somewhere outside the city, park the car at the Meyer Centre, ☎ (07) 3229-1699, on Elizabeth and Albert Streets, for an AU $7 and up daily rate.

By Taxi for about AU $30 by queuing up at curbside at the airport.

By Bus, also not a good idea, but if you are traveling light, go for it. No public buses are available, but grab a Coachtran at the curb for the trip and pay only AU $9 to the Roma Street Station or AU $11 directly to your hotel (discounts available for larger numbers of people traveling together). To get tickets, go to the service desk at either airport terminal or ☎ (07) 3236-1000.

PRACTICALITIES:

Whether you decide to walk or get some help from mass transit, wear comfortable shoes and clothing. It gets hot even in the winter and you can rest those feet on the well-manicured garden lawns, but most of the hike is on sidewalk. Put on sunblock even if it looks cloudy, and bring along a good pair of sunglasses and a hat. I would recommend a golf shirt, shorts, and sneakers for this trip. Bottled water is available along the way, so don't worry about packing that for this leg.

As you may pick up some goodies along the way, try to get a good-sized shopping bag if you buy something early. The Information Centre has a nice one to stash all your brochures and maps.

For further information, contact the **Information Centre** at Queen Street Mall, ☎ (07) 3229-5918, (07) 3006-6200, or **W**: ourbrisbane.com. Other good sources include **Queensland Tourism** at **W**: tq.au; **Brisbane Tourism** on ☎ (07) 3221-8411 or **W**: brisbanetourism.com.au; **Queensland Government Travel Centre** (a travel agency) on ☎ 13-88-33 or **W**: queens landtravel.com.au; or the **Brisbane City Council** on ☎ (07) 3403-8888.

FOOD AND DRINK:

To make it easier to choose from the mass of eateries in this part of the city, I will list a few selections from cheap eats to highbrow. You will find KFC, McDonald's, Hungry Jacks (Burger King), Subway, Pizza Hut, and Domino's in most areas. But why come all the way to Australia to eat US foods?

Most famous pub ($-$$): **The Breakfast Creek Hotel**, 2 Kingsford Smith Road, Albion, ☎ (07) 3262-5988. You must try this out as it's the only pub that still uses wooden barrels for its beer.

Take out (all $-$$): **Aladdin Doner Kebabs** in the Meyer Centre at 91 Queen Street for tasty kebabs, ☎ (07) 3229-4688; **Anzac Square Patisserie** on the corner of Edward and Adelaide Streets for quick eats, ☎ (07) 3229-2388; **Carvery Plus** for a sandwich at 12-40 Adelaide Street, ☎ (07) 3229-6445; **Croissant Express** for a sweet at three locations around Queen Street Mall, ☎ (07) 3229-4500; **Curry in a Hurry** for some spice at 170 Queen Street, ☎ (07) 3229-0144; **Go Sushi** for those who like it raw at Warf & Adelaide Streets, ☎ (07) 3211-7737; **King Pie** for an Aussie meat pie at 300 Queen Street, ☎ (07) 3211-1062; and **Wild Bites** at 123 Eagle Street, ☎ (07) 3838-9106.

Cafés (all $-$$): **Aromas** at several locations on the Mall for coffee and decadent deserts, ☎ (07) 3229-4041; **Bilby's Café** at 40 Tank Street, ☎ (07) 3236-2636; **City Rowers Fish Café** at 1 Eagle Street, ☎ (07) 3221-2888; **Ecco Bistro** at 100 Boundary Street, ☎ (07) 3831-8344; **Fasta Pasta** in the Wintergarden Mall, ☎ (07) 3210-1509; **Pig & Whistle** also on the Mall, ☎ (07) 3229-9999; and the **Zen Bar** at the Post Office Square, ☎ (07) 3211-2333.

Fine Dining (all $$-$$$): **Siggi's** at the Stamford Plaza on Edward Street, ☎ (07) 3221-4555; **II** (or Two) at Edward & Alice Streets for top dining, ☎ (07) 3210-0600; **Marco Polo East West Cuisine** at the Treasury Casino, ☎ (07) 3306-8744; **Armstrong's** for French/Asian flavors at 73 Wickham Terrace, ☎ (07) 3832-4566; **Circa** for pure French cuisine at 483 Adelaide Street, ☎ (07)

3832-4722; **Jameson's** for Australian Fusion at Queen Street Mall, ☎ (07) 3831-7633; **Michael's Riverside** for seafood on the river at 123 Eagle Street, ☎ (07) 3832-5522; **Pier Nine Oyster Bar and Seafood Grill** at 1 Eagle Street and one of my favorites, ☎ (07) 3229-2194; and **Green Papaya** for some Vietnamese food at Milton Road, ☎ (07) 3870-8850.

SUGGESTED TOUR:

Circled numbers correspond to numbers on the map.

One note to those who do not relish long city walks—all of the sites on this tour can be reached in an air-conditioned, narrated, and cushy bus. **City Sights Tours** (☎ 13-12-30) will cart you around in style for a full day and you can stop off at any of the attractions below. They will not follow the actual itinerary laid out for you, but they do a good job of getting you around the city. However, I would recommend the walking as you get to experience the smells, sounds, and flavor of the city much better.

To aid your sense of direction a little bit, the city streets are often listed for Kings and Princes (e.g., Edward and George) from north to south, and Queens and Princesses (Elizabeth and Ann) east and west.

If you decide to enjoy the sights on foot, fuel up with a bit of caffeine at one of the hundreds of coffee shops and get ready for a great day of touring. A favorite and familiar jet fuel-potency walking juice can be found at Starbucks right in the Meyer Centre block. Just follow your nose to the smells of freshly baked muffins. Begin your adventure at the **Visitor Information Booth ❶**, corner of Queen & Albert Streets on the Queen Street Mall. ☎ (07) 3221-8411, **W**: brisbane.qld.gov.au. Open daily 8:30–5. Look for the blue sign with the yellow **i**. There you can load up on free information, brochures, maps, and events schedules. They are great help and can give you all sorts of tips for your visit in Brissy. The **Transportation Hub** is right underneath the Mall; you can get information about public transport there.

Walk through this recently renovated shopping area and save the shopping until later so you don't have to carry all those goodies around all day. Pass the water fountain near George Street (it is an oversized table set with a flood of water flowing over the tabletop, onto the chairs, and into a stainless steel floor), and turn left onto William Street. Hike about 2-1/2 blocks to the:

*COMMISSARIAT STORES MUSEUM ❷, 115 William Street, ☎ (07) 3221-4198, **W**: rhsq.net. *Open Tues.–Sun. 10–4, closed holidays. Adults AU $4, children/seniors AU $2. Guided tours, self-guided tours. Gift shop. ৬.*

Brisbane's newest museum, opened after more than two years of historical renovation, sports a cool elevator that touches no part of the existing walls, suited for the fully disabled. Even if you are not a history buff, this repository will give you a chilling insight to the convict life in the early 1800s. The seven sections of the exhibition present Brisbane as it looked in 1838. The tour guide will show you a model of the town, a mini GPS rep-

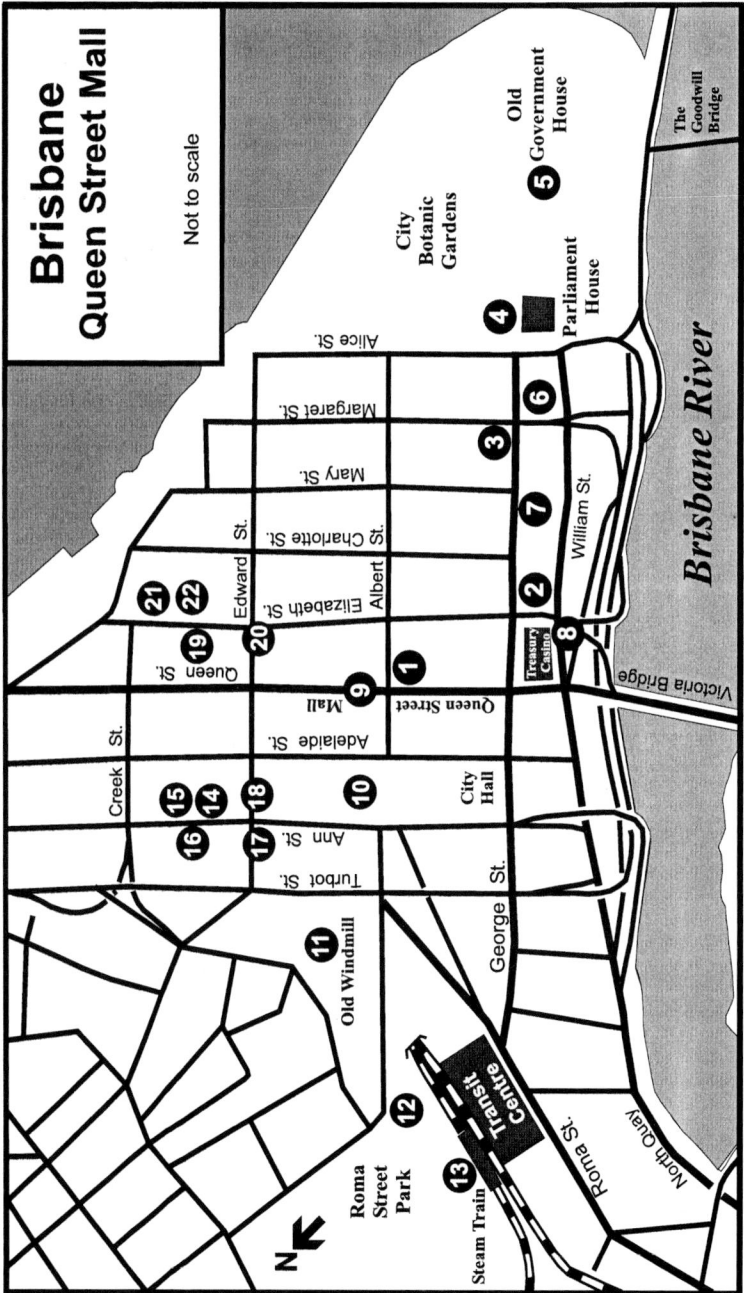

Brisbane
Queen Street Mall

Not to scale

City Botanic Gardens

Old Government House

⑤

The Goodwill Bridge

Parliament House

④

Alice St.

Margaret St.

⑥

Mary St.

③

William St.

⑦

Charlotte St.

Edward St.

②

Albert St.

Elizabeth St.

㉑ ㉒

⑳

⑲

Queen St.

①

⑧

Treasury Casino

Brisbane River

Victoria Bridge

Queen Street Mall

⑨

Adelaide St.

Creek St.

⑮ ⑭ ⑱

⑩

City Hall

⑯ ⑰

Ann St.

Turbot St.

George St.

Old Windmill

⑪

Roma St.

North Quay

Transit Centre

⑫

Roma Street Park

Steam Train

⑬

N

resented in 1:72 scale model buildings, laid out in the basement display. Each floor panel is numbered to identify where the artifacts were found and are now displayed in the glass cases on the first floor. Along with the descriptions of the penal colony and their interactions with the Aboriginal peoples are displays of how the store supported the community along with old newspapers, whips, chains, eating utensils, a straightjacket used for the insane convicts, and daily tools used in that era. Ask about the purpose of the bars on the windows, what is "tuff," did the wood in the building really come from Sherwood Forest, and how did they get the stone from Kangaroo Point. The answers may surprise you. Don't be too shocked at the desiccated rat staring at you from behind the glass, mates, and believe what you may about the murder that took place on the site. This second-oldest building in Brisbane, also called The Government Stores, is the home to the Royal Historical Society of Queensland.

If you are not interested in looking at the facades of old majestic ladies of brick and mortar, skip over this section, head to the Sciencecentre and stimulate your sensory circuits. But if you want to soak in how the city looked in the early 1800s, let's see some of the real buildings and varied architecture on the next few stops. The following sites do not have structured tours and some do not allow access to the buildings, but let your mind wander as you gaze on the varied styles of construction of the colony. Leave the Commissariat Museum and take a short jaunt southeast down William Street, turning left on Margaret and right onto George Street to:

THE MANSIONS ❸, 40 George Street, ☎ (07) 3221-1887. *Open Mon.–Fri. 9–5, closed holidays. Free. Gift shop. Restaurants.*
    The brick- and sandstone Victorian-style set of townhouses have ornate ironworks, mysterious verandas, and a carved stone cat guarding each end of the building. The six houses, built in 1890, are now home to several stores. The National Trust gift shop and a restaurant are worth a browse, but access to the majority of the building is restricted to staff.
    Continue east on George, making a quick right on Margaret Street, and a left on William until you reach one of the entrances to the Botanical Gardens, where you will see the:

STATE PARLIAMENT HOUSE ❹, George & Alice Street, ☎ (07) 3406-7562, **W**: parliamenthouse.qld.gov.au. *Open Mon.–Fri 9–4:30, closed holidays. Free guided tours are Mon.–Fri. 9:30, 10:30, 11:15, 2:30, 3:15, and 4:15. The 10:30 and 2:30 tours allow entrance to the house floor when the government is in session. Gift shop.* &.
    The French Renaissance home to the state government is a copper-topped beauty, and is pretty on the inside too. Don't miss the "good old boys" hangout in the O'Donovan Room. Parliament House is rated the number-one heritage building in Queensland, and is home to the 89 elect-

ed members of the only State Parliament in Australia that has a single leg-islative chamber. The cedar woodwork, Colebrooke balustrades, brass fit-tings, frosted glass, and marble decorated hallways can be toured with a group or just wander on your own.

Farther along the path in the gardens you will find the:

OLD GOVERNMENT HOUSE ❺, City Botanic Gardens, ☎ (07) 3229-1788, **W**: nationaltrustqld.org. *Open Mon.–Fri. 9–4:30, closed holidays. Adults/children: AU $4.*

At the far end of the government grounds is the current home to the National Trust. It was built in two years and opened in 1862 to house the early governors. Unfortunately, it is being annexed by Queensland University of Technology, so you may have to admire the old lady from the outside.

Right up the block on George Street find:

THE QUEENSLAND CLUB ❻, 19 George Street, ☎ (07) 3221-7072. *Closed to the public.*

The building is claimed to be the most elegant in town. Now a very exclusive gathering place for the well-to-do, it is a grand sight from the street. It is a mix of Old London and the tropics with intricate iron net-works protecting the guests from falling off its second-story verandahs, also designed to keep the building cool. Access is not allowed to non-members, but if you think you may want to join give them a tingle.

Backtrack towards the Commissariat Store, stopping at 110 George Street. If there is a bit of child in you, this halt will dazzle your brain.

*THE SCIENCECENTRE ❼, 110 George Street, ☎ (07) 3220-0166, **W**: sci-encecentre.qld.gov.au. *Open daily 10–5, closed holidays. For those who can't pass for kids AU $8, those who can (5–15) AU $6, under 4 AU $2.50, family passes AU $28. Guided tours, self-guided tours. Gift shop. Café. Special events.* ♿.

An interactive delight for the ageless kid. Keeping that in mind, it is primarily for school-aged children; if you are kidophobic with little toler-ance for shrieks of delighted munchkins, visit their website instead. But if you have a sense of adventure and want to take in the wacky world of sci-ence, this is the place. I'll borrow some of the tidbits from their brochure and tell you that there are three floors of fun, 170 hands-on exhibits, 20-minute interactive shows every day, permanent interactive space for 3–6 year old kids to launch rockets and play giant pianos, and a great gift shop. If you want to find out the best time to visit, call this campus of the Queensland Museum.

You may need a break at this point, so continue to backtrack up George and pick between one of the many cafés on Queen Street Mall or turn left onto William Street across from the Mall and try out the casino.

But if you have the inkling and love maps, there is a fantastic little shop at 187 George Street just along the way back. **World Wide Maps and Guides** has a great selection of road, city, boating, topographic, and antique maps for the rest of your journey in Oz, or to chart the memories of this trip. If you get lost before you find them, call on ☎ (07) 3221-4330 or **W**: worldwidemaps.com.au. At the corner of George Street and the Mall check out the:

TREASURY CASINO ❽, corner of George & Queen Street, ☎ (07) 3306-8888 or 1-800-506-888, **W**: treasurycasino.com.au. *Open daily 24 hours. Free (kind of) and discount meal, transport, and gaming vouchers available. Gift shop. Cafés and restaurants.* ♿.

An unmistakable building taking up a full city block and protected by bronze statues on the Queen Street side. The two entrances to this massive Italian Renaissance structure, a military barracks in 1824, are on Elizabeth Street and Queen Street. Once past the beefy security guards, you will find a very refined style of gambling establishment. Oh, sorry, gaming is now the kinder word here for gambling. With three levels of gaming, 1,200 pokies or slots, over 90 gaming tables, five restaurants, and seven bars, you will have plenty to choose from. There are no shows in this casino, and the dress code admits only those with collared shirts, long pants for men, and no sneakers.

For the serious shopper, the best is next. Stroll across the street to the shopping mecca and go for it.

***QUEEN STREET MALL** ❾, between George & Edward streets, ☎ (07) 3006-6290, (07) 3006-6291, or (07) 3229-5918. *Open daily 24 hours a day. The general shopping hours are: Mon.–Thurs. 8:30–5:30, Fri. 8:30–9, Sat. 8:30–5, Sun. 10:30–4. Dining areas stay open into the night.* ♿.

This is a mass of shopping stalls, cafés, and street vendors. Here you will undoubtedly hear the street musicians, buskers dressed in tattered garb with a cockatoo perched upon their bush hats, play an assortment of guitars, didgeridoos, and harmonicas. Although the Meyer Centre, David Jones, and the Wintergarden malls dominate the two-block pedestrian-only thoroughfare, it is teeming with novelty stores, souvenir stalls, and a wide variety of eateries. With that in mind, it would be best if you selected a copy of "The City Guide" brochure from the information booth to scout your way around the shopping maze. You might want to grab the brochure called "City on Sale" too as it lists specials, retail shops, hotels, restaurants, and has over $100 worth of discount coupons inside. The exchange rate is so favorable, there are some great deals to be found, but many of the souvenir items are less expensive on the Gold Coast in Surfers Paradise. The original site of the Mall was called *Mi-an-jin* by the indigenous peoples, meaning a place for resource gathering and special ceremonies. It was also the theater district in the early 1800s, the shopping precinct in the mid-1900s, and the redevelopment in 1999 has now made it a world-class place for resource gathering. The list and numbers of stores and cafés keeps changing (my current favorite is Pig N Whistle right smack dab in the middle of the Mall), but there are plenty to keep you busy for an hour or a week.

In addition to the main avenue of stores, you will find several hubs or separate malls off the main drag. **Broadway on the Mall**; **Brisbane Arcade**; **David Jones**, ☎ (07) 3243-9000, department store; **Myer Brisbane City Store**; the **Myer Centre**, ☎ (07) 3232-0121; **Tattersalls Arcade**, ☎ (07) 3221-8667; and **Wintergarden**, ☎ 1-800-351-445, will also delight the serious shopper. Broadway on the Mall and the Brisbane Arcade offer the standard wares, David Jones is a high-end department store as are the Myer stores, Tattersalls is an upscale leather and jewelry mall, and Wintergarden is the sophisticated shopper's hangout with leather couches and lovely paintings strewn about for your enjoyment. Food courts are sprinkled amongst the stores, so you will not go hungry. The hours are basically the same as the rest of the mall area, and some of the relevant web sites include **W**: wintergarden.net.au, **W**: davidjones.com.au, and **W**: myer.com.au

Once you stowed your goodies and rested, walk northwest past David Jones and onto Adelaide Street to the busy park across the street.

KING GEORGE'S SQUARE PARK, *THE CLOCK TOWER, BRISBANE CITY GALLERY AND CITY HALL ❿, between Adelaide & Ann streets, ☎ (07) 3403-8888, W: brisbane.qld.gov.au. Clock tower open Mon.–Fri. 10–3; building open Mon.–Fri. 8–5, and Sat./Sun. 10–4, closed holidays. Free.

The heart of Brisbane and the home to the statue of Steele Rudd (1868-1935), the great Aussie storyteller in Speaker's Corner. There are some statues worth a snapshot in the park, and you can just sit by one of the water features and watch the tourists and govies mix. Don't linger after dark as there have been some assaults in the area as of late. The real purpose of this stop is the trip to the clock tower; you will find the entrance to the building right in the center, under the six huge Ionic stone pillars. The elevator lift is just behind the information counter and to the left. Right now it's a free elevator trip to the lookout 250 feet above, but there are rumors to charge a fee to pay for the lift operator. But mates, he is well worth the few coins they will charge. He is a non-stop chatterbox with continuous banter and interesting facts about the building and tower like: the clock is 16 feet in diameter, the minute hand is 10 feet long and the hour indicator is 5'6", the hour bell weighs 4.3 tons, the viewing platform is a 25-square-foot, 360-degree Kodak moment, and the tower was originally opened in 1930 and reopened (after renovation) by "Their Royal Highnesses the Duke and Duchess of York in 1988." It is a great spot to look out over the city and get a perspective of how the river snakes around the town. You can see the needle at the top of the MLK Building, and get an idea of what the weather is going to be by the color code of the lights on the needle. Just make sure you get out when the bells toll; it's loud. The gallery is housed in a great hall on the first and second floors, where you can see the contemporary exhibits.

Cross over Ann Street, continue past the Brisbane Dental Hospital at Turbot Street and enter Wickham Park.

THE OLD WINDMILL ⓫, Wickham Terrace, ☎ (07) 3403-8888. *Open 24 hours daily. Free. Wheelchair difficult (very hilly).*

At the top of a winding path and through the park sits a grim reminder to the city's past. This oldest surviving building in Queensland is creepy when you hear of what went on there. Unfortunately the actual wind sails are no longer in place and you can't enter the building, but you can still almost hear the groans of the convict ghosts. The 1828 stone/brick building was the main source of ground flour and maize meal used to feed the surrounding penal colonies. History books that chronicle the convict life claim that being sent to the wheel was one of the worst punishments dealt out. Found guilty of a nuisance crime, a prisoner would be required to tread for up to 14 hours pulverizing grain. If he refused, he was hung. There were two pair of millstones (one for the windmill and one for the treadmill outside) and since the sails rarely worked (too heavy or often being repaired), there was a constant need for manual laborers. The tower of terror was converted to a signal station and fire lookout in 1861, occupied as a pioneer radio/TV station in the 1920s and into the 1940s, and is now a stark reminder of some of Australia's early history. Next to the windmill, also called the Observatory, is a series of dilapidated clapboard buildings that were the water reservoirs in the city, built in 1871. Not much to see, but worth a sticky beak (curious eye). Since the entrance to the top of the tower is now closed, you can see the beautiful stonework any time you like, and there is no fee to roam the grounds.

*ROMA STREET PARK ⓬, 1 Parkland Blvd., ☎ (07) 3006-4545, **W:** roma streetparkland.com. *Open daily dawn to dusk. Free. Café. Special events. Guided tours Thurs.–Sat. 11–2, ☎ (07) 3224-2714. ♿.*

Ready for a refreshing breath of air and a nice change of pace to the day's hike? Located just below the Old Windmill, the 35 acres of gardens are tucked into a diamond-shaped nook between Wickham Terrace, Parkland Boulevard, Albert Street, and the Roma Street Railway Station. Access to this world's largest subtropical garden in a city is via the Wickham Terrace gates near Gregory Terrace, from the Roma Street Transit Centre, or though the Albert Street walkway. It's best to come into the park from Albert Street as the Activity Centre has guide maps, information brochures, touch-screen computer screens for information, a first aid station, toilets, barbeques, water fountains, and a top-notch coffee shop to freshen up a bit. **The Parkland**, formerly called the Brisbane Terminus, was built in 1874 as a hub to move people and goods in the area. From 1884 to 1964 is was primarily used as a market of produce and live animals, and during WWII is was the site of air raid shelters and the home to an American Army clubhouse. The vast acres were basically ignored until 1999 when the Queensland Government decided to spruce them up and open up a garden walkway. Entering the gardens mixed with artworks, kangaroo paws, water displays, and playgrounds, you will be transported into Eden. The Parkland is easily enjoyed by meandering down the four walks and nine distinct features including the Spectacle Garden with its Lilly Pilly Garden, the Forest and its Fern Gully Bridge, the Celebration Lawn perfect for picnics, the Lake Precinct known for its Paper Bark trees and Wetlands surrounding the massive lake, the Activity Centre and its featured Carriage Shed, the Upper Parkland and the subtropical gardens near the amphitheatre, the Playground's sound boxes and dry bed creek for kids to explore, the Roma Street Parkland Bridges for sheltered walks, and the Public Art scattered in all the areas. There are Space-Age-looking fountains that are synchronized to squirt in a certain order, the walls are covered in saprophytic ferns, a stainless steel wave that is covered in multicolored potted plants, with Jetson-style street lamps guiding your way. Look for imprints of Aussie critters, leaves and branches in the concrete. There are also hidden statues of ladybugs and frogs in the flowerbeds as you enjoy the park and surrounds.

While in the area try out the:

BLUE BABY STEAM TRAIN ⓭, Roma Street Railway Station, ☎ (07) 3235-2219 or stop at the South Brisbane Station for tickets. *Sunday boardings at 10:00am, 11:30am or 1:00pm. Adult AU $8 and children AU $4.*

This special treat can be enjoyed on most Sundays from the Roma Street Station Park. It is a steam-filled one-hour journey around the Brisbane CBD, and the rocking-rolling ride is a good way to get a rounded view of the city. Additionally, it is staffed with volunteers who explain the sights and cityscapes as you ride the circumference of the river town.

For a bit of nostalgia and war history, double back to Ann Street by walking Albert Street, left on Ann and enter another park on your right.

*ANZAC SQUARE ⓮, Ann Street, ☎ (07) 3221-0722. *Open 24 hours daily. Free. Guided tours, self-guided tours. Special events.* ♿.

A hallowed ground to commemorate the men and women who have served and died in defense of their country. Enter either on Ann Street or on the lower level at the middle of Adelaide Street (between Edward and Creek streets). I think it's best to enter from the lower level to gain the best perspective of the history of the battles fought and heroes made. Then as your reach the shrine above, you can look back upon the history. Pass under the giant stallion mounted by a horse soldier to commemorate to heroes who fell in the South African Wars of 1899–1902, and enter the tidy park. Between the shade trees that look like huge tubers (turnips to be exact), are gut-gripping statues depicting snapshots of war in action. There is the "Fuzzy Wuzzy Angel" showing a Papua New Guinean (with fuzzy hair) aiding a soldier in the 1942–45 SW Pacific Campaign at the Kokoda Trail, a sandstone wall showing a parade of weary-looking warriors to remember those who lost their lives in The Great War of 1914–18, a statue for the dead in the Korean, Malaya, and Borneo battles from 1948–66, and a WWII sculpture with a wounded digger being tended to by a nursing sister. The icons commemorating the spirit and determination of those who fought are powerful, and the Aussies are just as patriotic towards their diggers as the Yanks are about their GIs.

Climbing the spiral steps to the rotunda takes you to the:

SHRINE OF REMEMBRANCE ⓯, Ann Street, ☎ (07) 3221-0722. *Open 24 hours daily. Free. Guided tours, self-guided tours. Special events.* ♿

Centered in the sandstone dome is the eternal flame to commemorate the war dead from WW I, with the inscription "For God, King and Empire." Looking through the Greek Classic Revival shrine down into the park presents a great vista, and is well worth a moment for reflection and a respectful photo.

Back down at the bottom of the stairwell is a long cool tunnel that directs you towards the Central Station railway and the:

SHRINE OF MEMORIES ⓰, Ann Street, ☎ (07) 3221-0722. *Open Mon.–Fri. 9–2:15. Free. Guided tours, self-guided tours. Special events.* ♿

The small museum holds memorabilia, photos, and bits of ground (called Forever Australia) brought back from the battlefields of WWII where blood was spilt. The memorial was built by the Queensland Returned and Services League of Australia (RSL), the Australian version of the VFW, to honor the men and women who served in the war. Her Royal Highness Princess Alexandra originally opened it in 1959. The highlight of the crypt below the eternal flame is the mosaic of over 140,000 tiny fragments of cut Venetian glass to commemorate the sacrifices made. Equally moving is the display of soils that have been transported from WWII cemeteries. In addition to the shrine, reopened in 1984, the hall is decorated with numerous plaques in honor of the units that served in the war to end all wars.

On the same side of the street, at the corner of Ann & Edward Streets, check out the huge building on the opposite side of the road. It is the:

PEOPLE'S PALACE, now called **PALACE BACKPACKERS** ⓱, corner of Ann and Edward streets, ☎ (07) 3211-2433, **W**: backpackers.com.au. *Open 24 hours. Free to roam around and get a feel of the international tourism atmosphere.*

This backpacker's delight was opened in 1911 as a low-cost lodge for the Salvation Army; today it's a cool-looking hotel and looks like it could fit well in New Orleans. It houses a young and friendly crowd, and if you are looking for information on backpacking in the region, they have a wall full of brochures and a helpful staff.

Exit the park from Ann Street and walk a half a block to the corner of Ann and Edward. Halfway there, on the opposite side of the street, check out the:

SCHOOL OF ARTS BUILDING ⑱, mid-block on Ann Street. *Closed to the public.*

This marvelous structure has a plaque at its entrance informing you of the building's colorful history—from a clearing-house for new domestic servants in 1865 to an art school; the intricate Queenslander is magnificent. Since the house is now home to several businesses, you may ask to browse around the inside of the building, but just the view from the outside is worth a gander. Completely restored in 1985, the balconies and tiered seating in the lecture hall are stunning, but the verandahs, roof trusses, and gingerbread decorations are my favorite.

Continue onto Edward Street, turn right on Queen Street and again right into the open-air plaza on the right.

THE POST OFFICE SQUARE ⑲, between Queen & Elizabeth streets. *Open 24 hours daily. Free.*

This plaza is worth a mention if only to take a look at the magnificent complex and enjoy the beauty of the surrounding buildings. The original residents of the current post office structure, in the late 1800s, weren't too impressed though. It was once the Female Factory Prison. There are some nice cafés in the square (one subterranean spot is called The Best Address), with the classy Brisbane Club Tower on one side, and Rowes Arcade with some more specialty shops (if you haven't had your fill of buying) on the other.

To continue the war theme, hop over to the corner of Queen and Edward streets near the Queen Street Mall.

MACARTHUR CHAMBERS ⑳, 201 Edward Street, ☎ (07) 3403-8888. *Open daily 9–4, closed holidays. Free.*

This was the home to the General during WWII, serving as headquarters for MacArthur and his staff in the battles of the Pacific region. Reopened in August 2002, the room in the current office building has had over $70,000 of restoration done, and is filled with wartime memorabilia and photos. Not too much to see right now, but the Queensland Premier is asking for loans or donations of additional items relating to the period of the General's stay in Australia. Brisbane was selected as HQ because the military (and politicians) were willing to sacrifice the territories above that parallel line, and it was relatively safe from Japanese bombing raids, unlike Darwin and Broome. One fact not revealed in the historic chamber is the record of the Battle of Brisbane, a fight between 4,000 American and Australian troops on November 26, 1942, where six Allied soldiers were shot and one killed. It has been kept quiet until recently, with news of the hostilities squashed during the war to keep Japan from using it as propaganda.

Let's change the pace a bit and walk left on Queen, right on Creek, and right on Elizabeth Street to:

ST. STEPHENS CATHEDRAL **㉑**, Elizabeth Street, ☎ (07) 3224-3111, Mass times ☎ (07) 3224-3107, **W**: stpauls.com.au. *Open Mon.–Fri. from 8 am, Sat. from 11:30 am, Sun. from 6 am. Book/gift shop.* ⟰.

This grand dame of churches reminded me of a medieval refuge. St. Stephen's is an Early English Gothic piece of architecture that originally opened its doors in 1850. The building cost £1,400 upon completion. The outside walls seemed to be built with brown sandstone blocks with a rough finish. Stepping through the glass front door you will be greeted by a cool drafty air carrying scents of recently burnt incense. The inside has a series of adorning flags stationed at each of the fourteen massive pillars lining the path to the altar. The royal colors, the Stations of the Cross painted in canvas, and stained-glass windows completed the picture in a glorious fashion. If you let your imagination float, the interior could easily be an ancient sanctuary with an introspective crusader knight kneeling at one of the pews. The most interesting, though not necessarily the most impressive, sight in the church is the cross with Jesus. It was suspended above the altar and it is not a completed cross, but a single wooden beam spanning His shoulders and arms. It appeared as though He was floating in mid-air as the cables are not noticeable in the dim lighting of the church. The candlelight does give a view of His face and I swear it looks like JFK.

Right next door is:

*ST. STEPHENS CHAPEL **㉒**, same as the Cathedral.

Not nearly as massive in bulk, but just as powerful. Just off to the right of the cathedral is the tiny chapel that houses the Shrine of Mary Mackillop. This is the oldest church in Queensland, with the first mass being held on May 12, 1850. Even now it holds its visitors in awe at the simple, but inspiring surroundings. To me it looks like a tiny abbey with its small upright organ, windows like slits to the outside, and very uncomfortable. The centerpiece of the small chapel is the sculpture of Australia's first "Blessed" carved from a hundred year-old camphor laurel tree. The sculptor, John Elliott, captured the figure of Mary Helen—Mother Mary of the Cross (1842–1909)—perfectly, and her kind eyes penetrate the soul. The ancient tree used was to represent the wooden slab hut she used as her first school in the Australian bush. Pope John Paul II beatified Mary for her work with the poor children and destitute women of the countryside. The four panels of wood, surrounding her shrine, are covered in drawings representing her work throughout her ministry. Don't miss the old piece of wood, set into stone near the shrine, as it is a piece of her original coffin. What is not revealed is the struggle she had in obtaining the support from the church, needed to assist the poor and itinerant. The bookstore has some interesting coverage of this; well worth a read.

The Riverside District

This is probably the most beautiful stretch of the city, with the relaxing gardens and gentle lapping sounds of the river wake on the shoreline. There is always something going on, whether it is a wedding in the park, an impromptu band playing on the street, or a concert in a public plaza. If you happen on the gardens in late October or early November, check out the jacaranda trees. With absolutely no leaves it is smothered in bright blue/purple flowers. A painting in the Art Gallery at South Bank features the jacaranda tree near the entrance of the Botanical Gardens.

GETTING THERE:

Since you are in town already, just put on your walking shoes and stroll northeast from the Queen Street Mall towards the Brisbane River. It is only a twenty-minute walk from the CBD to your first attraction, or you can hail a cab and start the tour fresh and ready to meander along the river. If a breakfast is not included as part of your lodging, enjoy a brekkie or brunch overlooking the river at the Customs House.

If you are traveling from the Gold Coast, take the Brisbane train from Robina or Helensvale (there the platform is called "Hogwarts Express Platform 9") for under AU $10.00 as a one-way, non-peak rate. Trains depart every half-hour each way. Exit at Vulture Street (also the first South Bank terminal) and cross the Goodwill Bridge to begin the tour in reverse order. You are able to bring bicycles onboard after the 9 am peak period. If you are driving from the Coast, get there early as parking is limited.

PRACTICALITIES:

The same guidelines apply as in Trip 11, though you will have much more shade and places to just sit and enjoy the views. The walk takes you along the river, where there are plenty of eateries, shops, and cool park benches. The Queen Street Mall Information Centre also has maps and brochures on this part of town, and there is a big blue i booth in the City Botanical Gardens near the café.

You can alter the tour in any way you like, but it can be best covered by starting at the attraction on the north end of the river and proceed along the muddy Brisbane River to the southern point near the Parliament House. This is an easy walk and can easily be completed in a half a day, depending on your pace, but you can stretch it out into a fair dinkum walkabout, soaking in the delights of the river and gardens over the entire day. If you walk in a straight line it is only about a five-mile stretch, but there are plenty of meandering pathways to explore and I would urge you to be adventurous.

An alternative to this (and any of the Brisbane day tours) is to cycle along the riverside pathways (refer to it as a push-bike or the locals will think you want a motorcycle). The city has over 240 miles of bike pathways, and you can take the bikes on the river ferries. Rent bikes at **Valet Cycle Hire** by calling ☎ 0408-003-198 or **W**: valetcyclehire.com. They offer guided tours too, starting at AU $30 for a half-day excursion. There are also rental shops listed in the Yellow Pages.

FOOD AND DRINK:

Depending on the time of day you start the tour and what you enjoy nibbling on, your choices are varied in this neck of the city. On Sundays (7am–4pm) the sidewalks are abundant with smells of Aussie food delights as the craft markets overwhelm the resident shops. Along Eagle Street are the terrace cafés with your pick of a simple café latte at Muffin Break to beautiful white linen service and gourmet foods at Pier Nine.

Here are a few recommendations for you to narrow the choices a bit.

Customs House Brasserie (399 Queen Street) International food overlooking the river. Their French toast is tops. ☎ (07) 3365-8921. $$

Cha Cha Chap (1 Eagle Street) Simple but delicious steaks. ☎ (07) 3211-9944. $$

Michael's Riverside (123 Eagle Street) Upscale Italian with great seafood and local favorites like Bouillabaisse of Local Seafood. Reserve, ☎ (07) 3832-5522. Lunch Mon.–Fri., dinner Mon.–Sat. $$ & $$$

Il Centro (123 Eagle Street) Another one of my favorite Italian/seafood eateries with great service—try their trademark Lasagna Alla Granseola loaded with sandcrab. Reserve, ☎ (07) 3221-6090. $$

Pier Nine Oyster Bar and Seafood Grill (1 Eagle Street) My favorite restaurant, with fresh scrumptious Moreton Bay bugs and the best brown-bellied mud crab you will ever taste. Reserve, ☎ (07) 3229-2194. Lunch daily from noon and dinner every night from 5:30 pm. $$ & $$$

Vino's Bar & Café (1 Eagle Street) Classy and comfortable with fantastic Tiger Prawns. ☎ (07) 3221-0811. $$ & $$$

Sushi Together (123 Eagle Street) Sushi and sake. ☎ (07) 3831-1138. $

McDonalds (1 Eagle Street) America's Embassy. ☎ (07) 3221-2440. $

Tognini's on Main (Kangaroo Point) Contemporary Northern Italian foods enjoyed on the opposite side of the river. Reserve, ☎ (07) 3895-8311. $$$

City Gardens Café (Botanical Gardens near Alice Street) Great setting for tea and sandwiches. It gets busy at noon, so get there a bit early to enjoy the peaceful setting. ☎ (07) 3229-1554. X: Sun. $

Fish Restaurant & Bar/ City Rowers (1 Eagle Street) Try the Northern

Territory barramundi and chips. ☎ (07) 3221-2888 ext. 221. $

II (Two) (Corner of Edward & Alice Streets) Top of the line mix of French/Mediterranean/Asian tastes. ☎ (07) 3210-0600. $$$

There are plenty of cheap eats, cafés and luxurious dining in this area, so don't be limited by my list; browse any of the brochures for more taste temptations. At the Riverside mall area there is a food court with sushi, kebobs, coffee shops, the Pig "N" Whistle Pub ("oink if you're thirsty") and variety stores. There are also several riverboat excursions that offer lunch and dinner cruises like the Kookaburra River Queen, though they are more for the view and entertainment than the food.

SUGGESTED TOUR:

Circled numbers correspond to numbers on the map.
Start you day of scenic strolling at the:

*CUSTOMS HOUSE ❶, 399 Queen Street, ☎ (07) 3365-8999, The Brasserie (07) 3365-8921, **W**: customshouse.com.au. *Open daily 10–4, closed holidays. The Brasserie daily 10–4, Tues.–Sat. dinner, and Sunday brunch. Free guided tours available Sun. 10–4. Free.*

This Heritage-listed building looks the part, with a huge crusty green copper dome hovering over Corinthian columns and fortified with stacked blocks of sandstone. Since it is also an art gallery and mini-museum, it also has the familiar old history smells too. If you time it right, you can enjoy a sophisticated brunch or a brisk cup of tea while staring across to the Story Bridge. The Customs House opened in 1889 and served as the city's duty collection center for river trade until 1988. It was renovated to its current grand status by the University of Queensland, costing over seven million dollars in three years. It now greets you as an art gallery with national and international exhibitions, wall displays that house memorabilia from its Customs Service period, a nice little gallery shop with unique gift ideas, and an exquisite terrace brasserie. On the last Sunday of each month you can also enjoy a free concert put on by the U-of-Q School of Music.

Walk around to the street side of the building, head left down Queen Street, and make a quick left onto Eagle Street (at the giant chrome hand with its index finger pointing to the sky). On your left, at the river's edge you will find a modern collection of glass and open-air shops, eateries and friendly street hawkers. If you do engage a street vendor, be prepared to have a nice long chat about, well, anything under the sun.

*RIVERSIDE CENTRE AND *EAGLE STREET PIER ❷, Eagle Street, ☎ (07) 3403-8888, **W**: brisbanetourism.co.au. *Open 24 hours. Free.* ♿

Enter a district and conglomeration of high-rise office buildings, fantastic restaurants and cafés, and a mishmash of boats moored at the curving dockside. I find this area to have some of the best mid-priced bistros

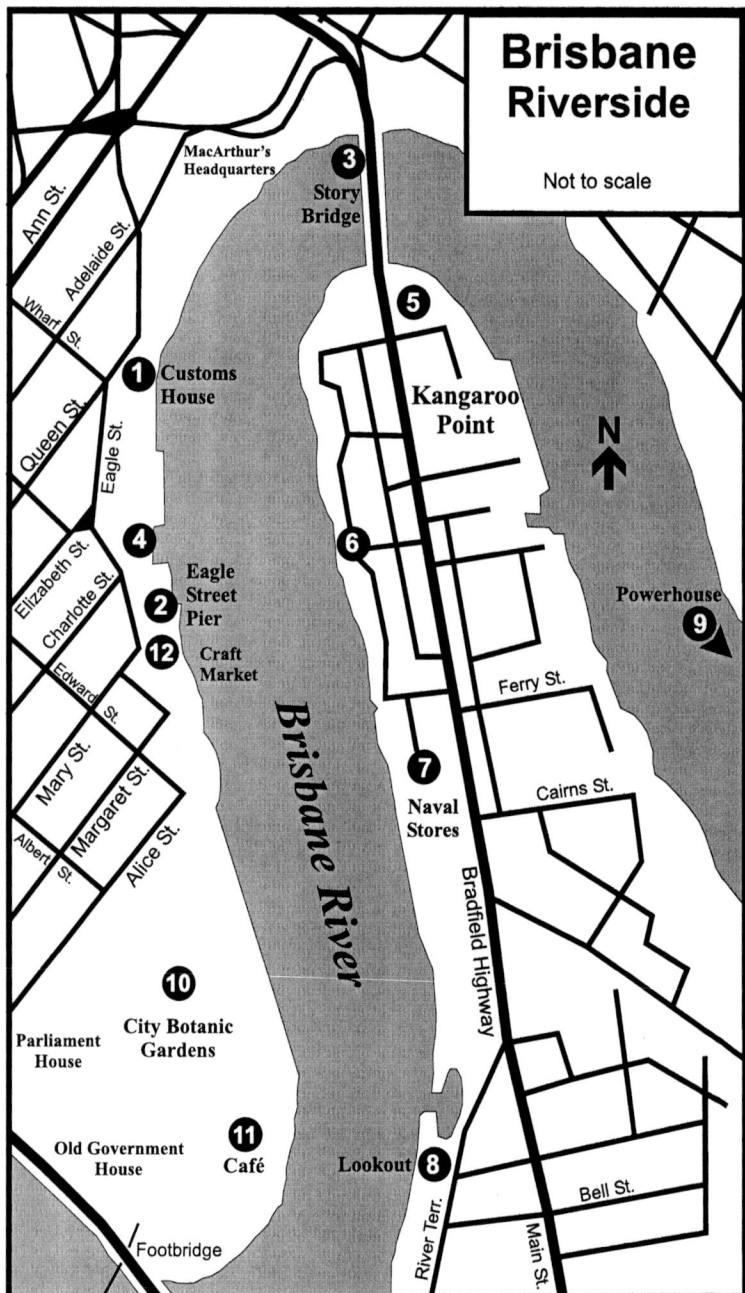

Brisbane Riverside

Not to scale

MacArthur's Headquarters

3 Story Bridge

1 Customs House

5

Kangaroo Point

N

4

2 Eagle Street Pier

12 Craft Market

6

Powerhouse **9**

Ann St.

Adelaide St.

Wharf St.

Queen St.

Eagle St.

Elizabeth St.

Charlotte St.

Edward St.

Mary St.

Margaret St.

Albert St.

Alice St.

Ferry St.

Cairns St.

7 Naval Stores

Brisbane River

Bradfield Highway

10 City Botanic Gardens

Parliament House

11 Café

Old Government House

8 Lookout

Footbridge

River Terr.

Main St.

Bell St.

in the city, and you certainly cannot beat the views. If at all possible, join the throngs of shoppers on Sunday from 7 in the bright morning sun till 4 o'clock teatime at the Eagle Street Market. It is probably the most extensive of the three city craft markets, a wonderland of sights, sounds, and smells. The place is crowded; if you don't like to be packed into narrow aisles of multicolored stalls with curious buyers or enjoy a good bargain or two, then avoid the mid-day activities and get there early. It is a fantastic place to buy local crafts and stock up on goodies to take home. Most vendors are happy to bubble wrap any fragile stuff if you ask. As you sit in one of the many cafés along the pathway, with your chilled glass of wine or frosty pint of beer, you can look upon the city's own Brooklyn Bridge and ponder your next purchase.

THE STORY BRIDGE ❸, ☎ (07) 3403-8888, **W**: brisbanetourism.co.au
   A significant landmark of both history and the city's landscape. Not quite as grand as the Sydney Harbour Bridge, it is a major traffic artery like its sister down south and was overseen by the same engineer—Dr. J.C. Bradfield. The bridge opened in July 1940 after over five years of construction in some of Australia's darkest economic times. This structure was initiated more for a need to stimulate the local economy and inspire the public than to improve transportation across the Brisbane River. The 922-foot span is a cantilever truss bridge, costing the government over three million Aussie dollars to complete. Today it is indeed a vital link between the New Farm and Kangaroo Point neighborhoods of the city, and is one of the significant icons of the river town.

   In the middle of the Riverside area are the docks for the CityCat and paddleboat tour vessels. Give your feet a rest now or later in the evening and book a cruise up the winding river with a meal, dancing, or just drinks. Stop at the River Cruise Wharves at Eagle Street Pier and take a cruise with:

*KOOKABURRA CRUISES ❹, 1 Eagle Street, ☎ (07) 3221-1300, **W**: clubcroc.com.au. *Daily 1-1/2-hour cruises depart at 12:15 am, nightly 2–3 hour cruises leave between 6:30 and 7:30 pm, jazz breakfast at the pier on Sundays from 7:30–10:30 am. Costs vary depending on your pleasure and gastronomic interests, from AU $22 for a tea-and-cookies lunch cruise to a AU $65 seafood platter. Children from 4–14 are half price. Coupons for AU $10 off some tours can be found in the free "Dining Out" magazines found in hotel lobbies and the information centers.* ⅋.
   I have watched the gangplank full of partygoers with the live entertainment wafting across the gently rocking paddle wheeler. Dancing is encouraged as the three-decked ships float past the city and all the riverfront homes. The best seats for viewing are on the left side of the ship as you are serenaded by a band at night and commentary and accordion by day. The boats are the only two of its type built in the last century. One was launched in 1986 and the other in 1988. Both are diesel, built with ironbark

keels and decorated with silky oak and Huron pine timbers that were aged for 60 years before shaped. Ask for a gent named Cole; he will fill you in on all the history and secrets of the area. Between dance partners, some points to be observed and noted for later jaunts include **Kangaroo Point** ❺, that can be reached by CityCat ferries at the Thornton, Captain Burke Park, or Dockside ports. Kangaroo Point is a popular spot for family bar-beques, abseiling the steep sandstone cliffs, and soaking up the rays of the subtropical sun. It wasn't so popular in the early 1800s as it was the quarry site for convicts put to hard labor. The rocks cut from the cliffs were the foundations for many of the city's landmarks. Look for the multi-colored metal sculptures that appear as frozen aerobic exercisers staring at the river. This is the home to the **Sculpture Riverwalk** ❻ that is well worth the effort, but is kind of out of the way. In the middle of the walk-way is the **Naval Stores** ❼ that was once the base for the warships in the late 1880s. It should be fully renovated and open to view the historic dis-plays at the time of this publication. At the southern tip of the walk is the **Kangaroo Point Lookout** ❽, where you can get a fantastic Kodak panorama shot of the city and the City Botanical Gardens.

Just as you are ready to pass under the Story Bridge, look to your right—the entire tip of the point is the park dedicated to an Irish rascal called Captain Burke. There are numerous folklores about the lad who arrived wearing a beat-up rum barrel and a grin. He became a wealthy shipping tycoon who could wear any barrel he chose after that.

Farther around the point and on the right is a huge building called Yungaba, for an Aboriginal term "land of the sun." It was established to provide shelter for immigrants and later served as a refuge for soldiers returning from the Boer War.

As you party on the river you can gaze at the current and know that it dumps its wealth of water seventy miles downstream into Moreton Bay, the original home to many poor convicts. The river holds the proud name of Sir Thomas Brisbane, who was the governor of New South Wales.

At the northern end of the cruise (depending on the tides and sched-ule of the ships) you may also get a glimpse of the **Dockside** ❾ marina cove and the grand remnant of the Powerhouse energy plant. Now that is definitely a must-see site and if you can work it out, try one of the funky performances there. But keep a very open mind, as it is quite abstract and bizarre. You will have to double back to due justice to New Farm's Arts Centre, and you have the choice of making an evening of it by taking a cab or ferry to tour the riverside building. The **Qtix** on ☎ 136-246, **Centrestage** pocket guide, the **City Council** on ☎ (07) 3403-8888, or any of the informa-tion booths can provide you with the entertainment schedule.

Continue your stroll southwards along the river to the entrance of the immaculate gardens just across from the Parkroyal Brisbane Hotel on Alice Street. You can enter the gardens via the Stamford Plaza Hotel foot-path, but the most impressive entrance is mid-block where Albert intersects Alice Street. Only a 15-minute walk from the center of town, or take the Circle Bus Number 333 and exit at Albert Street to the:

*CITY BOTANICAL GARDENS ❿, Gardens Point at the intersection of Albert and Alice streets, ☎ (07) 3403-0666 or (07) 3252-2979, **W**: brisbane.qld.gov.au. *Open daily, 24 hours. One-hour tours from the Rotunda near Albert Street Mon.–Sat. 11:00am or 1:00pm. Group tours also available. Free.* ♿.

Cleared by convicts in 1828 and opened in 1855, the 50 acres were originally the hunting grounds for Aboriginal peoples and later tilled as a produce site for the penal colony on Moreton Bay. It became a scientific grove to promote cultivating crops as tobacco, sugar cane, tropical fruits, and home of original macadamia, jacaranda, and pecan trees. A point of interest described on the tour was that the macadamia nut originated in Australia and was shipped to Hawaii for use as wind breaks around sugar cane fields. Stroll amongst the fragrances and colors, soaking in the history of the trees and events that mark this part of town, with just as colorful memories like the Paluma gunboat ramming the now children's playground or the floods that covered the entire area in 1974.

The two lily ponds in the park are part of a natural billabong that is over 68 feet deep. The lake nearest to the café, identified with the bearded man posing with two storks, was sadly once the bear pit and home to captive deer, monkeys, and aviaries. It now is the happy home to lungfish, carp, eels, sacred kingfishers, and kookaburras. The tour is well worth the time and will provide a gentle walk amongst the Lily Ponds, Bamboo Forest, Royal Palm Circle, the Formal Garden, the Walter Hill Fountain, Camellia Garden, Hibiscus Garden, the Tamarind Trees, Palm Grove, into the Rainforest, across the wooden Mangrove Boardwalk, Garden Domain, and finish at the River Stage and Amphitheatre. A secret told to me was of the rocks that form the rockery near the Bromelaids—the stones are gneiss brought from England as ballast in the old wooden sailing ships. For the botanist fans, see the experts at the Rotunda for some more detailed information about the garden species. If you visit in September, the gardens will be in full glory.

In the middle of Eden you can find an apple or scrumptious light meals at:

THE CITY GARDENS CAFÉ ⓫, City Gardens, Alice Street, ☎ (07) 3229-1554, **W**: stewarts.net.au/citygardens. *Partially* ♿.

Open seven days a week for breakfast, lunch, and dinner, the converted curator's bungalow offers tea and light meals. The food is delightful—and you are often joined by colorful, chatty birds, business folks enjoying a break, and surrounded by lush colorful flowerbeds. Table number two is my favorite; you can people-watch as well as get a great view of the surrounding manicured gardens. Plus you will be confident in your safety as the approach is protected by a dragon. The dragon tree, native to the Canary Islands, grows to 30 feet and lives for 400 years. This poor old dragon is supported by a few steel rods, but it is worth the look as this ancient is one of the two left. The red gooey sap, called dragon's blood, was used as medieval medicines and as an ingredient for the lacquers used to finish the famous Stradivarius violins.

At the end of the pathway you will find an interesting lounging area for the QUT students. The Domain is a hub for cyclists, walkers, and joggers as they navigate the Goodwill Bridge to South Bank. The footbridge was opened on Sunday 21 October 2001 amid the political storm over the need and cost of such a span. It is a nice walk and provides a southern view of the river and city.

*EAGLE STREET PIER CRAFT MARKET ⑫, Eagle Street, ☎ 0414-888-041, **W**: espcraftmarket.com.au. *Open Sunday 8–4. Free. ⅋ but crowded.*

Musicians will serenade you as you loosen your wallet to purchase some of the handcrafted goods displayed in colorful tents. The hawking is friendly and gentle, but the crowds may be a bit intimidating. So, go early to get the best deals and views (unless you prefer people-watching over shopping). Find some Aussie artworks, wooden toys, funky clothing, Aboriginal art, fruit & veggies, tasty foods, and good fun.

Brisbane Waterfront Beach at Southbank

South Bank District

Originally built to showcase Brisbane's World Expo in 1988, this is a brilliantly designed urban park, 40 acres of landscaped grounds complete with a Gondwanaland wildlife exhibit (the ancient super-continent of Australia, Antarctica, South America, India, and Arabia). You will enjoy the newly-created archways covered in lush green and purple vines, the swimming lagoon surrounded by sandy beaches and lifeguards, a Nepalese pagoda, cycling paths cutting a swath besides the river, and the myriad of eateries tucked in between sculpture gardens. It is one of the cleanest, safest parks I have ever walked through, complete with children laughing, waiting for dad to finish barbequing the deliciously aromatic snags. Stroll along the riverbank and stop in at the largest art galleries and museums in the state. If you are lucky enough to visit on the weekends, don't miss the markets.

GETTING THERE:

By Car, park in one of the underground lots. Just look for the parking lot signs on Little Stanley Street, at the Performing Arts Complex, and at Vulture Street. Early-bird specials apply, but it is by the hour (four hours or more is AU $9.90) and closes by 1 am.

By Bus, buses stop at Grey Street, near Victoria Bridge, and at the Vulture Street train station.

By Train, two stops include South Brisbane (South Bank) or Vulture Street (South Bank).

PRACTICALITIES:

This is an easy walking tour with lots of eateries, shade trees, and resting spots. Take a swimsuit if you choose to cool off at the South Bank Beach. A hat and comfy walking shoes still apply. The area is well laid out and maps/directories are easily located. You can browse the attractions in any order, but stop first at the Information Building to get a map of the area. Oh, and check out the MLC Building to see what weather the winds will bring. If the tower is white it will be a clear day, if it is red—sailors beware.

FOOD AND DRINK:

There are over 30 restaurants, fast food joints, and cafés spread out along this district. From fish & chips or ethnic foods to fine dining, you will have a wide selection here. Since they change frequently, check out the directories posted on the poles along the walking paths. My favorite for modern Australian fare on the river is the **River Cantina** ($$), but I also like the pushcart foods. A favorite for out-of-towners is the **Plough Inn** ($-$$) for steak and potatoes in a traditional pub. If you want the best ice cream, try the New Zealand Natural cart near the Central Cafés.

LOCAL ATTRACTIONS:
Circled numbers correspond to numbers on the map.

INFORMATION CENTRE ❶, corner of Stanley and Ernest streets, ☎ (07) 3867-2051, **W**: south-bank.net.au. *Open Sat.–Thurs. 9–6, Fri. 9–9, closed holidays.* ♿.

Heaps of free brochures and helpful staff will make your tour easy. There is even a Ticketeck station inside, and you can check out the performing arts agenda.

After picking up the South Bank map at the information center, make your way to the southern tip of the strip, just next to the Goodwill Bridge. From that point, you can work your way along the riverbank and see all the sights in a sequential manner and save those dogs.

MARITIME MUSEUM ❷, corner of Sidon & Stanley streets, ☎ (07) 3844-5361, **W**: qmma.ecn.net.au. *Open daily, closed holidays. Adults AU $5.50, children/seniors AU $4.40. Self-guided tours. Special events. Partially* ♿.

This is a gem on the tour, and although I'm not a sea dog by nature, it captured my interest. Kids of all ages will enjoy the hands-on exhibits, the military history, and the ability to climb aboard a real River Class Frigate. Welcomed by a real-life lighthouse beacon, the four galleries display a variety of early navigators, handcrafted models of ancient ships, a mock-up of a ship's bridge, navigation instruments, diving displays, a WW II Coral Sea exhibit, and a map of the sunken ships off the coast.

The main attraction is the dry-docked 1,420-ton **RMAS *Diamantina*** anti-submarine ship now stationed on the grounds out back of the museum. You are allowed onboard to see how the sailors lived on this WW II vessel that saw action in New Guinea and the Solomon Islands.

In addition to this grand lady is the *Forceful* tugboat (you can actually take a ride on her), a lighthouse, the bow of a Japanese yakatabune, and a giant torpedo. But do not miss my favorite—the *Happy II*. A mad Canadian sailed this 9-foot, aluminum sailboat from the east coast of his country, through the Panama Canal, across the Pacific, to New Caledonia, and finally Australia. Can you imagine?

Stroll through the Grand Arbor of 411 curved columns covered with 465 vines of bright magenta bougainvillea flowers and enjoy the meandering trail past Picnic Island, the Formal Gardens, around the Arbour

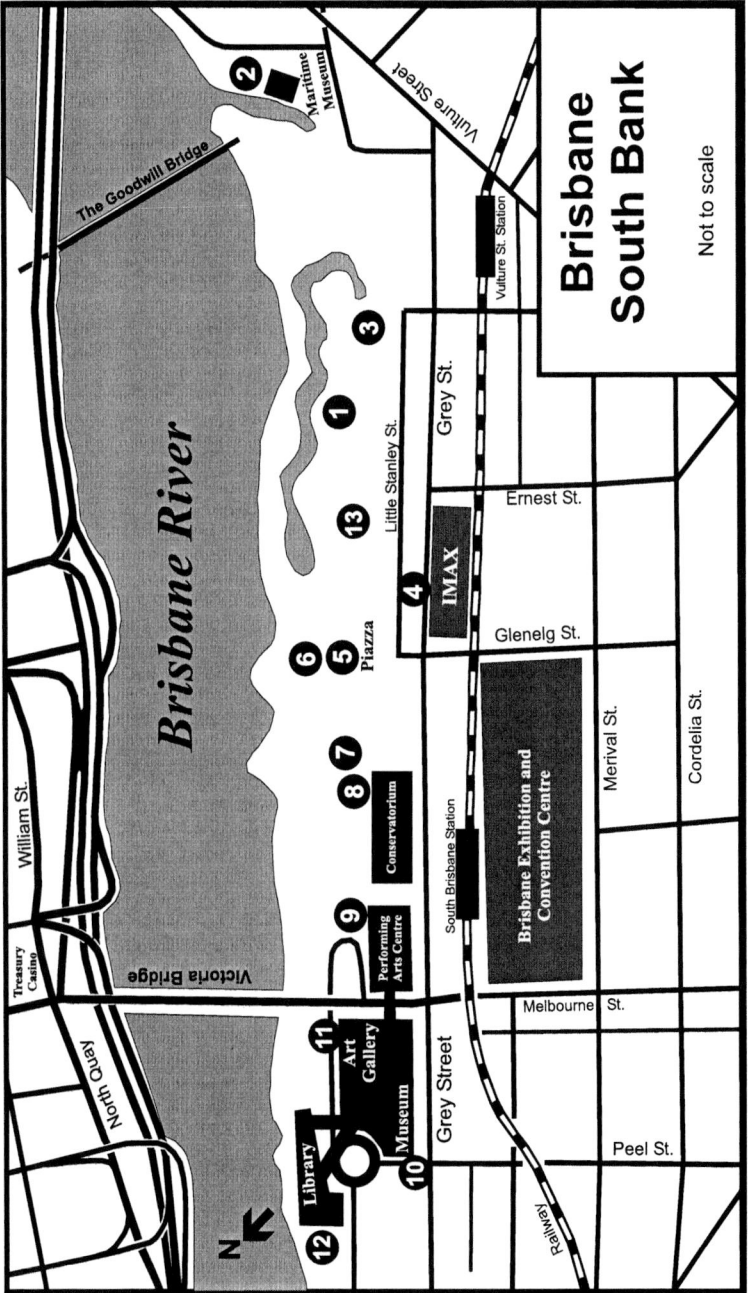

Brisbane
South Bank

Not to scale

Maritime Museum

Vulture Street

Vulture St. Station

Grey St.

The Goodwill Bridge

Brisbane River

Ernest St.

Little Stanley St.

IMAX

Glenelg St.

Piazza

Brisbane Exhibition and Convention Centre

Merival St.

Cordelia St.

South Brisbane Station

William St.

Conservatorium

Performing Arts Centre

Victoria Bridge

Treasury Casino

Melbourne St.

Grey Street

Art Gallery

Museum

North Quay

Library

Peel St.

Railway

N

View Cafés, and check out the South Bank Beach. This is an urban swimming hole complete with lifeguards, sandy beach, and bathing beauties. Browse the Stanley Street Plaza shops and make a stop at the:

ABORIGINAL ART CULTURE CRAFT CENTRE ❸, Shop PO 1, Stanley Street, ☎ (07) 3844-0255. *Open Mon.–Thurs. 9:30–5, Fri. 10:30–9:30, Sat. 10:30–5. Closed Sun. & holidays. Free. Gift shop. Special events.* ♿.

This is an Aboriginal-owned and operated center that allows you to get a personal view of the craft and culture of the most ancient of peoples. Things to do include: making your own didgeridoo, learn how to use a boomerang, listen to the deep drone of the didgeridoo musicians, watch authentic Aboriginal dancers, shop for crafts made by the local artists.

Exit into the colorful street and make a left onto Glenelg Street and hike two short blocks to the:

IMAX THEATRE ❹, corner of Ernest & Grey streets, ☎ (07) 3844-4222, **W**: imax.com.au. *Open daily from 10–10. Adults from AU $14.50, children from AU $9.50, students from AU$11.50, seniors from AU $10.50, family passes from AU $42. Gift shop. Snack bar.* ♿.

This 16-story screen gives you an action-packed, in-your-face show that has a pretty high wow factor. The 3-D movies are the best, and you will catch yourself ducking from objects spiraling out of control and off the screen. Call them or check the web site for the current shows.

With eyes fully adjusted to the sunlight, double back to the Parkland and see if there are any shows scheduled at the **South Bank Piazza ❺**. This open-air, covered stadium hosts special events throughout the year. If you luck out, you might catch one of the local groups singing their hearts out. Continue on the Arbour pathway and detour past the Riverside Restaurant area and check out the **Rainforest Walk ❻**. It is cool and shady with a gentle brook flowing under the boardwalk. Next door is the **Nepalese Pagoda**—a giant "souvenir" of the World Expo 88 events. Proceed towards the **Cultural Forecourt ❼**, and duck into the **Queensland Conservatorium ❽** to see if there might be a concert you would be interested in seeing. Then cross the court to the:

QUEENSLAND PERFORMING ARTS CENTRE ❾, Queensland Cultural Centre, ☎ (07) 3840-7444, **W**: qpac.com.au. *Open for performances. Tickets start around AU $46 for matinees. Gift shop. Café & restaurant. Special events.* ♿.

Good Shows, good food, and good shopping can be found within the walls of this performance center. From ballet, to musicals, to opera, the entertainment is some of the best found in Queensland. You have a choice of four venues—a 2,000 seater called the **Lyric Theatre**, the **Concert Hall** set up for 1,800, the medium-ranged **Optus Playhouse**, and the intimate 335-seat **Cremorne Theatre**. Each setting offers great views and top-notch performances. You will find it amazing to actually be able to get reasonably priced tickets to acts and shows untouchable in other countries. And the small playhouses offer unusual and interesting shows not found anywhere else. Stop in even if it is the day-of-show to catch a meal at the Lyrebird Restaurant and enjoy a show. The gift shop has some cool stuff too.

Stop at the Promenade Café and enjoy the cascading waterfalls as you sip your espresso or cross over (or through the safe and well-lit tunnel) to the:

*QUEENSLAND MUSEUM ❿, South Bank, ☎ (07) 3840-7555, **W:** qmuseum.qld.gov.au. *Open daily 9:30–5. Free. Gift/book shop. Special events and exhibits.* ♿.

This place has a high wow factor, mates, and it is very manageable to see all the nooks and crannies in this natural history museum in two hours. You could spend all day if you like to peruse the changing exhibits, but make sure you check out at least two spots. The first is the **Endangered Species Cavern** with its strange displays of cute, deadly, and rarely-seen animals. The second is **The Inquiry Centre** with experts on hand to answer questions and direct you to the giant magnetic termite mound, the 15′ redback spider, the 30-foot skin of a 506-pound anaconda, or some of the live exhibits. This is a touching museum, and you might never get out of this section. But do try because you should find the "Death on the Downs" exhibit with the Diprotodon and giant goanna to scare the young ones.

Around the corner you can absorb some highbrow culture at the:

*QUEENSLAND ART GALLERY ⓫, South Bank, ☎ (07) 3840-7303 or (07) 3840-7350, **W:** qag.qld.gov.au. *Open Mon.–Fri. 10–5, Sat.–Sun. 9–5. Closed Christmas and Good Friday, and half-day on Anzac Day. Free. Gift/book shop. Special events and exhibits. Café.* ♿.

With over 10,000 works in storage, the viewing of Australian and international paintings, sculptures, and photographs is ever rotating. There are a few permanent exhibits; my favorite being the Indigenous Australian Art section. It feels powerful and ancient. Free guided tours are available from the information desk and are staggered about every other hour during the day. Lectures are usually held every Wednesday at 10:30 if you desire intimate descriptions of the currently displayed works. This is also a great quiet spot for lunch; the **Bar Merlo** is surrounded by crashing waterfalls and posing statures—just watch out for the hungry birds as they will take food off your plate if you get distracted.

Right around the corner and at the intersection of Peel is the last building to explore.

THE STATE LIBRARY OF QUEENSLAND ⓬, ☎ (07) 3840-7666, **W:** slq.qld.gov.au. *Open Mon.–Thurs. 10–8, Fri.–Sun. 10–5. Special events. Library shop for gifts. Café. Free.* ♿.

Over 100 years old, the library has a host of goodies spread through its corridors. The staff provides workshops, lunchtime talks, films, and research services. You can get free internet access, check to see if any of your ancestors lived in Australia, check out maps of the area, research old sheet music, and enjoy the cartoon workshops for kids. It really is an undiscovered gem, off the beaten path for local and international tourists.

Finally, if you are lucky to be in the South Bank area on the weekend, do not miss the:

SOUTH BANK CRAFT MARKETS ⓭, Stanley Street/Little Stanley Street, South Bank, ☎ (07) 3846-4500, **W**: south-bank.net.au. *Open Fri. 5–10, Sat. 11–5, Sun. 9–5, Farmers Market every 3rd Sunday of each month from 6–noon. Food & drink everywhere. Free.* &.

Spread out amongst the purple flowers with throngs of folks looking for a treat, this is the spot to be on the weekends. Colorful, fun, and tasty sums it up—look for the mimes and strolling troubadours, or just sit and people watch.

OTHER THINGS TO DO ON SOUTH BANK:

Cycle Rides with a group leaving from the Maritime Museum (free 12-mile trek), Victoria Bridge underpass (free ride of 25 miles), or Riverside Green (AU $5 triathlon training program).

Rollerblade the parkland with **Blade Sensations**, Shop 2, 493 Stanley Street, South Bank, ☎ (07) 3844-0606, **W**: bladesensations.com.au. Daily 10–5. From AU $11.

Chinatown &
Fortitude Valley

Enter the ornate Chinese arch and journey into the Orient with rows of Peking Duck hanging in storefronts, smells of healing herbs wafting down tidy alleys, and chatter of vendors selling their wares. Formerly tea-tee lagoons that were converted to cornfields to feed the English settlers around 1827, the "new farm" area was converted to sugar refineries, wool stores, and a center for local energy. Now know locally as "The Valley," this seven-by-eleven cultural and entertainment sector of town includes the postcodes of Chinatown, Fortitude Valley, and New Farm. Set in the northern part of the city it is also the cosmopolitan heart and soul of Brisbane, and the multicultural hub of Queensland. Many tourists bypass the area, but it has the most diverse range of traders, retailers, pubs, clubs, and eateries possible in a compact neighborhood. It is also the home to the alternative scene, not to be passed over if you have an open mind. If you are into the alternative grunge music scene, this is the place to find the best clubs for your ears.

GETTING THERE:

By Car, the most central parking lot is just off of Wickham at 31 Duncan Street, ☎ (07) 3257-1367. Other choices include Kings Parking at Warner & Ann Streets on ☎ (07) 3257-3055 or Kings at 230 Brunswick Street on ☎ (07) 3852-1483.

By Bus, numerous stops in the area—grab any of the Brunswick Street buses.

By Taxi, there is a taxi rank on the corner of Ann and Brunswick streets as well as one on Wickham and Warner streets.

By Train, there is a station stop at Brunswick Street, only a 2–3 block hike to the center of Chinatown.

PRACTICALITIES:

If you want to blend and mingle with the locals, designer jeans and labels will not do the trick. Dress real casual and get into the groove. The distances between locations means you will probably have to either get behind the wheel or take public transportation. But as is the rest of the city, parking is tight. Wear comfy shoes and don't be alarmed to see people rolling cigarettes, it is actually tobacco (mostly). The main event in this area is the Powerhouse, but do enjoy strolls around the neighborhood, being a bit careful after dark. Shops are open from 9–5 (till 9 on weekends), restaurants till late, and nightclubs till very late. Festivals and special events occur throughout the year; check with the internet sites listed below for current details.

To get a glimpse of this bohemian area, click on **W**: valleyweb.com.au; **W**: newfarmneighborhood.org; **W**: ehatson.au; **W**: valleymalls.com; or the funky local rag at **W**: thebug.com.au

FOOD AND DRINK:

Restaurants come and go pretty quickly in this neck of town, but you will not have any problem finding food or drink. With streets packed with Chinese, Thai, curry, coffee shops, Vietnamese, Malay, and yes even an American diner (sort of)—you will have plenty of taste delights to choose from. I always try to sample the Peking duck at **China Sea** ($-$$) or **Enjoy Inn** ($-$$); or the fantastic Yum Cha for lunch ($$) at the **Chinahouse Seafood Restaurant** or the **Golden Palace Chinese Restaurant** when I visit the area.

LOCAL ATTRACTIONS:

Circled numbers correspond to numbers on the map.

*CHINATOWN MALL ❶, Duncan Street. *Open 24 hours. Free.*

The Asian aromas here are the most distinctive, and the coffee the most powerful in town. Saturday markets are the best, and you will definitely see a few tie-dyed duds, lots of piercing and fluorescent/spiked dog collars on modern-day hippies. The crafts are bizarre with hemp clothing and New Age paraphernalia prevalent, with the mainstream stores offering a bit of balance to the area. A short trip away from the Mall, on Wickham Street, just across the street is one of the best spots to buy hiking/camping equipment.

McWHIRTER'S BUILDING ❷, corner of Duncan & Ann streets. *Open 24 hours. Free.*

A huge redbrick structure was under construction at the time of this publication, but plans are for a mega shopping mall with apartments above. Drop in to see how it is progressing.

*BRUNSWICK STREET MALL ❸, Brunswick Street, between Wickham & Ann streets.

Another retail section in the Valley. Have a wander to see if anything catches your fancy. Make a night stop at the Empire Hotel and dance the night away to a mix of music or just enjoy a brandy and cigar at the Press Club. Around eleven art galleries along the footpath will draw you in for a gander during the daytime hours.

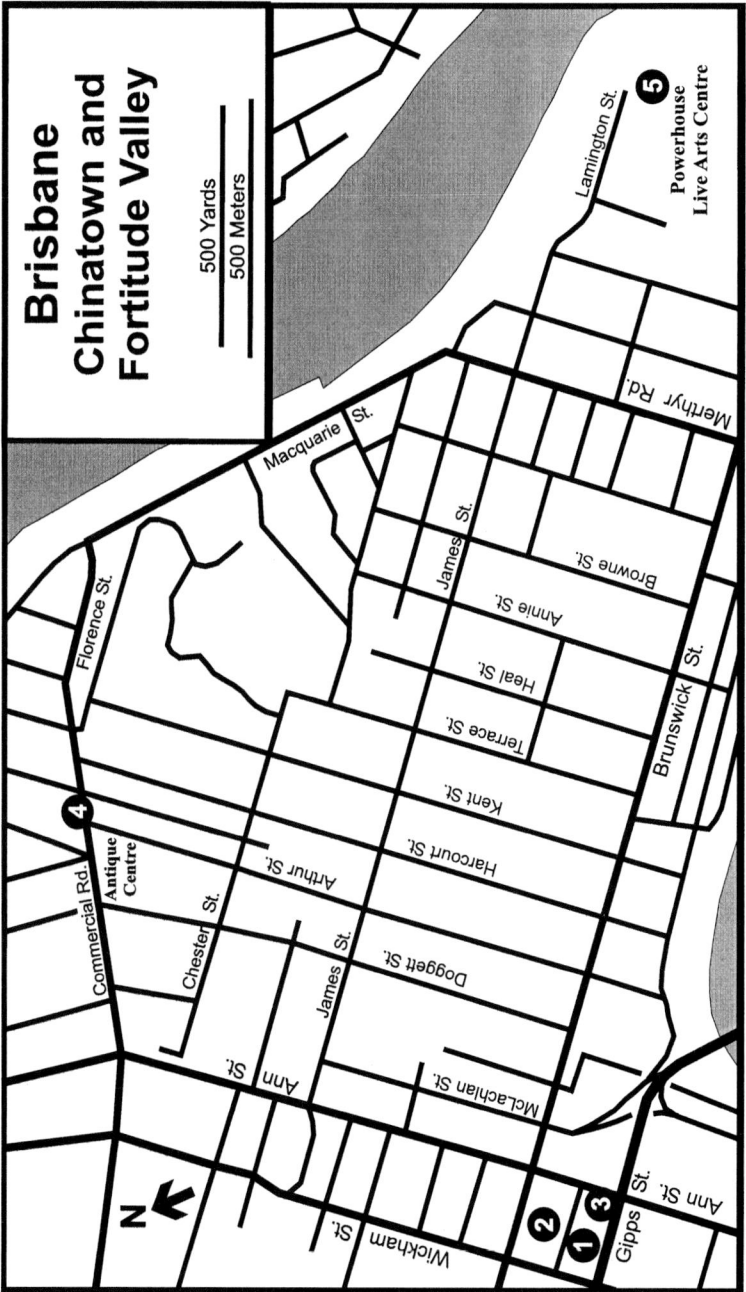

Brisbane
Chinatown and
Fortitude Valley

500 Yards
500 Meters

N

Powerhouse
Live Arts Centre

Lamington St.

Merthyr Rd.

Macquarie St.

Florence St.

James St.

Annie St.

Browne St.

Heal St.

Terrace St.

Kent St.

Harcourt St.

Brunswick St.

Commercial Rd.

Antique Centre

Arthur St.

Chester St.

James St.

Doggett St.

Ann St.

McLachlan St.

Wickham St.

Gipps St.

Ann St.

NEW FARM ANTIQUE CENTRE ❹, corner of Arthur & Commercial Road, New Farm, ☎ (07) 3852-2352. *Open: 9–5. Free.*

Housed in a heritage wool store, the building is almost as interesting at the antiques displayed inside. I found this bazaar to have better prices for antiques than anywhere else in the area. From Georgian to Art Deco to 1960's Retro, the variety is astounding. I am pretty sure that you will not walk out of this place empty handed.

*THE POWERHOUSE LIVE ARTS CENTRE ❺, 119 Lamington Street, New Farm. ☎ (07) 3358-8622 or (07) 3358-8600 for the box office, **W**: brisbanepowerhouse.org. *Open 9–5 weekdays and during performances. Spark Bar, Watt Restaurant,* ☎ *(07) 3358-5464. Free tours by appointment.* ♿.

This is Brisbane's newest performance center, and home to some of the most unique shows you might ever witness—like the Brisbane Queer Film & Video Festival or Circus Oz. They have some enlightening shows and weeklong events such as the Sacred Music Festival with chanting Gyuto Buddhist monks and Tibetan folk singers. The art gallery in the basement is an odd assortment of sculptures, paintings, and photography. It may offend some, so read the posting at the door before you enter the free exhibit. The building alone is worth the stop; it was built in 1928 to supply electricity for the tram system that provided mass transportation to the city in the mid-1900s. The bus system made the trams obsolete, so they and their power station were decommissioned in 1971. The renovated building proudly bears the graffiti of its day, and the three main structures—the **Turbine Building**, the **Boiler House**, and the **Stores Building** depict intricate cornices, huge casements of glass, incredible iron beams, and beautiful brickworks, making it a perfect venue for dance and music. The terrace level boasts an art gallery and a scrumptious menu at the Watt Restaurant.

OTHER STUFF:

Empire Hotel, 339 Brunswick Street, ☎ (07) 3852-1216, **W**: empirehotel.com.au

Sydney Street Theatre, 166 Sydney Street, New Farm, ☎ (07) 3395-6400. For out-of-the-ordinary theatre.

Geeta Enterprises, Shop 30, Wickham Street, ☎ (07) 3252-4937. Indian herbs and healing potions.

Sheepskin Warehouse, 281 Brunswick, ☎ (07) 3252-2903. Warm up with thick Aussie wool slippers or a car seat.

Chinatown Butchers, 3 Duncan Street, ☎ (07) 3252-2479. Just have a peek through the window and see if you can identify what is on display.

International Beer Bar, 206 Wickham Street, ☎ 07-3852-5660. Any beer from any country.

The Book Warehouse, 230 Brunswick Street, ☎ (07) 3257-0181. Books old and new.

Mt. Cooth-tha
and the Cosmos

A ll of the locations listed in this trip are within a 15–20 minute drive from any CBD hotel lobby. Some are accessible via the CityCat river taxis, and mass transit is relatively inexpensive. The drive can be a bit confusing despite our maps to guide you; the drive to Mt. Coo-tha will definitely test your roundabout skills. Each attraction could be a half-day or full day event and you can mix and match them to suit your schedule and interests.

Outstanding Attractions include Lone Pine Koala Sanctuary, Mt. Coo-tha Botanical Gardens, Mt. Coo-tha Scenic Lookout, the Australian Woolshed, Sir Thomas Brisbane Planetarium, and the Boondall Wetland Reserve.

GETTING THERE:

By Car, your first stop should take you about 15 minutes to drive to along Coronation Drive, following signs to Milton Road into Toowong and finally up the hill to Mt. Cootha Road.

By Bus, Bus 471 from Adelaide Street will get you there, or hop the great City Circle Bus 598 or 599.

PRACTICALITIES:

Just wear comfortable shoes, take the camera and enjoy. The walk is quite hilly in places and may be a bit strenuous, but there are lots of benches and shaded avenues to rest. The guides are fantastic and will be of great assistance with most of your questions and needs. If you drive up the mountain, get good directions and don't get frustrated if you get lost — I still do.

FOOD AND DRINK:

All food groups are covered on the way and on the mountain. There are some cool eateries in Toowong, and you may want to explore that tiny hamlet. On the mountain and at the attractions there are assorted fast food spots, ice creamery, a pub, and a very nice restaurant at the Botanic Gardens. If you have the energy and facilities, take a picnic lunch up and find a great view to enjoy the warm sun.

LOCAL ATTRACTIONS:
Circled numbers correspond to numbers on the map.

*BRISBANE BOTANIC GARDENS at MT. COOTH-THA ❶, Mt. Cooth-tha Road, Toowong, ☎ (07) 3403-2533, E-mail: vsomg@brisbane.qld.gov.au. *Open daily 8:00–5:30 (closes at 5 from April to August). Free. Picnic facilities, restaurant/café, tours. ♿, but not recommended; you can circle the gardens on Ring Road during weekdays.*

This giant gem, open since 1970, eluded me for years, but now it is a regular escape destination into 128 acres of a living museum. The area is named from the Aboriginal designation of "place of wild honey," and the pollen gatherers remain to help out the foreign and domestic flora. You have the choice of gathering all the brochures at the information booth at the entrance and having a walkabout, following the self-guiding interpretive walks, or asking for one of the volunteers to give you the hour tour. I recommend the tour, as the botany buffs will have some great tidbits found only in their bank of knowledge. Like pointing out the favorite hiding spots of the eastern water dragons or the hidden location of the dinosaur tree next to the 240-million year old fossilized logs. If you are lucky, you can experience a Japanese purification/wedding ceremony in the Japanese Garden based on the mountain-stream style of garden, and be welcomed by the sign that says, "Come into this garden and enjoy the blue of the water and the green of the trees." If you would rather just wander, here are a few tips: Drive the loop around the gardens first to get your bearings. Take a photo of the one of 38 known Wollemi Pines, also known as the Dinosaur Tree. Look for the tree in the **Tropical Dome** (open 9:30 am–4:30 pm) that has leaves shaped like hands. Stroll the **Japanese Gardens** that were originally planted in South Bank as a gift from the Japanese government for the 1988 Expo. Scout the new **Fern House** that opened in July 2002 and check out the 400 miniature trees surrounded by Rammed Earth Walls of the **Bonsai House**. If you get to the gardens early, park at the Lookout for a noontime picnic. Don't miss the National Freedom Wall with 16,000 plaques dedicated to those who died in the conflicts fought by Australia. It's eerie to look out and see the Toowong Cemetery across the valley. Take the kid in you to the waterhole playground of the dragons on the stone bridge near the Japanese Gardens. Get a sense of Australian, American, Temperate, Arid, Eucalypt, Wetland, Rainforest, and African zones in separate sections of the gardens that are listed on the free brochure. Finally, if you have time, check out the Herbarium and its library of over 600,000 plant specimens. Craft fairs are held on some weekends.

If you can break for lunch, I would recommend the **Lakeside Gardens Café** for a choice of two types of food, and free South-East Queensland Tourism or Westside News guides that will give you even more ideas to scout out the area. The Terrace and Café each look over the busy lake and

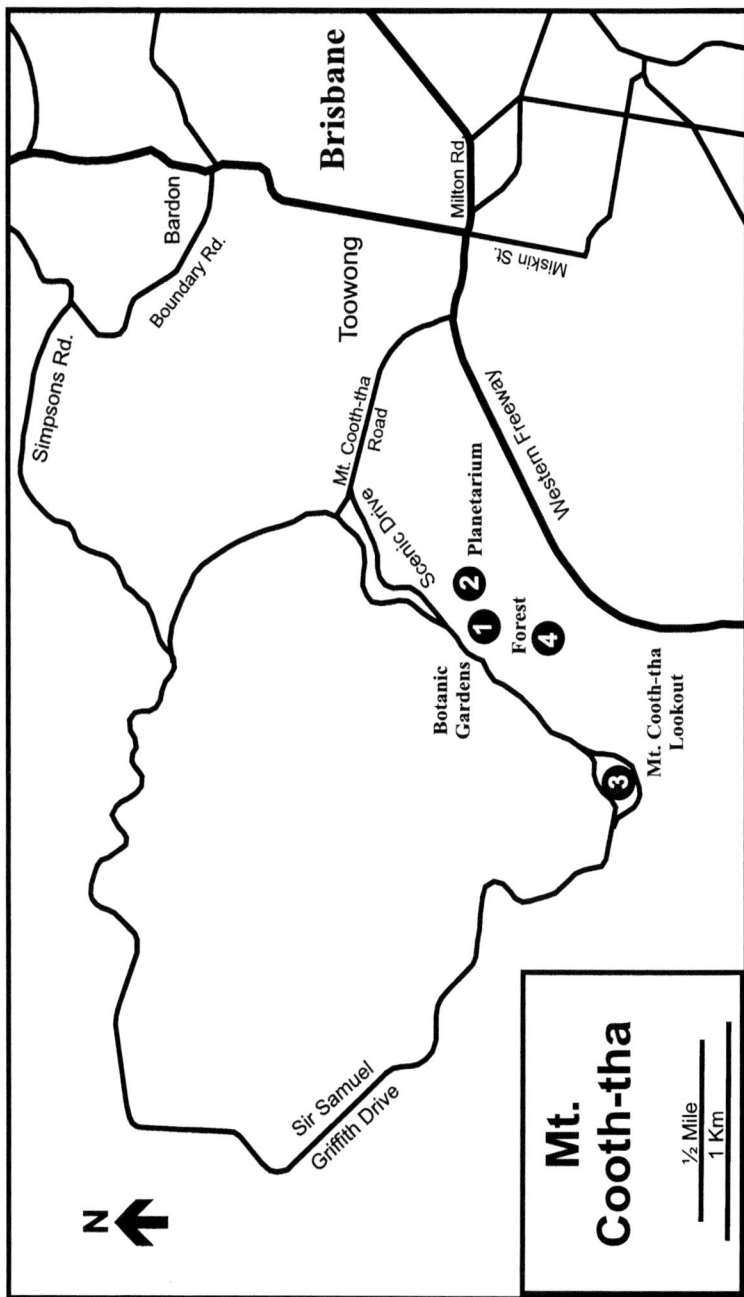

Brisbane

Bardon

Boundary Rd.

Simpsons Rd.

Toowong

Milton Rd

Miskin St.

Mt. Cooth-tha Road

Scenic Drive

Western Freeway

Planetarium

Forest

Botanic Gardens

Mt. Cooth-tha Lookout

Sir Samuel Griffith Drive

1 **2** **3** **4**

Mt. Cooth-tha

½ Mile
1 Km

N

offer delicious food, from burgers to pastas. Open daily for lunch from 9:30 am until about 5:00. ☎ (07) 3870-9506 or **W**: stewarts.net.au/lakeside
After a snack, drop in on the:

*SIR THOMAS BRISBANE PLANETARIUM and THE COSMIC SKYDOME ❷, Mt. Cooth-tha Road, Toowong, ☎ (07) 3403-2578, **W**: brisbane.qld.gov.au (look under planetarium). *Shows Wed.–Fri. 3:30 & 7:30 pm, Sat. 1:30/3:30/7:30 pm, Sun. 1:30 & 3:30 pm, closed Mon. & Tues. Observation sessions on a reservation basis; costs are the same as the shows. Adults AU $10.50, children AU $6.50, family AU $30.00, group rate discounts of ten or more available.*

This will give you a chance to sit and enjoy the stars after your hike around the gardens. The 40-foot dome was opened in 1978 to allow both the novice and buff to stargaze images of the Southern Cross skies. Guided by an astronomer, you will be given a chance to peek through the giant refractor or reflector telescopes. Groups of no more than eight are permitted, so reserve a time well in advance. Documentaries and special effects in the Skydome will dazzle even the uninterested astronomer, and the 45-minute show is changed on a regular basis. The gift shop and museum is chocker block full of ancient meteorites, books, educational packs, gadgets, and the original telescope owned by Sir Thomas himself.

For a grand view of the city, jump in the car and head up to the top of Mt. Coot-tha to the ***Mt. Coot-tha Scenic Lookout** ❸. Open day or night and free, this mountaintop tourist attraction provides breathtaking panoramic views of the city and surrounding landscapes. Parking can be tedious and it is often a mob scene, but it is worth a look. The area is adorned with attractive water features and hosts the Kuta Café, the Scenic Summit Restaurant, a small gift shop, bar, and an ice cream stand. There are several platform areas with different views of the valley below, and the gardens frame the sights with colorful blooms most of the year.

If you haven't had enough of the nature trail, point your car to Sir Samuel Griffith Drive (off of Mt. Coot-tha Road) and hike or drive the:

MT. COOTH-THA FOREST ❹, Sir Samuel Griffith Drive, Toowong, ☎ (07) 3403-2533. *Free. Not recommended for &.*

This forest backs to the Brisbane Forest Park, comprising over 74,000 acres watched over by the rare Powerful Owl. With more than 370 animal species keeping her company, and extensive walking tracks, it is a great place to explore and stretch those legs. Loaded with goshawks, parrots, whipbirds, white-striped freetail bats, and heaps of small mammals you will have a blast exploring the looping path.

Shipwrecks and Wild Dolphins

There are only two places in the world where you can hand feed wild dolphins, and the Tangalooma Wild Dolphin Resort is one of them. I would urge you to take the plunge and make this a two-night Beachcomber trip onto Moreton Island. The resort, opened in 1963, is also a marine research station, and you will be able to participate and interact with the loveable subjects. This ecological marine base was once a slaughterhouse for the dolphin's big brother, the humpback whale. Remnants of the whaling station remain on the island's eastern shoreline, and the jetty pylons, oil extraction platform, and butchering deck remain on the northern end of the resort's grounds. Now a natural reserve for whales, dolphins, and dugongs (like the manatee), the sand island of Moreton forms a wildlife haven about six miles wide and 21 miles long. The northern point of Moreton Island claimed over twelve ships, and they now create a protective reef that looks like a rusty graveyard.

GETTING THERE:

The jump-off point is near the Brisbane Airport, on the Brisbane River, and there are courtesy pick-up services from the airport and most of the hotels in the city. From there it is a 70-minute jaunt across Moreton Bay to a magical island surrounded by liquid opal waters and a whole host of friendly animals.

PRACTICALITIES:

I rate a camera above all else on this journey. You will have stories to tell and they won't be believed without proof. Shorts and long pants are recommended as well as a windbreaker or foul weather gear. The normal sun protection goes here, and hiking sandals or shoes. You can take food, but no alcohol onto the island. If you want to have your own snorkel/dive gear take it along, but the facilities offer all of that too. **Tangalooma Wild Dolphin Resort**, P.O Box 1102, Eagle Farm QLD 4009, ☎ 1-300-652-250 or (07) 3268-6333, Fax: (07) 3268-6299, **W**: tangalooma.com. *Open all year. From AU $35.00 for a five-hour Day Cruise to over AU $400.00/ night for families.*

Overnight Wild Dolphin Package for AU $158.00 per adult twin share, AU $58.00 for children, and AU $234.00 single adult. Best deals are off-season (anytime except 25 Dec.–12 Jan. and Easter weekend), breakfast included; tours are extra.

FOOD AND DRINK:

There is a grocery store on the resort grounds and plenty of BBQ stations for your own cooking. Most rooms have cooking facilities along with cutlery and tableware. There is a pub, a bakery, a café, and a great restaurant in the area too. And for an island resort the beer and tucker is reasonably priced.

SUGGESTED TOURS:

The activities are as varied as you might ever want with surf, sand, hiking trails, and helicopters in abundance. The wild dolphin contact is obviously the centerpiece attraction, but you can opt for the whale watching too if it's in season. Several guided tours are listed and you can do the four-hour **Northern Safari** to the Lighthouse and Honeymoon Bay that tours the WWII defensive bunkers and lighthouse built by the convicts. The Blue Lagoon is a favorite; it is rumored that a dip in the crystal-blue water will increase your life span. The **Desert Tour** takes you to the 100-acre sand blow (or desert) just south of the resort and offers an opportunity to toboggan down the sand dunes. The **Guided Quad Tour** looked like heaps of fun, but it's best to hoof it around the island and get a natural view of the surroundings. The self-guided tour of the **Tangalooma Wrecks** is as impressive as the desert walk. It only takes 20 minutes to hike north along the beach to the graveyard of 12 ships lined up near the shoreline. They now create an artificial reef where one old bugger has been resting on the bottom for over 100 years.

OTHER ATTRACTIONS IN THE BRISBANE SURROUNDING AREAS:

These three bonus sites are included to meet the local wildlife and cuddle a koala or two. You can drive the 15 minutes from the city, take the 430 Koala Bus from the Meyer Centre, or cruise up the river on the **Mirimar Boat, ☎** (07) 3221-0300.

*LONE PINE KOALA SANCTUARY, Jesmond Road, Fig Tree Pocket, Brisbane, ☎ (07) 3378-1366, **W**: koala.net. *Open daily from 8, Anzac Day from 1:30. Adults AU $15, children (3–13) AU $10. Special activities and tours available.* ⅖.

The world's largest koala sanctuary boasts over 130 of the furry critters plus many more of its friends too. Staff provides regular animal talks, and you can hand-feed most of the animals. You have the option to board the Wildlife Cruise from Queens Wharf at George Street in Brisbane.

Cruise up to Lone Pine from the city docks. The Mirimar steams the

Tangalooma Wild Dolphin Resort

12 miles up the river, past city mansions and the inner-city colony of fruit bats, then stroll Lone Pine for two hours. ☎ (04) 1274-9426, **W**: mirimar.com. Adults AU $25, kids AU $15.

AUSTRALIAN WOOLSHED, 148 Samford Road, Ferny Hills, Brisbane QLD. ☎ (07) 3872-1100, Fax: (07) 3351-5575, **W**: auswoolshed.com.au. *Open 8:30–4:30. Outback Adventure Pass (includes all attractions except the dance): Adults AU $22.00, children AU $14.50, family of 2 adults and 3 children AU $78.00. Restaurant or BBQ facilities.* ♿.

Enjoy the Outback setting only a 20-minute drive from the city, or take the train from the Ferny Grove Station. Step into your chaps and grab your shears mate, there's heaps to do at this action-packed sheep farm attraction. Here are a few treats to consider: Listen to Outback yarns while witnessing a Ram Show with shearing, dog herding, and hands-on animal farm complete with my favorite, the hairy-nosed wombat; Dance the jig and enjoy bush tucker at the Bush Dance & Variety Show; Cool off on the kid's favorite Waterslide or challenge them to a round of Mini Golf; Enjoy damper bread/Billy Tea and Outback delicacies at the Woolshed Dining Hall, the Drovers Camp Function Room, the Wattleseed Café, or Shelter Sheds. Look around the gift store for some fun goodies to take with you mate.

GOLD COAST & HINTERLANDS

I f Brisbane is considered the gateway to paradise, then the Gold Coast holds the key to Shangri-La. With pristine beaches listed as some of the best in the world, and nine tropical and subtropical parks to explore, the only limit to immersing yourself into this Aussie wonderland is time. The easy hour drive/train ride from Brisbane will transport you to a holiday resort-type environment. If you choose to spend a few nights on the Coast or make that area your base for the seabound trips, several accommodations are recommended. There are plenty of hotels and restaurants to select from.

This section will give you a taste of almost every aspect of the Australian lifestyle, from shopping at glitzy tourist spots, golfing with kangaroos, riding turquoise waves, witnessing the strangling figs, or simply shedding your clothes and soaking in the sun. This is Australia's playground and backyard holiday spot for the Pacific Basin, so join the locals and see the sights.

Several trips will be based on a body of water called the Broadwater. This is a local term for the tidal network that is a mixture of river, bay and ocean. Looking on a nautical map it is a stretch of water from narrow canals to bay-like sections that parallels the South Pacific Ocean and is protected from bashing waves by a landmass north of Surfers Paradise and farther north by the Stradbroke Islands. It is usually calm water, but storms and the two seaways in the area make it a body of water to be respected.

The references to The Spit and The Seaway in this portion of the book are related to the narrow strip of land that juts out into the ocean. The Gold Coast, like many coastal towns, has an area called The Spit. It is usually near an entrance to the sea and is also referred to as The Seaway. Another characteristic of seaside villages is to name the road that runs parallel to the ocean, The Esplanade or Marine Parade. It's kind of like Main Street.

Another common term used in this section and around Australia is hinterland. The dictionary describes hinterland as a district lying behind a coast or a remote, fringe area. This term, used commonly on the Gold Coast, is to depict the mountain ranges behind the coastline and includes the Tamborine and Springbrook forests.

The Gold Coast and its hinterland offers a mix of driving, boating, walking, cycling, and even aerial tours. The hinterland trips are only a 15–45 minute drive from the coast or 1 – 1-1/2-hours from the city, but many of the roads are narrow and will allow only the passenger the opportunity to see the beauty of the valleys. Remember you are also driving on the opposite side of the road mates. Commercial tours are available, and I have listed a few of them. If you are comfortable driving on the cliff's edge, it is much more fun to explore on your own. Of the sixteen daytrips offered in this section, many will not be found in most travel guides. These are designed as a cross-section of what is available to the traveler who wants non-tourist adventures.

Not to be outdone by Brisbane, one of the local mottos in this area is "Paradise one day, Paradise the next." A few good Internet sites give you a flavor of the area including: **W**: goldcoasttourism.com.au; **W**: surfersparadise.com; **W**: hellogoldcoast.com.au; **W**: destinationsurfersparadise.com.au; **W**: bestofthegoldcoast.com.au; **W**: pointout.com.au; **W**: goldcoastregion.com. My best experiences have been looking and booking through a local tourist information center called Wot's On. You can check out hotels, attractions and local hot spots on their web site **W**: wotson.com.au

For a comprehensive look at the region's hinterland national parks go to **W**: goldcoasttourism.com

GETTING TO THE GOLD COAST:

By Car: The exits for the Gold Coast are a straight and direct 40-mile shot down the Pacific Highway (or M1) from Brisbane. Turn off at the Smith Street or Southport/Nerang Road exits and drive east unit you dead end at the Gold Coast Highway, following that to your desired destination. Note that there is a strict 50 km speed limit in most residential or "built-up" areas. If you pass a van and see a flash—your photograph was taken and a speeding ticket will be sent to you in the mail. There are also police cameras at many stoplights.

From Brisbane to the Coast there are several stops you could make just off the highway. Attractions with easy on/off access include: **The Carleton Brewery** at Yatala (Exit 41 for free beers), tours at 10 am, noon, 2 pm, ☎ (07) 3826-5858. **Zorb Gold Coast** (Exit 49), open 9–5 daily, ☎ (07) 5547-6300, is a thrill of a lifetime by rolling down a giant slalom inside a ball. The **Le Mans Raceway** in Pimpama (Exit 49), open 10–5 daily, ☎ (07) 5546-6566. **Dream World** at Coomera (Exit 51), open 10–5, ☎ (07) 5588-1108 or 1-800-073-300, **W**: dreamworld.com.au. **Movie World** in Oxenford (Exit 60), open 9:30–5:30, ☎ (07) 5573-8485, **W**: movieworld.com.au. **Water World** at Oxenford (Exit 60), open 10–4, ☎ (07) 5573-2255, **W**: wetnwild.com.au

By Train: Hop any of the express trains to the Gold Coast or Robina stations. Avoid the local train as it stops at all stations in between. You may board at Central, Roma Street, South Brisbane, or South Bank stations in Brisbane; and sit back and enjoy the scenery on the one-hour trip to the Nerang Station. From there you can catch the Trainlink service or hail a taxi to the surf. Refer to the Queensland Rail map on page 00 for stations and routes.

By Bus: Try **Coachtrans** at ☎ 13-12-30 or (07) 5506-9777, **W:** coachtrans.com.au. Access is available at any of the Bus/Rail transport hubs in Brisbane, but the best is from Roma Street. Check the timetables for your destination of the Beach Road Stop in the heart of Surfers Paradise. It will take a little over an hour to smell the sea air, but it is the most economical way to head south with a one-way trip costing: Adults: AU $14 and kids: AU $11. An alternative bus service is **Kirklands**, ☎ 1-300-367-077, **W:** kirklands.com.au. The most attractive option is the **Surfside Buses** on ☎ (07) 5574-5111 or 1-300-655-655, or **W:** gcshuttle.com.au. They have a Freedom Pass with unlimited local travel, door-to-door theme park transfers, and airport transfers. The local route map is provided for your convenience.

By Plane: Luckily the Coolangatta Airport is just a 30-minute drive south of Surfers Paradise, and it is a short commuter fight from Brisbane. There are direct air routes into this small airport from most major Australian cities. When you arrive you can catch one of the many ground transport systems. To book ahead, try these two suggestions: **Con-X-ion**, ☎ (07) 5591-2525, AU $35; **Gold Coast Ecotours**, ☎ (07) 5559-0377 for about AU $25. Again, the Surfside Buslines are a great way to travel unless you require a door-to-door drop off.

ACCOMMODATIONS ON THE COAST:

If you decide to move your base to the Coast, the best locations are probably either the hectic Surfers Paradise or its quieter next-door neighbor Main Beach. There is a wide selection of accommodations in both locations centered around most of the activities and attractions in this section. For the mountain and rainforest trips you may want to book overnight stays in a hinterland resort to get the full benefit of what nature has to offer. In both the beach and mountain areas, mid-priced accommodations are suggested. A listing of accommodations can be found on **W:** goldacc.com, and you can book directly through the Wot's On website at **W:** wotson.com.au. Backpacker's accommodation can be viewed at **W:** surfersparadisebackpackers.com.au

MAIN BEACH:

The **Sheraton Mirage**, Sea World Drive, The Broadwater, Main Beach, QLD 4217. ☎ (07) 5591-1488, **W:** sheraton.com/miragegoldcoast. ***** Rooms start at AU $517 and go as high as AU $2,900 for a suite. Great location on The Spit and right on the beach if you want to pay that sort of money. Top-notch restaurants and a fantastic buffet breakfast; and dinner can be enjoyed downstairs.

Sea World Nara Resort, Sea World Drive, Main Beach, QLD 4217. ☎ (07) 5591-0000, **W:** seaworldnara.com.au. ***** Rooms starting at AU $238 and up to AU $320 for a suite. Geared towards the Asian tourist with good Japanese-style restaurants. On the Broadwater, at The Spit, and right next door to Sea World.

Sunbird Beach, 3540 Main Beach Parade, Main Beach, QLD 4217. ☎ (07) 5532-9888, **W**: sunbirdbeachresort.com.au. **** 1/2 Weekly rates are AU $649–$1,397. Right across the street from the surf beach and a great spot during the Indy Race. A nice high-rise complex with a heated indoor pool.

Aloha Lane, 11 Breaker Street, Main Beach, QLD 4217. ☎ (07) 5591-5944. **W**: alohalane.com.au. *** 1/2 Daily rates are around AU $90-155 and weekly prices from AU $517–$990. A three-story complex only a skip from the beach and a good value. A short walk to the Tedder Street restaurants or to Surfers Paradise.

Main Beach Tourist Park, Marine Parade, Main Beach, QLD 4217. ☎ (07) 5581-7722. **W**: gctp.com.au/main. A **** 1/2 caravan park with sites starting at AU $20 and cabins beginning at AU $110 a day or AU $600 a week. Surrounded by high-rise apartments, it has a pool and cooking facilities. The cabins are a good value and are just across the street from the beach.

SURFERS PARADISE:

ANA Hotel, 22 View Ave, Surfers Paradise, QLD 4217. ☎ 1-800-074-440 or (07) 5579-1060, **W**: anahotelgc.com.au. Rooms start at around AU $270 and suites at AU $385. In the heart of the action of Surfers, the ***** ANA has an international clientele, lots of extras and is only a block from the beach.

Mercure Resort, 122 Ferny Avenue, Surfers Paradise, QLD 4217. ☎ 1-800-074-111 or (07) 5579-4444. **W**: mercuresurfers.com.au. Starting at AU $160. This **** 1/2 resort boasts the best place to take kids. It is also in the heart of the city and near the beach.

International Beach Resort, 84 The Esplanade, Surfers Paradise, QLD 4217. ☎ (07) 5539-0099. **W**: internationalresort.com.asu. Starting at AU $77 to a weekly rate of AU $539. *** 1/2 beachfront property, and you will be right in the thick of the activities. Good breakfast deals too.

Surfers Paradise Backpackers Resort, 2837 Gold Coast Highway, Surfers Paradise, QLD 4217. ☎ (07) 5592-4677, **W**: surfersparadisebackpackers.com.au. Rates start with dorms for AU $22 and three-share rooms for AU $26. Rated one of the best hostels in Surfers, on the main drag and close to beach and clubs.

Surf-n-Sun Beachside Backpackers, 3323 Gold Coast Highway, Surfers Paradise, QLD 4217. ☎ (07) 5592-2263 or 1-800-678-194, **W**: surfersparadisebackpackers.com.au. Four-share rooms only start at AU $22. Free pick up from the bus station and the hostel backs onto the beach.

Trekkers, 22 White Street Southport, QLD 4215. ☎ (07) 5591-5616 or 1-800-100-004, **W**: trekkersbackpackers.com.au. Starting at AU $21 for dorm and AU $50 for twin-share. Friendly and unobtrusive, this hostel is off the beaten track and about a mile from the beach. Regular shuttles to the beach and bus station and rated high in the area.

GENERAL PRACTICALITIES:

The major issue in this area is water and sun safety. Swim between Red/Yellow flags and heed the signal flags that designate: Green = safe, Yellow = caution or dangerous conditions, and Red = do not enter the water. The ocean temperatures and water sweep (undercurrents) are usually listed on chalkboards in the center of the swim area. Again: Don't forget to slip on a shirt, slop on sunscreen, and slap on a hat.

Shorts and comfortable shoes are a must and the standard casual standards include thongs (flip-flops), a baseball hat, and a singlet (tank top). Beachwear varies from board shorts and sun-protective suits, to tiny Speedo-style swimmers, to cut-offs. Ladies wear little to nothing and going topless is acceptable. Nude sunbathing is not allowed, but the rules slip a bit as you trek towards the seaway Spit on the northern beaches.

Dinner attire is also very relaxed, and you can leave the ties in the bag, unless you need a headband. Shorts and collared shirts are usually OK, but you might feel uncomfortable in shorts at the higher-end restaurants. So slacks and a nice shirt would be appropriate. Oh, and mates, Hawaiian shirts are in vogue. Women's stockings are rarely seen and the short and tight is in vogue right now.

FOOD AND DRINK TIPS IN THE AREA:

According to the local tourism directories, there are over 500 restaurants in the Surfers business area. Many of them do turn over, but there are many eateries that are a Gold Coast tradition. The strip at Elkhorn and Orchid Avenues in Surfers has a wide variety of foods from fast food to gourmet dining. Mariners Cove at Marina Mirage has a popular selection of restaurants and fun nightclubs. Broadbeach also has great eateries and is the hangout for local diners. If you want to throw a shrimp or steak on the barbie, look to **Charis** ($) in Labrador (☎ (07) 5527-1100) for a wide selection of seafood and **Cavs Butchery** ($-$$) in Labrador (☎ (07) 5532-2954) for the best-aged meats. To escape the hectic pace on the main drag of Surfers Paradise, try Tedder Avenue on Main Beach and dine in some of the top restaurants the Coast has to offer. You can scan the dining scene at **The Gold Coast Dining Out & Entertainment Guide** site on **W:** diningout.com.au. Here are a few to start your mouth watering:

Domani's On Tedder (corner of Woodroffe & Tedder Avenue, Main Beach) Traditional and modern Italian with a nice pasta-and-bug plate. ☎ (07) 5571-0091, **W:** domanisrestaurant.com. $$ and $$$

Holy Mackerel (174 Marine Parade, Labrador) One of the best and freshest seafood meals offered on the coast. ☎ (07) 5531-1017, **W:** holy-mackerelrestaurant.com. $$

King Arthur's Table (F51/16 Raptis Plaza on Cavill Avenue, Surfers Paradise) Old English-style pub for local bush tucker treats, seafood, and steaks. ☎ (07) 5526-7855, **W:** kingarthurstable.com.au. $$

Bangles (38 Frank Street, Labrador) A favorite local Indian curry place. Intimate, cozy, and fantastic flavors. ☎ (07) 5591-7000. $-$$

Tandori Place (multiple locations on the Coast) Inexpensive and tasty North Indian & Tandoori taste delights. ☎ (07) 5592-1004 (Surfers); (07) 5526-2233 (Broadbeach); (07) 5532-6228, (Southport). $–$$

Little Buddha (corner of Musgrave & Kerr Avenue, Chirn Park) Probably the best, hidden gem on the Coast. Funky surroundings, innovative foods, and a wide range of vegetarian foods. ☎ (07) 5531-3311. $–$$

Saks (Marina Mirage, Main Beach) The in-crowd hangout that doubles for a nightclub. Right on the Broadwater and surrounded by yachts. ☎ (07) 5591-2755. $$

Lemongrass on Tedder (6/26 Tedder Avenue, Main Beach) The best Thai food I've eaten, and acclaimed by my Thai friend Rudi. ☎ (07) 5528-0289. $$

Dracula's (1 Hooker Blvd., Broadbeach) A horror-themed cabaret that is lots of fun. A bit risqué for children, but a good dinner show for most everybody else. ☎ (07) 5575-1000, **W**: draculas.com.au. $$–$$$

The Castle (412 Coolangatta Road, Tugun) You guessed it, a theater inside a castle setting. Fun and also a bit risqué. ☎ (07) 5534-3455, **W**: thecastletheatre.com.au. $–$$

Sushi Train (2769 Gold Coast Highway, Surfers Paradise) Sit on a barstool, pick the succulent pieces of sushi you desire as the dishes pass by on a model train, and pay by the plate. ☎ (07) 5592-4077. $

Omeros Brothers (corner of Ocean Avenue & Gold Coast Highway, Surfers Paradise) Maybe the best seafood on the Coast, and great service too. ☎ (07) 5584-6060. $$–$$$

Conrad Jupiter's Casino Restaurants (Broadbeach Island, Broadbeach) Choose from the nine venues for food and drink at the casino building. From the Food Fantasy Buffet to a pub meal to fine dining, there are great values and dinner show packages to enjoy $$–$$$. ☎ (07) 5592-8443 for Andiamo Italian $$–$$$ or the Charters Towers $$–$$$; ☎ (07) 5592-8181 for Zen Chinese. $$–$$$

Mikado (Imperial Plaza, corner Of Elkhorn & Gold Coast Highway, Surfers Paradise) High-end traditional Japanese dining. ☎ (07) 5538-2788. $$$

Food courts can be located at any of the shopping malls in the area and you can get fish & chips on almost every block. Just follow your nose.

SHOPPING:

Lots of good deals to be found on the Coast from trinkets, to high-end clothing, and electronic gear. Check out Trip 21 (Shop Till You Drop) for the grand tour of the shopping meccas.

Surfers Paradise & the Beach Scene

T his is Australia's sandbox; the Pacific Region's playground. Surfers Paradise is the heart of tourism in the Southeastern corner of Queensland, with all the benefits and disadvantages that go with that. There's entertainment for every age bracket, income group, and level of adventure seeker. But it is a bit crowded at times, though not compared to most US resort towns. This high-rise seaside town has lots of glitz. The beaches on the Gold Coast are some of the best in the world, and will satisfy the needs of families chock full of kids, the solitude-seeking couples, and those who are single and want some fun in the sun.

There is so much to do in the Surfers area that I have divided the entertainment areas into Beaches, Surfing, Shopping, Attractions, and Night Life. Mix and match your activities to meet your interests or focus on only one aspect that the Coast has to offer.

GETTING THERE:

By Car: The Gold Coast exits are a straight and direct 40-mile shot down the Pacific Highway or the M1 from Brisbane. Turn off at the Smith Street or Southport/Nerang Road exits and drive east unit you dead end at the Gold Coast Highway, then follow that to your desired destination.

By Train: Hop any of the express trains to the Gold Coast or Robina Station. Avoid the local train as it stops at all stations in between. You may board at Central, Roma Street, South Brisbane, or South Bank Stations and sit back and enjoy the scenery on the one-hour trip to the Nerang Station. From there you can catch the Trainlink service or hail a taxi to the surf.

By Bus: Call **Coachtrans**, ☎ 13-12-30 or (07) 5506-9777, or **W**: coach trans.com.au. The best connection is at Roma Street, but check at any of the Bus/Rail transport hubs in Brisbane for timetables and look for your destination of the Beach Road stop in the heart of Surfers Paradise. It will take a little over an hour, but it is the most economical way to head south with a one-way trip costing: Adults: AU $14 and kids: AU $11. An alternative bus line is **Kirklands**, ☎ 1-300-367-077, **W**: kirklands.com.au. The most attractive option is the **Surfside Buses**, ☎ (07) 5574-5111 or 1-300-655-655, or **W**: gcshuttle.com.au. They have a Freedom Pass with unlimited local travel, door-to-door theme park transfers, and airport transfers.

By Plane: Luckily the Coolangatta Airport is just south of Surfers Paradise and it is a short hop from Brisbane. There are direct routes from most major Australian cities. When you arrive you can catch one of the many ground transport systems. To book ahead, try these two suggestions: **Con-X-ion**, ☎ (07) 5591-2525, AU $35; **Gold Coast Ecotours**, ☎ (07) 5573-6080 for about AU $25.

PRACTICALITIES:

See the specific sections below, but follow the standard Aussie rules of sun protection, casual clothes, comfy clothes, and laid-back attitude.

FOOD AND DRINK:

You have a wide selection of fast food, cafés, and fine dining in the area.

THE BEACHES:

Kick off your shoes and get some pure white sand between your toes. If you want to bronze in the blazing sun, nap to the sounds of crashing waves, people watch, stroll for hours on end, body surf, take a chance on a board, or shop this is the place mates. The beach runs from the southern tip at Rainbow Bay and Life Station #01 to the northern most spot at the Seaway Spit and Life Station #45.

If you have a new style of bathing suit (swimmer or tog) to show off, then the beach off of Cavill Avenue and Station #34 is best for you, but if you want to mingle with the beautiful people then Main Beach at Station #40 is the spot. Dogs, solitude, and some nudity can be found north of Station # 41 and lots of dunes to laze and soak in the rays.

My favorite spot is just by Station #41 as it is quiet, has a wide beach, plenty of parking, showers and toilets in the park by the parking lot, and has the best fish & chips joint across the street. Peters Fish has a nice broiled filet and perfect chips. Plus you can have a wander at Marina Mirage Shopping center after a day on the beach.

A popular family spot is near Station #23 or Nobby Beach. Not sure why, but it is always loaded with kids with water wings strapped on their arms. Most areas are patrolled and have showers right on the beach. The entrance at Surfers Paradise has lockers too if you want to secure your valuables. The Gold Coast Guide & Map brochure, found at the information booths on the Coast, has a full listing of the beaches, patrolled times and Life Station locations.

To stroll the entire length of the beach would take all day, but a barefoot walk from Surfers Paradise to The Spit and back takes about two hours. If you are not used to walking on the soft sand of the coastline, you may be a bit sore the day after a stroll.

Oh, don't be too alarmed if people stare at you on a walk, it happens all the time and no offence is intended. The Australians often look you straight in the eye and have no worries in greeting people passing. And the guys will normally gape at the ladies—come to think of it the women do their fair share of flirting too. Please take both greeting styles as a compliment and not a threat. But it is in very poor taste to photograph people on the beach (especially the topless ladies) and you might get a few sharp words if you do.

Here are a few warnings on swimming conditions to take under consideration. If the wind is blowing off the water, take care for little buggers called blue bottles. They are a small, blue marine stinger that can make you quite uncomfortable. Don't swim at night and definitely not after a few drinks. Swim between the flags that are posted on the beach. Don't go in the water unless you see locals in swimming. If you do get in trouble, just raise your arm and help will be to you in minutes. I don't believe anyone has drowned between the flags.

SURFING:

There seem to be several spots along the coast that are favorites of the surfers. Taking a drive from The Spit to Burleigh Heads; scanning the coast will give you a pretty good indication where the best waves are breaking. Most newspapers and radios advertise the day's conditions and hot spots. The favored curls of the locals include South Stradbroke Island (you need to get a ferry or paddle across the Seaway to get there), The Spit at station #45, Narrowneck between Stations #37/38, Surfers Paradise at Station #34, between Kurrawa Station #28 and Mermaid Beach at Station #26, Burleigh Heads at #18, Kirra at #04, and Rainbow Bay at Station #01. There are quite a few surfing schools in the area; one that seems to be popular is **Surfing Schools** at ☎ 1-800-787-337, (07) 5526-7077, or **W**: australiansurfer.com. From AU $45 you can get a group lesson and maybe meet a cute surfing mate.

SHOPPING:

Circled numbers correspond to numbers on the map.

Surfers Paradise is a mass of shops, amusement spots, pubs, adult-dancing venues, restaurants, and street activities. It would not help you to list them all, but I will provide a cross-section of spots that may interest you. To get a full list and maps to locate your own favorites, start at:

*The GC Tourist Bureau ❶, Corner Cavill & Orchid avenues, Surfers Paradise, ☎ (07) 5538-4419. Get your maps, attraction brochures, accommodation listings, tour information, tickets for attractions, and friendly advice.

The major shopping centers are generally open between 9–5. Thursdays the shops are open until at least 9 o'clock. Some of the shopping spots include:

*Cavill Mall ❷, between Gold Coast Highway and the beach, Surfers Paradise. Open 24 hours. Trinkets, teens, titillating pubs, and taste delights are all centered around this shopping plaza. Probably has the best prices

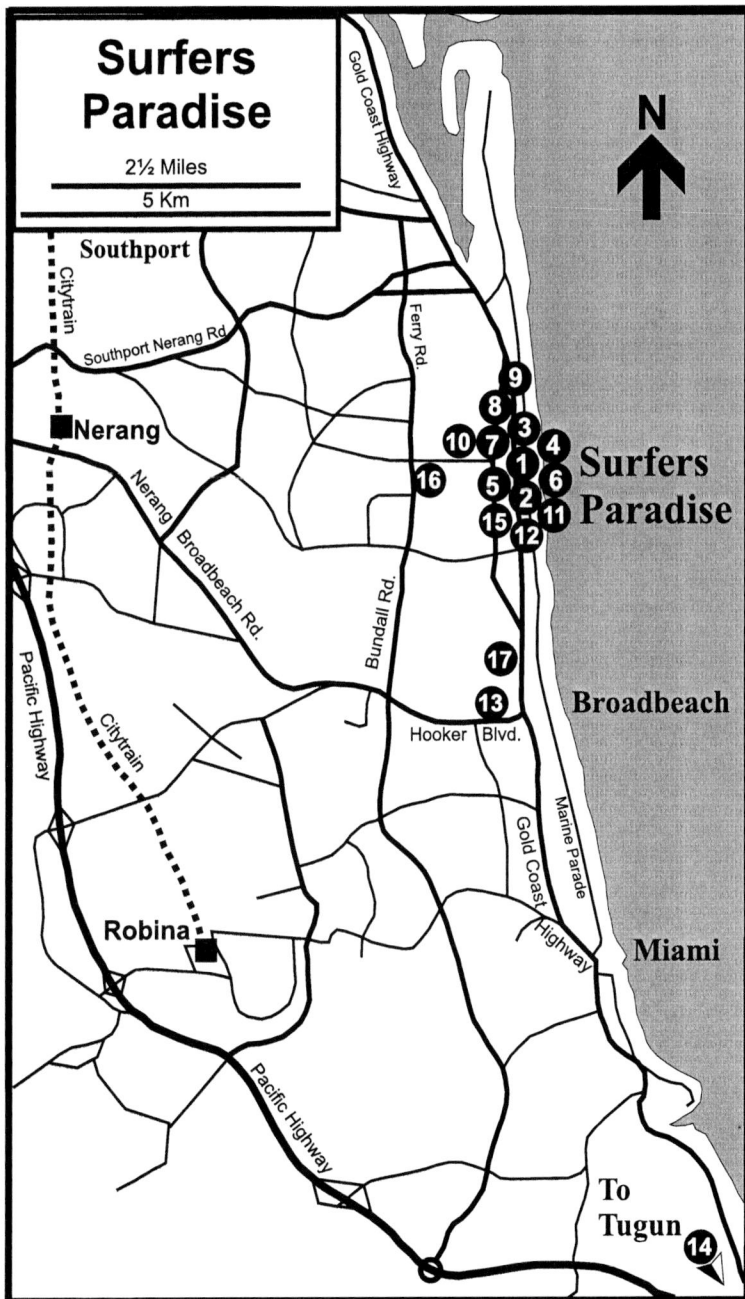

Surfers Paradise

2½ Miles

5 Km

Gold Coast Highway

N

Southport

Citytrain

Southport Nerang Rd

Ferry Rd.

■ Nerang

Nerang Broadbeach Rd.

Bundall Rd.

Pacific Highway

Citytrain

9
8
3
10 7
1
4
16
5
6
2
11
15
12

**Surfers
Paradise**

17

13

Hooker Blvd.

Marine Parade

Broadbeach

Robina ■

Gold Coast Highway

Miami

Pacific Highway

**To
Tugun**

14

for souvenirs like kangaroo "lucky pouches" and cane toad purses, but you might want to buy your opals up north for the best deals. There will be a listing of good spots to purchase opals in later sections.

Piazza on the Boulevard ❸, corner of Elkhorn and Orchid Avenue, Surfers Paradise. ☎ (07) 5592-1100, **W**: piazzaontheboulevard.com.au. Duty-free goods and high-end leather, jewelry, electronics, and fashion.

Le Boulevard ❹, between Orchid Avenue & The Esplanade on Elkhorn Avenue, Surfers Paradise. Duty-free goods and high-end leather, jewelry, electronics, and fashion.

Monte Carlo Arcade, **The Forum**, **Lido Arcade**, **The Mark**, **Centre Arcade**, **DFS**, and the **Dolphin Arcade** ❺. All laid out on the strip of Orchid Avenue between Elkhorn and Cavill avenues in Surfers Paradise. Shop till you drop for hats, T-shirts, opals, stuffed toy koalas, sheepskins, postcards, kangaroo leather goods, cane toad purses, cameras, and almost anything Australian.

The Raptis Plaza ❻, Raptis Plaza on Cavill Mall, Surfers Paradise, ☎ (07) 5592-2123, **W**: raptisplaza.cpm.au. Another information booth is located in the center of the mall along with novelty stores, a food court, and a giant nude statue of David.

*Chevron Renaissance ❼, corner of Elkhorn Avenue & Gold Coast Highway, Surfers Paradise, ☎ (07) 5592-5188, **W**: chevronrenaissance.com.au. The newest upscale shopping area on the strip with lots of high quality merchandise.

ATTRACTIONS:

From tacky tourist traps, to futuristic shows, to thrillers, it is all here in Surfers. I can't admit to entering all of the spots listed here, but all get good reviews (depending on age and thrill preferences). One note of interest before you go venturing into the attractions—grab a copy of the free "Wot's On" and "Point Out" brochures. They are loaded with discount coupons and they will save you some money for the pubs at night.

THE WAX MUSEUM ❽, Corner of Elkhorn Ave. and Gold Coast Highway, Surfers Paradise, ☎ (07) 5538-3975, **W**: australiagoldcoast.com. *Open daily until 10 pm. Adults: AU $22.50 ($14.50 for entrance to only the Chamber of Horrors) and kids: AU $15.50 ($10.50 for the Chamber only). 1/2 -hour guided tours and self-guided tours allowed.* ♿.

Noted as the largest wax museum in the southern hemisphere, it will be a treat for the kids with life-sized and somewhat realistic wax figures of royalty, explorers, villains, and famous people.

KING TUTTS PUTT PUTT ❾, corner of Gold Coast Highway & Pandanus Avenue, Surfers Paradise, ☎ (07) 5570-2277, **W**: kingtuttsputput.com. *Open daily until 10 pm. Adults AU $11, children AU $7, group: AU $28.80.* ♿.

A mix of mini-golf in Jurassic Park and Egypt. It has miniature courses and parties in its undercover/outdoor kids playground. Great place for the kids on a rainy day, with a laser shooting range, video games, and air hockey tables.

INFINITY ⑩, Chevron Renaissance Centre, Surfers Paradise, ☎ (07) 5538-2988, **W**: infinitygc.com.au. *Open daily 10–10. Adults AU $18.90, children under 12 AU $10.90, student AU $15.90, family AU $148.90. Self-guided tours. Gift shop.* ♿.

I can personally recommend this must-see trip into the constantly changing psychedelic worlds of special effects. Pass through the huge, round hatch with sparkling purple, silver, and azure blocks that form a gateway into the unknown. Explore for as long as you wish (most people take 45 minutes) the universes of: Inter-dimensional Space, Cyclotron, The Electron Maze, Infinite Star Chamber, The Mystery Zone, The Light Canyon, and The Infinite Kaleidoscope. The computer imagery and random light deprivation add a quality that twists the senses in a way that will keep you guessing between reality and imaginary.

RIPLEY'S BELIEVE IT OR NOT! MUSEUM ⑪, Raptis Plaza in Cavill Mall, Surfers Paradise, ☎ (07) 5592-0040, **W**: ripleys.com.au. *Open daily 9–11. Adults AU $12, children under 14 AU $8, groups over 10 people AU $8.50/$6.50. Self-guided tours. Gift shop. Partially* ♿.

Yep, there's one here too, and it has original shrunken heads to scare the young ones. But the highlights are the glass cases showing the Guinness Book of World Records like the tallest man, fattest man, and some really gross items. You can't miss the entrance with two huge crocs guarding the keg of beer. Not a must-see attraction, but always fun for the kiddies.

AUSTRALIAN SHOOTING ACADEMY ⑫, Level 1, Paradise Centre, Surfers Paradise, ☎ (07) 5527-5100, **W**: shootinggoldcoast.com.au. *Open daily 10–10. Free admission. No admittance under 11 y/o, 11–17 y/o must be accompanied by legal guardian.* ♿.

Strap on your six-gun, mates, and blast away at the targets. Supervised by a range instructor, you can shoot 50 rounds from a .38 revolver for as low as AU $95, and try the hand-held .50-caliber cannon for AU $75 (five rounds). They also have rifle ranges, trap shooting, and a total of 27 shooting lanes. All supervised, air-conditioned, and all safety equipment supplied in the price.

NIGHT LIFE:

The range for night entertainment is from family movies to raunchy "dance clubs." The recommended age groups are listed on each venue, but please check before you go if you have children. The standards are a bit relaxed here and some R-rated humor or skimpy attire is not normally considered offensive. It is all in good fun, so no worries. A sad fact of life in the bar scenes is the use of ecstasy and often unwanted spiking of cocktails. Keep your drinks with you, don't accept drinks from a new friend, and if it has a weird taste or looks funny, don't drink it. Sorry mates, it does happen.

*DRACULA'S CABARET RESTAURANT ⓭, Hooker Blvd., Broadbeach, ☎ (07) 5575-1000, **W**: draculas.com.au. *Open Tues.–Sat. from 6 pm to midnight. Admission AU $54 Tue-Fri. and AU $59 Sat. Must be 13 y/o to enter. Bar.* ♿.

This is a treat and a fun night out for the mature family with a good sense of humor. The 4-course dinner and 2-hour show is racy, innovative, and well done. The wait staff is in costume and you might be harassed and teased at your table while you order. Start at the creepy bar with air blasts coming from unknown spots, and then ride the ghost train to the crypt and the show. Expect an interactive night with odd but professional characters looming in the shadows.

*THE CASTLE THEATRE RESTAURANT ⓮, corner Coolangatta Road & Boyd Street, Tugun, ☎ (07) 5534-3455, **W**: thecastletheatre.com.au. *Open Thurs.–Sat., shows start at 6:15 and dancing until midnight. Admission AU $49 all ages. Bar. Partially* ♿.

Probably a PG 13-rated dinner show with a 3-course feast and entertainment. A fun medieval time warp with costumed actors mingling with the crowd. Shows change once a year, but they are all fantastic and a good belly laugh. After the entertainment, the dance floor and bar open up for continued partying. Shuttle transport available to/from your lodging on the Coast.

*SURFERS BY NIGHT PARTY CRUISE ⓯, Shop 158A Dolphin Arcade, Surfers Paradise, ☎ (04) 1249-9825, **W**: surfersbynight.com.au. *Nightly starting at 5:30. Adults only at AU $55 per person. Special events.* ♿.

Join the party crowd and have a mix-and-mingle with people from all over the world. The directors attempt to get a 50/50 mix of blokes and girls, but no guarantees. The festivities and drinks start at Billy's Beach House in Surfers Paradise, then a three-hour cruise on the Broadwater, a BBQ dinner, stops at The Bourbon Bar and Cocktails & Dreams. Free pizza and T-shirt at the end of the night too.

THE GOLD COAST ARTS CENTRE ⓰, 135 Bundall Road, Surfers Paradise, ☎ (07) 5581-6500 or (07) 5588-4008 for movies, **W**: gcac.com.au. *Open Wed.–Mon. 9–5, closed holidays. All ages. Gift shop. Café & restaurant. Special events.* ♿.

This is Australia's largest regional art and entertainment complex offering some great way-off-Broadway shows. Packed into a cluster of buildings are the two art galleries, a large and reasonably-priced performing arts theater (without a bad seat in the house), two cinemas, café, community rooms, a restaurant, and a fantastic shop that has over 20,000 costumes for rent when you want to arrive at a party as a famous star. Check out the cool sculptures; one of my favorites being of a surf lifesaving team in action. Movies are a delight here at the full-sized cinemas, and you can take your own bottle of wine along. Sip a beer and savor the salty popcorn as you watch first-run movies for AU $10 for adults or AU $8 for kids, seniors AU $6.50 (add a dollar for night shows). Budget Tuesdays are AU $7 for adults and AU $6 for everyone else.

*CONRAD JUPITER'S ⑰, Broad Beach Island, Broadbeach, ☎ (07) 5592-1133, **W**: conrad.com.au. *Open every day 24 hours. Family in most common areas, but adults only in the gaming areas.* ♿.

Under this flashy exterior is a nightlife extravaganza with five restaurants, buffet cafés, bars, and people dressed to thrill. The shows are fantastic, and if you are in the area for a while, look into a dinner/show package that mimics a Las Vegas event. Most people go for the gaming; there is plenty to choose from with 70 gaming tables, 1,200 slots, Keno, and two levels of gambling activities. Acres of tropical gardens and a host of bars, cafés and top-notch restaurants that will meet any culinary desire. The best deal is the Food Fantasy Buffet where you will walk away stuffed to the gills.

Nightclubs and dance show bars in Surfers Paradise include **Shooters Saloon Bar**, ☎ (07) 5592-1144, at 46 Orchid Avenue; **Fever Nightclub**, ☎ (07) 5592-6222 or **W**: fever.net.au, on Orchid Avenue; **Sugar Shack**, ☎ (07) 5592-4850, on Orchid Avenue; **Billy's Beach House**, ☎ (07) 5531-5666), on the corner of Hanlan & The Esplanade; **Melbas**, ☎ (07) 5538-7411, at 46 Cavill Avenue; **The Bourbon Bar**, ☎ (07) 5538-0668, on Orchid Avenue, **Cocktails & Dream**, ☎ (07) 5592-1955, at 3 Orchid Avenue; the **Drink Nightclub**, ☎ (07) 5570-6155, at 4 Orchid Avenue; **The Rose & Crown**, ☎ (07) 5531-5425, in the Raptis Plaza, and many more on Cavill Mall and Orchid Avenue. Adults only in all of these venues and IDs will be checked.

Theme Parks

The four worlds of the galaxy are at your fingertips on the Coast—and only a short hour from Brisbane. All clustered in convenient locations with public transportation available to/from each park, the only difficult question is which ones to see first. My personal favorite with a uniquely Australian flavor is Sea World, but they all offer a great day out. The best attribute of the parks is that they are each manageable in a day's outing and if you are quick smart, you can do a half-day then relax on the beach and catch a curl. Each theme park has its own major attraction draw with dolphins at Sea World, Tower of Terror and Big Brother at Dream World, Mammoth Falls at Wet 'n' Wild Water World, and Warner Bros. Movie World's Harry Potter Move Magic Experience, or the newest Scooby Doo Spooky Coaster (check for opening dates).

All of the parks have areas set aside for the youngest of the family members. Sea World and Wet 'n' Wild Water World have kid-friendly great spots to relax while toddlers can safely splash around. Warner Bros. Movie World is great for all ages, and Dream World has the best options for the thrill seeker. All provide food and resting areas when parents need a snack and a nap.

RACQ offers discount coupons, as do some of the local grocery stores. Check out "Wot's On" brochures for listings and deals too. A 3-Park Super Pass is also available, for AU $141 (Adult) and AU $91, that includes a bargain deal to enter three of the four worlds (Dream World not included).

GETTING THERE:

By Car: All parks are easily found by car, and all but Sea World are clustered around Exits 51 and 60 off of the M1 Pacific Highway. Sea World is on Main Beach's Spit at Sea World Drive.

By Bus: The following bus lines have service to the parks. From Brisbane it costs around AU $84 (including entrance fees to the parks), call **Australian Day Tours**, ☎ 1-300-363-436; or **Coachtrans**, ☎ (07) 3236-1000. From the Coast a ride alone is AU $2.20-$4.40 for a one-way trip, and packages are available. Call: **Active Tours**, ☎ (07) 5597-0344; **Coachtrans**, ☎ (07) 5506-9778,; **ConXion**, ☎ (07) 5591-2525; **Gold Coast Shuttle**, ☎ 1-300-655-655; **Surfside Buslines**, ☎ 131-230; **Surfers Holiday Tours**, ☎ (07) 5531-5888; or **Tram Tours**, ☎ (07) 5571-2711. Another attractive option is **Surfside Buses**, ☎

(07) 5574-5111, 1-300-655-655, or **W**: gcshuttle.com.au. They have a Freedom Pass with unlimited local travel, door-to-door theme park transfers, and airport transfers.

By Train: There are stops in Coomera for Dream World and at Helensvale for Movie World and Wet 'n' Wild.

PRACTICALITIES:

Each park excursion can be considered a full-day outing, though you can easily whiz through any of them in four or five hours. To manage the trips, it would be best to have a car; your second choice would be using one of the bus services. Though the parks are much more manageable than the mega-parks of the US, make sure you wear comfy shoes and wear a hat. Strollers are available for young ones and lockers are provided for a small fee. I would suggest taking treats for you and the kids, as food is a bit expensive. No alcohol allowed into the parks.

For a listing of almost all the theme parks in the area go to **W**: reflections.com.au/GoldCoast/ThemeParksandAttractions

FOOD AND DRINK:

All parks have plenty of food from junk to decent meals. It is always a treat to eat amusement park food, and there are new tastes awaiting you. Try the fairy floss or a Pluto Pup.

LOCAL ATTRACTIONS:

Circled numbers correspond to numbers on the map.

*SEA WORLD ❶, Sea World Drive, Main Beach, ☎ (07) 5588-2205, **W**: seaworld.com.au. *Open daily 10–5 with ticket sales starting at 9:30. Adults AU $54, children AU $35. Gift shops. Cafés and restaurants. Special events.* ♿.

Enjoy a full day of shows, movies, thrill rides, and exhibits at one of my favorite hangouts on the Coast. You will want to spend the entire day here, absorbing the marine wonders and seeing the newest polar bear cub at Polar Bear Shores. All animal shows and exhibits are eco-friendly, offering natural settings for our aquatic friends. Feature attractions include the acrobatic team at **Dolphin Cove**, the comedians in **Quest for the Golden Seal Show**, a learning center at **Reef Discovery**, the hilarious 3D adventure movie called **Pirates**, an extreme sports show called **Ski Challenge**, and the kids favorites at **Cartoon Beach**. Lots of rides and interactive programs are packed in here too. Some of the up-close-and-personal experiences like swimming with the dolphins or the rides on the Sea World helicopter are a bit extra. For these treats, the passes can be purchased at the ticket booths. Oh, and if your have the heart and the nerve, try the giant **Free-Fall Speedslide** in the water park section. It's a shocker.

DREAM WORLD ❷, Dreamworld Parkway, Coomera, ☎ (07) 5588-1111, (07) 5588-1122, or 1-800-073-300, **W**: dreamworld.com.au. *Open daily 10–5,*

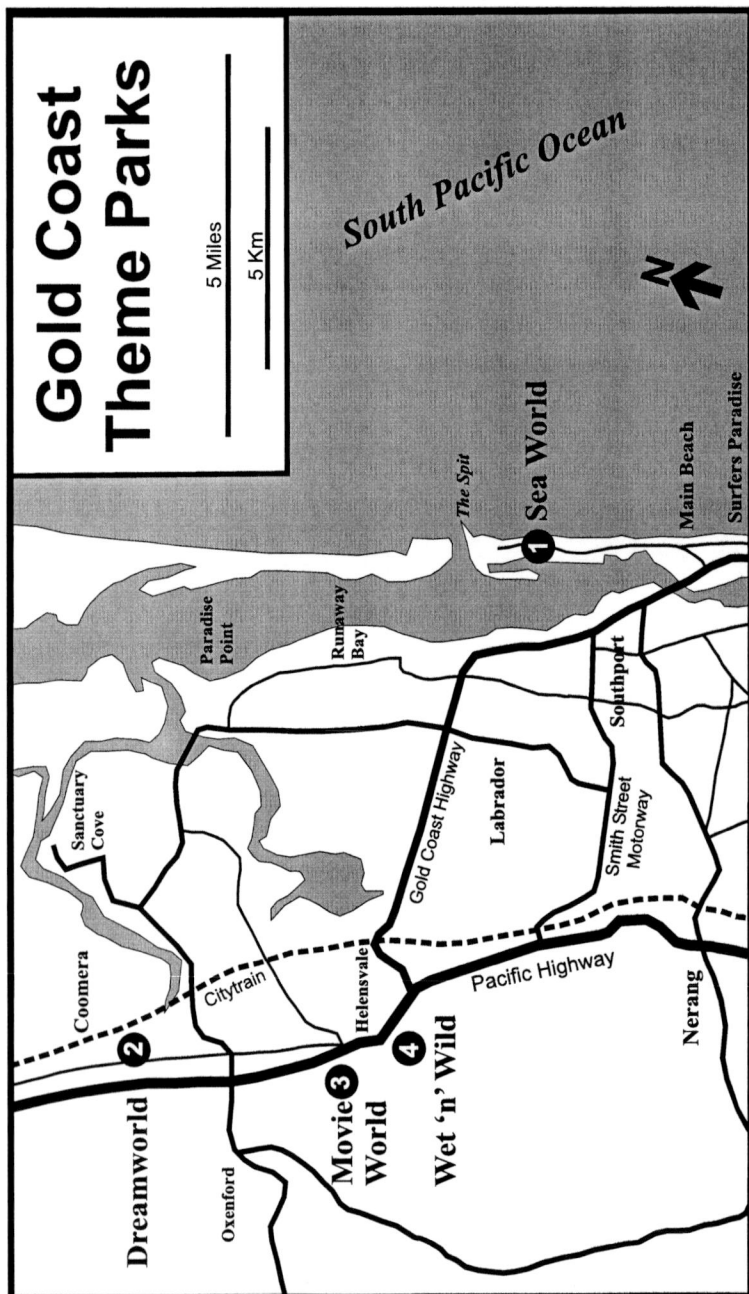

Gold Coast Theme Parks

5 Miles
5 Km

South Pacific Ocean

N

The Spit
1 Sea World
Main Beach
Surfers Paradise

Paradise Point
Runaway Bay
Southport
Gold Coast Highway
Labrador
Smith Street Motorway

Sanctuary Cove
Coomera
Citytrain
Helensvale
Pacific Highway
Nerang

2 Dreamworld
Oxenford
Movie World 3
4 Wet 'n' Wild

closed Christmas and at 1:30 on Anzac day. Ticket booths open at 9:30. Adults AU $54, children (4-13) & seniors AU $ 35, Groups of 20 or more 20% discount. Gift shops. Cafés and restaurants. Special events. ♿.

With an Aboriginal theme, Dream World is full of excitement and wild rides. The centerpiece of horror can be seen from miles around, and the **Giant Drop** and **Tower of Terror** are worthy of their names. Four G's and a breathtaking 394-foot drop will scare you into a smile. On the other side of the spectrum is **Kennyland** for the munchkins. Mini-rides, Kenny Koala, and gumnut fairies abound along with fun food for all. In the middle is a six-story **IMAX** show, a log flume ride—and the lumbering tigers will be a treat. The **Big Brother Studio Attraction** is also a hit here, where you can tour the television setting of the hit show Big Brother. But even if you are an oldie like me, do go see the **Dinky-Di Bush Band**, and have a sing-along at **Gum Tree Gully**—and don't forget to shout out your Outback greeting of "coo wee."

WARNER BROS. MOVIE WORLD ❸, Pacific Highway, Oxenford, ☎ (07) 5573-8485 or (07) 5573-3999, **W**: movieworld.com.au. *Open daily 9:30–5:30. Adults AU $54, children (4-13) & seniors AU $35, 1-Year Passes for AU $108/$70. Gift shops. Cafés and restaurants. Special events.* ♿.

Rub elbows with the stars, superheroes, cartoon characters, and even have lunch with the legends. This park is another favorite of mine and is a movie nut's heaven. You can get a behind-the-scenes peek at movie sets, participate in the filming of the Memphis Belle Airship, or sit back and watch the parade of all the Warner Brothers characters on Main Street. Thrills and chills can be had on the **Lethal Weapon** corkscrew, ride the Batmobile at the **Batman Adventure**, explore an old ghost town on the **Wild Wild West** flume ride, and come face-to-face with the world's bravest Great Dane at the **Scooby-Doo Spooky Coaster**. But do not miss the comical antics of the accident-prone cops at the **Police Academy Stunt Show** or the shoot-um-up and magical **Maverick Show**. The kids will fit in here too at the Musical Review in **Looney Tunes Village**, and in the 3D **Marvin The Martian Movie** as he tries to take over the galaxy.

*WET 'N' WILD WATER WORLD ❹, Pacific Highway, Oxenford, ☎ (07) 5573-2255, **W**: wetnwild.com.au. *Open daily 10–4 or 5 (depending on the season), Anzac Day opens at 1:30. Adults AU $33, children (4-13) & seniors AU $21, group rates available. Gift shops. Cafés and restaurants. Special events.* ♿.

Strap on the goggles, chill out, and dive into the cool waters at Wet 'n' Wild with over 12 deliciously wet rides, about five eateries, and lots of shopping. Good for every age and aquatic skill; you can dare your friends to risk the **Terror Canyon**, **Mammoth Falls**, **Double Screamer**, or **Twister** (I didn't dare this one). Race to the bottom of **Super 8 Aqua Racer** or laze down the gentle currents at **Calypso Beach**. It's all up to you, but the coolest spectacle is the **Giant Wave Pool**. By wading in over your head or riding the churning waters in an inner tube, you will feel as though you have been thrown into a giant washing machine. It is a totally different feeling and a fun frolic. At dusk, you can hang around and float in a tube while watching a premier movie—fair dinkum! They have a huge movie screen at the deep end of the pool and you can check the movie, times and hours on their web site or call them.

Surfers Paradise at Cavill Avenue and the Beach

Golfing with the Kangaroos

Venture out into the bushland and drive into the scenic foothills of Springbrook just beyond the town of Mudgeeraba. There you will find a quaint woodchoppers' village, old neatly painted Queenlsander homes, a true blokes Aussie pub, aromatic forests of eucalyptus trees loaded with koalas (though they are difficult to spot), out-of-this-world resorts, and good grub.

It is a bit of a hike from Brisbane, but a short hop from Surfers Paradise. Consider it a full day's outing to see it all, but if you just choose to hit the golf ball around you can easily do that in a 2–4 hour walk around the course. I guarantee that you will never have an experience on the links like this; make sure you take your camera in the golf bag. Oh, they do rent clubs if you left yours at home.

There are heaps of side trips available in this area, but the Springbrook Mountain tour will bring you past this neck of the bush again and you can pick them up later. If you select only this trip to venture out into the hinterland area, make sure you spend at least a day exploring this wonderful section of Queensland.

GETTING THERE:

By Car: The Pacific Highway (M1) is the best and most direct way to access this area. From both Brisbane and Surfers Paradise, take the highway south towards Coolangatta. It will be about a 70-minute drive from Brisbane and a 15–20 minute commute from Surfers Paradise. After passing the "shark teeth" sound barriers at Nerang you will exit the highway at Exit #79—also called Mudgeeraba/Robina Exit. Follow signs to Mudgeeraba-Springbrook until you come to a "T" junction. Turn right onto the Link Highway, bear left at the next roundabout towards Springbrook. Driving on the Gold Coast-Springbrook Road (#99) you will notice signs for the Boomerang Farm. Drive about 3 miles (5 kilometers) and turn right onto Boomerang Road and an immediate left onto Johns Road.

By Bus: Some tour operators do offer customized trips. You can organize a tour into the Mugerabba area and select your specific destinations. Check with the golf farm to book a bus. See page 130 for a list of operators.

PRACTICALITIES:

I recommend using a car and a good map (provided) for this trip. It is pretty easy to navigate this section of the hinterland, but if you get lost, you will really be lost. Regularly check the big brown road signs that provide distance markers to the various attractions in the area.

In addition to the sunscreen, hat, and sunglasses, you might want to take some bug repellant. Mossies (mosquitoes) are not bad until dusk, but then they swarm. Golfing shoes suited for hilly terrain, shorts, and a golf shirt will accommodate most daytime and evening activities. If you feel awkward wearing shorts and sneakers for dinner, pack a change of clothes—but not too fancy mates.

One thing to keep in mind on this and all of the hinterland trips—the animals are wild. Even if they look cute and huggable, don't try a cuddle. Kangaroos are capable of doing serious damage, especially if a Joey (baby roo) is nearby or the boomer (large male) is wooing his girlfriend. And don't even think about picking up the poisonous cane toad.

FOOD AND DRINK:

I have recommended **Woodchoppers** ($$-$$$) as a favorite local eatery, listed as Attraction ❻. Other selections include: The **Wallaby Hotel** ($-$$), 45 Railway, Mudgeeraba, ☎ (07) 5530-5600, for a truly Aussie pub setting with photos of local celebrities plastered on the walls, heavy cigarette smoke, and a clientele that would look at home in a biker bar. The patrons are friendly, the beer is cold and inexpensive and it is really worth a stop. **Panchos Mexican Restaurant** ($-$$), Springbrook Road, Mudgeeraba, ☎ (07) 5530-4433, is supposed to be the best Mexican eats on the Coast. It is a run-down looking building with tacky signs welcoming you into the small café. But everyone raves about the food. **The Windmill Restaurant** ($-$$), 410 Gold Coast-Springbrook Road, ☎ (07) 5530-4950, has just changed hands and is no longer an Italian restaurant tucked into the confines of a windmill. It now serves curry or Indian cuisine. There are also plenty of cafés, bakeries, and fast food joints in the shopping village at Mudgerabba.

LOCAL ATTRACTIONS:

Circled numbers correspond to numbers on the map.

*BOOMERANG FARM ❶, 54A Johns Road, Mudgeeraba, ☎ (07) 5530-5231, **W**: boomerangfarm.com.au. *Open dawn to dusk. Nine holes cost AU $15.50, 18 holes is AU $25, and club rentals are AU $8. Anyone eleven or younger must be with an adult. Gift shop. Clubhouse pub. Book ahead to make sure you can get on.*

For a fun-filled golf outing geared towards the not-too-serious hacker, try hitting the ball around some unique hazards—kangaroos. Boomerang Farm is a double nine-hole course right out of a Disney set. The entrance has gates that look like they were taken from the film

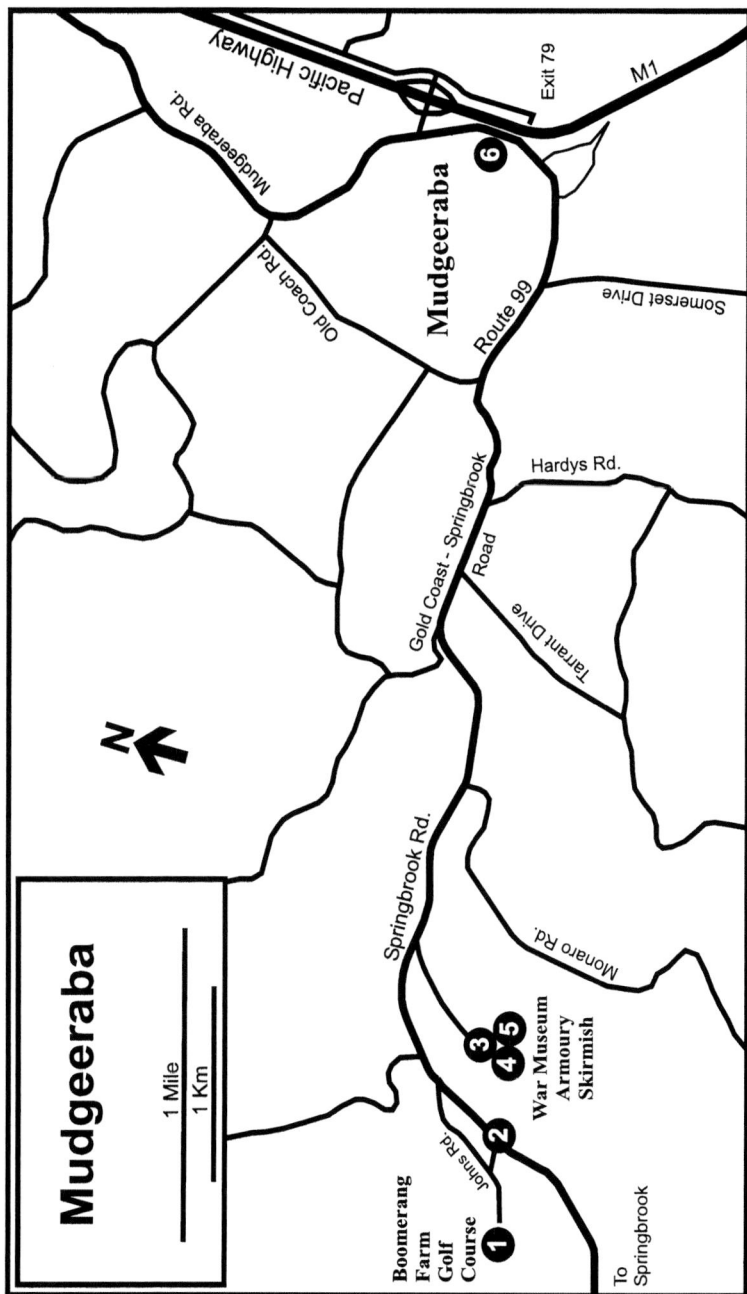

Mudgeeraba

1 Mile
1 Km

Mudgeeraba

Pacific Highway

Mudgeeraba Rd.

Exit 79

M1

6

Mudgeeraba

Old Coach Rd.

Route 99

Somerset Drive

Hardys Rd.

Gold Coast - Springbrook Road

Tarrant Drive

Springbrook Rd.

Monaro Rd.

3
4 5

War Museum
Armoury
Skirmish

2

Johns Rd.

1

Boomerang
Farm
Golf
Course

To
Springbrook

N

Jurassic Park. The kangaroos are real and considered hazards with a two-stroke penalty if you strike them with a ball. You are strongly advised not to kiss the cane toads as they are poisonous; and it is as scenic, lush, and full of wildlife as it is funky golf. You do not have to be a pro to whack the ball at this 5,193-yard, par 67 course—so go out and enjoy. Among the purple jacaranda trees, dense palms, and screeching cockatoos you will have just as much fun just being on the fairway as scoring a par on every hole. I find early morning and dusk are the best times for a Kodak moment with the kangaroos. The local gang usually hangs out at the fifth and sixth holes, but they do move around a bit each day. After the game, relax in the rustic clubhouse pub built in 1902 (it looks much older), roam amongst farm implements, and sit on old timber logs with a cold beer and a meat pie.

On your way out of the golf course, on the right side of the road, you might want to stop and visit the hosts of a pyramid at:

THE SUMMER HOUSE ❷, corner of Gold Coast-Springbrook & Boomerang Roads, Upper Mudgeeraba, ☎ (07) 5530-4154, **W**: themelodge.com.

Although it is not technically an attraction, it is a unique, themed eco-lodge resort worth mentioning. If you decide to stay the night, this is the place. It offers deluxe escapes to the 1/20 scale Pharaoh's pyramid, the earthy feel of the American Indian lodge called Inela Yunka, the Aboriginal Karringal House spa room, the scented Rose Lodge, the Casa Amore Lodge with Mexican accents, the Valentine Lodge for lovers, and look for the new African hut nestled by the pond. Prices start at AU $155/night (per couple) to AU $930 for a couple to enjoy a 5-night getaway. This place is worth at least a look around.

On the way back to Mudgeeraba, and only a few miles on the right is the triple delight of the:

*WAR MUSEUM ❸, 42 John Rogers Road, Mudgeeraba, ☎ (07) 5530-5222, **W**: warmuseum.com, collectorsarmoury.com.au, or skirmishgoldcoast .com.au. *Museum open daily 9–5. Adults AU $7, children AU $3. Self-guided tours. Gift shop. ♿. Skirmish open 10 am & 1:30 pm, AU $39 per player (includes game, gun, and 56 paintballs).*

The **museum** has a collection of Australian war memorabilia that includes tanks, aircraft and a huge display of weaponry. The two large military-looking buildings house various displays of battle equipment. The main attraction is the fully operational **Scorpion Combat Tank** in the center. Surrounded by a range of armored personnel carriers, it is the only one of its kind in Australia. Another display with lots of wow power to it is the assembled **Spitfire**. The kids love this and can easily imagine a dogfight with tracers flying past their ears. Look in most of the free Coast brochures for free entry coupons. Every item in the museum is for sale; imagine coming home with the AU $75,000 tank and saying, "Honey guess what I have in the driveway?"

The **Collectors Armoury** ❹ shares an entry with the War Museum and has an impressive array of full-sized replicas, helmets, swords, canons, flags, wanted posters, gas masks, dog tags, knives, deactivated mortars and bombs, and even armored vehicles. It also boasts a huge selection of German, American West, and Cold War paraphernalia for the war buff. It's kind of creepy, but very impressive. The weapons have been deactivated and are legal to take away. But be careful if transporting back through Customs, and ask the helpful staff for the best way to ship the stuff home if you decide to buy.

Skirmish ❺ is also in the same building, and is not for the faintheart-ed. But everyone is welcome to give this paintball battle game a go. It is safe with a full-face mask, dog tags, pyrotechnic effects, and instructors. Two teams are set up; the goal is to capture the opposing team's flag. The cool thing about this site is that there are real army tanks, combat heli-copters, and authentic vehicles scattered throughout the wooded playing field. Environmentally safe, colored gel "bullets" sting a bit when they hit, but you only have to stop, back up 30 paces and start over again. There are several game formats, including Blow the Bridge, The Tank Destroyers, Defense of the Fort, and Terminator. It is a strategic exercise, and many local corporations use the facility as team building outings for their staff. It's a blast—so to speak.

Though I usually stop at the **Wallaby Hotel**, at 45 Railway Street, ☎ (07) 5530-5600, for a pint with the larrikins at the pub, you probably worked up a fierce hunger by now and need some hearty grub and a calming glass of wine. One of my favorite pit stops for excellent kangaroo is the:

WOODCHOPPERS INN ❻, 66 Railway Street, Mudgeeraba, ☎ (07) 5525-3500. *Open daily for lunch noon–2:30; dinner from 6–9:30*, $$–$$$.

Unlike the olden years, you are not expected to grab an axe or cross-cut saw and compete in a wood chopping competition before dinner, but you can see the remnants of the champion axe men. And if your make your entrance at the right time, you might just see the local horse patron drinking a beer from a bowl—fair dinkum! The quaint colonial restaurant offers a nice arrangement of foods and local wines. Greeted in the lobby by the hostess and beautiful hand polished furniture (some for sale), you will be seated in a cozy wing of the building that looks out onto the hin-terland foothills. If you are lucky, the local possum will join you as he/she feasts at the platform situated outside near the wall of windows. Two good treats are the Seafood Fettuccine Bugs, Scallops & Prawns, or the scrump-tious Loin of Kangaroo marinated, char-grilled to a perfect pink, and served with mango and peppercorn sauce. Try either for a nice local taste.

If you have steam left in the engine, you can stop by **Conrad Jupiter's Casino** for a few rolls of the dice, a show, or a nightcap.

Golfing with The Shark

It would not surprise me if the local myth was true that they had to build a dam just to irrigate all the golf courses in the area. With Jack Nicklaus, Arnold Palmer, and Greg Norman-designed courses, no wonder some of the world's best competitions are held on the Gold Coast. The added beauty is that they are reasonably priced and are not closed to the public. Some of the five-star courses offer package deals of golf, lodging, and meals; and they are good programs if your goal is improving your handicap. You can book a tour of golf outings and even get a package that allows unlimited golf at selected courses. For an easy course that's close to Surfers Paradise, try Parkwood International. If you want tight, narrow, and beautifully groomed go for Robina Woods. Closer to Brisbane and greatly underrated is Gainsborough Greens located in bushland. This former home of the Queensland PGA title is loaded with huge kangaroos and gorgeous settings. Royal Pines has two courses to choose from with great facilities when you are done playing. Sanctuary Cove is for members only or guests of the Sanctuary Cove Hyatt. It's top-of-the-line, tough, and a tricky course. Southport is one of the best on the Coast, and you must be invited to play by a member. Hope Island is a tough course with heaps of bunkers. Finally the Glades is the newest and designed by The Shark— Greg Norman. Surrounded by wetlands with unbelievable bunkers, expect a challenge here.

A general listing of Gold Coast courses is provided below. It does not mention each and every spot in the area, but gives you a varied array of choices. I have made the rounds at most of the courses, but my helpful hints wouldn't be of much assistance. The courses change with the weather conditions and what may be good advice one day might be off the next. One thing that is fairly standard is the greens are hard and fast.

GETTING THERE:

Some courses offer transportation services and many buses offer packages, but the best bet in this section is to use a car. The courses are spread all over the Coast, and lugging your bag around on public transportation is not a good way to get into your zone or end a pleasant day on the links. The pro shops usually provide good directions and landmarks to help you find them.

PRACTICALITIES:

Most courses rent clubs, carts, and buggies, so you don't have to bring your favorite putter along. The majority of the transport systems do accommodate well for the mega-bags you might want to bring along. Soft spikes are almost universally the rule, and proper golf attire is expected (but rarely enforced except at the very plush resorts). Sun protection, hat and sunglasses are a good idea.

Koala Golf Day, ☎ (07) 5591-6181 or **W**: australiangolftours.com.au, has four different golfing packages available. Since their prices are scheduled to change before this guide is available, check their website for current deals. Another opportunity to get the most of your golfing dollar is to access **Golf Bank**. For overseas visitors there is no joining fee and you can get package deals at between 20–50% off the regular greens fee prices. They are Australia-wide and offer access to over 66 courses. Check them out on **W**: golfbank.tv or ☎ (07) 5561-1411. You will probably have to drive to each of the courses, but if you are staying on Gold Coast, you can check with the hotel for pick-up options.

FOOD AND DRINK:

All the clubs have a 19th Hole hangout, and most are pretty flash. The fine food is usually good and the fast food even better. The beer is cold and tasty everywhere and some guys drink it mixed with lemon squash (lemonade). Give it a go, as it is really refreshing.

A FEW LOCAL COURSES:

Circled numbers correspond to numbers on the map.

The Glades is the highlighted course as it is one of the newest and most challenging. Additional information is provided to entice you for a few rounds there. The range of prices for a round of golf in the area start around AU $22 for 18-holes to around AU $100 for the higher end, resort-style courses. Greens fees vary depending on season, times and specials are usually available.

EMERALD LAKES ❶, 3 Alabaster Drive, Carrara, ☎ (07) 5594-4400, **W**: emeraldlakes.com.au. $$

A new facelift and maintenance program has put this course in line with other locals, although it can be soggy in wet seasons. It's a par 72 and is 6,680 yards.

GAINSBOROUGH GREENS ❷, Yawalpah Road, Pimpama, ☎ (07) 5546-6003, **W**: gainsboroughgreens.com.au. $$

I like this 568-acre wildlife sanctuary-style golf course, but it doesn't like me. With seemingly long fairways it is usually hot, has the biggest darn kangaroos around, and has one of the best clubhouses. A 6,635-yard par

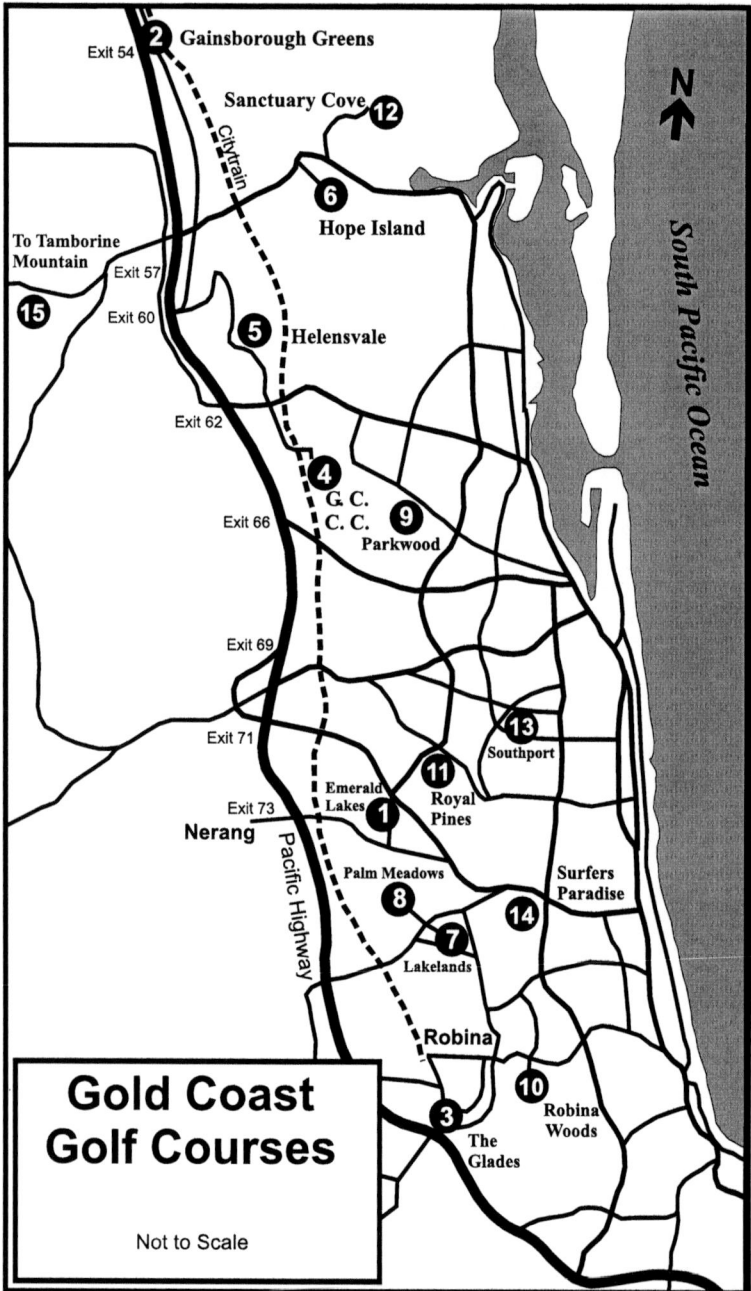

Exit 54
2 Gainsborough Greens

Sanctuary Cove 12

Citytrain

6
Hope Island

To Tamborine
Mountain
Exit 57

15
Exit 60

5 Helensvale

Exit 62

4
G. C.
C. C.
Exit 66
9
Parkwood

Exit 69

Exit 71

13
Southport
Exit 73
Emerald
Lakes   11
Royal
Pines
1
Nerang

Pacific Highway

Palm Meadows   Surfers
Paradise
8
7   14
Lakelands

Robina

10
Robina
Woods
3
The
Glades

South Pacific Ocean

N

Gold Coast
Golf Courses

Not to Scale

72 beauty.

*GLADES ❸, Ricerwalk Way, Robina, ☎ (07) 5569-2222, 1-800-452-337, **W**: glades.com.au. $$$

This is the one to try if you are a Greg Norman fan and want the very best that the Gold Coast and maybe Australia has to offer. This is no easy walk on the greens mate, and the par 72, 6,420-meter course has bunkers that will have you waking in a cold sweat. In 2002, this resort course was ranked #1 in Australia and is one of the favored hangout of the pros. The course meanders along creeks and has breathtaking views of the not too distant hinterland. If you are not a serious golfer, I would pass this one by. But if you want a memorable outing—this is the place. It is in excellent condition; even for a young course, and the resident owner Ian Baker-Finch keeps a close eye on his investment.

GOLD COAST COUNTRY CLUB ❹, Discovery Drive, Helensvale, ☎ (07) 5573-2940, **W**: goldcoastcountryclub.com.au. $$$

A 6,847-yard par 72, the course is home to many PGA Championships. A few do-or-die holes sprinkled in for good measure, but not too difficult.

HELENSVALE ❺, 16 Wandilla Drive, Helensvale, ☎ (07) 5573-1329. $$

This one has recently improved but can be swampy in wet weather. A fun 5903 par 70 with lots of water hazards.

*HOPE ISLAND ❻, Oxenford-Southport Road, Hope Island, ☎ (07) 5530-9000, **W**: hir.com.au. $$$

One of the best courses on the Coast and difficult to get tee times. If you get on expect lots of pot bunkers and a fair bit of water in play. A par 72 7060-yard well-groomed course.

LAKELANDS ❼, Gooding Drive, Merrimac, ☎ (07) 5579-2450, **W**: lakelandsgolfclub.com.au. $$$

Another beauty with a Jack Nicklaus design to it. Take a few extra balls, as there are some tough water holes on this 7095 par 72.

PALM MEADOWS ❽, Palm Meadows Drive, Carrarra, ☎ (07) 5594-2450, **W**: palmmeadows.com.au. $$

Watch for the giant bamboo clusters, and the water, and the bunkers, and more water. A tough 6909-yard par 72.

PARKWOOD INTERNATIONAL ❾, Napper Road, Parkwood, ☎ (07) 5594-6388, **W**: parkwoodgc.com.au. $$

A good, fair course. One of the best values on the Coast and easy to get tee times. Some manageable water holes, but avoid the houses that crowd around the out of bounds. Try to finish around dusk to witness the screeching howls of the cockatoos that inhabit the grounds. A 6607-yard par 72.

*ROBINA WOODS ❿, Ron Penhaligon Way, Robina, ☎ (07) 5593-1766, **W:** americangolf.com (under Robina Woods). $$$

A tight, unforgiving course with lots of banking greens. I still like this classy course, but a it's a bit pricey. A par 71 6645-yard tree-lined course.

*ROYAL PINE RESORT ⓫, Ross Street, Ashmore, 4214, ☎ (07) 5597-1111, **W:** royalpines.com.au. $$$

It's best to stay at the resort and play. With two courses to choose from you can get great overnight packages that are cheaper than just showing up for golf. Home to the Australian Ladies Masters, it has lots of good holes. You have a good chance of finding lots of stray balls along the way, as the overseas visitors here tend not to pick any out of sight. The East Course is par 72 7183-yard and the West Course is 6817-yard par 71.

*SANCTUARY COVE ⓬, Casey Road, Sanctuary Cove, ☎ (07) 5577-6151, **W:** sanctuarycove.com. $$$

A top-notch course that also boasts being one of the toughest in Australia. Access to the Pines is allowed only if you say at the Hyatt, use one of the package deals, or know someone with a membership. The Palms has social access. Pines is a par 72 7305-yard and the Palms is a par 71 6377-yard course.

SOUTHPORT ⓭, Slayter Avenue, Southport, ☎ (07) 5532-1577. $$$

You need a friend to play here, and it is a top quality, tight course. A par 71 6316-yard course.

SURFERS PARADISE ⓮, 1 Fairway Drive, Clear Island Waters, ☎ (07) 5572-6088. $$

A well-worn course, but fun and inexpensive to play a round or two. It is a par 71 with 6432-yard challenge.

TAMBORINE MOUNTAIN ⓯, Golf Coarse Road, Tamborine Mountain, ☎ (07) 5545-1788, **W:** tamborinemountain.com. $

One of the most spectacular panoramic views of any of the courses with challenging (undulating) greens. If you are not a Billy goat, you may want to take a cart instead of walking—it has some steep climbs. A beautiful par 70, 5813-yard walk in the woods.

Shop Till You Drop

The Aussie currency may be great to look at with its fun colors, but you will love it even more because of the current exchange rate. You will almost double you money with the plain-looking but mighty American greenback. This section will help you spread around that funny money and enjoy the major duty-free, discount, and upscale market areas. It will also list the local craft fairs that offer unique Aussie goods, foods, and other fun stuff.

Outstanding shopping malls include the largest center at Pacific Fair, the largest discount mall at Harbour Town, the manageable Australia Fair, the very upscale Marina Mirage (your money will vanish before your eyes here), the new and trendy Chevron Renaissance, the largest duty-free shop in Queensland at DFS Galleria, the compact Robina Town Centre, the waterside marina mall at Sanctuary Cove, and the Oasis at Broadbeach. Plenty of cafés and bistros are available at each mall to keep your strength up. For great Australian-made gifts try the Sunday markets along the beach. The schedules are listed and the varieties of goods will please even the toughest shopper. Carrara Markets are open every weekend and it is a 500-stall market with everything from antiques, junk, veggies, and good tourist gifts.

GETTING THERE:

By Car: The only reasonable way around is by car—and one with plenty of space in the boot (trunk). See the map provided and directions for each shopping area.

By Bus: You can call around to the tour bus centers mentioned, but it will be inconvenient and cumbersome to use a bus for this section. See page 134 for details of what service does exist.

By Train: The best area for a train stop is Robina Town Centre with a station a short walk from the entrance. Surfers Paradise malls are accessible from the train/bus hub in the heart of town.

By Water Taxi: If you want to arrive in style, forget the Benz and go by speedboat. Pacific Fair and Marina Mirage have ports for the taxis to drop you off. It is expensive, but it is something special to add to that postcard note. Call **Gold Coast Water Taxis** at ☎ 0418-759-789, **Gold Coast Water Tours** on ☎ 0418-611-999, **Gold Coast Ferries** at ☎ 0411-711-274, **J&J Broadwater Ferry** at ☎ 0412-179-582, **Ocean Taxi** on ☎ 0411-411-422, or **Pacific Water**

Taxis on ☎ 0410-504-669.

PRACTICALITIES:

As a typical shopping excursion, prepare for lots of walking. Allow for at least three hours at each location, and you can spend the entire day mulling around Surfers Paradise and Broadbeach. Make sure you put your goodies in the trunk of the car and out of sight. Petty theft happens here like anywhere else.

FOOD AND DRINK:

Good food is found at all the locations and, surprisingly, some fairly good restaurants. Fast food outlets are prevalent and Australian outlets that serve kabobs are everywhere.

LOCAL SHOPPING HOTSPOTS:

Circled numbers correspond to numbers on the map.

*PACIFIC FAIR ❶, Hooker Boulevard, Broadbeach, ☎ (07) 5539-8766, **W:** pacificfair.com.au. *Open Mon.–Fri. 9–5:30, Thurs. 9–9, Sat. 8:30–5:30, Sun. 10:30–4. Movies and restaurants closing later. Cafés & restaurants.* ♿.

If you like maps and mazes, this place is for you. I get lost every time I go to "Pac Fair" and always rely on the information maps posted throughout the mall to get my bearings. It is one of the biggest malls in Australia with over 6 major department stores, 260 specialty shops, 12 cinema screens, 14 restaurants, a food court, bank outlets, and tons of services. With over 5,000 spots in the car park you may have a hike at peak shopping hours, but you can take the Surfside Buslines from most spots on the Coast and get dropped off at the underground stop at the mall's California Avenue. Tour coaches and taxis also service Pac Fair and you can call the Customer Service Desk at ☎ (07) 5539-8774 for the best way to get there. It is only a 15-minute drive from the heart of Surfers. The information billboards are located near the lake and the Target Department store or in the Riverside Court at the ground floor escalators. From the accounts of inbound tourists I have met, this is the granddaddy of the shopping meccas.

AUSTRALIA FAIR ❷, Marine Parade, Southport, ☎ (07) 5556-6600, **W:** australiafair.com.au. *Open Mon.–Fri. 9–5:30, Thurs. 9–9, Sat. 8:30–5:30, Sun. 10:30–4. Movies and restaurants open longer. Cafés & restaurants. Special events.* ♿.

A smaller version of Pacific Fair, it has two main shopping levels with good ole Kmart as the major department store draw. The Information Booth is located near the food court right across from the New Zealand Ice Cream stand. Major draws to this mall are the cinemas and grocery stores, but it does have a nice blend of stores and fashion boutiques. Think of it as your day-to-day shopping center only 10-minutes from the

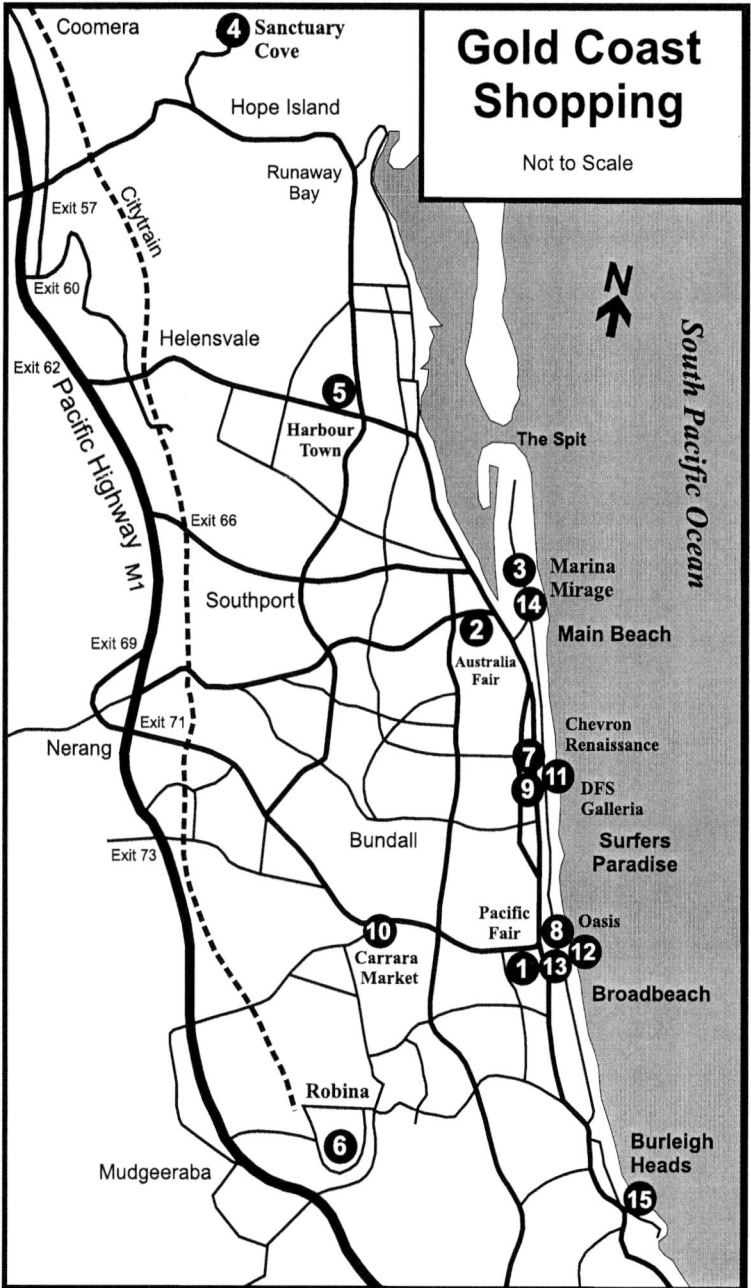

Gold Coast Shopping

Not to Scale

Coomera

4 Sanctuary Cove

Hope Island

Runaway Bay

Exit 57

Citytrain

Exit 60

Helensvale

Exit 62

Pacific Highway M1

5

Harbour Town

The Spit

Exit 66

Southport

3 Marina Mirage

14

2

Australia Fair

Main Beach

Exit 69

Exit 71

Nerang

Chevron Renaissance

7

9 11

DFS Galleria

Exit 73

Bundall

Surfers Paradise

10

Carrara Market

Pacific Fair

8 Oasis

1 13 12

Broadbeach

Robina

6

Mudgeeraba

Burleigh Heads

15

South Pacific Ocean

N

heart of Surfers. Check out the giant fig tree in the food court and have a cuppa while you rest your feet.

*MARINA MIRAGE ❸, 75 Seaworld Drive, Main Beach, ☎ (07) 5577-0088, W: marinamirage.com.au. *Open daily from 10–5 with restaurants and nightclubs closing much later. Café & restaurants.* ♿.

You can't miss this place with giant white sails shimmering in the bright Coast sun and brightly lit at night. The area looks as though there is a giant ghost ship docked in Mariner's Cove. It is the classiest, and the prices reflect it too. But the glamorous international shoppers love the leathers and lace, the high fashions and fabulous eateries it has to offer. To get an idea of the style, their brochure suggests that you arrive by **Hughes Limousine**, ☎ (07) 5531-1411. Only a 10-minute drive from Surfers, it is well worth the stop. You can also dock your yacht among the multi-million dollar ships or make your entrance by water taxi. Oh, and you can stroll next door to Palazzo Versace for a taste of the bubbly if you get stressed. Boasting over 80 stores and great restaurants, it does live up to its reputation and has many major labels for you to choose from. It is a small two-level mall with a great aviary in the center with squawking tropical birds. You can drop the kids off inside the bird sanctuary and stroll at your leisure. Outside are rows of sailboats, cigarette speedboats, and huge cruisers that accent the mall quite well. To top it off, check out the 17th- and 18th-century statues cast about the mall—they are real mates!

SANCTUARY COVE ❹, Casey Road, Hope Island, ☎ (07) 5530-8400, **W:** sanctuarycove.com. *Open daily 9–6, movies and restaurants open longer.* ♿.

With around 80 specialty shops, eateries and businesses lining the harbor cove, it makes for a quaint and relaxing outing. About 25 minutes north of Surfers and less than an hour from Brisbane, it is a bit out of the way but worth the excursion. Trains and buses do link to the shopping cove; the best stop is at Coomera. There is street entertainment on weekends, you can view opal cutting, and there are heaps of exhibits like a car show, boat shows, and just good fun. If you are not into the shopping, no worries as you can take a tour of the **Gold Coast Brewery** micro-brewery for a mere AU $7, ☎ (07) 5577-9262, and taste a honey brewed Beez Kneez, a 7% alcohol Cane Toad or some tasty Duck's Nuts beers. If you want to just veg-out, stop in for a movie at the old-time-looking **Village Theatre**, ☎ (07) 5577-8999. The restaurants are fantastic—one of my favorites is **George's Paragon** for a bargain brunch. To burn off the calories from the fine cuisine, try strolling around the marina or take a sightseeing tour on the M.V. *Kilkie* ferry and see inside the waterfront homes of the well-to-do. If you want to make a full day of it, there are some great getaway packages that include golf, massages, fishing, fully equipped health club/spa, and tennis for around AU $100. For those who are curious, you can also try your hand a lawn bowls game. It's kind of like refined bocce ball.

*HARBOUR TOWN ❺, Corner of Gold Coast Highway & Oxley Drive, Labrador, ☎ (07) 5529-1734, **W**: harbourtownshopping.com.au. *Open Mon.–Sat. 9–5:30, Thurs. 9–7, Sun. 10–5, closed Christmas, Good Friday, extended hours near Christmas and restricted times on Anzac Day and Labour Day. Theater and restaurants open longer. Cafés & restaurants.* ♿.

The Coast's premier outlet shopping center with up to 60% discounts on name brand merchandise. David Jones is the major department store here, but Nike, Oroton, Calvin Klein, City Beach Surf Australia, Polo Ralph Lauren, Waterford, and Mikasa outlets are favorites. I consider the cinemas the best ever at Reading Cinema's Regency lounge theater with lounge seating and food service. The avenues weaving amongst the stores and eateries are lined with huge palms, and the sidewalk is studded with stars. Tour buses do stop here and the plaza even has a tourism lounge. It is a good 20-minutes from Surfers Paradise and about an hour from Brisbane.

ROBINA TOWN CENTRE ❻, Robina Town Centre Drive, Robina, ☎ (07) 5575-0480. *Open Mon.–Fri. 9–5:30, Thurs. 9–9, Sat. 8:30–5:30, Sun. 10:30–4. Theater and restaurants open longer. Cafés & restaurants.* ♿.

A boutique-style shopping center, it has three major department stores in David Jones, Kmart, and Target. The Information Booth is in the center of the mall at Town Square near the entrance to the food markets. It is a pleasant venue with different fashion boutiques and unique retailers. The kids will enjoy the Pop Jet Fountain; and two good outlets are Target Home and Rebel Sports.

*CHEVRON RENAISSANCE ❼, 3240 Gold Coast Highway, Surfers Paradise, ☎ (07) 5592-5188, **W**: chevronrenaissance.com.au. *Open daily, shop times vary but are generally open from 9–5. Café & restaurants.* ♿.

The newest addition to Surfers Paradise and definitely a major upgrade to the area. It has an open-air attitude with a touch of Rodeo Drive. Classy, sassy, and fun to just hang out, it has become a favorite for the locals as well as the international travelers. If you do pass by, make sure you at least look into Infinity. It is a bizarre high-tech fantasy amusement attraction that is worth the investment.

OASIS AT BROADBEACH ❽, Broadbeach Mall, Victoria Avenue, Broadbeach, ☎ (07) 5592-3900, **W**: oasisshoppingcentre.com. *Open daily, shop times vary but generally are 9–5.* ♿.

With over 100 specialty shops, it is close to the beach and has some fun places to browse. Good food, fine fashions, and great gifts are to be found in this small center. And if you get bored, hop the Oasis Monorail (8–midnight) to Conrad Jupiter's Casino and try your luck at the pokies (slots).

DFS GALLERIA ❾, Corner Cavill Avenue & Gold Coast Highway, Surfers

Paradise, ☎ (07) 5570-9401, **W**: dfsgalleria.com.au. *Open daily, 11–10:30.* ♿

Just across from the Hard Rock Café and the Paradise Centre Shopping & Entertainment Area is the huge duty-free building well marked with the worldwide logo of DFS. With a money exchange, FedEx counter (AU $80 to ship a package anywhere on the planet), and several floors of shopping, you will find anything you need to take home. Take along your passport and departure tickets to confirm you tax-free status in stores like The Gap, Ralph Lauren, and Banana Republic. You can buy a wide range of liquors and wines (spirits are usually cheaper in the States), find the latest fashion styles, pick up bags of beauty products, and even buy Cuban cigars (though you probably have to smoke them before you board the plane).

CRAFT MARKETS:

There are quite a few good markets, and the Carrara Market is the most consistently best and largest. Many of the stalls are hosted by many of the same faces at each of the regional markets and the prices are also similar.

*CARRARA MARKETS ❿, Nerang-Broadbeach Road, Carrara, ☎ (07) 5579-9388, **W**: ion.com.au/~holiday/carraramarkets.htm. *Open Sat.–Sun. 6am till the vendors feel like leaving. Cafés & fast food.* ♿

This is a wild market and if you can make the 20-minute drive from Surfers, do it. You will see knickknacks, inexpensive clothing, and people of every shape, size, and personality. If you go just to people watch and have a snag (sausage) you will be happy. Over 500 stalls of antiques, Buddhist prayer beads, pottery, fruits and veggies, and five acres of pure bargains; this is the largest permanent market in Queensland. A standout stall from the hippie days is Billy's Bong Shop, and for the kiddies there is a snake show on the pathway near Dandenong Street (see the hand-out map at the market). If you hear a strange bird in the area, it's just the hawker selling whistles. There are courtesy buses from the resorts in Surfers Paradise—just call ☎ (07) 5579-9388 to catch a ride out. Really, do this if you are in the area on the weekend. Courtesy buses run from the larger resorts in Surfers Paradise from around 7:30 am and return until about 2:30.

Other mobile markets can be found around the Coast and times may vary so check out the brochures from the **Information Booth** at Cavill Mall, ☎ (07) 5533-8202 or **W**: artandcraft.com.au. Here are a few to look in on:

SURFERS PARADISE BEACHFRONT ⓫. The Esplanade at Cavill Avenue, Surfers Paradise. *Starts at around 5 o'clock at night.*

This is a small set-up on Friday nights near the entrance to Cavill Mall. It is a double line of vendors that stretches about two blocks along the surf. One regular artist has some great miniature paintings of Australian landscapes that are precious.

BROADBEACH ⑫. *Held in Broadbeach near the surf, starting at early morning and ending at 10 pm on the first and third Sunday of each month.*

This is a bit larger in scope than the Surfers market, but a lot of the vendors are at both. Held in Kurrawa Park, it is a bit more spread out and easier to get around and have a sticky beak (nose around).

BROADBEACH LANTERN MARKET ⑬. Broadbeach Mall, Broadbeach. *Open Friday nights from 6–10 pm from September to May.*

Similar to the one at Cavill Mall, with many of the same vendors.

*MARINA MIRAGE FARMER'S MARKETS ⑭. 75 Seaworld Drive, Main Beach, ☎ (07) 5577-0088, **W**: marinamirage.com.au. *Starts about 7am and runs until noon. Currently held on the first and third Saturday of the month at the Marina Mirage Shopping area.*

One of the newest additions to the market scene and a great place to pick up green grocer produce as well as gourmet breads, yabbies, olives, sauces, sweets, and meats. Some of the outside vendors have hot plates and cook some unusual goodies. Try the emu on a stick for an interesting taste or sample the bush lemons. Don't be afraid to ask what some of the odd looking stuff is in the stalls. You will get a full and friendly description. It does get very crowded so go early and have a sample or two.

BURLEIGH HEADS ⑮. The Esplanade, Burleigh Heads. *The last Sunday of the month from 8–2:30.*

On the last Sunday of the month, the tents pop up at The Esplanade in Burleigh Heads right on the beachfront. I think it is the best of the weekend markets, but maybe that's because I head right for the nut lady and buy a huge bag of macadamia nuts for a great price.

A Three Hour Tour, A Three Hour Tour

D raw straws to determine who should captain your tinnie (aluminum boat) and who should be Gilligan. The Coast is a boating paradise—and the best way to navigate the estuaries is by renting a small boat and exploring the crystal-clear bay called the Broadwater. You can beach the boat on the isolated South Stradbroke Island and wander over to deserted beaches, or locate the local fishing holes and wet a line. It is safe, easy to get around, and you can even get a close look at the multi-million dollar homes with super yachts docked at their back doors. Take a fishing rod if you like that sport, and just watch where the tinnies are huddled around a spot for the best anchor point, or check the local newspapers for the day's favorite fishing holes.

GETTING THERE:

By Car: Depending on the boat rental service you use, you will probably have to drive or take a cab. It is worth the 6-mile drive from Surfers Paradise to board one of **Ahoy Tinnie Hire's** (☎ (07) 5577-5077) boats as the prices seem the best by far. You will want to call ahead and ask for the most convenient boat ramp. The main spot for them is at Paradise Point and is marked on the map as ❶. Some hire companies allow you to tow the boat to your choice of boat ramps, but why waste time negotiating on the road?

Other boat hire options on the Coast include: **Cove Hire Boats** in Sanctuary Cove, ☎ (07) 5577-9477; **Lofty's Watersports** at Marina Mirage, ☎ 0410-505-669; **Mac's Boat Hire** on Marine Parade in Southport, ☎ 0408-762-516; **Popeye Boat Hire** at Marina Mirage, ☎ (07) 5591-2553 or (07) 5591-2553; and **Shane's Watersports World** on the Broadwater in Labrador, ☎ (07) 5591-5225).

By Bus: Check the **Surfside Buses**, ☎ (07) 5574-5111 or 1-300-655-655, or **W**: gcsshuttle.com.au. They have a Freedom Pass with unlimited local travel, door-to-door theme park transfers, and airport transfers.

PRACTICALITIES:

It can get a bit choppy in the Broadwater, and the bigger boats can make life a bit difficult too. So be prepared to get some sea spray on your face and wear clothes that you aren't terribly fond of. A hat that covers ears is best as the reflection off the water will burn every exposed part of you; many people forget their ears. Load on the sunscreen, and sunglasses are a must. Wear junky sneakers or deck shoes because your feet will get wet. And take along some sort of waterproof windbreaker just in case the sun disappears and it cools off. If you plan to spend most of the time out on the boat or beached on Stradbroke Island, take water and some food— something about sea, sun, air, and sand makes one hungry. A good trick is to freeze your water the night before so it is nice and cool (and keeps your food good). You can buy inexpensive eskies (coolers) for under AU $15 (see any of the Crazy Clark stores), which might be worthwhile. Don't forget to ask for a map of the Broadwater before you go. It will help you navigate around sandbars and will point out the main sights. If you do run into trouble, there are plenty of boats nearby to offer assistance. But it might be smart to take along a mobile phone in case of an emergency. No license is required to rent most of the boats. Finally, a security deposit is usually requested and a picture ID must be shown. Prices generally start around AU $45 for a half-day trips in midweek to over AU $300 for a full week rental. The prices do vary a tad bit depending on the season.

FOOD AND DRINK:

It would be good to take some snacks, but there are plenty of convenience stores and fast food joints on your outing venture. There are two spots I can recommend when you are in this area. The first is **Charis Seafoods** ($), open every day except Monday, at 6 Marine Parade in Labrador, ☎ (07) 5527-1100. It is a waterside family park with good fish & chips as well as a wide range of takeout seafood items. There are plenty of park benches, shade, and a small lagoon for the kids to splash around, as well as a local flock of pelicans (over 100 show up at to be fed by the staff at 1:30 every day it's open) ready to share a few leftovers with you. The second dining choice is **PP's Bistro** ($$) at 21 Hansford Road in Coombabah, ☎ (07) 5577-5477. Pete can thrill your taste buds with what he calls an à la carte menu. To me it's a wonderful mix of Italian, Thai, and Australian flavors that will make it a meal to remember. But you can stop whenever you get hungry or fry up that fish on a beach barbeque.

LOCAL ATTRACTIONS:

Circled numbers correspond to numbers on the map.

First stop is to pick up your aluminum yacht. There are several options listed above, but I have used Ahoy Tinnies several times and have been quite pleased—as have friends. The choice is entirely up to you as the costs are similar at the rental places. However, at the date of going to press, Ahoy Tinnie had the best prices by far for the party boat.

A great option to renting a small tinnie is to hire a Crabb's Barby Party Boat from Ahoy Tinnie Hire. The 23-foot pontoon barbeque boat is fully equipped for a party of up to 8 people. Partially covered from the sun, the

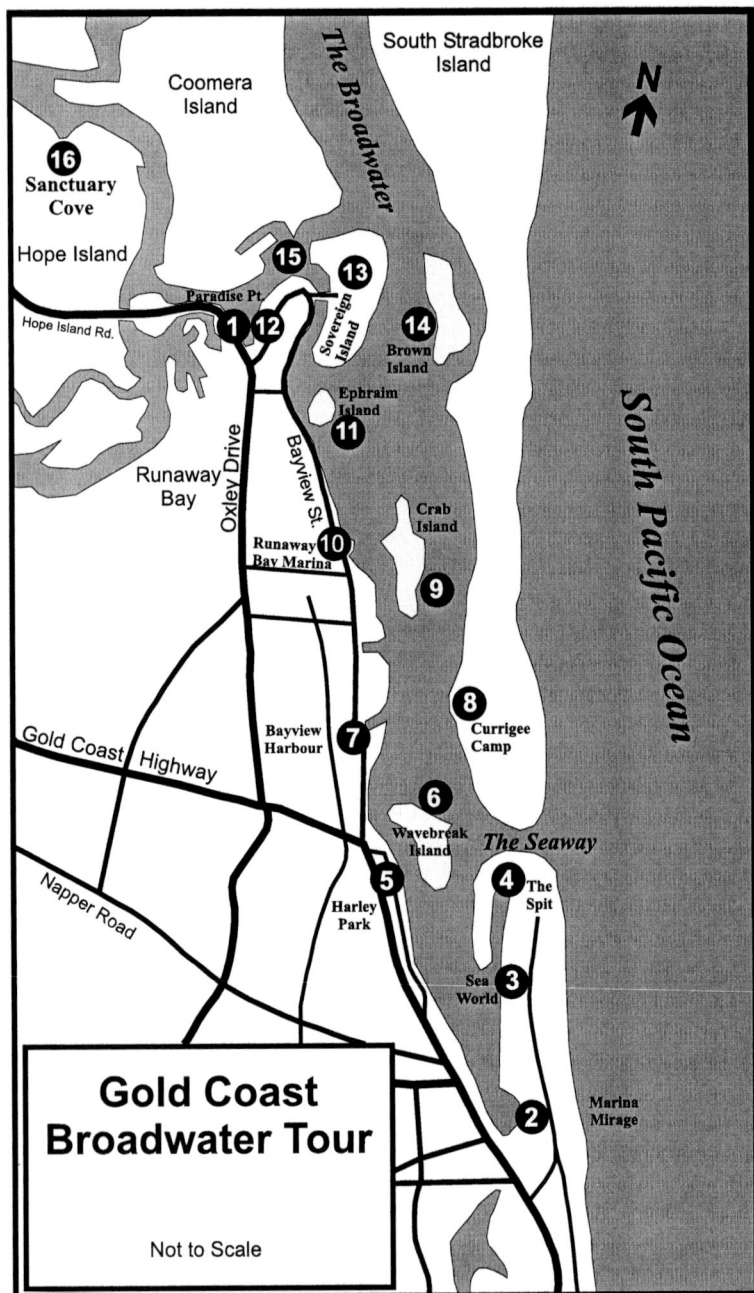

Coomera Island

The Broadwater

South Stradbroke Island

N

16 Sanctuary Cove

Hope Island

Hope Island Rd.

15

13

Paradise Pt

1 **12**

Sovereign Island

14 Brown Island

Ephraim Island

11

Oxley Drive

Bayview St.

Runaway Bay

Crab Island

Runaway Bay Marina **10**

9

South Pacific Ocean

Gold Coast Highway

Bayview Harbour **7**

8 Currigee Camp

6

Napper Road

Wavebreak Island

The Seaway

5

Harley Park

4 The Spit

3 Sea World

Gold Coast Broadwater Tour

2

Marina Mirage

Not to Scale

runabout has a stereo system, iceboxes, a gas BBQ, paper plates and cups supplied, snorkel gear upon request, flush toilet, and a shower. I have gotten rave reviews about this excursion that originates from Paradise Point. Anchor nearby in the safe harbor of Brown Island and explore the Stradbroke bush on the 4WD tracks that are surrounded by wallabies and kangaroos. Hike to the surf beach and have a look or motor around the Broadwater and Coomera River system. The stops listed below apply to either the party boat or small tinnie; the selection should be based on the number of people joining you, the desired outcome (party or sightseeing), and your mood that day.

*AHOY TINNIE HIRE ❶, #8 Cavell Road, Birkdale, ☎ 0408-066-446; or in the Paradise Harbour Store at 16 Paradise Parade, Paradise Point, ☎ (07) 5577-5077 or (07) 3207-4359. *Open daily early to late. Tinnie hires start at AU $45 for a half-day in midweek, a whole day (7–5:30) is AU $60. Weekend rates are AU $50 and $75 respectively. The Crabb's Party Boat price is AU $125 for a full day, plus fuel (expect $10–15).* ♿.

This could be one of your favorite tours—you will definitely get a different perspective of the Coast from a small boat. All boat rentals have at least a 6hp outboard, a canopy, navigation lights, seat cushions, sturdy anchor, and safety gear. They seat between 2–6 people and are in pretty good nick (well maintained). You have your choice of destinations and stops along the way and I will supply you with a few suggestions. Generally, you will want to travel only the distances between Marina Mirage or the southern tip of Wavebreak Island to the area near Tipplers Island. Take care not to venture into the seaway on the eastern side Wavebreak, or into the seaway at Jumpinpin. Both channels are rough and treacherous for even larger boats. But don't worry, there is no strong current to sweep you into those areas and they are clearly identified from a safe distance.

The following areas are pointed out on the map; you might enjoy exploring them. To travel the entire length of the waterway on the map requires about a full day in good weather. Allow enough time to get back to port by sunset as I would strongly recommend you not attempt the trip after sundown. This is a very safe body of water if you follow the safety tips. As far as navigation, all you have to remember is that South Stradbroke Island is on the east and the mainland is on the west. Remember that drinking laws apply on the water too and the water police do patrol the area. Finally, there is rumored to be a nudist colony somewhere on South Stradbroke Island. It is not listed on any map I've seen, but I assume you will know it when you see it.

Ask at the rental agency for the times of the tides and plan to motor with the tide—it's quicker and much smoother. At low tide be very careful of sandbars and have a spotter in front to look for shallow waters. Starting from the southern most section of the map and working north, here is a variety of nooks and crannies to look for buried treasures:

Marina Mirage ❷. You might feel a bit inadequate in a small aluminum skip at this marina as you putt past the super yachts and rich people's toys, but it is a great stop. Either gawk at the sailboats, powerboats, and tourist launches or stop and have a browse in the shops. The cafés and restaurants are fantastic, certainly worth a go. You may notice some odd-looking vessels in this area with a floating chapel, a hut on pontoons, and various planes bobbing on the tides. Keep the camera ready.

Seaworld ❸. You can spot this theme park miles away, just look for the flames spouting from the volcano and listen for the screams of delight. Not much to see in the cove there, though.

*The Spit Cove ❹. If you navigate into the protected point at the Spit, you will find a host of locals sunbathing, swimming with their dogs, or frying up some recently caught fish on the barbie. It is a favorite area that has recently been beautified with walkways and newly planted trees.

*Harley Park and Charis Seafood ❺. Another hangout for the local team. I would recommend you stop for at least a look around. The fish & chips stand is rated one of the best in town, and it seems there are an equal number of pelicans and bathers at this protected swimming hole. Take your camera into the fish market and snap a few of the incredible display of seafood packed on ice. Here you will see what Moreton Bay Bugs really look like in the raw, as well as the other taste treats from the South Pacific Ocean. There is a boat/jet ski rental tent in the car park, and you can book a good time at Shane's Watersports.

*Wavebreak Island ❻. Just a landmark, but an important one. This man-made island was built to protect the area from the strong tides of the Seaway. I would strongly recommend staying on the western side of the sandbar. Many boaties beach their boats on the northwest side of the island to party and enjoy some time on the sandbars. This island is currently causing a major controversy with plans by developers to put a cruise ship terminal on the island, complete with a huge resort. There is a great spot to drop anchor and snorkel on the northeast side of the island. Just near the rocky outcropping you will see a protected cove with a sandy beach—give it a try.

Bayview Harbour ❼. As you proceed north you will see a series of white-and-blue high-rise apartment buildings called Bayview Towers. The Coast Guard station is located at this inlet; you can pick up advice or maps here. This is a good navigation landmark as you continue up the Broadwater.

*Currigee Camp ❽. Ready for a stop? This is a good place to throw the anchor onto the beach and have a walkabout. I'm told by my local mate Trevor that it is not a worry about having the boats "borrowed" as the rentals have distinctive markings and theft is extremely rare. This stretch of pure white beach is on the western shoreline of South Stradbroke Island. It is safe to swim and soak up the rays here. If you are adventurous, you can hike the half-mile across the island to the eastern surf beach. Look for an area where lots of people have beached their boats because that is probably the narrowest spot to cross over. But be very careful if you decide to swim on the eastern beaches. The rips are strong and you are basically on your own out there.

Crab Island ❾. Here is where you will find lots of salty dogs with a fishing line in one hand and a beer in the other. The best spot seems to be on the east side of the usually submerged mangrove island. It is also a calm area where lots of people anchor in the protected area between the island and South Straddie.

Runaway Bay Marina ❿. If you need fuel or want to stop for a coffee, you can pull into this marina that is about the halfway point on this tour. Not much doing there, though.

Ephraim Island ⓫. Bought by Japanese developers in the real estate boom of the 1970s and 80s, it is now deserted and a good place to drop anchor and watch the world go by. It is scheduled for development in the next year or two.

*Paradise Point ⓬. This is a quaint town with a good variety of eateries and lots of ethnic restaurants. There is a netted swimming area (to protect from marine stingers), a beach, lots of barbeques, and a small fishing ramp for use by all.

Sovereign Island ⓭. Meet the rich and famous on this exclusive residential isle. If the homes don't amaze you, the yachts will. There are several inlets to explore and access is open to all if you abide by the speed limits. Some of the ships moored adjacent to the mega-million-dollar homes are almost as large as the houses themselves.

*Brown Island ⓮. Directly east of Sovereign Island is a tiny inlet that is another favorite spot for anglers. A rundown marine research boat that looks creepy guards the entrance to the banana-shaped inlet. On the western shoreline is a quiet cove to have a stroll on sandy shores. If you do wade around the beaches, either wear surf shoes or drag your feet when you walk. It is difficult to see the stingrays that are nested in the shallow waters. Ahoy Tinnie Hire has posted a yellow marker/stake on the beach for the best spot to anchor and hike across to the eastern shoreline of South Stradbroke Island.

Coomera River ⓯. If you have the time, spend a whole afternoon puttering up this winding river, framed by sprawling mansions and mangrove inlets. It is a good area to explore if the Broadwater is a bit rough or windy.

Sanctuary Cove ⓰. On the Coomera River is the Sanctuary Cove Marina and shopping center. A great place to stop and have lunch and spend some of you pocket change. See Trip #21—Shop Till You Drop.

Twenty Nautical Miles Out

I f you have a hankering for real fishing, try one of the charters that will take you to the reef for some serious angling. It can be a bit rough, but the catches are usually worth a bump or two. There are quite a few to choose from, and I will recommend several options. I have featured the one that helped me land a snapper big enough to feed my wife and I for a whole week, and it also seems to be a popular charter. To decide if this trip is for you, here are some highlights to consider.

The local sports news regularly shows the catch of the day brought in from between 20–25 nautical miles off shore. The reef fish you might expect to catch include snapper, squire, pearl perch, kingfish, flathead, mahi mahi, amberjack, and maybe a black marlin. The boats normally leave around 6 in the morning and get back about 3 in the afternoon. The fishing beds cover the areas between Byron Bay (40 miles south) to Point lookout (about the same distance to the north) and the fish finder usually finds schools over the reefs at the continental shelf. You normally don't loose sight of land and the trip out takes only 20 minutes or so. The crew will gut your catch and some will ready it for the barbeque for a small fee. If you catch a whopper, it often takes 20–30 minutes to land it and it is hard work. If the ocean is rough, expect to get wet and bounced around a bit, but it is quite safe. It is a blast and a good day out on the seas.

GETTING THERE:

By Car: Just off the Gold Coast Highway on Marine Parade, it is directly across from the Smith Street Motorway. The red BAIT & TACKLE sign is easy to see from the highway, and the building is between the Southport Olympic Pool and the train (it's a locomotive in the park next door).

By Bus: The bus station stops about six blocks away. You can easily find it by walking towards the Broadwater and turning right.

By Train: Take the train to the Nerang Station and hop the Trainlink bus service to Surfers Paradise, look for a bus to Southport Bus Station or grab a taxi.

PRACTICALITIES:

Plan to get wet and a bit fishy, so wear old clothing if you can. As all the other water sports, wear sunscreen, a hat, and sunglasses. Depending on the weather you might be smart to pack a slicker or windbreaker. It would be wise to pack spare clothing and leave them at the dock. If you have a tendency of motion sickness try any of the over-the-counter products as they seem to work quite well. Toilets and a lower cabin is available if you catch a chill.

For a comprehensive listing of charters Australia-wide, check out **W**: australianfishingcharters.com to add to the options listed below. Another good site is **W**: ausfish.com.au, which provides weather, fishing spots, tackle advice, and charters available.

FOOD AND DRINK:

Food and soft drinks are provided as part of the package. The sandwiches are tasty and the drinks taste great on a hot trip.

LOCAL CHARTERS:

Here are a few companies that have been recommended by local fishermen and at some of the bait & tackle stores in the area. The list is not comprehensive and the Yellow Pages has three pages of charters. **Reel Action Fishing Charters** in Southport, ☎ (07) 5596-5546 or 0412-761-188, **W**: ausfish.com.au/reelaction; **Gone Fishing** from Marina Mirage, ☎ (07) 5530-3804 or 0408-061-944, **W**: gonefishing.net.au; **Hooker Charters** from Marina Mirage, ☎ (07) 5528-6469; **BK's Fishing Charters** in Labrador, ☎ 0414-293-034.

*NEV HOWARD'S SEA PROBE, Marine Parade at Howard's Landing, Southport, ☎ (07) 5531-2333, **W**: seaprobe.com.au. *Open daily. Prices from AU $135 per person to AU $990 for the entire boat (9 person limit).*

The family-owned business has been in operation for over 30 years and is based in a small block fishing shop at Howard's Landing. They have two 35-foot Flybridge Norcats that cruise out to the fishing grounds at 20 knots. You can book a trip on their offshore daytrip that runs from 6am–3pm, the full-moon journey from 4pm–11pm, or even a dive adventure if you choose. If you are queasy about baiting your hook, no worries as the crew will set you up and even remove that record-breaking fish from your line. All fishing gear is provided including Wilson rods and Penn reels. I have never heard of a trip coming back empty-handed, though they do hold to all the bag limits/sizes. When the fish finder locates the fish, you get your orders to drop the lines (often to around 500 feet) and the fun begins. One word of advice is that if the fish looks ugly as sin, don't touch it as it is more than likely poisonous. The crew will deal with these types of fish. If you are lucky, you will get to meet the crew's mate, called Scarface. He is a rouge dolphin with lots of battle scars. They will stop the boat and offer him a hearty hello and a good feed of fish. You may also see whales jumping around the boat—in the distance. There are strict rules of engagement, but you will get a clear look if they are running.

Just the ride out into the bluish-green South Pacific is a fantastic experience and bringing dinner home makes it even better. One additional thrill is breaching the seaway at the Spit. The currents and eddies make the beginning of the journey exciting.

After the trip you can relax (after showering of course) in one of the fine restaurants at Marina Mirage. Choose between the trendy **Grumpy's Wharf** ($–$$) or the top quality (and expensive) seafood at **Omeros Brothers** ($$–$$$). As you dine on a scrumptious meal you can look over the marina and dream of the big one that got away.

Nev Howard's Sea Probe Catch of the Day

Walk on the Wild Side

You have two main selections to meet the Aussie animals on this tour, but I have also included a bird garden and a beehive colony in case you are more of a bee/bird lover. Of the two main attractions, one will offer a smaller and more natural environment and the other will be large and more hands-on with the critters of the wild. Both have guided tours with qualified rangers and nature conservationists. If you have the time, visit each park. David Fleay Wildlife Park has elevated boardwalks that keep you safely from the jaws of the crocodiles and almost within reach of the loveable kangaroos. This environment allows you to feel like you are with the animals without interfering with them, but you can get a photo holding a koala if you wish. Currumbin Wildlife Sanctuary is the larger sister to Fleay's and is geared more towards the younger kids with lots of shows and feedings. Right next-door is the giant beehive where you can actually walk into the queen's colony protected by a glass wall. At night, ride the free bus and catch a show across the border at Club Banora or Twin Towns Services Club.

GETTING THERE:

By Car: Both locations are about a 20-minute drive south of Surfers Paradise and a little over an hour from Brisbane. Fleay's is just off the Pacific Highway. Exit at Burleigh Heads/Tallebudgera Valley exit and follow the signs. Currumbin is accessed from the Pacific Highway and exiting at the Palm Beach ramp. Then follow Palm Beach Avenue to the Gold Coast Highway and turn left at the huge sign. Olsen's is on Currumbin Creek Road, just off the Gold Coast Highway and only 15-minutes from Surfers Paradise.

By Bus: Surfside buses run up and down the coast. There are stops near both attractions, but you may want to take a cab to Fleay's as it is a steep hike after departing the bus. Coachtrans also have shuttle service in the area. No service to Olsen's.

By Train: Exit at either the Robina or Nerang Stations and access the bus/rail links. No access to Olsen's.

PRACTICALITIES:

This is an easy walk, lots of shade, and plenty of places to sit and relax. Don't forget the camera as there will be some good close-ups of Australia's best characters. Don't wear any blue accessories unless you want a close encounter with the thief called bowerbird, but more of that later. You can spend a whole day at each of the parks, and if you have a particular interest in an animal that is dear to your heart, call ahead for the day's feeding or presentation times. If you have the time, split this into two days and see each of the main attractions as a full daytrip. When the schedule is tight, see Fleay's first, then Currumbin, the Superbee Honeyworld, and finally Olsen's. If you are driving, that is the order that you will come upon them off of the Gold Coast Highway from Brisbane and Surfers Paradise.

FOOD AND DRINK:

All areas provide café service and fast food is available in abundance. Fleay's café is small but adequate. Olsen's has a quaint little tearoom for refreshments. And you can dip your fingers in the honey jar all day at the bee colony.

LOCAL ATTRACTIONS:

Circled numbers correspond to numbers on the map.

*DAVID FLEAY WILDLIFE PARK ❶, West Burleigh Road, Burleigh Heads, ☎ (07) 5576-2411, E-mail: fleays@env.qld.gov.au. *Open daily 9–5, closed Christmas. Adults AU $6.50, children AU $3.35, seniors AU $4.25, families AU $16.50. Guided tours, self-guided tours. Gift shop. Café. Special events.* &.

This is a cool place even before you actually get inside the park. Entering amongst a mass of eerie mangrove trees you climb up to the friendly ranger who stamps your hand for entry. As you step into the rainforest setting, the sounds of the inhabitants, as well as bush smells, will immediately catch your attention. But wait! Make sure you get a copy of the mud map that lays out the terrain ahead of you. The walk around the park is a giant oval with exhibits (in order) starting at the **Munch Zone** (food kiosk and gift shop entranceway) and working your way clockwise. **Treetop Zone** is where you will find the koalas, wombats, and can get that great photo to send home of you holding a koala (for AU $8.95). Around the bend is **Culture Zone** with Aboriginal presentations and your chance to hold a (non-poisonous) snake or two. Up next is **Rare Zone** and one of the oddest birds you'll see anywhere—the colorful and deadly cassowary. The **Flight Zone** is home to tree kangaroos (no, they don't fly), eagles, and elusive owls. The best spot here is the **Rainforest Aviary** and my buddy the bowerbird. This small and bold fowl showers his attention to his lovers by stealing anything blue and hiding it in his nest. I saw the pigeon-sized pipsqueak carry a guy's blue hat off his head and tuck it into his nest at the far end of the aviary. Up the steps, through the **Eucalyptus Forest** (look for koala scratchings on the trees) and into the **Danger Zone**. Here you must keep your hands to yourself or the dingoes and crocodiles will remove a few fingers. Past the Ring and Moon Dams you enter the **Roo Zone**. Finally,

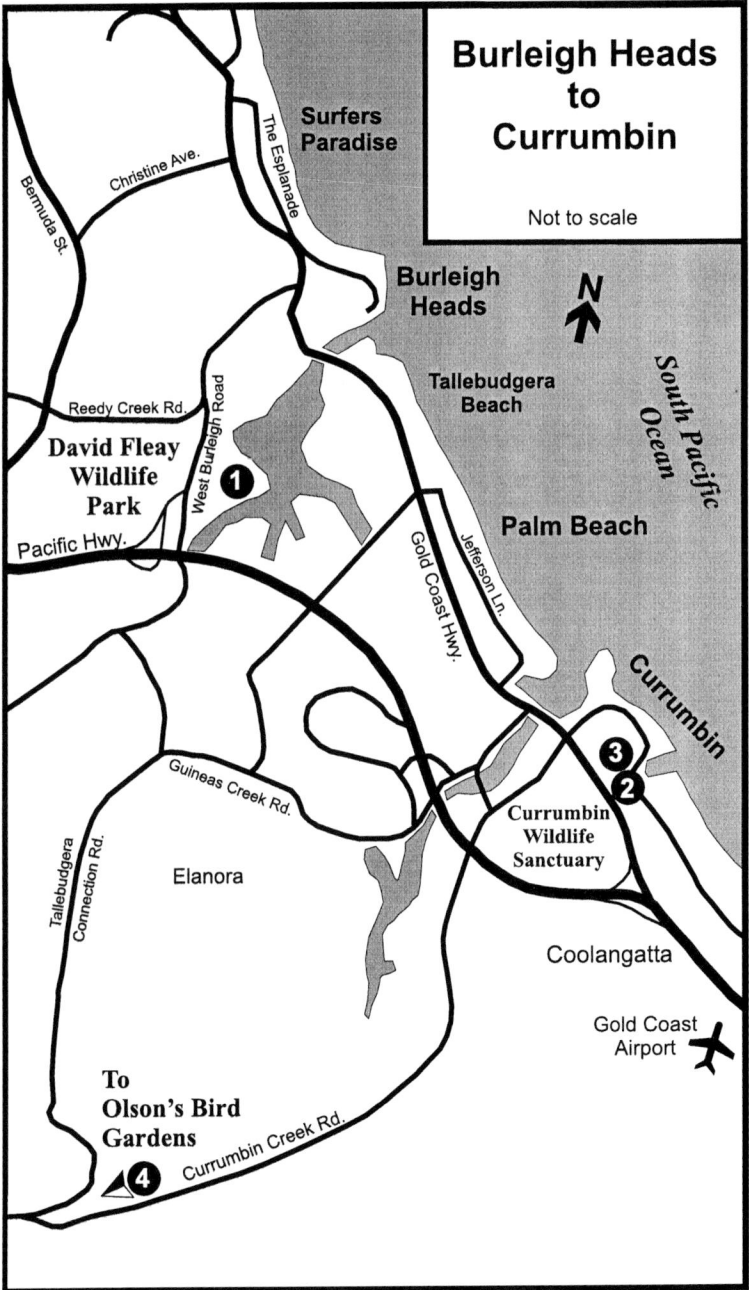

Burleigh Heads to Currumbin

Not to scale

Surfers Paradise

Burleigh Heads

Tallebudgera Beach

South Pacific Ocean

N

The Esplanade

Christine Ave.

Bermuda St.

Reedy Creek Rd.

West Burleigh Road

David Fleay Wildlife Park

Pacific Hwy.

Palm Beach

Jefferson Ln.

Gold Coast Hwy.

Currumbin

Guineas Creek Rd.

Tallebudgera Connection Rd.

Elanora

Currumbin Wildlife Sanctuary

Coolangatta

Gold Coast Airport

To Olson's Bird Gardens

Currumbin Creek Rd.

delve into the **Twilight Zone** with its platypus, quolls, bilbies, and bats. The ranger-assisted tours and presentations are really worth it and they are free. Finally, the gift shop has some interesting posters, educational activity books, and unique stuffed toys.

*CURRUMBIN WILDLIFE SANCTUARY ❷, Gold Coast Highway, Currumbin, ☎ (07) 5534-1266 or (07) 5598-1645, **W**: currumbin-sanctuary.org.au. *Open daily 8–5, closed Christmas, closes at 1pm on Anzac Day. Adults AU $19.50, children AU $11.50, seniors AU $13.50. Guided tours, self-guided tours. Gift shop. Café. Special events.* &.

Enter a 66-acre wildlife wonderland with free-roaming mammals, reptiles and birds. Many of the 1,400 critters in this largest collection of Australian native wildlife are touchable—if you dare. Or simply stroll the grounds and watch the regular activities. Ranger-led educational shows run throughout the day and you can even see the wildlife hospital where over 4,000 native animals are cared for each year. Be prepared to duck when the lorikeets swarm at 8 am and 4 pm and stop at the crossing when the miniature train passes by. The air is full of laughing children with background sounds of nature calling. The list of activities is unending and the park is geared for all ages and levels of curiosity. Aboriginal dances, hand feeding animals, playgrounds loaded with emus and kangaroos, costumed characters tickling the youngsters fancy, conservation exhibits, and even a nighttime adventure are all found at this sanctuary for people and our animal mates. The eateries are varied and very accessible and the gift shop is a good place to pick up some memories. If there is a logical method to touring this park, I haven't found it, but you may want to take the train ride first to get your bearings. Have a wild time!

THE SUPERBEE HONEYWORLD ❸, 35 Tomewin Street, Currumbin, ☎ (07) 5598-4548, **W**: superbee.com.au. *Open daily 8–5.30. Closed Christmas Day. Show Times: Daily on the hour from 10–4, duration 30 minutes. Free admission to the main display. Live Bee Shows cost: Adults AU $6, child AU $4.50, family pass and group discount available for AU $18.50. Bee Brave Experience is an extra AU $5.00 per person. Great gift shop.* &.

Right across the street in Currumbin's parking lot is this hive of activity. You probably won't see it advertised anywhere, but it is a very good tour—and don't think it's for kids only. Protected by glass or netting at all times, you actually enter a huge beehive and are surrounded by over a million bees. It is weird being in the midst of the droning hum of the live bees. With the help of the keeper and his flashlight you will meet the queen herself. In the **Bee Brave Experience**, you can suit-up and volunteer to help the keeper smoke and handle the bees. See how the honey is extracted and bottled. Over 25 varieties of honey are available, at factory prices, including the popular Propolis and Royal Jelly.

OLSON'S BIRD GARDENS & SUBTROPICAL RAINFOREST ❹, Currumbin

Valley, Currumbin Creek Road, Gold Coast, ☎ (07) 5533-0208. *Open daily 9–5. Adults AU $10, children AU $5, seniors AU $8, and families for AU $28. Guided tours, self-guided tours. Gift shop. Café. Special events.* &.

Roam the 20 acres of botanical gardens and come nose-to-beak with some of the world's most exotic birds. Specialties include the plum-headed parakeets from the Himalayas, the brilliantly colored South American conures, New Guinea parrots, pheasants from Asia, and the raucous pink and ret-tailed cockatoos. Not limited to aviaries and swarms of lorikeets, the gardens are loaded with roses, gingers, palms, ferns, and the most popular—**Lillypilly Maze**. Lillypilly is a rainforest tree with glossy green leaves and pink edible fruits. This six-foot puzzle is a favorite for everyone under six feet tall. You can make a day of it or wander for an hour or so. Barbeques and a café are on-site or you can enjoy scones and jam at the tearoom that is surrounded by tropical ferns.

Currumbin Wildlife Sanctuary – Dinner for the Kangaroos

Extreme Recreation

For the adrenalin junkies, I have a few treats for you. Choose your poison mates. All the thrillers are within the reach of the Surfers Paradise CBD, can keep you busy for a full day, and most are within walking distance of the main strip at Cavill Mall. Hold onto your shorts and give some of these a go. Please call ahead before getting your juices flowing as the liability insurance problems have arrived in Australia and some attractions have closed shop until things quiet down. I really have no favorites to offer for this section and it really depends on what excites you.

GETTING THERE:

By Car: The Gold Coast exits are a straight and direct 40-mile shot down the Pacific Highway or the M1. Turn off at the Smith Street or Southport/Nerang Road Exits and drive east unit you dead end at the Gold Coast Highway and follow that to your desired destination.

By Train: Hop any of the express trains to the Gold Coast or Robina Station. Avoid the local train as it stops at all stations in between. You may board at Central, Roma Street, South Brisbane, or South Bank stations. Sit back and enjoy the scenery on the one-hour trip to the Nerang Station. From there you can catch the Trainlink service or hail a taxi to the surf.

By Bus: Coachtrans at ☎ 13-12-30 or (07) 5506-9777, **W:** coachtrans.com.au, is a good option. Check at any of the Bus/Rail transport hubs in Brisbane, but the best is from Roma Street for timetables. Get off at the Beach Road stop in the heart of Surfers Paradise. It will take a little over an hour, but it is the most economical way to head south with a one-way trip costing: Adults: AU $14 and kids: AU $11. An alternative bus line is **Kirklands**, ☎ 1-300-367-077, **W:** kirklands.com.au. Another attractive option is **Surfside Buses**, ☎ (07) 5574-5111 or 1-300-655-655, **W:** gcshuttle.com.au. They have a Freedom Pass with unlimited local travel, door-to-door theme park transfers and airport transfers.

By Plane: Luckily the Coolangatta Airport is just south of Surfers Paradise, a short hop from Brisbane, and there are direct routes from most major Australian cities. When you arrive you can catch one of the many ground transport systems. To book ahead, try these two suggestions: **Con-X-ion**, ☎ (07) 5591-2525, AU $35; **Gold Coast Ecotours**, ☎ (07) 5573-6080, for about AU $25.

PRACTICALITIES:

Make sure you use extra strength denture grip, wear a strap around your glasses, and hold on to your hat. Other than that, dress to suit the weather.

FOOD AND DRINK:

All types of cafés, coffee shops, restaurants, and fast food joints will surround your fast-paced outing. If your stomach can take it, that is. But since you probably will have used up all of your energy and need lots of iron, try a big juicy steak at **Cav's Steakhouse** at 30 Frank Street in Labrador, ☎ (07) 5532-2954. This informal setting offers the best premium aged steaks I have eaten in Oz.

LOCAL ATTRACTIONS:

Circled numbers correspond to numbers on the map.

FLY-COASTER ❶, Cypress Avenue, Surfers Paradise, ☎ (07) 5539-0474, **W**: flycoaster.com. *Open daily 10–10, 3-person fly AU $29, 2-person AU $35, solo AU $39, video AU $20, photo AU $10, and kids 8-minute mini-fly AU $10.* ♿.

This giant sling makes it look like you are Superman or Superwoman as you fly 80 miles an hour from a 12-storey pendulum platform. It looks like loads of fun, and the regular shrieks of delight sort of confirm it. The youngsters can strap on a bungee harness and enjoy acrobatics on the trampolines.

SLING SHOT ❷, corner of Palm Avenue & Gold Coast Highway, Surfers Paradise, ☎ (07) 5570-2700, **W**: funtime.com.au. *Open daily 10–10, costs AU $30 per person in a 2-seat capsule, videos are AU $20.* ♿.

Now this one looks scary and I'm not about to try it. You get strapped into a thing that looks like a roll cage. Bungee straps are stretched to the contraption from a tower over 262 feet above your head. The countdown begins and you are launched straight up at nearly 100/mph. The videos are funny to watch as the faces contort at a 6 G shock.

BANZAI BUNGEY ❸, corner of Palm Avenue & Gold Coast Highway, Surfers Paradise, ☎ (07) 5526-7611, **W**: banzaibungey.com. *Open daily 10–10, prices are AU $80 a jump.*

What can I say—it's a daredevil event?

SKYDIVE QUEENSLAND ❹, PO Box 2696, Nerang, ☎ (07) 5574-7777, **W**: skydiveqld.com.au. *Open daily, prices AU $390 for a jump out over the ocean and AU $270 over the hinterland mountains.*

Here's one of the rare chances to jump out of a helicopter or seaplane over the surf. After 15 minutes of instruction, you can tandem jump with a

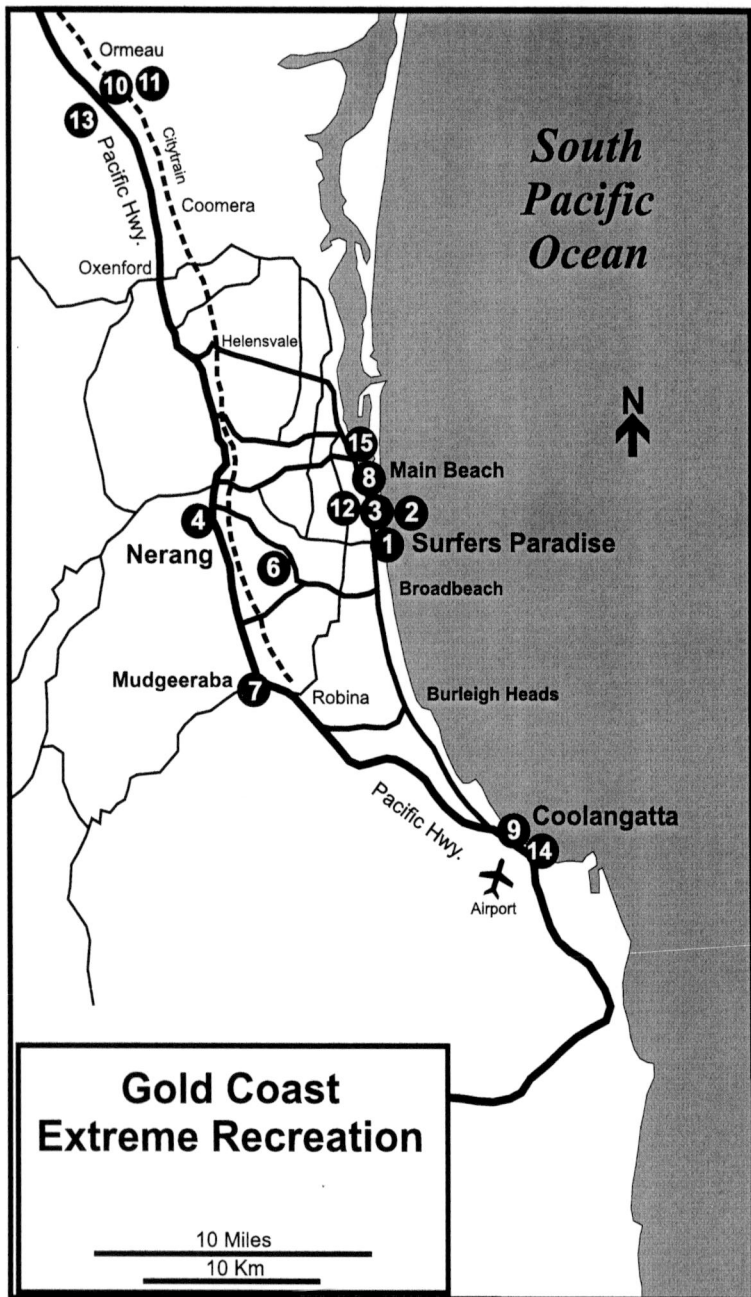

Gold Coast
Extreme Recreation

10 Miles
10 Km

world champion skydiver. The drop over the South Pacific is a chance of a lifetime.

TANDEM SKYDIVE ❺, no permanent address, ☎ (07) 5599-1920. *Open daily, prices: AU $275.*

Take a tandem freefall from 10,000 feet and pop the chute at 4,500 feet to enjoy the sights of the Coast as you fly like a bird.

HOT AIR BALLOONING ❻, 13 Lakeview Drive, Carrara, ☎ (07) 5593-3291, **W**: balloonaloft.net. *Open daily. Prices AU $230.* ♿.

A one-hour sunrise flight over Surfers Paradise is topped off by a champagne toast when the basket touches back to Earth. This is Australia's oldest and largest ballooning company.

BALLOON DOWN UNDER ❼, 4 Coastview Crescent, Mudgeeraba, ☎ (07) 5530-3631, **W**: balloondownunder.com. *Open daily, prices AU $175 for a half hour, AU $230 for a full hour; children AU $145 and AU $175 respectively.* ♿.

A 6 am liftoff will take you over the hinterland rainforests while floating quietly in the thermals above the national parks. Champagne and nibbles are waiting for you when you land.

ST ELMOS LIGHTNING CRUISES ❽, Gold Coast Bridge, Main Beach, ☎ 0404-466-909. *Open daily. Prices start at AU $19 and the top end is about AU $145. Guided tours.* ♿.

Choose an **In A Flash To The Surf** with a speed dash to the ocean for AU $41/$21. **Thunderbolt Surf Cruise** takes you further out into the ocean for a possible sighting of whales and dolphins for AU $83/$41. Speed up the Broadwater and catch the sights in the **Fast Boat To Wilderness** at AU $145/$72. Check out the canals and huge homes in the **River Spinning Tour** for AU $28/14. Or charter the boat for AU $165 an hour.

BARNSTORMERS AUSTRALIA ❾, Coolangatta Airport, Coolangatta, ☎ 0412-078-869. *Open daily. Prices: AU $50 for 10 minutes, AU $85 for 20 minutes, AU $105 for 35 minutes, AU $160 for 1 hour.*

Choose a ride, a stunt trip, or just a scenic tour in this new Super Waco replication of a 1935 barnstorming biplane.

LE MANS ❿, Old Pacific Highway, Pimpama, ☎ (07) 5546-6566, E-mail: janjlemans1966@bigpond.com. *Open daily 10–5. Prices AU $37.50 for 10 laps and AU $60 for 16 laps at a faster pace.* ♿.

Check your lap times against the clock and beating the 53-second lap speed allows you to get behind the wheel of a supercharged cart.

ZORB GOLD COAST ⓫, Exit 54 at 232 Old Pacific Highway, Pimpama (right behind Le Mans), ☎ (07) 5547-6300. **W**: zorb.com. *Open daily 10–5. Prices AU $38–$66.*

Roll down a sculptured slalom course while strapped in a huge inflated ball. You can add to the thrill by adding water and a few friends inside for the ride.

OCEAN RAFTERS ⑫, Appel Park Wharf, Surfers Paradise, ☎ (07) 5502-6976, **W**: oceanrafters.com. *Open daily, departures at 11 am, 1 pm, and 3 pm. Price is AU $60.*

This 80–90 minute Kodiak-style speedboat ride flies over the waves at 50 knots. Expect a bouncy ride as you go airborne over the surf.

TIGER MOTH JOY RIDES ⑬, PO Box 224, Broadbeach, ☎ (07) 5502-7855 or 0418-787-475, **W**: tigermothjoyrides.com.au. *Open daily. Prices run from AU $75 to AU $360.*

Jump into the cockpit of a DH82 Tiger Moth and enjoy an open-air ride above the Gold Coast. Choose from 10-minute to 1-hour flights over Tamborine Mountain, a Surfers Paradise flyby, or a Springbrook Rainforest ride. All provide different perspectives of the area, and you can truly see the change from beach to bushland. Geoff Stillman, your pilot, also offers "In Formation" flights as you nearly touch the wingtips of your mate's plane. If you think your harness is tight enough, the aerobatics will begin and you can experience "the Immelmann."

GLIDING ADVENTURES ⑭, PO Box 1004, Coolangatta, ☎ (07) 5599-2877, **W**: glidingadventures.com. *Open daily from 9:30–4. Prices: AU $195 for an hour or AU $95 for a 20-minute trip.*

You get to take the stick on this soundless flight over the hinterland or coastline. The glider has a motor to get you up to soaring heights. Then cut the engine to enjoy the serenity in the clouds as you float to Earth.

HELICOPTER JOYFLIGHTS ⑮, D Dock, Marina Mirage, Main Beach, ☎ (07) 5591-8457, E-mail: helitour@onthenet.com.au. *Open daily 9 till dark. Adult/child prices: AU $44/33 for 5 minutes, AU $77/44 for 10 minutes, AU $110/77 for 15 minutes, AU $137/93 for 20 minutes, AU $203/115 for 30 minutes.* ♿.

Whirl over the beaches and enjoy the sights below. Charters are available on their 2/3/6-seater birds.

Broadwater Cruises

A re you ready to work the upper body a bit mates? If so, this will be a grand chance to paddle around the local islands, explore Aboriginal sites, and smell the aromas from muddy mangrove islands. You can even tip over and have a swim or snorkel along the way. If you are not quite so adventurous, I have listed a bunch of motorized cruises to choose from. Included is a nice variety to meet your interests.

GETTING THERE:

By Car: The Gold Coast exits are a straight and direct 40-mile shot down the Pacific Highway or the M1. Turn off at the Smith Street or Southport/Nerang Road Exits and drive east until you dead end at the Gold Coast Highway, then follow that to your desired destination.

By Train: Hop any of the express trains to the Gold Coast or Robina Station. Avoid the local train as it stops at all stations in between. You may board at Central, Roma Street, South Brisbane, or South Bank stations and sit back to enjoy the scenery on the one-hour trip to the Nerang Station. From there you can catch the Trainlink service or hail a taxi to the surf.

By Bus: ☎ 13-12-30 or (07) 5506-9777, **W**: coachtrans.com.au for a **Coachtran Bus**. Check at any of the Bus/Rail transport hubs in Brisbane, but the best is from Roma Street for timetables, and look for the Beach Road stop in the heart of Surfers Paradise. It will take a little over an hour, but it is the most economical way to head south with a one-way trip costing: Adults: AU $14 and kids: AU $11. An alternative bus line is **Kirklands**, ☎ 1-300-367-077, **W**: kirklands.com.au. Another attractive option is the **Surfside Buses**, ☎ (07) 5574-5111 or 1-300-655-655, or **W**: gcshuttle.com.au. They have a Freedom Pass with unlimited local travel, door-to-door theme park transfers, and airport transfers.

By Plane: Luckily the Coolangatta Airport is just south of Surfers Paradise. It is a short hop from Brisbane, and there are direct routes from most major Australian cities. When you arrive you can catch one of the many ground transport systems. To book ahead, try these two suggestions: **Con-X-ion**, ☎ (07) 5591-2525, AU $35; **Gold Coast Ecotours**, ☎ (07) 5559-0377, for about AU $25.

PRACTICALITIES:

Depending on the season, you will want to be prepared with a layered approach. The Broadwater can be cool in the morning though the winds are usually non-existent, then it warms up quickly with the rising sun. Sun protection, hat, and shoes (that you don't mind getting wet) are essential. If it is cool out or if you prefer some additional protection for the suggested tour, you might want to consider renting a wet suit for the trip. You can find them at most dive shops in the area or ask when you phone for a booking. The featured tour group does offer free pick-up and return transportation in the Gold Coast area.

FOOD AND DRINK:

Food and drink is provided on most of the cruises, but check ahead if you are not sure. If you are hungry after the tour try out **Holy Mackerel Seafood Restaurant** ($$-$$$) at 174 Marine Parade in Labrador, ☎ (07) 5531-1017. A good choice in this area if you are in the mood for fresh seafood, it is upscale casual and has one of the best hot/cold seafood platters in the area. Another set of options is across from the launch site in the **Grand Hotel** complex at 360 marine Parade. There is **Mano's Bistro**, **Phuket Thai**, **Café Riviera**, **Kokonut Willy's Bar & Restaurant**, all with different and interesting menus at a $$ price tag.

MAIN ATTRACTIONS:

Circled numbers correspond to numbers on the map.

*KAYAK ECO-ADVENTURES ❶, Gold Coast, ☎ (07) 5502-8219 or 0412-940-135, E-mail: dkubeda@bigpond.com. *Open daily from 6:30 am. Prices: 3-hour Dawn or Sunset Tour AU $40, Half-day Kingfisher Tour AU $60, and Full-day Tipplers Tours AU $110. Guided tour.*

Of the three options on this water-based adventure, I recommend the half-day **Kingfisher Tour** for several reasons. If you are not used to flexing certain muscles, a half-day is enough to test them; and you can soak in plenty of the surrounds in four hours or so. Plus, you will be doing another kayaking excursion on a later trip, and you might want to save some energy for that one too. But you can go for it and enjoy the full-day or two-day trips and really see it all. This is what to expect on the half-day paddle: Rub those eyes and get ready to experience the coast from a totally different perspective.

The aquatic adventure starts on the beach at **Charis Seafoods ❶** at 6 Marine Parade in Labrador. There you will meet the smiling Dave, your marine biologist guide for the day. After ten minutes of safety instructions, fitting you out with snorkel and fins, and a quick demonstration of kayak maneuvering, you hop aboard the colorful 12-foot plastic kayaks. Not to worry mates, Dave uses the most stable kayaks made and the water is usually very calm. He also picks the easiest route for the day, based on the tides. As you are getting your sea legs, he softly points out the landmarks, provides a history of the Broadwater, and expertly hovers over specific aquatic specimens for you to gawk at. The water is only about 2-1/2 feet

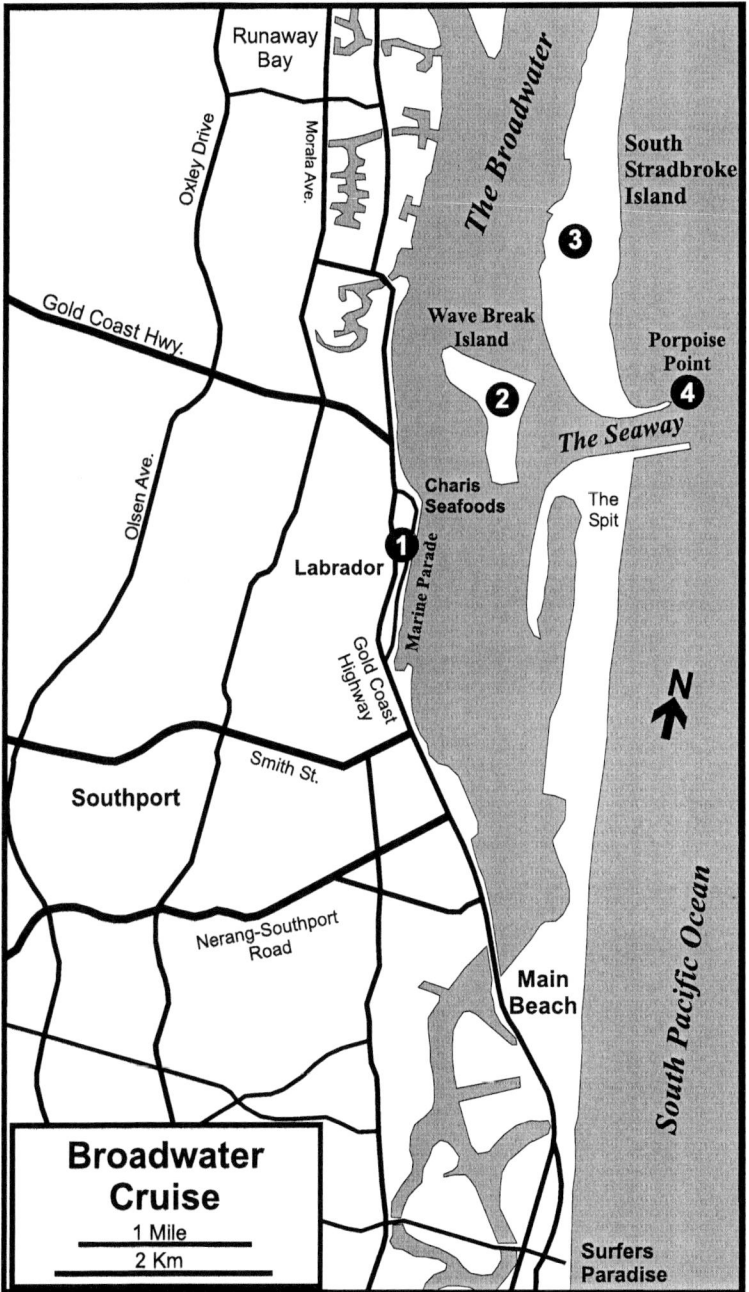

Runaway
Bay

Oxley Drive

Morala Ave.

The Broadwater

South
Stradbroke
Island

3

Gold Coast Hwy.

Wave Break
Island

Porpoise
Point

4

2

The Seaway

Olsen Ave.

Charis
Seafoods

The
Spit

1

Labrador

Marine Parade

Gold Coast
Highway

Smith St.

Southport

Nerang-Southport
Road

**Main
Beach**

South Pacific Ocean

N

**Broadwater
Cruise**

1 Mile

2 Km

**Surfers
Paradise**

deep at this point as you float over stingray beds (look for round divots in the sand) and see the tiny holes that are home to yabbies. If you are lucky, you will get a pleasant surprise if a stingray jumps out of the water to dislodge parasites from its gills.

On the western side of **Wave Break Island** ❷, your scout will point to a sandbar for you to beach your ship. At this juncture, he will offer binoculars, a wide range of information on the area, a dissertation of the ecosystems (17 different types of mangroves), and a description of the wildlife floating, flying (check out the oyster catcher birds and huge pelicans) and swimming (715 different species of fish) by. Back in the water, you will paddle around to enjoy the serenity, cruise by clusters of boats moored for the weekend, say a g'day or two to the sleepy boaties, and avoid the speeding jet skis. On the northern side of Wavebreak Island (or a safe harbor in the area), it's time for brekkie and a yarn or two. Something I learned was that North and South Stradbroke was once a single island and was split apart in 1896 by a ship called the *Cambus Wallace* that was loaded with dynamite and had crashed on the eastern beach. As you devour his homemade baked goods, cereals, fruits, and juices he opens his wildlife books, explains the history of the Aboriginal tribes that lived along the water, and prepares you for the indescribable beauty you will see on the snorkel part of the tour. He talks of the sand dunes, the oxygenated sand bars, and the varied land creatures we will track after tea.

Saddled up and ready to go, you will round the tip of Wavebreak Island and catch the strong current (not much paddling here mates) to South Stradbroke Island ❸. You will pull your kayaks up onto the soft white sand and hike across the island towards the surf beach on the opposite side. During the short half-mile walk you begin the tracking. Dave points out the wallaby footprints, marks made by lace monitor tails, the twitty honey eater birds, the she oak trees, and the wonders of this isolated island.

In a short time you will hear the thundering waves and crest the dunes to see a mass of black-suited surfers riding the waves at **Porpoise Point** ❹. Expect a sudden stop or two along the beach as he picks up some strange sea critter and calls a huddle to explain it. He varies his walks on this 15-mile stretch of pure white beach, but is careful to answer any and all questions of the area. Back in the kayaks and a short trip back to Wave Break Island for a snorkel. The dip will bring you face-to-face with millions of swarming fish. In the short time I swam, I saw lacey damselfish, spiky puffers, giant silvery bream, huge schools of baitfish, huge angels, and a deep-sea flute mouth fish that looked like a flat eel. Depending on the time of day, sun conditions, and water temperature, the water can be a liquid blue opal, emerald green, or a mix of aquamarine in color. As the day gently passes, it is time to paddle back. Now you can expect some rolling waves created by the tide and increased boat activity. It makes for a fun ride; before you know it, your back at the starting point—ready to do it all over again.

OTHER POPULAR TOURS:

AQUABUS SAFARIS, 7A Orchid Avenue, Surfers Paradise, ☎ (07) 5539-0222, **W**: aquabus.com.au. *Open daily 8:45–5:50. Adults AU $27, children AU $21, seniors AU $24. Guided tours. Souvenirs onboard.* ♿.

This amphibious vehicle is a popular treat for tourists and is always crowded. The distinctive truck/boat takes you along the beach to the Spit, past Marina Mirage, and then into the Broadwater to cruise the varied shoreline.

ADVENTURE DUCK, P.O. Box 1078, Surfers Paradise, ☎ (07) 5557-8869, **W**: adventureduck.com. *Open daily, 8:30–5:15. Adults AU $28, children AU $22, seniors AU $24. Guided tours. Gifts onboard.* ♿.

The Duck aquatic ATV looks like a duck and takes a similar route as the Aquabus.

SHANGRI LA CRUISES, Marina Mirage, Seaworld Drive, Main Beach, ☎ (07) 5557-8888, **W**: shangrila.com.au. *Open daily 8–5. Prices range from AU $34 for a canal cruise to AU $74 for a dinner/show night sail. Guided tours. Gifts and souvenirs available.* ♿.

This is a calm water cruise line that offers a wide range of cruises and sightseeing tours. Most trips serve refreshments and a diverse set of sights to choose from.

GOLD COAST GONDOLAS, Mariners Cove, 60 Seaworld Drive, Main Beach, ☎ (07) 5529-1513 or 0419-790-221. *Open daily 8–late. Prices from AU $50–$100, Guided tours.*

Charter your own gondola and enjoy a romantic cruise complete with champagne, fine foods, and music. Choose from breakfast cruises, mid-day jaunts, twilight sail, or under the stars.

TOP CRUISE "RANI", Pier 'A' Runaway Bay Marina, 247 Bayview Street, Runaway Bay, ☎ (07) 5529-5588. *Open daily 9–3:45. Adults AU $29, children AU $15 (4–14 y/o), hotel transfer AU $6. Guided tours. Gifts on board. Special events.* ♿.

Calm water cruise out to South Stradbroke Island Resort and a day of relaxing, water sports, tractor rides to the surf beach, shopping stopover at Sanctuary Cove, canoeing, slot machines, and plenty of grog (beer and wine).

ISLAND QUEEN SHOWBOAT, PO Box 1225, Surfers Paradise, ☎ (07) 5557-8800, **W**: islandqueen.com.au. *Open daily 8:30–6:30. Adults from AU $23 to AU $74. Guided tours, Gift shop on board. Special events.* ♿.

A combination of cruises are available on this well-established cruise line. From morning tea sightseeing trips to a seafood buffet night cruise, the tours are narrated and offer water sports and a host of activities.

Stopovers ports are along the Broadwater, and the ride is smooth and calm. The only wild thing about it is the party.

TALL SHIP, Marina Mirage, 74 Sea World Drive, Main Beach, ☎ (07) 5532-2444 or 0413-871-711, **W**: tallship.com.au. *Open daily 9–midnight. Price range AU $32–$229, partially* ♿.

Board the Australian Tall Ship *Sir Henry Morgan* and settle under flapping sails as you are whisked over the Broadwater to one of several destinations. Evade the pirate ships with a glass of champagne and search for gold on the beaches of McLaren's Landing Resort. Or just sail amongst the coves of the calm waters of the coast.

War Canoe Races on the Broadwater

Cycle the Beach
to Burleigh Heads

Scout the beach scene on this 30-mile roundtrip from Surfers Paradise to Burleigh Heads. It is an easy ride and most of the trek is made on a bike path just adjacent to the surf, so you will have a fantastic view all the way. This trip will take you through some of the older neighborhoods of the Gold Coast, past Millionaires Row, through sprawling parks, and around some formidable rock formations. The ride is flat and is more of a tour than a race, so you can plan a half a day for the round-trip tour. Or linger at a beach that appeals to you and make a full day of it. The only hassles will be the oblivious walkers who don't seem to want to share the pathway. But with the smell of the surf, warm sun, and beautiful sun worshipers packed on powder-white sands, how could you have any worries about a few obstacles? At either end of the tour, you can build up your tan, catch a few waves, or rest at a café. If you want more exercise, you can ride farther up to The Spit and ride through the dune park called Federation Walk, or hike the national park at the end of the bikeway in Burleigh Heads. The best time of day to jump into the saddle is early morning as the winds tend to pick up in the afternoon; if you get a headwind on the return trip your legs will get an excellent workout.

GETTING THERE:

By Car: The Gold Coast exits are a straight and direct 40-mile shot down the Pacific Highway or the M1. Turn off at the Smith Street or Southport/Nerang Road Exits and drive east unit you dead end at the Gold Coast Highway. Follow that to your desired destination.

By Train: Hop any of the express trains to the Gold Coast or Robina Station. Avoid the local train as it stops at all stations in between. You may board at Central, Roma Street, South Brisbane, or South Bank stations, then sit back and enjoy the scenery on the one-hour trip to the Nerang Station. From there you can catch the Trainlink service or hail a taxi to the surf.

By Bus: See page 134 for details.

PRACTICALITIES:

Firstly, your do not have to be a tri-athlete to do this ride; it is flat, easy to pedal with lots of stops along the way. Most hotels rent bikes or you can hire one at a shop in Cavill Mall. A few in the area include: **Rent A Bike** in Surfers Paradise, ☎ (07) 5531-5411; **Hire A Bike** in Labrador, ☎ (07) 5528-8227; **Bicycle World** in Southport, ☎ (07) 5591-5883; and **Broadbeach Cycle Centre** in Broadbeach, ☎ (07) 5539-0188. Take water, sunscreen, a helmet, and your swimmers. If you are an avid cyclist, purchase a copy of *Bob's Bike Book* at the City Council, ☎ (07) 5581-6000 or (07) 5582-8211; or from a local bike shop. It will outline biking trails in the area, when/how to utilize the trains in combination with your rides, and regional riding conditions. The local government also has a *Gold Coast Cycling Guide* that provides a few very good maps, local laws, instructions on interpreting road/bike signs, and bike club contacts. Although you will be in a metropolitan area with plenty of phone booths, packing a mobile phone is a good idea.

FOOD AND DRINK:

There are heaps of cafés, fast food outlets, fine restaurants, and fish & chip stands along the ride. The majority of the eateries are clustered at Cavill Avenue, The Oasis Shopping Center in Broadbeach, and in Burleigh Heads.

TOUR DE GOLD COAST:

Circled numbers correspond to numbers on the map.

You have several kick-off points for this bike trek. If you are renting, you can start from the rental place and improvise on this point-by-point tour. You can also drive to one end and just start pedaling. If you want a longer ride, you can extend the tour on the northern end of the path up to The Spit or up into Paradise Point and beyond. And if you don't like any of my suggestions, hop a train and go to a remote location and explore. Just take a map and water. If you do extend up to the seaway Spit, refer to the map for that added section and follow Seaworld Drive left onto MacArthur Parade. Follow this until it turns into Main Beach Parade, and finally on The Esplanade with the bike path. It is perfectly safe on the roadway up there, but due to the dunes and scrub trees, it can be hot and lacking exciting scenery. There is plenty of parking at The Spit, showers, a good beach area, and a good café with tasty ice cream. If you decide on a ride farther north into Paradise Point, follow the Gold Coast Highway. There are bike paths most of the way that weave around the Broadwater thru Runaway Bay and into Paradise Point. It will add about five miles to the ride.

But for the majority of you all, we will start at the **Narrowneck Surf Life Saving Club** (SLSC) just north of Cavill Avenue in Surfers Paradise. I choose this over some of the other options because it has public toilets, showers, and a parking lot that usually has plenty of free parking available. To

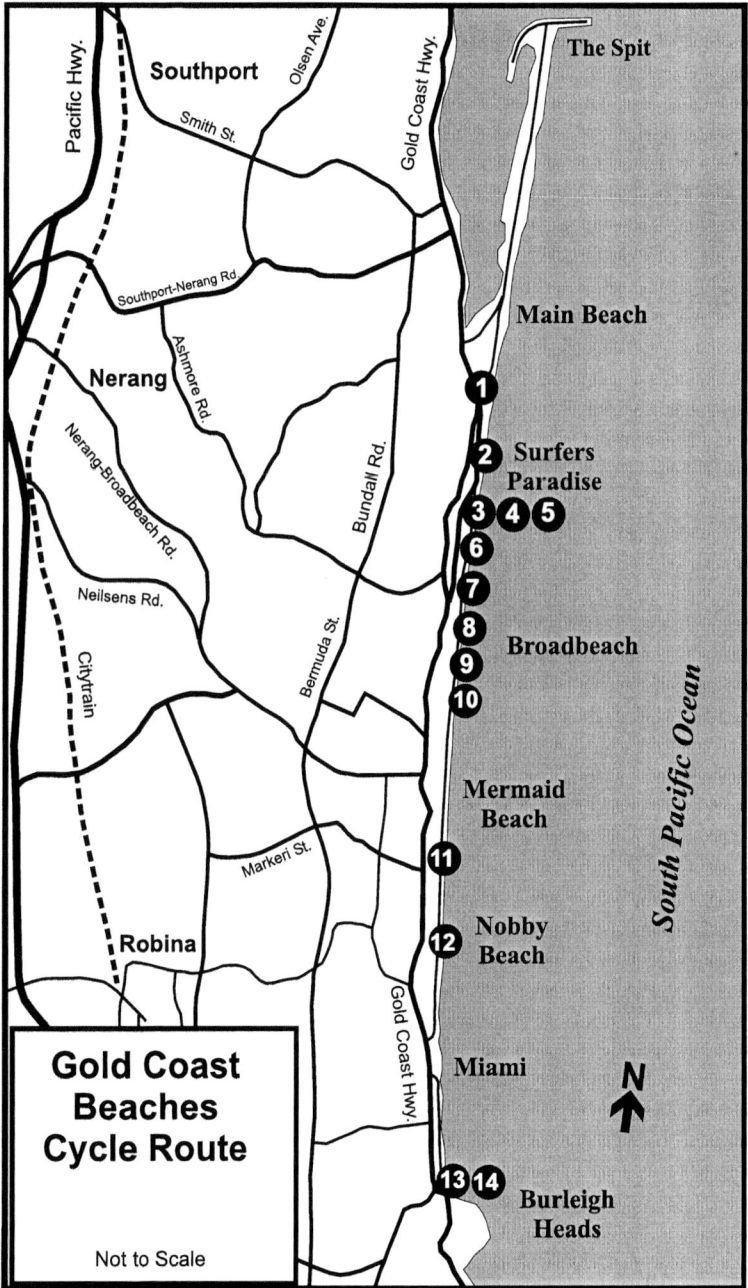

**Gold Coast
Beaches
Cycle Route**

Not to Scale

enhance the trip, I have included some commentary of the neighbor-hoods and local insights provided by my good mate Rollo. He is a fair dinkum Australian Queenslander who knows the area and has surfed this neck of the beach for decades. Take your time and enjoy the ride mates.

As you slip on your helmet your senses will be heightened to the sound of the waves pounding the beach, the smell of the sea spray, and the sights of beautiful bodies soaking in the Australian sun. Every day is a good day for a bike ride, and only the headwinds and baking rays will be a worry. Start your trek at the **North Narrowneck SLSC Station 38 ❶**. To the left of the parking lot (facing the beach) is one of the best views of the South Pacific in Surfers Paradise. If you haven't enjoyed the panorama of the surfers riding the waves, breach the dunes and give it a quick look before you start. Then ride into the shade of the bike path and head south towards Surfers Paradise. As you roll past the exercise stations and water fountains along the way, check out the newly-groomed park between the bike path and the beach. The council has renovated the area and made a pleasant transition from roadway to sea grass dunes with a well-mani-cured lawn. On your right will be the **Chateau Beachside Hotel ❷** (at Elkhorn Avenue). This is a favorite spot for food bargain seekers and those trying to vanquish a late night hangover with an all-you-can-eat buffet breakfast. Only a few minutes and you will enter Surfers Paradise central marked by hobbit-like huts that are the public toilets. At this point there are signs painted on the blacktop indicating right-of-way guidelines. Just into Surfers Paradise you will see Suncoast Rentals across the street. There you can rent mini dune buggies that are equipped for the road. They are funky two-seaters great to get around quickly and cheaply, but not partic-ularly safe. As you near Cavill Mall, look for King Arthur's Table Restaurant, and the fast food joints of McDonald's and Hungry Jack's.

On your way back, save some room for a beauty of an ice cream at New Zealand Natural ice creamery, and try the Spotty Dog or Cookies & Cream. At **Cavill Mall ❸** you can delight in the aluminum surfboards stuck in the sidewalk, and the giant clock that counted down the beginning of the new millennium. In the center of the plaza near the beach is a great spot to take a tourist photo under the aluminum banner of "Surfers Paradise." Be wary of the crowded path at this point due to the increased activity at the main entrance to the beach. One word of warning now, peo-ple simply do not move out of the way. And pedestrians have the right of way, so be wary and overly polite. Just past the mall on the left is a strange set of Maui-looking abstract sandstone sculptures. **The Elements ❹** are worth a look and maybe another photo. At that point near the beach you can rent surfboards or check out the local icon—Al's Beach Service. Rollo said that this sun-baked old gent has been renting beach chairs, umbrel-las, boogey boards, and offering free fresh air & clean water for decades. He looks like he's been in the sun since birth.

Next view to the left and on the beach is the beach volleyball court for anyone wanting to show some athletic prowess. Near the path here is the triangular monument that commemorates the service men/women with the common Aussie phrase—"Lest We Forget." But a mighty impressive bronze statue is just ahead in the middle of the path at Trickett Street. **Peter John Lacey** ❺ was a famous local lifesaver; the life-sized bronze statue is of him running into the surf with rescue gear being dragged behind. At this section the path splits. Take either route as they rejoin in 20 yards. Here the road and sidewalk narrow. I recommend using the road, but be very careful of cars and buses coming from behind. Next big attraction is the construction site of the world's tallest residential tower right across from the Watermark Hotel. The **Q1** ❻, **W**: qtallesttower.com, on Clifford Street will be a monolith over 1,057-feet tall, with 80 storeys, 527 apartments, and a 400-person observation deck that will look out onto the surf and hinterland.

If you chose to remain on the sidewalk, now is a good time to get off and ride the road as the path gets very bumpy. Straight ahead, as you approach **Aquarius Hotel** ❼, bear right and glide down a gentle grade. At the next roundabout, bear left onto Old Burleigh Road. Keep your eyes and ears open here as it is a bit busy on the road. About a half a mile on Old Burleigh Road, you will be entering Broadbeach. This is where many of the original Gold Coasters live, and it is loaded with quaint units and cottages. It is undergoing major renovations and a bit of a facelift. You will find some neat shops and cafés in this area if you want to have a wander.

At First Avenue, bear left and after one block you can continue along the beach road and pick up Broadbeach Boulevard. As soon as you see the park, follow the roadway past **Dr.Geoffry Cornish Walk Park** ❽ on the left and stop for a peek across the water onto the skyline of Coolangatta and Tweed Heads. The ride will once again be peaceful, with both the road and the parks opening up for a good view. The scene changes again with small bungalows being the preferred living space. Many are buildings just waiting for the wrecking ball to be replaced with multi-story rental units. A bit along the roadway on the right is a cute little art gallery called the **Royal Queensland Art Society**. You can take art lessons or just check out the local talent there.

Past the Broadbeach SLSC jump the curb and get back onto the bike path at **Neilsen Family Park** ❾. This is where the weekend markets are held on the first and third Sunday of the month. It is a great place to take a break, sit on a picnic bench, and watch the surfers. Just across the street from the SLSC is **The Oasis Shopping Centre** ❿. If you fancy, lock the bikes up and do a bit of shopping in the area or have a light meal at one of the cafés. Next landmark is the Kurrawa SLSC on the left, then the path opens up into rolling parklands. The wind from the beach is reduced here by a row of casuarinas trees. These hearty evergreens have distinctive needles or leaves and are resistant to salty sea spray. Appearing to have braided green horsetails as leaves, the "needles" are actually an extension of the branch with the leaf sprouting at the very tip. Now you will enter a land of giggling children, exercise stations along the path, wide-open spaces good for cricket, and sandy playgrounds under bright blue sails. You will pass by Stella Maris Catholic Church on the right and then enter the street at Hedges Avenue.

As you enter this area, half of the road is closed to allow for cyclists to have a worry-free ride. This is an interesting neighborhood termed **Millionaires Row ❶**. There are some impressive homes lining the beach line; even the old fibro-shacks (fiberboard) are worth at least three million. The value is actually in the beachfront land. Now even though you can't see the ocean at this point, it is a nice stretch of bike path and good for gawking at the houses. Next up is Mermaid Beach and more parklands and the sea views start again. At **Nobby Beach** you can stop at the convenience store for a drink or continue until you are confronted by **The Knob ❷**. I'm not sure that is the correct name, but that's what I call it. It is a huge brown boulder that jutes out into the water and blocks the path. If the tide is low you can walk on the beach around it or take the vertical steps to heaven and soak in the grand view up and down the coast. But we will be diverting around it on the street side.

After passing the families pushing strollers (this is a favorite for family getaways), turn right at Hythe Street. Go a block and you will come to the Gold Coast Highway. Before you get to the stoplight, turn left onto the sidewalk and stay behind the green protective fence. It is only a short ride to Kelly Avenue, and at the Tandori Place Indian Restaurant make a quick left until you dead end into Ocean Beach Tourist Park and **Mick Schamburg Park**. You will see a pub on your right with lots of young people soaking in beer and sun. Here on The Esplanade the views really open up and you will have a choice to stop at the North Burleigh SLSC or trek on to the final destination. Passing through Rotary Park (home to the Burleigh markets) you must pay attention as the bike path separates from the pedestrian footpath. A short distance farther and you will reach Burleigh Heads. It gets very busy here. Watch for the kids as you pedal through the park, and lock up the bike for a swim and some lunch. You can continue on to the **Burleigh Heads National Park ❸** to end the ride. From that point, walk along the pathway and stroll until you reach Tallebudgera Creek. On top of Big Burleigh (at the park near Hill Haven Resort and at the entrance to the park) get the camera out and set it on panoramic view. It is a stunning vista looking back onto Surfers Paradise.

My suggestion at this point is to go to the Burleigh Heads SLSC, change into your swimsuit, and have a swim. After soaking and catching some rays it is a good idea to eat. I have lots of favorites in this area and you can wander around the shops for a café that appeals to you or try the sophisticated **Mermaids** (you will be within feet of the crashing waves), **Oskars** (right above Mermaids and you can look down onto the beach and have a more far-reaching view), or if you want to try my mate's favorite spot do try **The Burleigh Beach Hut ❹**. Famous for their low-fat burger, mingle with the true locals and soak in the atmosphere. One insider secret—order the baked potato. It's not on the menu and it is fantastic. Save some energy for the ride home, and just backtrack until you reach Surfers Paradise.

Couran Cove Island Resort

This half-day or full-day trip to an award-winning and environmentally friendly resort on South Stradbroke Island is a great place to escape. Only 30 minutes from Surfers Paradise, it will invigorate your body and soul. Great for kids, singles and couples looking for a natural retreat near the ocean, it has as much or as little in the way of activities as you wish. This is a classy getaway and well worth an overnight stay. I would not recommend it for those who just want to chill out as there is jut too much to do and see on the island. Some of the Olympic athletes from Australia hang out there, and lots of people go out to enjoy the pampering spas and sports facilities. But if you just want a look around, you can try one of the island escape tours for a daytrip.

GETTING THERE:

Use the directions to the Gold Coast; the departure terminal is at 247 Bayview Street in Runaway Bay. From there, just sit back and enjoy the short trip across the Broadwater to the resort.

PRACTICALITIES:

Generally casual clothes, beachwear, sunscreen, shorts, and golf-style shirts are the norm. You should take a pair of long pants and a business casual set of clothing for dinners. It's not a bad idea to pack an extra towel and maybe a light jacket for evenings.

FOOD AND DRINK:

There are several food packages available, or you can wing it with four restaurants, numerous cafés and bars to choose from.

LOCAL ATTRACTION:

COURAN COVE ISLAND RESORT, 247 Bayview Street, PO Box 224, Runaway Bay, OLD 4216, ☎ (07) 5597-9000 or (07) 3854-3000, **W**: couran.com, E-mail: enquiry@couran-cove.com.au. *Open daily. Prices start* *at AU $55/$30 and run up to around AU $900. Guided tours, self-guided tours. Gift shops. Cafés and restaurants. Special events.* &.

When you make your reservations, you will receive a map of the island retreat's offerings. Since you will want to explore at your own leisure, I have simply listed the options available to you with a bit of commentary along the way. You will be greeted at the Arrival Hall at the Inner Marina. From there you can wander the walkways near the waterfront villas and scout out the duck pond or continue out to the calm **Water Sports** beach on the Broadwater. An alternative is to walk across **Spa Island** and check into the **Community Activities Centre** and book a game or two. Continue through the exotic **Livingston Rainforest** and hike out to the **Surf Club** on the ocean-side of the island. Oh, you can hop a ride if you want to save your energy for sports later. With over 14 miles of isolated beaches, you can have a wander on your own or share the beauty with a mate.

For the ambitious there is an **Adventure Ropes Course**, rock climbing, running track, tennis courts, an Olympic-style gymnasium, and bikes to hire. For the more relaxed sportsperson try lawn bowls, put a hook in the water, putting around the greens, or fly a kite—really. Now if you want to tone it down even more then explore the **Spa and Total Living Centre** for a rubdown or relax and enjoy the four restaurants. Family fun can be found at the **Aboriginal Heritage Centre** or just drop the munchkins off at the **Play Ground** or **Kid's Camp**. For the water lover stop in at the **Water Sports** hut and grab a catamaran cruiser or jet ski. I prefer one of the relaxing pools on the grounds. For eats you can rough it and get some grub at the **Wilderness General Store** or try the famous seafood dishes at the **Oceanman Surf Club** on the dunes, or sample nibbles at the **Poolside Café**, or maybe sip a cool drink at the **Boardwalk Bar**, but do try to sample the food at **The Restaurant** by the marina. And yes, there is plenty of shopping to do out there too.

The Natural Arch

This 30-minute drive into the Coast's hinterland will transport you into a dense rainforest. My mate Shaun introduced this wonder to me; and the first time you step into this wonderland, I expect you will experience the same thrill. Witness a roaring avalanche of water pouring from Cave Creek into the cave once used as shelter by Aboriginal tribes and read the signposts that explain this natural phenomenon. The easy walking paths will accommodate most hikers, but is not wheelchair accessible. For a real treat, wander up the mountain at dusk, following the path with a flashlight, to witness the phosphorescent glow-worms hanging from the ceiling of the cavern.

GETTING THERE:

By Car: The best way to access this natural wonder is by car. Follow the directions to the Gold Coast from Brisbane and exit at Nerang. Continue on the Nerang–Tamborine Road to Cave Creek Road and watch for signs to the arch. It's about a 1-1/2-hour drive from the city and 40-minutes from Surfers Paradise.

By Bus: There are bus tours to/from the Natural Arch. Check out the listings in the beginning of this section for names and numbers of the operators.

PRACTICALITIES:

Even if it is hot on the Coast, take a jacket as it gets quite cool amongst the giant strangling figs, goannas, bandicoots, lorikeets, and wallabies. The paths are easily walked and running shoes or hiking boots are best. If it is wet or has rained, avoid brushing against the bush as there may be a few leeches waiting for a feast. This is an easy walk with lots of steps and the loop is a little over a half-mile long. My recommendation is to walk the path in a clockwise direction as it is a bit easier climb out of the basin. If you want to call ahead to get maps and fast facts on the park, contact The Ranger on ☎ (07) 5533-5147.

FOOD AND DRINK:

There are several cafés along the way; my favorite is **The Natural Arch Café Restaurant** ($-$$), ☎ (07) 5533-6140. From Devonshire teas, homemade muffins, sandwiches, burgers (very delicious), steaks, seafood, and cool wine & beers, it is also known as Two Pines Café. An old gas pump is outside and the building was once the telephone exchange for the area. The food is great, there are good souvenirs to be found, but the best part is the spectacular view from the veranda dining area. There are barbeques at the park if you want to cook a few snags.

LOCAL ATTRACTIONS:

THE NATURAL ARCH/BRIDGE, Springbrook National Park, Cave Creek Road, Mudgeeraba, ☎ (07) 5533-5147. *Open Daily. Free. Self-guided tours. Toilets.*

Welcome to the hinterland, or as termed by Gold Coasters—"The Green Behind the Gold." It is a mountain range formed by the Mount Warning lava flow, a rarely advertised treat full of varied forest terrain and wondrous wildlife. This section of the national park is home to over 100 miles of bush walking trails and some of the oldest sections of rainforest in the world. It is a mix of humid rainforest, subtropical stands, fertile valleys, and crashing waterfalls. One of the spectacles that will make you stop and stare is the huge and eerie giant strangling figs. Your senses will also be opened up to the aromatic eucalypt trees that proliferate the area. The Aboriginal tribes lived on this remote plateau for over 6,000 years until they suddenly disappeared. The local myth is that the exodus is attributed to an ill omen like a comet or a rumbling from the now dormant volcano of Mount Warning.

The main attraction for this outing is the cave waterfalls, created by the drilling action of the water and boulders that broke through a deep cavern. One of 500 cascades in the park, it is a favorite of locals looking for a cool waterhole and a break from the coastline crowds. The .621-mile (1km) sealed hiking path takes you right amongst the strangling vines, and the first giant is cordoned off now to protect it from damage. If you lean over the railing you can see right up the inside of the tree. Formed by seedlings germinated on the treetop branches of the host tree, they slowly strangle their original landowner. Finally, the tree inside rots out and leaves a hollow tube. As you descend to the valley floor, you will spot some of the dozens species of parrots and a scrub turkey or two, and hear lots of scramblings in the bush. Bring a slow-speed film as the forest is an array of shadows in colors of green velvet, gray barks, and brown trunks. As you enter the cave you will feel the chill—heightened as you see the bats hanging from the creviced ceiling. The level of roar of the crashing waterfall will depend on recent rains, but it is majestic even on a slow day. At night the glowworms are the center of attention, and it is estimated that over 10,000 of them are hanging out. These fungus gnats weave sticky webs on the roof of the cave, luring small bugs by creating an internal bright blue glow. The amount of oxygen released in their digestive systems regulates the light in the cave. Please follow the rules in the cave as these critters are very sensitive to changes in their environment (no smoking).

Tamborine Mountain

Drive to this plateau some 1804 feet above the coastline and visit the flora and fauna sanctuary. Hike the national park trails, stop at one of the many craft stores on Gallery Walk, or just sit and have a cuppa overlooking the Gold Coast. Named "a place of yams" by the Aboriginal inhabitants and now being re-introduced as the Gold Coast Mountain Range, it is a popular tourist stop. Tamborine Mountain is about four miles long, two miles wide, and was created be a lava flow over 22 million years ago. Commercialization of the area began in the late 1800s, but was declared a Flora and Fauna Sanctuary in 1908. The locals are very independent and do not like being clumped in the same category as their Brisbanite and Gold Coaster cousins. It's almost a modern pioneer spirit flowing on top of that plateau, and the residents are loads of fun to chat with. I would suggest splitting your time between hiking amongst the waterfalls and browsing the shops of the hilltop towns. You will find natural wonders in the national parks and some good gifts hidden on the shelves of the unique stores. The hill is dotted with B&Bs, cottages, craft stalls, and lush gardens.

There are three main settlements on the top of the mountain. They are North Tamborine, Mount Tamborine, and Eagle Heights. I try to avoid the market days on the first, second, and last Sunday of the month as it is mobbed with tourists. It's much better to explore at your leisure during the weekdays. The trail at Witches Falls is a short hop from the main street of Tamborine, and you should have the park to yourself for most of the hike. Almost all the local people I have met insist that you stay up on one of the western peaks at the mountaintop and watch a sunset. With the ocean-laden air and cooling thermals rising up the slopes, it is indeed fantastic as the sun lights up the heavy sky.

GETTING THERE:

By Car: The best way to access this area is by car. Follow the directions to the Gold Coast from Brisbane and get off the M1 at Exit 57 Oxenford (Dream World). Continue on Tamborine–Oxenford Road until it turns into Macdonnell Road and park anywhere along Gallery Walk. It is about 50 minutes from Brisbane and 35 minutes from Surfers Paradise.

By Bus: Bus service is available on weekdays from the Beenleigh

Railway Station, Helensvale Station, and from the Gold Coast. **Tamborine Trolley Tours,** ☎ (07) 5545-2782 or **W**: tamborinetrolley.com.au, has passes from AU $10 and tours from AU $50. **Tamborine Tourist Shuttle,** ☎ (04) 1700-5184, has shuttle service available seven days a week.

By Train: Take the Gold Coast train to Beenleigh, Helensvale, or Gold Coast Stations. Then hop one of the buses to the mountaintop.

PRACTICALITIES:

The drive up the mount is a curving challenge, so I would strongly recommend you keep your headlights on so the few cars coming in the opposite direction will see you. The village walk is easy, but the hike down to Witches Falls will be a bit more strenuous. It is cooler up on the mountaintop, so do the layered thing. It would be advisable to take a bottle of water if you hike the falls. I have set this section out as two independent walking tours that should easily take half a day each. Please keep in mind that some of the stores and shop owners will change over time, but the major landmarks will remain static. The very enthusiastic folks at the information center insisted that you plan to spend a night or two when you explore their neighborhood. If you have the time, enjoy the hospitality, wood fires, fine foods, and feather beds.

For a glimpse at the area, go to the **Tamborine Mountain Getabout Promotions** site at **W**: tourismtamborine.com.au, ☎ (07) 5545-1161; the council's site at **W**: tamborinemtncc.org.au, ☎ (07) 5545-0944; or visit the information center at the entrance to the village.

FOOD AND DRINK:

Good food and plenty of places for a glass of wine can be found up on the summit. Most eateries are casual cafés, but you can find both fine dining and cheap eats up on Tamborine Mountain. The local scoop for food (recommended by several shop keepers) includes but is definitely not limited to **Sam's Chilli Den** ($-$$), ☎ (07) 5545-3666, at 3B Main Street, North Tamborine for a mix of Mexican and Thai. **Chef Jacques** ($$-$$$), ☎ (07) 5545-1499, at 21 Southport Avenue in Eagle Heights has fine dining with awards to match its food. For something different and for those who want to catch the magnificent sunsets, try the **Ozen Dining Room** ($$-$$$) for Japanese fusion treats served at the Witches Falls Cottages, ☎ (07) 5545-4411, in North Tamborine.

LOCAL ATTRACTIONS:

Circled numbers correspond to numbers on the map.

Once you exit the Pacific Highway (M1) turn left at the first roundabout, right at the second one, and follow RT 95 and signs to Tamborine Mountain. You will be entering a new type of terrain, so open your windows, turn off the radio, and soak it all in. During your 16-mile drive the car windows will be filled with deep gorges, the air will be laden with fra-

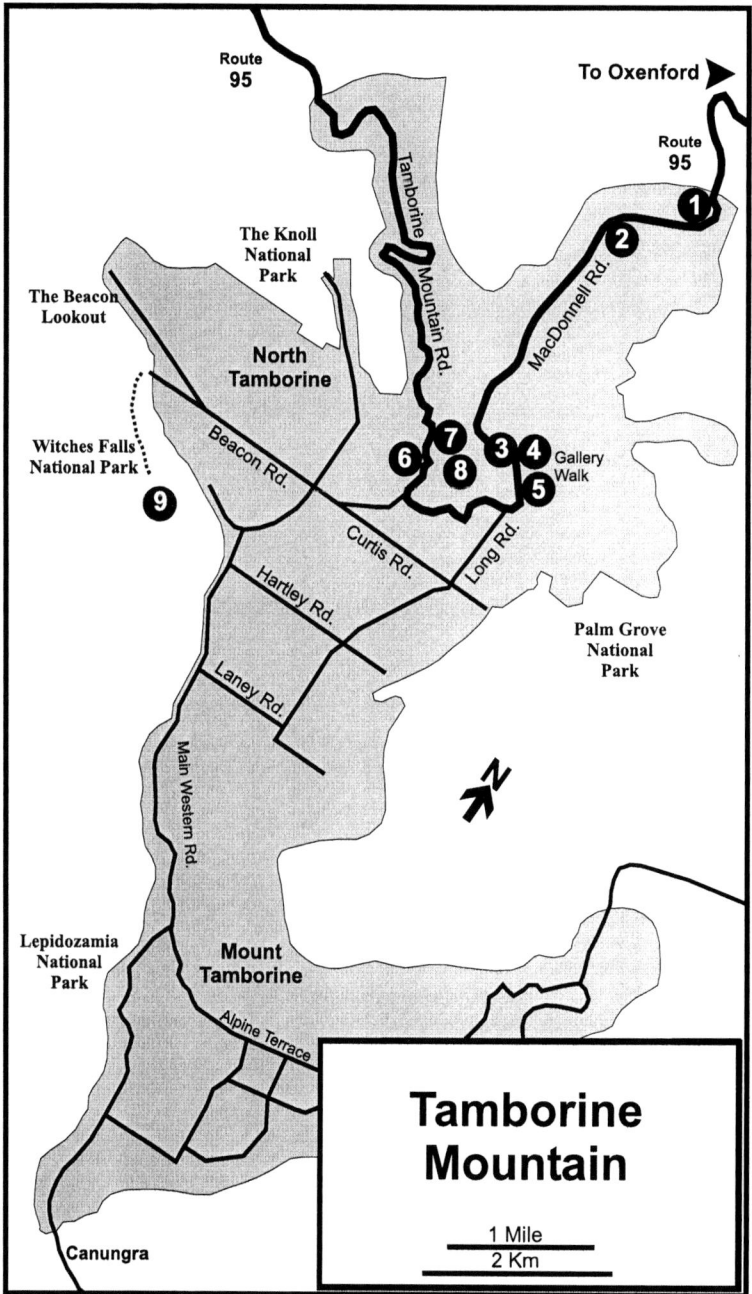

Route 95

To Oxenford

Route 95

1

2

The Knoll National Park

The Beacon Lookout

Tamborine Mountain Rd.

MacDonnell Rd.

North Tamborine

Witches Falls National Park

9

Beacon Rd.

6 7 3 4

8 5 Gallery Walk

Curtis Rd.

Long Rd.

Hartley Rd.

Palm Grove National Park

Laney Rd.

N

Main Western Rd.

Lepidozamia National Park

Mount Tamborine

Alpine Terrace

Tamborine Mountain

1 Mile

2 Km

Canungra

grant bushland smells, and you will hear nothing but ever-present wildlife songs. Look for the kangaroo crossing signs, the bear eating a hamburger at the Hungry Bear Café, roadside vegetable stands, multiple wineries, antique stores, and horse farms. After you pass the Fire Danger Billboard, that indicates the level of fire hazards, don't be alarmed if you see a smoky fire near the roadway or notice lots of charred trees and shrubs. It is customary to burn-off the excess bush to avoid large bushfires. The trees and most of the foliage do survive the heat. In fact, many Australian trees need the heat to crack their seed shells for germination. Even before you reach the summit, make a stop at the nut house that's nine miles (14 kilometers) from the highway.

THE NUT SHED ❶, 1459 Tamborine/Oxenford Road, Wongawallen, ☎ (07) 5545-1799. *Open daily 10–5:30. Free to all who love macadamia nuts. Self-guided tours. Gift shop. Café.* ⴷ.

Boasting and roasting the freshest plantation macadamia nuts, it has vacuum-packed nuts to please any whim—from raw, roasted, hickory, honey, garlic, and even wasabi-flavored.

INFORMATION KIOSK ❷, 17 kilometers (11 miles) on Macdonnell Road in Eagle Heights.

This is number 10 of the 11 "You Are Here" maps that have the locations of businesses, attractions, and towns in the immediate vicinity. The kiosk also has a map of all the wineries in the area.

*TAMBORNE MOUNTAIN TOURISM ASSOCIATION KIOSK ❸, 10 Macdonnell Road, Eagle Heights, ☎ (07) 5545-1161, **W**: tourismtamborine .com.au. *Open daily 10–5:30. Gift shop.* ⴷ.

Grab a few leaflets that detail the Gallery Walk shops and scan the information that maps-out the hiking trails in the parks. The staff is extremely helpful and there is even a "QUINTOUCH" touch-screen computer that can answer any other queries. The center has additional books for sale that provide details of the rich history of the mountain. If you want to check out the listing of all the shops in the area before you mount the mount, look at **W**: tamborinemtncc.org.au/tourist craft shops.htm

THE AUSTRALIAN ARTS CAFÉ or WATTLE BRAE ❹, 10 Macdonnell Road, Eagle Heights, ☎ (07) 5545-4484. *Open Wed.–Mon. 10–5:30. Gift shop. Café.* ⴷ.

This is a cool place to start your browsing, and a fanciful spot to photograph the plastered car, stalking statues, a movie prop shop, and odd structures. It has good coffee too.

At the next roundabout, at the Fig Tree, you want to exit onto Gallery Walk and find a parking spot. From this point you can browse to your hearts content. Here are a few of the goodies to look for:

*GALLERY WALK ❺, Eagle Heights, QLD. *Most shops open daily 10–5:30, some cafés and restaurants open until late. Guided tours, self-guided tours. Gift shops and cafés. Special events. Partially &.*

Like a mountaintop peddler's village, this street is loaded with woodworking stores, Aussie-made clothing, pottery, porcelain dolls, art galleries, cookoo clock nest (enter through the face of the clock), crafts, crystals, and heaps of eateries.

Some of my favorites spots on this street include: **The Crafters Gallery** for beautiful woodcrafts and a strange gift item called a gumnut. **Roseleigh Cottage** has gifts I've never seen anywhere else, and the kite shaped like a colorful sailing ship is a great gift idea. **Ballard House Art Gallery** is a mini-mansion tucked behind a pea gravel driveway with a great array of local (high-end) art. **The Country Café** that looks like a mix between a wood cabin and Queenslander with two spires and green tin roof. **The Pioneer Homestead**, **W:** pioneerhomestead.com, has a show every day at 11 o'clock, and for AU \$12.50/\$9.50 you can participate in the cow milking, cross-cut sawing, sheep shearing, bush songs, Dinky-Di Dunny races, and optional tours of the area.

Other unadvertised attractions in the area that are worthy of a stop include: the ***Mt. Tamborine Wildlife Sanctuary ❻** at Thunderbird Park on Tamborine Mountain Road, ☎ (07) 5545-3625 or **W:** cedarcreeklodges.com.au/wildlife.htm. For AU \$8.80/\$5.50 you can hand feed the huge 5-foot kangaroos, spot the blue-winged kookaburras, and meet all the other natives. But avoid the bird-eating spider. Do not miss the internationally acclaimed ***Tamborine Mountain Distillery ❼**, ☎ (07) 5545-3452 or **W:** home.austarnet.com.au/tmdistillery, and sample the schnapps, fine liqueurs, and spirited fruits and chocolates all created from a small pot still and carefully sealed in hand-painted bottles. The **Fingertip Gallery & Coffee Plantation ❽**, ☎ (07) 5545-3856, at 66 Alpine terrace in Mt. Tamborine is a family-owned coffee plantation where you can see how the beans are harvested, dried, and roasted—not to mention sample the freshest cup of java you will ever taste. A favorite way to safely sample the local wines and tour the numerous wineries is to take one of the wine tasting bus trips that cost less than AU \$100. Several operators offer this half-day or full-day trip. Look to **Cork'n'Fork** at ☎ (07) 5543-6585, (04) 0714-4396 or **W:** corknfork.com.au; or **Winery Escape Tours**, ☎ (07) 3299-5075, (04) 1965-7907 or **W:** wineryescapetours.com.au

If you are up for a walk, drive to the roundabout at Eagle Heights Road, cross over onto Long Road, turn right onto Hartley Road, left onto Main Western Road, and park at the lot designated for Witches Falls National Park.

*WITCHES FALLS NATIONAL PARK ❾, Tamborine Mountain National Park, Main Western Road, ☎ (07) 5545-1161, **W:** qldwalking.org.au/walks/tam bor.html. *Open daily dawn to dark. Free. Self-guided tours. BBQs. Not ♿.*

If you want the complete lowdown on the hiking paths in the area, visit the **Tamborine Mountains Natural History Association** at Doughty Park in North Tamborine. Call ahead on ☎ (07) 5545-3200 or stop in and check out the local lore from 10–3 daily. A stream that drops over the side of the mountain and pools into a rocky crevice 326 feet below forms the falls. The name originated years ago when the local cattle ranchers would be herding their cows after dark and many would claim to have seen strange apparitions that stalked them up the hill. The weird thing is that many tourists have claimed the same sensations if they waited until dusk to reach the summit. But I have never seen anything strange—well, maybe. It was first opened in 1908 and is Queensland's first national park. The park is 324 acres of pure fascination and changing views as you descend to the falls.

You will first notice the formation off on the western horizon called the Great Dividing Range. Far below the land is a patchwork of horse farms and planted fields. The track meanders through open forests and winds sideways along the cliff side into thick eucalypt stands. The tree trunks are often bleached white and look eerie as the sun washes through the thick canopy. The path is wide, but you may encounter fallen vines or branches on the trail. I usually carry a walking stick to brush aside the spider webs and just in case of an uncommon encounter with a brown snake. Several areas have swampy lagoons, and you will end the journey at the boardwalk platform about a mile into the gorge. It is cool at the bottom, but you will be wet with perspiration when you reach the top of this moderately easy hike.

O'Reiley's Rainforest Retreat

This is a dizzying drive 3,000 feet above sea level with many of the blind turns being one-lane only. To top it off, cattle roam onto the roads at some places, so be prepared to stop. I swore that I would not drive it again after the first 3-hour roundtrip, but it is just too beautiful to be missed. If you have the time and some extra change, stay at the guest-house, as it is a luxury mountain lodge with fantastic activities and guided hikes planned all week. The only problem with this trip is the number of tourists who will be sharing a small hilltop with you. But if you are into serious hiking, this is a grand spot and you can hike for days on the well-marked paths. The lodge is a masterpiece; at least take a look around and browse the library. The gardens that surround the lodge are magnificent, and the views are the best around. The caretakers have incorporated several short hikes around the lodge and even a suspended bridge that takes you to an eagles-nest lookout.

For over 85 years this resort has been greeting visitors and introducing them to the World Heritage Lamington National Park. You can ask for a walking map or arrange to join one of the nature walking tours that are guided by one of their botanist/guides. But if you want a quick treat, walk the gardens, feed the crimson lorikeets, and soak in the oxygen-rich air.

GETTING THERE:

By Car: From **Brisbane**, take the Pacific Highway (M1) southbound to the Beenleigh turnoff, follow signs for Beaudesert (Beenleigh/Beaudesert) Road, after a half-hour you will reach a town called Tamborine Village, bear right (not towards Mt. Tamborine). At Mundoolan Connection Road turn left and drive to Canungra, turn right into Kidston Street, go past the Canungra Hotel and follow Lamington National Park Road for about 5 miles and it is on the right. Just follow the signs to continue up to the Alpaca Farm and O'Reilly's.

By Car: From **Surfers Paradise**, take the Pacific Highway southbound to Nerang, follow the Beaudesert–Nerang Road until you see a large sign for O'Reilly's and turn right, go to Canungra, turn left at Kidston Street, follow the Lamington national Park Road for 5 miles and it's on your right. Just follow the signs to continue up to the Alpaca Farm and O'Reilly's. See the map for directions to Binna Burra.

By Bus: There are several tour buses that visit O'Reilly's and Binna Burra including the **Mountain Coach Company**, ☎ (07) 5524-4249. One organization that does a nice job in covering almost all of the attractions listed is **Australian Day Tours,** ☎ 1-300-436, (07) 3236-4155, or **W**: day-tours.com.au. For AU $66/$35 they will pick you up either in Brisbane or Surfers Paradise and give you the grand tour of Canungra, the winery, the Alpaca Farm, and O'Reilly's.

PRACTICALITIES:

It is much cooler up on the mountain, so a sweater or light jacket is recommended for this trip. Even if you are walking under the rainforest canopies, it is always good to wear a hat and even a bit of sunscreen. Comfy walking shoes and shorts are acceptable, but take a pair of long pants just in case it's cooler than you expect. One strong suggestion—if you hike up there make sure you keep to the paths. If you want to explore beyond the marked trails, check with a ranger and be prepared with the appropriate navigation equipment and supplies. You can buy seed or take a bit with you if you want to feed the birds. You will be amazed at the great photo-ops you will get as the blue/yellow/red birds cover you. I would not start this trip in late afternoon as the roads zigzag all over the place and some of the roads run through the middle of cow paddocks. Plus you will want to sample some of the local wines. Plan a full day for this trip and take your time.

FOOD AND DRINK:

Food is served at the resort, and you can get quick foods at the café. Fine dining is also available at the lodge's restaurant. Many people pack a lunch. If the place is mobbed, you can travel a bit down the mountain to the Alpaca Farm, the winery, or in Canungra for a quieter meal.

LOCAL ATTRACTIONS:

Circled numbers correspond to numbers on the map.

*CANUNGRA INFORMATION CENTRE ❶, 12-14 Kidston Street, Canungra, ☎ (07) 5543-5156, E-mail: canungrainformation@bigpond.com. *Open Sun.–Fri. 9:30–4, Sat. 9:30–2.* ♿.

First stop and a good place to get last-minute directions up the mountain. Helpful volunteers will provide hints for the drive, recommend their favorite store in town, and offer brochures for your adventures.

DOWNTOWN CANUNGRA ❷, Canungra.

The name of the town is based on three Aboriginal words that express the description of the area—*Kununguh* (a type of iron-wood tree that boomerangs were made from), *Coonoongra* (small grey owl or good

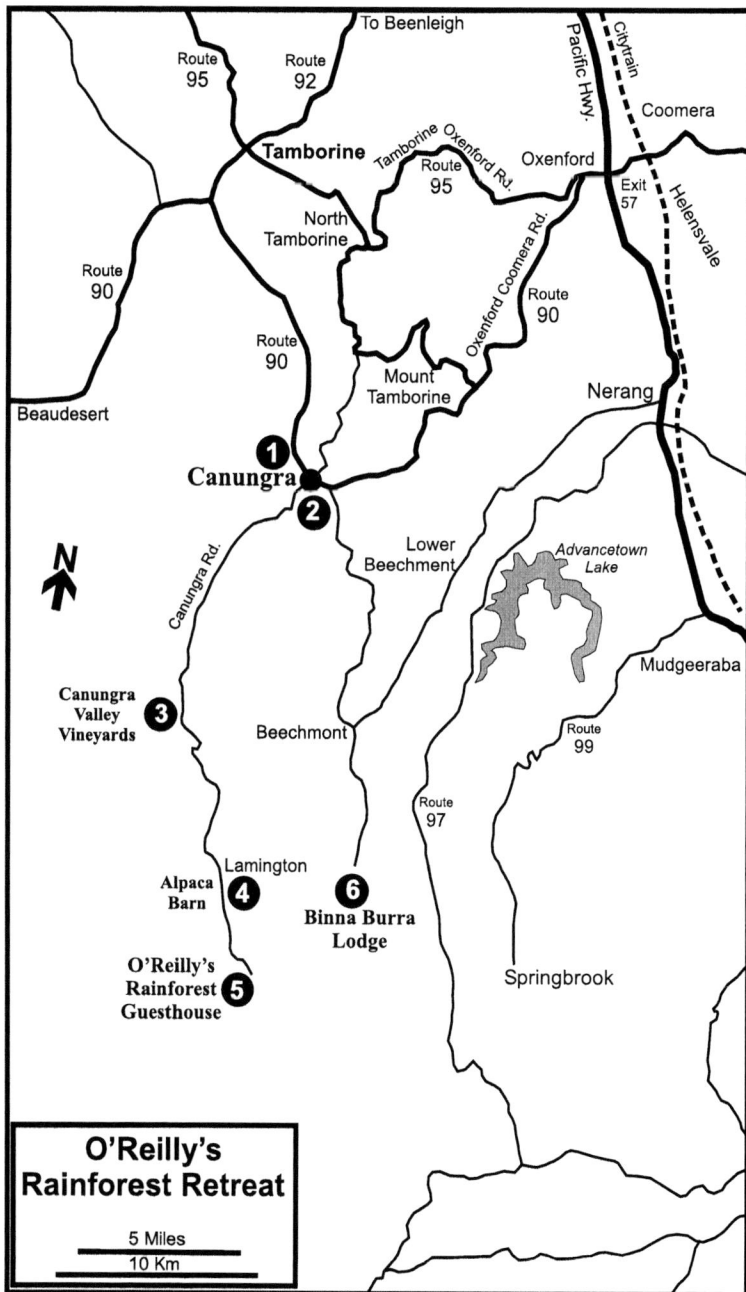

O'Reilly's Rainforest Retreat

place with lots of game), and *Gunungai* (the flat part of a plain). It has a great market day if you are lucky to pass through on the first Sunday of each month; the rodeo in June is a blast, and the Canungra Pie shop has some tasty Australian treats. Make sure you check your petrol levels here before heading up the mountain.

***CANUNGRA VALLEY VINEYARDS ❸**, Lamington National Park Road, Canungra, ☎ (07) 5543-4011, **W**: canungravineyards.com.au. *Open daily 10–5, tours at 11. Wine tasting for AU $3 (free if you buy a bottle). Guided tours, self-guided tours. Gift shop. Café. Special events. ♿.*

I love this vineyard even when I'm not in the mood for wine. The 1858 Queenlsand mansion is surrounded by seven acres of Chambourcin and Semillon vines and is picture perfect. It has a resident ghost, a former owner who died before the home was relocated to this site. As the story goes, the young woman had a photo taken of her daughter—alone. Before the negative was developed, the woman died. A short time after she passed away, the photograph was developed and her image strangely appeared in the picture. Now the staff regularly notices that items in the house have been moved after locking up, pictures knocked off walls, and coffee pots smashed. But the real draw card, other than the American award-winning wines, is the Platypus Pool right behind the house. A family of six is regularly seen basking along the creek, especially if you get there early morning and late afternoon.

***ROSEMOUNT ALPACA STUD BARN & RAINFOREST GALLERY ❹**, Lamington National Park Road, Canungra, ☎ (07) 5544-0107, E-mail: georgerose@bigpond.com.au. *Open daily 9–5. Free. Guided tours, self-guided tours. Gift shop. Café. Special events. Partially ♿.*

This will be one of the most spectacular views of the trip, and that includes the great sights from the top of the mountain. It looks like the opening scene from *Bonanza* as the view pans out to an unobstructed view of the valley below. To add to the rustic feel is the flock of black, brown, and white alpacas lazily munching on grass. Sip a cup of coffee in the Rainforest Gallery as you switch your gaze from fine art works to Mother Nature's canvas outside. On your way out you may want to check out the shop full of alpaca hats, capes, jackets, socks, and teddy bears. You can also buy up to 22 different colors of raw wools and fleeces ready to spin.

***O'REILLY'S RAINFOREST GUESTHOUSE ❺**, Lamington National Park Road, O'Reilly's Plateau, ☎ (07) 5544-0644, **W**: oreillys.com.au. *Open daily. Free. Overnight accommodations start at AU $70/night to AU $220/night. Guided tours, self-guided tours. Gift shop. Café and restaurant. Special events and lectures. ♿.*

Family owned and operated since 1926, the resort is surrounded by nearly 50,000 acres of rainforest. You will share this isolated peak with bright blue/red Crimson Rosellas, huge king parrots, yellow/black thief called the Bower Bird (he will steal anything blue), Red-necked Pademelons, and enough frogs to keep any princess kissing 24 hours a day. But when you walk into the rainforest paths you will be amazed by the massive Antarctic Beeches, the moss-covered Brush Box Trees, the gnarly Strangling Figs, and the most-deadly Stinging Tree. This dangerous specimen is well off the pathway and is pointed out to you by a sign. This bugger can knock you out, and horrible pain from the needles injected from the leaves will last for up to two years. Cross the suspended bridge, through the canopy tops, and climb about 3-storeys straight up to a platform at **Tree Top Lookout.** If you dare and are in good physical condition, organize a guide and hike to the famous site of the 1937 Brisbane-to-Sydney **Stinson Plane Wreck** deep in the shrouded rainforest. The hiking paths that originate at O'Reilly's extend for short 15-minute walks around the botanical gardens to over 12 miles along the New South Wales Border Ranges. Refresh at Gran O'Reilly's for lunch, and I think the gift shop has some great presents.

BINNA BURRA MOUNTAIN LODGE ❻, Beechmont, ☎ (07) 5533-3622, **W**: binnaburralodge.com.au. *Open daily. Free, overnight accommodations available. Guided tours, self-guided tours, workshops. Gift shop. Café and restaurant. Special events.* ♿.

An alternative to O'Reilly's is Binna Burra, a resort deep in the Green Mountains of Lamington National Park. With nearly 100 miles of walking tracks that pass by 2,000-year-old Beech Trees, across pure streams and into wind-carved caves, you have the choice of 15 different paths to follow. The local ornithologist can point out the Rufous Scrub Bird, the Paradise Rifle Bird, as well as the creepy crawlers underfoot. The lodge limits the availability of clocks, phones, radios, or televisions to help you forget the hectic life below. They also offer interpretive walks, bird-watching expeditions, abseiling, and gourmet cooking lessons.

Trip 32
Gold Coast Hinterlands

Springbrook Mountain, Enter the Volcano

This is a gentler drive than to O'Reilly's, but no less fantastic. Taking about two hours for a roundtrip, you may still want to stay overnight at one of the B&Bs right near the gorge. This area is a remnant of a huge volcano where you actually descend into the ancient core to view waterfalls cascading into the valley. The sights of the 2,000-year-old Antarctic beech trees and waterfalls are incredible, but beware of leeches. If you observe one of the many maps of the area, you will get a good perspective of how enormous this hole in the ground is. After the 50-mile wide Mt. Warning Volcano blew its top and the basalt lava poured over the area, subsequent rhyolite flows and erosion created the sheer cliffs at Springbrook.

Springbrook National Park has five different forest types within its boundaries, and all are within walking distances of this tour. You will enter the mysterious closed canopies of the Subtropical Rainforest filled with strangling figs and rocks covered in velvet-like mosses. The two distinctive Eucalypt forests include the white-trunked Flooded Gums and prehistoric Tree Ferns in the first group. The Blue Mountain Ash and New England Blackbutt hover over colorful heath plants in the second. Both Warm and Cool Temperate Rainforests are present in the confines of the park, too. The higher regions have the Brush Box and Coachwoods with plenty of lichen to spare. The lower and warmer areas are jungle-like and have my little friends the leeches.

GETTING THERE:

By Car: the M1 or Pacific Highway is the best and most direct way to access this area. From both Brisbane and Surfers Paradise, take the highway south towards Coolangatta. It will be about a 90-minute drive from Brisbane and a 45-minute commute from Surfers Paradise. After passing the "shark teeth" sound barriers at Nerang you will exit the highway at Exit #79—also called Mudgeeraba/Robina Exit. Follow signs to Mudgeeraba-Springbrook until you come to a "T" junction. Turn right onto the Link

Highway, bear left at the next roundabout towards Springbrook. Driving on the Gold Coast–Springbrook Road (#99) you will follow signs to Springbrook.

By Bus: Some tour operators do offer customized trips, and you can organize a trip into the Mudgerabba area and select your specific destinations. Check with Wot's On to book a bus tour. Also try **Bushwacker Ecotours**, ☎ (07) 5525-7237 or **W**: bushwacker-ecotours.com.au, starting around AU $50/$30; **Scenic Hinterland Day Tours**, ☎ (07) 5545-2030 or **W**: imagetech.com.au/hinter.tour.

PRACTICALITIES:

It will be cool up on the plateau even in the summer months. Take layered clothing, closed-toe/comfortable walking shoes, and a hat. If it has rained or is damp, plan on leeches so take some salt or matches to get them off easily and pack some antiseptic. It really is not that big of a deal, but some people have a thing for the little suckers (me included). For free maps and National Park information call The Ranger at ☎ (07) 5533-5147 between 8–4. It is a good hike from Brisbane, and you will be a bit weary after hiking the trails, so you may want to think of lodging up on the mountain. My favorite B&B is the peaceful and regal **Springbrook Mountain Manor Resort**, ☎ (07) 5533-5344 or **W**: maguires.com/spring.com, for about AU $200/night. You will be treated like a baron/baroness in courtly surroundings. **The Mouses House**, ☎ (07) 5533-5192 or **W**: mouseshouse.com.au, for around AU $325/2-night minimum; and the **Mountain Lodge/Cabins**, ☎ (07) 5533-5366, for less than AU $70/person/night are two other popular accommodations. But there are heaps of B&Bs tucked in around the basin.

FOOD AND DRINK:

Mostly fine dining up on the mountain, and many of the best meals are to be had at the B&Bs. But a very good spot is **Canyon View Café & Guesthouse**, ☎ (07) 5533-5120, $$, only yards away from the cliff side at the Canyon Lookout. A good $ eatery is **Kimba's Kitchen**, ☎ (07) 5533-5335, and make sure you say g'day to Feral Cheryl The Chook. She is the pet rooster who cleans up scraps around the place. There is one winery in the vicinity, the **Springbrook Mountain Winery**, ☎ (07) 5533-5300, worth buying a bottle just for the interesting labels—and the wine is pretty good, too.

LOCAL ATTRACTIONS:

Circled numbers correspond to numbers on the map.

The best way to introduce this venture into this *Lost Continent* atmosphere is to simply provide an overview of what you might expect on your journey into the depths of Gondwanaland. See the mud map that is provided with the roads that rim the giant cavern and markings that indicate the walking path entrances. An overview and descriptions of each of the four circuits is presented to help you make your choice of paths to

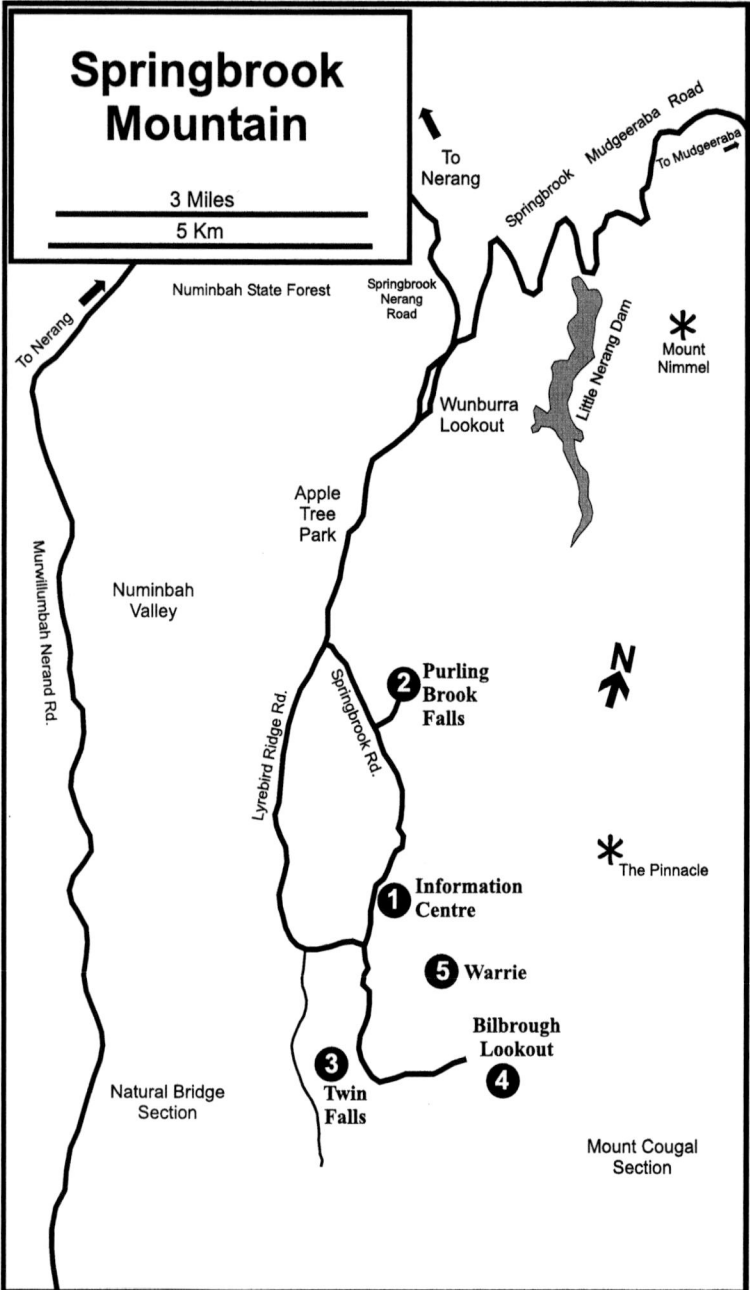

Springbrook Mountain

3 Miles

5 Km

To Nerang

Springbrook Mudgeeraba Road

To Mudgeeraba

Numinbah State Forest

Springbrook Nerang Road

To Nerang

Mount Nimmel

Little Nerang Dam

Wunburra Lookout

Apple Tree Park

Munwillumbah Nerand Rd.

Numinbah Valley

Lyrebird Ridge Rd.

Springbrook Rd.

② Purling Brook Falls

N

The Pinnacle

① Information Centre

⑤ Warrie

Bilbrough Lookout

④

Natural Bridge Section

③ Twin Falls

Mount Cougal Section

hike.

This former home to the largest volcano in the southern hemisphere is surrounded by 7,299 acres of rainforest and sheer cliffs with rainbow-laden, cascading waterfalls. You can still see the outline that was once the rim of the volcano from the three viewing platforms—Wunburra, Canyon, and Best of All Lookouts. Expect to fill your nostrils with primeval earthy scents, feel warm thermals rushing over your skin as they search for escape, and a surround-sound track of screeching, singing and laughing birds. Your path will cut through house-sized boulders, under crashing vertical streams up to 918-feet high, and around lichen-covered trees that would dwarf most giant sequoias. Animals are shy, but you might catch a fleeting glimpse of a rainforest wallaby, a pademelon, brushtail possum, sugar glider, koalas, goannas, skinks, carpet pythons, and more than 100 species of birds. The trip will allow you to swim in the herb-scented pools (though very cool) or just soak in the oxygen-rich environment. The following options will give you a choice of treks with varying degrees of length, sights, and difficulty.

*INFORMATION CENTRE ❶, 2873 Springbrook National Park, Springbrook, ☎ (07) 5533-5147. *Open Mon.–Fri. 8–4. Free information, mud maps, brochures.* ♿.

Though not usually staffed, the posted maps and free brochures will be a help to navigate the area. If you want a detailed history on the area, ask the Ranger about the local who wrote a detailed account. The book is only about AU $20, and it is a good read.

PURLING BROOK FALLS ❷, Forestry Road, Springbrook National Park, Springbrook. *Open daily. Free.*

This is a 2.5-mile (4km), 2–3 hour hike with many good views of the various waterfalls. Expect to see massive stands of eucalypt forests and a number of "downunder" views of the falls. This one has a great picnic area and is home to several cafés and shops.

TWIN FALLS ❸, Springbrook Road at the Tallanbana Picnic Grove, Springbrook. *Open daily. Free.*

Follow this 2.5-mile (4km) 1-1/2-to-2-hour path in a counter-clockwise direction to be able to read the signs describing the environment. This one is a favorite of my wife's. You get to walk under two waterfalls and see the largest one in the park. One section has a 3-story rock wall covered in moss that is weeping with moisture. Another part you must squeeze between boulders to gaze upon a black pool of water.

BILBROUGH LOOKOUT ❹, Springbrook Road at the Goomoolahra Picnic Grounds, Springbrook. *Open daily. Free.*

A 1.8-mile (3km), 2–hour hike with a pretty good incline. On a clear day you can view Byron Bay to the south and Moreton Island to the north.

WARRIE ❺, Springbrook Road at the Canyon Lookout, Springbrook. *Open daily. Free.*

For the ambitious and fit, this 10- 1/2 (17km), 5–6-hour journey is claimed to be the best of all. Warrie means "rushing water" and that's exactly what you will get. At the lowest point called Meeting of the Waters, all the canyon's streams join. Do not start this one in the afternoon.

Natural Bridge/Arch Cave View

Section V

Daytrips in

Southeast Queensland & Northern New South Wales

This corner of heaven includes border tours in the southeastern tip of Queensland and the northern-most part of New South Wales (NSW). The mix of water, mountains, and desert environments assures a very diverse set of trips—and most escapes are only 3–4 hours southeast of either Brisbane or Surfers Paradise.

The selected tours include climbing the largest inactive volcano in the Southern Hemisphere; taking a trip back to the 60s in the hippie town of Australia; catching the big one in the fishing town named edible shellfish by the Aboriginals; kayaking the waves over sharks, turtles, and mantas; whale watching from the most eastern point of Australia; riding out to the bushrangers' hideouts in the Outback; and tasting sugar right off the cane.

The trips offered in this section require some difficult driving over the Continental Divide, but the views are spectacular and the diversity of landscape will make it very enjoyable. To allow you to fully enjoy each area, I have laid out accommodation recommendations in four specific hubs. The most southern trip will be staged from Yamba, the second stop will be in Byron Bay, the last layover in NSW will be Uki, and the final tour of this section will be on a ranch in Warwick.

PRACTICALITIES:
An interesting web site that covers both the Gold Coast and Northern NSW region is a tourist organization's page at **W**: aussiegateways.com.au, where you can book accommodations and check out the attractions. An internet spot specific to the area south of the Queensland border is **W**: bayweb.com.au

YAMBA TRIPS

This is the farthest south to be explored in this section, about 2–3 hours south of Brisbane and Surfers Paradise. I chose this area as it is recorded as having the best climate in the world by Stanford University and CSIRO. But more importantly, it is not mentioned in any travel guides that I have seen; and this type of fishing village, with its old-time feeling, will not be around forever. This tiny town was called "edible shellfish" by the original inhabitants; after a day or two in the area, you will understand why. You can spend between two and four days to adequately cover Yamba and its neighbors—Maclean & Iluka. But if surfing and fishing are priorities, you may want to extend that amount of time. This place really feels good—even if you have teenagers tagging along, there is plenty to do.

Yamba was originally inhabited by Bundjalung, Yaegi, Baryulgil, and Gumbaynggirr Aboriginal tribes (for 60,000 years) until Matthew Flinders landed in 1799. Rich in cedar, farmland, and fishing, the area began to boom in the late 1800s. Then tourism took hold in the early 1900s and the town never looked back. Luckily, the local councils have controlled growth and the village is a comfortable yet fun place to hang out.

General information can be found at the **Ferry Park Tourist Complex** on the Pacific Highway near Maclean, ☎ (02) 6645-4121; or from **Clarence River Tourism**, ☎ (02) 6642-4677 or **W**: clarencetourism.com, at the Information Center on Yamba Street. Three other good websites to check out before you go is the Yamba site at **W**: yambansw.com.au, a tour magazine site on **W**: tropicalnsw.com.au, and the **NSW National Parks & Wildlife Service** site at **W**: npws.nsw.gov.au, or call them for maps at ☎ (02) 6641-1520.

SPECIAL EVENTS:

January has the Surf Carnival, July has the Family Fishing Classic, September is the Cane Harvest Festival, and October brings the famous Seafood Expo. This a small, but really festive affair. The Yamba Markets are every 4th Sunday and Iluka's are every 1st Sunday. In Maclean the Highland Gathering is at Easter, the Power Boat Regatta is in August, and the Community Markets are held in the CBD parking lot every 2nd Saturday of the month. The clans gather in town at 11am on the Sunday following Easter to have their tartans blessed in celebration of the lifting of the "Act of Proscription of 1747." This British law forbids the Scots from wearing their colors, speaking Gaelic, or playing the bagpipes.

GETTING THERE:

The southbound journey from the Gold Coast is a drive that will take you less than two hours, and into sugar cane country. From Brisbane, plan on 2–3 hours and about a 186-mile ride (depending on your choice of routes). The Pacific Highway (M1) is the main route into New South Wales, but you can take one of the inland roads for a scenic, if not more time con-suming trip. All the stops in this section split off from the Pacific Highway and are less than 15 minutes from the M1.

By Car: From Brisbane, hop on the Pacific Highway through Nerang, past the Coolangatta Airport, across the New South Wales border, past Byron Bay and into Yamba. It is a straight line to the Yamba Exit. Then fol-low signs along Yamba Road to the river's edge and the Blue Dolphin Holiday Resort. Please note that a new highway has opened and is called the **Pacific Highway** and the older route is called **Tweed Valley Way** or the **Old Pacific Highway**. Friends that pass through the area claim that the old route is much better with the truck traffic being diverted onto the new highway. The old road is also more scenic.

By Bus: Most of the main bus companies service the area, but stop only in Maclean or out on the Pacific Highway near Maclean. Contact **Greyhound Pioneer,** ☎ 13-20-30 or **W**: greyhound.com.au; and **Coachtrans**, ☎ 13-12-30 or **W**: coachtrans.com.au, for details on service to the area. **King Brothers Bus Service** seems to be the local transport provider; you can reach them on ☎ (02) 6646-2019.

By Train: The nearest train station is in Grafton about 45 minutes south of Yamba and costs about AU $56 for a one-way ticket. From there you would have to catch a bus north. Contact **Country Link Trains,** ☎ 13-22-32, E-mail: gfnctc@tpg.com.au, or **W**: countrylink.nsw.gov.au. This method will take you lots of time and is a bit inconvenient.

By Plane: You can fly into Grafton City Airport about 45-minutes south of Yamba and arrange for ground transport at the Yamba Airport Shuttle inside the airport.

ACCOMMODATION IN YAMBA:

There are lots of caravan parks for camping/cabins and many are right on the water. Hotels, motels, and pubs abound too. To get a complete list-ing of the accommodations available, see the local web site at **W**: yam bansw.com.au. I will offer two very classy spots to try out. The first one changed my mind about campgrounds and the clientele I had been accus-tomed to at trailer parks. Here in Australia, they are normally clean, bright-ly lit, tidy, and very middle-class. The **Blue Dolphin** is a 4-1/2-star resort that would be 5-star if it had valet parking. You will be bunked in a new-look-ing cabin right on the Clarence River, and the resort offers a full range of boating rentals, a heated pool, recreation and video rooms for kids, fish-ing jetty, free movies, and a café. The place is clean, friendly, quiet, and a bargain.

A second choice is the brand new and luxurious **Angourie Rainforest Resort**. The villas are nestled between the dunes of the South Pacific and the lush rainforests of NSW. It is a higher-end resort, but with what I have planned, you may want some pampering at the end of the day. Run by the same family that manages the Blue Dolphin, the staff is well trained and the surroundings are well apportioned.

THE BLUE DOLPHIN HOLIDAY RESORT, Yamba Road/PO Box 21, Yamba, NSW 2464, ☎ (02) 6646-2194, **W**: bluedolphin.com.au, E-mail: bludolp@nor.com.au. Camp sites from AU $28–$53/daily or $168–$371/weekly, cabins from AU $49–95/daily or $294–$665/weekly, units from AU $57–130/daily or AU $342–910/weekly, 2-bedroom villas from AU $78–$170/daily or AU $468–1190/weekly, deluxe villas from AU $120–210/daily or $720–1470/weekly.

Located in the midst of all the activities slated for Yamba, it is set up in a way that provides quiet room to stretch out. The 15-acre, eco-friendly resort offers 93 cabins, 53 cabins with master bathrooms and spas, 170 powered campsites, and two-bedroom deluxe villas. Each cabin is surrounded by tropical foliage, many face the Clarence River, and most have full kitchens and a television. The gated resort has a giant community entertainment building, two pools (one heated) with waterslides and fountains, tennis courts, a cool colorful castle for kids to play in, and video games galore. For the fisherperson, there is a fleet of boats to choose from, or just fish off the boat pier that is guarded by a flock of 20 pelicans. There are also jet skis, canoes, and paddleboats for hire. If it sounds like I am selling this place, I am—it is the best park I ever visited, though some say it gets a bit busy in high season.

ANGOURIE RAINFOREST RESORT, 166 Angourie Road, Angourie, NSW 2464, ☎ (02) 6646-8600, **W**: angourieresort.com.au, E-mail: enquiry@angourieresrt.com.au. 1-bedroom villas start at AU $120–200/daily or $720–1,400/weekly, 1-bedroom deluxe villas start at AU $130–$220/daily or $780–1,540/weekly, 2-bedroom villas start at AU $140–$240/daily or $840–1,680/weekly, 2-bedroom deluxe villas start at AU $150–$270/daily or $900–$1,890/weekly.

This new resort, still in the Yamba area, is tucked right next to a 1,482-acre rainforest and smack in front of the Angourie Beach. It is an upscale oasis with a knack for accommodating children and adults alike. Quiet and secluded, with lagoons, waterslides, and spas spread throughout the complex makes it a perfect hideaway. Cocktails, lunch, and dinners are served overlooking the lagoon with sounds of the ocean surf—at no extra charge. If you need even more solitude, walk into the Yuragir National Park right next door and get lost in time or take a dip in The Blue Pool (a freshwater pool that was once a rock quarry).

Some other accommodations in the area include: **Yamba Ocean View Inn** on Clarence Street, ☎ (02) 6646-9411; **Moby Dick Resort** on Yamba Road, ☎ (02) 6646-2196; **Inca Sun Motel** at the corner of Wooli & Claude Streets, ☎ (02) 6646-2144; **Oyster Shores Motel** on Yamba Road, ☎ (02) 6646-1122; **Yamba Beach Motel** on Queen Street, ☎ (02) 6646-2150; **East S Calypso Holiday Park** on Harbour Street, ☎ (02) 6646-2468; and **Yamba Waters Caravan Park** on Golding Street, ☎ (02) 6646-2930.

PRACTICALITIES:

Plan on a wide mix of activities and weather variations, but normally casual wear with one set of dress-casual clothes should do the trick. Since the area is known for its rivers, parks, and beaches bring along swimming gear, sun protection, good walking shoes, and definitely bug spray—the mosquitoes are big and hungry.

FOOD AND DRINK:

Straight from the ocean or rivers, the prawns, oysters, and fish are out of this world. Even the fish & chips taste better here. Like most small seaside towns, you have a wide choice of fast foods (no chains though), pub meals and a few really good restaurants. My top choice is Gorman's with a fantastic seafood platter with an old-timer playing the piano. Most resorts have facilities for cooking-up your daily catch and The Blue Dolphin is top notch with cleaning facilities and BBQs right near your cabin. The following is just a sample for you to choose from.

Gorman's Restaurant at Yamba Bay, ☎ (02) 6646-2025. You can't go to Yamba without trying this place and one of their famous Seafood Platters. Straight from the trawlers onto your plate, this is some of the best seafood you will find anywhere. The dining room is decorated with hanging plants and the food is served in giant clamshells. Located right off Whiting Beach, you can also watch the boats bring in more goodies. $$

Restaurant Castalia on Clarence Street, ☎ (02) 6646-1155. Another seafood eatery that is featured in the annual seafood festival. Open for breakfast too. $$

Neptune's Seafood Café, 11 Yamba Street, ☎ (02) 6646-2260. I think it has the best fish & chips in town, and you could live on the pile of chips they serve—for a week. $

Two Fat Men on Yamba Street, ☎ (02) 6646-2619. A small and fun café for quick and tasty food. $

Coldstream Italian Restaurant & Pizza on Coldstream Street, ☎ (02) 6646-8259. Pasta and pizzas are the best bets, but they do have seafood dishes and the Chili Garlic Prawns are tasty. $

Pacific Hotel Pub on Pilot Street overlooking the beaches, ☎ (02) 6646-2466. The local hangout and a true pub with pub vittles. $

Blue Dolphin Café on Yamba Road, ☎ (02) 6646-2194. Good home-cooked-style food in a diner setting. $

Yamba Bowls Club at 44 Wooli Street, ☎ (02) 6646-2305. Choose the Riverboat Restaurant for outdoor buffet-style dining or enjoy the Dunes Coffee Shop for casual treats. $$

Yamba Shores Tavern & Pelican's Restaurant at 64 The Mainbrace, ☎ (02) 6646-8055. A-la-carte meals overlooking the water or bar food in the tavern section. $$

Trip 33
Yamba

River Exploration

Since this location is where several rivers meet the deep blue sea, it's best to get your sea legs right off the bat. You will be able to explore a section of the nearly 250-mile-long Clarence River to get a good overview of the history of the river, the surrounding towns, wildlife, and the friendly residents. The River Explorer II and Iluka Ferry provide cruise tours along the Clarence River and among the islands in the area. Both include a tour and a chance to discover some of the island treasures. The highlight of this trip is delving into the natural wonders of the Iluka Nature Reserve and the isolated Iluka Beach.

LOCAL ATTRACTIONS:
Circled numbers correspond to numbers on the map.

*RIVER EXPLORER II ❶, PO Box 135 Yamba, ☎ (02) 6642-3456, Email: great-timecruises@bigpond.com.au. *Open for bookings daily. Adults from AU $139 for 2 days. Guided tours, self-guided tours. Special events.* ♿.
This is a bit different, but to see all the stuff around Maclean and Yamba, this is the trip to take. On the two-day tour, you will be boarded in the town of Grafton (30–40 minutes south of Yamba) and begin the history lesson, games, food, and absolute fun aboard the *Explorer*. The captain is a hoot, and you can participate in trivia quizzes about Australia and the region as you cruise up the river system. If you decide to pass on the games, there are five videos that are archival renditions of the Clarence River and surrounds. The trip will take you from Grafton to Ulmarra for a stopover, tea and antiquing in the town where the mini-series "Fields of Fire" was filmed. Then back on board you trek up to Lawrence and land at Maclean for lunch and a tour of the Scottish highlights and Yamba's goodies. A sleepover in a local motel allows for a fresh start to the second day of Iluka forest treks, seafood tasting, prawn farm tours, and sugar mill expeditions. After picking up the resident Aboriginal elder, a tour of the local islands and the ancient sites of Aboriginal cultures will commence. The price includes all food, lodging, transfers, tours, and booby prize awarded to the winner of the onboard games. The boat is fully licensed, so you can enjoy a bottle of wine along the way. During school holidays (see up front section for dates), the River Explorer does sail from the Yamba Shores Tavern for shorter, but just as much fun, tours of the Yamba/Maclean area. But for both tours, call in advance to get a seat and

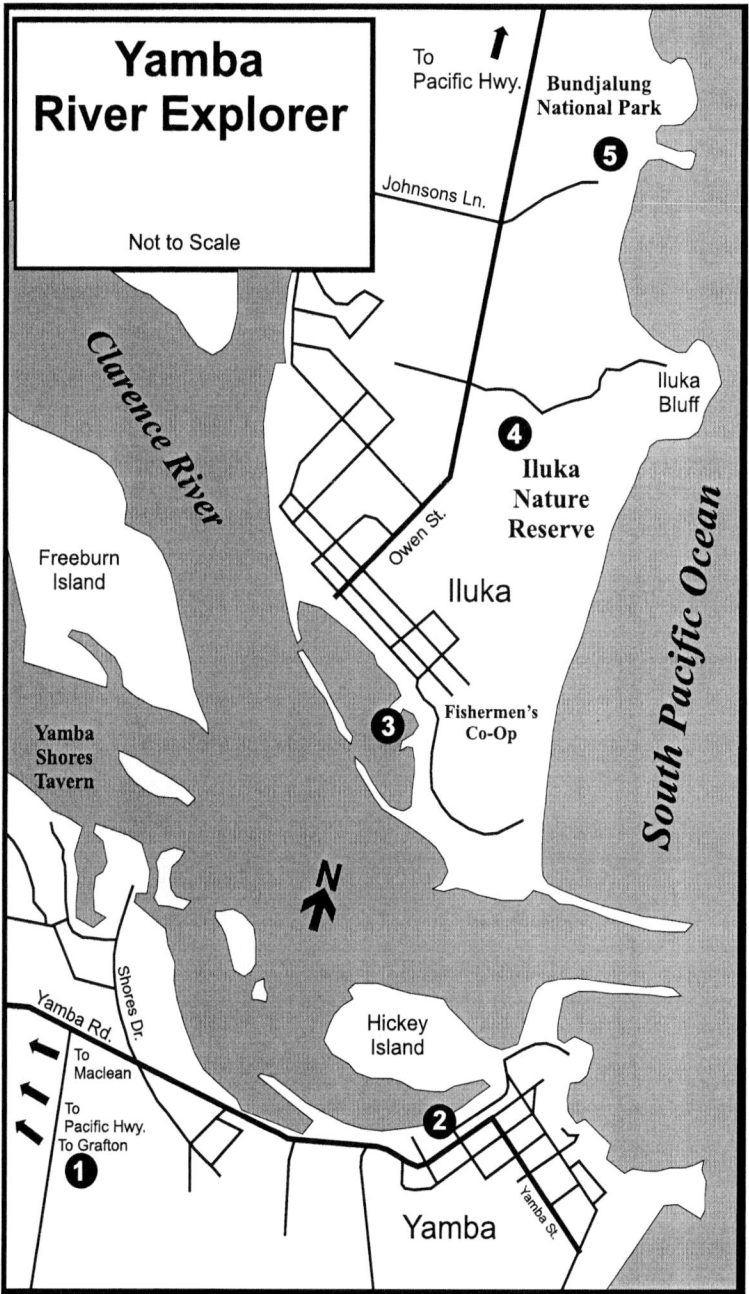

Yamba
River Explorer

Not to Scale

To Pacific Hwy.

Bundjalung National Park

❺

Johnsons Ln.

Clarence River

Iluka Bluff

❹

Iluka Nature Reserve

Freeburn Island

Owen St.

Iluka

South Pacific Ocean

Yamba Shores Tavern

Fishermen's Co-Op

❸

N

Shores Dr.

Yamba Rd.

To Maclean

To Pacific Hwy.
To Grafton

❶

Hickey Island

❷

Yamba St.

Yamba

ticket to the past.

CLARENCE RIVER FERRIES ❷, River Street at Ferry Wharf, Yamba, ☎ (02) 6646-6423 or (04) 0866-4556. *Ferry Timetable: Daily: 9:30, 11:00, 3:15, 4:45; return from Iluka: 8:45, 10:15, 2:30, 4:00. Closed Christmas. Adults AU $3.90 each way, children AU $1.95 each way.* **Harwood Island Cruise Schedule:** *Wed., Fri., and Sun. at 11:00–3:00 from Yamba or at 11:45–2:30 from Iluka. Adults: AU $16 (Yamba) or $14 (Iluka), children half price and seniors: $13/$11. Wednesday Night BBQ Cruise Schedule: Wed. between Dec. 26–Jan. 26, Yamba in Dec. from 4:45–7:00, Iluka in Dec. from 5:15–7:30 or Yamba in Jan. from 6:15–8:30, Iluka in Jan. from 6:45–9:00. Adults from AU $16, children half price.*

This is basically a ferry with extended services provided in the way of two different cruises. The ferry sails to Iluka, where you are basically on your own to hike into the parks and over to the beach. Maps of the reserve and descriptions of the pathways can be obtained at any of the visitor centers or by calling the **National Parks and Wildlife Service** at ☎ (02) 6642-0613. But if you prefer a catered affair, choose between the Harwood Island Cruise and the Wednesday Night BBQ Cruise.

The **Harwood Island Cruise** is a four-hour trip up the Clarence River, with the jolly captain on the horn narrating the cruise. After loading up between 45–150 passengers, he navigates along the Rock Walls, past the islands and up to the historic iron bridge. You will hear the interesting tidbits like the river was only navigated by vessels with 13′ draft and how the river traffic grew due to the increased New England wool industry, timber, fishing, and now tourism. He may even point out the graveyards of some of the shipwrecks. *Josephine* was a schooner that sunk off of Hickey Island in 1879, the *Marama* was a steam tug boat that sunk just off of Palmers Island in 1972, right off of Turners Beach the fishing boat *Nina Meg* was put to rest by a cyclone in 1917, and the skipper was killed in the 1979 swamping of *Sea Dreamer* just off the Yamba Bar (the keel is now displayed at the Story Hours Museum. Tea, sandwiches, and alcohol are served on the cruise, but the real treat is riding the currents that were once loaded with old riverboats and hearing the tales associated with them. During the Christmas holidays, a similar trip is offered along with an onboard BBQ taste treat.

FISHERMANS CO-OP ❸, River Street, Maclean, Queen Street, Iluka, Yamba Road, Yamba, ☎ (02) 6645-0955, **W**: crfc.com.au, E-mail: meverson@crfc.com.au. *The retail sites are open daily 9–5.*

The Clarence River Fishermen's Co-operative (CRFC) is one of the largest jointly-owned fishing organizations in New South Wales. Some 240 commercial fishers participate in the co-operative. Their sea and estuary-based fleets maintain initiatives based on the sustainable management of the wild fish resources. They embrace strict regulations of fishing times and locations, managing the by-catch (waste) returned to the waters, and promoting a clean/green environment. While attending the Seafood Expo, I was amazed at the complexity of the fishing operations handled by this co-operation. They are one of the major providers of fish to the Sydney Market and the auction house there (See the Darling Harbour Tour in The Sydney Section). The now-famous Yamba Prawn is a delicacy sought by many of the best seafood restaurants in Sydney, and they also handle a wide range of seafood including crabs, lobster, fish, octopus, and oysters. Visit one of their local retail sites and sample the fresh goodies. You will be delighted that they are doing their best to ensure their product remains available. If you are lucky enough to visit the area during the Seafood Expo, have a chat with the gang at the Co-op tent and learn even more (plus you will see the bounty of the sea unique to this area). Take a camera too, as the display of fish and shellfish is incredible. There are plans to open a full-blown tour program at the Queen Street docks. Call ahead to see if it is up and running.

*ILUKA NATURE RESERVE ❹, entrances at Hickey Street, Long Street, or from Clarence Head Caravan Park, Iluka, ☎ (02) 6642-0613 or (02) 6641-1500, **W**: npws.nsw.gov.au, ilukansw.com.au, or tropicalnsw.com.au. *Open daily, 24-hours a day. Free. Special events in October for kids. Partially* &.

It is only a short jaunt up from the Ferry Wharf and the Fisherman's Co-op to the entrance at the park, so it's best to eat and pick up a bottle of water before entering the largest shoreline rainforest in NSW. There are several walking paths cut amongst the 336 acres of chirping birds, with croaking frogs and fantastic varieties of vegetation. You will have stepped into a rare ecosystem that has the ability to survive a mixture of salt ocean winds, harsh soil, and former sand mining operations. Oh, and cyclones, fires, and off-road vehicles too! The **Rainforest Walk** is a straight 1-1/2-mile stroll to a car park near Iluka Bluff. It is an easy hike, and if you have the energy, you can ride a few waves at the far end at the **Bluff Beach**. The beaches there are patrolled during holidays. If you take the normal precautions, the water is safe. But take your time under the thick canopies of Tuckeroo and Banksia Trees near the sand dunes, soak in the coolness under the even taller Riberry and Broad-leaved Lilly Pilly Trees, and scope out the noisy crack whip bird hidden in the foliage. For the bird-lovers, two rare birds have taken refuge in this World Heritage forest—the white-eared monarch and the barred cuckoo shrike. But as warned in other areas of this book, avoid the Stinging Tree with its shiny leaves loaded with poisonous hairs and be aware of the possibilities of leeches and mosquitoes.

*BUNDJALUNG NATIONAL PARK ❺, entrance at Johnson's Lane and Iluka Road, Iluka, ☎ (02) 6627-0200 or (02) 6646-6134, **W**: npws.nsw.gov.au, ilukansw.com.au, or tropicalnsw.com.au. *Open daily, 24 hours a day. Free to walk in, cars AU $6/day pass.*

With over 43,000 acres and 24 miles of gorgeous beach line, this national park is a huge wonderland mix of inland waterways, thick forests, lagoons, cypress stand, wetlands, Aboriginal camps, and diverse flora and fauna specimens to gape at. It is so overwhelming that you could spend weeks amongst the varied environmental landscapes. The Parks Department allows for canoeing, surfing, fishing, camping, and hiking all along the parkland sections. The Esk, a coastal "wild river," is protected within the park's boundaries and it is a beautiful sight. Some 4WD beach access is permitted, but make sure to follow the guidelines set out by the rangers and pre-register.

Yamba Beach Scene

Fishing for Flathead

Hire a tinnie at the Blue Dolphin, chug around the Middle Wall sea break, and wet a line. If you're smart, check out the locals, drift near them, and you will be sure to catch a flathead for dinner. They taste like butter. By staying away from the seaway entrance, the river system is very safe and heaps of fun to explore on your own. One hint though—take mosquito spray and a cooler full of beer, water, or soft drinks. It can get hot out on the water and it takes about 20 minutes to get into port at most places. One neat thing that often occurs on this tour is when you are sitting still in the boat and gliding along with the current, you may be visited by the local pods of dolphin. As they feed, they will check you out by crisscrossing in front of the boat. If you're lucky, one will do a flip for you or come close enough to see them eye-to-eye. Even if you choose not to take the angler's approach, the wildlife and serenity of the waterways are very calming.

Oh, flathead is an ugly fish and it has a totally pancake-sized head with huge dorsal fins. It's greenish/brown and gets up to about 25 pounds. Right now the daily limit is 10–20 (depending on what variety you pull in) and the minimum size is a bit over a foot (33 centimeters).

GETTING THERE:

By Car/Boat: Drive to any of the parks, boat ramps, or wharves that rent boats or check out the Yellow Pages. I recommend taking one of the 10-foot aluminum fishing boats from The Blue Dolphin Resort. They reside on Yamba Road near town. Boat rentals start around AU $40 for two hours, $50 for a half a day, and around $90 for all day. Fuel and life vests are included.

PRACTICALITIES:

The water is fairly calm, but it can get choppy. Make sure the boat is equipped with life vests just in case of an emergency. The fishing license is usually included in the boat rental, but confirm that with the rental staff. A mobile phone is a good idea, but there are plenty of boats nearby and within shouting range. Try to get a boat with a canopy for shelter from the blazing sun or cooling rains. Wear clothes you don't care too much about and plan to get wet even on a calm, sunny day. Sunglasses, hat and sunscreen are a must. Sloppy shoes or flip-flops are a good idea; I wouldn't recommend going barefoot. Rods can be rented, bait can be bought everywhere (and each place has "insider tips" of what to use), and for a bait bucket just recycle a plastic milk jug by cutting the top off. You will need to take spare hooks and sinkers too as well as a good sharp knife. The river system is pretty easy to navigate, but grab one of the maps that indicate where certain fish can be found and you will be much better off. The maps will also provide the current fishing "bag limits," size requirements, and recommended bait. If you do run into trouble, the **Yamba Coast Guard** number is ☎ (02) 6646-6311.

A cool web site to check out before you launch your boat is the fisheries page on **W**: fisheries.nsw.gov.au., or contact the fisheries officers at ☎ 1-800-043-536.

FOOD AND DRINK:

I usually pack some easy-to-eat foods and even take a few sandwiches if the word is out that the fish are biting. My brother will not let me off the boat if we are catching fish, and you will not want to leave the waterways if you are landing fish either. There are fast food places near most of the docks in Yamba and Iluka, so don't panic if you don't take food along.

SUGGESTED TOUR:

Circled numbers correspond to numbers on the map.

After organizing the boat rental, hop aboard your tinnie and crank up the engine. Unless you have a boating license to operate larger craft, your maximum outboard size will be 9 horsepower, but that will be plenty for this body of water. The map provided indicates the hot spots for fish, the major land/river navigation points, and areas where I have spotted the dolphins. The river system is safe and relatively calm, but avoid the seaway entrance by Moriarties Wall and give the fishing boats plenty of leeway as they enter/exit that area. Travel into the several water systems to witness a different set of sights, sounds, and treasures. The rivers and estuaries include Coldstram River, Esk River, Sportmans Creek, Yamba Bay, Oyster Channel, Lake Wooloweyah, and the mighty Clarence River. If you are not into fishing, the trip can be very relaxing with interesting sights and plenty of bird watching spots. The fishing stocks include mullet, jewfish, blackfish, flathead, bream, mackerel, whiting, and the occasional crab. I think the best bait is squid and prawns, but you can try worms or yabbies. Good luck, and for good measure here are two alternatives for renting a boat for the trip: **Oyster Channel Boat Hire** at ☎ (02) 6646-0263 or **Yamba Marina,** ☎ (02) 6646-9245.

Blue Dolphin Marina and Fishing Pier ❶. Tucked right on the water and just off of Yamba Road is the wharf full of tinnies and fishing gear. Check in at the front desk and they will set you up with all the gear necessary. The gas station right next door has tackle, bait, and foods that will be perfect for the trip. Past the boom gate and straight back to the riverbank is the

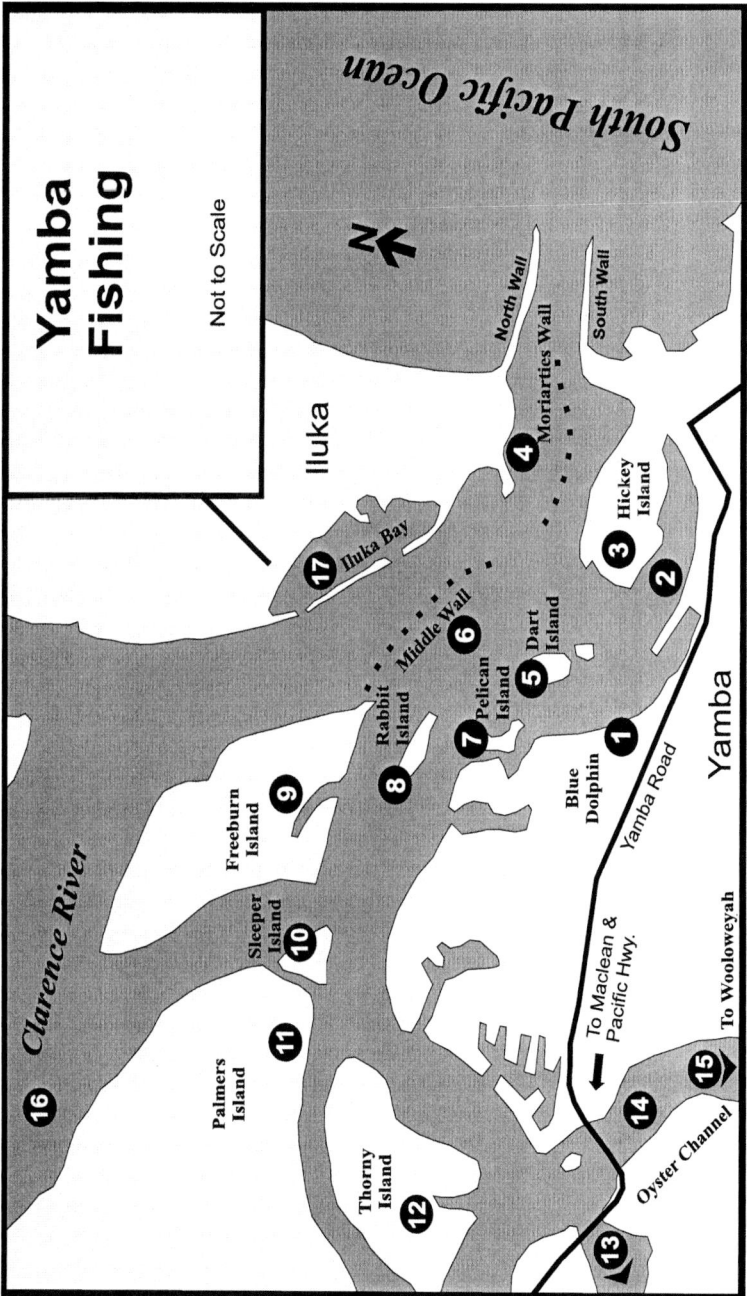

Yamba
Fishing

Not to Scale

South Pacific Ocean

Iluka

North Wall

South Wall

Moriarties Wall

4

Hickey Island

3

2

17 Iluka Bay

Middle Wall

6

Dart Island

5

Rabbit Island

Pelican Island

7

8

9

Freeburn Island

1

Blue Dolphin

Yamba Road

Yamba

Clarence River

Sleeper Island

10

11

Palmers Island

To Maclean & Pacific Hwy.

14

15

To Wooloweyah

16

Thorny Island

12

13

Oyster Channel

pier with the moored boats. At the wharf is a station to clean your fish and a big tree where you can tack your trophy flathead head next to all the other monsters. It is apparently a tradition to post your prized catch for all to see.

Yamba Bay ❷. Calm protected waters and home to the Marina Wharf. Several boat ramps and cafés can be seen from the water. Good spot for bream and very calm water to be found here.

Hickey Island ❸. Flathead and more calm waters found west of this outcrop. If you get tired of the water, there is a good walking track around this point. Flathead, whiting, and tailor are more prevalent on the side closest to the seaway.

Moriarties Wall ❹. Stay clear of this entranceway to the ocean as the currents and boat traffic make it a bit dangerous. The wall is adjacent to where many of the prawn boats and sports fishing boats exit into the South Pacific Ocean, and though they are cautious, their wakes may make your pop around like a top if you get too close.

Dart Island ❺. This is a small island in the middle of the main fishing channel. Most fish can be landed in this area; just watch for the gulls diving into the water for the best spot to drop your line.

Middle Wall ❻. This seems to be the favorite spot, but beware of losing hooks and tackle in the rocks. It is pretty deep here with dart, bream, and whiting schooling near the rocks. At high tide you can actually pick a spot where it is safe to cruise over top of the wall, but watch others do it first to make sure you will have clearance. The tidal pull is strong here and your will need to pay attention to the nearby rocks.

Pelican Island ❼. Flathead are plentiful in this shallow section of the water and between this spot. You can spot the fish on the bottom in many sections around the island, and it will probably be where you see your first flathead schools.

Rabbit Island ❽. Between this tiny island and the Middle Wall is where my brother Ron spotted the dolphins feeding. We found the best location to visit with the beautiful mammals is near the northeastern tip of this landmass.

Freeburn Island ❾. A large island shaped like a giant whale's tail. Home to flathead hideouts, and is the landmark that splits the Clarence River in two. If you bear to the left of the island, you will be heading towards Oyster Channel and the lake.

Sleeper Island ❿. Now you are heading into slower moving water where jewfish may start biting. The mangroves are a tempting choice to drop a line here; just make sure you don't get tangled on the spiky root systems of these natural filtration systems.

Palmers Island ⓫. This is a large island cut off from the mainland by a several channels. The Clarence River Resort is on the northern banks, where you can stop for a stroll or a refreshment on the banks of the Clarence River. The Wynyabbie House, right on the riverbank, is famous for its Devonshire teas and scones (with real cream and jam). Flathead can be found in the hook of water on the south-central section of the island waters.

Thorny Island ⑫. Now you are getting into the backwater, where the mosquitoes will be a bit fiercer. The estuary fishing is good, but it didn't seem too popular with the locals when I wandered back there.

Romiaka Channel ⑬. Right behind Thorny Island is a channel with flathead, but not much else up there other than being an neat and eerie waterway to explore.

Oyster Channel ⑭. Floating under the Oyster Channel Bridge, you will see the Oyster Cove Resort and Sports Centre on your left. This is a nice spot to walk around and plan your retirement days.

Lake Wooloweyah ⑮. Bream and flathead are found in these calm waters, but I don't think it is worth the journey back into this neck of the woods unless you just want a day out putting around the waterways.

Clarence River ⑯. The massive river flows into the Pacific Ocean, and the fishing is good along the banks of the seawalls and shallows of the islands. Cross over the Middle Wall to get into the main flow of the Clarence and motor against the current to moor and try you luck here. Some sizeable ships cruise these waters, but the scenery is magnificent. Plan to go up to Maclean and have a look around this small Scottish town.

Iluka Bay ⑰. Sheltered from the currents, and a nice spot to have a break and some food is the harbor area at Iluka Bay. The Fisherman's Co-op is located there, so you might get a tip or two on where the big one might be found. It is a good place to fish when the fish from the trawlers is being unloaded. If your luck is not running, you can purchase fish after 9 am—right off the docks.

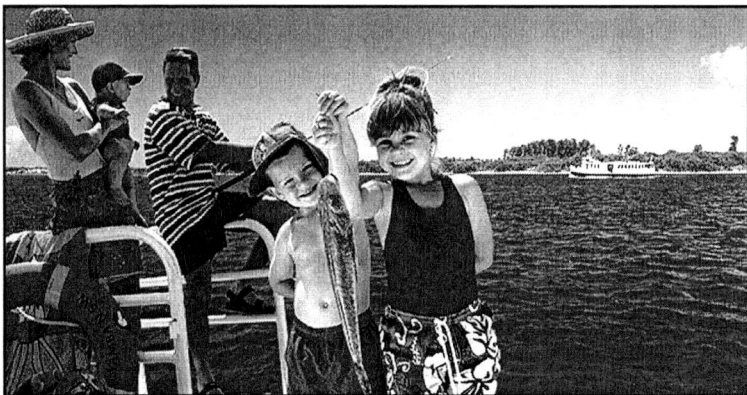

Fishing for Flathead

Trip 35
Yamba

Twin Town Walks

It's possible to walk to the CBD in Yamba from most of the resorts; however you will see more if you take the car along and make several stops. I would love to make this a walking or cycling trip, but the hills are formidable and the distance between attractions best accommodate motorized transportation. Yamba and its sister town Maclean are small, friendly and welcome strangers. You will not see any of the American-style fast food joints; the local eateries put them to shame anyway. There is only a small shopping district in each town, but you will find some interesting regional crafts that are not found in larger towns. And it will bring back fond memories if you take home a trinket or two from this area. Now the stores do change hands fairly often, but if the kite shop on one of the side streets is still there, it's a must see. The Story House Museum is a good stop as is the Pilot Hill & Lighthouse, the beaches, and chipping around at the Yamba Golf Club. Further afield is the Yuraygir National Park and the cute town of Maclean with its telephone poles painted in clan colors. Maclean, only a couple of miles west of Yamba, is very different as the town has a distinctive Scottish culture. Just wander the little town and see the Scottish Cairn in Herb Stanford Memorial Park (built by rocks brought over from Scotland), check out the prawn fleet headquarters, hike up to the strange rock formation and a cave network at The Pinnacle, look over the vast sugar cane fields at Maclean Lookout, get a historical perspective at the Bicentennial Museum, and visit the gallery at the information center.

For the beach-lovers and surf fanatics, you are in luck with 11 beaches in the area to choose from. Whiting Beach is a good spot to take the kids with little worry, Turner's Beach has rock pools and is protected from the winds, Main Beach is a popular hangout and has a built-in saltwater rock pool, Pippi Beach is the surfers' spot and is a good one for long walks.

GETTING THERE:
By Car: Follow the main artery (Yamba Road) into town and park anywhere on Yamba Street for free. To enjoy Maclean, drive west on Yamba Road towards the Pacific Highway and follow the signs. It's only a 15-minute drive at worst.

PRACTICALITIES:

You may want to do some beach time between the hiking, so take along a towel and swimming suit. The same common sense sun protection rules and water safety guidelines apply. Bicycles can be rented at **Yamba Squash & Cycles,** ☎ (02) 6646-2237 or (04) 1764-8978.

FOOD AND DRINK:

Fish & Chips shops abound and the **Pacific Hotel** is a great spot to have an inexpensive meal and mingle with the local crew. If you get hungry in Maclean, try the **Clarence Hotel** and **The Bottom Pub** for a counter meal, the **Clarence River Seafood** shop or the **Maclean Hotel** for "the best beer in town."

LOCAL ATTRACTIONS:

Circled numbers correspond to numbers on the map.

YAMBA WALK/DRIVE:

*YAMBA STREET SHOPPING ❶, Yamba Street, Yamba. *Generally stores are open between 9–5 and restaurants close much later. Free (unless you find some goodies to buy).* &.

This is only a short twelve blocks, with most of the shops clustered between Harbour Street and Church Street. Fishing stores, camping supplies, novelty shops, New Age vendors, and eateries line both sides of the street. It will only take an hour tops to wander around this section.

*STORY HOUSE MUSEUM ❷, River Street, Yamba, ☎ (02) 6646-2316. *Open Wed., Sat., Sun. 2–5 (4:30 in the winter), closed holidays. Adults AU $3, children AU $ .50. Self guided tours. Gift shop. Special events.* &.

A small building that was once the bowls club, it houses memories of the past, with over 1,000 photographs, relics, and models. The Art & Craft Exhibition is held here the first week of December. If you are a history buff and want a taste of Yamba's rich traditions, pick up the free pamphlet "Historical Walk Around Yamba" and put it to good use. The guide and map provides a 1–2-hour, 4-mile trek past sites such as beaches, Mathew Flinders Monument, the Star of the Sea Convent, the art deco Pacific Hotel, the various parks, and the cemetery. This walk is a good way to become familiar with the town and local landmarks.

YAMBA LIGHTHOUSE ❸, Clarence Head Point, Yamba. *Open 24 hours daily. Free. Partially* &.

Not too much to see of the lighthouse and you can't access the tower, but the views 135 feet above the surf are spectacular. The tower sits right above the channel at the South Wall, where you can see the surf crashing on Whiting Beach as well as the surfers at Turner's Beach. It is also a popular picnic stop.

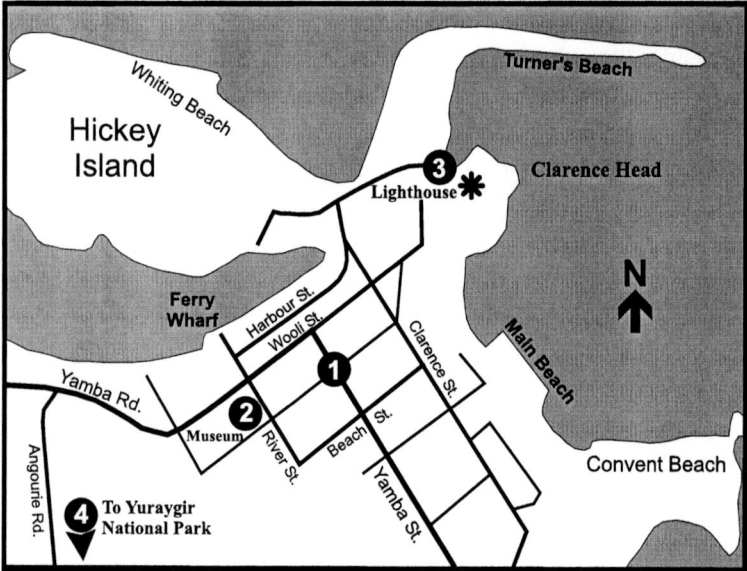

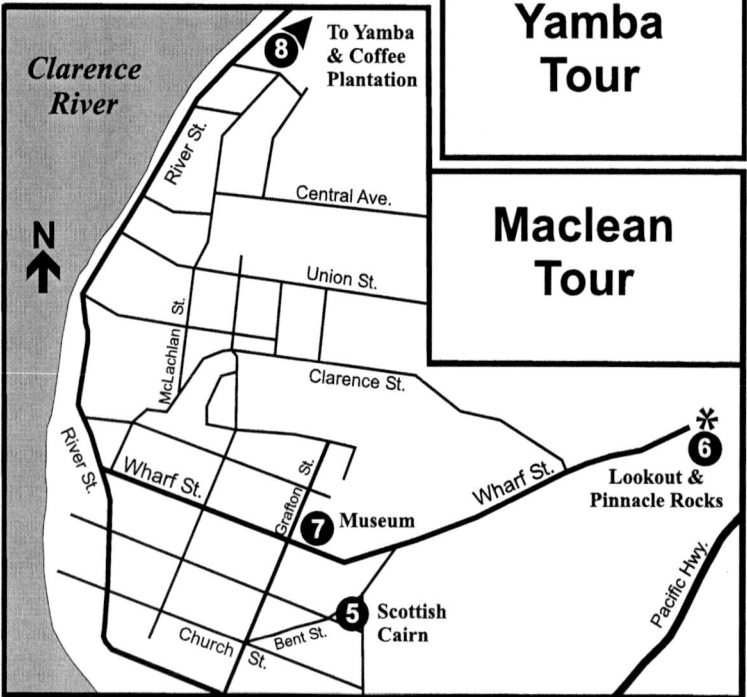

*YURAYGIR NATIONAL PARK ❹, off the Pacific Highway, Angourie, ☎ (02) 6641-1520, **W**: npws.nsw.gov.au. *Open daily, 24 hours a day. Parking fee is AU $6/day for a carload, overnight camping is AU $5 for adults and $3 for children. Self-guided tours. Partially &.*

You can spend a few hours amongst the lands of the Aborigines or stay for a week and still not see it all. The park is separated into a Northern, Central, and Southern Yuraygir sections. Hike, canoe, or swim through the park to experience a perfectly peaceful setting. The remnants of spiritual sites and middens (rubbish heaps) can be found in the area, while the Dreamtime stories abound about the area and how it was created. Check out the local **Visitor Information Centres** for maps of the sites and the ancient yarns. There are quite a few walking paths cut amongst the swamps, woodlands, and forests; and they range from a mile long to over 5-mile circuits. The brochures at the Park's entrance will map-out the paths and what to expect along the way. The area is loaded with eastern grey kangaroos, cute sugar gliders, wallabies, and a host of small carnivore mammals. But the real treats are the emus and goannas that may come close to inspect you. The bird population is overwhelming and quite loud. Make sure you avoid "Jock the Croc," but do ask the locals about this reptile that allegedly lived there in 1939. There are heaps of campgrounds and picnic areas, but you have to take your own food and water in. On the northern tip of the park, you should check out the Blue and Green Pools at **Angourie Point**. Despite warnings against diving from the cliffs into the deep blue waters, you will probably see a few kids doing so. The rock formations in the area are fascinating and worth a look.

Over to Maclean now for a wander around in the town originally called Rocky Mouth. One sight that will take you aback when you enter town is the Tartan Power Poles. The early settlers have been commemorated near their original business sites by having their tartan colors painted on the telephone poles. The town has also placed metal plaques at most of the historical sites in town and they provide a good way to identify the special spots to see. An information sheet is available at the **Clarence Visitor Centre** or at any of the stores in town displaying the **i**. If you want to select a few of your own tartans or Scottish gear, stop in at **The Scottish Shop** on River Street (Mon.–Fri 10–4 and Sat. 9–11) and maybe find one of your relatives.

MACLEAN WALK/DRIVE:
*SCOTTISH CAIRN ❺, Herb Street Memorial Park, Maclean. *Open 24 hours daily. Free. Special events. &.*

This is a memorial built from stones collected and donated from Scots throughout Australia and Scotland. A stonemason by the name of George Kerridge built the memorial that is dedicated to Maclean's Scottish pioneers.

*THE LOOKOUT & PINNACLE ❻, Wharf Street, Malcean. *Open daily 24-hours. Free. Self guided tours. Not ♿.*

Two great natural wonders that offer a panoramic view of the surrounding cane fields, river, and town. They are only a mile from the center of town, and the Pinnacle is a pile of rocks precariously balanced over a network of caves.

*BICENTENNIAL MUSEUM & STONE COTTAGE ❼, Wharf Street, Maclean, ☎ (02) 6645-3416. *Open Wed. & Sat. 1–4, Fri. 10–4, closed holidays. Adults AU $3, children AU $1. Self-guided tours. Gift shop. Special events. ♿.*

This 1879 stone cottage was built from local sandstone and depicts the traditions and living conditions as they were in the late 1800s. The museum has displays of an early hospital ward, a schoolroom, and a series of changing exhibits. Both the museum and cottage have educational working models depicting ways of yesteryear.

WOOMBAH COFFEE PLANTATION ❽, Woombah Coffee Plantation, Woombah, ☎ (02) 6646-4380, **W**: hotkey.net.au/~woombah/, E-mail: woombah@hotkey,net.au. *Open daily 10–5, Free. Guided tours, self-guided tours (call ahead). Gift shop. Café. Special events. ♿.*

Established in 1982, the organically-grown coffee plantation produces some of the tastiest coffees in the area. Records show that coffee was nurtured nearby as early as 1889, and now the onsite factory process has been refined to produce flavorful cups of coffee. Joy and Joan, the two owner/operators of the plantation use the same methods used by the early growers, with a few tricks of their own. Nestled in a corner of paradise, enjoy a cuppa or take a packet home with you for AU 25/kilo.

BYRON BAY TRIPS

The point at Cape Byron and the home to the national landmark lighthouse occupy the most eastern point of the continent. This area was originally the site of the oldest known Aboriginal camp and pippi midden (a disposal spot for mollusk shells). Now a 452-acre reserve, it is the first land use indigenous parks in the nation, and is part of the Arakwal National Park. Organized tour operators will point out the varied and rare plant life like the Acronycia (only 100 found in nature), the stinky Cryptocarya, and a variety of the Palm Lily. But more people come to see the whales, dolphins, turtles, manata, sharks, and overhead osprey from the cliffs.

Byron Bay is a real trip in every sense of the word, and a very popular tourist location for Aussies and overseas travelers alike. Since the heydays of the 60s, the freaks have moved in and forgotten to reset their clocks. This hippie capital of Australia is a small seaside town noted for its psychedelic peace buses, tie-dyed bell-bottoms, and black light posters. Beyond the alternative lifestyles, abundant in town, the area offers the sports-minded experiences such as sea kayaking, hiking the lighthouse trail, diving the Julian Rocks, and surfing the nude beaches at Tallow Beach.

Since this is only a short hop from either Brisbane or the Gold Coast, you can make this a daytrip—a long day trip. Or you can satisfy your karma in three to four days at Byron Bay, but you may never want to leave. The beaches alone are worth a few days of doing nothing but staring at miles of beach and opal-colored surf. The only problem with Byron Bay is that it has become commercialized and development has run rampant. Yuppies from Brisbane are buying properties and pushing out the local and often long-term residents. It's still a good place to chill out and reminisce about the lost years of youth. Prepare for a flashback or two mates.

No trip to Byron is complete without a day of sun worshiping. There are several beaches to choose from, but the best is Tallow Beach with its seven-mile stretch of absolutely stunning white sand and clear blue waters. You can stroll the beach to Cibum Margil Swamp and hike the wetlands that were once Aboriginal camps. If you are into surfing or tanning this is the place to be. But this beach is not patrolled, so if no locals are in the water - don't swim.

SPECIAL EVENTS:

Everyday is a special event in Byron Bay, but some of the other goings-on include: Community Markets every first Sunday of the month, the popular East Coast Blues and Roots Music Festival over Easter, January's Sculpture Show, the Writer's Festival in August, and a food extravaganza in September called The Taste of Byron.

GETTING TO BYRON BAY:

By Car: If you skipped the Yamba tours and are driving from the north, you will pass lush banana groves, miles of sugarcane fields, and over the steep Dividing Range as you enter New South Wales. Bryon Bay is a 109-mile, 2-1/2-hour drive south of Brisbane. From Surfers Paradise it's only a 1-1/2-hour or 62-mile trip on the well-traveled Pacific Highway. Although the drive is fantastic with black soils of the cane fields and ominous shadows from Mount Warning, the road is a bit tricky when you cross the Great Dividing Range. On the way south, make sure you stop at the Moo Moo Café—right off of the Pacific Highway. You will not miss it with spotted cow signs covering the roadside. It has great coffee and burgers, plus some good shops to browse and buy.

By Bus: Most major bus companies stop at Byron Bay. The local buses include **Kirklands**, ☎ 1-300-367-077 or (02) 6622-1499; and **Blanch's**, ☎ (02) 6686-2144.

By Train: Country Link stops right near the Visitor's Centre. You can organize a trip on ☎ 13-22-32 or **W**:countrylink.nsw.gov.au.

By Air: The closest airports are Coolangatta on the Gold Coast or in Ballina (a 30-minute drive from Byron). I don't recommend either for this trip.

PRACTICALITIES:

The laid-back approach is the way to go here and that applies to food, attire, and attitude. Take a set of "business casual" clothing, but most restaurants have little if any dress code. Surf wear, sun protection, good attitude, and warm weather gear is recommended. Exploring Byron Bay requires a bit of driving, but you can hike the entire area from the lighthouse, to the beaches, around the shopping hub, and beyond if you have the time and energy.

The Byron Bay website is fantastic, and you can view almost any aspect of the town including accommodations, attractions, tours, maps, and listings of the local businesses. Have a look on **W**: byron-bay.com or call the **Visitor Centre** at ☎ (02) 6680-9271. A local newspaper is found on **W**: echo.net.au

FOOD AND DRINK:

Jonson Street and its offshoots, from the beach out to Marvel Street are loaded with all sorts of cafés, bistros, ice creameries, and good eats. Just have a stroll and let your nose and stomach make the decision on food. Oops, I mean let your karma choose. The eateries change pretty regularly, but I will list a few of my favorites and include a variety that were current on my last jaunt to the area.

The Famous Old Piggery Restaurant & Cinema, The Arts Factory, Byron Bay. Great pizza and gourmet food as well as a movie, but beware of flying pigs. ☎ (02) 6685-5828, **W**: piggery.com.au. Open daily after 5:30. $$

The Beach Café, Clarks Beach, Byron Bay. This is a must-do for breakfast. You are sitting amongst the waves, dunes, and sea spray. The coffee is deadly and the food is piled high. ☎ (02) 6685-7598. Open daily from 7:30–3 on weekdays and till 4 on weekends. $–$$

The Rails Bar, Jonson Street, Byron Bay. Only a couple of yards from the railroad tracks, this is a cool hangout with good pub food. It is one of the favorite backpacker's hangouts and the bands at night are good. ☎ (02) 6685-7662. Open daily from around noon until late. $

Hogs Breath Café, 4 Jonson Street, Byron Bay. Good food in a perch over the center of town. Great burgers, salads, and fantastic ribs. You will recognize a few license plates on the walls too. ☎ (02) 6685-5320. Open daily for lunch and dinner. $–$$

Oh Deli Tandori, 3/4 Bay Lane, Byron Bay. A nice option when your palate is crying out for good curry. Good service too. ☎ (02) 6680-8800. Open daily for dinner. $–$$

Fins Restaurant, at the Beach Hotel, Byron Bay. Innovative foods with a good view. Seems to be a local favorite. ☎ (02) 6685-5029. Open daily for dinner. $–$$

Raving Prawn, Jonson Street, Byron Bay. Probably the best seafood in town. Make sure you make a reservation in advance if you want to get in. ☎ (02) 6685-6737. Open Tues.–Sat. from 6pm. $–$$

ACCOMMODATIONS IN TOWN:

There is a good range of lodging to choose from in town. I found the B&Bs to be really nice, but generally overpriced at AU $200+/night. Contact the **Visitor Centre** on ☎ (02) 6680-8558, **W**: visitbyronbay.com, and they can arrange a place that suits your needs. Here are a few to start you off:

Aquarius Backpackers Resort, 16 Lawson Street, ☎ 1-800-028-909 or (02) 6685-7663, **W**: aquarius-backpack.com.au. $

Lord Byron Resort Motel, 120 Jonson Street, ☎ (02) 6685-7444, **W**: lord byronresort.com. $$–$$$

Oasis Resort, Scott Street, ☎ (02) 6685-7390, **W**: byronbayoasis.cpm. $$–$$$

Waves Motel, 35 Lawson Street, ☎ (02) 6685-5966, **W**: byron bay.com/waves. $$

Ruskin House B&B, 131 Jonson Street, ☎ (02) 6685-6144. $$

Seaview House B&B, 146 Lighthouse Road, ☎ (02) 6685-6468, **W**: byron bayseaviewaccommodation.com. $$$ (AU $220 and up per couple per night).

**Trip 36
Byron Bay**

Cape Byron Lighthouse

Cape Byron is one of the most beautiful places in the world, with sheer cliffs dropping into the clear blue ocean that is teeming with whales, turtles, huge manata rays, flipping dolphins, and the occasional shark. The foundation of the lighthouse rests on the remnant of a 20-million-year-old volcano flow that spewed from Mount Warning. This hardened magma crept as far north as Brisbane and south to Ballina—the creation of the largest volcano in the Southern Hemisphere. The 150 acres that surrounds the lighthouse is a reserve peppered with feral goats balanced precariously along the cliffs. The Cape Byron Lighthouse towers 72 feet above its base and is around 308 feet above sea level. Built in 1901 from pre-cast concrete blocks, it was established to reduce the hazards encountered by ships navigating that stretch of coastline. The beam has the power of 2,200,000 candles and the light is one of the most powerful south of the equator. Flashing every 15 seconds, the tungsten-halogen lamp has a range of 27 nautical miles. The lens is 6-1/2 feet in diameter and floats in a mercury bath to reduce the risk of fire. Walking tracks, around the white tower, create a path that circles the entire point with at least five lookout platforms and spectacular views.

GETTING THERE:

It is a 5-minute drive out of town to Lawson Street and then onto Clark's Beach Caravan Park. Just follow the signs to the Lighthouse. If a walk is in order it is a 15-minute stroll along the water at Main Beach to the starting point.

PRACTICALITIES:

If you choose to walk the entire course, be warned it is strenuous with heaps of stairs and winding trails. It is best to hike the full circuit, but if your legs aren't up to it, you can park at the summit and walk around the lighthouse lookouts only. To make things a bit easier, I will lay out the best way to trek the walking tracks. You might want to stuff your bathing suit and towel in a bag and carry it along as it will get warm and there are plenty of spots to take a dip in the crystal-clear ocean. Pack some water if you decide to do the full tour, and you might want to take a pair of binoculars to zoom in on the possibility of a whale sighting. Shorts and sun protection are a good idea too.

FOOD AND DRINK:

The information area at the top does have a small selection of food, but you would be smart to take an energy snack along for the trip. There are two good little beachside cafés along the way.

SUGGESTED TOUR:

Circled numbers correspond to numbers on the map.

For the long haul, start your walking tour at **Captain Cook's Lookout ❶**, right at Clarks Beach and just off of Lighthouse Road. Hiking in either direction to the top of the point is OK, but if it's hot, the clockwise direction is a bit cooler with breezes off of the ocean. Or you can decide to bag the inland section and hike down the road instead if it gets too hot. If you want only to view the lighthouse and take a shorter walk, drive up to the top where you can find limited parking for a small fee. There is another parking lot about 100 yards down from the summit that is marked as **Lighthouse Road Parking ❷**. It is free, but also usually crowded. From either spot you can take and easy hike to the areas that interest you the most up there.

Following along **Clarks Beach** you will see a spot to look over an Aboriginal site and a tiny island just offshore. **The Pass ❸** has a little café with great espresso and breakfasts. You can stop there for a dip with showers and toilets right near the beach. Next point of interest is the **Palm Valley Drive Lookout ❹**. This will be your first glimpse at the protected cove of Wategos Beach. A bit farther, passing the guesthouse called Rae's On Watego's, you can actually hike along the soft sand here. Test the water to see if you are up for a dip. Continue along the shoreline to an intersecting path at **Little Wategos Beach ❺**.

Remain on the path to the beach and the farthest point that juts out into the sea. This is a great location for spotting whales and looking over to the Julian Rocks Aquatic Reserve. The tides will be rushing over the reefs at this favored spot for scuba enthusiasts. You can feel the sea mist as the waves break over the rocks only yards away. I'll call this spot **Julian Rocks Lookout ❻**, and one of the plaques in the area will describe the Aboriginal lore of how the rocks were formed. But the best story and one to scare the kids with is of a newlywed couple that took a scuba trip out to the rocks with a group of divers. No sooner did they enter the water than a huge great white shark came in, took the husband, and disappeared under the surf. No trace was ever found of the man (not even his wet suit) or the shark despite extensive air and sea searches.

Doubling back along the path and the scrubby bushes, start up the long stretch of steps. Take your time on this section and stop regularly along the way. Pausing and standing quietly will be rewarded with lots of

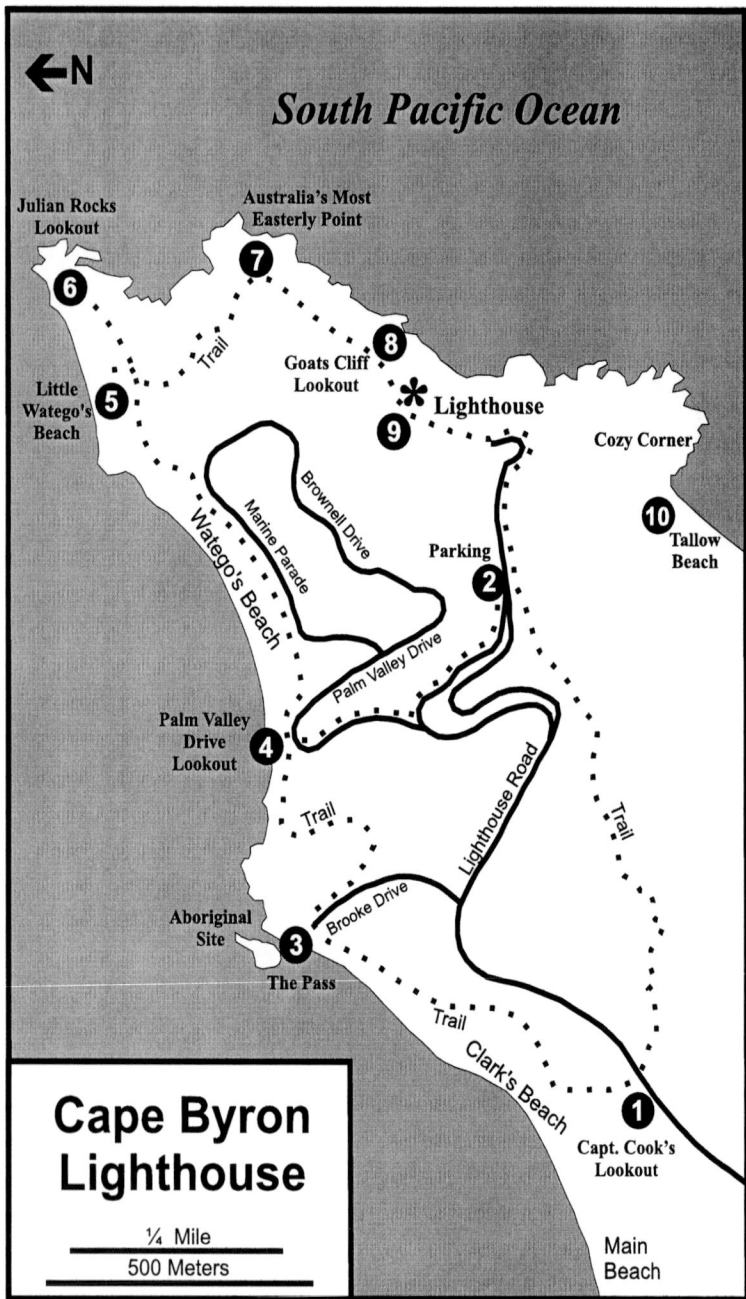

←N

South Pacific Ocean

Julian Rocks
Lookout

Australia's Most
Easterly Point

7

6

Trail

8

Goats Cliff
Lookout

＊ Lighthouse

Little
Watego's
Beach

5

9

Cozy Corner

Brownell Drive

10

Tallow
Beach

Marine Parade

Parking

Watego's Beach

2

Palm Valley Drive

Palm Valley
Drive
Lookout

4

Lighthouse Road

Trail

Trail

Aboriginal
Site

Brooke Drive

3

The Pass

Trail

1

Clark's Beach

Capt. Cook's
Lookout

Cape Byron
Lighthouse

¼ Mile

500 Meters

Main
Beach

interesting bird sounds and rustlings in the bush. The trailside plaques will help you identify them. At the second headland point you will reach **Australia's Most Eastern Point** ❼. Why not take out the camera and get a picture of the marker that identifies this landmark? It was one of the most popular spots during the ticking over of the new millennium as this (and Mount Warning) is where the first ray of light hits the continent. This is also a good vantage point to scan the horizon for sea creatures. The water is so clear here that you can see the sand washing on the bottom of the ocean.

Up a few more steep steps you will see one more lookout platform that I will call **Goats Cliffs Lookout** ❽. This is usually where the goats hang out; getting close-up photos of the scraggly beasts is possible here. There is a story that they practice population control by bumping the old and weak of the herd off the side of the cliffs. Apparently there is limited food available and survival instincts prevail.

Next up is the top of the hill and the **Cape Byron Lighthouse** ❾. Here is an information center, a small gift shop, and a place to get some refreshments. It is worthwhile to spend a bit of time relaxing and soaking in the clean air. Huge container ships and tankers can be easily seen from this point, and there is plenty to study in the form of plaques and brochures from the information counter.

Starting back down from the summit, you will hike along Lighthouse Road adjacent to **Tallow Beach** ❿. Don't get too absorbed in the hang gliders floating overhead after launching from the cliffs nearby. The road becomes narrow, and there is a bit of car traffic, so please keep your eyes and ears open. It will be an easy downhill trek from here, and you will branch off the road and onto hiking trails until returning to Captain Cook's Lookout and your car.

All told, you will probably need at least 3–4 hours to hike this path, but I think it is at least a half-day tour, especially if you want to take a swim or savor the natural wonders up there.

Find Your Groove

The downtown shopping area is a maze of head shops, New Age vendors, and now lots of mainstream stores. But you will find cool stuff like leather goods, earrings, sarongs and good quality opals. There are sidewalk chess games galore, and there is usually a festive air about the place. The cafés and eateries are varied too, and you will find lots of herbal concoctions to soothe the soul. You can easily spend a full day shopping and relaxing on Main Beach at the end of town or whiz through the shops in a few hours and settle in to get your hand read or something like that. The vendors change pretty frequently, but the wares are similar and despite the recent upscale facelift and money being poured into the place, there are still bargains to be found. You might get a whiff of some marijuana floating in the air, but don't think that everyone who is rolling their own smoke is getting to fire up a joint. It is common practice to hand-roll tobacco cigarettes, though there are a few who use the illegal stuff too.

This shopping portion is best accomplished by just wandering—let the force be with you and find your own way. But for the less adventuresome, here is a general outline to follow. Start at the Visitor Centre on Jonson Street and work your way towards the beach. From that point, start back from Bay Street, along Jonson, and weave in and out of Lawson, Byron, Marvell, Carlyle, Kingsley, Ruskin, and Browning Streets. The majority of the shops are in little malls in the side streets just off Jonson. And let me know if you find that black-light lava lamp with the Jimi Hendrix poster.

GETTING THERE:

It is a short walk into town from almost all of the accommodations. Avoid driving into the CBD as parking is limited. There are lots near the train station and one down by the beach off of Jonson (good luck there though).

PRACTICALITIES:

All you need is a good attitude and a bit of cash in your pocket.

FOOD AND DRINK:

Health food, fast food, and good restaurants are on every block. My favorite in town is the Hogs Breath Café.

MAJOR ATTRACTIONS:

Circled numbers correspond to numbers on the map.

Depending on where you landed in town, it will be best to start at the Visitor Centre, grab a map, and some brochures.

VISITOR CENTRE & TOURIST OFFICE ❶, 80 Jonson Street, Byron Bay, ☎ (02) 6680-8558, **W**: visitbyronbay.com. *Open daily 9–5. Gift Shop.* ♿.

Hanging out in the middle of the Transit Hub and only a hop from the Railway Pub, is this small cabin that is bursting with good information. Plus they have great postcards and some local crafts for sale there. I think they have some of the best T-shirts in town, made by local craftspeople. They can organize tours and accommodations for you too. If you want a detailed view of the town and local shires, buy the map for AU $2.50 and you will be set. One bit of warning, they have become a bit commercial and depending on the individual who is behind the counter, you will get either fantastic insights of the area or an indifferent attitude staring you in the face.

In the same parking lot area is one of the favorite watering holes and just a cool bar with fishing gear on the walls, a chart of recent record catches, and an airplane diving from the ceiling.

*THE RAILS PUB ❷, ☎ (02) 6685-7662, **W**: byronbayentertainment.com.au. *Open daily 10–midnight. Special events and great bands.* ♿.

The barmaid calls the place "Rockin on the Rails" and she is spot on. You may want to wait until later in the day to quench your thirst. In fact they do have specials of Hahn and Carlton Bitter beers; last time I was there you could get a Hahn hat if you drank 10 beers at one sitting. The bands come on later in the night, and during the daylight hours you can enjoy good food and even better beer. The bands play every night and the flavor of the music is world, jazz, and folk. In my queries of hot spots and off-the-beaten-path sights, the bartenders were friendly, helpful, and willing to go the extra mile to assist you finding your way around. In fact, I would recommend you pass over on the city council sites and the Visitor Centre (except to pick up a few brochures and free maps) and enjoy a beer while you get the best information in town at this pub.

Across the street is the once-popular photo op that has been flashed in many tourist magazines and on many travel shows:

COMMUNITY CENTRE ❸, 69 Jonson Street, Byron Bay, ☎ (02) 6685-6807. *Open daily 9–5. Free. Special events.* ♿.

This was one of the most photographed spots in town. The entire streetside wall used to have a mural of whales, local "dignitaries," and beach scenes painted across it. The wooden clapboard artwork sort of summed up the attitude of the town. The last time I checked, it was being

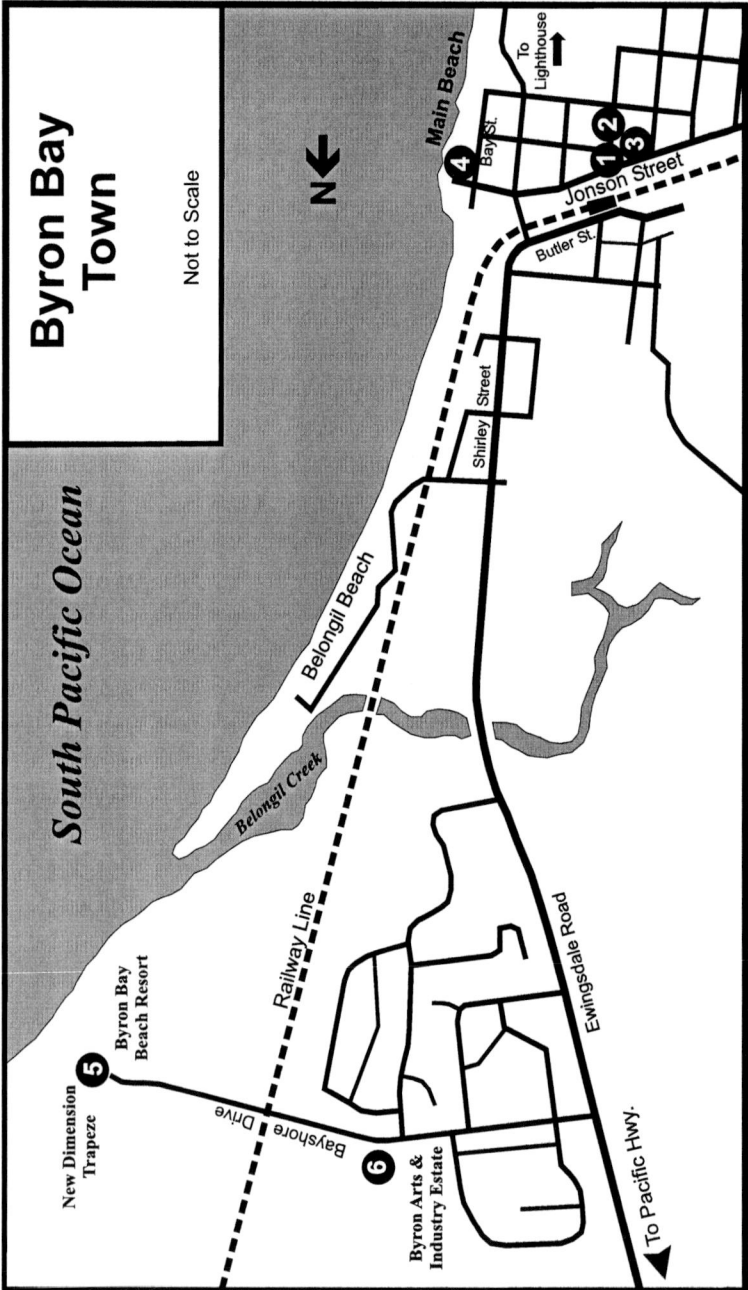

Byron Bay Town

Not to Scale

N

South Pacific Ocean

Main Beach

To Lighthouse

Bay St.

Jonson Street

Butler St.

Shirley Street

Belongil Beach

Belongil Creek

Railway Line

Ewingsdale Road

To Pacific Hwy.

Byron Bay Beach Resort

New Dimension Trapeze

Bayshore Drive

Byron Arts & Industry Estate

painted over and I'm not sure if the local council plans to re-do the mural. They have restored it to its original 1920's heritage look and have even installed a veranda over the front section. Unless you are interested in some of the local issues or community programs, there is no need to go inside. It is the home to the literary society, has a large amphitheater in the rear, and you may get some good information about local happenings that are posted on the wall outside.

All the way at the end of Jonson Street and near the beach is the turn-around point of the shopping tour. You can now start back into the heart of town—after a wine or beer maybe at the:

BEACH HOTEL ❹, corner of Bay and Jonson streets, Byron Bay, ☎ (02) 6685-6402. *Open early to late.* ♿.

Touted as the most easterly pub in Australia, it is probably at least the most popular watering hole on the beach. The corner bar has a comfortable al fresco setting right across from Main Beach. There are plenty of stories about the place including that one owner is none other than Crocodile Dundee. This is a good place to be seen and see the pretty people from the cities.

From this point on, it is best to just have a wander around Lawson, Byron, Fletcher, and Jonson streets to pick the stores that interest you. The renovation, increasing rents, and changed attitudes have chased many of my old favorites out of town, and apparently the changes continue. So, I could be misleading if I listed all the current shops in the heart of the town. But there are plenty of goodies to be found and last check, you can find some of the best black opal at **Byron Opals** on Jonson Street, get your karma checked at the **Byron Medicine Wheel** at 84 Jonson Street, call **Sieghart Rohr** on ☎ (02) 6685-4699 to attend astrology classes, grab a bag of nuts at **The Native Nut Shop** on Bay Lane, and get a free didgeridoo or fire twirling lesson at **Gowdwana Gifts** on Byron Street. Or why not stop at one of the many tattoo shops and buy something a bit more permanent?

A short drive out of town along Ewingsdale Road, turn right at the BP gas station, onto Bayshore Drive, and follow signs to the Byron Bay Beach Resort. Stop at the reception desk and ask for:

NEW DIMENSION TRAPEZE ❺, The Byron Bay Beach Resort, Byron Bay, ☎ (04) 1707-3668, **W**: byronbaybeachresort.com.au, E-mail: trapflyer@yahoo.com. *Open daily for lessons, but call ahead. A two-hour session is AU $40 for all ages. Café. Special events. Not* ♿.

Join the circus mates! This is for real and you can take a safe, well-monitored, 2-hour session to learn the basics of flying through the air with the greatest of ease. You will learn the knee hang and participate in a mid-air catch. That is—if you dare. Hanging upside-down 25 feet off the ground might look easy from the ground, but wait until you see it from the air. The facilities are extremely safe with nets, safety harnesses, and expert coaching. For the truly young at heart, there is a Circus School and Show during school holidays.

If you have any energy left in your body, the last stop for this expedition is nestled in a reinvigorated industrial site on the way back to town. It is best to drive around this shopping mecca as it is spread out over a large area. The stores are a collaboration of artsy, eco furniture, and surfing gear outlets. It looks like a typical discount mall with a hippie twist. You might find just the right gift to take home from:

*THE BYRON ARTS & INDUSTRY ESTATE ❻, off of Ewingsdale Road between Banksia Drive and Tasman Way, Byron Bay. *Open daily 10–5. Gift shops. Cafés.* ♿.

With a nice mix of goods and services displayed in this huge industrial shopping mall, you might find a bargain or two. There is a helpful map of the area in the center of the free "Byron Guide" found in most of the accommodations and at the Visitor Centre. Stores offer lingerie, swimwear, surfboards, honey and beeswax products, rustic wood furniture, blown glass treasures, funky hats, and baked goods. It is worth a spin around, but definitely drive this section.

Sea Kayaking
with the Dolphins

This is not as scary as you might think, and the instructors keep a watchful eye on everyone in the kayak pod. It is a bit of work but the sights, sounds, and surf rides are too good to miss. The choice of two guided tour companies both assure that you get out to the dolphins and offer half-day morning and afternoon trips. Morning is best because the wind is down and the surf is calmer. Both operators offer marine tours and an on-going narrative of the sea life below your tiny one- or two-person boat. The water is incredibly clear, so you will indeed see huge sea turtles, manta rays, and dolphins. In whale season they will come in close enough to smell their breath (for real—and it smells like rotten anchovies). It looks shallow, but if you get a chance, dip your paddle into the water and it just keeps going. Over 20-feet deep in the protected areas of Main Beach, it gets much deeper on the point just under the lighthouse.

The competing operators offer similar tours, wave surfing, promises of seeing dolphins up close and personal, and a morning or mid-afternoon tea break on one of the protected beaches. The trips start on a protected section of Main Beach, and you are expected to drag your kayaks down to the water. During the wave-riding portion of the outing, you sit in rolling waves while you wait for the right wave to ride in. It takes a bit of a knack to get it right. My wife and I had only one decent ride. You receive detailed instructions before you go out and even get to try tipping over on purpose to learn how to right the kayak and re-board. It is quite a sight riding the waves under the towering lighthouse above—the only sounds you hear are people laughing as they catch a good wave. In the background is the crashing of the South Pacific against sheer rocks and beaches. The surf can get a bit rough when you pass the point and cross over into the eastern side of the peninsula, but you can stay back in the protected area if you wish.

Half way through the trip, you will be given instructions to head for the beach. At either Wategos or Clarks Beach the boats are marooned amongst the sea-worn rocks and smooth sand. Teatime consists of sweets, fruits, tea/coffee, and good stories. Apparently in the Wategos Beach area, pregnant Aboriginal women would come to the edge of the ocean, wade out knee-deep, and deliver their children in the water. After tea you are invited to splash around in the spectacular surf and cool off while the guides stow the gear in the holds of their kayaks. Then it is a gentle paddle back to Main Beach where a satisfied feeling will wash over you. During the course of the trip you will have probably covered about 3 miles along the coastline.

GETTING THERE:

There is a parking lot at Clark's Beach, just off of Lawson Street, and you can usually find a spot there. I would probably walk it as it only takes about 5 minutes to hoof it along the beach.

PRACTICALITIES:

You should be relatively fit to go on this tour, and if you get motion sickness, take something before you go out. All protective gear, including helmets are provided, but you would be wise to wear a swimming suit as well as lather up with sunscreen. Speaking of the lotion, you are warned against touching any of the sea critters as it damages their skin and could burn their eyes. The exception is sharks—you can pet them all you want.

FOOD AND DRINK:

Refreshments are provided for this tour so you need not go away hungry if you like good healthy foods.

TOUR OPERATORS:

DOLPHIN KAYAKING, Main Beach, Byron Bay, ☎ (02) 6685-8044 or (02) 6685-8040, **W**: dolphinkayaking.com.au. *Open daily, weather permitting. Tours are 3 hours long, starting at 9am or 2pm. Prices for each person AU $40. Guided tours. Not ♿.*

BYRON BAY SEA KAYAKS, Main Beach, Byron Bay, ☎ (02) 6685-5830, **W**: byronbayadventureco.com. *Open daily, weather permitting. Tours are 3+ hours long starting at 8:30am and 1:30pm. Prices AU $45. Guided tours. Not ♿.*

Byron Surrounds

You can choose your make this a daytrip or blend some of the activities in with the other tours. Three days in Byron Bay proper is plenty, but on your way out of town, you may want to see some of the surrounding countryside and visit a few of the peripheral attractions. The best things to do are in the eco-tours, and getting right into the dirt and breathing in the natural wonders in the area. You can search out some of the tour operators in the brochures and Yellow Pages, but I have chosen one operator (with two styles of adventures) that has gotten consistent top ratings by people I interviewed in the industry and some who regularly take their tours. I admit to not taking their tours, but have been to most of the places they tour and they seem to be very comprehensive and a good value.

ROCKHOPPERS ADVENTURE CO., corner of Jonson & Marvel streets, P.O. Box 1169, Byron Bay, ☎ 0500-881-881, **W**: rockhoppers.com.au. *Open for tours daily from around 8:30. Tour prices start at AU $69 to about AU $150. Guided tours, self-guided tours. Special events. Not &.*

GRASSHOPPERS, corner of Jonson & Marvel streets, P.O. Box 1169, Byron Bay, ☎ 0500-881-881, **W**: rockhoppers.com.au. *Open for tours daily from around 8:30. Tour prices start at AU $69 to about AU $150. Guided tours, self-guided tours. Special events. Partially &.*

GENERAL TOURS:

The teams above offer some really interesting trips for the active person. If your preferences are to sit back and let others do the work—this is not for you. But if mountain biking, whitewater activity, and rock climbing tickle your fancy, you are in the right section of the book. The titles of the tours, **Downhill Rainforest Biking**, **Extreme Adventure Abseiling**, **Waterfall Canyoning**, and **Rock Climbing** sort of say it all. This series of well-organized and professionally-guided tours are for the adrenalin junkies. They have the latest gear and safety equipment to make the trip as easy as they can without doing the exercise for you. The cool part of these exhilarating trips for the fitness-minded it that you will be engrossed in the lush and pristine surroundings as well.

For the more laid-back approach, the Grasshoppers offer eco-explorer tours on a comfy bus, so sit while you enjoy the scenery. The most strenuous activity is to plant a eucalyptus tree (the tree is supplied) in support of the environment and to provide future food for the koalas. The tour winds along the beautiful mountains around Nimbin, and you will get to park your bum on a bar stool and chat with a new friend, dip a toe or two in the hidden swimming holes, and hike a few of nature's trails. There is an optional BBQ trip, or just hang out in one of the parks.

Both organizations support environmental efforts and donate a portion of their proceeds to local efforts in maintaining the eco-systems.

Final Ascent of Mt. Warning

UKI & TWEED VALLEY TRIPS

Sitting smack dab in the shadows of Mount Warning is the tiny town (population 250) of Uki. Even though it's only two hours south of Brisbane and an hour from Surfers Paradise, it's not listed in most guides or travel books. The locals don't have the money for slick promotions and just can't compete with the larger towns. Though I did see one tiny ad in a local newspaper about Uki and all it could say was that it has a strong community spirit. And that sort of sums it up mates. When you enter this area you will realize that you are well off the beaten track—a suburb of Murwillumbah—itself a small river town hardly mentioned. The town consists of a primary school, one church, a petrol station, general store, pub hotel (of course), fruit & veggie stand, a hairdresser, one café, and an auto-body shop. Uki means something like "edible fern root" in Aborigines. I chose this series of tours because it will show you parts of real Australia with town folk just as curious about you as you are of them. Once the g'days are out of the way, you will be welcomed, sitting down for a beer or two, and exchanging yarns with at least one of the residents. The other good reason for this location is that it is in sight of the climb planned on the next tour and you will not be willing to go far after climbing its summit. For those who prefer a bit more action (and it will be only a tiny bit), I have included an option of staying closer to the Pacific Highway in the midst of the cornfields at Murwillumbah.

The Tweed Shire is a rich mix of beach, World Heritage rainforests, massive river systems, and cane fields stretching over flat green plains. It is an ideal setting for the lover of outdoors and those who enjoy physical activities. Or just come to love the scenery and drive through the mountains and onto the beaches.

Refer to the specific tours for directions, practicalities, food, accommodation, and special events.

Trip 40
Uki & Tweed Valley

Hike the Volcano

Mount Warning is located within a 5,461-acre World Heritage rainforest park and is home to over 100 species of birds and strange subtropical plant life. The original height of this 23-million year old spewing mount was 6,560 feet; its lava covered over 3,105 square kilometers of land. It is now significantly stooped by age, but it remains a 3–5 hour hike labeled strenuous by local guides. You can see the misshapen mountain from pretty far away as it has two peaks or "shoulders" with one summit much higher and knobby-looking. It is well worth the effort, and if you take your time, very doable. The view is magnificent, the flora and fauna unique to the area. It was once called Wollumbin by the Aboriginal peoples, which can be translated into "fighting chief of the mountain" (others claim it was "cloud catcher"). The defining lightning and thunder, still present today, was thought to be fighting warriors battling out their differences. The landslides found along this burnt-out volcano, still visible, were considered the wounds resulting from the wars fought above.

Then along came old Captain Cook in 1770, who decided the best name for the landmark was Mount Warning. He wrote that name on his maps to caution mariners to watch for the offshore reefs adjacent to the mountain. It is now the site for daytrippers who want to hike the hill, to the ferals who camp nearby and live off the land, and the birdwatchers who visit on a regular basis. The volcano core (the core—not the shell) is half the height it once was in its heyday, but it is still a healthy walk up. This was the largest shield volcano in the prehistoric world. The area is now protected by the national parks of Australia and is included in UNESCO's World Heritage Listing. Over 100 bird species can be seen on the hike including rufous scrub-bird, wompoo pigeon, marbled frogmouth, and Albert's lyrebird. The vegetation includes strange and old survivors like the figs, booyongs, carabeens, flame trees, and the painful giant stinging trees. The hike includes steep and rocky track conditions. Do not start the climb after 2pm in the winter (due to darkness) and never climb in a storm (warring chiefs, you know).

GETTING THERE:

By Car: In either direction from the Pacific Highway, exit at the roundabout at Murwillimbah and follow Kyogle Road west for about 7-1/2 miles (12km), turning onto Mount Warning Road and driving 3 miles (5km) to

Korrumbyn Creek Picnic grounds. Proceed past the park for about a mile (1.5km) and park in the Breakfast Creek Parking Area.

By Bus: Check any of the tour operators from either the Gold Coast, Murwillimbah, or Byron Bay for options, but I have never seen a bus up there.

PRACTICALITIES:

This is a strenuous climb with steep and rocky sections. If you are not in shape, walk the shorter Lyrebird Track. If it has recently rained, it will be a muddy slog up the path. Do not start the climb after 2 o'clock in the winter months because you will run out of daylight. Keep to the track at all times and please carry your cigarette butts and litter back to the bins at the bottom of the park. The most important item of clothing will be good hiking shoes meant for gravel, dirt, and some rock climbing. Layering your clothing might be a good idea as it is often a quite different temperature at the top of the old volcano. A bottle of water is an excellent idea as there are no water or toilet facilities past the park's entrance. Bug spray might be good, but since you will be under thick canopy for most of the hike, sun block is probably not necessary. There are warnings about locking your car and stowing any valuables out of sight. Even people at the nearby town reported to me that car break-ins are fairly common.

If you want to join a group of people and be led up the mountain by a guide who will explain the terrain as you climb, look to **Rockhoppers** at ☎ 0500-881-881. You can choose between a Sunrise Trek and start at 2am with flashlights, enjoying a champagne breakfast on the summit, or do a Day Trek and have lunch at the top. Both cost about AU $55 and include guides, food and bus ride to the base.

For information before you go to the mount, you can contact the **National Parks & Wildlife Service** at ☎ (02) 6627-0200 or **W**: npws.nsw.gov.au

FOOD AND DRINK:

There are no eateries in the area, but there are plenty of BBQ facilities if you want to pack a cooler with goodies. You can make your way back and try a healthy meal at **Uki's Solstice Café** ($), relive your hike over a cold beer at the **Mt. Warning Pub** ($), or enjoy dinner in the outdoor **Beer Garden** ($) at the pub.

ACCOMMODATION:

The towns that surround the mountain offer a variety of lodging, but I am going to recommend two very different types of retreats. The first is quite rustic, out in the middle of nowhere. Its name includes the word hideaway, a perfect description. The second is a high-end accommodation with the most interesting decorations you will ever see.

MOUNT WARNING FOREST HIDEAWAY, 460 Byrrill Creek Road, Uki, NSW 2484, ☎ (02) 6679-7277, **W**: foresthideaway.com.au. *Prices range from AU*

$88–$120. Partially &.

The small but adequate rooms are decorated with hand-polished timber furniture (available for sale), the headboards of which are just incredibly beautiful wooden masterpieces. There are over 100 acres of woodland, creeks, waterfalls, and cooling pool if you haven't had enough walking. You will not need any wake-up calls as the abundant wildlife will make sure you don't miss the first light of dawn. The best aspect of this motel is the friendly family atmosphere. Local information as well as great home-style care is abundant.

WOLLUMBIN PALMS RETREAT, 6 Mt. Warning Road, Murwillumbah, NSW 2484, ☎ (02) 6679-5063, **W**: wollumbinpalms.com.au. *Prices range from AU $230–$245. Partially &.*

With lodges named Sir Joseph Banks and William Wordsworth, you know this secluded B&B is top notch. It is not only one of the most peaceful places to put your feet up, it is incredibly interesting to witness the inspired architecture. The main areas are a 12-sided Mongolian-style hut, a Javanese palace, and a lodge with a fish tank built into the toilet tank. The three lodges are separate and surrounded by thick rainforest, so privacy is assured.

LOCAL ATTRACTIONS:

You can choose between the 4–5 hour hike or the much easier and almost as scenic. Here is what you can expect on your climb into the clouds:

SUMMIT TRACK.

As you hike up the paved lot at Breakfast Creek Park, you will come to an information kiosk. I would urge you to read the suggestions and guidelines laid out on the boards. There is a bit of interesting information about the mountain and what to expect on the climb. Toilets can be found just up to the left; they are the good old dunny-style (outhouse). You will immediately enter a thick treetop canopy that blocks most of the direct sunlight, but allows pinprick beams of light onto the thick underbrush.

Entering the **Mount Warning Summit Track**, the gravel path will gently rise, the air becomes noticeably cooler and oxygen-rich. Along the path small placards identify some of the more interesting trees. Ascending the one and only path up the slope, timber stairs and root-covered sections will break your walking cadence. You will immediately feel the thermal breezes looking for an upward escape through the leaves above. Your nostrils will be filled with earthy smells of rotting leaves, rich humus, and exotic flowery perfumes. Your ears will fill with lots of chirps, tweets, twangs, and unnerving sounds coming from the bush. The birds are a busy lot in the surrounding forest and the scratching noise is no worry, as it is only bush turkeys busily scavenging for food.

Making way towards the former magna core, you will first enter the

Subtropical Rainforests, with lush palms and undergrowth. Strangling Figs are present most of the way up, a scene right out of a bad movie with huge tentacles wrapped around a host tree until it choked it to death. The scenery will discretely change into **Temperate Rainforest, Wet Sclerophyll Forest, Heath Scrubland**, and **Barren Rock Faces**. You will notice a mix of palm trees giving way to evergreens and deciduous-looking giants. The path now seems to become one switchback after another, with about five spots to have a rest. Halfway up the mount a marker will indicate your position on the trail, reminding you to turn around if it is too late in the day. The path winds up and around the circumference of the mountain, giving you several opportunities to have a glimpse of the villages, plains, sea, and forests below.

Near the top of the mountain, the foliage changes to coarse and spiky-shaped ferns that look a bit like Yucca trees. Unless the Parks Department cut them back recently, you will have to duck and weave through an obstacle course of sharp leaves. But the effort will pay off as the next turn provides a great view of the **Pacific Ocean**, complete with a well-deserved blast of cooling air.

About 5–10 minutes past that point a bench will appear at the end of the path. This will be a good spot to rest those weary legs and check out the information plaques before the final assault. Described as the **Final Rock Scramble**, the last leg upwards is a craggy path to the top. Luckily, several years ago the park service sunk steel posts in the former lava flow and strung a chain between them to allow hikers the option of pulling their hulks up the mount. It is only a hundred yards up this section, but you had to watch every step to avoid twisting an ankle or letting loose a flurry of rocks onto the climbers below.

Your reward should be a fantastic view at the **Mount Warning Summit**. The panoramic view of the lighthouse at Byron Bay and the patchwork of farms surrounded by smaller mountains is described by metal signs bolted to the viewing platforms spaced around the top. From this vantage point you'll surely get an idea of how huge this volcano really was. To think that it was twice the size it is today, and that you are only standing on the eroded core of the thing. Rest a bit before you start your descent, as it will be a bit less strenuous, but you will be using totally different muscles.

If you decide to enjoy an easier path, the **Lyrebird Track** will give you a taste of the mountain and its beauty.

LYREBIRD TRACK .

This short 200-yard stroll will lead you across a rippling brook, through a palm forest and to a Viewing Platform. This is a great trek for kids and those not able to endure the long trip to the top of the mountain. Stay awhile and enjoy the serenity.

Trip 41
Uki & Tweed Valley

Explore the Tweed Valley

The Tweed area is known for its beaches, entertainment hub, intricate waterways, and World Heritage National Parks. It is relaxed river country, and the recommended driving tour will allow you to pick and choose your stops or simply drive on by and just take a scenic ride. There are a few interesting places to visit in this area, a mix of the natural, industrial, and bizarre attractions.

GETTING THERE:

By Car: From Brisbane it's about a 90-minute drive south off the old Pacific Highway, exiting at any of the Tweed–Coolangatta ramps for the information booth. If you want to drive straight into the Valley, turn left onto Cane Road (at the Condong Sugar Mill), left onto Nimbah Road, and follow signs to the starting point of Crystal Creek Miniatures. If you are bypassing this attraction, you can start your tour at the sugar mill and improvise from there using the map provided. Coming from the south and the Byron area, it is only a 30–45-minute hop up the Pacific Highway, exit at the Murwillumbah Roundabout, and bear left onto Kyogle Road to your selected stops.

By Bus: Contact **Greyhound Pioneer** on ☎ 13-20-30 or **W**: greyhound.com.au, and **Coachtrans** at ☎ 13-12-30 or **W**: coachtrans.com.au, for details on service to the area.

SPECIAL EVENTS:

Monthly Markets and events are held at varying villages. Call the **Tweed Heads Visitor Centre** at ☎ (07) 5536-4244 or (02) 6672-1340 for current schedules. Tyalgum Music Festival (September), Visions of Nimbin (September), Rainforest Week (September–October), Harbour Town Festival (October), Kingscliff Main Street Festival (October), Tweed River Agricultural Show (November), Mooball Fish & Nana (May), Winter Sun Festival (June), Banana Festival & Harvest Week (August), and Doug Moran National Portrait Prize (December-January).

PRACTICALITIES:

It can get quite hot and humid in this area, and the mosquitoes are glad to greet you. If you are driving, there are plenty of fuel stations to tank up, but if you are heading into the national forests, keep it topped up. For the walking bit, good shoes and some layered clothing are a good idea. If you decide on the boating gig, check on the need for licenses, and river maps (usually provided) are a must.

If you want to bypass this area altogether, I would urge you to pick up a copy of the Tweed–Coolangatta Visitors Guide and at least follow one of the driving tours mentioned in the free booklet. The area is stunning, so it would be a shame to miss some of the spectacular sights along the Border Ranges. You can obtain a copy of the publication from the visitor's center at their Tweed Heads location in the **Tweed Heads Mall** on Wharf Street, ☎ 1-800-674-414 or **W**: tweed-coolangatta.com; or from the visitor booth in Murwillumbah at the corner of the Pacific Highway & Alma Street in Murwillumbah, ☎ (02) 6672-1340. The staff at both locations is extremely helpful, and you will have every question satisfied. Oh, you can book your accommodations and some of the attractions through these lovely folk too.

FOOD AND DRINK:

There are cafés, good restaurants, and fast food outlets peppered along your route as well as small grocery stores. Other than the Moo Moo Café in Mooball (on your way up from Byron Bay), I don't have any recommendations for a quick and easy meal. To get a wide selection of foods, the Coles Shopping Centre in Murwillumbah has it all. If you are coming from the north and the Gold Coast, the Tweed Heads area is full of good eateries, and its streets are lined with bistros and restaurants. Most of the attractions serve good food; if you want a different experience, try stopping at one of the bowls clubs for lunch or dinner. They usually welcome guests and charge only around a dollar to "join the club" (to actually be served alcohol).

ACCOMMODATIONS:

If you decide to stay overnight and start early to Warwick (3–4 hours northwest) or beyond, a good location is one of the popular eco lodges in the area known as Tree Tops. I have listed Treetops as one of the points of interest due to its eco-attraction, but it is a cool place to have a sleepover. Another interesting spot to rest your head is in a houseboat on the Tweed River. The houseboat rentals are usually a 3-night-minimum, so keep that in mind with your travel schedule. See the second stop below for details.

LOCAL ATTRACTIONS:

Circled numbers correspond to numbers on the map.

Only about a 15-minute, 6-mile jaunt from the either the Pacific Highway or Mount Warning areas, you will arrive at a spot where tiny crea-

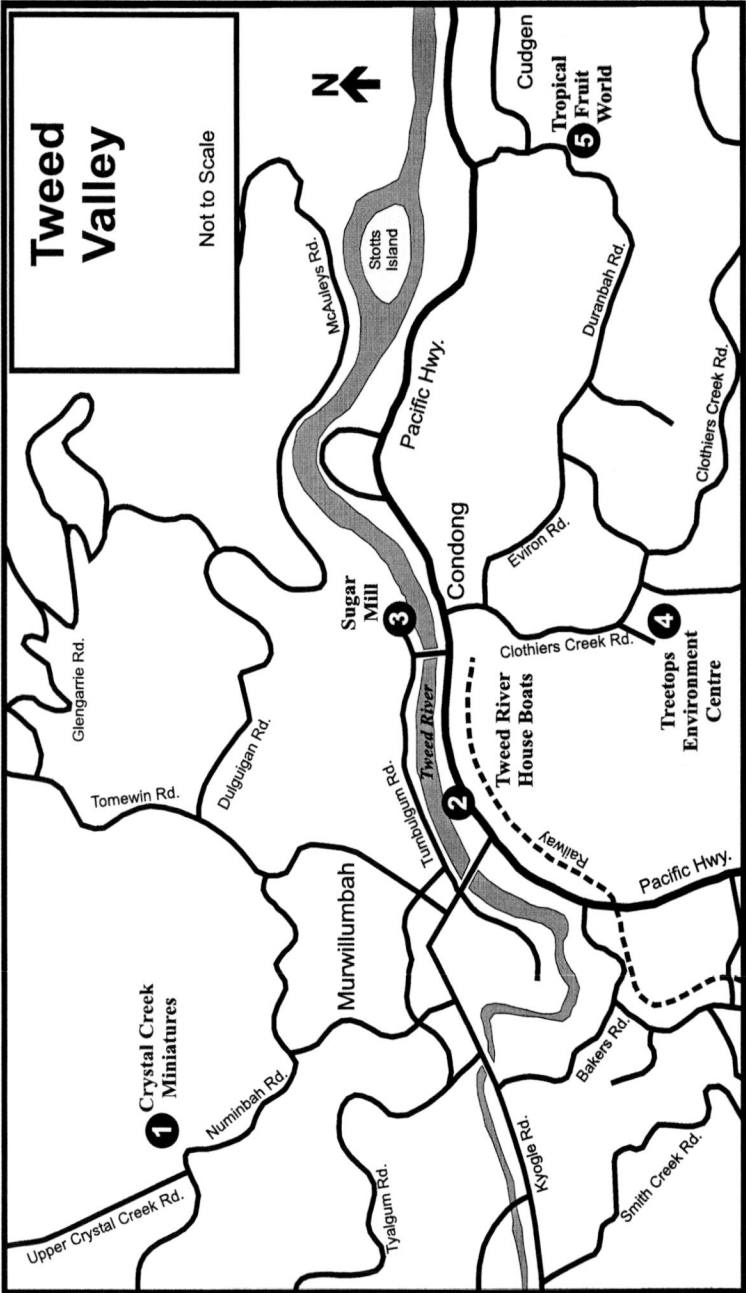

Tweed Valley

Not to Scale

N

Cudgen

5 Tropical Fruit World

Stotts Island

McAuleys Rd.

Pacific Hwy.

Duranbah Rd.

Clothiers Creek Rd.

Condong

Eviron Rd.

Sugar Mill 3

4 Treetops Environment Centre

Clothiers Creek Rd.

Glengarrie Rd.

Tweed River House Boats

Tweed River

Dulguigan Rd.

Tumbulgum Rd.

Railway

2

Tomewin Rd.

Pacific Hwy.

Murwillumbah

Bakers Rd.

Crystal Creek Miniatures 1

Numinbah Rd.

Kyogle Rd.

Smith Creek Rd.

Tyalgum Rd.

Upper Crystal Creek Rd.

tures abound. There are several roads that approach the park on Nimbah Road; the two most direct are North Arm Road (from the west) or Cane Road (from the east).

CRYSTAL CREEK MINIATURES ❶, corner of Numinbah & Upper Crystal Creek roads, Murwillumbah, ☎ (02) 6679-1532, **W**: minianimals.net. *The hours are a bit confusing, so call ahead before you drive out. Adults AU $15, children AU $7.50. Guided tours, self-guided tours. Gift shop. Café. Special events.* ♿.

With over 100 miniature animals to greet you, this is a haven for kids. The farm/attraction is a stud farm and a park that showcases some amazing miniatures. The best way to see the place in a reasonable amount of time is to hop aboard the tractor train. Guided tours offer insights to the animals, breeding, and stops to let the young and old pet the friendly, furry critters. They even provide feed to allow you to give them each a treat on your visit. The range of different animals includes huge slow-moving turtles, tiny braying donkeys, wee mooing cows, miniature horses, and even a nursery to explore.

The next stop is designed for hearty souls who want a day or two on the Tweed River. You can rent a houseboat from a station on the river by the old Pacific Highway. My brother, who loves fishing, crabbing, and the tranquility of the water would definitely stop in to charter a houseboat at:

TWEED RIVER HOUSEBOATS ❷. 161 Tweed Valley Way (Old Pacific Highway), Murwillumbah, ☎ (02) 6672-3525, **W**: tweedriverhouseboats.com.au. *Open daily from early till late. Three-night prices range from AU $375-595 (sleeping 2–8 people).* ♿.

See the world from a different perspective on one of their luxury floating bedrooms. You can be the designated captain, cook, skipper, or passenger on the variety of boats available. No license is required to take the wheel, and you will be rewarded with the freedom to find a good fishing hole, dive off the side and cool off, bake on the upper decks, or motor along to see the sights of the ancient river way. The team at the rental office will give you in-depth instructions, fuel you up, and provide river charts and tide guides for your journey. They also have plenty of tips on how to fill the cooking pot with a mudcrab for dinner. To make sure you have a fighting chance, they also supply a dinghy, crab pots, hand lines for fishing, and free parking.

Continuing eastward and right on the Old Pacific Highway is the unmistakable:

*CONDONG SUGAR MILL ❸, McLeod Street, Condong, ☎ (02) 6670-1700, **W**: nswsugar.com.au. *Open Tues.–Thurs. 9–3, closed holidays. Adults AU $7, children AU $3.50, group rates available. Guided tours. Souvenir shop. Partially* ♿.

This imposing hulk of a building houses an impressive operation of crushing cane and producing sugar, molasses, and cane by-products. The 120-year-old mill still uses some of the steam equipment originally installed. There is a full tour of the production process after a 25-minute video called "Crystal Clear" that provides a thorough overview of the history and processes involved in the sugar industry. But be prepared for a bit of noise as you enter the main section of the factory, especially if you visit during crushing season from around July to November. After seeing the operations around you, your next teaspoon of sugar will be appreciated much more. The mill and all the supporting operations, involved in manufacturing the white gold, employ one of the largest single groups in the region. There is a pretty even split between cane growers and the mill workers, but the farmers usually outnumber the factory folks by a small margin. The revenues realized by the co-operative run a little over AU $230-million annually.

Ready for some peace and quiet? Just up the road from the mill is an eco-retreat with some interesting sights, good food, and fantastic shopping. Find Clothiers Creek Road near the mill (you really can't miss the huge sign along the road), turn right onto Hindmarsh Road, and up the gravel road to:

*TREETOPS ENVIRONMENTAL CENTRE ❹, Clothiers Creek Road, Condong, ☎ 1-800-027-242, W: treetops.com.au. *Lodge & restaurants open daily for breakfast, lunch, and dinner. Stores and tours operate between 10–4 (tours allowed anytime to those staying over). B&B prices range from AU $120–$165. Tour costs about AU $2.50 (free if you buy stuff or have lunch/dinner there). Self-guided tours. Gift shop. Café. Special events.* ♿.

Ah mates, you should definitely check this place out and spend a few hours with fantastic hosts and beautiful surroundings. If you sleepover, you will be absorbed in rustic timber lodges and sounds of nature, overlooking a pond with over 100 acres of native animals. Polished wood floors, furniture of unique design, and cozy beds will shake off the worst of road wear. If you are just passing through, make sure you say howdy to the greeting peacock and visit the working shed out back. The woodworker's barn is an incredible mix of old and new with rich smells of naturally harvested woods. You walk above the lathes, bandsaw, and stacks of ancient timber; and if you're lucky they will be working on more furniture for the showroom. Now that you have an appreciation of the effort to hew the giant logs into workable planks, visit the **Griffith Furniture** showroom. For lovers of timber products and the smells of finished woods, your eyes and nose will be ecstatic. The jewelry and art fans will be in their glory by walking across the patio to the **Griffith Galleries**. There is a wide range of art to wear or hang on the wall. The prices are extremely reasonable, and there is a wide range of one-of-a-kind bracelets in this store. Finally, treat yourself to a gourmet lunch or dinner at the **Verandah Restaurant** before you finish this section of touring. At night the possums scamper around the outer handrails and stare forlornly from a safe distance.

The final stop is an attraction advertised as having the largest selection of tropical fruits in one spot. Near Tweed Heads just off the Old Pacific Highway and on Duranbah Road you will see the home to the Big Avocado at:

*TROPICAL FRUIT WORLD ❺, Duranbah Road, Duranbah, ☎ (02) 6677-7222, **W**: tropicalfruitworld.com.au. *Open daily from 10–5, closed Christmas. Adults AU $25, children AU $15. Guided tours, self-guided tours. Gift shop. Café. Special events. Partially ♿.*

A fruity theme park with lots of educational value, this world of over 500 varieties of fruits has the possibility of consuming a good half-day—especially if you have young ones. Considered a sanctuary for research and development of healthy products, the park is a major tourist attraction in the area. Supposedly, the special and essential oils from the avocado will vanquish 10 years of aging from your skin. If you are only 10 years old, skip this part. There are tractor tours of the facilities, themed gardens, boat cruises, a Koi fish dam, a petting farm, plantation safaris, and cafés galore. I would recommend taking the tractor ride first and then vote on the areas that interest you the most. But seriously, try out some of the fruit products developed at the horticultural research labs and taste some delicacies that taste like chocolate, ice cream, and champagne. For real!

If this tour doesn't do it for you, other areas of interest in this region include: A tour of the **Madura Tea Estate** at Clothiers Creek Road, or take a **Crab Catching Cruise** on the Tweed river with **Tweed Endeavor Cruises**, ☎ (07) 5536-8800 or **W**: goldcoastcruising.com

If you are really willing to go to the fringes, make a quick stop at the "Alternative Capital of Australia." Also home to the annual cannabis festival, **Nimbin** is a small town in the rainbow region of NSW. But be prepared for a shocker as drugs are prevalent here (it actually has a marijuana museum), and despite the beautiful surrounding area, it is a bit run down. However, there are plans underway to renovate the main street. Check it out at **W**: nimbinaustralia.com.au

WARWICK TRIPS

Southwest of Brisbane is the gateway to the Outback. The little town of Warwick is a grand spot to get a taste of the cattle and open ranges that are becoming more popular with overseas visitors. The scenic drive seems long, but there are Revive/Survive stops along the way that offer free cups of coffee. And no need to pull over at the road inspection stops; they are setup for the cattle cars traveling to/from the district to prevent transportation of unwanted pests into the region. With a population a little over 12,000 (and probably way more numbers of cattle), Warwick began in 1847 as a sheep station, but its notoriety is now based on its roses and rodeos. For those not interested in either of those, you can try out the gold, silver and petrified wood fossicking (prospecting) popular in the area. Warwick is also known for its historic sandstone buildings, though I am just as impressed by the fancy timber Queenslanders. But the most impressive sight is the lack of litter on the streets. Appropriately named as it holds the title of a "Tidy Town." You will find the people the biggest draw card; they are some of the most genuine folks I've met anywhere. Another fun aspect of the area is its rich history. From the 1892 record-breaking shearing of 321 sheep in one day (with hand shears), the "egging" of the Prime Minister in 1917, the 3-Bullet Pub where an American soldier ordered a beer by firing his rifle into the ceiling, and the new 15-ton granite frog to honor the Aboriginal legend called Tiddalik. For more information on the Warwick area try the **Visitor Information Centre** at 49 Albion Street, ☎ (07) 4661-3122 or **W**: qldsoutherndowns.org.au; and the **Warwick Shire Council** on Fitzroy Street, ☎ (07) 4661-0300 or **W**: warwick.qld.gov.au

A bit out of town and the site of the stage two of this segment is a ranch called Cherrabah Homestead Resort. This 5,000-acre property is set in the middle of bushland and is surrounded by majestic and craggy mountains. Set up as a farmstay experience, it's sort of like a dude ranch. The name of the area is derived from the Aboriginal word for fresh water. This region was also home to some famous bushrangers, and some of Captain Thunderbolt's treasures have been found on the resort by ranch hands. I have been to the place twice and both times it was a blast. You will be treated to open plains, plenty of horseback riding, bullwhip classes, bronco riding if you choose, a chance to shear a sheep, and getting up close and personal with at least one of the thousands of kangaroos running wild. But don't go cornering any of the 4-foot goannas running around in the scrub.

Refer to the specific tours for directions, practicalities, food, accommodation, and special events.

Guns & Roses

S trap on your six-shooter and smell the roses. This town is a strange mix of Queensland's rodeos and the red "City of Warwick (Artofuto) Roses." Now you probably won't see a cowboy with a rose in his lapel, but both are prevalent around this tidy town in the center of Queenlsand's Southern Downs. The region is famous for establishing the State's first free settlement and promoting the initiation of the wool industry. The history is as interesting as its mix of sandstone federal-style buildings, grand pubs, and little Queenslanders. People of the town were so disrespectful to the unpopular Prime Minister (president) Billy Huges that someone launched an egg at his face when he tried to promote his WWI draft for the war. The local and state police refused to arrest the perpetrator on the grounds of "no jurisdiction" and the PM stormed back to his federal seat to establish the Federal Police Force. A second and just as notable tale is of the young lad, raised by a circus acrobat on a local station, who set a record for sheep shearing. Because he regularly ripped the sleeves off of his shirt, and his feat made him a living legend, the first singlet (or tank-top) was named "The Jackie Howe." These irreverent and independent attitudes are beautifully maintained today.

This is a great town for a bicycle tour, with only a few hills, wide streets, and very little traffic on the side streets. The parks are well maintained and there are several museums to browse and learn more history of the area. There are plenty of shaded picnic areas, streams, and dams stocked with loads of fish, golf courses, and fields of wide-open spaces. One thing not to miss is the local cheddar, camembert, and brie cheeses produced locally by Dairyfields. Washed down with a local Stanthorpe wine (the reds are better than the whites), they are the perfect companions to pack in your bicycle basket on this trip. You can choose to drive the route if you want to see a wider range of terrain. There are driving tours laid out in the free Warwick Shire brochure found at the information/visitor centers in town.

GETTING THERE:

By Car: from Brisbane, it is about a 2-1/2-hour drive (102 miles southwest) straight out the Cunningham Highway. From the Gold Coast, a 3-

hour, drive (192 miles west) out through Beaudesert, over the Great Dividing Range, along Route 15 and a short hop down the New England Highway.

By Bus: Both **Greyhound**, ☎ 13-20-30 or **W**: greyhound.com.au, and **McCaffertys**, ☎ 13-14-99 or **W**: mccaffertys.com.au, bus lines run to/from Brisbane to Warwick out of the Warwick Transit Centre (twice a day). The cost is about AU $35 for the 2–3 hour journey.

By Train: Travel Train, ☎ 13-22-32, passenger service to the area has been discontinued.

SPECIAL EVENTS:

Autumn Flower Show (March), National Rock Swap and Gem Show (April), Warwick Picnic Races (April), Gardening Extravaganza (June), Veteran's Day Horse Race (August), Spring Horse Show (September), Rose & Rodeo Festival (October), Rodeo & Campdraft (October), and the Scots PGC Highland Gathering (December).

PRACTICALITIES:

You are now entering cowboy country so you will be trading your flowery shirts, flip-flops, baseball caps, and shorts for checkered shirts, boots, Akubra hats, and jeans. Actually, you can wear shorts and golf shirts without standing out too much. The food will be transformed from seafoods to hearty beef and pork products. The beer is just as cold and tasty and the people are equally as friendly. Sun protection still goes out here and, seriously, take along some long pants and a hat.

FOOD AND DRINK:

I think the best foods are in the pubs, but there are a good selection of cafés and pie (meat) shops. If you want upscale, there are fine restaurants too. From the food court in the Rose City Shoppingworld on Grafton & Fitzroy streets, to a coffee shop setting at Bryson's Place on Palmerin Street, Wen's Thai restaurant on Palmerin Street, and at the fancy Cloisters in the Abby of the Roses on the corner of Locke & Dragon Streets.

ACCOMMODATION:

You can do the daytrip in Warwick, then head out to Cherrabah to stay overnight, but you might want to pack a full day in town and crash there. If you stay in the CBD area, the Fitz Cottage is my pick as the B&B. They provide bikes, offer walking/biking maps, and the small cottage is close to all the attractions.

FITZ COTTAGE B&B, 106 Fitzroy Street, Warwick, QLD 4370, ☎ (07) 4661-3806, **W**: travelau.com/southerndowns/. *Prices range from AU $60/double for the apartment to AU $40/person for the cottage.* ♿.

If you get a chance to reserve the cottage, do so as it is a cute little self-contained house that reminds me of a gardener's home smack in the middle of a well-manicured flowerbed. The owners advertise a quiet and friendly atmosphere—and that is a modest description. The apartment and cottage are off the main street and back upon open fields. A major appeal to my wife and I was the mini-library in the flat. It provided a history of the area, current eateries, and recommendations of what to see. The homemade breakfast treats include jams, honey and fruit, and many other personal touches to enjoy. They even have a working gramophone! You can sit in the cottage to savor the foods provided or picnic under the giant mulberry tree in the back yard (October–November). Rita and Mal treat you like newly moved-in neighbors and as well as offering their bicycles, they laid out a touring map of the town. I am borrowing part of it for the bicycle tour below.

Other lodging can be found at **National Hotel** at 35 Grafton Street, ☎ (07) 4661-1146; **Cromer Guest House** at 90 Oxenham Street, ☎ (07) 4661-8381; **Warwick Motor Inn** on Albion Street, ☎ (07) 4661-1533; **Burckaroo Motor Inn** at 86 Wood Street, ☎ (07) 4661-3755; **Darling Downs Hotel** at Sandy Creek Road, ☎ (07) 4661-3413; and if it is still operating, a former convent called **Abbey of the Roses**, ☎ (07) 4661-9777. Any of the pubs have good and inexpensive rooms too, but **The Criterion**, ☎ (07) 4661-1042, is the home to the Three-Bullet bar and a doozy of a hotel.

SUGGESTED CYCLING TOUR:
Circled numbers correspond to numbers on the map.

This is an easy ride and should only take about a half a day if you stop and smell the roses, break for lunch, explore the museums, and gab a bit with the townsfolk. Many of the buildings are Heritage Listed and are not open to the public. The historic sites that are open, have plaques on the front doors/gates as to the times and days available for inspection.

Start your ride at the **Fitz Cottage** ❶ and the first Heritage-listed house on the route. Then strap on a helmet, exit right from the driveway, and cruise down Fitzroy Street to **Kerong Cottage** ❷ at the corner of Fitzroy & Dragon streets. It was the sandstone-and-cedar home to a local artist, built in 1869. The small building is a bit plain, but the twin towering chimneys add a unique touch. Right next door and on the same side of the street is the bold **St Andrew's Uniting Church** ❸. The sandstone used to construct this house of worship was lugged by wagon from the distant quarry at Mt. Tambo. Opened in 1870, it has intricate spires and a wooden bell tower attached to the main structure.

Across the street at the corner of Fitzroy and Guy streets you will find the **Court House** ❹. This stately building, used to dish out justice, was built for merely £3,700 and was completed in 1886. The clock tower allows the locals to set their watches from any direction of town and make it to the pub on time.

Continue on Fitzroy and appropriately, right next door is the **Warwick Police Station** ❺. Even if you get the willies from police stations, this is a

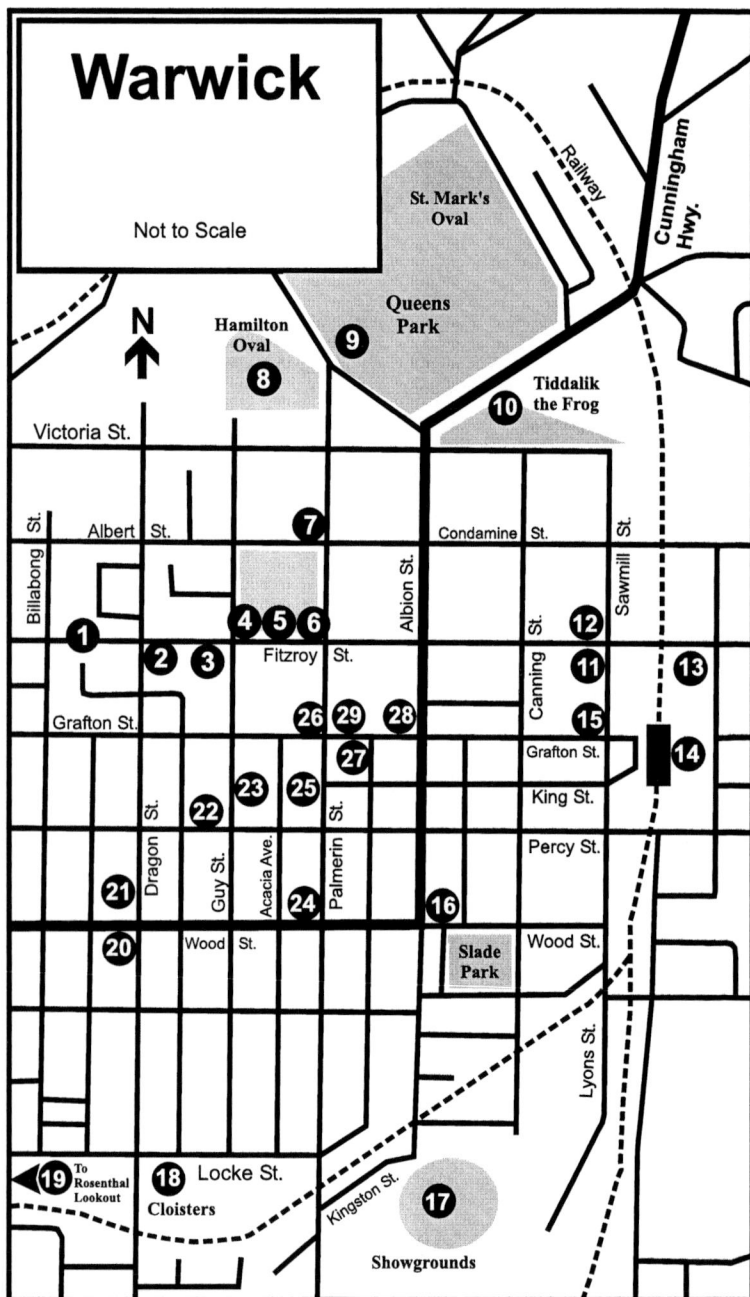

Warwick

Not to Scale

N

St. Mark's
Oval

Queens
Park

Hamilton
Oval

9

8

Tiddalik
the Frog

10

Victoria St.

Albert   St.

7

Billabong St.

Condamine   St.

Albion St.

Sawmill   St.

4 **5** **6**

12

Fitzroy   St.

Canning   St.

11

13

1

2 **3**

26 **29** **28**

15

14

Grafton St.

27

Grafton St.

Dragon St.

23 **25**

King St.

22

Acacia Ave.

Palmerin St.

Percy St.

Guy St.

21

24

16

20

Wood   St.

Slade
Park

Wood St.

Lyons St.

19 To
Rosenthal
Lookout

18 Locke St.

Kingston St.

17

Cloisters

Showgrounds

Railway

Cunningham Hwy.

cool building. It has housing, cells, stables, and a jailer's residence as part of the stone structure. In the roundabout at the intersection of Fitzroy & Palmerin streets are the structures built to honor the warriors of WW I, WW II, Vietnam, and other Australian conflicts. The War Memorial, Gates, and **Leslie Park ❻** have names of the fallen inscribed on plaques as you enter the park, and there is a large monolith in the center. The gardens are a nice place to have a wander too with swing boats for the kiddies and roses everywhere.

Exit the park at either end to cycle past the **Aquatic Centre ❼** to **Hamilton Oval ❽** on Palmerin Street. Both areas are for the sports-minded, where you can have a swim, take in some hydrotherapy to ease the muscles, or try you hand at cricket. Last time I ventured past, there was a very proper game going on and both sides were in their finest whites and cricket hats. If a game is on as you roll past, spend a few minutes watching.

Next stop is at the intersection of Palmerin & Alice streets, revealing the stately old rivergums that welcome you into the *****Queens Park & St. Marks Oval ❾**. You can ride through, but it's best to walk and smell the flowers of the season. The garden beds are immaculate and as a side fact, Mal, at the Fitroy Cottage, is the supervisor of all the gardens in the area. Again, you can exit at several spots along the parkway, but it is nice to wander along the Condamine River. The slow moving stream is bordered by willows and teaming with loons, water dragons, butcherbirds, and fish. If you are a keen observer you will notice the family of possums that have taken up residence along the muddy banks. But the star attraction is yet to be seen.

Rounding the park is Jackie Howe Drive. You can ride this loop or just follow the river under the Madsen Bridge to *****Tiddalick The Frog ❿**. This 15-ton, granite-carved frog is the Aboriginal Dreamtime culprit who drank all the water from the streams and created a drought. To get the full story, check out the billboard adjacent to the giant amphibian. It is a great photo spot and makes an impressive shot to send home to friends.

Double back to Albion Street. Two blocks down that strip you will see the Information Center off to your right. You can stop in for a chat or browse the award-winning art pieces if you reach them during opening hours. Turn left onto Fitzroy Street and two blocks on the right will be the next heritage-listed building on your path. The **Connolly Residence ⓫** is now privately owned by the family, but was originally designed and built by a famous local architect, Daniel Connolly. The quaint little one-story house has a long and popular history. Across the street is the **Warwick National School ⓬**, which really will satisfy your mind's eye of what an old school should look like. It is the oldest school building in Queensland, a timber and brick whitewashed structure, and has 10-foot verandas to cool the classrooms.

Now for a bit of fun history as you ride towards Hamilton Street and enter the *****Historic Railway Precinct ⓭**. Even though there will be little activity around the old railroad platforms, you can still hear the sounds and feel the energy from the locomotives, cattle being herded onto cars, and the smells of steam and oil from the old boilers. It seemed abandoned, but a local community organization is working to reinvigorate the area to support tourist travel to the area. The lonely site was once the home to over 50 steam locomotives and over 350 railway staff. A bit farther on Lyons Street at Grafton Street, you will approach the *Warwick Railway Station ⓮. Spend some time here and read the plaques describing the events that changed the nation. Although it is now strictly a base for freight transportation into the area, it was the site where the angry egg thrown at the Prime Minister initiated the act to create the Commonwealth Police. It really is a good story and depicts one aspect of the Outback spirit.

Turning your back on the station you will be staring at a building which, if it could talk, would have you spellbound with tall tales. The **National Hotel** ⓯ is a grand old Queensland-style pub with rooms to let above. It is now a dilapidated building but you can see the grandeur of its roots with pressed metal ceilings, tall wrapping verandas, and intricate railings. If it is open when you pass by, do have a cold one in memory of the rail workers who must have leaned on the bar rail over a few good stories.

Riding down Lyons to Wood Street, turn left and pass-by Slade Park on your left, and stop in front of **Aberfoyle** ⓰. The 1910 private residence has been completely renovated and is a fantastic photo opportunity. From the heritage booklet description, it is an example of how the Federation brick-and-tile buildings were transformed into timber-and-tin construction. The mailbox is even a great design.

Turn left at Kingsford Street. On the left will be the **Showgrounds** ⓱, home to rodeos and county fairs. Some of the homes surrounding the grounds are worth a look too, with a strange mix of ferns, gardens, and evergreens. Double back to Locke Street and follow it until you reach the hangout for the nuns. The *Cloisters ⓲ was originally called Our Lady of Assumption Convent and was the home to the Sisters of Mercy. This huge sandstone complex, with stained windows, magnificent staircases, and impressive spires, is now an on-again-off-again restaurant/B&B. If you happen upon town on the weekend of the town's market day, you will be able to wander through the grounds and building—maybe even make a quiet confession.

At this point, if you are full of energy and want a bit longer ride, continue down Locke Street, make a left onto the New England Highway for a block, and turn right onto Glen Road for a about a mile to **Rosenthal Lookout** ⓳. There are some moderately steep climbs to the top, but it will provide you with a good vantage point to scope out the tidy town. Otherwise, at the roundabout on Dragon Street, turn right and proceed two long blocks to the *Pringle Cottage Museum ⓴. The two-story sandstone was believed to be a home, then a school, and is now a museum. It is utilitarian in design, and if it is open, the small fee to enter is worth it.

Crossing over the Cunningham Highway, **The Commonage** ㉑ will be on your left. This is a plain-looking structure, but interesting nevertheless. It was constructed in the early 1870s using hand-made bricks, and has been upgraded with a tin-roofed, front porch and some snazzy accented paint. Continue on Dragon Street, turn right onto Percy Street and look for the **Warwick Central School** ㉒. The L-shaped block structure is neat with tiny dormers popping up from the roof. It was set up with separate wings for boys, girls, and infants. Detouring slightly onto Guy Street and riding only a short distance will bring you to one of the most grand of all Masonic Buildings in the country. The **Saint George's Lodge** ㉓ is stunning. It had springs installed under the ballroom decking, the foundation stone has treasures of 1800's coins, newspapers, and a scroll, and the announcement of "We fear the Creator of the Universe" carved above the huge sandstone pillars at the front door.

Two of my favorites are coming up. For these, you will need to go back on Percy street, pick up Palmerin Street to ***Old St. Mary's Church** and **St Mary's Catholic Church** ㉔. The older and smaller one was the first sandstone church in town and was opened in 1865. The grander, but with no greater feeling of religious power, is the more modern church built in 1926. The outside spire is pretty impressive though. If you have an opportunity, spend a few minutes inside to appreciate the silence in one of the pews.

On the other side of Percy Street on Palmerin Street is another pub called the **Langham Hotel** ㉕ that is now home to the sports club. The unique aspect of this watering hole is the design of a woman in a gown seen in each of the cast iron panels surrounding the balcony. The bottle shop is a good place to pick up a nice wine for the after-ride toast. At the intersection of Grafton and Palmerin Streets is the outstretched hand of Thomas Byrnes. The **Byrnes Monument** ㉖ is a marble testament to one of the local heroes. He was a very popular scholar and political figure on the late 1880s.

Still on Grafton Street is the **Post Office** ㉗. I think it matches the grandeur of George's Lodge as it looks like a grand government building typical of the 19th century. It has covered verandas with large arches looking through to windows that house the mailmen and women. On the corner of Grafton and the Cunningham Highway is the final church on the tour. ***St. Mark's Anglican Church** ㉘ has some of the most stunning stained-glass windows I've ever seen. See if you can determine which archangel is represented in one of the panes.

Finally, the end of the tour and what a great place to stop. You might think that I had ulterior motives for parking the bike against the rails at the **Criterion Hotel** ㉙ and you'd be right mate. I like this pub, whose history alone is worth at least one cold beer. This is where the Yank came in and shot up the pub. In fact, the three bullet holes are still very evident in the metal-pressed ceiling. Ask the barmaid about the event or just read the plaque at the entrance to the bar. And if that doesn't interest you at all, look for the face of the Virgin Mary looking down on you (it may take more than one beer) or check out the owls and rams watching from the stained-glass windows. The food isn't too bad either and the crowd will usually be happy to fill you in on the latest weather and stock prices.

Cherrabah Homestead Shearing Shed

Searching for Bushrangers

You don't have to be a champion rider to enjoy this place, but you will get a feel of the terrain on the back of a gentle horse. It is rumored that the feared bushranger Captain Thunderbolt hid his loot in the hills around the area, and you are free to try and find it. A bushranger is described in the Australian Oxford Dictionary as "a person who engages in armed robbery, escaping into or living in the bush in the manner of an outlaw." Advertised as providing a taste of the real Australia, it certainly seemed like it to me. The ranch is west of Warwick and much of the roadway is dirt and gravel, so don't wash your car before you go. If you don't have the time or energy to drive out to this farm, a sister ranch is located near Surfers Paradise.

You will need at least one night at Cherrabah, but it is best to do a two-night stint as there is so much to do. I found that the two horse rides are different enough to warrant saddling up both days. They have activities going all day long, from sheep shearing demonstrations, to boomerang throws, to bullwhip contests. At night they have entertainment, even giving you a ride on a mechanical bull. This is a real hoot and they will only crank it up as fast as you yell out. For the real adventurous, they sometimes allow you to ride a real bull.

The nice part about this resort is they don't treat you like a city slicker, and are very patient with those who have problems riding horses. And sometimes allowing you to ride a bit harder if the group is small and evenly matched in riding expertise. The narration during the rides and at the various demonstrations is provided by guys and ladies who ranch for a living. Most of the guides are local ranch hands on neighboring properties that come over to help out and have some fun too.

The rooms are basic and adequate. Believe me, when it is time to turn out the lights and sleep, you will be out as soon as you hit the pillow. You can be busy all day long with varied levels of physical play or just relax on the porch and listen to the animals play. Oh, if you get a chance say g'day to my girlfriend out there. Her name is Missy and she is a small 14-year old kangaroo that has been adopted by the farm. She hangs out near the cabins in the early morning and she will let you pet her. Another good mate is Madison, who is a giant white Maremmas dog that protects the sheep and goats on the farm. He looks fierce, but loves a scratch behind the ears and will be your friend for life for that treat.

GETTING THERE:

By Car: Cherrabah is 20 or 30 minutes, or 19 miles past Warwick just down Cunningham Highway and onto Killarney Road. This road is not paved on the last half-mile and can be a bit bumpy. Beware of the cattle grates in some sections of the road. If driven over too fast they can damage a car's suspension.

By Bus: Call the ranch to arrange pick-up. They do have courtesy buses from certain locations.

PRACTICALITIES:

Huge blowflies are pesky during the day and mosquitoes come out at night, so bug repellant is a good idea. A trick that I learned, but haven't shared it with anyone out there, is to wear a pair of padded cycling shorts under my jeans when riding the horses. Even with the extra cushioning, you will be a bit sore after two days of riding. The water is from a local spring and it tastes a bit tinny, so you may want to pack some bottled water.

The other resort, **Paradise Country**, is about 15-minutes from Surfers Paradise. Contact them at ☎ (07) 5578-4077 to book a similar tour. The major differences are no overnight stays, and it will be more of a touristy spot with crowds and not nearly as scenic. I don't think they have the horseback riding tours either.

FOOD AND DRINK:

Food is included in the package deal; you will not want for nourishment. There is a bar to buy alcohol, with reasonable prices. A sample of what to expect for your meals is:

Breakfast (7:30–8:30) includes a full buffet of cereal, fruit, toast, juices, eggs, bacon, sausages, and muffins. You can usually see the kangaroos lining up on the golf course early in the morning—right outside the windows.

Lunch (noon–1) will be welcomed with an all-you-can-eat BBQ, salads, and desserts served on the verandah overlooking the ranges.

Dinner (6:30–7:30) is a feast of country specialties including roasts (ask for cracklin), veggies, a pasta/potato/rice accompaniment, and a good selection of desserts.

CHERRABAH HOMESTEAD RESORT, Elbow Valley via Warwick, QLD 4370, ☎ (07) 4667-9177, **W**: cherrabah.com.au, E-mail: cherrabah@bigpond.com. *Open daily. Price ranges are for room only AU $70–$160/night, for the package that includes meals and all activities is AU $160/night. Guided tours,* *self-guided tours. Gift shop. Café. Special events. Partially ⅙.*

OUTSTANDING ACTIVITIES:

Since this is a package and the programs vary from day-to-day, instead of providing an itinerary, I will list some of the best things to do at your stay in the Outback. Here goes:

An Outback-style 9 hole **golf course** offers plenty of kangaroo hazards (a two stroke penalty if you hit them). It's not the flashiest course and on some holes it's difficult to tell where the fairway ends and the green starts, but it is fun to putt around the roos and the squawking parrots. The two tennis courts are surrounded by shade gums and laughing kookaburras. The court just below the cabins is adjacent to the golf course, and just above the dam. Heaps of **hiking trails** and the mud map shown gives you choices of Snake Gully, Bee Sting, and Peter's Poole. The pistol of Captain Thunderbolt was found off of one of the trails on the resort; it is rumored that some of the bushranger's gold is also buried in the area. A refreshing **saltwater pool** looks out onto the Cunningham Valley and the dry, brown mountain ranges that encircle the area. A fantastic program of **horse riding** takes you through the valley and up to Balancing Rock, the giant Fig Tree, Hillcrest, Whale Rock, The Caves, Hidden Valley, Norma's Lookout, or Split Rock. The best trip is to ride up to Balancing Rock, tie off your horses, and hike to the boulder that is the size of a large house. It is in one huge piece. Behind it is a smaller balancing rock, and from all reports, my brother has been the only one who successfully rocked the giant marble—go ahead and try it! Fun and educational **animal shows** down by the stables, and sheep shearing demonstrations. You can volunteer to try your hand at **shearing**—it is no easy task. An animal farm that has goats, sheep, chickens, and the guardian named Madison. Chances to wet a line and try your luck at a **fish** or two in the lake or paddle across to the barbeque shed named New Cabin. **Dancing** and music at night, but for the brave ones—the **Deadly Mechanical Bull**. They also had pool tables, videos, games, and other stuff in the lounge, but why stay inside at an action-packed place like this? But at the end of a hard day's ride, relax in the Squatters Chairs (they have planks that pull out so you can stretch your legs straight out) on the veranda and watch the sun set over the range.

Section VI

Daytrips Along
The Sunshine Coast

Well, if you want to meet Stevie the Crocodile Hunter, this is the place. The Australian Zoo is his home base, and the area is loaded with sights unique to the world (and that's no exaggeration). Even though the Sunshine Coast is only an hour northeast of Brisbane, the scenery changes dramatically and will present prehistoric photo opportunities. Passing through the Glass House Mountains and the glittery facade of long-dead volcanoes, you will be delighted with the national parks, monumental spectacles like Aussie World, Ettamogah Pub (based on a famous Australian cartoon), the Big Pineapple, the Big Shell, the Big Fish—and the "Big" list goes on. Most are worth the stop, but it is hard to top Mother Nature in the 20-million-year-old driving/hiking trails that surround the "Bigs."

The driving and walking tours wind past the aromatic Ginger Factory, the magic of the Pacific deep at Underwater World, a replica Norman Castle (complete with a dungeon and torture chamber) at Bli Bli, and unforgettable sights of Hells Gates and the Fairy Pools in Noosa National Park. The highlight of this section, 152 miles north of Brisbane, is Fraser Island—the land of dingoes. This largest sand dune island in the world boasts the purest strain of dingo anywhere, lakes so clean that they will not support any life, rainbow-colored beaches, remnants of sunken luxury liners, and miles of just empty beaches.

Buderim is centrally located to all of the tours and offers a quiet, accessible accommodation right off of the highway. If you decide to stay in this area, the lodging selections will be listed in Trip 44—The Glass House Mountains. If your preference is to move around a bit, accommodations can be selected in three different areas to allow the best opportunities to experience everything without stressing too much over driving. The first layover can be at the foot of the Glass House Mountains at a quiet B&B, the second may be in the glamour town of Noosa, and the final stop before heading north to the Capricorn Coast might be the magical Fraser Island.

The tours in each area are designed to allow a mixing and matching of attractions for flexible planning of one-day excursions. Fraser Island is best seen by scheduling three days of touring and at least a two-night sleepover with the dingoes. The three-day, organized tour highlights the best things to see and do. The attractions vary greatly and offer a combination of natural openness, shopping madness, and ocean wilderness. Although it is probably the second or third major tourist center In Queensland, it is not overly crowded yet and you shouldn't expect long queues for any of the attractions, restaurants, or even on the roads (after you leave the Brisbane area).

GETTING THERE:

By Car: The drive is a straight shot up the Bruce Highway. The Sunshine Coast region begins at about Bribie Island (an hour from Brisbane's center), and the northern end at Fraser Island is about three hours north of Brisbane. All attractions can be reached from the Bruce Highway, and they are well marked along the way. All major rental car agencies operate in the area. Beware of a bit of a bottleneck that usually occurs heading north about 15–20 minutes past the Brisbane Airport. It creeps for about two miles during peak hours of the weekend before clearing out.

By Bus: **SunAir Bus Service,** ☎ 1-800-804-340 or **W**: sunair.com.au; and **Sun Coast Pacific,** ☎ (07) 5491-2555, operate between the Gold Coast, Brisbane, and points along the Sunshine Coast. **Greyhound Pioneer,** ☎ 13-20-30 or **W**: greyhound.com.au, and some of the other national bus lines operate to/from the area also. The local bus service is **Sunbus,** ☎ (07) 5492-8700 or 13-12-30. For road service, call **RACQ,** ☎ 13-11-11.

By Train: **Queensland Rail,** ☎ 13-12-30, provides transport to the area. Refer to their maps in Section IV—Brisbane & Surrounds—for more details.

By Air: There are two small airports in the area. **Caloundra Airport** in the town with the same name as well as the **Sunshine Coast Airport** near Mudjimba can be contacted on ☎ 1-800-804-340. Currently, **QANTAS Link** and **Sunshine Express** provide daily service to the two airports. But since the airline industry is a bit shaky, call either **QANTAS,** ☎ 13-13-13 or **W**: qantas.com.au, or **Virgin Blue,** ☎ 13-67-89 or **W**: virginblue.com.au, for flight information.

PRACTICALITIES:

The number of roads is limited to/from the major hubs, so pack water just in case the roads shut due to an accident. The weather is a bit warmer and more humid as you drive north, but not noticeably until you reach Cairns. Sun protection, good hiking shoes, and a dressy set of clothing is in order for this section.

Because there are options for your hub selections, I provided general directions to the Sunshine Coast, an overview of the practicalities, food opportunities, accommodations, and special events. Each trip will also have specific recommendations. For general information before you head to the northern playgrounds off the Coral Sea, check out the following visitor and tourism sites: **Sunshine Regional Guide**, **W**: sunshinecoast-tourism.com; **Blackall Tourism**, ☎ (07) 5478-5544; **Cooloola Information Centre**, ☎ (07) 5483-5554; **Maroochy Tourism**, ☎ (07)-5479-1566; **Caloundra Tourism**, ☎ (07) 5491-0202; and **Noosa Information Centre**, ☎ (07) 5447-4988. I think the best comprehensive guide available is the free "Discover Queensland's Sunshine Coast" handed out at most of the information and tourist centers.

SPECIAL EVENTS:

January—Ginger Flower Festival in Yandina, Buderim Australia Day Parade, Dunny Races at Aussie World. February—Queensland Surf Life Saving Championship in Peregian. March—Noosa Longboard Pro-Am. April—Kilkivan Great Horse Ride, Orchid Show in Caloundra. May—Noosa Picnic Races & Ball, Gympie Show, Malaney Show, Calaundra Show. June—Noosa Boat Show, Sunshine Coast Show in Nambour, Queensland Air Museum Show, Motorbike & Hot Rod Show. July—Race the Rattler in Gympie, Home Garden Show in Nambour, Rainbow Beach Fishing Classic, King of the Mountain in Mt. Cooroora, Caloundra Arts & Crafts Festival, National Aboriginal & Islander Day in Caloundra. August—Sugar Festival in Nambour, National Country Music Muster in Gympie, Noosa Country Show. September—Noosa Jazz Festival, Maleny Scarecrow Festival, Kenilworth Show, Rodeo, Arts Expo. October—Model Railway Show, Doll Show, Coolum Kite Festival. November—Sunshine Coast Rodeo, Sunshine Coast Wine Festival. December—Woodford Folk Festival, Mountains to the Sea Festival.

FOOD AND DRINK:

Heaps and heaps of eateries will be found along the way. The range is unbelievably good, and you could spend a month at Noosa and still not have sampled all the fine foods. Most petrol stations have a cafeteria-style restaurant; the food is usually pretty good if not entirely healthy. Look for the gas stations with the largest number of trucks in the parking lot—that's a good indication of the quality of food served. BBQs and picnic areas are plentiful and small grocery stores are a good supply for cheap eats.

ACCOMMODATION:

This is a haven for B&Bs, with plenty of motels/hotels along the way also. Your best lodging choices are the B&Bs. I have tested the two listed below and found them to be in perfect locations, great value, and well appointed. The hosts were very accommodating in each spot and had lots of good insider information about the surrounding activities. The third description is of a mid-priced motel in Noosa that provides the best value in that area. The final listing is of the beachside resort on Fraser Island.

Again, it is not the least or most expensive, but offers the best deal. One resort that may be a good option for Fraser Island is the ****1/2-Star **Kingfisher Bay Resort & Village**. It is a classy, eco award-winning hotel that is the most popular with overseas tourists. It is a bit pricier than the other resorts on the island, but gets rave reviews. You can look for yourself at **W**: kingfisherbay.com or call them to book, ☎ (07) 4120-3333.

For the full contingent of B&Bs and hotel/motel descriptions and prices check **Queensland B&B Association Getaways**, ☎ (07) 3321-8780 or see the listings on **W**: bnb.com.au. Two other good sources are the **Discover Queensland's Sunshine Coast** booklet and their website on **W**: sunshinecoasttourism.com; or the **RACQ Automobile's Experience Queensland** manual, ☎ 1-800-629-501, (07) 3361-2802 or **W**: racq.com.au.

For the Sunshine Coast trips, all tourist points can be reached from any of the accommodations listed below—with the exception of Fraser Island. The most central to the first three spots, and my favorite, would be the Main Creek Bower B&B and is a perfect retreat after each day of touring. The Fraser Island trip is a 2–3 day excursion and it's best to stay at one of the resorts on the island.

MAIN CREEK BOWER B&B, 123-125 Main Creek Road, Tanawha, QLD 4556, ☎ (07) 5476-8327, **W**: babs.com.au/maincreek, E-mail: mcbower@bigpond.com. *Prices range from AU $66–$132, children (2–12) AU $33, and small dogs/cats free. Not ৬.*

This is a perfect central hub for at least the first three trips around the Sunshine Coast. It is close to the Bruce Highway and has easy access to all the attractions, but distant enough to feel like you are in the middle of a rainforest. Actually, the tastefully converted 1920–30 church hall is indeed in the middle of a rainforest full of red cedars, ferns, palms, and colorful (and chatty) bird life. It is a top-notch, private, feel-good B&B, with a fantastic array of home-cooked meals delivered to your door each morning. Your hosts will make you quite comfy in their hideaway "bower" (country dwelling). Most attractions, from the coast to the Blackall Range, are within a 10–30 minute drive.

GLASS HOUSE MOUNTAINS B&B, 76 Kings Road, Glass House Mountains, QLD 4518, ☎ (07) 5493-0031, **W**: bans.com.au/glasshouse, E-mail: ghbb@bigpond.com.au. *Prices are around AU $130/couple. Not ৬.*

Though not quite as central to the attractions as the first recommendation, it is a grand spot tucked in behind pineapple plantations and fragrant pines. The upstairs bedrooms are lushly decorated and there is polished wood everywhere. Food for brekkie is provided in the fully-equipped kitchen, and all the rooms are spacious. This is a good spot if you decide to hike one of the Glass House Mountains or spend the majority of your time around the Blackall Ranges.

CARIBBEAN NOOSA, 15 Noosa Parade, Noosa Heads, QLD 4567, ☎ (07)

5447-2247, **W**: caribbeannoosa.com.au, E-mail: carribeannoosa@big-pond.com. *Nightly prices from AU $85–$110/room.* &.

The ***1/2-Star rooms are off the hectic Hastings Street, but only a five-minute walk to all the shops. The split-level flats are decorated like a ship's cabin with rope handrails, sailcloth accents, polished wooden stairs, and the queen-sized bed tucked in the crow's nest. If you decide to spend a bit more time in this ritzy upscale town instead of touring around, this is a good hub for a few days.

EURONG BEACH RESORT, Eurong, Fraser Island, QLD, ☎ (07) 4127-9122, **W**: fraser-is.com, Email: frasertours@whalewatch.com.au. *Prices range from AU $80–$190. Guided tours, self-guided tours. Gift shop. Café and pub. Special events.* &.

Right on the 75-mile surf beach, this is a great mid-ranged, all-inclusive, holiday resort. It has it all, and the daily tours run right from your doorstep. The units are not all that flash and it is a Caribbean-style, laid-back kind of place. You can book directly with them or arrange it through the very helpful **Information/Booking Service** located in Noosa, ☎ (07) 5474-9166, **W**: auusiemail.com.au, E-mail on noosa@palmtreetours.com.au.

The Glass House Mountains

A s you enter the Blackall Ranges, spectacular rock needles magically appear off to the left, welcoming you to the first touring location. The 13, odd-shaped, 24-million-year old volcanic plugs, dotted on the western horizon, were first described in Aboriginal Dreamtime stories, and each is identified with a name. As the legend goes, Tibrogargan and Beerwah (mother and father) had nine children—Beerburrum, Coonowrin, Coochin, Elimbah, Miketeebumulgrai, Ngungun, Tibberoowuccum, and the Tunbubudla twins. There were also Round and Wildhorse, but they are just mentioned and seemed not to participate in the grand scheme. The information center at Caloundra has the sheet describing the torment, dislocated shoulders, tears, pregnancies, and floods related to the ancient myth. All the events in the tale are applied to the shape, size, and location of each of the pinnacles that cover the ranges.

But in 1770 a new description took hold that is applied even today. Captain Cook spotted the eroded volcanic mountains made of trachyte and rhyolite, and in his ship's log described them as glass houses. Now I have heard two stories why he thought of them as glass houses. The first is based on the silica chips that cover the sheer cliffs—when the sun hits them, they look as though they are made of glass. The second and more credible is that they resembled the factory buildings in London that were built to produce glass.

Any way you choose to look at the history, the current views of the formations are spectacular. If hiking is in the cards, it's best to stop, consult with the Ranger on Roys Road or call the reserve information line on ☎ (07) 5499-9907 to obtain maps and directions. For the rest of us, there are four lookouts that provide ample opportunity for photos and viewing pleasures. This trip is designed as a driving tour that allows for shopping and snacking along the way. Shopping detours will be made at Maleny and Montville; both are small towns that can be walked in an hour or two each. They are chock-a-block full of good crafts, candies, and artwork.

GETTING THERE:

By Car: Driving is simple, with only one real turn to reach the first destination. There are two options in exiting the Bruce Highway to access the Glass House Mountains Tourist Drive. The first exit will be the scenic route towards Beerburrum (the preferred exit) and the second ramp is at Jonston Road. Both are well marked and easy to navigate. From that point, just follow the signs to your favorite lookout. If you decided to come directly from Warwick, the drive will take about 3–4 hours, and from Brisbane only an hour or about 45 miles.

By Bus, you can sit back and let the driver do all the work and enjoy your window seat.

PRACTICALITIES:

Most activities require driving in a half-hour radius and then stretching your legs with moderate hikes. You can choose to climb the volcanic plugs, but I would advise in finding a guide as many people do get injured on the cliffs. The shopping portions will require a bit of tramping, and comfortable footwear is suggested.

FOOD AND DRINK:

Food is found at every stop along the way, and some mighty tasty eats too. There are a few fancy restaurants in Maleny and Montville that look over the valley, while the zoo has a host of snacks and fast food items available. You will not go hungry on these trips.

SUGGESTED DRIVING TOUR:

Circled numbers correspond to numbers on the map.

Prior to starting the looping drive, it might be good to obtain a map of the area from the ***Blackall Range Business & Tourism Information Centre ❶** in Montville. Open daily 10–4, closed holidays. They can be contacted at ☎ (07) 5478-5544 or on **W**: montvillevillage.com.au. The B&Bs in the area usually have a spare map or two also. There are several approaches to this scenic drive and depending on your interest, it can be a half- or full-day trip. **Kenilworth Drive ❷** is a full circle, shaped a little like Africa, about 100 miles around. To capture the full beauty of the valley, range, and weird-shaped mountains, it is best to do the whole loop, but if time is short the leg between Maleny and Montville will do the trick. There are lookouts all along the way and I think the best is at ***Mary Caincross Park ❸**. It is a picnic area with a ranger tower accessible to the public. It has plenty of parking, and the small mount offers 360-degree views, making it a good location for a bit of a walkabout. There are gently sloping paths that make for an easy stroll. With over 100 acres in the reserve, there are rare plants, trees to be photographed, and a few crittes to meet too. Before you have a wander, cruise through the educational center to get a feel of the area and what it has to offer. There is a 3/4-mile wheelchair track, a one-mile

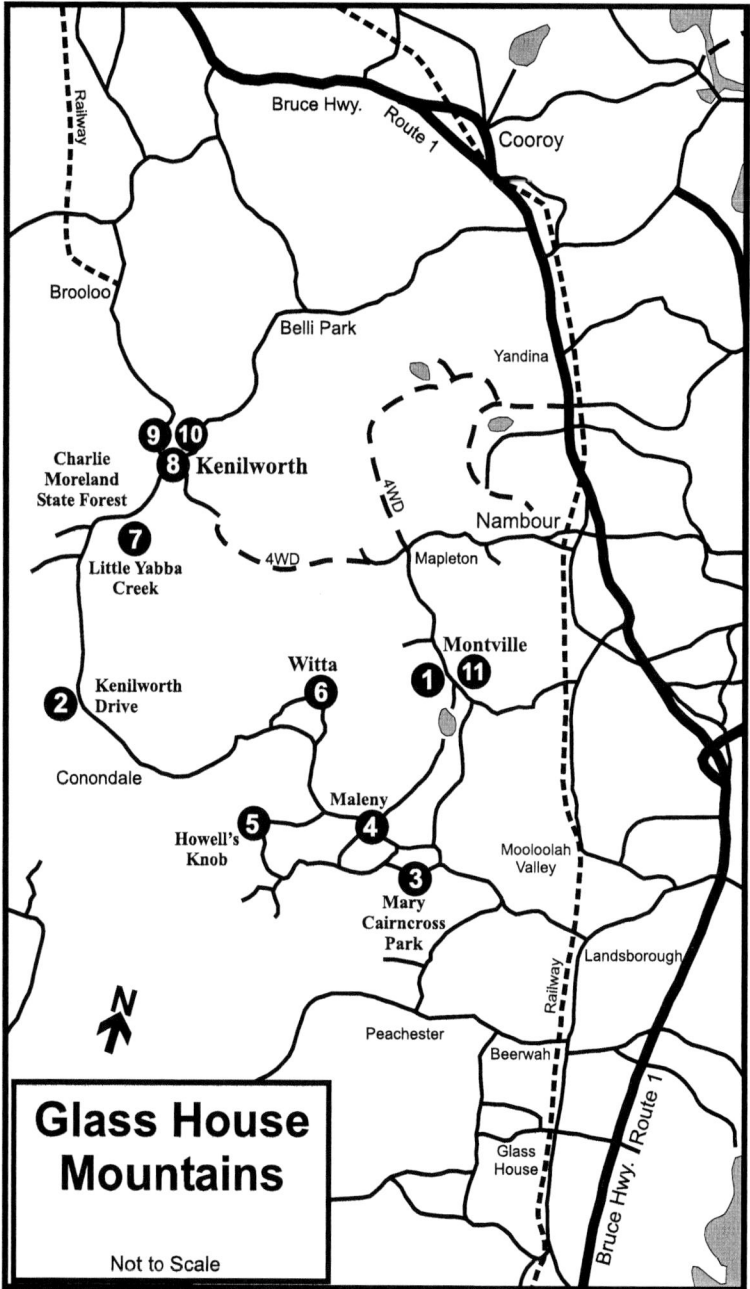

Glass House
Mountains

Not to Scale

path, and a full trek of a little over a mile around the tower. The track has strangler figs, sassafras, cedars, rose gums, and ancient lianas to greet you on your walk. For a more strenuous series of hiking trails, locate the "Walks in the Glass House Mountains" brochure stocked at most of the information centers in the surrounding areas.

After stretching the legs, hop into the car for a short drive to **Maleny** ❹. This sleepy town began as a lumbering center, harvesting cedar, hoop pine, and beech for ultimate use as furniture and building materials. When the timber was cleared, the natural progression was to dairy farming and cheese making. Now it is a tourist spot and haven for artists. There isn't too much to see in town, but a few stores and art galleries might pique your interest. The **Bushman's Warehouse** has great clothing made for country wear, a wide range of leather goods including saddles, and all-around interesting gifts not seen in Macy's. **Bold in Gold** jewelry, **Maleny Toyworld**, and the **Craftery** all have interesting displays of gifts, artwork, and novelties. The antique stores, sprinkled along the street, have indescribable curiosities. When I was browsing, I dared not even ask what some of the dusty old goods were in **Georde Lane Antiques & Tearoom**. It was fun trying to figure them out, though. The **Black Forest Clock Centre** has some of the best cuckoo clocks I've seen. For a hinterland community, it offers interesting cuisine. Fine dining can be found at the **South African Figtree Cottage**, upscale meals and great views at the **Terrace Seafood Restaurant** right on the edge of a the cliffs, and nearby Bavarian delicacies can be sampled at **King Ludwig's**, **W**: kingludwigs.com.au, also on the Cliffside. But the real charms of this location are the buildings and the old-time feel to the area. You will not require much time to wander the few streets, but do have a look and try it out. The craft markets are held every Sunday and most of the shops are open from 9–5 weekdays and 9–3 on weekends. Information can be obtained at **W**: malenyqueensland.com, or call the town's **Information Centre**, ☎ (07) 5499-9033.

From this juncture, the road continues on to Kenilworth, past some excellent lookouts, parks and picnic areas or you can double back to roam Montville. If the shorter path is your decision, jump to Montville and pick up the tour there. Following a clockwise path, you will come upon **Howell's Knob Lookout** ❺. This is the most southwestern view of the ranges and is also a good place to have a hike. Several other points of interest include the **Witta General Store** ❻ where you can ask about trail rides in the area, **Little Yabba Creek** ❼ where you can wander the forest trial, or hike into **Charlie Moreland State Forest Park** (same number) across the road. There are a few nice creeks and rivers in the area to have a look at too. Continuing on the tourist drive, you will enter the town of **Kenilworth** ❽. This is a central spot for many artists and the **Lasting Impressions Gallery of Fine Art** ❾ at 6 Elizabeth Street is where most of the potters, painters, and sculptors hang their works. Browse on **W**: lastingimpressionsgallery.net before dropping in to get an idea of the fabulous displays awaiting you. There is a wide range of affordable pieces and the gallery is open daily from 10–5. For the outdoors minded, try a stroll into the **Conondale Ranges National Park** or a paddle up Mary River.

But my personal favorite spot in this country town is the ***Kenilworth Cheese Factory ⑩**, ☎ (07) 5546-0144 or look for the cheese factory at **W**: coolum.com.au. If you have any love for cheese, the factory tour and tasting is absolutely a must and the history of the factory is enthralling. They are open Mon.–Fri. 9–4 and weekends 11–3. A Dane by the name of Peter "Poppa" Hansen left his home about 100 years ago and ended up on a dairy farm in the hinterland of the Sunshine Coast. He was so successful that he could not sell all his milk. So, he began experimenting with cheeses and wound up with his tasty Malling Red and Roma-style brands (named after the first town he settled in here). The handcrafted, award winning, cheddar cheeses can be tested at the factory on 45 Charles Street in Kenilworth.

Completing the exploration here, drive eastward towards **Mapleton**. The road can be a little rough on this leg and may still be unpaved in areas, so take it easy or reverse direction and go back through Maleny. From Mapleton head south to Flaxton then onto Montville. One stop worth checking out on the way towards Montville is the **Maleny Touch Wood** mill and shop at 58 Maleny-Montville Road. The carved, shaped and turned wood products are fantastic and they have a ruler (in metric) that has a sample of each of the woods produced in the area. It is a good gift for the Dad (like mine) who is a master woodworker and loves woods.

*Montville ⑪ is the last stop and probably the best location to pry open the wallet/purse. There is a blend of over 80 stores, eateries, attractions, and lodgings listed in their village directory. The town is rich in history and it appears as though the Kabi tribe regularly visited and swapped goods here way before the Europeans arrived. Since the area was rich in foods and loaded with the Bunya Pine Fruit (Bonyi Bonyi), the tribe would meet at Obi Obi Creek near Baroon Pocket and have a party. Later the climate and timber brought the loggers and farmers. It is still the home to many macadamia, pineapple, avocado, and citrus plantations. Now a tourist and shopping town, the English hamlet-style village was established in 1887 and the **Information Centre** in town, ☎ (07) 5478-5544 or **W**: montvillevillage.com.au, offers walking maps and a list of the shops and eateries that await you. Expect to run into a knight or two, as the streets do appear to be similar to those of a small village outside a castle. The town has a strange mix of clock towers, Tudor designs, chalets, Queenslanders, and a mill with a working waterwheel attached to it. The walk is a bit hilly, but the art, crafts, artifacts, and foodstuffs will delight even the hardened shopper. The coolest thing I purchased there was a picture frame set made of banana leaves. I never saw anything like it before or since. The bakery is a great stop and the **Sunshine Candy Kitchens** have some hilarious sweets, like the bag full of chocolates with Koala Poo, or Kangaroo Droppings stamped on the outside. They are great gift ideas for kids. Take your time in this village and try to at least window shop in front of each store. Luckily the stores are all laid out on the Main Street and are easy to find on the directory provided by the Information Centre. If you want to avoid the shopping spree scramble, take a gentle stroll along the **Blind Senses Trail** or gaze over the valley at **Razorback Lookout** across the way from the main shopping street.

Steve Irwin's Australian Zoo

The Crocodile Hunter's Hideout

The Australian Zoo in Beerwah is indeed Steve Irwin's home — and the pride of his conservation park site. With over 100 staff members to care for the animals as well as making sure visitors get a memorable experience, it is a good daytrip excursion. The Zoo opened in 1970 and is now a very sizeable (and growing) tract of land dedicated to the protection of animals as well as the education of people in the marvels of Australian wildlife. The self-guided tour will take between 3–6 hours, with shows spread out from 10:30 until 3:30. If you are lucky enough to see Stevie do a show, it will be a memorable spectacle. When the crocs aren't cooperating and don't have an agro attitude, he takes his boots off and climbs in the water to taunt them — for real, I've seen it! The one catch phrase that you will hear over and over at the park is: "Crocs Rule!"

The second portion of this tour will be spent in the vicinity of the strange concoction of a building called the Ettamogah Pub and Aussie World. The pub is a leaning structure that prides itself in exactly mimicking the pub in the comic strip it's named for. It is a huge pub with pool tables, games, music, good food, and the oddest public toilets I've entered. Out back is the amusement area with rides, shows, and shops to wander through. The pub is a grown-up hangout, and Aussie World is a family and kid's theme park. The park is small, free, and takes an hour or two to see it all.

Finally for the shopper there are a few vendors in the vicinity that are worth a mention. Some of the best opal deals are to be found next to the pub, there is a sheepskin shed, and the novelty stores in Aussie World have good-value Aboriginal products to take home with you.

GETTING THERE:

By Car: All the attractions in this area are within minutes of the Bruce Highway and are well marked. The Australian Zoo is in Beerwah along the Glass House Mountain Tourist Route, the Aussie World and shopping spots are in Palmview (right on the highway), and parking is free and available at each location.

By Bus: Bus tours are available from most of the resort towns; the

Information Centres at each spot can arrange the tours for you. There is also a free courtesy pickup at Sunshine Coast locations.

By Train: There is a "Crocodile Train" that runs from Brisbane to the Australian Zoo (7:50am from Brisbane and return from Beerwah at around 3pm for AU $16.50 for adults and AU $8.30 for children). Contact **Queensland Rail and City Train** on ☎ 13-12-30 or **W**: qr.com.au.

PRACTICALITIES:

The attractions have plenty of shade, but a hat and sun protection are good to take along. The parks are all suited for an easy walk; comfortable shoes will help. It will get warm, so wear light clothing.

FOOD AND DRINK:

Food is found everywhere on this leg of the journey. I think the best grub is upstairs at Aussie World's **Ettamogah Pub**. Or try out the **Dingo Diner** at the zoo. There are eateries and grocery stores nearby, and restaurants at most of the gas stations.

LOCAL ATTRACTIONS:

Circled numbers correspond to numbers on the map.

*AUSTRALIAN ZOO ❶, Glass House Mountains Tourist Route, Beerwah, ☎ (07) 5494-1134, **W**: crocodilehunter.com, E-mail: info@australiazoo.com.au. *Open daily 8:30–4, closed Christmas. Adults AU $23, children from 3–14 for AU 14, seniors AU $18, and family of five for AU $65. Self-guided tours. Gift shop. Café. Special events.* ♿.

For foreign visitors, this is a great place to see the koalas, pythons, the oldest living Giant Galapagos land tortoise (Harriet), a 1-ton 20-foot croc (Acco), and a host of snakes, dingoes, wombats, and Tasmanian devils. The big events are the feeding of the crocodiles scheduled throughout the day. Each of the large lagoons is occupied by a resident croc, and has bleachers set around the fenced-in area to witness the feeding of the reptiles. To add to the authenticity, they smell like swamps with murky water and have well-manicured foliage to accompany the scene. The shows are fantastic, enhanced by crazy handlers searching the waters with wide eyes, crouched stance, and head whipping from side-to-side looking for their adversary. I give them credit, they know how the animals will react and don't (as far as I could see) have any backup to stop an attack. They enter the cage alone with only one other spotter to keep track of the crocodile's girlfriend. When I was there with my wife we saw Steve, and because Graham wasn't cooperating, he took his boots off and waded into the water to aggravate the monstrous croc. But at one point in the show he said that it was probably too dangerous to be in the enclosure as it began to rain and he couldn't spot the crocs underwater. Apparently, that's where the brute could wave his tail and launch out of the water with no warning and jump about 6–8 feet in the air. The thriller is when they

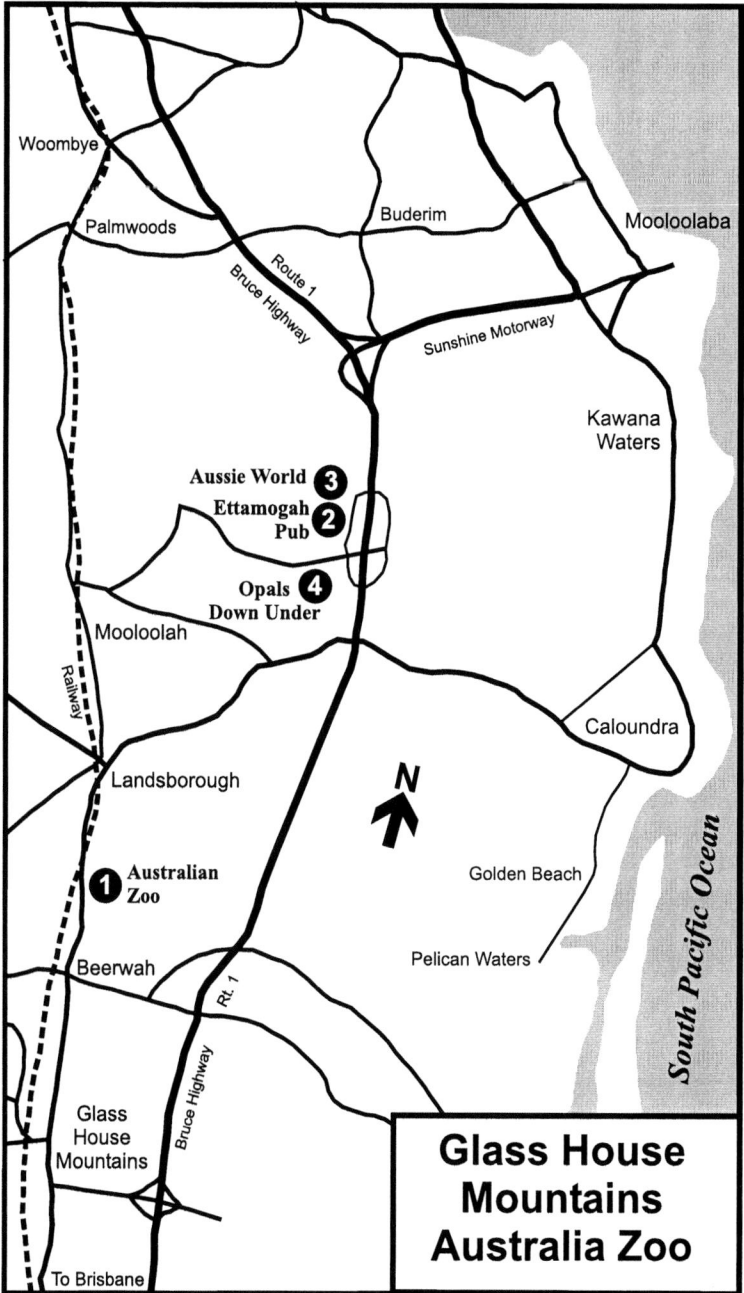

Glass House
Mountains
Australia Zoo

demonstrate the power of the thrashing beast by dangling a piece of meat over the murky water. The other animals are a hoot, and you can get close and touch many of the people-friendly ones. The half-day can include sitting on the 50-foot wooden crocodile named Coot-tha, strolling past the 40-foot wall of Steve memorabilia called the **Croc Hunter Museum**, sit in one of the Crocodile Hunter's jeeps for a photo-op, feed the albino kangaroo, and get underwater views of Murry and Molly as they launch an attack, picnic amongst the over 500 animals, have a photograph wearing a huge python necklace, and finally wander the gift shop with clocks of Steve, dolls of Steve, movies of Steve, posters and heaps of goodies to share with friends back home.

Nearby is the strange cartoon-inspired building fondly known throughout Australia as the:

*ETTAMOGAH PUB ❷, Bruce Highway & Frizzo Road, Palmview, ☎ (07) 5494-5444, **W**: aussieworld.com.au. *Open daily 9–late. Free entry. Gift shop. Special events. Partially* &.

I think the pub was built to demonstrate the Aussie attitude of nonconformity and independence (of a comical sort). Apparently, there is not a straight, level, or plumb piece of construction in the place. The doorways look like parallelograms, the windows are crooked, and supporting posts are leaning at odd angles. The urinals are made from halved beer kegs and the entrance to the toilet listed some of the nicknames of the men's room, including Throne Room, Dunny, Loo, Outhouse, and Thunderbox. The pub is modeled after a cartoon strip first shown in the Australian Post that ran until 1998. Samples of the comics are plastered along the walls and staircase—framed, all askew, and are similar to the Dogpatch series. The pool table is made of hand-carved timber that looks like white walnut. It has a huge goanna carved in the side right above a sign that declares, "No smoking or drinking over the pool tables—THANKS MATE." Overhead is a green biplane near the wooden rafters. The rustic wood makes the place feel like a lodge in the Catskills. **Bluey's Restaurant** is upstairs and is named for either a swag, (the outer blanket carried was usually blue), a coat, or a red-haired bloke. In the back of the pub is an arch leading to **Jackie Howe Bar**, honoring Australia's sheepsheering legend. The huge room is equipped with slot machines, pool tables, a jukebox, rows of arcade games and a stage. Don't leave until you say g'day to Ace, the carved wooden dog that barks as you passed by, see the giant water barrel painted with "Welcome—Don't be a drip, Drop in mate . . . Tanks!" and the statue of a bloke hanging by his bootstraps welcoming all to the Pub for Grub at Bluey's.

Just behind the pub is a maze of Australian and Aboriginal activities to be enjoyed.

AUSSIE WORLD ❸, Bruce Highway & Frizzo Road, Palmview, ☎ (07) 5494-5444, **W**: aussieworld.com.au. *Open daily 9–5, closed holidays. Free entry,* *some activities require an entry fee. Self-guided tours. Gift shops. Cafés. Special events. Partially ⅃.*

This theme park is geared towards kids, but there are great shops and attractions for adults as well. Some of the rides include a wild mouse, carousels, motorized boats to maneuver around watery obstacles, bumper cars, and most of the standard rides found in amusement parks. But there are unique and fun things for adults too, like the **Aboriginal Cultural Centre** with good educational exhibits and shows, a working **Blacksmith Shed** where you can actually make a horseshoe yourself, the **Giraween Track** where you will learn about bush tucker and Outback medicines, and the typical sheep shearing and pony rides. But if the place is hopping, check out the Dunny (outhouse) Races and maybe try your endurance at the Pie Eating Contest or Keg Lifting Competition. I do recommend the shops in the fairground. The prices are very competitive, and you will find some different souvenirs.

About a half a mile from Aussie World are a few good shopping stops to consider, including:

*OPALS DOWN UNDER ❹, 11 Ballantyne Court, Palmview, ☎ (07) 5494-5400, **W**: opalsdownunder.com.au. E-mail: istein@bigpond.com. *Open daily 9–5. Free entry. Audio/video presentation. Gift shop. Café. ⅃.*

This is where I buy my opals, since it generally has the best quality and fairest prices for a wide range. They buy direct from the mines, and you can watch them cut the precious stones from behind a glass partition. With the patience of a saint, they will explain in detail what opals are, how they are presented (solid, doublet, or triplet) and the different colors available. My favorites (and most expensive, it seems) are the black opals. They also have nut opal, boulder opal, crystal and milky opal to choose from, depending on your budget. For the kids, there is a bin full of semi-precious stones, where you can fill a small bag of the multi-colored gems for very little money.

The other small shops to have a peek at in the same vicinity are: **The Skin Thing** with sheepskins and wool products, the **House of Herbs** for healing, aromatic and cooking plants, and **The Crayfish Farm** with its ponds of succulent shellfish.

Trip 46
Sunshine Coast

Underwater World

How do you feel about being immersed in a giant aquarium and appearing to be a tasty morsel to a hungry shark? Trust me on this one—it will be a real thrill as you are only inches away from the jagged jaws of these ocean predators. This pulse enhancer of an attraction will be at least a half-day tour, and more if you read every wall display, see each show, and check out every tank. The entrance to the aquatic adventure is on The Wharf in Mooloolaba Harbour. New-looking shops and cafés are stacked on pylons over the Mooloolaba Harbour, with sounds of creaking boats and smells of the day's catch. The colorful series of shops and milling people make for a pleasant atmosphere to soak in the sun. This tourist area is not very big, so you can shop the boardwalks in less than two hours. Save your time and energy for the highlight of Underwater World. If you have time to spare, the beaches are a great diversion and place to recharge the batteries.

GETTING THERE:

By Car: Exit the Bruce Highway at the ramp marked for Mooloolaba, drive east on the Sunshine Motorway for about 10 miles, turn left onto Brisbane Road, right on River Esplanade, and park at the Wharf's parking lot. The signage is good all the way, and it is a straight shot to the ocean attractions. From the Main Creek Bower B&B, drive east on Mooloolaba Road until it turns into Buderim Road, turn right onto Alexandra Parade (when you reach the ocean), turn right on Venning for a block, right on Walan Street and into the Wharf parking lot.

By Bus: The local bus service is **Sunbus**, ☎ (07) 5492-8700 or 13-12-30. Tours can be arranged through **Storey Line Tours**, ☎ (07) 5474-1500 or **W:** storeylinetours.com.au

PRACTICALITIES:

No major hiking here mates, as the area is shaded or under cover for most of the day. If you choose to visit the beach the sun-and-surf safety rules apply. There are a few fancy restaurants that you might want to pack some nice eveningwear for.

For more information on the area call the **Wharf Information** line, ☎ (07) 5444-8088; visit the town's **Information Booth** at the corner of Brisbane

Road and First Avenue, ☎ (07) 05478-2233, or look at the town's internet site on **W**: mooloolababeach.com

FOOD AND DRINK:

It is absolutely loaded with all food groups, so you will not go hungry unless you are too distracted with the sights and sounds in store for you. There is a spud place that stuffs potatoes with a variety of goodies—one alone is a complete meal.

LOCAL ATTRACTIONS:

Circled numbers correspond to numbers on the map.

*THE WHARF & UNDERWATER WORLD ❶, The Wharf at Parkyn Parade, Mooloolaba, ☎ (07) 5444-8488 or (07) 5444-8088, **W**: underwaterworld.com.au. *Wharf open daily 24 hours and free, Underwater World open daily 9–6, closed Christmas, limited hours on Anzac Day. Adults AU $22, children AU $13, seniors AU $15, students AU $16, family 2/2 AU $59. Guided tours, self-guided tours. Gift shop. Café. Special events.* ♿.

I had to control myself and not push the little kids out of the way when I entered this aquarium-filled attraction. Check on the feeding times before you start on the tour and try to plan the non-scheduled activities around your favorites. The first stop is the baby stingray reef with hands-on feeding of the baby mantas and rays. The demonstration allows the kids to hold a spear with a piece of fish on the end and actually feed the swimming phantoms. Next to the Rocky Shore Touchpools are small ponds where you can reach in and handle certain species of sea critters under the supervision of a staff member. Farther into the maze of hallways are exhibits of freshwater billabongs with crocodiles, the 400-seat arena with a seal show, the cold-water habitat display, and the otter encounter. After learning all about frogs versus toads (frogs are slimy and jump / toads are dry, warty and walk, a bunch of frogs are called an army / the same number of toads are called a knot) you get to go under the sea.

Descending into a cool dark cave you will be bathed in strange underwater sounds of melodic whales, chirping dolphins, and bubbles. A short distance from the bottom of the ramp/stairs, you turn a sharp corner and are suddenly underneath 2.5 million liters of water protected only by 3 inches of Plexiglas. The curved dome hovers overhead as you make your way around the circular tunnel. Fortunately you can focus all attention on the sharks, mantas, and schools of fish since the 80-yard moving walkway moves through different scenes laid out above. Sharks swim within three feet of your heads, and I can't imagine what it must be like to face those jaws in open water. The circuit takes about ten minutes and is so eerie—the place even had a smell of the sea about it. Hiking up the carpeted ramp to the surface are a series of shark facts that include the sad truth that many shark species are becoming extinct and that over 100 million

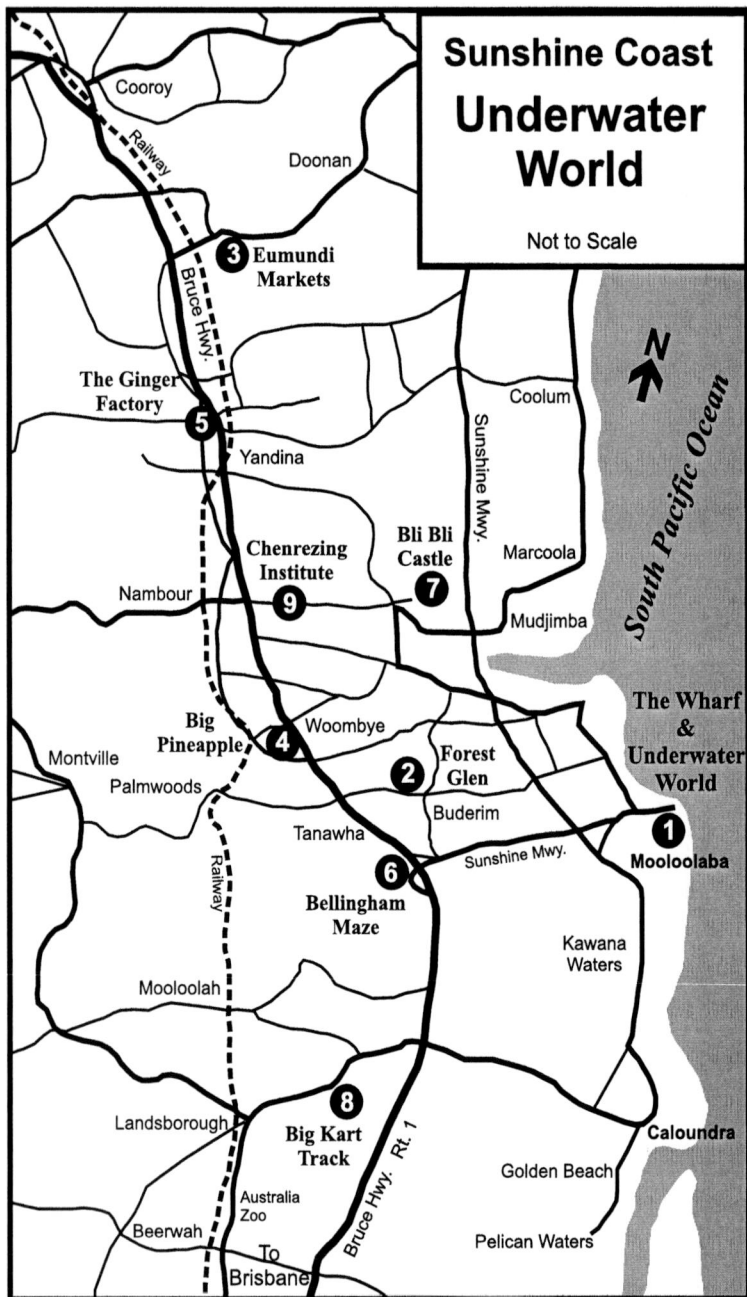

Sunshine Coast
Underwater World

Not to Scale

Cooroy

Railway

Doonan

Bruce Hwy.

3 Eumundi Markets

The Ginger Factory

5

Yandina

Coolum

Sunshine Mwy.

Chenrezing Institute

Bli Bli Castle

7

Marcoola

Nambour

9

Mudjimba

South Pacific Ocean

Big Pineapple

Woombye

4

Montville

Palmwoods

2

Forest Glen

The Wharf & Underwater World

Tanawha

Buderim

Railway

6

Sunshine Mwy.

1

Mooloolaba

Bellingham Maze

Kawana Waters

Mooloolah

Landsborough

8

Big Kart Track

Australia Zoo

Bruce Hwy. Rt. 1

Caloundra

Golden Beach

Beerwah

To Brisbane

Pelican Waters

N

sharks are killed each year. It is easy to lose time in the wild blue ocean displays, but there is one more stop before you can shop.

The **Virtual Dolphin Ride** is a flight simulator-type attraction that swims along with the dolphins as you sit in the strapped in comfort of a padded chair. When the lights flash and the seat begins to vibrate, be prepared for a jolt into the virtual water world as you flip, jump, and cut through the waves. It is pretty intense, a great ride, and is included in the pass into Underwater World. One suggestion: try to get tickets way ahead of time as they tend to fill up the pod rather quickly.

Pop the sunglasses on as your exit the ride and have a nice stroll through the shops and past the cafés on The Wharf. It is a small, but boutique style of shopping, with additional stores across the street from the parking lot. But satisfy the kid in you by stopping in the store called **Amazen Puzzles and Games**. I believe you will find an unfamiliar game or two as well as some old-time favorites (Lincoln Logs and Pick-up Sticks). The women's clothing and jewelry stores are fantastic, too, with many handcrafted bobbles and fabrics.

For the sun-seeker, head for either the Mooloolaba Beach just behind The Wharf, the Alexandra Beach, or Maroochydore Beach off of Alexandra Parade. All are patrolled and offer good surf to cool off.

OTHER LOCAL ATTRACTIONS:

The Sunshine Coast and its hinterland are loaded with other attractions for the active, the curious, and the nature lover. I tried to list a variety of activities that might appeal to a broad range of interests. Here are just a few within a 40-minute drive for you to consider:

Forest Glen Sanctuary ❷, ☎ (07) 3321-5199, in Forest Glen is open daily 9–5, closed Christmas and until 1 o'clock on Anzac Day. Entry is AU $13.90 (adult), AU $6.90 (5–15), AU $ 3.90 (2–4), and AU $9.90 (seniors). This 60-acre, family-style park is full of kangaroos, emus, koalas, deer, and rainforest critters. Hand feeding of the local residents is encouraged, and tours are provided through the park. **Eumundi Markets ❸* in Eumundi is free on Wednesday, Saturday, and Sunday, ☎ (07) 5442-8581. With almost 300 stalls of handcrafts, sculptures, artwork, leather products, and farm fresh food, it's like a Woodstock gift shop. The town opens the park and clears the sidewalks to host "The Best Saturday on the Coast." Locally, it is known as the market under the trees and it is recognized by the rich coffee aromas, sounds of local blues and rock bands, and a mix of hippies, city slickers, and tourists.

*The Big Pineapple ❹, ☎ (07) 5442-1333 or **W**: bigpineapple.com.au, in Woombye is open from 9–5 daily, with limited access on Christmas and ANZAC Day. The plantation costs nothing to enter and pay-as-you-go for the rides and attractions in the park. Prices for the rides run from AU $3.65 to AU $23.60 and a family pass is around AU $70. The unmistakable 53-foot high pineapple is a good Kodak opportunity; the rows and rows of pineapple trees are impressive too. The options for fun include a sugar cane train ride, an interactive Nutmobile trip into macadamia orchards and the macadamia factory, educational boat rides, animal nursery interactions, and a wild wildlife garden stroll. This is a Sunshine Coast landmark.

The **Ginger Factory** ❺, ☎ (07) 5446-7096 or **W**: buderimginger.com, is open every day 9–5, closed Christmas. It's free to enter the factory, but if you choose to take the Ginger Train Tour, it costs AU $6.50 (adults) and AU $4.50 (kids). The train offers a historical trip through the ginger fields to inhale the spicy scents, shop for ginger candies, ginger beer, and sample the jarred ginger at the popular Gingertown heritage village. Learn the medical uses of the ancient plant and the current cooking properties. The **Bellingham Maze** ❻, ☎ (07) 5445-2979 or **W**: bellmaze.com, is open Fri.–Wed. 9–5 and every day during school holidays. Although it costs only AU $6 (adult), AU $5 (child) and AU $20 (family of 4) to enter, they were not clear on the price to get out. It is a puzzle made to confuse those who enter the large hedge and takes about 20 minutes to find your way out.

Bli Bli Castle ❼, ☎ (07) 5448-5373, is open daily from 9–4 and costs AU $10 (adults), AU $5 (kids), and AU $9 (seniors). Built on solid granite over-looking the Maroochy River, it is a replica of a Norman Fortress. The drafty castle displays mediaeval armor, a doll museum with miniatures dressed in native costumes, and toys dating to the mid 1800s. The **Big Kart Track** ❽, ☎ (07) 5494-1613 or **W**: bigkart.com.au, drops the checkered flag from 9–5 for around AU $44 for a 30-minute drive and a Bungy Bullet launch. There are 50 carts to choose from, or just try the slot car racing.

The Chenrezing Institute ❾, ☎ (07) 5445-0077 or **W**: chenrezig.com.au, is a center for Buddhist studies and home to the resident Tibetan lama Geshe Tahsi Tsering. The grounds are peaceful, the temple is interesting, and the gift shop has some cool prayer wheels, meditation books, and clothing. It is free to wander around and center your karma by yourself, but classes and prayer sessions can be arranged at the office.

Noosa

Noosa, or more properly Noosa Heads, is the most northern point of the Sunshine Coast and is on the southern tip of the Great Sandy National Park. This compact shopping mecca for the rich and famous is not really a typical Australian town, but it is a blast. It probably has the highest density of wealthy vacationers anywhere on the continent. This sophisticated and charming place has plenty of things to keep you busy for two to three days. I look on the area as an upscale Key West with a nice mix of hippies, surfers, artsy-fartsy types, and yuppies pushing baby carriages.

This tour is divided into two sections and can be easily accomplished in one day. But if you want to spend lots of beach/hiking time or are really a shopaholic, then divide the trips between the two specific interests. I really think the emphasis is best focused on the National Park hike and the spectacular views on the headland, but the shopping and cruising Hastings Street is pretty OK too.

The first (or maybe second) excursion will lead you to the main street of Hastings. Both sides of the street are peppered with shops and a few mini-malls packed with high fashion, food, artworks, and a few pubs and nightclubs. The ocean-side is adorned with a curving boardwalk that connects the parklands at either end. This walk along the small beach might be favored over the congested stroll on Hastings Street and my favorite restaurants face Laguna Bay and the ocean. The area recently underwent a facelift and many of the stores moved around, but the aromas of coffees will keep you alert and actively finding great deals. I think the prices are a bit high, but there are gifts and jewelry found nowhere else.

The other leg of the excursion leads to the Noosa National Park and the angry sea beating against rock, Hells Gates where the sheer cliffs drop into foaming sea froth, nude beaches, and crisscrossed trails through dense forests. The five walking tracks allow easy half-mile treks or three-mile jaunts. It can be a bit confusing on the trails, but the signs allow you to get your bearings at most of the crossroads. This is an impressively beautiful walk. At minimum effort, take the short part from the Information Centre, at the park's entrance, past Tea-Tree Bay, and to Hells Gates. It has breathtaking views all along the cleared path.

GETTING THERE:

By Car: Drive about 90 miles north of Brisbane on the Bruce Highway. Exit at Eumundi and travel west on Eumundi Road for about 8 miles until it turns into Gibson Road. It gets difficult here and keep your eyes open for signs to Noosa Heads at each roundabout. Turn left at Weyba Road, and another left onto Noosa Parade into town. The 45-minute drive from the Glass House Mountains will get you into town in time for some shopping, hiking, or just relaxing of the beach.

By Bus: SunAir Bus Service, ☎ 1-800-804-340 or **W:** sunair.com.au; and **Sun Coast Pacific,** ☎ (07) 5491-2555, operate between the Gold Coast, Brisbane, and points along the Sunshine Coast. **Greyhound Pioneer,** ☎ 13-20-30 or **W:** greyhound.com.au, and some of the other national bus lines operate to/from the area also. The local bus service is **Sunbus,** ☎ (07) 5492-8700 or 13-12-30. Estimate the price for one-way to be AU $21 from Brisbane and AU $38 from Surfers Paradise (through Brisbane).

By Train: Trains are not an option.

PRACTICALITIES:

Beach and hiking gear will be needed for this tour as well as at least one set of dress-up clothes. Though the dress remains casual, it is a spot where looks and style count.

Accommodations vary greatly along the busy Hastings Street from high-end to backpackers. I have selected a quieter approach and I think you will enjoy the nautical touch of Caribbean Noosa just 200 yards from the main street. For more options, contact the information centers or **Accom Noosa** on ☎ 1-800-072-078 or at **W:** accomnoosa.com.au. The **Sheraton Noosa** is the American-style resort on Hastings; ring them on ☎ 1-800-073-535 or check it out on **W:** Sheraton.com/noosa

Information in the area is easy to find, and the local resources are the **Noosa Enterprise Group,** ☎ (07) 5474-9377; the large **Hastings Street Tourist Information Centre,** ☎ (07) 5447-4988 or **W:** tourismnoosa.com.au; and my favorite—**Palm Tree Tours** on Hastings Street, ☎ (07) 5474-9166 or **W:** ozemail.com.au/~noosaptt. There is a good little booklet packed with information called "Hello Noosa Visitor Guide," which has the latest version of shops, eateries, tours, and maps. But do go to the Information Centre and ask for the Queensland National Parks and Wildlife Service map of the Noosa National Park/Headland Section or call the ranger service, ☎ (07) 5447-3243. Or simply follow the map provided in this section.

FOOD AND DRINK:

The agenda, venues, and players change regularly, but you will have plenty of choices along Hastings Street and in the neighboring towns. And don't pass up the surrounding eateries as they often offer a bit lower-priced meal. There are lots of walk-up stalls, too, and two great ice cream shops to pick from. Barbeque and picnic areas are plentiful in the parks, but they do fill up quickly. If you like a nice dry martini, the Sheraton

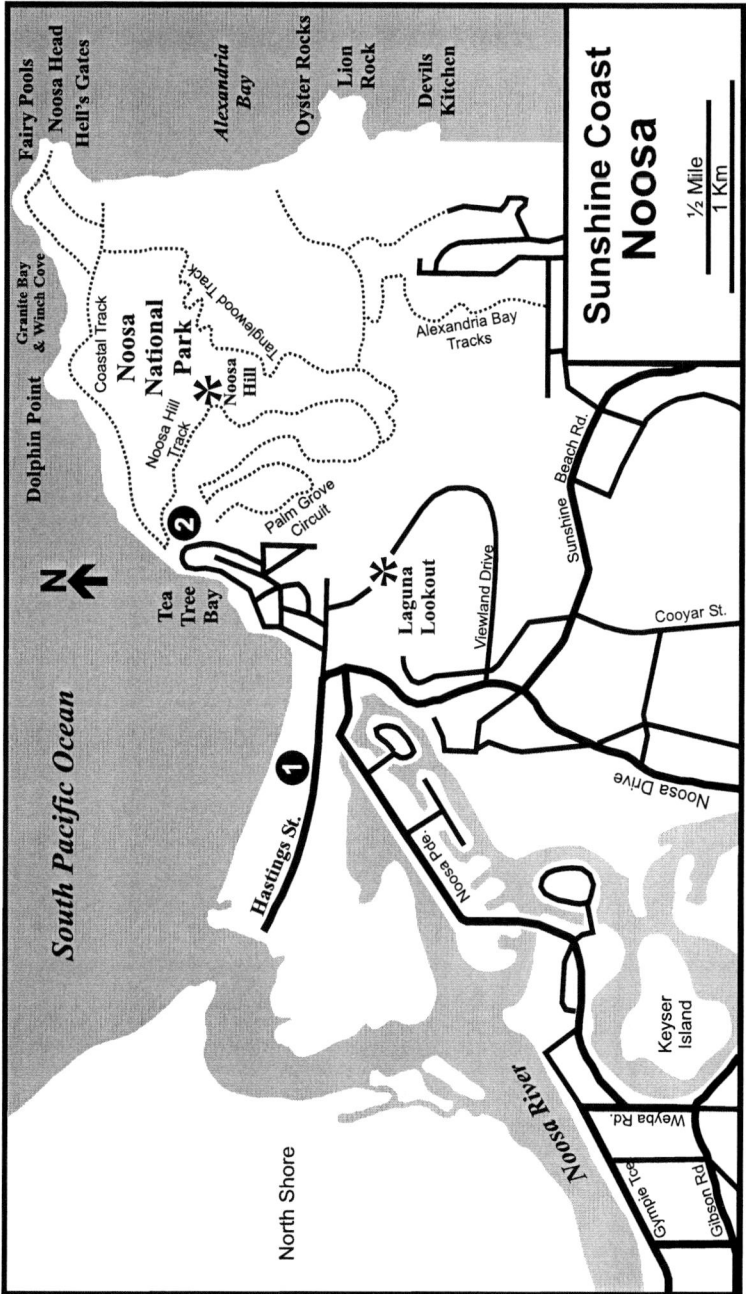

Sunshine Coast
Noosa

½ Mile
1 Km

South Pacific Ocean

Fairy Pools
Noosa Head
Hell's Gates

Alexandria Bay

Oyster Rocks

Lion Rock

Devils Kitchen

Granite Bay & Winch Cove

Dolphin Point

Coastal Track

Noosa National Park

Tanglewood Track

Noosa Hill

Noosa Hill Track

Alexandria Bay Tracks

Palm Grove Circuit

Tea Tree Bay

Laguna Lookout

Viewland Drive

Sunshine Beach Rd.

Cooyar St.

Hastings St.

Noosa Drive

Noosa Pde.

Keyser Island

Weyba Rd.

Gympie Tce.

Gibson Rd.

Noosa River

North Shore

serves them shaken or stirred. At night, just listen for the joint that emits your favorite tunes and join in.

LOCAL ATTRACTIONS:
Circled numbers correspond to numbers on the map.

*HASTINGS STREET ❶, *Open daily 24 hours a day, with shops generally open 9–5 with extended hours on Thursdays.* ⅃.

The strip is only a few blocks long, but it is packed with good shopping and fantastic eating. Supposedly there are over 100 pubs and restaurants listed. **The Bay Village** at 18 Hastings Street is the largest mall area with a food court, internet cafés, and "elegant European" styles. It is always bustling and is a great central point of the street stroll. Many of the larger hotels have snazzy shops, too, so don't forget to have a browse. There are a few bargain stores and the news agency has some good stuff. But the art and jewelry are pleasant to the eye and may be good choices for reminders of this northern coast.

Walking about a mile along the boardwalk, the entrance of the National Park can be found. You can drive up to the spot, but be warned that open parking spaces are hard to find. As mentioned earlier, you can do this portion before, after, or in-between the shopping spree. If it is the hot season, it might be best to hike in the morning and get back by early afternoon. Take a bottle of water and enter the:

*NOOSA NATIONAL PARK HEADLAND SECTION ❷, Park Road, Noosa, ☎ (07) 5447-3243. *Open daily 24 hours. Free. Self-guided tours. Toilets at picnic areas. Not* ⅃.

The park covers 1,179 acres of land on the tip of Noosa Heads and is a variety of dense forests, powder-white beaches, high cliffs with Neptune smashing his angry waters against the walls, and private protected coves that would be perfect for a pirate brigantine. The hiking choices include the half-mile **Palm Grove Circuit** with a rainforest stroll; the **Tanglewood Track** that is a 3-mile walk to Hells Gate by an inland trail through woodlands; the 2-mile **Noosa Hill Track** that takes you to the center of the rainforests and offers a view of the coast; a 2-mile **Coastal Track** to Hells Gate via the shoreline; and the **Alexandria Bay Tracks** for a 1-1/2-mile trek to the pristine nudist beach of Alexandria Bay.

For an idea of what is in store for you, I have mixed a few of the hikes into one suggested walk. There is a kiosk, showing the paths at the Information Centre, just above the parking lot. The order and directions of the walk can be changed any way you choose. The suggested trip offered here is probably the best way to see it all in a few hours and still have time to jump into the Coral Sea at Alexandra Beach. Whether you wear a suit to swim is entirely up to you!

Laguna Lookout is at the top of the parking area, and you will begin the trip through dense vegetation. The bush turkeys are abundant in this area, probably due to the scraps left by messy picnickers. After starting the journey around the tip of land jutting out to the right of Laguna Bay, follow a sandy footpath that offers stunning sights of **The Boiling Pot** and **Tea-Tree Bay** near Dolphin Point and look for the brave (or foolish) surfers daring the sharp, jagged, black rocks at **Granite Bay** and **Winch Cove**. **Picnic Cove** appears below, where you can descend to the beach and laze on the shoreline. **The Fairy Pools** are next with smooth pockets of rock laden with fresh saltwater left from the last high tide. In contrast, the following spots are as vicious as there names implied—**The Boiling Pot** with its churning washing machine-agitated waters, **Winch Cove** that has round, black, soft-ball-sized rocks covering its shoreline, **Hells Gates** and its sheer cliffs that drop about 400 feet down into the Coral Sea, and **Alexandria Bay** with its secluded, calm lapping waters and bright beach.

It might be a god idea to cool off in the protected waters of Alexandria Bay. The water is usually calm and you can just splash around or float on the salty waves. It is usually sparsely populated near the Hells Gate portion of the beach and the emergency radio-telephone is nearby if you would need help. But do be careful as this beach is not patrolled and it would be quite a long time before anyone could come to the rescue. You can walk for another two hours past Oyster Rocks, Lion Rock, Devils Kitchen, and through the dense bush of the center of the park. It offers a different perspective to the coastline path, and you will have a better chance to see some of the wildlife near Noosa Hill. I recommend going back through the center, but pay attention to the directional markers.

TWO OPTIONAL ATTRACTIONS:

If there is any spare time in the schedule, these two side trips will provide plenty of material for that e-mail back home. **Camel Safaris**, ☎ (04) 0871-0530 or **W**: camelcompany.com.au, at Beach Road near Noosa has a 2-hour **Beach & Bushland Safari** for around AU $45, a 1-hour **Bushland Safari** for about AU $30, and a 1-1/2-hour **Beach Bush Safari** for around AU $38. If you have never ridden a camel, the time is now. The second tour requires at least a two-day layover to be able to ride into the sunset with **Clip Clop Treks**. You can book your trusty steed for a 2/4/6-day ride on ☎ (07) 5449-1254 or **W**: clipcloptreks.com.au. The rides take you around Fraser Island (nest tour), into the hinterlands and to the pubs, or along Noosa River to Lake Weyba. Food for thought.

Fraser Island and the Dingoes

This two-day tour of the world's largest sand island, and home to the planet's purest dingoes, will be a trip you will never forget. The recommended bus tour will stop at the colored sands at Rainbow Beach, offer a swim in dune lakes so pure they will not sustain life, stop at the shipwrecked hull of the luxury passenger liner the Maheno, and allow for hikes across desert dunes.

Located in Hervey Bay and just 155 miles north of Brisbane, the sand island is part of the Great Sandy National Park. It is the most visited site in Australia (beating out Ayers Rock) and has the only highway that's also an airstrip. This third-largest island off the Australian coast averages 9 miles wide and is 77 miles long. It is 1-1/2 times the size of the Sahara Desert! Overall it is 403 square acres of blowing sand dunes, thick rainforests, crashing waves, freshwater lakes, murky-looking swamps, pristine beaches, and incredible flora and fauna. Built up over 800,000 years, the sand has been swept north from New South Wales and deposited on the coffee rock base (a brown mix of clay and decomposed vegetation). Between the cyclones, erosion, high winds, droughts, and pulling sea currents, the island is continuously changing shape. Because of that feature, sailors are wary of the area around the island. Inland streams constantly dump millions of gallons of prehistoric water into the sea. And there are 40 lakes of varied size, shape, and character; one is so pure that no life can be sustained in it.

It was originally believed to be an Aboriginal camp due to the massive amounts of food available. But that changed quickly due to the discovery of gold, and the local Butchalla tribe was driven out in the 1830s. The island was converted to a quarantine station for people coming to pan for the metals on the mainland. As a result of the smallpox, influenza, and alcohol introduced to the tribe it diminished from over 2,000 to 150. The last of them were removed and put on reserves.

First named The Great Sandy Island by Captain Cook in 1770, it was later changed to Fraser in memory of a shipwrecked party led by James Fraser. Well, to be totally accurate, the first name of the island was K'gari (pronounced *gurrie*). Logging took over and the Giant satinay (turpentine) trees were removed and used to build the Suez Canal, and were also utilized as pylons to reconstruct the British docks after WW II. Next came the Z Force commandos and their training for war. The camouflage used today was based on the colorations found on Fraser. Then the sand miners arrived and removed as much of the rutlie, zircon, and ilmenite-rich sand as they could before being asked to leave by the government. Finally today, the island is a nature wonderland for tourists from all over the globe.

The reserve has no kangaroos, but there are many nocturnal critters such as spiny anteaters, gliders, bats, bobucks, bandicoots (cat-sized rat), and of course dingoes. Horses, brought in by timber cutters, have been reduced to only a few brumbies (wild horses). But birds are everywhere! From majestic sea eagles to noisy lorikeets and disliked ibis, spoonbills, ducks, and a variety of kingfishers. The island has enough brown snakes, death adders, taipans, and red-bellied black snakes to wipe out a small town. But I've not met anyone who has seen any of them.

GETTING THERE:

By 4WD: Please don't bother. Some people choose to hire a 4WD vehicle and explore this island with no roads, but I warn you against it. It is difficult to navigate and very expensive if you get stuck. If you do attempt it, read the small print of the rental contract.

By Bus: There are several bus tours available and are based your timeframe, the money you want to spend, and what you desire to see. You can book directly, but to have it all laid out for comparisons, contact **Palm Tree Tours** in Noosa, ☎ (07) 5474-9166 or **W**: ozemail.com.au/~noosaptt. I preferred the 3-Day **Adventure Safari**, ☎ (07) 5447-3845, that provides pick-up at your accommodation in Noosa, handles all tours and lodging at the Eurong Beach Resort—for AU $249/twin share. Tour options include: **Trailblazer Tours**, ☎ (07) 5444-6957, for around AU $130-$229; **Fraser Venture Tours**, ☎ 1-800-249-122, for AU $82/day, **Fraser V.I.P. Tours**, ☎ 1-800-649-988, for AU $220-$286; and the **Wilderness Lodge Tours** from Kingfisher Bay Resort, ☎ 1-800-072-555, for AU $225–$285.

PRACTICALITIES:

Hiking clothes and footwear appropriate for rainforest and sand treks are recommended. Sunscreen and bug spray is a must, and take along treatments for bug bites. It's not a good idea to swim unless the area is patrolled. The waters are dangerous for lots of reasons. There are free-roaming animals and they are wild despite their tame appearance. Dingoes can be a real threat and have killed children and attacked adults in the past. Follow these guidelines on the island:

   * Always stay with your children.
   * Walk in groups and keep your distance—watch quietly but do not attract, encourage, or excite dingoes.
   * NEVER feed dingoes—they are naturally thin and don't be tricked to

think they are hungry. It is illegal (AU $1,500 fines and up) to feed them or leave food where they can reach it.

* Lock away all food supplies and scraps—even clean BBQs and lock up dirty dishes.
* If you feel threatened by a dingo—stand up at your full height, face the dingo, fold your arms and keep eye contact; if in pairs—stand back to back, confidently call for help, calmly back away, do not run or wave your arms.

The sources for some of this information was gleaned from Australian Geographic and a book called "Fraser Island" by Angela Burger. I would recommend both of them as a good source for further biographical, geographical, and natural history insights. But also check out **W**: fraser-is.com, **W**: env.qld.gov.au/cyberrangers, or **W**: unesco.org/

FOOD AND DRINK:

Most tours supply all food and refreshments. The resorts have cafés, pubs, bakeries, grocery stores, and restaurants onsite. Picnic sites are located in most of the highlighted stopping spots.

LOCAL ATTRACTIONS:

Circled numbers correspond to numbers on the map.

The tour operators will organize the best schedule to see what you want on the 2–3 day tour. Normally, the guides pack two days full of options and allow a day to chill out or take in additional (for additional costs) sights. The goodies listed below are an example of some of the exotic adventures in store at the island.

Before the skip across the Great Sandy Strait, the tour will stop at **River Heads ❶**. The break allows passengers to stock up on treats and water at a small grocery store on the shoreline. It isn't necessary to clear the shelves as plenty of food and drink will be available on the entire trip. I think the main reason is to allow the drive to drop the tire pressure to 18 pounds as required to navigate the sands of Fraser. The large 4WD bus then lumbers through foot-deep sandy ruts, across a narrow strip of beach, and onto the ***Fraser Venture ❷***. The ferry is shaped like a sloop and the mass of busses, 4WDs, and passengers are loaded in minutes. This low-slung ship is clean, offers a whiff or two of diesel exhaust, and has about 5 feet of steel above the waterline. On the short 5-mile journey from the mainland, tea, biscuits, muffins, and coffee are served. Even on a calm day expect some sea spray mixed in with your drinks as you cross over. You might notice the absence of seagulls at this point. Apparently the sand is pure silica and the gulls need sea grit to allow the digestion of food. On the entire trip the coach captain will be spouting facts and trivia about the island and its inhabitants. Like the dingo is actually a Singapore wolf originally brought to the area by seamen who used the animal to

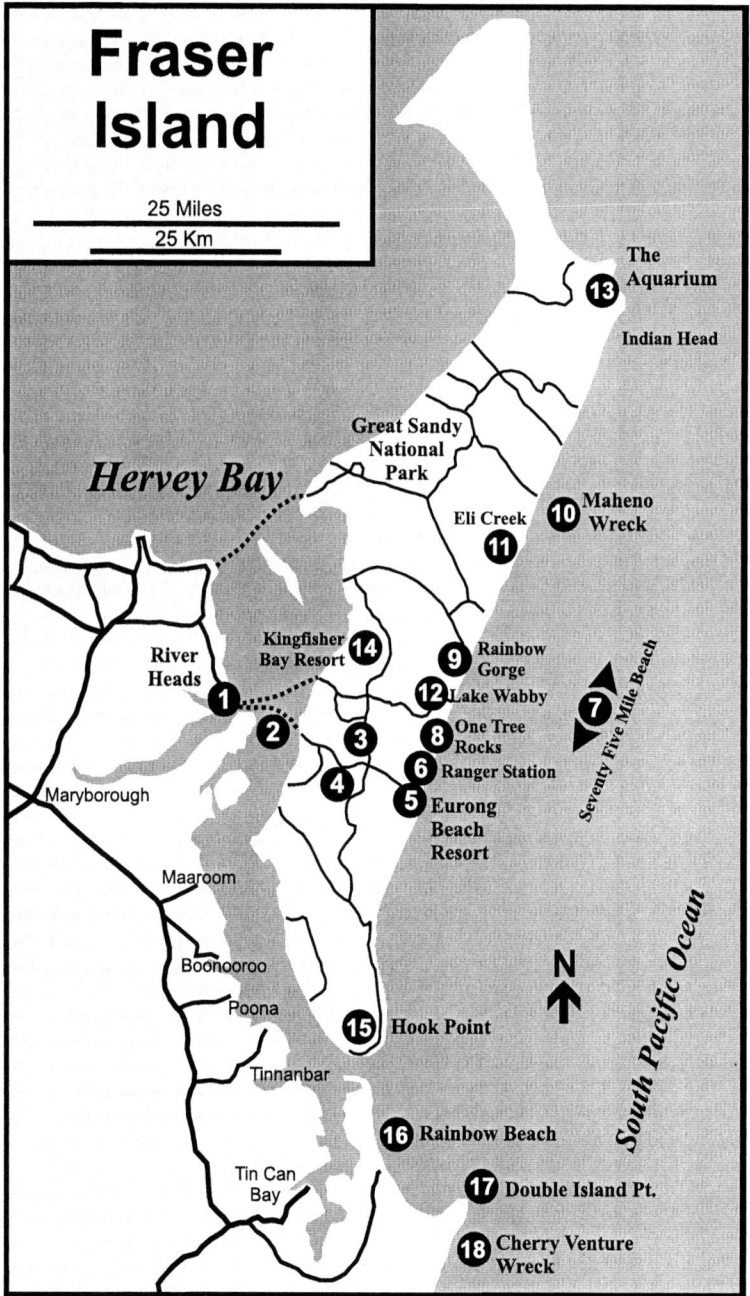

Fraser Island

25 Miles
25 Km

The Aquarium

Indian Head

Great Sandy National Park

Hervey Bay

Eli Creek

10 Maheno Wreck

11

13

Kingfisher Bay Resort

River Heads

14

9 Rainbow Gorge

12 Lake Wabby

1

2

3

8 One Tree Rocks

6 Ranger Station

4

5 Eurong Beach Resort

7 Seventy Five Mile Beach

Maryborough

Maaroom

Boonooroo

Poona

Tinnanbar

15 Hook Point

South Pacific Ocean

N

Tin Can Bay

16 Rainbow Beach

17 Double Island Pt.

18 Cherry Venture Wreck

locate land. Supposedly they can smell land from 300 miles out from shore.

Weaving around obstacles and oncoming vehicles the bus heads along the sand track called Mine Road. There are several different paths used to transverse the island, and this is one of the main tracks that cuts across the island. The first destination on Fraser is **Lake McKenzie** ❸. The lake is so pure, with a ph of 4.0, that it will not sustain any form of plant or animal life. It is about 70 degrees F, is a light green color around the sandy beach, and cools off into a deep dark blue color about 20 yards out. You're not supposed to drink from the lake, but I did and it tastes like distilled water. The freshwater pond is surrounded by dense green trees, is about a mile in diameter, and ringed with dazzling white sand.

After about an hour's swim, the bus is loaded up and heads to **Central Station** ❹. The driver will fill heads up with more yarns—and some pretty good ones at that. The station was once the main logging camp on the island with many of the timber-cutter's cabins and facilities well preserved. It wouldn't be at all surprising to see a lumberjack stroll from one of the log huts and say "g'day." The driver will switch hats and begin a walking tour along the rainforest filled with Satinay pines, 300-year-old king ferns, orchids, and palm trees. You will be warned of the dangers lurking 30 feet above. The bush pineapples are known to drop and do serious damage if you happen to be directly underneath. As you follow along the boardwalk, check out the stream running alongside the path—**Wanggoolba Creek.** It looks to be covered in Jurassic-age slime, but in fact it is so clear that you can see the green leaves on the bottom. Walking under the 150-foot trees and breathing in earthy scents feels as close to Eden as it gets.

Two more stories and you will arrive at **Eurong Beach Resort** ❺. The 3-star, absolute beachfront accommodation is a ten-acre refuge with luxury apartments, cottages, motel-style rooms, cabins, and family flats. It is a casual place with a general store, two pools, a karaoke pub, a gas station, a gift shop, and one of the few public phones to be found. Oh, mobile phones are basically useless on most parts of the island. The food is basic, but tasty and the beer is cold as is the fine selection of wines. You will be served cafeteria style and can go back for seconds and thirds.

The first tour on the eastern side should begin with the **Ranger Station** ❻ about 100 yards up the beach from the resort. It is loaded with great posters, maps, a small display of the island and its creatures, and friendly advice. Really do try to make it there first and get some background information on what else is in store for you. When the Mad Max Bus is ready to roll, the driver will count his wards and head north along **Seventy Five Mile Beach** ❼. If your guide/driver sees something worthwhile, he or she will pull over and explain what's happening. There will be quite a few stops along this official highway called Route 1. You may notice the driver will often look to the sky—remember that this patch of sandy road is also a landing strip for the commuter planes and all vehicles must give right of way.

The transport will come to an abrupt stop at **One Tree Rocks** ❽ if the dingoes are hanging out when you pass by. It seems to be a popular hang-out for the yellow dogs. If they are shy, the trip continues up the beach to the first notable attraction, called **Rainbow Gorge** ❾. The dunes on Fraser Island are called "continuously forming sand dunes" because they are constantly building on themselves and are affected by the changes throughout the millennia. Like archeological digs that unveil the layers of history, Rainbow Gorge reveals a layered-cake view of different sand types, clays and minerals. The rainbow effect is created from a mix of inorganic and organic materials being exposed to the air and bleeding the colors for all to see. The Aboriginal legend of the gorge goes something like this: Wuru, a young girl, was to marry an old man named Winyer. But Wuru was in love with a handsome boy named Wiberigan (that means rainbow). When the old man found out about this competitor in love, he hunted Wiberigan and killed him at the gorge with his boomerang. The boy fell and died on the spot, his blood covered the gorge and formed a rainbow. In all honesty, the sands are not very rainbow-like nor are they all colors of the bloody rainbow. They have a dappled texture with the predominant color being yellow or tan. But you can definitely see the layers and the gorge looks like Spielberg created it for a *Star Wars* desert scene.

Next up, **The *Maheno*** ❿. This wreck of a luxury liner may jog a memory, as it is a standard backdrop for many bikini-clad calendars. The giant boat looks like a rusted erector set in the shape of a battleship. The ship was used to treat passengers to an elegant trip between New Zealand and Australia in the early 1900s. It was a 459-foot triple steam-engine powered boat used as a hospital ship in WW I and in 1935 she was sold for scrap to a Japanese company. While being hauled from Australia, the towline from the Oonah tugboat snapped in a vicious cyclone and she ran aground on Fraser. Apparently, they took the screws off the Maheno to lighten the load and she was dead in the water. Being too damaged to refloat, the salvage company stripped off the valuables and left the hull there to rust into oblivion. It does look like a skeleton with ribs poking from the depths of the sea of blinding white sand with only ghosts responding to commands of abandon ship. It is now the sand-bound flagship for fisherpersons from all over the area. Supposedly it is a hot spot for tailor and hundreds of anglers line up for a nibble.

Eli Creek ⓫ is a great spot to stretch, have a walk and maybe float down the freshwater stream a few times. Halting at Eli Creek you can change into a swimming suit and take the plunge. Warning—despite what the guide says, the water is bloody cold! This second largest creek on the island has a water flow of almost 1 million gallons per hour. The water is supposed to be somewhere around 200 million years old (though the literature claims 80-million). You can doggy-paddle along the curvy stream with fellow tourists and scramble over a few shallow spots until approaching the beach about 80 yards from the beginning. At the wooden bridge that crosses over the little stream is a sign that details the area and the creek. Don't read it before you jump in the water though. It is loaded with eels hiding in the vegetation along the banks, and keelback snakes too. But they are not supposed to be a threat, just like the striped rocket frog and empire gudgeon fish. Tall grass-covered creek beds surround the slowly rippling water of the creek until it dumps onto the beach where it pools up into a 40-yard, round, wading pool. At this point the driver may fill you in on the dangers of getting stuck in the sands of Fraser, especially near the creeks that flow onto the beach. Some of the creeks dump as much as 1-1/2 million gallons of fresh water onto the beach every hour. If you happen to get stuck near or on the flows, it takes only two hours to swallow your vehicle whole. Remember the warning about not renting a vehicle for this trip—the island consumes quite a few trucks each year.

This will probably be the extent of the first day's activities, and you will be escorted back to the resort for a meal, drinks and a party at the pub.

The next day will most likely start on the beach again and a drive to **Lake Wabby** ⑫, a body of water known as a barrage lake. That means that a sand blow, a moving dune of sand, blocked a creek to create a lake. The fish-laden Wabby is loaded with Salmon Tailed Catfish, and the dominant turtle is called Kefts. But first you must cut a swath between the scrubby trees on the ocean-side dunes across about a mile-wide desert. The mirage of heat waves will break into a greenish lake with a 25-yard embankment that dives straight into the water. The lake is in a basin with dense bush and trees on the foreshore. There is clear evidence of the sand blow activity with treetops sticking from areas of the dunes. The tops, looking like small shrubs, are actually large trees that have been covered in twenty feet of sand. The wind whips from the beach area and pushes the sand inland in slow waves to encroach on anything in its way. Eventually the lake will be overtaken and covered by the sand.

If you choose to continue up the beach **The Aquarium** ⑬ is waiting to greet you. Also called the Champagne Pools, they are a great place to relax, sit in the rock pools, and watch the world go by. Another notable landmark and a great place to sneak over to for dinner is the **Kingfisher Bay Resort** ⑭. It is an eco-friendly accommodation with fine dining and luxury rooms. It's worth a look if you can find a ride to the western side of the island.

That should fill the second day and the final glorious trip on day three will take you south along Seventy Five Mile Beach, past **Hook Point** ⑮. A ferry will transport you over the narrow causeway and back onto the mainland at **Rainbow Beach** ⑯. The left side of the bus will be filled with four-story cliffs of multi-colored sand formations etched in their face. It looks like Mother Nature's graffiti with swirls and markings of all colors. The sand is crunchy around the base of the cliffs with small pools of life huddled in the shade. There are 72 different colors of sand, and they are supposedly over 40,000 years old. The "dream-time" story related to the cliffs talks about a beautiful maiden called Murrawar who would sing to the cliffs each morning. But a bad man attacked her one day and threw his boomerang at her. The girl's faithful rainbow came to the rescue and both the boomerang and the rainbow were shattered. The cliffs and beach are the remains of the great battle.

Rounding the point at Rainbow Beach is the landmark that deceived Captain Cook when he was navigating the area. Because the two knobby rock formations look like two separate islands from the ocean, he named this **Double Island Point** ⓱. The bus will cut a bit off the point as it enters Cooloola Beach, 40-Mile Beach, and the home to The MV *Cherry Venture* ⓲. This was a cargo ship that came ashore over 20 years ago, and its single steam stack is slowly sinking into the sand. It looks a lot like the other wreck described earlier, but it is loaded with local graffiti.

The final stretch will be driven through the logging forests, through a few small towns and back to your accommodation.

The MV Cherry Venture *Shipwreck*

Section VII

Daytrips in
The Queensland Outback

This section will expose you to the incredible vastness of Australia's "Sunburnt Country." The television shows, photographs, and verbal accounts of so harsh a land will in no way prepare you for what is to be seen, heard, smelled, and touched in the Outback. Not even many Australians venture out into the areas where trees survive the parched conditions by pruning their own limbs to conserve water, the red earth is cracked into a maze of criss-crossed fissures from years of drought, drenching rains create a plain of rivers flowing over miles of land, only animals with superior survival instincts exist, and a love of the land and the freedom it brings creates a special (and colorful) breed of people. Since the Outback is indeed simultaneously so harsh and beautiful, it will either capture your heart and soul or make you want to rush back to the lush coastline and waterfront cities.

When driving into this region, you will appreciate the pioneering spirit permeating all aspects of life—even now. Just traveling the expansive and dusty roads is an eye-opening adventure. Traveling straight in from the coast and along the 1,242 miles of the infamous Route 66, the landscape quickly changes from the hustle and bustle of Rockhampton's city life to an unimaginable vastness. Even if you decide to ride in luxury aboard Queensland Railroad's "Spirit of the Outback," you will stare into a world like nothing you've seen before. It is not comparable to the midwestern plains of the United Sates as this stark horizon is straight out of a scene from Mad Max (literally). But when you take the time to look closely, there is a wonderful and amazing world waiting to greet you.

2002 was designated as the Year of the Outback; a celebration of the true grit, innovative approach, and adaptive manner in which the people of the Queensland Outback live in harmony with this magnificent land. Realizing there is no conquering nature in the Outback, residents and visitors alike learn quickly to respect the surroundings and rely on each other for survival. This has created an atmosphere unlike any I've seen anywhere.

On your journey, you will cross the Tropic of Capricorn, taste Bundy Rum right from the barrel, enjoy what might be the best steak in the world at Rockhampton, see miles of chocolate-colored dikes protecting precious acres of cotton fields, venture into the rubble of abandoned mining camps as you prospect for sapphires and rubies, learn the history of the Outback at the Stockman's Hall of Fame and the Waltzing Matilda Museums, soak in artesian waters gushing from ancient underground rivers, and maybe even adopt a Tambo Teddy.

But above all things you will appreciate the generous, genuine, gutsy, and openness of the people along the way. Unlike the coastal populations, the extremes of this part of the country have tempered a character only described as proudly Outback. These tours should provide a great cross-section of the life many would never leave. I have only scratched the surface of things to be seen and people to be met, but the main attractions are included.

I believe the best way to gain the full perspective of the trips is to drive Route 66 (the Capricorn Highway) and stop at the selected towns for a look around. It is the most economical, will help you appreciate the distances, and will give you more flexibility to pick and choose your interests. On the other hand, the rail coach option will ease you into the atmosphere and eliminate the long drive times necessary to get to each stop. The drive is indeed brutal and you can expect to be in the car on average four hours a day.

GETTING TO THE OUTBACK:

By Car: From Brisbane, the first stop is about 300 miles north to Bundaberg. The main road is the Bruce Highway that cuts a straight swath up the coast. Rockhampton is another 93 miles north along the coast, also on Bruce Highway. At that point, all attractions are due west along the Capricorn Highway, also known as Route 66. From Rockhampton to the farthest point in Winton is about 534 miles. Driving west should take about 10–14 days with 1–2 day layovers at each major town. The trip back south, on Matilda Highway to Brisbane, is about 836 miles and will take you a good 2–3 days.

By Bus: Not very attractive because of the limited departure/arrival schedules and the lines only allow for a 2-stop layover from Rockhampton to Winton. The estimated cost for a trip from the coast to Winton is about AU $140 (20% less for kids). If you want to give it a go, call one of the two primary Australian bus lines: **Greyhound Pioneer**, ☎ 13-20-30 or **W**: greyhound.com.au; and **McCafferty's**, ☎ 13-14-99 or **W**: mccaffertys.com.au. The booking agent for both transportation organizations is **Travel Coach Australia**, ☎ 13-14-99.

By Train: This is a serious option and they run specials in the summer months (up to 50% off). If you don't desire to get the grit in your teeth and want the tour planned out for you, **Queensland Rail** (QR) can do the trick. The *Tilt Train Service* and the *Spirit of the Outback* services (both QR) have prepared a package deal requested for the Daytrips' traveler. The following option incorporates train travel, a listing of attractions listed by Queensland Rail, estimated departure dates/times, and layover estimates. You can get assistance for all train travel and suggested itineraries by contacting **Traveltrain Holidays**, ☎ 1-800-627-655, (07) 3235-7802, or **W**: traveltrain.com.au. For connections and tours at the towns where layovers are stipulated, see the specific section for suggested tour operators. Or simply shop at **Tourism Queensland's** web site, **W**: queensland-holidays.com.au

This is the sample provided courtesy of Queensland Rail for Daytrips. It includes most of the tours mentioned and adds a few from their own tour operators:

DAY 1   Brisbane to Rockhampton
Departs 10.30am (Departs everyday except Saturday from Brisbane)

QR's high-speed *Tilt Train connects* visitors to major tourist destinations from South East to Central Queensland. As the fastest train in Australia, it travels at speeds of up to 100mph and is outfitted with state-of-the-art facilities and catering services. The 7-hour trip between Brisbane and Rockhampton meanders through lush green walls of sugar cane, scenic Glasshouse Mountains, and quaint regional towns.

DAYS 2–3   Rockhampton
Arrives 5.30pm

Rockhampton is the capital of the Capricorn Region and provides a gateway to the Capricorn Coast, central highlands, gemfields, and the rural hinterland. Founded in 1853, Rockhampton boasts fine examples of colonial architecture dating back to the early pioneering days.

DAY 4   Rockhampton to Emerald
Departs 4.35am (Wednesdays/Sundays)

The *Spirit of the Outback* offers a unique insight into the history and culture of early Australia. Themed carriages such as the Stockman's Bar, Tucker Box Restaurant, and Captain Starlight's Lounge reflect the rich heartland that it travels through, further enhancing the Australian Outback holiday experience. The scenery of the Outback makes train travel a truly marvelous experience, capturing the changing terrain and wildlife that makes the Outback so quintessentially Australian.

DAYS 5–7   Emerald & Carnarvon Gorge
Arrives 9.18am

Emerald is the center of the Central Queensland Highlands region. While in Emerald visit the sapphire gem fields, take an underground mine tour, fossick for your own sapphires, and visit Lake Maraboon that is 3 times the size of the Sydney Harbour. Emerald is also the gateway to Carnarvon Gorge, approximately a 90-minute drive outside of town.

DAY 8   Emerald to Longreach

Departs 9.18am (Wednesdays?Sundays)

Back on board the *Spirit of the Outback* heading farther west to Longreach and other outback towns such as Barcaldine and Winton. On arrival to Longreach you will be met by one of the local tour operators "a true Outback character," who will show you the sites of Queensland's Outback. Your host can transfer to your accommodation.

DAY 9   Barcaldine

See the sights at Barcaldine including the Tree of Knowledge, Australian Workers Heritage Centre, and enjoy lunch at the Ironbark Inn's 3L's Restaurant. Visit the historical Langenbaker House, Folk and Transport Museum, and the Wellshot Hotel.

DAY 10   Longreach

Arrives 5.58pm

Today you will visit the Longreach Pastoral College, Australian Stockman's Hall of Fame, and Oakley Station. Finish the day with a sunset dinner cruise along the Thomson River. Overnight Longreach.

DAY 11   Longreach

Enjoy an optional sunset safari. Visit Banjo's Outback Theatre and Shearing Shed, and the Longreach School of the Air. You will also see the Qantas Founders' Outback Museum and enjoy a Herbert Range safari. Savor a camp oven dinner in a magic setting. Overnight Longreach.

DAY 12   Winton

Head west to Winton and explore Rangelands Station's scenic Rift Valleys, lookouts, and remnants of Gonnaway Plateau. At Winton you will see the Opal Walk, Open Air Theatre, Prehistoric Dinosaur Diorama, and the famous Waltzing Matilda Centre. A great finale with the Wildlife Safari Awards and farewell dinner. Overnight Longreach.

DAY 13

Your tour concludes this morning in Longreach. You will be transferred to the Longreach Railway Station or Airport to take you to your next port of call, after experiencing a truly memorable Queensland Outback Experience.

By Plane: This is OK if you have big bucks and little time to get a flavor for the Outback. **Qantas Link** is about the only airline available, with a few competition prospects waiting in the wings. Contact **Qantas**, ☎ 13-13-13 or **W**: Qantas.com.au, for schedules and prices. Try **Planet Aviation**, ☎ (07) 4922-7255 or **W**: planetaviation.pm, for some comparison-shopping. Planet Aviation is based in Rockhampton, offers scenic tours locally (from AU $100) or charters to most Outback destinations (starting around AU $1,000), and can be a personal sky guide. It has been announced recently that **Virgin Blue**, ☎ 13-67-89 or **W**: virginblue.com.au, will be providing service to selected towns in the Outback.

ACCOMMODATION IN THE OUTBACK:

Since the distances are so great between trips, I have picked several layovers to permit reasonable driving times and allow periods for relaxing exploration at the key attraction sites. The primary stopovers are at Bundaberg, Rockhampton, Emerald, Sapphire, Longreach, Winton, and Mitchell. Plan on a day or two at each base with about 4 hours of driving between each spot. As all of our trips, you have the option of skipping over spots, combining tours, or staying longer at a favored location.

The accommodation choices are varied, but I think the best sleep-overs are to be found at the B&Bs. I found them to be the quietest, most comfortable, and the best source on the local (and often unadvertised) hidden secret attractions. The next best night's sleep can be found in the cabins at the caravan parks (trailer parks), but some require a two-night minimum. The pubs and motels are also usually a bargain as are the back-packer accommodations found in almost all towns. There will be options selected for each tour, but if you desire to do some additional research try these sources: **Bed and Breakfasts,** ☎ (07) 4097-7022 or **W**: bnbnq.com.au; **The Accommodation Centre,** ☎ 1-800-807-730 or **W**: accomcentre.com.au; **Backpackers,** ☎ (07) 3236-4999 or **W**: yha.com.au; **Peter Pan Backpackers,** ☎ 1-800-252-459 or **W**: peterpans.com; **Caravan Parks, W**: qparks.asn.au

PRACTICALITIES:

Be prepared—the Outback can be unforgiving country. The trips out-lined will not take you into the remote areas where most of these rules apply, but it is good to heed them anyway. Firstly and most importantly—drink lots of water, protect yourself from the sun, and keep a map with you. Mobile phones have limited range and are not reliable unless they are a satellite version. There are plenty of sources for drinkable water, but if you are finicky about the taste (some places have very sulfur-smelling/tasting water), stock up on bottled water or carry along a water filter. From there use these as guidelines for safety as well as showing respect for the landowners:

* Keep the fuel tank topped up (though the gas stations are rarely more than 150 miles apart.
* If you do have vehicle problems—stay with the car and wait for help.
* Livestock and wildlife frequent the roadsides, especially at dawn and dusk. Slow down and pay attention if they are nearby.
* It is wise to keep your headlights ON. The distances are deceiving and this will let the opposing vehicles better judge your position.
* When a large truck (roadtrain) approaches, slow down and stay away from the center of the road. Being 164-foot long, having 36 wheels, and are up to three trailers connected to a "pull cab", they cannot stop quickly.
* If you come upon a gate across the road—leave it the way you found it (if it's closed, close it behind you or leave it open if that's how you found it).
* You will see signs reminding you to "Buckle Up in the Bush." It's the

law.

* Fires are a real hazard and once started can rip across the plains. Don't throw any cigarettes out the window, light campfires only in designated areas, and keep an eye out for fires on the horizon.
* Don't feed, hassle, or touch the native animals. They are wild — take a picture instead.
* If you explore off the beaten path, let someone know where you are going and when to expect you back.

There is a ton of reference material on the Outback in the form of brochures and web sites. Each trip provides the contact data for the local information center and relevant web sites to have a peek prior to the journey. Before heading west, you might want to obtain the following magazines, brochures or information packages: R.M. Williams **Outback Travel Guide** magazine, ☎ (02) 9908-8050 or **W**: outbackmag.com.au, for about AU $10; the free **Travel Action Matilda Country** magazine, ☎ 1-800-061-414, ☎ (07) 4685-2266 or **W**: action-graphics.com.au; **Queensland's Outback Traveler's Guide**, free by ☎ 1-800-247-966 or **W**: outbackholidays.tq.com.au; the independent traveler's magazine of **TNT Magazine**, free on ☎ (02) 9299-4710 or **W**: tntmagazine.com; the **Western Round-Up** magazine, free at most information centers; the free **Queensland Motoring Holiday Guide**, ☎ 1-800-222-689; and the free **Guide to Queensland's Roads**, ☎ (07) 3883-8711.

SPECIAL EVENTS:

The dates may vary a bit, so check with the local information centers to confirm an event you are intent in seeing. Events are listed in their relevant touring section.

FOOD AND DRINK:

For the most part, the pubs are the best value, and you can meet some local characters at these watering holes. The food is good, the beer is very good, and the crowds are fascinating. There are also cafés, restaurants, and some fast food outlets along the way. The highway gas stations usually have a small eatery or at least a cooler with quick eats. There are a few gems along the way too, and the B&Bs mentioned all have fantastic food.

SHOPPING:

The main attractions have gift shops with trademark goodies and fun locally created products. Each town has a fair selection of shops catering to the local needs. For the shopping maniac, this is not the series of trips for you, but there are some good buys along the way.

Bundaberg's Rum & Turtles

Bundaberg (or Bundy) is noted for its rum, turtles, sugar cane, whale watching, and being the southern tip of the Great Barrier Reef. Bundaberg is the epicenter of the sugar industry and a small comfortable town; only 9 miles to the Coral Sea and the wonders of the ocean. From August to October the humpback whales migrate from Antarctica to Bundy's warm waters, where you can hop aboard a guide boat to witness their grandeur. Arriving in November–February (nesting season) or January–March (hatchlings appear), you must get out to Mon Repos Beach to take a guided tour of the nesting sites and the turtle scramble to/from the ocean. If you haven't had enough of the water sports you can take daytrips out to Lady Elliot Island, Lady Musgrave Island, or Fitzroy Reef Lagoon. For the landlubber, the highlighted tour will focus on the rum distillery and samples of Australia's pride and joy - Bundy Rum. If you never tried their rum, then you haven't lived.

This flat area just south of the Tropic of Capricorn has rich volcanic soil that is perfect for sugar cane. During planting season the fields, full of mounded rows, look like powdered chocolate. When the cane peaks (between July and November), you are completely surrounded by lush green stalks. At harvest time, the sky is a swab of soot as the cane is burned off in an orange glow. The crop is torched to remove unwanted foliage, and the stems then harvested. Cane trains are everywhere too, and you will pass over numerous rail crossings on the rumble roads around Bundy.

A full day in Bundaberg is plenty of time to experience both tours, enjoy a nice meal at the ocean-side pub, and have a good rest in the middle of a sugar cane field. But if you are as enamored of the place as I was, you might want to stay for a couple of days to soak in the friendly little series of towns in and around Bundaberg.

GETTING THERE:

By Car: A straight shot up the Bruce Highway it's about 300 miles or three hours north of Brisbane.

By Bus: Either **Greyhound**, ☎ 13-20-30; or **McCafferty's**, ☎ 13-14-99, travel to Bundaberg. The cost would be about AU $60 and take about four hours.

By Train: Take the *Spirit of Capricorn,* the *Queenslander,* the *Sunlander,* or best of all the *Tilt Train.* Call **Queensland Rail** at ☎ 13-22-32 or on **W**: traveltrain.qr.com.au. The cost for all services is approximately AU $56 for a one-way adult fare.

GETTING AROUND:

This is a small area, and if you arrived by coach or train, you can easily walk or cab around to the various attractions. During the week the local bus line, **Duffy's Coaches,** offers transportation, and during the weekends just hail a cab.

PRACTICALITIES:

The heat will increase as you proceed north and west. The temperature range will generally be comfortable with the coldest in July with lows near 50 degrees Fahrenheit to the heat of summer in January with 86 highs. The turtle tours will require sun protection and beachwear. The rum trip is basically inside with lots of stairs to climb. Take a cab if you really like rum.

Some helpful contacts to assist in coordinating your visit include: The **Bundaberg Regional Visitor Centre** at the corner of Bourbong & Mulgrave streets, ☎ (07) 4153-8888, 1-800-308-888, or **W**: bundabergregion.info; the **Bundaberg Region Limited** at 271 Bourbong Street, ☎ (07) 4152-2333; whale and turtle data at ☎ (07) 4159-1652 or **W**: epa.qld.gov.au; **Bundaberg Rum Distillery,** ☎ (07) 4131-2999 or **W**: bundabergrum.aom.au; **Lady Elliot Trips,** ☎ 1-800-072-200 or **W**: ladyelliot.com.au; and **Lady Musgrave Island,** ☎ 1-800-072-110 or **W**: imcruises.com.au

SPECIAL EVENTS:

January—Australia Day celebrations; March—Wild Scotchman Bushranger and Heritage Festival; April—Easter Country Music Roundup; May—Agro Trend Field Day, Regional Show; June—Orange Festival; July—Multicultural Food, Wine and Performing Arts Festival; August—Whale Watching, Pottery Group Exhibition, Quilter's Biennial Patchwork & Quilting Exhibition, Doll and Bear Fair; September—Bundy in Bloom Spring Celebrations, Orchid Society Spring Show, Garden, Home, Leisure, and Boat Expo, Style Spectacular Fashion Awards, Heritage Festival; October—The Rodeo, Festival of the Arts, Axeman's Woodchop Festival, Lifetime Jazz and Blues Festival, Graphic Arts Exhibition; November—Bundy Thunder Power Boat Classic, Midtown Marinas On the Water Boat Show, Turtle Nesting Season, Surf Girl Contest; December—Light Up Celebrations, Pageant of Lights, Carols by Candlelight, Country Queensland Disabled Centre Challenge.

FOOD AND DRINK:

Not that there aren't good places to eat in Bundy, but I recommend the beachside eateries in Bargara Beach. The **Bargara Beach Hotel/Motel** ($-$$), at the corner of Bauer & See Streets, ☎ (07) 4159-2232, provides a fantastic array of foods from Thai, to seafood, to pub counter meals. Plus, the view is right over the ocean. **The Spinnaker Restaurant & Bar** ($-$$), ☎ (07) 4152-8033, on Quay Street in Bundaberg is also fantastic for seafood and looking over the Burnett River. Don't worry about breakfast as the feast provided at the **Dunelm House B&B** ($-$$) will keep you going most of the day. Beyond these choices, there are heaps of pubs, fast food outlets, cafés, and ethnic restaurants to select for a fine meal.

ACCOMMODATION:

As mentioned at the beginning of this section, the B&Bs seem to be the best choices as they give good value, provide hearty meals, and offer great insights to the local attractions. I have listed my preference in the Dunelm House B&B. Also included are a few other options to suit your particular interests.

THE DUNELM HOUSE B&B, 540 Bargara Road, Bargara Beach, QLD 4670, ☎ (07) 4159-0909, **W**: bedandbrekky.com/dunelm. *Prices range from AU $50–$75. Not* ♿.

Smack in the middle of a sugar cane field is this quaint cottage with ensuite bedrooms, a pool, air conditioning, common television room, great breakfasts with homemade breads and jams, and walls full of interesting paintings. Make sure you stick a pin in the map to mark your hometown. The great advantage of this 4-1/2-star B&B is not only the hospitality, but also its central location to most of the attractions in the area.

Other lodging suggestions include the **Reef Gateway Motor Inn** (Best Western) at 11 Takalvan Street, ☎ (07) 4153-2244. This 4-star lodge costs about AU $85–$145/night. **Whiston House** at 9 Elliott heads Road, ☎ (07) 4152-1447, is a 3-1/2-star B&B, also a bargain at AU $70–$90. The 3-star **Turtle Sands Tourist Park & Holiday Retreat** at Mon Repos Beach, ☎ (07) 4159-2340, has beachfront campsites and units for AU $17–$70/night.

LOCAL ATTRACTIONS:

Circled numbers correspond to numbers on the map.

*THE BUNDABERG RUM DISTILLERY ❶, Avenue Street, Bundaberg, ☎ (07) 4131-2999, **W**: bundabergrum.com.au. *Tours run every hour Mon.–Fri. 10–3, Weekends 10–2, closed Christmas. Adults AU $7.70, children AU $2.20, groups of 15 or more AU $5.50. Guided tours. Gift shop. Pub. Special events. Not* ♿.

The region began producing sugar commercially in 1872, and in 1888 a consortium of sugar farmers established the Bundaberg Distilling Company. It was created as a way to utilize the byproduct of sugar manufacturing—molasses. The sugary extract is now the base for the famous

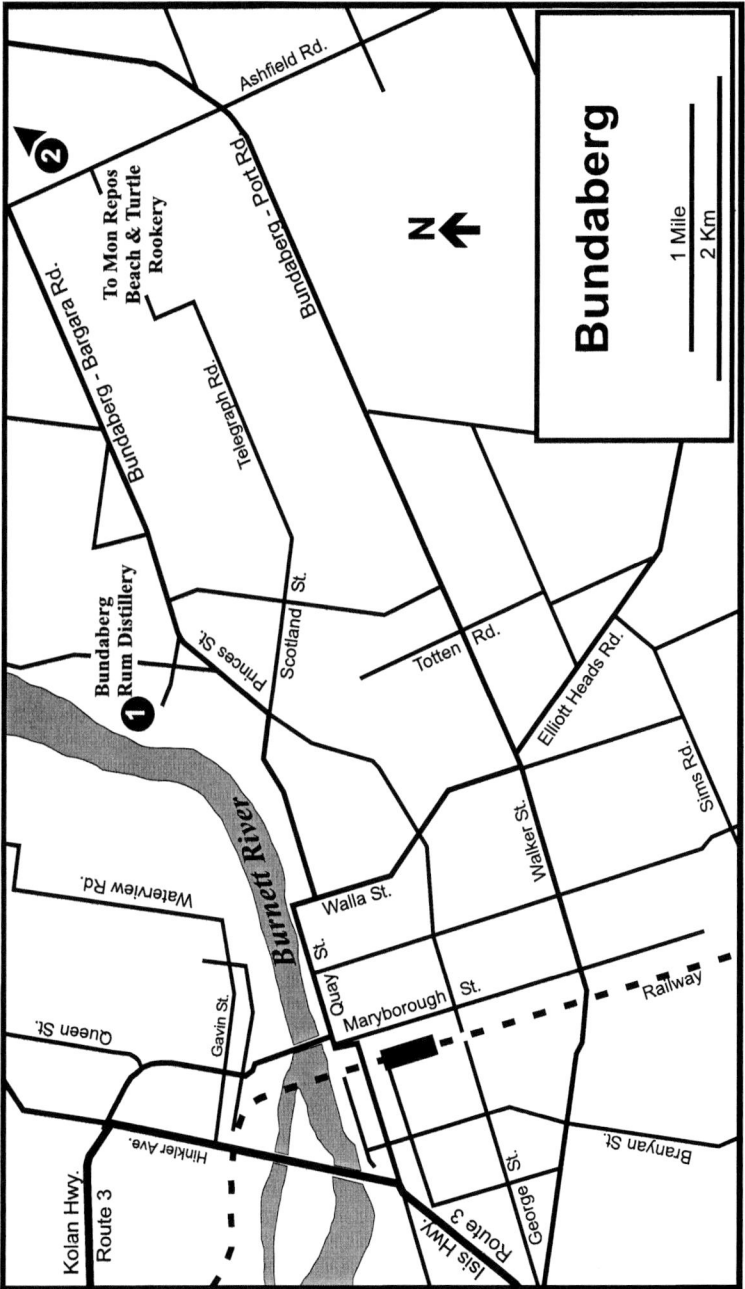

Bundaberg

1 Mile
2 Km

N

Ashfield Rd.

Bundaberg - Port Rd.

To Mon Repos
Beach & Turtle
Rookery

Bundaberg - Bargara Rd.

Telegraph Rd.

Bundaberg
Rum Distillery

Scotland St.

Princes St.

Totten Rd.

Elliott Heads Rd.

Sims Rd.

Walker St.

Burnett River

Waterview Rd.

Walla St.

Quay St.

Gavin St.

Queen St.

Maryborough St.

Railway

Branyan St.

Hinkler Ave.

Kolan Hwy.
Route 3

Isis Hwy.
Route 3

George St.

❶ ❷

Bundy Rum. When you arrive at the parking area of the factory, you will immediately smell the burnt molasses permeating the air. The first rum was distilled in the 16th century around the Caribbean, then Australia used the spirit as barter currency in the 18th century, and now it's the most popular spirit drunk in Oz.

The tour will take you through all phases of the processing, and into a maze of molasses vats that look as though they are filled with warm molten lava. You can also peek into huge barrels that store up to 10 million liters of dark, light, and red rums. One barrel of White American Oak might be maturing 60,000 liters of spirit in controlled temperatures. It takes between two and ten years to age the rum and is only produced five months a year. There is AU $5 million worth of rum in each barrel, and you will be hard-pressed to see the end of the barrels tucked away in the warehouse (there are supposed to be over 200). The fumes are so intense on the tour that all cameras, lighters, matches, mobile phones, and any electrical devices are stored at the front desk before the show starts.

It takes only an hour to complete the tour—from the introductory video of the region, to the viewing platform watching 5,000 bottles an hour whip by as they are filled, labeled and boxed, to the final and anxiously-awaited taste testing. Even if you aren't a rum fan, try a sip of the chocolate liqueur, or the new draft rum and cola. You do get a free sample after all, and discount prices for as many bottles as you wish to purchase. The gift shop has some great goodies to eat, wear, or carry and the fudge is out of this world. Finally say g'day to the smiling Bundy Polar Bear. He/she is the trademark that symbolizes the "liquid sunshine" called Bundaberg Rum, boasting it "can keep out the wickedest cold."

*MON REPOS TURTLE ROOKERY ❷, 108 Mon Repos Beach, ☎ (07) 4159-1652, **W**: env.qld.gov.au. *Open daily 7pm–11pm (when rangers are available, so call first). Adults AU $5, children AU $2.50. Guided tours only. Gift shop. Café. Special events. Partially &.*

If you arrive at Mon Repos Beach on the off-season, there will be no turtle encounter, but the center is well worth the price and the educational value is immeasurable. If you are lucky enough to appear on their beach in laying and hatching season (Nov.–Feb. and Jan.–Mar.), a ranger will help you strap on a miner's helmet or better yet carry a light stick for the wander onto the beaches. Flashlights can be taken along, but not used anywhere near the turtles. Groups of 1–70 people are ticketed and timed to go near the nests one at a time. Beaches are closed from sunset to sunrise and access is only permitted in the company of a ranger. The most populous turtle is the endangered Loggerhead, but the Green and Flat varieties also come in to lay eggs. There is a great audiovisual presentation in the outdoor theater starting at 7:30 at night, and a nice environmental display in the building.

A few hints that will help you better see the nocturnal critters (and they will be reinforced by the rangers during orientation). Keep the use of lights (including your headlights in the parking lot) to a minimum, move slowly when near the turtles, photos are allowed only when the ranger says OK, you must wear your assigned number to assure you are with the correct touring group, the total night viewing time may take up to six hours, no smoking on the beach or along the boardwalks, and no alcohol is permitted.

OTHER LOCAL ATTRACTIONS:

The **Bundaberg Coastal Leisure Trail** (see the Visitor Information Centre for a map and directions) begins at the Information Centre and includes a 4-hour beachside walk, a swim, and maybe even a picnic lunch. It will take you past some significantly historical sites like The Basin, Kelly's Beach, Mon Repos Rookery, and Bundaberg Port. Right next to the distillery is **Schmeider's Cooperage & Craft Centre** at 3–7 Alexandra Street, East Bundaberg, ☎ (07) 4151-8233, with barrel making, woodturning, glassblowing, pottery, paintings, and woven products being made right on site. The free pavilion is open Mon.–Fri. 9-5 and weekends 9–3. The free **Botanic Gardens** in North Bundaberg, with over 65 acres of lakes and manicured lawns, has a steam locomotive puffing through the grounds. **Hinkler House Memorial Museum**, ☎ (07) 4152-0222 or **W**: aceflyer.com/hinkler, has a collection of Hinkler memorabilia displaying the feats of this famous Aussie test pilot for a mere AU $4 adult, AU $2 kids, and AU $9 family pass. If you want to see the three museums near the gardens including the Hinkler, Fairymead House (sugar museum), and the Historical Museums, you can purchase a combined pass for only AU $14. The **MV** *Spirit of Musgrave* **Whale Watching Cruise**, ☎ 1-800-072-110, (07) 4159-4519, or **W**: imcruises.com.au, is a tour of Platypus Bay staged to greet the humpback whales for around AU $42-$85. The **Mystery Craters** are a big draw too, and these 25-million-year-old rock formations are open daily 8–5. Entrance to the phenomenon listed as one of the unsolved mysteries of the world is only AU $5 adult, AU $2.50 for children, and AU $12.50 for a family of 2/2. At Lines Road in South Kolan (20 minutes from Bundaberg) you will witness 35 craters of varied size that may have been created by meteorites, volcanic activity, aliens, or is the roof of a subterranean lake. Who knows?

Entrance to Rockhampton Cattle Town

Cattle Town of Rockhampton

Rockhampton has everything for the cowboy/cowgirl in you, but don't think that the area offers only saddle sores and steaks. Although you can see your share of rodeos, bull & quarter horse auctions, and cattle drives, there is so much more to experience in this Tropic of Capricorn city. The town has recently taken a hit in the cattle industry with the largest slaughterhouse closing down and many people out of work. You might find the city to be a bit of a ghost town, but the main attractions have not been affected. The cattle are still a main focus for the town and at times over three million head pass through the area. Other industries include the farming of paw paws, pineapples, custard apples, and lots of pine timber. It's sister city of Yeppoon is the gateway to some of the island retreats on the Great Barrier Reef. I have listed those options if you haven't had enough sea spray, but the focus of this entire section will be the Outback experience.

A day or two is plenty for this leg and that will give you sufficient time to delve into the bat caves, find a thunder egg or two, and soak in the charm of this city with the widest streets I've ever seen. An obligatory activity is to snap a few photos of the six giant bull statues stationed at each major intersection coming into town. They represent the main breeds of the area. The city council has stockpiled re-attachable organs for the massive bulls as it appears to sporting to remove them late at night.

The beef capital of Australia will be a good spot for possibly the best steaks in the world (no mad cow here mates), enjoying a cool beer, and touring the magnificent buildings of town. This will be the last major city you will see for over a week, so stock up on supplies and take it easy for a day or two.

GETTING THERE:

By Car: The 400-mile trip from Brisbane up the Bruce Highway will take about 9 hours. Leaving Bundaberg, it's only 165 miles and about two hours north. Either way it is a straight shot with no turnoffs. Just follow the road signs.

By Bus: The two primary Australian bus lines are **Greyhound Pioneer**, ☎ 13-20-30 or **W**: greyhound.com.au, and **McCafferty's**, ☎ 13-14-99 or **W**:

mccaffertys.com.au. The booking agent for both transportation organizations is **Travel Coach Australia**, ☎ 13-14-99. The estimated one-way adult fare is AU $83.

By Train: The *Tilt Train*, *Spirit of Capricorn*, and the *Sunlander* run to/from Brisbane. The best and quickest choice is the *Tilt Train*. All services cost about AU $88 for a one-way adult fare.

By Plane: Contact **Qantas**, ☎ 13-13-13 or **W**: qantas.com.au, for schedules and prices. Try **Planet Aviation**, ☎ (07) 4922-7255 or **W**: planetaviation.pm, to compare pricing. The fares change so dramatically, that it would be unfair to list any. It has been announced recently that **Virgin Blue**, ☎ 13-67-89 or **W**: virginblue.com.au, will be providing service to selected towns in the Outback.

GETTING AROUND:

Some of the attractions offer pickup from your hotel. **Olsen's Capricorn Caverns** offer a good deal with half- and full-day tours that include food, botanical gardens, cultural center, and cave tour. Pick up is in town and tours cost around AU $33–$64 adults and AU $16–$32 for kids. Tour operators include **Get-About Tours**, ☎ (07) 4927-5977; **Taxi Tours**, ☎ (07) 4922-7111; and **Why Not Tours**, ☎ 1-800-353-717.

PRACTICALITIES:

Nothing special needed for this section except the usual well-worn hiking shoes, sun protection, and lots of water. The city has Civic Guide Map Kiosks conveniently placed around town that list the attractions and their locations. For a pocket map, call ☎ 1-800-033-502.

The information centers in and about town are fantastic, and the staff extremely helpful. The main center is in the grand **Customs House** at 208 Quay Street, ☎ 1-800-805-865, (07) 4922-5339, or **W**: rockhamptoninfo.com. Ask for the free "Rovin Round Rocky Region" guide for a good quick reference newsletter of attractions and activities.

SPECIAL EVENTS:

January—Australia Day; February—Central Queensland "O" Week; March—St. Patrick's Race Day; April—Horrors in Rocky; May—Rockhampton Eisteddfod; June—Rockhampton Show day & Winter Racing Carnival; July—Chinese Festival; August—Multicultural Fair and Rocky Swap; September—Founders Day, Big River Festival, and Big River Jazz Festival; October—Rocky Barra Bounty, ABC Arts in the Park, and Brahman Week; November—Summer Street Party; December—Summer Solstice, Carols by Candlelight, and Four Day New Year's Eve Bash & Ball. For a complete event guide, call ☎ (07) 4927-4111 or see **W**: venuesandevents.com.au. The **Rocky Markets**, ☎ (07) 4922-2400, are at 132 Denison Street every weekend from 7:30–noon. The **Kern Arcade Carpark**, ☎ (07) 4926-6844, variety markets are held every Sunday from 8:30–12:30.

FOOD AND DRINK:

It's time to start on the pub meals mates. Several offer great meals (and fantastic steaks at $–$$ prices). Try **O'Dowd's Irish Pub** ($-$$) on the corner of William & Denison Streets, ☎ (07) 4927-0344 or **W**: odowds.com.au; the **Great Western Hotel** ($-$$) at 39 Stanley Street, ☎ (07) 4922-1862, with live bull rides in the back of the pub; the upscale **Kershaw House** ($-$$) on Glenmore Road in North Rockhampton, ☎ (07) 4922-0922; or one of the three eateries in the **Jungle on East** ($-$$), ☎ (07) 4922-2882, complex at the corner of William and East Streets. The specialties are the barramundi fish and beef, but most ethnic foods can be found in the Yellow Pages. There are the typical American fast food outlets if you want a quick familiar meal.

ACCOMMODATIONS:

The top end selection is the **Cattle City Motor Inn**, ☎ (07) 4927-7811, at 139 Gladstone Road. This 4- 1/2-star rating Best Western chain is only around AU $84 for a room or $146 for a suite and is close to the attractions. **Club Crocodile Motor Inn**, ☎ (07) 4927-7433, offers *Tilt Train* specials with one- to three-day stays and courtesy pick-up at the train station. The cabin option is **Southside Holiday Village**, ☎ (07) 4927-3013, at Lower Dawson Road. There are 10 cabins and 10 villas from AU $51–$64/day. The pub selection is **Ollie's Pub**, ☎ (07) 4922-1853, for AU $30/night. A farm stay resort about 40 miles south of town is called **The Langmorn Station**, ☎ (07) 4934-6562. The B&B-style ranch has riding and nature surrounds for around AU $120/person/night.

LOCAL ATTRACTIONS:

Circled numbers correspond to numbers on the map.

*OLSEN'S CAPRICORN CAVERNS ❶, 30 Olsen's Caves Road, The Caves, ☎ (07) 4934-2883, **W**: capricorncaves.com.au, E-mail: capcaves@cqnet.com.au. *Open daily 9–4. Adults AU $14, children AU $7. Guided tours. Gift shop. Café. Special events. Partially* &.

Enter caverns with odd-named sites like "Headache Rock," "Rhino Passage," "Fat Man's Misery," and "Camel Cave." John Olsen found these in the early 1880s, and the limestone caves were initially explored using candles and long ropes. They were blasted asunder at one point to mine bat manure or guano. Entering with your guide, the hour of commentary points out the rock formations, shares the history of the 13 caverns, and directs you through the five corridors. Don't worry when the guide tells you of cave-ins as you enter the cool darkness—the last one occurred during the Ice Age. The fig roots that you will notice dangling from the ceilings are the culprits and some squeezed through yards of seemingly solid rock to weaken the structure. About 350-million years ago the caves began forming from the flowing of an underground river. As the water drained, surface water seeped in and created the marvels of the caves. On the tour

Rockhampton

1 Mile

2 Km

To Olsen's
Capricorn
Caverns
25 Km

Route ·1

Railway

Bruce Hwy.

Fitzroy River

N

To Mt Hay Gemstone
Tourist Park
35 Km

Capricorn Hwy.
Route 66

Bruce Hwy.

Route 1

To Brisbane

you will see the sections of the cave mined for bat dung, be able to identify the shapes of a camel, the continent of Australia, a bat, and see the
tunnel of lights from vents. The amazing end of the excursion is the
Cathedral Chamber where weddings are actually performed underground.
At this point, the lights will be extinguished as organ music bounces off
the surrounding walls. With the power back on, you have the choice of
walking to the surface with the guide or venturing along one of the corridors with only the light of a candle. The candle is the way to go mates.
One last item—if you are in the area around Summer Solstice (December
and early January) try to go for the 11am tour, but book ahead. There is a
section of the caves where a shaft is directly in line with the sun's rays and
there is a ceremony in that area every year.

The remaining day can be spent relaxing or seeing the following
attractions in the area:

OTHER LOCAL ATTRACTIONS:
Have lunch under a giant Banyan tree (planted in 1895) in the midst of
the **Botanical Gardens**, ☎ (07) 4922-1654, and the **Rockhampton Zoo** on
Spencer Street. Gardens are open from 6–6; the Gardens Tearoom operates from 8–5, closed Christmas; the Zoo can be visited from 8–5 (feeding
starts at 3:30). They are great spots to relax, let the kids run free and stroll
the 96 acres of stunning landscapes. Stop by the living museum at the
*Rockhampton Heritage Village, ☎ (07) 4936-1026, on Boundary Road and
see how life was enjoyed between 1850–1950s. The tour is worth the time
and you will get to ride in period-aged transportation too. Open weekdays
9–3 and weekends 10–4, the costs ranges from AU $5.50 for adults and AU
$1.10 for kids. **Mount Archer**, ☎ (07) 4936-8000, has free walking tracks and
observations lookouts that look down upon the city 24 hours a day. There
are tracks of varied lengths and difficulty to choose from peaking at 1,981
feet. Switch gears and learn of the local tribes at the **Dreamtime Cultural
Centre**, ☎ (07) 4936-1655, on the Bruce Highway. Open Mon.–Fri. 10–3:30.
With tours starting at 10:30, the prices range from AU $12.10 adults, AU
$5.50 children, and AU $8.25 seniors. The **Archer Park Station & Steam Tram**,
☎ (07) 4922-2774 or (07) 4936-8191, is on Denison Street. Open Tues.–Sun.
10–4. Costs AU $5.50 adults, AU $2.20 kids, and AU $3 for seniors. This
open-air museum is home to the Purrey Steam Tram that is supposed to
be the only one in the world. There are great historic photographs, displays, and surround-sound exhibits that will delight every history buff. If
you still need more relaxation, head over to the **Kershaw Gardens**, ☎ (07)
4936-8254, off the Bruce Highway. The free park is a reclamation area set
up to depict the natural Australian bush environment. It's a great place for
a BBQ or to let the young ones play on the park toys. Finally, a highly recommended spot to while away an hour is a gardener's haven called **St.
Aubins Village**, ☎ (07) 4927-5676, on Canoona Road. The little nursery is
crammed full of 12th-century plants, herbs, and the largest range of fragrant roses in Australia. I went to see the Brahma bull, but was mesmer-

ized by the personal tour Michael Bleines gave my wife and I. We sampled plants that taste like mushrooms, smelled pungent spiced leaves, and were treated to a plant that is 100 times sweeter than sugar. Before you leave, pick up some handmade Flutter by Fudge. Trust me on this one.

If you want to play a few days on a nearby Barrier Reef Island try:

ISLAND ATTRACTIONS NEAR ROCKHAMPTON:

The Keppel Islands are only 35 minutes east from Rockhampton. Arrangements can be made through **Capricorn Tourism, ☎** 1-800-676-701 or **W**: capricorntourism.com.au. Beautiful unspoiled beaches surround the **Great Keppel Island** with 90% of the island covered in untouched bushland. The short ferry ride from Yeppoon departs at 9:15 am and 6:00 pm every day. Best pick for lodging is the mid-priced Beachfront Units of the **Great Keppel Island Resort, ☎** (07) 4939-5044. This is a spot for the party animals and is a bit on the rustic side. Another new resort called **Contiki, ☎** 1-300-305-005, is another option for a less hedonistic approach to relaxation, but also a bit pricier. Expect lots of white, sandy beaches, snorkeling, diving, kayaking, bush walking, and a visit to the **Koorana Crocodile Farm**. Claimed to be the best resort island on the eastern coast of Queensland, **Heron Island, ☎** (07) 4972-9055, is a classier resort. The downside of this option is the 40-mile trip out by ferry from the mainland and the two-hour trip on the high-speed catamaran can be a bit rough. The option to accessing the island is to charter a helicopter for about $400 round-trip. There are excursions to see the thousands of green turtles, whale watching tours from July to October, snorkeling the crystal blue waters, bird watching tours, and taking an underwater reef ride in a submarine.

When you are ready to move westward into the barrenness of the Outback, drive 23 miles west on the Capricorn Highway to:

*MT. HAY GEMSTONE TOURIST PARK ❷, 3665 Capricorn Highway, Wycarbah, **☎** (07) 4934-7183, **W**: mthaygems.com.au, E-mail: aradon@roc-net.net.au. *Open daily 8:30–4:30. Prices are $16.50 for fossiking, guided tours are AU $14.50 adult and AU $9.50 for children. To get the gems cut/polished it runs about AU $.65/$15. Guided tours, self-guided tours. Gift shop. Partially &.*

Time to search for the 120-million-year-old Thunder Eggs! These spheroids that look like potatoes are gems formed from a gentle lava action (probably from a vent and not blasted from the core) that are primarily an agate. The silica and minerals inside the crusty-looking rocks create spectacular shapes, colors and images. The biggest thunder egg ever found weighed in at 110 pounds, was found by a Brisbane schoolboy, and has never been cut. Expect to find a decent bagful of marble to baseball-sized eggs in one of the piles of dumped excavated soil. Right now you cannot go into the mining area to dig in the tunnels. The crew now dumps large amounts of the dirt for you to scavenge around in. It's dirty, hot, thirsty work. But is it ever fun. You are marched out near the edge of the mining area, handed a pick and protective glasses, shown what to look for, and released to dig away. Gwen Kayes and her husband Bert have run this place for 28 years, and it's one of the few mines that will cut the eggs as you wait.

Bus Tours of the Queensland Outback

**Trip 51
Queensland Outback**

Cotton Fields
of Emerald

E merald is a cotton town, but many get hooked on the fossiking (prospecting) in the surrounding areas. I originally intended to make this a gem-searching trip, but found that the charm of the cotton farm was too difficult to dismiss, and the enjoyment of the vast holdings had more to offer. Plus the next stop will allow you to search to your heart's content with a pick and shovel. The area around Emerald will ease you into the vastness found in this Queensland Outback. The real gems in this area along the highway are the people.

The actual attractions offered in this neck of the bushland will not take very long to cover, but as you slow to the Outback pace two days will easily do the trick here. If you get antsy and want to wander far and wide, the information center in town (in Discovery Park) has a sheet of tours called, "The Way To Go!" It will outline several three-day tours into the outlying areas. But after the drive from Rockhampton, you may want to chill out and relax amongst the acres of cotton. If you consider fishing a relaxing sport, then you'll be happy to know there are heaps of fishing holes in the area. Fairbairn Dam and the surrounding streams are stocked full of catfish, sleepy cod, golden perch, and grunters. The "Recreational Freshwater Fishing" guide at the information booth will share all the hotspots with you.

GETTING THERE:

By Car: The drive is about 165 miles or three hours due west from Rockhampton, but there are some good sights along the way, so plan on an easy four-hour trip. You will now start getting a flavor of the Outback as you motor along Route 66 (Capricorn Highway).

By Bus: Take either **Greyhound Pioneer,** ☎ 13-20-30 or **W**: greyhound.com.au; or **McCafferty's,** ☎ 13-14-99 or **W**: mccaffertys.com.au. Schedules will become a bit less frequent, so check before you plan each stage from here on.

By Train: Take the *Spirit of the Outback* by calling **Queensland Rail,** ☎ 13-22-32 or **W**: traveltrain.qr.com.au. The cost is approximately AU $48.40

for a one-way adult fare from Rockhampton, but you could get as much as a 50% discount during summer months. Right now trains depart on Wednesdays and Saturdays from Rocky.

By Plane: Contact **Qantas**, ☎ 13-13-13 or **W**: Qantas.com.au, for schedules and prices. Try **Planet Aviation**, ☎ (07) 4922-7255 or **W**: plane-taviation.pm, to compare pricing. It has been announced recently that **Virgin Blue**, ☎ 13-67-89 or **W**: virginblue.com.au, will be providing service to selected towns in the Outback.

GETTING AROUND:
Emerald Coaches, ☎ (07) 4982-4444 or **W**: emeraldcoaches.com.au; **Car Hire**, ☎ (07) 4982-3591; or see **Central Queensland Travel Link** at the railway station, ☎ (07) 4982-1300/1399. Tours run from AU $25–$150, depending on what you want to see. If you have the cash to spare, helicopter flights can be arranged by calling ☎ (07) 4987-5400.

PRACTICALITIES:
The sun is hot during the day, and the flies and mosquitoes are in full glory at night. Unless you decide on the gemfields, you will be OK with just comfortable shoes, light clothing and sun protection. If you do go searching in the fields, let people know where you are going and when you plan to be back. Take plenty of water and make sure you get the proper permits to go into the fields. I would recommend a tour operator to go fossicking; suggestions are provided below.

The **Queensland Fisheries Management Authority** has a good web site at **W**: qfma.qld.gov.au/qfma. Visitor information can be gathered at **Central Highland Tourism**, ☎ (07) 4982-4142, on Clermont Street; **Capricorn Tourism**, ☎ (07) 4927-2055; **Emerald Chamber of Commerce** at **W**: emdchamber.com.au; or **Central Queensland Travel Link**, ☎ (07) 4982-1399.

FOOD AND DRINK:
You're now getting into serious pub-meal territory, but there are other good eateries in town, and some fantastic bakeries. You will be treated very well at the **B&B** (below) with a full stock of eggs, fruit, breads, cereals, juices, and more waiting for your hunger. If you also want dinner to be included, let Terre know ahead of time. For other options in town, try the **Maraboon Tavern** ($–$$), ☎ (07) 4982-0777, on the corner of Hospital Road & Esmond Street for a good dinner by the pool; **Capella Star Café** ($–$$), ☎ (07) 4984-9512, at 65 Peak Street for casual dining; the **Emerald Meteor Motel** ($–$$), ☎ (07) 4982-1166, at the corner of Opal & Egerton Streets; the **Gateway Steakhouse** ($–$$), ☎ (07) 4982-3899, at the corner of Hospital Road & Theresa Street for a giant T-bone; and **Kesorn's Thai Takeaway** ($–$$), ☎ (07) 4987-7300, on the Capricorn Highway for an ethnic flavor.

ACCOMMODATIONS:
My top pick is the **Brearley Downs B&B Farmstay** at Wills Road,

Emerald, QLD 4720. Call ☎ (07) 4987-4266, (04) 1872-5022 or email on athj-mann@tpg.com.au to book your stay in the middle of a cotton farm. The price of AU $75 per double includes breakfast, the pool, free companion-ship of the family dog (if you want it), and good company. This might be one of the highlights of your trip along the Capricorn Highway and the self-contained cabins (you have three—sleeping quarters for up to six people, a recreation cabin, and a bathroom section) are well done with cotton farm accents that make you feel part of the family. The biggest attraction is being in the midst of a working cotton field and learning what it's all about. But your hosts may even cook dinner over an open fire in a camp oven (cast iron pot) with bread pudding included.

Other accommodations include: The top-end **Emerald Explorers Inn**, ☎ (07) 4982-2822, on Gregory Highway for AU $89–$120/night; the mid-ranged **Emerald Meteor Motel**, ☎ (07) 4982-1166, at the corner of Opal & Egerton streets for AU $90-$109; and to get near the fishing the **Lake Maraboon Holiday Village Cabins**, ☎ (07) 4982-3677, on the Fairbairn Access Road for a mere AU $50-65. Another good B&B in the area is **Braeside B&B**, ☎ (07) 4987-6868. The hostel in town is the **Emerald Hostel**, ☎ (07) 4982-4938, is on Hospital Access Road.

FESTIVALS:

Sunflower Festival on Easter, Ag-grow Agricultural Festival in July, Gemfest and Festival of Gems in August, and Heartland Festival in October.

LOCAL ATTRACTIONS:

Circled numbers correspond to numbers on the map.

*BREARLEY DOWNS COTTON FARM ❶, Wills Road, Emerald, QLD 4720, ☎ (07) 4987-4266, (04) 1872-5022, or E-mail athjmann@tpg.com.au. *Tours free upon request (and as the workload permits). Guided tours, self-guided tours.* ♿.

You don't have far to go on this interesting tour. Either hop in your own car to wander around the dirt roads and soak in the magic of the cot-ton fields, or ask Terre or Alan Mann for a tour. There will be sights never witnessed before, and you will get a better appreciation for those cotton briefs mate. Like learning how many hours it takes to cultivate, that cotton is a form of hibiscus, it grows to four feet, and the flower turns several col-ors until it becomes fluffy white boll.

Here's what's in store for you as you get your toes either muddy or dusty: Ride along smoothly past either fields of snowy cotton, deep green stalks, colorful flowers, or deep dark brown rows of rich dirt (depending on the season). The dark soil looks almost gray at spots due to the mixing of remnant cotton and the black dirt. If you are lucky you will get to find and pluck a boll weevil from its feeding nest on one of the stalks. The huge machinery mesmerizes most people, and descriptions of the plows,

To
Brearley
Downs
Cotton Farm

Braeside Rd.

Gregory Hwy.

Park Ave.

Emerald

½ Mile
1 Km

Railway

Cameron St.

Loch St.

Racecourse Rd.

Moody St.

Campbell St.

Hogan's Rd.

Baker St.

Dundas St.

Hospital Rd.

Harris St.

Esmond St.

Retro St.

Ruby St.

Theresa St.

Bonilla St.

Opal St.

Pioneer
Cottage

Emerald
Cabin &
Caravan
Village

N

Capricorn Hwy.

Anakie St.

Church Ln.

Yamala St.

School Ln.

Egerton St.

Station

Clermont St.

Capricorn
Highway

Railway

King St.

Roberts St.

New St.

Botanic
Gardens

Gladstone St.

Gray St.

White St.

Long St.

Barton St.

Riverview St.

Botanic
Gardens

Campbell Ford Dr.

Nogoa River

Andrews Rd.

seed, and harvesting monsters will be shared with you. For the adventurous, you might actually get a chance to get hands-on experience of starting a siphon in the irrigation channels. The most amazing aspect of the tour is the incredible maze of irrigation streams flowing through the fields. Water is routed from miles away, passes through a metering wheel (to calculate the daily need and to estimate the water charges), and then siphoned over the channel banks into the rows of thirsty cotton. If you can explore with Alan, please take him up on the opportunity. It will provide a lasting impression.

There are a few interesting spots to visit in town, but this walking tour will only take an hour or two. So, go slow, enjoy the sights, and stop for a coffee or maybe a cool drink as you meander through town.

*EMERALD TOWN WALK ❷, Central Highland Tourism, ☎ (07) 4982-4142, on Clermont Street. *Open daily. Free (except where specified otherwise). Self-guided tour.* ♿.
Start at the information trailer set on the corner of Discovery Park and grab a city map or look for the "Business & Services Directory" with a map and listings of the town's establishments. From there, walk behind the building and follow the **Centenary of Federation Mosaic Pathway**. The sidewalk describes the area's history in mosaic tiles titled the "100 years in 100 metres." Starting at Creation, past the Aboriginals, into the Exploration years, then Settlement, and continuing into The Future, a collaboration of artists depicted the spirit of the people and their land. Even if you are not a fan of Van Gogh, you should not miss the **Big Easel** and the **Giant Sunflower Painting, W**: the big easel.com. This huge replication of one of Van Gogh's masterpieces is painted on 24 sheets of plywood, with 13 gallons of paint, and stands on an easel 82 feet high. Exit the park, cross over Clermont, and follow Ruby Street for one block, turn right onto Egeton Street, then left onto Anakie Street. On the corner will be the 250-million-year-old **Fossilised Tree** standing guard over Town Hall. The rock was donated by BHP from the local Gregory Mine. Continue on Anakie Street until it dead ends (six blocks), turn right on Harris Street for two blocks, turn left onto Centenary Drive, and stop in at the **Emerald Pioneer Cottage & Museum**, ☎ (07) 4982-1050. Tours start at 9 o'clock Mon.–Fri. and 10 on Sundays. Admission is AU $5.50 adults and free for kids. The price will admit you to the largest pit-sawn, drop-planked construction home in Australia. You will not find a nail in the walls as mortises were used to hold the place together. Double back to Opal Street and hike back to Clermont Street (about 11 blocks) to the **Emerald Railway Station**, ☎ (07) 4983-8386. This grand station was built in 1900, and is a beautiful structure. The still functioning rail stop is a good spot to take a photo as it is claimed to be the "most handsome railway station in Queensland." From the station, continue on Clermont Street, past the Memorial Club and Emerald Plaza to the **Botanical Gardens**, ☎ (07) 4982-8333. This 16-acre park is home to 62

species of Eucalyptus, palms, ferns, and cypress trees. The playgrounds, BBQs, and rose gardens make a perfect place to nestle in with a book and relax. And let me know if you figure out what the Yarn Pit is all about. Another goody near town is **Kiely's Farm & Animal Sanctuary**, ☎ (07) 4987-6700, located about 5 miles east of Emerald. Open mid-April to late September from 8–5 daily, with prices of AU $7.50 adult, AU $5.50 student, AU $3.50 kids, and AU $20 family. Here you can hang out with the ostriches, emus, and parrots, camels, dingoes, and kangaroos.

THE HIGHLAND ADVENTURE TOURS ❸, Central Highland Tourism, ☎ (07) 4982-4142, on Clermont Street. *Open daily. Free. Self-guided tours.* ᚻ.

The tours are laid out as a mix of car and walking tours, and the starting point is the Information Centre in Discovery Park. There you will find a one-page flyer titled "THE WAY TO GO," which will map out 22 different locations to visit. The one-hour to three-day tours cover the areas from Emerald and its surrounding districts, as well as the gem fields, and ranges as far as Longreach. I would suggest sticking with the one-hour, two-hour, and half-day tours. On the one-hour tour, you will visit the Emerald Pioneer Cottage, the Fossilized Tree, and the Emerald Railway Station. You can actually walk most of this and have a 2–3 hour stroll, actually meeting some of the town folk. On the two-hour driving tour, you will venture out to Capella and the Pioneer Village, have a cool drink at The Wombat and see the piano in a tree at Clermont, visit the site of the 1961 train wreck in Bogantugan, gaze upon the clapboard murals in the town of Alpha, and wet a line in Lake Maraboon. The half-day excursion will focus on driving to the lakes, do the "short triangle" and drive gravel roads through parts of the gem fields, and basically have a wander at each location.

Into the Gem Fields of Sapphire

Beware—this trip has addicting features—and you may not come back from the gem fields until you find the big one. But before we go there you need the description of what you will be doing for the next 2–3 days. To fossick, as defined in "The Australian Macquarie Dictionary," is "to search unsystematically or in a small way for mineral deposits, usually over ground previously worked by others." But you still need to get a permit to hunt around the area, and it is best not to wander into unknown territory. Claim jumpers are know to get shot at from time to time—seriously.

The chances are that you will be lucky enough to find a few memorable stones to have cut. In 1993 a couple of novices found a sapphire worth AU $300,000. Now do you have the fever? Also found was a 202 ct. Stonebridge parti-colored sapphire, and the famous Heads of Presidents that were cut to busts of Lincoln, Washington, Eisenhower, and Jefferson. They now rest in the Smithsonian Institute. To top it off, this area has the largest producing commercial fields of sapphire in the Southern Hemisphere. It is backbreaking work, and you will probably walk away with the blisters to prove it. It's also great fun to get out in the middle of nowhere and scratch the dry riverbeds looking for that gleaming stone. There are also rubies and a six-sided crystal called a Tomahawk Tiger to be found. You need not be fit to pan for jewels though. There are plenty of parks that provide the wash. You just have to stand and sift the materials. But, rumor has it that that the dirt is screened first and any big valuable stones are removed.

The area around Sapphire, Rubyvale, and Anakie will appear as true frontier towns. You will see piles of rubble stacked in giant mounds along the road, abandoned equipment rusting next to huge mining holes, and horses calmly strutting in the middle of the street with not a care in the world. It is a barren part of the planet with few shade trees, and even fewer gardens. But it has an appeal that is undeniable.

GETTING THERE:
  By Car: It is only about 40 miles from Emerald, just off the Capricorn

Highway. Turn right at the crossroads of Capricorn Highway and Anakie Road that marks the way to Sapphire and Rubyvale. It's only a 10-minute trip to Sapphire and about 15 minutes to Rubyvale.

By Bus: Take either **Greyhound Pioneer,** ☎ 13-20-30 or **W:** greyhound.com.au; or **McCafferty's,** ☎ 13-14-99 or **W:** mccaffertys.com.au. Schedules will become a bit less frequent, so check before you plan each stage from here on.

By Train: Take the train to Emerald or Longreach and then transfer to a coach line.

By Plane: Contact **Qantas,** ☎ 13-13-13 or **W:** Qantas.com.au, for schedules and prices. Try **Planet Aviation,** ☎ (07) 4922-7255 or **W:** planetaviation.pm, to compare pricing. The local airport can be contacted on ☎ (07) 4982-1133. It has been announced recently that **Virgin Blue,** ☎ 13-67-89 or **W:** virginblue.com.au, will be providing service to selected towns in the Outback.

GETTING AROUND:

There are heaps of tour organizations that will pick you up from your accommodation or at the **Big Sapphire & Gemfields Information Centre** at Anakie Road & the Capricorn Highway, ☎ (07) 4985-4525. A listing of the major tour groups is in the free magazine called "Queensland's Central Highlands & Sapphire Gemfields," and a few include: **Rubyvale Gem Gallery,** ☎ (07) 4985-4388 or **W:** rubyvalegemgallery.com; **Miner's Heritage Walk-in Mine,** ☎ (07) 4985-4571; **Pat's Gems,** ☎ (07) 4985-4544; and **Fascination Gems & Crystals,** ☎ (07) 4985-4675. The best option is the combined B&B and tour offered by **Sapphire Safari Tours & Fossickers Rest Accommodation,** ☎ (07) 4981-0076. Other operators include **Central Queensland Day Tours,** ☎ (07) 4982-1399.

PRACTICALITIES:

The first thing you need to know is if you see a sign that says "KEEP OUT," heed the warning. Secondly, if you want to go off on your own (I would not recommend it), you need a license, tools, and maps. Sorry, no dynamite. Fees start at AU $5.10 for 1 month (family is AU $7.20/month) and AU $30.90 for a year. If you take one of the tours, the license, tools, and insider tips are included. Another option is to buy a sack of gem-bearing soil and sift a selected bag for $7, or buy a gem for half-price at one of the many outlets in the area.

It is a very hot, dry and forbidding territory, so water and sun protection is extremely important. Sturdy hiking shoes, light clothing, and mosquito protection is recommended. Eye protection is also a good idea, and do not dig underground unless you are with a licensed tour operator.

For an educating read before you start in the area try: "The Queensland Fossicking Guide" by the Queensland Government (AU $12), "The Central Queensland Sapphire Experience" (AU $6), and the free "Gemfields Gazette." All are found in the stores, tour centers or the information center.

SPECIAL EVENTS:

In the middle weekend of June the Iron Man Wheelbarrow Derby is held in the area. It's a 50-person, 11-mile, race pushing a wheelbarrow filled with a pick, a shovel, and a "Billy boulder" weighing 22 pounds. In the second week of August, the Gemfest—Festival of Gems celebrates the sapphire industry. Held in Anakie, it is the largest display of gems in Australia; you can have a glimpse on **W**: gemfest.com.au.

FOOD AND DRINK:

The B&Bs supply a great breakfast spread to prepare you for the trek into the bush, and some home-baked goodies are usually included in the package. Otherwise there's not a whole lot to choose from, but here are a few recommended spots to pull up a chair. **Rubyvale Hotel** ($–$$) gets the best ratings. In addition to pub-style counter meals, they serve tea in their gardens, and the stone building is cool. Pub meals can also be found at the **Anakie Hotel Motel** ($–$$). Other cafés, takeaways, and grocery supplies can be located at **Andrea's** ($–$$) in Sapphire, the **Big Sapphire Information Centre** ($) on the Capricorn Highway, the **Blue Gem Van Park** ($) in Sapphire, **Muggachinnos Internet Café Lounge** ($–$$) in Sapphire, **Rubyvale Gem Gallery** ($–$$), **Rubyvale News and Main Street Café** ($), the **Sapphire Trading Post** ($), and the **Thai and Chinese Take Away** ($–$$) in Sapphire.

ACCOMMODATIONS:

The **Fossicker's Rest**, ☎ (07) 4981-0076, (04) 0905-0742, or (07) 4985-4566, is a great place to stay. This B&B also runs a fossicking tour. The choices include a huge cabin that will sleep a small army of 8, or a more intimate cabin for two. The prices range from AU $75–$85 per double and $15 for each person over. The place is a fantastic value with lots of room in a custom-built cabin with fascinating features like stained-glass windows, polished timber floors, and a wide porch to sit and watch the world go by. The next-best option is the **Rubyvale Hotel & Cabins**, ☎ (07) 4985-4754, for about AU $85–$95 (with a spa); **Gemini Cabins**, ☎ (07) 4985-4280, for about AU $25–$50; **The Castle Casuarina Hill**, ☎ (07) 4985-4118, for AU $55–$80; and the B&B of **Ramboda Homestead B&B**, ☎ (07) 4985-4154, for AU $32–$67.

LOCAL ATTRACTIONS:

*SAPPHIRE SAFARI TOURS**, PO Box 345, Sapphire, QLD 4702, ☎ (07) 4981-0076, (04) 0905-0742, (07) 4985-4566, E-mail: Jarrett@ozzi.com.au. *Three-hour Sight Seeing Tour (9:15 pickup) AU $38 adult, AU $19 child. Half-day Digging Tour (1–5) AU $58 adult, AU $35 child with all food and equipment. Full-day Digging Tour (9:15–4:30) AU $96 adult, AU $54 child. All but the* *sightseeing tour is not* &.

Since most people aren't used to the heat and pick & shovel work, I'll recommend a half-day tour to give you a taste of fossicking without too much stress. Hopping aboard the Range Rover, the ride will show you the black-barked trees and struggling shrubs eking out an existence. It's amazing that anything grows in the red dirt and tan gravel soil. About half of the trip will be on sealed tar roads, but then the fun begins. The road abruptly ends and you will be on a rumble-strip, one-lane, dirt road. Then it gets even starker, the trees crowd out the path, and you will bounce off the seat as you ford dry creek beds. The driver will be giving you the history of the area and answers questions as you creep along the trail. When you reach the Sapphire Safari's claim, everyone (usually 4–6 people) pile out into the gully full of hidden treasures.

The pans, sieves, picks, shovels, water drums, and marked areas are awaiting you as instructions on how to properly dig are recited. The trick is to pick a spot near the creek bed, clear away 4–6 inches of the topsoil, then pick away at the "Billy boulders." These are the rocks about 8 inches in diameter that are mixed with fist-sized or smaller rubble. This is where the gems are deposited. "Billy boulders" refer to the rocks used to create a campfire to boil water for your Billy tea. When you create enough of a pile, you throw shovel loads onto the screens that are set up in strategic areas. As the bucket underneath the screen fills up, it's over to the sieving area. After the dust is sorted out, you place the sieve into a dunking contraption and wash your dirt. Then dump the remaining contents onto an overturned barrel and start the hand search. If the sun is up, the gems should pop right out at you. The guide usually seeds each pan with one sapphire (that you get to keep) to show you what to look for. A sapphire is the second hardest natural substance, comes in blue, green, gray, yellow, gold, pale pink, orange, violet, brown, and even clear.

It's wise to fossick in a shaded area, but the guide will actually point out the best spots to work where they have mining rights. When you do find your rubies or sapphires, slip them into the small bag provided and the leader will sift through your find and tell you what is a real "cutter" and what is just quartz. Half way through the tour, it's Billy teatime with homemade pasta, sandwiches, and sweets. You will sit around the campfire and share the excitement of this adventure with your fossicking comrades.

At the end of the day you drive back to town, and if you're lucky enough to have found some good gems, there are several places to get them cut. One of the preferred places is **Pat's Gems**, ☎ (07) 4985-4544, in Rubyvale—right next to the Fossicker's Rest B&B. They charge about AU $25 to cut each gem and can either mail them to you or you can pick them up in a day or two.

On the second day you can trudge back into the fields or check out some of the sights in the three towns. Here are a few to choose from:

Pat's Gems in Rubyvale has a section to buy a bucket of wash and try your hand at the gems under shaded areas, **Bobby Dazzler Fossicking Park**, ☎ (07) 4985-4170, in Rubyvale has an underground mine to tour—just look for the giant statue of a miner kneeling and holding a huge rock. The **Rubyvale Gem Gallery**, ☎ (07) 4985-4388 or **W**: rubyvalegallery.com, has some of the best quality gems in the area, and if you don't mind the price, they are precious. **Miners Heritage**, ☎ (07) 4985-4444, in Rubyvale boasts the largest underground sapphire mine in Australia. **Fascination Gem Fossicking**, ☎ (07) 4985-4675, in Sapphire offers self-drive day tours and will rent you all the equipment you need.

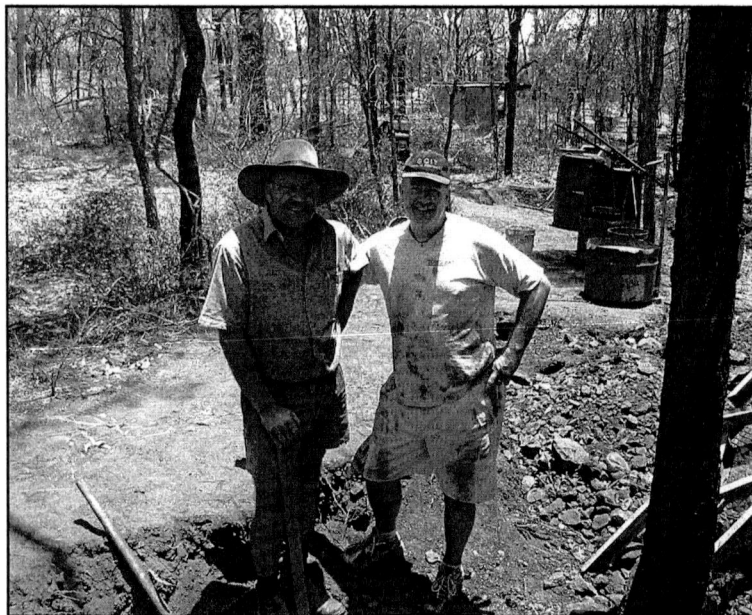

Digging for Sapphires in the Gem Fields

Longreach and the Stockman's Hall of Fame

D riving westward towards Longreach, crossing over the Drummond Range, past Alpha (good spot for a break), and onto the plains, brings dramatic terrain changes. The range here is full of 3-foot termite mounds, brown spiky spinifex grass covering large tracts, emus strutting in the bush, herds of cattle looking for a bit of protein, kangaroos (live and road kill) everywhere, and very few cars. Don't be alarmed if you drive through some smoky bush burn-off areas, get stuck in a traffic jam caused by drovers moving cattle right down the middle of the highway, or small dust devils swirling near the road. It's all part of the experience.

Some say that Longreach is the most influential town in the country due to its history of cattle ranching and being the center of Mitchell grass country. This only natural-grass region in Australia started the cattle boom in Oz. In addition, it is the first home of Qantas Airlines (Queensland and Northern Territory Aerial Services), the second-longest serving airline in the world. The best reason to visit this remote town, though, is because every Australian I met insisted that visitors see the place. And mates, that's a very good recommendation. You could spend a full day just seeing the Stockman's Hall of Fame.

This is the heartland of the Outback, and former haunts of the famous bushranger Captain Starlight, home to the serious drovers, and a great place to learn the history and tales of this part of the country. There is not too much to cover in this town of around 3,700 kindly souls, but the few attractions will keep you busy for at least two days.

On your way to Longreach, you will pass the small town of Barcaldine. It's worth stopping in to see several of the attractions there as well. You will find the Australian Workers Heritage Centre, Mad Mick's pioneer village, and the Tree of Knowledge. If you want to spend a bit more time in Barcaldine, you can opt to go back for a daytrip as it is only an hour east of Longreach.

Believe it or not, the Longreach district has great billabongs loaded with fish. You can cruise the Thomson River or just take one of the boat rides to see the inland waterway. There are some real characters out there; do yourself a favor and have a chat with a few of them. You will learn lots of facts and hear some stories that stretch the truth a bit, but both are interesting.

GETTING THERE:

By Car: Follow the Capricorn Highway about 100 miles west of the Gem Fields straight into the town.

By Bus: Take either **Greyhound Pioneer**, ☎ 13-20-30 or **W**: greyhound.com.au; or **McCafferty's**, ☎ 13-14-99 or **W**: mccaffertys.com.au. Schedules will become a bit less frequent, so check before you plan each stage from here on.

By Train: Organize the *Spirit of the Outback* by calling **Queensland Rail**, ☎ 13-22-32 or **W**: traveltrain.qr.com.au. The cost for all services is approximately AU $68.20 for a one-way adult fare from Emerald, but you could get as much as a 50% discount during summer months.

By Plane: Contact **Qantas**, ☎ 13-13-13 or **W**: qantas.com.au for schedules and prices. Try **Planet Aviation**, ☎ (07) 4922-7255 or **W**: planet aviation.pm to compare pricing. It has been announced recently that **Virgin Blue**, ☎ 13-67-89 or **W**: virginblue.com.au will be providing service to selected towns in the Outback.

GETTING AROUND:

Two great options include **Outback Aussie Tours**, ☎ 1-300-78-78-90, (07) 4658-3000, or **W**: outbackaussietours.com.au; or **Longreach Outback Travel**, ☎ (07) 4658-1776 or **W**: longreach.net.au/biz/lotc. **Central Queensland's Travel Link**, ☎ (07) 4982-1399, also operates in the area.

PRACTICALITIES:

With temperatures ranging from 46°–100° F, it's wise to hydrate and protect yourself from the sun. Most of the tours are in air-conditioned complexes and are easy walking, but if tours in the bush are decided upon, take precautions against the heat and dryness.

A great option to see the general area, including Longreach, Winton, Barcaldine, the Dinosaur Footprints, some of the local cattle stations, meet the historical and living legends, and even enter Mt. Isa's mines, is by organizing a tour or two with **Outback Aussie Tours and Travel**, ☎ 1-300-787-890, (07) 4658-3000, E-mail info@outbackaussietours.com.au, or **W**: outback aussietours.com.au. I would strongly recommend their tours because it's a no-brainer, they organize all the passes, provide transport along the way, have great coach captains (bus drivers) who offer comical and informative narrative of the area, and have access to areas not open to the general public. They offer one-day (AU $99–$129 adult or AU $69–$89 for child), three-day (AU $399 adult, AU $299 child), five-day with lodging and most meals (around AU $804–$952 adult), six-day with accommodation and most meals (around AU $999–$1184 adult), and nine-day tours with lodging and most meals (around AU $1899–$2240 adult). The only issue is the amount of time you have to spend in the area, the schedules of the tours (they are only available certain days of the week), and your budget. I think the three-day tour called the **Best of the West Touring Pass** is the best value and will give you all the attractions listed below (and more), and provides you plenty of time to see them all. If you want more, the longer trips offered will take some of the travel stress off you (especially if you are driving this leg) and allow you to relax and see the sights from an elevated seat on an air-conditioned bus. They are truly the way to go.

I have split this trip into two days with a listing of additional attractions if you want to hang out in town a bit longer. As with the other sections, you can easily mix and match the attractions to suit your tastes and timeframe. Visit the **Information Centre** at Eagle Street, ☎ (07) 4658-3555 or **W**: longreach.qld.gov.au for brochures and general information about the area.

SPECIAL EVENTS:

January—Australia Day; March—Easter in the Outback; April—Longreach Campdraft; May—Stockman's Hall of Fame Drover's Reunion, Longreach Agricultural Show, Desert Uplands Festival; July—Diamond Shears National & South Pacific Shearing Championships, Longreach Rodeo; August—Bronco Branding; December—Christmas Mardi Gras & Street Party, St. Andrews "Christmas Tree" Festival, Carols By Candlelight.

FOOD AND DRINK:

There are five decent restaurants in town, but if you want a real gourmet treat in a quaint establishment decorated as a bush-shack, try the fine food at the **Bush Verandah Restaurant** ($–$$), ☎ (07) 4658-2448 or **W**: bushveranda.com.au, on the corner of Swan & Galah Streets. The fabulous five-star quality eatery has meals starting around AU $14. With red checkered table cloths, handwritten notes written on the walls, and electric bush lanterns lighting your table, you can enjoy ribeye steak topped with blue-vein cheese, chicken stuffed with olives and sun-dried tomatoes or fresh oysters. I would strongly recommend at least one meal here. Five fast food places ranging from pizza, Chinese, and café-style are available along the main strip of town. Add to it nine pubs, five coffee shops/bakeries, and two grocery stores, you will be in good shape for food. The **Golden Gate Café** ($) has a great breakfast in a 50's-style local hangout.

ACCOMMODATIONS:

My first pick is **Aussie Beta Cabins**, ☎ (07) 4658-3811, at 63 Sir Hudson Fysh Drive, about 3/4 of a mile from the main street of town, but near most of the attractions. You get your own tidy cabin, kitchen, TV, air-conditioning, and a pool for only AU $59–$68. **The Commercial Hotel**, ☎ (07) 4658-1677, at 128 Eagle Street received good ratings by the locals at only AU

$28–$39 for a room over the pub and AU $50-75 for the quieter rooms in the West Wing. **The Town Lodge B&B,** ☎ (07) 4658-1516, at 161 Crane Street is a nice quiet choice for a mere AU $33–$66/night, but there are shared bathrooms. There are five motels listed and the prices range from AU $60–$78/night, and they are all 3- and 4-star quality. **The Albert Park,** ☎ (07) 4658-2411, on Sir Hudson Fysh Drive is the best bet, and has a good restaurant too. If you want a bit more of an adventure, try one of the farmstay resorts. **Toobrack Station,** ☎ (07) 4658-9158, about 37 miles out of town (on a dirt road) is a working sheep ranch with lots of activities to keep you busy. The other Outback choice, also 37 miles out a dirt road, is **Honan Downs,** ☎ (07) 4658-9516, a cattle station for about AU $ 50 adults and AU $10 for kids. The bush walking tours are free and you even get to ride along with the hands as they do their daily chores to see how the ranch operates. You have your own self-contained house to enjoy the day too.

LOCAL ATTRACTIONS:
Circled numbers correspond to numbers on the map.

DAY 1:
*AUSTRALIAN STOCKMAN'S HALL OF FAME ❶, Landsborough Highway, Longreach, QLD 4730, ☎ (07) 4658-2166, **W:** outbackheritage.com.au, E-mail: librarian@outbackheritage.com.au. *Open daily 9–5, closed Christmas. Adults AU $18.50, children under 18 AU $8.80, family AU $40. Guided tours, self-guided tours. Gift shop. Café. Special events.* &.

Opened in April 1988 by Queen Elizabeth II, this sandstone building with 9,840 feet of space under roof is a masterpiece with just as magnificent displays housed in slate, Tasmanian Oak, and wool. The three levels of exhibits are packed full of interesting facts, replicas, and memorabilia that more than matches anything I've seen on the American Wild West. The adventure begins with a 15-minute movie (on the half-hour) in the Theatrette. It provides a brilliant overview of the people of the Outback. As you wind around the ramps you will find that a shepherd's 6-week rations were called 10/10/2 and consisted of that amount (in pounds) of flour, meat, and sugar; get to walk through an 1860 settler's hut; see the most prized Scobie Stock Whip made of kangaroo hide (costing a drover equivalent to AU $500); learn that the four methods of mustering cattle include helicopter, 4WD, motorbike, and horse; watch videos of musters moving 7,000 head of cattle; browse the library's archives for specific details; learn that ringers are specialized drovers who select good stock while keeping wild animals away from the "mob" (herd); and get to play with the touch screen computers.

The sections to be covered include **Water—The Key to Survival** and its full-sized display of an artesian bore; **Opening to the Inland—Explorers** with the equipment, extensive use of camels, and documentaries of the hardships; **The Settler's Hut** with an audio story told by a selector's (farmer) wife; the **Blacksmith Corner** with a shed and forge built to the standard of

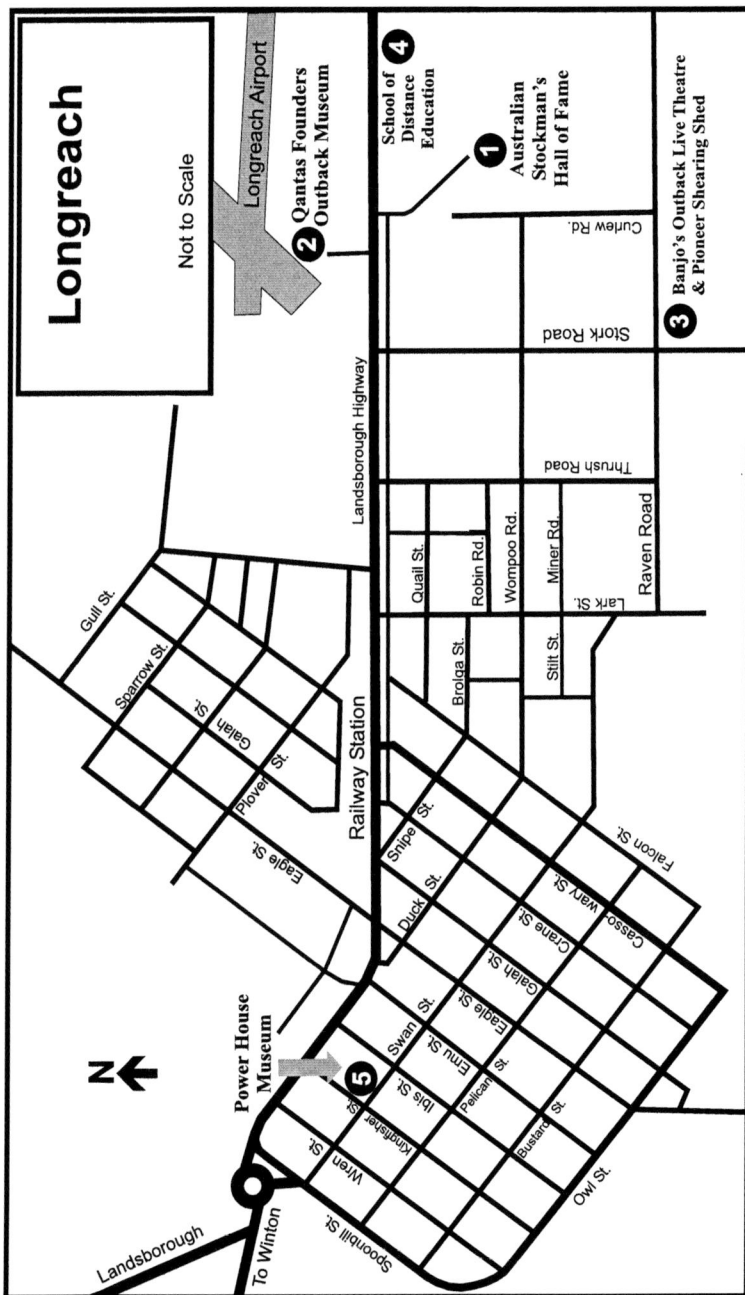

the 1800's; **Getting About—Transport** and its photo gallery; **The Hawker's Wagon** is a must-see with a wagon stuffed with all the necessities needed by the Outback people; **Life Wasn't Meant to be Easy** with descriptions of bushfires, rabbit plagues, dust storms, floods, and cyclones; **Droving—Life in the Saddle** with a fantastic talking drover in a darkened room made to look like a campfire scene; the **Golden Fleece** and its descriptions of the wool industry; **Bush Communications** and the long-distance innovations used to connect the Outback to the vital resources of the cities; a 1920's **Kitchen—Focus of the Home** and an actual display with a wooden sink, food safe, and the fire stove; **The Modern Age** of solar power and distance education programs; the all-important **Sporting Life** with scenes of horse racing, bush cricket, rodeos, and Polocrosse; and finally a hall of memories called **Recording the Past.**

When you need a break from the information overload, take a cup of tea in the cafeteria, browse the souvenir stand, and snoop in the bookshop.

*QANTAS OUTBACK FOUNDERS HERITAGE MUSEUM ❷, Landsborough Highway, Longreach, ☎ (07) 4658-3737, **W**: qfom.org.au, E-mail: qfom@tpg.com.au. *Open daily 9–5, closed Christmas. Adults AU $7, children AU $3.50, senior AU $5, family AU $14. Self-guided tours. Gift shop. Café. Special events.* &.

The **Queensland and Northern Territory Aerial Services** (Q.A.N.T.A.S.) began in Winton with operational headquarters moving to Longreach in 1921. Fysh & McGuinness were the pioneers who started the organization, and the museum documents their exploits. The huge hangar-like building is filled with memorabilia, old flight logs, mail run contracts, tools, models, and photos of Australia's most successful airline. It's best to first see the eight-minute video to get the history of the organization and its beginnings. The museum is quite small and can be covered in about an hour. It is packed with glass displays, an open-cockpit 1921 Avro 504K plane, a Model T Ford used to navigate the country to find landing strips for The Great Air Race of 1919, model planes flying overhead on a track, and a museum shop in one hangar. Right next door is the original 1922 hangar used to launch the airline. You can have a walk through, with roped-off areas depicting the old machine shops, and it will only take 15 minutes to see it all.

After five or six hours of museum coverage, it's time to get some nice and hot fresh air. For the rest of the day/night, it might be best to stroll around town to do a bit of shopping, have a cool drink and snack, and stop in at the **Information Centre,** ☎ (07) 4658-3555, at the corner of Duck & Eagle Streets or at QANTAS Park. Do try to get to the upstairs **Longreach Arts & Crafts Gallery** at 111 Ibis Street. It has locally designed paintings, pottery, silver products, fabrics, and leatherworks. There are clay spoonholders that have been formed by pressing flower leaves into the soft material and the veins and textures appear on the finished product. The jams and cookies are a real treat, but not nearly as enjoyable as chatting with the older folk who hang around as volunteers. There is also a cool memorabilia room with antique medical equipment. The **Gumnut Craft Cottage**, ☎ (07) 4658-2224, at 113 Eagle Street has a good selection of local souvenirs too. If you feel like a 15-minute drive, try out the historic village of Ilfracombe, have dinner at the Wellshot Hotel, and see the 40-minute Stockmanship Show.

DAY 2:
*BANJO'S OUTBACK THEATRE AND PIONEERING SHEARING SHED ❸, near the crossroads of Thrush & Raven Roads (book at 106 Eagle Street), Longreach, ☎ 1-800-641-661 or (07) 4658-2360. *Open daily with shows staring at 9:30. Adults AU $12, children AU $6. Stage show. Gift shop. Café. Special events.* ♿.

Welcome to Mulga Bill's Stockman Show and a hilarious medley of singing, shearing, and wool pressing. The event is held in a large, tin shed and begins with a "smoko" of Billy tea and cookies. If the breeze is blowing, the shed talks to you with rattling corrugated panels shuddering in the wind. When the camel bell chimes, old Alan "Banjo" Blunt announces the beginning of the stage show. His first claim is that you will be participating in the only shearing shed & theater combination in Australia. From there the tall tales continue and he rips off a few songs, recites a couple of bush poems, and dances a jig or two. Settling into a rugged chair, the grin appears and he begins his renditions of life in the bush. He talks of cattle rustling, the loneliness of the trail, and includes a few good jokes. The beauty of this show is that the man actually lived the life he explains and has a first-hand perspective of the harshness and humor of the Outback. Some of the famous Banjo Patterson bush poems are explained in detail after he recites them, making it easy to understand the slang used—like the "Drover's Dead Boy." Apparently it was a common occurrence for a drover (cowboy) to take an Aboriginal wife and cut her hair short to assume the identity of a boy. The couple would then camp apart from the rest of the gang and have their private time without any danger of reprisals from the group. When the "boy" in the story died, the gang couldn't understand why the old drover cried in fits, not realizing it was his wife. He tells the stories of Chinese laborers burning all their shearing sheds when they realized they were being shortchanged, and there were better wages to be made in the gold fields. The old gent who is a mix of bush poet/drover/boxer/snake oil salesman/sheep shearer/showman, is joined by a lovely lass that assists him in shearing a sheep and pressing the wool. Not only entertaining, the show is educational, like learning about the jute bags used for shipping wool. They were originally made in Pakistan and weighed 11 pounds. The worn out bags were cut into shoes and bedspreads, but were eventually replaced by plastic bags.

SCHOOL OF DISTANCE EDUCATION ❹, Sir James Walker Drive, Longreach, ☎ (07) 4658-4222. *Tours Mon.–Fri. at 9am and 10am, closed public holidays. Adults AU $3, children AU $1. Guided tours.* ⅙.

This is the largest classroom in the world (covering over 250,000 square miles), but has only about 200 students. Serving the remote and rural sections of Western Queensland, the class consists of radio contact, home visits, mail, and a curriculum developed from the school systems in Brisbane. The system relies on the home tutor, usually mum, and she ensures that the homework is not neglected for any reason. Classes are split into two groups for live, half-hour, on-air classes each school day. The teachers and students are united several times a year and the weeklong school sessions are held in Longreach so students can get a feel for the classroom rigors.

LONGREACH POWER HOUSE MUSEUM ❺, Swan Street, ☎ (07) 4658-3933. *Open daily April–October from 2–5, closed holidays. Check with the Information Centre for off-season openings. Price is a small donation. Self guided tours.* ⅙.

The original power-generating station is now the history museum. It will only take 15–20 minutes to see it all, but it's worth the stop.

OTHER OUTSTANDING ATTRACTIONS:

Starlight's Lookout is 31 miles northwest of town. It was the hill used as a vantage point by the famous Harry Redford (Captain Starlight) who, in 1870, stole 1,000 head of cattle, drove them 1,500 miles, selling them, and was arrested. He was miraculously found innocent. That is—when he agreed to return the stolen herd.

Toobrack Station, ☎ (07) 4658-9158, about 45-minutes out of town, is a sheep station open for tours. With 42,000 acres of property, the 100-year-old homestead is a good getaway.

Billabong Boat Cruises, ☎ (07) 4658-1776, are fun-filled rides down the Thomson River. Dinner cruises are also available.

Yellowbelly Express River Cruises, ☎ (07) 4658-9158, is a boat trip on the Yellowbelly River that is an Outback nature tour with live entertainment.

A **Thomson River Fishing Expedition** can be arranged by calling **Longreach Great Outdoors Centre**, ☎ (07) 4658-3229, at 106 Eagle Street in town, or just pick up gear and the "Fishing Mud Map" for the right spot on the banks of the river.

Pamela's Dolls & Syd's Outback Collector's Corner, ☎ (07) 4658-1958, at 19 Quail Street in town has teddy bears, fossils, coins, antiques, porcelain dolls, and matchbox cars.

Barcaldine (66 miles east of Longreach) can be seen on a daytrip from Longreach and is included on some of the tours offered by the local operators. If you are traveling by train, now is the time to stop and see this town. For the hearty car travelers, you can catch it on the way back to Brisbane on your way south on the Matilda Highway. Either way, try to catch the *Australian Workers Heritage Centre, ☎ (07) 4651-2422, on Ash Street for AU $9.90 adult, AU $5.50 children, AU $7.70 seniors and AU $27.50 families; *Mad Micks Hoppers & Huts Funny Farm, ☎ (07) 4651-1172, at 84 Pine Street for a hilarious show of Outback living for AU $8.50 adult, AU $5 kids, and AU $7.50 seniors; and the free display of the Tree of Knowledge on Oak Street that was the meeting place for the Great Shearer's Strike of 1891.

Stockman's Hall of Fame Museum

Winton and Waltzing Matilda

N ear Winton the scenery turns into real prairie, with round green/silver-leaved trees dotted among the herds, emus, and kangaroos. The sight of far-off mountains will come and go, the road trains become more frequent, and there are humorous signs warning of dinosaur crossings. I heard that there are trees with the world's hardest timber, called waddi trees, dotting the landscape. It's claimed that they break saws, turn axes into useless hunks of metal, and can barely be drilled. Welcome to the land of Banjo Patterson's song of the Outback wanderer and his anthem of "Waltzing Matilda." There are two main themes in this little Outback town—dinosaur tracks and Waltzing Matilda memorabilia. But if you look a little deeper, you will find this to be one of your favorite stopovers. It is like stepping back into the Old West, with wide streets, friendly nods, and life centered on the saloons (pubs). It's a one-horse town with lots of character and the people, though some may look a bit imposing, are fantastic to meet.

The town was established in 1876 as Pelican Waterhole. During the Shearer's Strike of 1891 and again in 1894, the town was put under martial law. When the traveling poet/songwriter by the name of Banjo Patterson stopped to whet his whistle and meet up with friends at Dagworth Station, he was told the tale of a swagman's death resulting from the strike. He later performed his song at the North Gregory Hotel and the legend began. Wandering out of town, you will be spellbound by the sight of a preserved dinosaur stampede. Grab a tour bus and take a daytrip to the Lark Quarry Dinosaur Trackways.

If you are in a sightseeing frenzy, you can easily see this area in two days, even if you include the dinosaur trek. But a slower pace of three days would be your best bet to relax and enjoy the feel of the Outback. This trip is the most remote part of the Outback planned before heading south to Brisbane. So, stay a bit and mosey around the one-of-a-kind attractions in town.

GETTING THERE:
By Car: Follow the Capricorn Highway for another 1-1/2-hours or 110 miles past Longreach. It is a straight and uneventful drive, but stay alert for

kangaroos, cattle, and emus. I would avoid driving at dawn and dusk, as the animals tend to graze near the roadway.

By Bus: Take either **Greyhound Pioneer**, ☎ 13-20-30 or **W**: grey hound.com.au; or **McCafferty's**, ☎ 13-14-99 or **W**: mccaffertys.com.au. Schedules will become a bit less frequent, so check before you plan each stage from here on.

By Train: Organize the *Spirit of the Outback* by calling **Queensland Rail**, ☎ 13-22-32 or **W**: traveltrain.qr.com.au. The cost for all services is approximately AU $68.20 for a one-way adult fare from Emerald but you could get as much as a 50% discount during summer months.

By Plane: Contact **Qantas**, ☎ 13-13-13 or **W**: qantas.com.au for schedules and prices. Try **Planet Aviation**, ☎ (07) 4922-7255 or **W**: planetaviation.pm to compare pricing. It has been announced recently that **Virgin Blue**, ☎ 13-67-89 or **W**: virginblue.com.au will be providing service to selected towns in the Outback.

GETTING AROUND:

Two great options include **Outback Aussie Tours**, ☎ 1-300-78-78-90 or **W**: outbackaussietours.com.au; or **Longreach Outback Travel**, ☎ (07) 4658-1776 or **W**: Longreach.net.au/biz/lotc—both can be arranged from Longreach. **Diamantina Outback Tours**, ☎ (07) 4657-1514, 1-800-625-828, or **W**: dotours.com.au, has a wide range of tours from Winton. Some include tours, food, and entry fees, while others provide field guides in and around town. They do have exclusive touring rights in the Merton Escarpment and at Lark Quarry Environmental Park—home of the dinosaur tracks. Prices start from around AU $95/day.

PRACTICALITIES:

More hot and sunny days and cool nights. Sun protection, comfortable walking shoes, and lots of water are appropriate—especially if you venture out to the surrounding areas and the dinosaur track area. If you do head out of town, it's best to organize a tour to get the most out of the experience. One word of warning, the water tastes pretty horrible in most places, so stock up on bottled water. And if you go to the pub and there is a giant of a man, with a Mohawk haircut, tattoos, and earrings—say g'day. He was great fun to talk to and friendly as can be.

Information can be found at the **Waltzing Matilda Centre**, ☎ (07) 4657-1466 or **W**: matildacentre.com.au, and at most of the convenience stores around town. The best buy in the store is the brown-covered "Mud Maps of Winton and Matilda Country." It has all the attractions listed, hotels, pubs, maps, and six tours laid-out from one to 535 miles long. Costing about AU $4, it's a handy tool as well as a good pamphlet for the memories.

SPECIAL EVENTS:

The Bronze Swagman Bush Poetry Festival in April and the Outback

Festival in September.

FOOD AND DRINK:

There are four pubs in town, three on the main street of Elderslie and one on Werna Street. An equal number of cafés are available as well as a Chinese takeaway and a few clubs that are open to the public. There are also several small grocery stores, and a fast food eatery at The Waltzing Matilda Centre.

ACCOMMODATIONS:

There is not a whole lot to choose from besides the hotels in town, though they are a good deal and very inexpensive. The choice I made was the 3-star **Banjos Motel & Cabins**, ☎ (07) 4657-1213, at the corner of Manuka & Bostock Streets. It is comfortable, quiet, and only a 15-minute walk from the heart of town. Expect to pay about AU $52–$61. If you want to sleep with the legends, try **North Gregory Hotel-Motel**, ☎ (07) 4657-1375 or 1-800-801-611, at Elderslie Street. This is the site where Waltzing Matilda was first performed, and rooms are only AU $33–$55/night. For a cabin-style night's sleep, try **Matilda Country Caravan Park**, ☎ (07) 4657-1607, at 43 Chirnside Street for around AU $50/night.

LOCAL ATTRACTIONS:

Circled numbers correspond to numbers on the map. You can mix and match the places you want to see, but I would split the dinosaur trek into a separate day trip.

*THE WALTZING MATILDA CENTRE ❶, Elderslie Street, Winton, ☎ (07) 4657-1466, **W**: matildacentre.com.au, E-mail: matilda@thehub.com.au. *Open daily 8:30–5, public holidays 10–4, and closed Christmas. Adults AU $14, children AU $12, family AU $30. Self-guided tours. Gift shop. Café. Special events.* ⚊.

The museum is dedicated to the "the story, the song, and the spirit of Australia." The recommended tour time is about 2–3 hours, and it is a fun-filled historical walk through the air-conditioned corridors. There are nine sections dealing with the area and it's famous characters. Don't think of this place as a hick town museum—it's high-tech, interactive, and uses incredible light shows and holographs to replicate authentic scenes of the Outback. The center court is a life-sized billabong with a pond, and a swagman surrounded by police to re-create the heart of the song Waltzing Matilda. For those who don't know what it means, here is what you will learn about. Matilda is another name used for a swag or bedroll for lack of a better translation. This is where the swagman would carry his worldly possessions in a bundle, usually slung over one shoulder, and was very heavy. The phrase "waltzing Matilda" refers to the walking motion (waltz) that was created by lugging this load across the Outback. So if someone would say, as the song goes, "Come a waltzing Matilda with me," it was

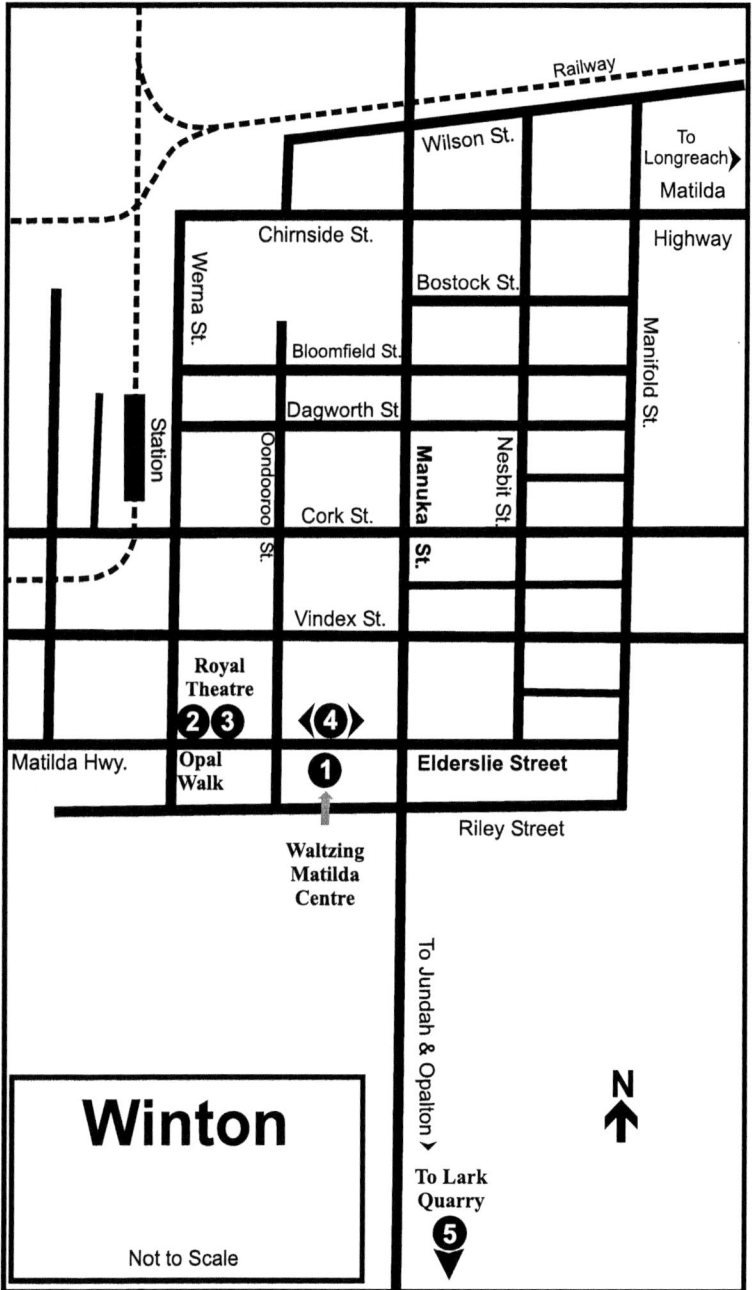

Railway

Wilson St.

To Longreach ▶

Matilda

Chirnside St.

Highway

Bostock St.

Werna St.

Bloomfield St.

Dagworth St

Station

Oondooroo St.

Cork St.

Manuka St.

Nesbit St.

Manifold St.

Vindex St.

Royal Theatre

❷ ❸

◀❬❹❭▶

Matilda Hwy.

Opal Walk

❶

Elderslie Street

Riley Street

Waltzing Matilda Centre

To Jundah & Opalton ▶

Winton

Not to Scale

N ↑

To Lark Quarry

❺ ▼

meant as an invitation to go for a long hike in search of work and food. The sadness of the song is that the swagman burned a wool shed down as part of the Shearer's Strike, escaped and camped at the Combo water hole, then killed a sheep for food. Troopers surrounded him and since the penalty for his crimes was hanging, he tried to swim the billabong to elude then and drowned. Banjo recorded the story in song, and it has been recorded over 500 times. It still brings a tear to some of the old blokes when it's sung. The museum has some very innovative ways of communication. As you enter **Legend Room**, you lift Billy cans to hear an audio presentation of the displays and learning about "Never Never"—the land out there that stretches on forever. At the water barrel, there are listening tubes sticking out at strategic points on its corrugated skin. There you hear poems, yarns, and a few true tales. Next is a cool **Spectra Vision** show with an animated character talking of the changes in the Outback country. The buildings adjacent to the main structure are still part of the museum and have heaps more displays and glass cases of artifacts.

*OPAL WALK ❷, Elderslie Street, Winton, ☎ (07) 4657-1296. *Open Mon.–Fri. 9–5, Sat. till noon, closed holidays. Admission is AU $2. Self-guided tours. Gift shop. Café. Special events. Partially ♿.*

Enter a dark, narrow hallway that is designed to look like a tunnel in an opal mine. On each side of the passageway are lit displays of local opal, tools, photos, and handmade gifts. Don't miss the Human Trap that was used to snare and maim any claim jumpers who dared to wander onto another man's territory.

ROYAL THEATRE OPEN AIR PICTURE SHOW ❸, Elderslie Street, Winton, ☎ (07) 4657-1296. *Open Wednesday nights from April–September. Adults AU $5.50, children AU $3.50.* ♿.

This is an old time, 1918, outdoor movie theater. You can tour the grounds during the day as part of the Opal Walk, but the movies are spectacular. Sitting in swayback canvas seats, munching on popcorn, you get to see the stars as well as a good "Movie of Yesteryear." Because the 700-seat theater was so popular when it opened up, seating was purchased on a permanent ticket basis. In front of the screen is a skating rink that was once used as a boxing ring for amateur and professional fights. You can tour the projection room and see the three huge projectors, 2-foot-diameter film reels, and all the gear used to run the old movies.

WALTZING MATILDA CENTENARY STREET THEME ❹, Elderslie Street, Winton. *Open daily 24 hours a day. Free. Self-guided tours. Shops, cafés, and pubs. Special events.* ♿.

Just wander along the three blocks of downtown to witness the various statues, displays, and memorabilia along the footpath and in the center grass strip. Check out the dinosaur trash bins and the saddles waiting for a horse to roll into town. Your walk will reveal the North Gregory

Hotel, the general store called Corfield & Fitzmaurice Store, the site of the first building in town, and Arno's Wall with a collage of household tools.

Day two you can relax and just prepare for the trip to Brisbane or check out the:

*LARK QUARRY DINOSAUR TRACKWAYS, Lark Quarry, Winton Jundah Road, ☎ (07) 4657-1466, **W**: matildacentre.com.au, E-mail: matilda@the-hub.com.au. *Tours start around AU $95, but are essential. Guided tours, self-guided tours. Special events. Partially* &.

Thirty-three miles south of Winton is the 93-million-year-old site with over 300 different types of dinosaur footprints. The theory is that a giant Carnosaur attacked a herd of Coelurosaurs and Ornithopods near the edge of an inland lake. When the frantic alarm was sounded, the herds stampeded, escaping across a muddy prehistoric flat. The scene fossilized, was discovered in 1960, and is now a protected site. The trip takes between one to two hours one-way and is not recommended for standard car traffic. Please take one of the tours unless you are into the 4WD thing.

The drive south towards Brisbane will take about two to three days and you can break the drive at several towns along the way. I will recommend an overnight stay in **Mitchell**, ☎ 1-800-648-243-55 for the information center, to soak in the artesian waters. It will take you within 372 miles or 4–5 hours from Brisbane and is about halfway from Winton. The best option for lodging is the **Berkeley Lodge Motor Inn**, ☎ (07) 4623-1666, at 20 Cambridge Street in town. There are several pubs to choose from too, but I recommend them for dinner instead of sleep. Make sure you spend at least an hour or two soaking in the ***Great Artesian Spa**, ☎ (07) 4623-1073, right around the corner from the motel at 2-3 Cambridge Street. It costs about AU $12 adults and AU $8 for children and is open daily (except Christmas and 1/2 day on Anzac Day) from 8–7. The ancient waters come to the surface from 4,000 feet below, are said to contain minerals with healing abilities, and are so hot that it they have to be cooled before you take the plunge.

One last suggestion on your drive south. Stop in the tiny town of **Tambo** and adopt a Tambo Teddy. They are sheepskin bears of every shape size and dress. Beginning in 1922, a group of ladies began the hand stitching and the bears have become a great success. The best ones are those dressed in the swag gear with leather hat, bullwhip, and smile for only AU $162–$218. And yes, you really have to sign adoption papers and promise to give the little bear a good home.

Section VIII

Daytrips in
The Tropical North

The steaming tropics bring you to what is commonly described as a living museum, a world of prehistoric times, and the hub to exciting excursions. Cairns (pronounced *Cans*) is your next home for a few days, and for an international destination you may find it a surprisingly small town. The port and harbor area is a central kick-off point for most of your local daytrips. It is surrounded by rainforests, macadamia groves, sugar cane fields, and pineapple plantations. Formerly known as the Barbary Coast and home to Southern Hemisphere pirates, it's now a haven for treasure seekers of a different lot—those looking to capture the natural beauty of the rainforests and reefs. Just offshore is the largest natural wonder in the world—The Great Barrier Reef. There are several options to find your daytripping treasure—The miles of Reef with more than 1,000 islands and thousands of individual reefs, or The Wet Tropics Rainforests with over two million acres of protected vegetation hiding the deadly crocodile and all the wonders of the jungles. But don't expect glamorous beaches near the town center. The city parks stop at a seawall and beyond that is either mudflats or brown bay water—depending on the tides.

The area is a magnet for international tourists and Daytrips should give you an edge in seeing the best of the natural environments while avoiding the tourist traps. The center of town is a bit seedy and geared towards the casual tourist looking for trinkets. Though most of the reef excursions originate at the Marlin Marina in Trinity Bay, I would suggest you spend your hours exploring the natural wonders rather than the city streets of Cairns. But there is a great casino, good art galleries, fine museums, and heaps of shopping in town if you desire.

Your wild wonderland tours include a crocodile safari along muddy mangroves, diving with the sharks on the Reef, visiting the hilltop Aboriginal village of Kuranda, hiking and riding horseback through dense rainforest trails, learning about Aboriginal herbal medicines at Flecker

Botanic Gardens, tunneling into an ancient volcano tube, and just chilling out on a slow fishing dingy.

GETTING TO CAIRNS:

By Car: It is a long 1,058-mile drive from the Brisbane base, and even if you drive from the Capricorn Coast it's at least a two-day haul. But, if you have the time and love to drive, head north on Route 1 and follow the signs. Have a look at **W**: queenslandholidays.com.au/driving for more info.

By Bus: The 2–3 day trip can be organized by calling **Greyhound**, ☎ 13-20-30 or online at **W**: greyhound.com.au. **McCafferty's**, ☎ 13-14-99, provides service too. The buses run about six times a day, and the estimated price is AU $192 or AU $364 for a round trip from Brisbane.

By Train: There is a two-day rail trip from Brisbane to Cairns. The fare is AU $176 (one-way) and can be booked from **Queensland Rail**, ☎ 13-22-32 or **W**: qr.com.au; or ☎ 1-800-627-655 or **W**: traveltrain.qr.com.au. The two Brisbane/Cairns train excursions are called *The Queenslander* with regular seats or first-class berths only; and the *Sunlander* with seats, economy, and first-class berths available. There are packages that combine reef, tropics, and resort accommodations available also. **Sunlover Tours**, ☎ 1-300-36-1915 or **W**: sunlover-holidays.com.au, have a wide range of deals that include rail travel. Don't get sticker shock though, with prices starting around AU $700.

By Plane: After a two-hour flight from Brisbane, you arrive at Cairns International Airport and take the ten-minute taxi ride to your selected hotel.

ACCOMMODATION IN CAIRNS:

Being a typical international destination, there are heaps of accommodations at varying star ratings as well as backpacker bunks. Most major hotel chains are represented and are primarily close to the waterfront. They are a bit more expensive than the locally-owned resorts, but offer regular deals. Almost all the accommodations can organize tours, and you can often get discounts that way. I have listed four options to choose from and they vary in price, location and type. For general information on the backpacker availabilities contact **YHA Queensland**, ☎ (07) 3236-4999, E-mail: yha@yhaqld.org, or at **W**: yha.com.au. **Bed and Breakfast** selections can be found at ☎ (07) 4097-7022 or **W**: bnbnq.com.au. General accommodations can be viewed/booked at **The Accommodation Centre** on ☎ 1-800-807-730, (07) 4051-4066, or **W**: accomcentre.com.au

THE PACIFIC INTERNATIONAL, corner of Spence Street & The Esplanade, Cairns QLD 4870, ☎ (07) 4051-7888, **W**: pacifichotelcairns.com, E-mail: pacific@cairns.net.au. *Prices are AU $220 and up, but ask if there are any specials for a more attractive rate.*

Right across from the marina and in the middle of the shopping district is this *** 1/2-star hotel that is part of the Quality chain. I think it's worth the extra bucks to stay in this classy place. They are very helpful in organizing all the tours (including the ones listed below) and courtesy buses are provided for airport and attractions.

OASIS INN, 276 Sheridan Street, Cairns, QLD 4870, ☎ (07) 4051-4073, **W**: oasis-cairns.com.au. *Prices range from AU $64 to AU $116, and weekly rates from AU $451 to AU $770.*

It is not very fancy, but it is away from the hustle and bustle of downtown. You can easily walk to town, but it is a good mile to the CBD along the waterway. It does have air conditioning and it is a very relaxed place to crash. They have BBQs and are also very helpful in arranging tours.

JENNY'S HOME STAY, Brinsmead Valley, Cairns, QLD 4870, ☎ (07) 4055-1639, **W**: bnbnq.com.au. *Prices range from AU $65-AU $90/night.*

It's a 12-minutes drive from town, but it is situated near the Kuranda Skyrail and Train Station. Quiet and peaceful, the quaint house is nestled in 14 acres of manicured lawns and rainforests. Rooms with bathrooms are available if you don't care to share.

UPTOP DOWNUNDER LODGE, 164 Spence Street, Cairns 4870, ☎ (07) 4051-3636, **W**: uptopdownunder.com.au, E-mail: uptop@uptopdownunder.com.au. *Prices range from AU $33 to AU $54.*

Clean and close to all the action, it is a bargain. It does have a pool and BBQ facilities. No air conditioning, but there are ceiling fans.

PRACTICALITIES:

It is advised that you visit from May to October because the rest of the year is unbearably humid. What you wear is vital to enjoying this area of Australia. Hiking shoes or sturdy sneakers are advisable and if you plan visits to the reefs and reef islands, a pair of reef shoes is strongly recommended. Most of the walking tours are on gravel or paved trails, so you will not have difficulty navigating around the forests. Light clothing is a must and a selected piece of lightweight raingear is a good idea. Shorts and high socks along with a hat is also standard dress for rides and hikes. Sunglasses and sun block are also very important. If you plan frequent hiking outings, pack bug repellent, matches or cigarettes (for leeches), and a product to soothe bug bites. It's not that bad, but they could come in handy if you are stung.

Heed warnings for the box jellyfish, do not swim near streams and avoid wandering off the paths. Read the signs at the entrances of parks for special instructions. It is safe if you pay attention and use common sense, but you are in the natural habitat of some worthy predators. Respect them and you will be OK. The parks in the city can be a bit intimidating with a number of homeless souls camping and drinking near the picnic areas. Be alert and avoid any boisterous groups in the park adjacent to Trinity Inlet and along the Esplanade.

To obtain additional information before you arrive, contact **Tourism North Queensland** on ☎ (07) 4051-3588 or see their website at **W**: tropicalaustralia.com.au. The **City Council** has a web site too at **W**: cairns.qld.gov.au. When you check into your accommodation, browse the lobby for brochures, clip out the discount pages, and you will save between 10–15% on some of the attractions mentioned here. A great publication is the "Tropical North Queensland Holiday Planner" found in most resorts and at the Information Centre at 51 The Esplanade. To book all your tours in one spot, try **Tropical Horizons** at ☎ (07) 4058-1244 or **W**: tropical-horizons.com.au. Diving tours can be arranged before you go to Cairns: at **Reef Watch** on **W**: reefwatch.com for air tours to the reef; **Diversion Dives** at **W**: diversionoz.com; **Down Under Dives** at **W**: downunderdive.com.au; or **Undersea Explorer** at **W**: underseaecplorer.com.au

SPECIAL EVENTS:

January—Fitzroy Yacht Race; May—Cairns Tropical Garden Show; July—Cairns Showday, September—Kuranda Spring Fair; October—The Reef Festival. Mud Markets at The Pier are every weekend and Rusty's Markets Friday–Saturday. Kuranda's markets (the best around) are Wed.–Fri. and Sunday.

FOOD AND DRINK:

The food establishments in the area are very relaxed. Choices are understandably focused around seafood, but there is a good variety of taste delights and plenty of ethnic restaurants. Here are a few that I have personally tested and liked.

Dundee's Seafood, Steak and Pasta, 29 Spence Street, Cairns. Make reservations early in the day (it fills quickly) and you will be treated to a variety of tropical and standard fare. The informal atmosphere and reasonable prices will allow you to try crocodile, emu, and barramundi along with less exotic foods. A chatty host in the form of a cockatoo called Micky will probably greet you. ☎ (07) 4051-0399 **W**: dundees.com.au. Open seven nights from 6 pm. $$

Fishlips Modern Australian Seafood, 228 Sheridan Street, Cairns. Off the beaten path, this small bistro serves up great à la carte meals. The barramundi is the featured plate and the pasta is fantastic too. When you enter this establishment, expect fine service and quality cuisine. ☎ (07) 4041-1700 or **W**: fishlips.com.au. Open daily from 5:30 and lunch on Friday from noon. $$–$$$

The Pier Market Place Restaurants, on the Esplanade, Cairns. The waterside shopping center hosts a food mall and a series of fine eateries. You have your choice of fish & chips, to ethnic foods, to fine dining. **W**: thepier.com.au. Open daily for breakfast till late dinner. $–$$$

Hogs Breath Café, 64 Spence Street, Cairns. For an easy-going pace, cold beer, and great steaks. This Australian-owned pub-style eatery is great for family meals. ☎ (07) 4031-7711 or **W**:

hogsbreath.com.au/launch.htm. Open seven days from 11–2 for lunch and 6 till late for dinner. $$

Rattle n Hum, 67-69 The Esplande, Cairns. This is a fun-filled, pub-style, rocking eatery with hearty meals. It is one of my favorites for lunch or a quick and simple dinner. Try this one out for late night partying too. ☎ (07) 4031-3011. Open daily from 11 am until late. $$

Bangkok Room Thai Restaurant, 62 Spence Street, Cairns. Some say that hot and spicy foods cool the body down. If you believe that, try out the delicious treats here. It is a small and plain eatery, but the cuisine is fantastic. ☎ (07) 4051-3135. Open daily from 6pm until late. $–$$

Perotta's At The Gallery, corner of Abbott & Shields streets, Cairns. For a sophisticated meal, street-side, this is an elegant café serving fine foods and one of the best Chicken Caesar Salads in town. Try a stroll around the art gallery afterwards. ☎ (07) 4031-5899. Open daily from 8am–12pm. $$–$$$

SHOPPING:

There are three major shopping malls and a maze of street shopping in Cairns. You will find some interesting stuff that is geared towards tropical wildlife like crocodile leathers and ocean oddities. Kuranda has the best value for the croc goods and even some interesting semi-precious gems. The prices are similar to the other shopping districts listed in the book, and the range is comparable too. The city's shopping plazas include: **Cairns Central** at the corner of Mcleod & Spence streets, **W**: cairnscentral.com.au, with Myer, Target, movies, food, and 180 boutique stores; **Orchid Plaza & Cosmos Arcade**, Lake & Abbott streets, with 45 fancy specialty shops; and **The Pier Marketplace**, **W**: thepier.com.au, open 9–9 daily on the marina with over 100 stores, Oceanarium, food courts, restaurants, and the Mud Markets.

Crocodile Hunting in Cairns

You don't have to look far in the Cairns area to find a wide-jawed dinosaur staring at you. These reptiles populate the local mangroves, rivers, and even parts of the ocean. A recent newspaper photo depicted a croc actually riding a wave into the beach—fair dinkum! Rumors have it that there is one over 28 feet long in the area and he is supposed to weigh over 2,300 pounds. You might not find that brute, but you will probably meet Agro. If you do—just smile and call him "sir." Keep the safety on your camera in the off position for this trip and you will get some memorable shots.

Although you will be completely safe in the luxuriously air-conditioned boat with windows at every seat, it is a bit creepy having such dangerous creatures close enough to touch with a ten-foot pole. And when you walk amongst them at the crocodile farm you can even smell their breath. Though these 70-year-old crocs can run six miles an hour, you will be secure behind heavy-gage fencing. It is truly a humbling feeling to be surrounded by such formidable hunters.

GETTING THERE:

Leave the car at the hotel and walk to the Wharf Pier. You can arrange a free pickup at your hotel, ☎ (07) 4031-4007 for Terri-Too, to start the tour at the Marlin Marina.

PRACTICALITIES:

Light clothing and that's about it. Most of the trip will be shaded and under cover. A bit of extra cash if you want to purchase some crocodile products—and a camera is a must. Not even much walking on this one, so no need to worry about hiking gear.

FOOD AND DRINK:

Snacks and drinks are provided on the tour, and you will get to sample some crocodile meat at the Crocodile Farm. Yes it does taste like chicken. If you want to have the energy for the trip, start with coffee and breakfast at one of the pier-side cafés. Afternoon lunch is easily found on the upper level of the Pier Market Place.

LOCAL ATTRACTIONS:
The tour begins at the Pier Wharf Docks.

TERRI-TOO CROCODILE ADVENTURE CRUISE, The Pier Marketplace at the "A" Finger Terminal, Cairns, ☎ (07) 4031-4007 or **W**: totaltravel.com/local-guides/cairns/activities. *Open daily, 10:30 am and 2:30 pm tours. Prices start at AU $34 and go to AU $54, half fare for 4–14 year olds and free for younger kids. Group rates and concessions are available. Guided tours, gift shop, and café.* ♿.

You have the option of a 2-3/4 hour morning or afternoon **Harbor Everglades Cruise** or **Cruise & Crocodile Cruise**. Go with the croc cruise mates, it is the better of the two. The tours include either lunch snacks or afternoon tea, and the 50-foot cruiser provides a safe viewing platform to see the crocodiles lining the riverbanks. The ship has a two-story observation deck with tinted windows, cushy seats, and a trademarked quiet motor designed to sneak up on the dozing crocodiles. If you are lucky, you'll get to see Custer and Agro—but keep your distance.

The tour operators guarantee that you will see crocodiles on the cruise; there are plenty sunning themselves along the mangrove swamps on this 21-mile ride up the murky Smith's River. But the skipper will point out a whole host of interesting sights along the mangroves or "Forests of the Sea." It is fascinating to watch the undisturbed activities of the storks, sea eagles, fruit bats, mudskippers, and reptile life as you cruise up to the largest crocodile farm in the country. The guided boat tour unlocks some of nature's secrets about the mangroves—the eco system of the estuary system. On the ride, you will witness 25 of the 30 species of mangroves in Australia, learn that this habitat is a nursery to 75% of commercial and recreational fish, observe how the twisting river creates a filter to sift out debris before it is dumped into the sea, and chuckle at the crocodile lore dished up over a cuppa tea and an ANZAC biscuit.

The red mud banks hide the ancient dinosaurs, but the crew will find a few for you and as they slow the engines to silently creep up on the giants—you will get the opportunity to snap some great photos. As the ship pauses in an area, you get the true feeling of the area with pungent smells emanating from the mangroves, screeches of bird life above, and critters swarming all around the water.

You will smell it before you see it, but the **Cairns Crocodile Farm** is the largest commercial crocodile farm in Australia. With over 7,000 of the hungry critters swarming around, you will feel safe behind the protective glass of the minivan transport. But there is no escaping the odor of musky swamp, scented eucalyptus, and rotting flesh that permeates the grounds. It does add to the intrigue and is really not that bad.

A croc specialist will guide you around the reserve and point out the various stages of the crocodile growth and how they accommodate the increased aggressiveness of the growing animals. Don't be alarmed when the tracker asks you to leave the van for a bit of a walkabout. It will be the highlight of the tour for those of you that make it back in one piece (only kidding). I won't give away the big surprise, but it will delight all but the faint of heart.

You will get to hold a small crocodile (with its mouth safely secured with a rubber band), watch the daily feeding ritual and frenzied fight for food, observe the nesting mounds of the adult female crocs, and receive a great overview of the habits and life of these grand creatures.

At the various holding pens, the guide will explain the various uses of the crocodile, and that most of the organs and skin are sent to the Orient for medicinal purposes. Not one piece of the critter is wasted. If you choose to take a belt or leather product out of the country check the Customs rules and make sure you have the proper document to declare any item.

The guide will provide all sorts of information like: Crocodiles are believed to be at least 200 million years old and are called Archosaurs or Ruling Reptiles. There are 22 species of crocodiles with the notable exterior body armor. About 80 percent of saltwater croc eggs never hatch and about 50 percent of the hatchlings die the first year. Crocodiles live for more than 70 years and can survive to celebrate their 100th hatch day. Since 1969 this reptile has taken only eleven people. Crocodiles can run up to 6 miles and hour, but usually walk at 1 mph. They can stay underwater for over an hour waiting for you to dip your toes in the water. Crocs have large stones in their bellies, eaten purposely to aid in digestion and to act as ballast to keep their body underwater with only eyes above water to look for prey. The jaw of the croc is very powerful and can crush the skulls of its victims. However, if you tie a string around its mouth, it will not be able to break it.

At the end of the farm tour, you will have the opportunity to taste some cooked or barbecued crocodile and purchase fine leather goods, books, and souvenirs. But ask about Agro before you leave and get at least one photo of this granddad of all crocodiles. I will bet that you never see another one so huge. He apparently weighs in (who weighs him, anyway?) at 2,000 pounds and is around 18 feet long. The old boy is used only for breeding now. I think his aggressive days are over and it's only loving now.

When you arrive back at Marlin Marina, it will be a perfect time to do a bit of shopping at **The Pier Mall**. Open seven days from 9–9 and full of fine fashion and great artworks, it's a two-story shopping center with a food court. There are art galleries, a cool surf wear shop called Shark Attack (take your camera for a bloody shot), heaps of bargain to expensive jewelry stores, and local crafts. The malls have a higher-end range of selections than do the vendors along the streets. But they are all fun to hang out in if it's raining or just too hot to be outside.

Hiking and Riding in the Rainforests

Are you ready for a little exercise? If so, follow me into the steamy tropical rainforests just outside of the city of Cairns. You can visit other rainforest retreats and huddle around a tour guide walking and talking about the surrounding wilderness at the more popular nature reserves (Paronella Park, the Rainforest Habitat), or you can pull on your walking shoes and explore on your own at Mount Witfield. Since you will have plenty of opportunities to mingle with the tourists on some of the other tours, try this quiet stroll for a change of pace.

Wander the groomed gardens of Flecker Botanic Gardens and learn all about the northern native plants, then enjoy a wonderful lunch in the Botanic Gardens Café surrounded by lush trees decorated with multi-colored birds. This part is an easy walk, and if you prefer to avoid the hike up the mountain, at least wander through these gardens.

Finally, share an amusing ride into the sunset with the team from Blazing Saddles—for real. The gentle ride is OK for anyone who can get up into the saddle. You can trot at one section if you like, but it is a slow and steady ride under tropical canopies. Standard damper bread and bullwhip demonstrations will be offered and the staff is pretty funny with a love for showing you a good time.

This trip will be split into two different modes of transportation, each providing a totally different perspective to the terrain covered. The walking tour takes about 2–4 hours and the ride is an easy half-day. As most of the tours, you can also split the hiking and walking into two separate days to allow time for a bit of shopping or maybe even trying your hand at the tables in the Reef Casino. Plus, if you are an avid rider and would prefer to have the horse do the entire day's work there is an option for a full-day ride. Blazing Saddles also offers an ATV ride through the rainforest if you have an aversion to horseflesh. I believe it is best to do a bit of walking though, and get a closer perspective of the rainforests in the area. The forests on each of the tours in the book have their own unique smells, sounds, and feel to them. You will even note the differences between the three neighboring tracts of forest in this section.

I would recommend the morning for the stroll, saving the heat of the day for the horses. That way you have that nice horse aroma at the end of the day and can rinse off right after the ride.

GETTING THERE:
The parks and botanical gardens are about a 15-minute drive towards the airport. Head out of town on Sheridan Street and turn left at Collins Avenue. You can arrange for a cab for a return trip or have Blazing Saddles pick you up at the gardens and then return you to your accommodation. If you decide on Blazing Saddles first, arrange a free pickup at your hotel, ☎ (07) 4059-0955.

PRACTICALITIES:
Since this is a mix of walking and riding, I'd recommend shorts and carry a pair of long pants for the ride. It really isn't necessary to cover your legs on the ride, but it is a bit more comfortable. Bug repellant is a good item to take along, especially for the hikes. It will be mostly shaded and cool on both trails, but there are sections that are sunny and hot. If you worry about hair hygiene, take a hat to wear under the mandatory helmets worn for the horseback ride.

FOOD AND DRINK:
The **Botanic Gardens Café** (9:30–4:30 daily) serves fantastic food in the middle of a secret garden. The cuisine is healthy, interesting, and reasonably priced. Light snacks of damper bread (with honey or jam) and Billy tea are served at Blazing Saddles.

LOCAL ATTRACTIONS:
Circled numbers correspond to numbers on the map.

MT. WITFIELD CONSERVATION PARK ❶, Collins Avenue & Crowley Creek Road, Cairns, ☎ (07) 052-3096. *Open daily dawn to dusk. Free. Self-guided tours. Not &.*
Walking quietly will open a new world for you in a rainforest, especially in this out-of-the-way park. Only the scratching of scrub fowl near the path and the often-hilarious birdcalls will break the tranquility. After applying generous amounts of bug repellant and reading the postings at the entrance, you will step into a canopy of lush green, air of earthy sweetness and calming peace. If you walk quietly you may see scrub turkeys, agile wallabies, tiger quolls, and tree kangaroos near the pathway.
Only about three miles from Cairns CBD, the 740-acre park is also the breeding grounds of the endangered cassowary. This giant bird looks like a huge emu, a blue-and-red head with fleshy folds of skin like that of a turkey, a short and serious beak, impressive size of eight feet, with talons extending three inches on each toe, and a crown of bone on its head. Like the other potentially dangerous creatures in the area, use common sense

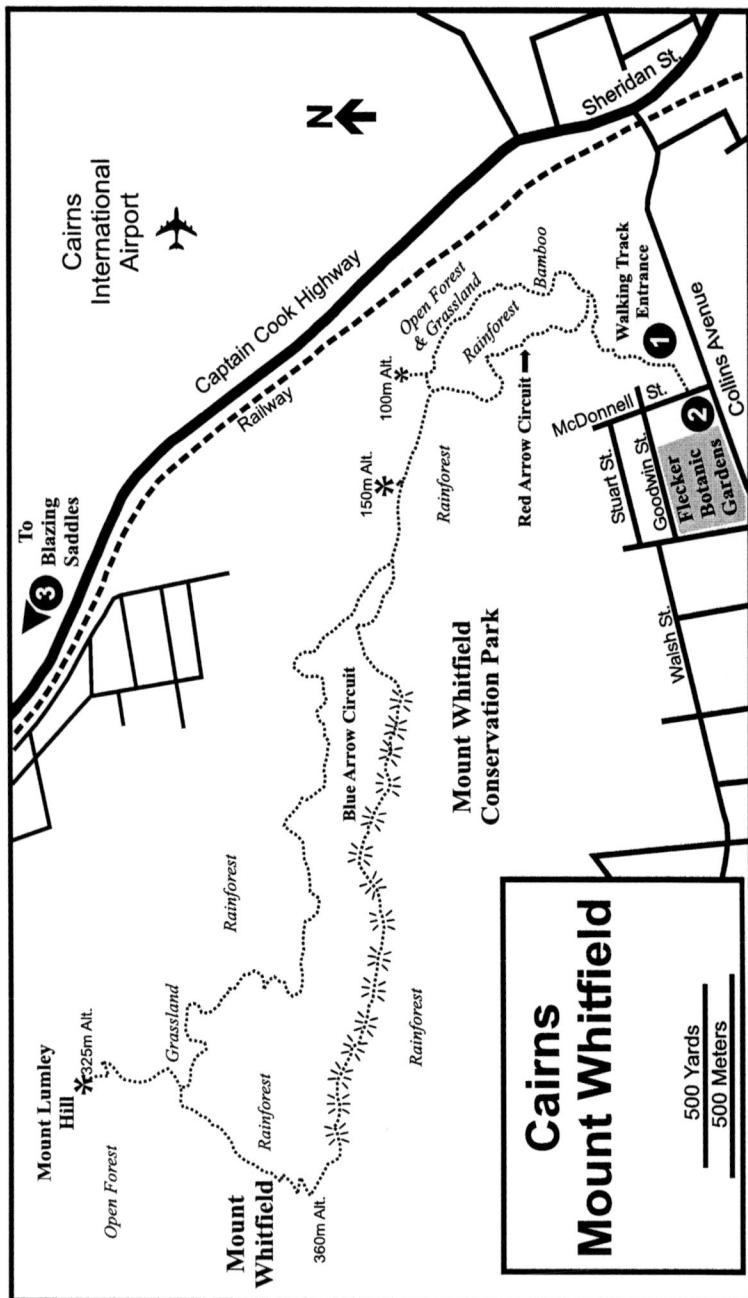

Cairns
Mount Whitfield

500 Yards
500 Meters

if you come upon the cassowary. They are only aggressive when they are protecting their young. Read the carefully worded signs that instruct your behavior in dealing with these birds. Your heart will beat a bit quickly if you see one, but it is a great experience.

You have your choice of two walking trails; the shortest is .8 of a mile of easy walking. Just follow the Red Arrows into the forest and enjoy the walk. The slightly more difficult Blue Arrow walk is about 3- 1/3 miles long and is worth the extra effort. Both wind amongst dense tree stands, rippling streams, bamboo groves, and eucalypt grasslands.

At the far end of the path there is an observation platform that looks out over Trinity Inlet, Mt. Yarbah, and the city of Cairns that was once called Gimuy by the Aboriginal Bama tribe. The lookout has signs posted that point out landmarks on the horizon, and several stone observation towers that were once used as a lookout for raiding pirates.

After a short 10-minute walk next door to the park you will see the iron gates and smell the fragrant flower arrangements of the:

FLECKER BOTANIC GARDENS ❷, Collins Avenue, Cairns, ☎ (07) 4044-3398 or **W**: barrierreefaustralia.com/sight_seeing/flecker_botanic_gardens.htm. *Open Mon.–Fri. 7:30–5:30, Sat. & Sun. 8:30–5:30. Free, but a donation is appropriate. Guided tours, self-guided tours. Gift shop. Café open 9:30–4:30. Partially* ♿.

Just a half-mile west of the Conservation Park is a secret garden loaded with native and exotic vegetation. Eugene Fitzalan, a botanical collector, established the gardens in 1888, and the park was named after a naturalist named Dr. Hugo Flecker. The botanic gardens have flourished and are a nice place to while away a hot afternoon. I would suggest it as a good mid-morning cooling off spot. The café might be a good place to start your relaxing stroll.

As you enter the stone-and-iron gateway, follow a brick trail that meanders past the **Orchid House**, the **Aboriginal Plant Use Section**, freshwater lakes, and the café. The sights include some strange-looking plants and trees like the bright red flame of the forest, the purple, spiny, cluster called Malay apple, the sunburst of yellow named the native tamarind, the beacon of red known as the Cairns torch ginger, and the numerous orchids that delight the nose. There are three separate gardens that are controlled by the soil composition and water applied to the vegetation. Along the boardwalk the signs will designate the **Tropical Palm Forest**, the **Lowland Paperbark Forest**, and the **Pandanus Swamp Forest**. At some stage of the walk, close your eyes and take a deep breath. Note the sound and scent differences between the forests.

I found the **Aboriginal Garden** the most interesting with the strange and toxic plants used for food, medicine, tools, and decorations. The Flecker brochure reveals the marvels of botanical uses including: river lily bulbs that were used for antiseptic and a dressing for leprosy, palm lily roots acted as a contraceptive, wait-a-while relieved cold symptoms and stopped dysentery, and fishtail lawyer cane that cured headaches.

The most fascinating plant of all the native plants is the gympie gympie, also known as the stinging tree. It is usually at ankle or arm height, grows near tracks and clearings, and is extremely painful if touched by bare skin. It has been known to knock horses off of their feet. It has dull-green, fuzzy-looking leaves that are shaped like a heart (how ironic) with small hollow hairs on the surface of the leaf that penetrate the skin and causes burning, swelling and intense pain.

Have a satisfying lunch in the café while resting and absorbing the oxygen-rich air. The menu might include a unique tuna sandwich that is spiced with sweet chili powder, Worchester sauce, and limejuice, making it quite refreshing. If you have some time to spare before the horseback section of the tour, make a stop next door at the **Tanks Art Centre**, ☎ (07) 4032-2349, for some very diverse art expressions.

BLAZING SADDLES ❸, PO Box 83, Clifton Beach, ☎ (07) 4059-0955, **W:** blazingsaddles.com.au. *Open daily with half-day (four hour) rides starting at 8:30 am or 1:30 pm. Full-day trips and ATV buggies are also an option. Adults AU $85, children AU $65. Full day is AU $195 and AU $175. Pick-up and transfers are included in the price. Guided tours. Gift shop. Café. Not* ♿.

The Blazing Saddles van will pick you up in front of your lodging, and the adventure will begin there with a faint smell of horses and trail dust floating off chaps. This really is a ripper of a trip—even if you don't feel like going out, please try this ride. You will have a blast and see things up on the horse you will never notice on foot. Even if you never rode a horse before, this will be a piece of cake as the guides are all expert riders with years of assisting greenhorns in the saddle. In addition, the stirrups are quick release "Peacock" style to avoid any twisted ankles.

Getting into the spirit of things, you will be introduced to a genuine "smoko," also known as tea and damper bread (a staple of Outback folk). While munching on the sweetened cake, your trail boss will saunter in with a crooked smile and a mischievous attitude. I think he likes the ride more than his wards. Depending on the schedule, you may get the bull-whip demonstration before or after meeting your ride. The horses are all retired trotters, well fed and passive. If you drop your reins they will stop or just follow the horse in front of them. Some of the inclines will be a bit steep, but the horses know what they are doing and the saddles are cat-tleman-style with Mickey Mouse ears right in front of your thighs (it makes it easy to hold on with your legs). You will probably be broken into teams of 10–15 riders, usually separated by the language of the riders as there are lots of Chinese, Japanese, and English participating.

On the trails you will be passing giant termite mounds, areas of dark rainforest, tinkling streams, and bright open pastures. In one of the cleared spots, the ranch hands do a bit of trick riding and let you trot a bit if you are so inclined. At the far end of the trail, the views are spectacular as you dismount and hike a short 30 yards to the pinnacle peak at 1,197 feet. There the guide will point out Spout Head Island, Double Island, and Shark Alley. The stories then start to fly and you will get a "real" history of the area. These Aussies can sure tell a good yarn or two. But one fact that seems like a fib is that if you can find the right ant hanging from a branch and plop it in your mouth, it tastes like lemonade. My brother tried it and thought it was similar to a lemon fizz drink. When you return to the barn and stomp off the dust, you are treated to another meal or refreshments — depending on what program you signed up for. The ride will give you a good excuse to use the spa/pool back at your hotel.

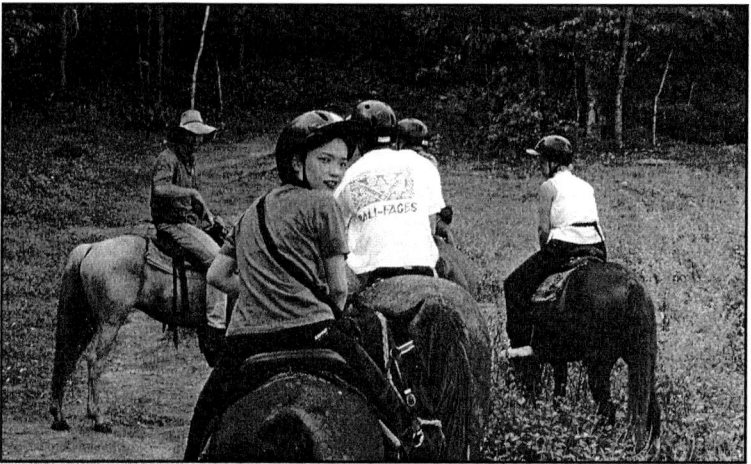

Riding the Rainforest with Blazing Saddles

Trip 57
Tropical North

A Dip in the Great Barrier Reef

You really have to experience this trip to realize the beauty of the largest living organism on Earth. The colors are right out of a children's coloring book and the flowing landscape is a Disney fantasy. But this will be more than a daytrip out to the world's largest coral reef for a splash around in lukewarm waters with colors beyond your imagination. It will be a once-in-a-lifetime tour worth sharing with a good mate, and a memory to last forever. It is an unbelievable journey to an underwater world seen by the fortunate few. But even more importantly, it will be a learning experience. The marine biologists and the protectors of this diminishing wonder will fill your head with the urgency of saving this huge reef system.

Because the Great Barrier Reef stretches along a large section of Queensland's east coast, it is so big that it is clearly identifiable from space. Actually the reef is not "a reef," it is over 2,900 reefs strung out in a line stretching over 1,250 miles. The living organisms that create the spectacular colors are the coral polyps and they are in danger of dying out. The white, bony part you will see on the trip is the dead part of the coral. It is unfortunate that more and more white structures are being seen due to the recent onslaught of the Crown of Thorns starfish, reckless boaters who drag anchors across the reefs, pollution, sun bleaching, and careless divers who touch or break off pieces for souvenirs. The good news is that you will not see many, if any, sharks on your trip out to the reefs. It's water is too shallow for them to maneuver properly, and they stick to the deeper waters outside the reefs. Enter a new world with five hours on the reef, lunch, glass-bottom boat tours with a marine biologist, snorkeling, and a free introductory scuba dive.

GETTING THERE:
Leave the car at the hotel and walk to the Wharf Pier. You can arrange a free pickup at your hotel, ☎ (07) 4031-1588, to start the tour at the Marlin Marina.

PRACTICALITIES:

Pack plenty of sunscreen, a swimming suit, towel, hat, and if at all possible, wear one of the UV-protective shirts sold at most surf stores. You can rent a wet suit on the boat for a few bucks, and the rest of the gear is provided.

Three good websites to check out are: **W**: gbrmpa.gov.au; **W**: greatbarrier-reef.com; and **W**: nationalgeographic.com/earthpulse/reef/reef1 flash.html. Or just do a simple search on "The Great Barrier Reef" and you will get all sorts of hits.

FOOD AND DRINK:

There is a healthy variety of food and soft drinks served on board, included as part of the package. The seafood/luncheon meat, fruit, and veggie buffet is great.

LOCAL ATTRACTIONS:

Just meet the boat on the Wharf Pier Docks and let the captain do the rest.

REEF MAGIC, Shop 13, Hides Corner, Cairns, ☎ (07) 4031-1588, **W**: reef magic.com.au, E-mail: reef.magic@altnews.com.au. *Tours run daily from 9–5. Adults AU $109, children (4–14) AU $69, family passes start at AU $320, 2-days from AU $196, 3-days from AU $278, and 4-day from AU $370. Check the website for specials before you book. Guided tours and self-guided swims. Gift shop onboard. Semi ♿.*

The 72-foot *Reef Magic* is all white and is decorated with the Aussie flag, the blue Reef Magic logo, and Outer Reef Cruises painted below a red, white, and blue racing strip just under the 22 waterfront windows. After climbing down past the galley for a cuppa you will settle into an air-conditioned cabin that seats about 100 people. As the captain pushes the throttle forward to the 24-knot cruising speed, the keel will rise out of the water for the 1-1/2 hour ride to the reef. The crew will provide excellent information on this natural wonder and watch you like hawks in the water. Another key factor in choosing this operator is that they are licensed to moor at ten different reefs including Norman, Saxon, Hastings, Michaelmas, Flynn, Milln, Moore, and Thetford Reefs. This is a valuable asset to the daytripper who is limited in the days set aside for the reef as they are able to choose the calmest (and clearest) waters near one of their moorings. Whatever cruise you take, make sure you pack the sunscreen, a sun-resistant shirt, sunglasses, and shark repellant (only kidding). I strongly recommended a wet suit because it will protect you from the sharp/poisonous coral, and the buoyant material will help you stay afloat while snorkeling. And if you have absolutely any problem with motion sickness, pop a few seasick pills before you go out. It's a fair way out and even though it is basically calm, it can get rough on the trip to the outer reefs.

Your day's activities on the reef include: a morning and afternoon snorkel with instructions for those needing assistance, an inflatable donut to hang onto if you are not the greatest of swimmers, a glass bottom boat cruise with ongoing descriptions of what you are floating over, a free introductory scuba dive, plenty of food, additional scuba for those who are certified, and all the equipment. The underwater show is fantastic; enhanced by the presentation by the resident marine biologist. A sample of what you can bring back is the knowledge that there are three types of reef—Fringing Reef that attaches to a continental shelf, Ribbon Reef that is on the outer part of the water just before it plunges into deep ocean troughs, and Patch Reef that is in the middle of the two. If you happen to stop at Saxon Reef, look for the giant clam that weighs in at 630 pounds.

There are several other island and reef trips and here are a few others to choose. But I would avoid the trip to Green Island, **W**: greenislandresort.com.au, as the waters around the island have been overused and lack clear viewing opportunities. If a mass of tourists doesn't worry you, call **Big Cat Cruises**, ☎ (07) 4051-0444 or **W**: bigcat-cruises.com.au. It costs about AU $54 adult and AU $32 kids for the return transport and a glass bottom boat tour. If you want to trek the rainforests or let the kid's run around safely, then it is a good spot for that. **Fitzroy Island** is one worth visiting if you want a bit of peaceful beach time or quiet walks around Secret Garden. The beaches are generally made up of coral pieces and you will need to wear surf shoes or sandals to walk along the shoreline. Try Nudey Beach for some isolated sunbathing. **Sunlover Cruises**, ☎ (07) 4050-1333, ☎ 1-800-810-512 or **W**: sunlover.com.au, can whisk you out to the island on one of their fast cats. The cost for a daytrip is about AU $36 adult, AU $18 kids, and AU $90 for family of 2/2 of each. **Great Adventures Reef and Islands**, ☎ (07) 4051-0455, ☎ 1-800-079-080 or **W**: greatadventures.com.au, have package deals to the reefs starting around AU $150 adults and AU $80 children. **Ocean Spirit Cruises** sail out to the reefs, and you can line up a trip with them on ☎ (07) 4031-2920, ☎ 1-800-644-227, or **W**: oceanspirit.com.au for around AU $150 and up. Your hotel, backpacker lodge or B&B will have a large of brochures to look for other options.

Kuranda Adventures

This trip will immerse you into the ancient rainforests of the northern wet tropics. These forests are considered to be a living museum and cover an area of over 2 million acres. It has primitive and prehistoric life living in today's modern world, and humans have not disturbed some of the areas for millions of years. According to the pamphlets, unidentified species of birds, insects, and mammals are still being discovered.

You can start or end at the Tjapukai Aboriginal Cultural Park and participate in the shows, learn to throw a boomerang, and immerse yourself in the holographic story of creation. It is well done, and the shop has great gifts that directly benefit the indigenous peoples.

I think the ride to and from the mountaintop village is actually more interesting than most of the activities in Kuranda. There is a train or a Skyrail that transports you from the base of Smithfield to the peak of the mount. I would suggest the train up and the Skyrail back because the train is slow and informative, while the Skyrail is quiet—so you can return at any pace you like. Each had unique features and the round-trip fee covers either mode of transport.

Kuranda is called the "Village in the Rainforest," and is 1,100 feet above sea level. Inhabited by the Djabuganydji people, it is on the edge of the Great Dividing Range of Northern Queensland. The traditional name of the village is Ngunbay, meaning the "place of the platypus." Other than the markets, it's not too exciting—it is very touristy and the local population is obviously quite poor. You will find some unique gifts from the local merchants; my personal favorites are the crocodile goods.

GETTING THERE:

By Car: it's about a 15–20 minute drive to either the train or Skyrail stations. Drive past the airport and follow signs off of Captain Cook Highway to Kuranda. It's best to have the hotel call you a cab though, and it's only about AU $15–20.

By Bus: If you book the tour, the bus pickup is included. Bus pickups are available or contact **Coral Coaches**, ☎ (07) 4098-2600 or **W**: coralcoaches.citysearch.com.au

PRACTICALITIES:

Easy walks and shaded strolls allow for almost any dress code. There will be some good photo opportunities, so take plenty of film.

FOOD AND DRINK:

Both the Cultural Park and the mountaintop village offer a good variety of food. I would suggest you wait until you get to Kuranda, because the views are fantastic and the dining options wider.

LOCAL ATTRACTIONS:

Circled numbers correspond to numbers on the map.

*TJAPUKAI ABORIGINAL CULTURAL PARK ❶, Aboriginal Cultural Park, Cairns, ☎ (07) 4042-9999, **W**: tjapukai.com.au or **W**: kuranda.org. *Open daily 9–5. Adults AU $61–$149 depending on options selected, children from AU $44-$75. Guided tours, self-guided tours. Gift shop. Café. Special events.* ♿.

Travel over 50 thousand years back into indigenous cultures and join the generations of Tjapukai as they share the evolution of their rich culture. The elders have reviewed and approved the presentations, and the local community benefits from the proceeds of the park. The name of the park means "People of the Rainforest" and includes several different peoples from the area. The center has a fantastic holographic story of creation that details Aboriginal heritage. Your admission will include entrance to **The Creation Theatre**, **The History Theatre**, **The Traditional Dance Show**, **Spear and Boomerang Throwing** (you can give this a go mates), and **Didgeridoo** playing. You can while away a full day here, but a half-day will be plenty. The gift shop has some unique items and you might want to purchase some goodies here as it benefits the indigenous programs.

Right next-door is the entrance to the Skyrail, but since it is recommended to take the train up the mountain, arrange for a ride to the train terminal at the front desk or next-door at the Skyrail Centre. You can, of course, decide to reverse the order and take the gondolas up instead and ride the train down.

*THE KURANDA EXPERIENCE ❷, Cultural Rainforest Village Ngunbay, Kuranda, ☎ (07) 4042-9999 or **W**: tjapukai.com.au for the Cultural Center; ☎ (07) 4038-1555 or **W**: skyrail.com.au for the Skyrail; ☎ (07) 4031-3636 or **W**: traveltrain.qr.com.au for the train; or **W**: kuranda.org for general information. *Kuranda is open daily generally from 9–5. Free to shop and walk around. A Skyrail/Train/Cultural Park package costs AU $91. If you decide on bus transfers from Cairns or Port Douglas figure between AU $50–$250 for one-way trips. Some attractions are a nominal extra charge. One-way/Return Skyrail and train prices are: AU $31/$44 adult, AU $23/$40 seniors, AU $15/$22 child, and AU $77/$110 family. Self-guided tours. Gift shops. Cafés. Special events. Partially* ♿.

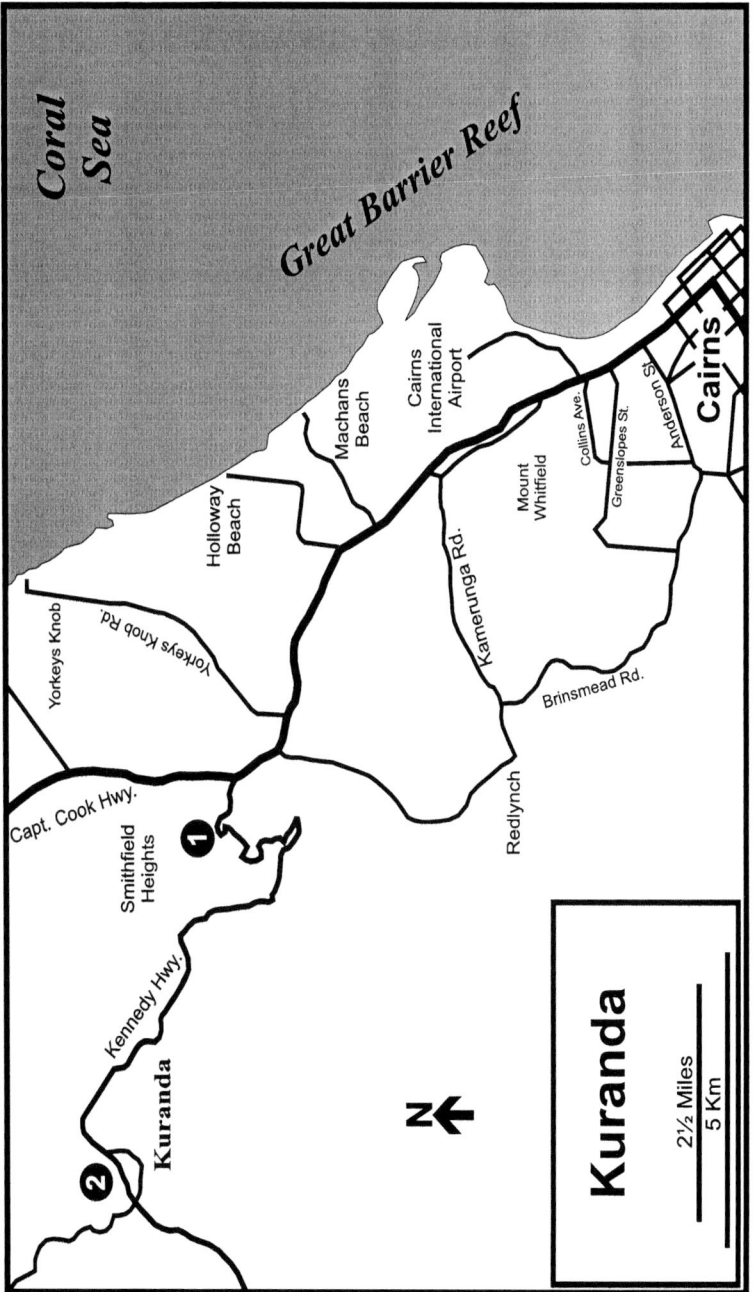

Coral Sea

Great Barrier Reef

Cairns

Machans Beach

Cairns International Airport

Anderson St.

Greenslopes St.

Collins Ave.

Mount Whitfield

Holloway Beach

Kamerunga Rd.

Yorkeys Knob

Yorkeys Knob Rd.

Brinsmead Rd.

Redlynch

Capt. Cook Hwy.

Smithfield Heights

1

Kennedy Hwy.

Kuranda

2

N

Kuranda

2½ Miles

5 Km

*The Train:

All aboard the **Cairns-Kuranda Railway** for a rocking and rolling ride along cliffs, over gorges, through tunnels, and under cascading waterfalls. The train is a grand old lady with ornate, wood-slatted cars painted barn red. Her coaches are decorated with rounded silver roofs and wide green accents. Hearing the throaty bellow of the whistle signals the beginning of the ride to the top of the mountain. The railway was built to create employment for starving miners between 1882–91. Earning 85 cents a day for backbreaking pick-and-shovel work, many men dedicated years of their lives to the effort. The rails opened up 47 miles of track that rises from 18 to 1,073 feet above sea level. There are 15 tunnels, 42 bridges, and the rails rise three feet every 164 feet. You will hear the commentary about this train system as the diesel engine chugs past sugar cane fields, horse pastures, and lush green rolling hills. Check out the watering troughs for the cows and horses. It's a great innovation using old bathtubs for the thirsty beasts. The train stops for a few photo-ops and a chance to stretch the legs, but make sure you use the toilet before starting the journey as the toilets are crammed at the stops along the way.

Kuranda Village:

When you exit the train at the top of the mountain you will climb a steep path to the beginning of the town. A five-minute walk passes by the Police Station, a backpacker's hostel, a few small shops, a restaurant, and an arts & crafts store. The majority of the shops and eateries are on either side of Condo Street (Main Street), and the markets are at the far end of town near Therwine & Thoree streets, by the park. The markets, with over 90 tents and stalls, are held every Wednesday to Friday and Sundays from 9–3. There are several scenic walks by the Barron River and Jum Rum Creek as well as a forest walk near Thongon Street. The 45-minute ***Kuranda Rainforest River Tours**, ☎ (07) 4093-7476, start right next to the train station across the footbridge and run about AU $12 adults, AU $6 kids, AU $30 family. **Birdworld Kuranda**, ☎ (07) 4093-9188 or **W**: birdworld-kuranda.com, at Rob Vievers Drive has a full stock of snakes, frogs, crocs, and the wild-colored birds flying overhead for around AU $10. The **Butterfly Sanctuary**, ☎ (07) 4093-7575 or **W**: australianbutterflies.com, is supposed to be the largest butterfly enclosure in Australia, and for AU $12 adults, AU $5 kids, and AU $38 family you can let your heart flutter around the 2,000 butterflies. Family passes for the attractions are also available. Or for a walk on the wild side, try the **Rainforestation Nature Park**, ☎ (07) 4093-9033 or **W**: rainforest.com.au, on Kennedy Highway for, well rainforest walks!

The stores change quite a bit, but you will find crocodile products, good opals, fine artworks, and good food among the three blocks of hilly streets. Look for the free "Kuranda Visitors Guide & Map" when you board either the Skyrail or train. It has opening times and directions to each of the 30 attractions and stores, **W**: kurandaline.com.au/market, on the hill. Every year in late October the 2-day Kuranda Festival electrifies the village and comes alive with shoppers and local festivities.

*The Skyrail:
For the 90-minute trip over the MacAlister Range, with the sparkling-blue Coral Sea in the foreground, jump into the Skyrail gondola. Despite the Greenies (environmental group) attempt to prevent the construction, the AU $35 million, American-designed, Skyrail opened in August of 1995. It is the largest gondola cableway in the world and was built over the rain-forest with no roads built to support the one-year it took to construct the project. The journey over the canopy of the lush World Heritage tropical rainforest is absolutely quiet. The only break in the solitude is the occasional cackling of a multi-colored fowl. There is also a smell of rich humus. There are 44 tons of galvanized steel rope used to carry the gondolas along the towers, and the 114 gondolas, purchased from Sweden at the price of $30,000 each, carry six people. At 11 miles an hour, you have the option of getting off at two different stations. Explore the magnificent forests on easy walking wooden boardwalks that weave amongst the trees. Here is what you might expect to see on the side trips: **Red Peak Station** is named for the red rock face nearby and is the highest point on the route at 1,788 feet above sea level. The well-documented boardwalk signs at this stop describe the struggle of the twisted vines, palms, and crawling creatures. Because only one percent of all sunlight reaches the forest floor, survival is based on what plants get their bit of sunshine. The Kauri Pines are the largest of the trees in Queensland, 164 feet high and there are heaps of them in this national park called Barron Gorge. Closer to the ground the low-light ferns such as the Fishbone Fern and Robbers Fern dot the landscape. An adaptive fern, called the Basket Fern, attaches itself to the side of large trees and creates a home for itself and the snakes, possums, and bats that live in them. They are also called epiphytical plants because they live on a host, but do no damage to that host. On the way back to board the gondola is a sign pointing out the dreaded Giant Stinging Plant. An adjacent sign notified you of another danger in the jungle—the cassowary. Although there are only 1,500 of the birds left in the wet tropics, they are very territorial and they have the size and clawed feet to do considerable damage. At **Barron Falls** the gondola crests the mountaintop to reveal the green canopy of treetops of the **Atherton Tablelands**. This area is rich in Aboriginal lore and is the home of the Djabuganydji Bama tribe's Rainbow Serpent (carpet snake). Barron Gorge is a huge cleft in solid rock that transforms the mellow Barron River into a roaring cascade of white water. The water crashing into the abyss creates a series of dancing rainbows in the misty valley below. This site is also the base of a hydroelectric plant with a series of dams that divert water into massive turbines.

For additional information on the Skyrail and the sights along the way, call the **Wet Tropics Management Authority**, ☎ (07) 4052; the **Department of Environment and Heritage**, ☎ (07) 4052-3092, or take a look at the Skyrail's web page at **W**: skyrail.com.au. If you care to have a tour company arrange everything, try **Tropic Wings Coach Tours**, ☎ (07) 4035-3555 or **W**: tropicwings.com.au, for the whole shebang.

Fishing the Estuaries

By rising early from your snug bed, you have a marvelous day on the water to look forward to. If you have any skill or luck, you will land a grunter, king salmon, queenfish, barramundi, mangrove Jack, fingermark, or trevally. There are several charters to choose from, and you can either ask at your accommodation front desk, or simply browse the waterfront piers for the boat that looks right. The prices vary a little bit, but they usually depend on how far upstream you wish to go. By taking a charter, you need not worry about licenses, and most supply drinks and light snacks during the half-day trips. Unless you go way into the mangroves, the bugs aren't too bad, but you will need a hat, sunscreen, and sunglasses.

GETTING THERE:
Leave the car at the hotel and walk to the Wharf Pier. You can arrange a pickup at your hotel, ☎ (07) 4031-4444, to start the tour at the Marlin Marina.

PRACTICALITIES:
Sun protection and grubby clothes are in order. If you think you'll be catching a record-breaker, take a disposable camera for the shot. The water is calm, so no need for motion sickness prevention.

FOOD AND DRINK:
Some charters provide food and drink, but it might be best to fuel up at one of the Pier Market cafés before you head out.

LOCAL ATTRACTIONS:
All the trips originate at the Wharf Pier.

CALM WATER FISHING, Marlin Marina, Cairns. Boardwalk Travel and Charters can arrange for any type of fishing trip you desire at ☎ (07) 4031-4444 or **W**: ausfish.com/crcs/. *Full or half-day sport fishing adventures start as early as 6:45. Cost is from AU$69. Alternatively, just go to the Marlin Jetty Pier and size up the boats and choose one on your own.*

If you love angling, you can look forward to the estuary fishing because you might land fish that you have never seen (or even heard of) before. All the skippers you have to choose from are men of few words, take their chartering seriously, and on their days off—they fish! Most of the boats are about 15 feet and move pretty slowly over the shallow harbor where you begin the day by throwing bait nets out near the mudflat walls at the Esplanade. The prawns and red herring caught are destined for your hooks and are deposited in a built-in compartment for the half-day jaunt. You will be protected from the sun by a weathered canvas roof over the aluminum-hulled boat while motoring up towards the bay shoreline and Chinaman's Creek. Most of the fishermen use Regal reels with 12-pound line attached to six-foot Ultra CastPro rods. To increase you odds of catching fish, let the captain set your rigs and bait your hooks. They all know what they are doing, and will let you know when the underwater creatures will begin to strike. When the tide changes, get ready to start reeling and wait till until the tip of your rod points straight into the water. The captain will also remove the fish for you—I would advise that especially since some of the critters have poisonous spines. You can take your catch along with you at the end of the day or the captain will be happy to take it home for his own dinner.

After scrubbing up a bit and changing into neat casual attire, you might want to try your hand at the pokies (slots) at the:

REEF HOTEL CASINO, 35-41 Wharf Street, Cairns, ☎ (07) 4030-8888, **W**: reefcasino.com.au. *Open daily 24 hours, Casino open Mon–Thurs. 10–4 and 24 hours a day Fri.–Mon. Free. Gift shops. Café and restaurants. Special events.* ♿.

Even if you choose not to risk your cash, take a stroll around the hotel and through the casino floor. There may be a few games you have never seen like Sic-Bo, Reef Routine, Paradise Pontoon, or the Reef Money Wheel. Nothing like Atlantic City or Vegas, it has a tropical appeal with a huge arboretum on the balcony of the top floor that is used as an entertainment center for luncheons or weddings. It is packed full of tropical plants, steaming ponds, and quiet walkways that look out over the city. The two levels of gaming floors are loaded with over 500 slot machines and your choice of vices. It doesn't have the same smoky, worn-out feel as most casinos do. Or try a bit of fine dining at one of the three restaurants with Pacific Region flavors, Asian/Western fusion style, and pub meals. Better yet, while away the hours at the Vertigo Bar for music and cocktails or the Casino Nightclub 1936 for an all-night party.

The Undara
Lava Tubes

The Undara Lava Tubes were caverns formed by a huge volcanic eruption in the McBride Province of Queensland almost 200,000 million years ago. Hot molten lava flows poured from the monolith and, as it cooled, created a blanket of hardened rock. Since the lava takes the easiest route, it began to flow under the surface, though softer sections, and creating underground rivers of magma. Because the volcano slowly reduced its output instead of blowing its top and cooling, the underground rivers were able to drain to create the tunnels. The 100-mile network of tubes is the longest lava flow in the world, and the word Undara means "a long way" in the Aboriginal tongue.

Several tubes have collapsed, some have not yet been explored, and all offer interesting eco-systems of animal and plant life. From the literature about the area, of the 300 roof collapses only about 68 individual cave sections have been identified. The bat caves are a big draw, and hikes in and around the tunnels can be arranged through the touring company. But if you fear the winged creatures, avoid the October–March tours of Barker's Tube. Millions of "micro-bats" take flight for the nightly feed.

The area is a wilderness experience with all the comforts of a soft warm bed, gourmet cuisine, and professional guided tours. One of the most impressive and memorable experiences will be an overnight stay in one of the restored early 1900's railway coaches that sleep under giant gum trees. The pool and resort facilities will be a welcomed sight after a day of hiking.

GETTING THERE:

By Car: Drive about 4 hours (170 miles) southwest from Cairns on Route 1, Kennedy Highway. The access road into the area is sealed, but there are sections (about 6 miles worth) of gravel and it can get a bit rattling. But there's no need for a 4WD vehicle.

By Bus: Most bust tours start at 8am from Cairns and take the scenic route to the tubes. The tours usually return back to Cairns at around 7:30 in the evening. I recommend the bus tour, as it will be a long daytrip to drive. Sit back, relax and enjoy the scenery. Pickup from most hotels or designated locations is available in the city.

By Train: The *Savannalander Train* is currently running, and the AU $500+ tour includes food and lodging.

PRACTICALITIES:

This will be a long day on the road and if at all possible, spend at least one night at the Lava Lodge. Especially if you are a keen hiker as you will want to spend a day or two strolling at your own pace along the self-guided paths. Hiking gear is appropriate, but if you are sticking to the guided tours of the tubes, just wear comfortable shoes. It will get hot and humid, but parts of the caves may be cool and the evenings get crisp. Take layers just in case. Sun protection goes here too. If you hike unaccompanied, take a map, let the staff know where you are heading, take water, and if you get lost, sit tight until help comes.

Check out the web page, **W**: undara-experience.com.au, to get a good perspective of the size of the tubes and the diversity of this Gulf Savannah region.

FOOD AND DRINK:

Food is provided on the tours and if you self-drive, there are spots along the way (pubs) to grab a quick and hearty meal. The restaurants at the lodge are good value and are moderately priced. The menu of the Fettler's Iron Pot is on the web site if you want to plan your meal. A real treat is to dine in one of the restored railway cars. But if you want to rough it, there are BBQs and campsites available.

LOCAL ATTRACTIONS:

UNDARA EXPERIENCE ❶, Lava Lodge, Mt. Surprise, ☎ 1-800-990-992 or (07) 4097-1411, **W**: undara-experience.com.au, E-mail: res@undara.com.au or infor@undara.com.au. *Tours daily from 8:00. Lodging from AU $6 (campsite), AU $18 (swag tent), AU $24 dorms in the Wilderness Lodge), and AU $121 (B&B in the rail coaches). Prices for the tours are around AU $33 (2-hour Tube), AU $63 (1/2-day Tube), AU $38 (Wildlife at Sunset), and AU $93 (full-day). Package deals run from AU $350–$577. Guided tours, self-guided tours. Gift shop. Café and restaurants. Partially ♿.*

Once you arrive at the Mt. Surprise area, there are several options to see the marvelous surrounds, tubes, swamps, forests, and wildlife. There are five self-guided hikes that range from 2-1/2-miles long and about 1-1/2 hours to a bit over 5 miles and 2-1/2-hours. The **Atkinson's Lookout** is an easy trek over a ridge and rock formations to a great view to the south. The **Bluff Walk** is also an easy hike through gullies and up to a lookout area that reveals the woodland lava plains. The **Bush Walk** is easy and meanders across grasslands, through a swampy area, and fields of wildflowers. Choosing **Flat Rock**, you will have a 2-hour stroll near the swamp, along a service road, and onto—Flat Rock with its 360-degree view of the lava fields and the ancient cones in the distance. Finally, the **Swamp Track** is an hour jaunt along the interesting wetland areas called the One Hundred Mile Swamp.

All explorations of the tubes must be with a tour guide. The organized trips are a fantastic value and the choices are varied enough to suit most daytrippers. The benefit of the tours is the detailed descriptions of the geological formations, the highlighted views of the wildlife, and the history of the region. The tours are carried out in air-conditioned buses, and food is provided along the way. If you are in a hurry, there are aerial tours available from the coast in a twin-engine Shrike AC 500 with bubble windows for best viewing. There is currently a rail tour that runs from Cairns, but there is talk of discontinuing this trek. Check with the booking agent if you have an interest in that one.

The Tubes are amazing, each different, have varied animals hanging around and crawling about the floor, and smell different (depending on the airways and types of cave-ins). They look big enough to drive a huge dump truck through in certain sections and could easily be mistaken for long entrances to nuclear bunkers. Several are described as wind tunnels, but the cool colors of the rock, the fallen ceilings, and imagining the volume of lava that flowed through these giant wormholes is unfathomable.

Section IX

Appendix

HELPFUL HINTS BEFORE YOU GET STARTED

Since you are probably traveling from another part of the world and will want to make the best of your walkabout in Australia, here are some good tips to think about before you book your trip. They might also be helpful while exploring the Land Down Under. The Internet sites provided are particularly helpful in getting a lay of the land.

It is important to plan around **public holidays** as operation hours, access to eateries, and attractions may be limited. Plus most restaurants tack on an additional fee during holidays. School holidays are to be taken into consideration if you don't want to deal with the often crazy Schoolies Weeks (like spring break), or the masses of Aussie families packing the roads. And **daylight savings** is something to watch for in all states except Queensland.

Not to be underestimated, but don't focus too much on it as it changes so quickly, is **weather**. The forecasting is not what you might be used to, and the general guidelines below will help you make some of your travel decisions.

One thing to always keep in mind is the phrase **Slip, Slop, Slap**—and that goes for the cities, beaches, Outback and rainforests. The phrase is to warn people of the dangers of this southern hemisphere's sun and skin cancer dangers. It means slip on a shirt, slop on sunscreen, and slap on a hat. It is a good rule to follow even if you have a tan or don't usually burn. The sun is bloody hot here mates.

Not to scare you off, but one important thing to remember when you are on any of the **beaches**—Swim Between the Flags! Not many Australians drown, and that's mainly because they know the surf can be tricky and it's best to swim where the Surf Lifesaving Clubs patrol. And if you don't see any Aussies in the water—do not go in. It is their backyard and they know if it is unsafe to swim.

Another good tip is to plan ahead for your **toilet breaks** when in Oz, especially if you have kids along or have special needs. Don't assume that all cafés, stores, and restaurants will have toilet facilities. Usually a shared public toilet is nearby and generally only the US-based fast food joints have toilets inside. Public toilets can be found in most parks (and there are parks everywhere), in the majority of museums, are closeby in shopping areas, and at tourist attractions.

A valid English-language **driver's license** will allow you to rent a car and get behind a wheel—no need for an international license. Remember that cars travel on the opposite (left) side of the road here, the gearshift is on the left and the wiper/turn signal sticks are reversed. Plus the highways and streets are full of roundabouts (known as Jersey Circles in the US), so slow down and follow the lead of the other drivers. A good rule to follow is to stay in the left lane unless passing, look both ways at all stops until you get used to cars coming at you from the opposite direction, and follow the markers painted on the road at the circles.

Some good reference materials can be found at the RACQ stores located in most shopping centers. You can also get **maps and guides** at the bookstores; Angus & Robertson has the top selections. The best, most comprehensive, and easiest-to-use road atlas is called "Discover Australia Road Guide," published by Lifetime Distributors.

You will be happy when you exchange you greenback for the colorful **Australian dollar**. At the time of the publication you will be almost doubling your bucks. If you are planning to purchase travelers checks before heading south, try to get them in Australian dollars. The banks should not charge you a conversion fee if they have already been changed over. Some financial institutions charge a hefty fee to make foreign exchanges. Major credit cards are accepted almost everywhere. If you do bring your own currency, stalls that exchange money are easy to find, but again there is a fee.

GETTING TO AUSTRALIA:

You have your choice of directions in getting to the Land Down Under from America. The first is through the western gates of the United States. I prefer San Francisco over Los Angeles, as the airport is more manageable and less crowded. However, during the foggy seasons it could be a risk in getting out on time. I recommend the midnight departure because you have a better chance of getting some sleep on the 13-hour leg and it will put you into sync with local Oz-times.

The second is through Hong Kong. Many friends have recommended this eastern journey as it offers the possibility of stopping for some custom-made clothing. I have been warned that the connections are not always desirable, it is about 4–8 hours longer, but is a tad less expensive.

Check with your travel agent for security issues, and allow plenty of time for clearing customs in both directions. Even though the airlines allow for an hour between connections, I would recommend at least two and probably three hours. If you miss a connection at the international terminals, you may sit for 12 hours before the next possible flight across the Pacific.

If you have frequent flyer miles, use them to **upgrade** on the trans-Pacific leg of the trip. It is worth using the points to have a bit of legroom in Business Class. Check with your doctor on this one mates, but it might be advisable to take a half of aspirin a day at least three days before flying. It will reduce the risk of Economy Class Syndrome or DVT (Deep Vein Thrombosis). Don't laugh this one off if you are a young traveler. Recently, a young Aussie cricket star came down with the clots and lost half a season of play. And even if they do now provide lots of water on the trip, take a bottle along to drink as you need it, and they will gladly fill it up for you too.

Most flights come into Sydney, so plan to explore that city at the beginning or end of your Australian trek. My suggestion is to do Sydney first, shoot down to Melbourne, and finish up with Queensland. Flights to/from Queensland and Melbourne's Victoria are frequent and now the choices are basically between Qantas and Virgin Blue. **Qantas** is the largest, full-service carrier and **Virgin Blue** is the discount carrier. Ansett is no longer in operation. You will have to check with your regular carrier to see if either of the Aussie airlines offer points to any of your plans.

Finally, ask about the **Boomerang Pass Program** or the **One World Air Pass Program** offered by Qantas. They are coupon-based tickets that allow various multi-city stops, saving you lots of money if you plan to hop around a bit when you are in Oz. You must purchase the Boomerang Pass before you arrive in Australia. The One World Air Pass can be purchased in Australia, but you would be better off including it in your overall flight plan.

PUBLIC HOLIDAYS AND SPECIAL EVENTS:

State abbreviations are:

ACT	Australian Capital Territory (or Canberra—like Washington DC)
NSW	New South Wales (capital is Sydney)
NT	Northern Territory (capital is Darwin)
QLD	Queensland (capital is Brisbane)
SA	South Australia (capital is Adelaide)
TAS	Tasmania (capital is Hobart)
VIC	Victoria (capital is Melbourne)
WA	Western Australia (capital is Perth)

General holidays are:

January 1	New Year's Day
January 26	Australia Day
February 11	Regatta day—TAS only

February 27	Launceston Cup—TAS only
March 4	Labor Day—WA only
March 11	Labor Day—VIC only
March 11	Eight Hour Day—TAS only
March 18	Canberra Day—ACT only
March 29	Good Friday
April 1	Easter Monday
April 25	Anzac Day
May 6	May Day—NT only
May 6	Labor Day—QLD only
May 20	Adelaide Day—SA only
June 3	Foundation Day—WA only
June 10	Queen's Birthday—Except in WA
August 5	Bank Holiday—NSW and ACT only
August 5	Picnic Day—NT only
August 14	RNA Show Day—Brisbane only
September 30	Queen's Birthday—WA only
October 7	Labor Day—ACT/NSW/SA only
October 10	Launceston Show Day—TAS only
October 4	Hobart Show Day—TAS only
November 4	Recreation Day—TAS only
November 5	Melbourne Cup Day—VIC only
December 25	Christmas Day
December 26	Boxing Day—Except in SA
December 26	Proclamation Day—SA only

SCHOOL HOLIDAYS:

Schoolies Week is in mid-December to the end of January. The roads are crowded, hotels fill up, and many businesses charge extra fees for service. This summer vacation for the kids varies a bit from state to state, but generally that is the time to stay away.

You may also decide against travel around the other school breaks, generally around the following dates: Late June to mid-July; Late September to mid-October; Late December to early February; Early April to mid-April

GENERAL WEATHER CONDITIONS:

Australia is known as the Sunburnt Country, but it has a wild mix of weather conditions, which can be a major factor in traveling to certain parts of the country. It is generally tropical in the north and temperate in the south. Spring or autumn is the best time to tour, when the temperatures are a bit more moderate.

Sydney's nearly four million residents enjoy mostly warm weather, and it is cool, not cold in the winter. Melbourne is so unpredictable that most of the locals prepare for rain, hot, cold, and snow in the same day. Queensland is warm to hot most of the year, so shorts and golf shirts are the norm.

It's best to see Queensland between April and October when it is dry, not too hot, and safer to swim in the Northern Tropics. The rainy seasons will not impact travel much as they are similar to Florida's showers/sun/showers and sun again with plenty of humidity in between. It is bearable for most people. Just dress in light clothing and keep a light-weight rain slicker and hat handy.

The southern capitals of Sydney and Melbourne are also best visited in spring and autumn. The flowers and gardens are picture perfect and you will not have to cook or freeze between day and night. But Melbourne is the weatherman's nightmare, so do the layer thing. Which reminds me — be wary of the weather predictions here, they are not spot on most of the time.

GENERAL TIPS:

* If you drive, remember that there are often great distances between service stations and toilet stops. Always keep water bottles in the vehicle, and it would be wise to keep a mobile (cellular) phone with you.

* **Mobile phone service** — You have several options including: **1**) bring your own phone (must be a tri-band phone) and Vodafone (☎ 1-800-501-052 or **W**: vodafone.com.au/fastfone) can possibly assign a new Australian number for a fee in addition to connection rates starting about AU $3/minute; **2**) purchase a phone with a pre-paid card starting at around AU $200 from Vodafone, **Optus** (☎ 1-300-301-937 or **W**: optus.com.au/prepaid-mobile) or **Virgin Mobile** (☎ 13-33-23 or **W**: virginmobile.com.au); and finally **3**) rent a phone and pay for services from **Cellhire** (☎ 1-800-144-340 in Australia, ☎ 1-888-476-7368 from the US, or **W**: cellhire.com) for around AU $15/day with charges for calls starting at AU .70/minute. Cellhire might be the best deal and you can possibly use your own phone if it has GSM 900-1800 band capacity.

* **Wildlife** can be a road hazard and especially kangaroos. Keep alert especially at dawn and dusk.

* Respect the **environment** when camping, traveling in pastoral areas and parks, and care for wildlife. Fire is a particular worry, so obey the guidelines at park entrances.

* If you are **hiking**, keep to the pathways or find a guide. Many people get lost here by being careless. Pack a compass and tell the rangers or friends where you are going and when to expect you back.

* Slip/Slop/Slap when in the sun and for goodness sakes, SWIM BETWEEN THE FLAGS MATES! If you do get stung by a marine stinger, get to the lifeguard immediately for first aid.

* Hiking can bring you in contact with various wildlife and insects. Heed any posted warnings; if you respect your surroundings you will have no worries. Pack **insect repellant**, matches, or salt for leeches, as well as a small first aid kit if you are out for long walks in rainforest environments. Look for a product called Savlon or Stingose

to ease most bites, cuts or stings.
* Basic **metric conversions** are:
  Celsius to Fahrenheit—multiply c by 1.8 and add 32.
  Kilometers to Miles—multiply km by .621.
  Meters to Feet—multiply m by 3.28.
  Kilograms to Pounds—multiply kg by 2.2.
  Liters to US Gallons—multiply l by .264.
* **Tipping** is not necessary, but a 10% gratuity is appreciated. Gratuities are sometimes added and corkage fees do apply if you bring you own alcohol.
* **Electric power** is 240 volts AC. Don't even bother bringing your hair dryer or electric razor—even with the conversion kits they tend to burn up.
* North American **time zones** are about 10–14 hours behind. To **phone home** dial: 0011-1-area code-number. To call to Australia dial: 0116-1-last digit of the area code-number.
* The **emergency number** throughout Australia is 000.
* **Drinking and driving** is strongly monitored with "drink driving" roadblocks set up randomly all over the place—even in mornings and mid-day. Don't risk getting locked up.
* Speaking of drinking **beer**—a "stubbie" is a 375ml (12oz) of lager, a "pot" is a 284ml (8oz) glass, and a pitcher of beer is called a "jug."
* Keep copies of you **passport/visas** in a separate location from the original. It is much easier getting replacements if you have a copy.
* If you plan to stay in Australia for a few months or more, think about buying a used car and reselling upon leaving. It will be cheaper than renting if you don't mind the hassle of haggling. But do get a RACQ membership for breakdown service.

TOURIST INFORMATION:

General phone numbers and/or web sites for Australia tourism-related offices are provided below. Information associated with specific trips will be listed in that section.

Medical & Inoculation Information:
World Health Organization **W**: who.int/wer
Center for Disease Control **W**: cdc.gov/travel
Travel Doctor **W**: tmvc.com.au
Travel Vax (vaccinations) **W**: travelvax.com.au
The Australian Travel Doctor **W**: thetravellersdoctor.com.au
Aviation Health **W**: aviation-health.org

Australia Wide:
Police/Ambulance/Fire   ☎ 000
Operator ☎ 12455
Long Distance Operator ☎ 1234
Overseas Operator ☎ 1225
US Direct Dialing ☎ 0011-1-area code-number

Yellow Pages **W**: yellowpages.com

US Embassy ☎ 06-270-5000 , 02-34-9200

City Search Maps & Directions **W**: citysearch.com.au

Aussie Travel Information **W**: seeaustralia.com.au

Where It Is Maps **W**: whereitis.com

Public Toilet Locations **W**: toiletmap.gov.au

Youth Hostel Association **W**: yha.com.au

Eco Tourism ☎ (07) 3229-5550 or **W**: ecotourism-australia.info

Qantas Airlines ☎ 13-13-13 or **W**: Qantas.com.au

Virgin Blue Airlines ☎ 13-67-89 (Domestic) or 617-3295-2296 (International), **W**: virginblue.com.au

Greyhound Bus lines ☎ 13-20-30 or **W**: greyhound.com.au

Aussie Business Directory **W**: aussie.com.au

Australia Net Tourism **W**: ants.net.au

Explore Australia **W**: exploreaustralia.com.au

Australia Online Magazine **W**: Australia-online.com

CIA World Fact Book **W**: cia.gov/cia/publications /factbook/index.html

City Search Australia **W**: citysearch.com.au

Aussie Cities Information   ☎ 13-11-11 or **W**: wishyou werehere.com

RACQ (Like AAA) **W**: racq.com.au

RACQ Road Information **W**: roadsafety.net

Aussie Internet Travel Info   **W**: http://travel.bigpond.com/ travel.asp

Online Events in Oz **W**: thisweekinaustralia.com

GLOSSARY

Australian English is a bit different than the American or British version. As a rule, words are shortened and an "ie" (or a vowel) is added to the end (Christmas is Chrissie, breakfast is brekkie, afternoon is arvo, and present is pressie). The slang and colloquialisms are called "Strine," which is like a slurred version of Australian. The hardcore slang and regional dialects are dying out (thanks to American television), but the old timers and people in remote areas keep the traditional words alive. These words have been explained to me, and some of the clarifications have been verified in various Australian dictionaries.

ANZAC - Australian and New Zealand Army Corps
Arvo - afternoon
Abo - derogatory term for an Aboriginal person
Aussie - Australian
Banana Bender - resident of Queensland
Barra - barramundi fish
Bathers - swimming costume
Bikie - biker
Bickies - biscuits or cookies
Billabong - backwater or pond in an otherwise dry stream
Billy Tea - tea made by boiling water in a tin can over an open fire
Bitumen - blacktop on roads
Bloody - term of disapproval
Bloke - a man
Blotto - drunk
Bonnet - hood of a car
Boot - trunk of a car
Blowies - blow flies
Bludger - a lazy or ungrateful person
Blue - fight or argument
Bluey - nickname for a red-haired person; also a type of
    Australian dog
Brekkie - breakfast
Bugs - short version of a tasty crustacean (like a cross between a
    crab and a lobster), which is a shortening of Moreton Bay Bugs
Bushranger - outlaw or bandit, usually in the Outback
Busker - street performer
BYO - ("bring your own") to take your own alcohol to dinner
    or a party
Caravan - trailer home
CBD - Central Business District or middle of a city or town
Chemist - pharmacy
Chips - French fries

Chockablock - full or crowded
Chook - chicken.
Chrissie - Christmas
Coach - bus, usually a tour bus
Coach Captain - bus driver
Cobber - old term for mate
Cozzie - bathing suit
Crikey - exclamation of astonishment
Crisps - potato chips
Crook - sick or ill
Cuppa - usually a cup of tea (or now coffee) or a tea break
Damper - unleavened bread traditionally cooked on a camp fire
Digger - an honest man, a hard worker, a patriot
Dinkum - honest, genuine, true
Dinky-di - the real thing
Dob in - to inform or turn in to the law
Drover - cowboy who herds sheep or cattle
Dunny - toilet
Entree - an appetizer (main course is called a main)
Esplanade - a walking path near the sea
Fair Dinkum - usually to confirm or question a statement as
     being true
Fairy Floss - cotton candy
Feral - wild, un-kept (often homeless) person
Footpath - sidewalk
Fossicking - to search for gold or gems on land usually a
     bandoned by owners
Galah - silly person, also a noisy pink-breasted cockatoo
G'day - hello, hi
Gurgler - drinking water fountain
Hinterland - an area situated behind the coast
Ice Block - popsicle or snow cone
Jackaroo - male ranch trainee
Jug - pitcher (of beer)
Jumbuck - sheep
Jumper - sweater
Lamington - dessert made as a cube of sponge cake covered in
     chocolate icing and coconut powder
Lolly - candy
Long Black - a standard black cup of coffee
Mate - a friend, fellow worker, or merely a greeting to a man
     (now women too)
Mexican - anyone who lives south of Queensland
Milk bar - corner store
Mob - usually a herd of cattle
Mossie - mosquito

MP - Member of Parliament
Muster - roundup of sheep or cattle
Never Never - remote area or far away
Nipper - child
No worries - no problem, not a problem
Outback - remote and sparsely inhabited areas
Oz - Australia, also Aus
Partner - either member of a married (or unmarried) couple
     (hetero or homosexual)
Pavlova - a dessert made of meringue, cream and fruit
     (usually passionfruit)
Piss - beer
Pissed - drunk or tired
PM - Prime Minister, similar to a president
Polly - politician
Poo - a bowel movement
Pom - an English person (supposedly an acronym for Prisoner
     of Mother country)
Postie - mailman
Pot - 284 ml (8 oz) glass of beer
Promanade - walking path along the sea
Pushbike - bicycle
Queue - a waiting line
Rellies - relatives
Ripper - word of admiration or enthusiasm for someone
     who has excelled
Road Train - a huge tractor trailer with up to three trailers
Root - tired or sexual intercourse (never "root" for your sports team)
Sanger - sandwich
Serviette - table napkin
Schoolies - school holidays
Sheila - a woman - not used much anymore
She'll be right - not a problem, don't worry
Short White - a small cup of coffee with cream/milk
Shout - usually to a buy a round of drinks
Sickie - to take a day off work (supposedly from being sick)
Singlet - tank top
Slab - case of beer
Smoko - tea-break, break for a cigarette, or short rest from work
Snags - sausages
Spit - a narrow strip of land jutting into the ocean
Stubbie - small 375 ml (12 oz) bottle of beer
Surgery - term for a doctor's office (general practitioner)
Swag - item used for sleeping outdoors
Ta - thank you
TAB - an off-track betting office (Totalisator Agency Board)

Takeaway - take out food
Taxi Rank - taxi stand
Tassie - Tasmanian
Tea - this can be morning tea, afternoon tea break, or most often
    referred to as the evening meal
Thongs - flip flops
Tinnie - can of beer, or small aluminum boat
Togs - swimming costume
Toilet - rest room facilities - do not call toilets bathrooms
Tucker - food
Uni - university
Ute - utility, pick-up truck
Veggies - vegetables
Vegemite - the diet of all Aussie kids
Walkabout - to go stroll around or disappear for a period of time
Wanker - an idiot who thinks he is self-important
Wet - rainy season
Witchetty grub - little white worms that are traditional
    food of Aboriginals
Wog - immigrant or foreigner
Woop-woop - a remote place or far away
Yank - American
Yobbo - beer swigging uncouth lout or ruffian
Yabbie - small freshwater crayfish
Yakka - hard work
XXXX - fourex beer

Index

Special interest attractions are listed under their category headings.

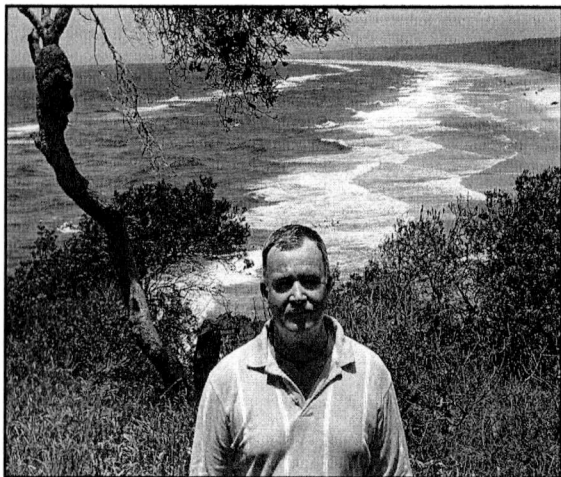

ABOUT THE AUTHOR

Jim Postell and his wife have discovered many interesting and varied tours through their extended stay in Australia. A six-month visit has turned into a lifetime love affair with this magnificent country and its people. All of the tours in his book have been hiked, kayaked, swum, cycled, driven, bused, and taste tested by Jim and Ann.

Jim has incorporated his varied travel experiences into this guide, and contributes stories to local Australian magazines and publications. His humorous insights, learning the culture from a perspective of an American expatriate, will ease you into a "no worries" tour of a wondrous country.